ANCIENT INDIAN TRADITION & MYTHOLOGY

Translated by
A BOARD OF SCHOLARS

And Edited by
Prof. J. L. SHASTRI

VOLUME 5

ANCIENT INDIAN TRADITION AND MYTHOLOGY SERIES

[PURĀṆAS IN TRANSLATION]

VOLUMES

ŚIVA 1-4

LIṄGA 5-6

BHĀGAVATA 7-11

GARUḌA 12-14

NĀRADA 15-19

KŪRMA 20-21

BRAHMĀṆḌA 22-26

AGNI 27-30

VARĀHA 31-32

BRAHMA 33-36

VĀYU 37-38

PADMA 39-48

SKANDA, PARTS I-XI, 49-59

VOLUMES UNDER PREPARATION

SKANDA, PARTS XII-XXV

BHAVIṢYA

BRAHMAVAIVARTA

DEVĪBHĀGAVATA

KĀLIKĀ

MĀRKAṆḌEYA

MATSYA

VĀMANA

VIṢṆU

VIṢṆUDHARMOTTARA

THE LIṄGA-PURĀṆA

Translated by
A BOARD OF SCHOLARS

PART I

MOTILAL BANARSIDASS PUBLISHERS
PRIVATE LIMITED • DELHI

First Edition: Delhi, 1973
Reprint: Delhi, 1982, 1990, 1997

ISBN: 81-208-0340-x

Also available at:

MOTILAL BANARSIDASS
41 U.A. Bungalow Road, Jawahar Nagar, Delhi 110 007
8, Mahalaxmi Chamber, Warden Road, Mumbai 400 026
120 Royapettah High Road, Mylapore, Chennai 600 004
Sanas Plaza, Subhash Nagar, Pune 411 002
16 St. Mark's Road, Bangalore 560 001
8 Camac Street, Calcutta 700 017
Ashok Rajpath, Patna 800 004
Chowk, Varanasi 221 001

UNESCO COLLECTION OF REPRESENTATIVE WORKS—Indian Series
This book has been accepted in the Indian Translation Series of the UNESCO Collection of Representative Works, jointly sponsored by the United Nations Educational, Scientific and Cultural Organization (UNESCO) and the Government of India.

PRINTED IN INDIA
BY JAINENDRA PRAKASH JAIN AT SHRI JAINENDRA PRESS,
A-45 NARAINA, PHASE I, NEW DELHI 110 028
AND PUBLISHED BY NARENDRA PRAKASH JAIN FOR
MOTILAL BANARSIDASS PUBLISHERS PRIVATE LIMITED,
BUNGALOW ROAD, DELHI 110 007

PUBLISHER'S NOTE

The purest gems lie hidden in the bottom of the ocean or in the depth of rocks. One has to dive into the ocean or delve into the rocks to find them out. Similarly truth lies concealed in the language that with the lapse of time has become obsolete. Man has to learn that language before he discovers that truth.

But he has neither the means nor the leisure to embark on that course. We have, therefore, planned to help him acquire knowledge by an easier course. We have started the series of *Ancient Indian Tradition and Mythology in English Translation*. Our goal is to universalize knowledge through the most popular, international medium of expression. The publication of the Purāṇas in English translation is the step towards that goal.

PREFACE

The present volume contains *Liṅgapurāṇa* Part I in English translation. It is the fifth in the series of fifty Volumes on *Ancient Indian Tradition and Mythology.*

The project of the Series was envisaged and financed in 1970 A.D. by Shri Sundarlal Jain, the veteran interprizer in the field of Oriental Publication and the leading proprietor Messers Motilal Banarsidass. Hitherto six volumes of the series (that is, four vols. of the Śivapurāṇa and two vols. of the Liṅgapurāṇa completing both the Purāṇas) have been published and made accessible to the reader.

The present English translation is based on the Sanskrit text of the Liṅgapurāṇa published in India by Messers Kṣemarāja Śrīkṛṣṇadāsa. This text, constructed on the collation of Mss. is fairly reliable, although here and there it suffers from certain lapses and defies our efforts for accurate translation. But these lapses are few and far between and they do not vitiate the quality of translation as a whole.

In this translation we have followed the text as closely as possible but at places we have been a little freer with a desire to maintain the spirit of the language in which the original is so rendered. At the same time we have excluded all far-fetched, forced or fancied interpretations including those that are suggested by the author of the Śivatoṣiṇī, though we have often quoted him in the footnotes.

The reader will find that the Purāṇa deals with a variety of subjects—geographical, historical, philosophical, religious and the like which need elucidation. This task could not be accomplished by a mere translation. We have therefore provided footnotes on these topics. The footnotes are very brief but illuminative. They supply the background without which the exegesis of the text would not be possible.

We have prefixed to this Part a critical introduction which discusses, besides other topics, the nomenclature, authorship, authenticity, date and general characteristics of this work. Wc have suffixed to Part II a general index which lists among other words the names of persons, tribes, places, rivers, lakes, mountains etc. of which the identity already discussed in the footnotes is marked here by introducing a letter of abbreviation put within the bracket against the name. But we have eschewed all unnecessary repetitions and therefore have included the constantly recurring names, as those of the deities, kings and sages, only when there is some special reason for specifying them.

Before closing, it is our pleasant duty to put on record our sincere gratitude to Dr. S.K. Chatterjee, Dr. V. Raghavan, Dr. R.N. Dandekar, Shri K.R. Kripalani and the authorities of the UNESCO for their kind encouragement and valuable help which render this work more valuable to scholars than it would otherwise have been. We must also thank Shri T.V. Parameswar Iyer for his valuable spade-work which lightened our labours especially in their initial stage.

In fine, we avail of this opportunity to state that any critical suggestions and advice for improvement are welcome and will receive proper consideration from us.

Translators and Editor

ABBREVIATIONS (Foot-notes)

AB	Aitareya-Brāhmaṇa
AG	Ancient Geography of India : Cunningham
Agni	Agnipurāṇa
AIHT	Ancient Indian Historical Tradition : Pargiter
Amara	Amarakośa
AU	Atharva-Upaniṣad
BD	Bṛhaddevatā
BG	Bhagavadgītā
Bhāga	Bhāgavatapurāṇa
Bhaviṣya	Bhaviṣyapurāṇa
Brahmāṇḍa	Brahmāṇḍapurāṇa
Devī Bhāga	Devībhāgavatapurāṇa
Droṇa p.	Droṇa Parva of the Mahābhārata
GAMI	Studies in the Geography of Ancient and Medieval India : D.C. Sarkar
Garuḍa	Garuḍapurāṇa
GD	Geographical Dictionary of Ancient and Medieval India : N.L. Dey
G. Dh. S.	Gautama-Dharmasūtra
GEAMI	Geographical Encyclopaedia of Ancient and Medieval India
GP	Geography of the Purāṇas : S. M. Ali
H. Dh. S.	History of Dharmaśāstra : Kane
HG	Hiraṇyakeśi-Gṛhyasūtra
HM	Hindu Mythology : Dawson
Harivaṁśa	Harivaṁśapurāṇa
Hyp	Haṭhayogapradīpikā
JIH	Journal of Indian History
JRAS	Journal of the Royal Asiatic Society (Great Britain)
KP	Kālikāpurāṇa
KRS	Koṭirudrasaṁhitā of Śivapurāṇa
KU	Kaṭha Upaniṣad
KŪ	Kūrmapurāṇa

Liṅga	Liṅgapurāṇa
Mārk	Mārkaṇḍeyapurāṇa
Mbh	Mahābhārata
Mbh. Ādi. P.	Mahābhārata Ādiparva
Mahān. U.	Mahānārāyaṇa Upaniṣad
Manu (MS)	Manusmṛti
MP	Matsyapurāṇa
MP. —A Study	Matsyapurāṇa—A Study: V.S. Agrawal
Mark.	Mārkaṇḍeyapurāṇa
Matsya	Matsyapurāṇa
N.	Nirukta
PE	Purāṇic Encyclopaedia
PGS	Pāraskara Gṛhyasūtra
Rāmā	Rāmāyaṇa
RV.	Ṛgveda
SG	Śivagītā
Sk	Skandapurāṇa
SK	Sāṅkhya Kārikā of Īśvarakṛṣṇa
ŚP	Śiva-Purāṇa
ŚRS	Śatarudrīyasaṁhitā of Śiva-Purāṇa
ST	Śivatoṣiṇī, a commentary on the Liṅga-purāṇa
SV	Sāmaveda
Śvet	Śvetāśvatara Upaniṣad
TA	Taittirīya Āraṇyaka
TB	Tattirīya Brāhmaṇa
TS	Tattirīya Saṁhitā
TU	Taittirīya Upaniṣad
Vā, Vāmana	Vāmana purāṇa
Varāha	Varāhapurāṇa
Vāyavīya (VS)	Vāyavīya saṁhitā of Śivapurāṇa
Vāyu	Vāyupurāṇa
Viśva	Viśvakośa
Viṣṇu	Viṣṇupurāṇa
VS	Vājasaneyisaṁhitā of Śuklayajurveda

CONTENTS

Introduction xiv

Liṅgapurāṇa (*in translation*)

Section I

1. Introductory 1
2. Index of Content 4
3. Primary Creation 8
4. Inauguration of Creation 12
5. Creation 16
6. Glory of Śiva 20
7. Esoteric secret of Śiva 22
8. Yogic Zones 27
9. Obstacles and Portents 37
10. Means of Direct Perception 43
11. Sadyojāta 47
12. Glory of Vāmadeva 48
13. Glory of Tatpuruṣa 50
14. Origin of Aghora 51
15. Glory of Aghoreśa 52
16. Glory of Īśāna 55
17. Origin of Liṅga 58
18. Viṣṇu's praise of Śiva 64
19. Enlightenment of Viṣṇu 68
20. Enlightenment of Brahmā 69
21. Eulogy of Śiva 76
22. Creation of Rudras 84
23. Kalpas 86
24. Incarnations of Śiva 90
25. Method of Ācamana and Ablution 100
26. Procedure of Sacred Ablution 103
27. Worship of Liṅga 107
28. Mental worship of Śiva 111
29. Victory over Death 115
30. Story of Sage Śveta 122
31. Hymn to Śiva 125
32. Hymn to Śiva 129

33.	Statement of the sages	130
34.	Praise of the Yogin	133
35.	Defeat of Kṣupa	136
36.	Dialogue between Kṣupa and Dadhīca	139
37.	Grant of boons to Brahmā	145
38.	Creation of Brahmā	148
39.	Specific Dharmas of Four Yugas	150
40.	Extent of four Yugas	156
41.	Nativity of Brahmā	164
42.	Origin of Nandīśvara	169
43.	Coronation of Nandīśvara	172
44.	Coronation of Nandīśvara	176
45.	Description of Nether worlds	179
46.	Dvīpas and their lords	181
47.	Bhārata sub-continent	184
48.	The mountain Meru	187
49.	Ilāvṛta sub-continent	190
50.	Abodes of Devas	195
51.	Continents	197
52.	Geography of the World	200
53.	Geography of the World	205
54.	Movements of Luminaries	209
55.	The Sun's Chariot	215
56.	Description of the Moon	221
57.	Movements of the planets	223
58.	Coronation of the Sun and others	226
59.	The form of Solar rays	227
60.	The Solar Sphere	231
61.	The situation of the planets	233
62.	Situation of Dhruva	238
63.	Origin of Devas and others	241
64.	Grant of boons by Pulastya	248
65.	Thousand names of Śiva	258
66.	The narrative of Yayāti	287
67.	The narrative of Yayāti	293
68.	The race of Jyāmagha	296
69.	Śrīkṛṣṇa, his birth and life	299
70.	Various Creations	306
71.	Statement of Nandikeśvara	333

72. Construction of Rudra's Chariot 347
73. Glory of Worshipping Śiva 364
74. Description of Śiva Liṅgas 366
75. Monism of Śiva 369
76. Installation of Śivā's image 373
77. The Temples of Śiva 378
78. Scrubbing and cleaning the shrine of Śiva 387
79. The mode of worship of Śiva 389
80. The holy Pāśupata rite 392
81. The holy rite for the release of Paśus 397
82. Hymn of purification 402
83. The holy rites of Śiva 411
84. The holy rite of Umā-Maheśvara 416
85. The glory of the five-syllabled Mantra 422
86. The sacrifice of meditation 441
87. Suppression of delusion 455
88. Review of Pāśupata yoga 458
89. Characteristics of good conduct 466
90. The expiatory rites of the ascetics 478
91. Portentous phenomena 480
92. Glory of Śrīśaila 486
93. The narrative of the Asura Andhaka 502
94 Uplifting the Earth 504
95. The Exploits of Nṛsiṁha the Man-lion 507

INTRODUCTION

Purāṇas : Origin and Development

According to the *Viṣṇupurāṇa*[1] the sage Kṛṣṇa Dvaipāyana Vyāsa compiled a *Purāṇasaṁhitā* from the various ancient episodes and imparted it to his disciple Romaharṣaṇa. The latter composed his own *Purāṇasaṁhitā* and among his disciples Kaśyapa, Sāvarṇi and Śāṁśapāyana composed their own. These four were the original *Purāṇasaṁhitās*. The *Vāyupurāṇa* specifies the number of the Purāṇas as ten. This represents the second stage in the development of the Purāṇas. The traditional number eighteen is the final stage.

The traditional list as given by several Purāṇas comprises the following : (1) Brahma, (2) Padma, (3) Viṣṇu, (4) Vāyu, (5) Bhāgavata, (6) Nāradīya, (7) Mārkaṇḍeya, (8) Agni, (9) Bhaviṣya, (10) Brahmavaivarta, (11) Liṅga, (12) Varāha, (13) Skanda, (14) Vāmana, (15) Kūrma, (16) Matsya, (17) Garuḍa, (18) Brahmāṇḍa.

The Purāṇic scholars are agreed upon the authenticity of the seventeen Purāṇas but in regard to the eighteenth there is a difference of opinion. Majority of the Purāṇas include *Śivapurāṇa* in the list while a few others substitute Vāyu for Śiva.[2]

The Liṅgapurāṇa—Contents

The *Liṅgapurāṇa* is divided into two sections comprising respectively 108 and 55 chapters.

Section I describes the evolution of Liṅga, a phallic form of Śiva. It records traditions about the rise of Liṅga cult, modes of worshipping Liṅga, principles of its ritual, efficacy of its worship illustrated by myths, legends and anecdotes. It provides a graphic account of the geography of the earth with seven continents, their flora and fauna, their people, mountains, oceans

1. *Viṣṇu* III. 6.

2. **For detail, see introduction to *Śivapurāṇa* Part I, English Translation P. xiii.**

and rivers. It describes the size of the earth, stars and planets, their positions and movements in the heavens. It recounts the genealogies of some famous monarchs of the solar and lunar dynasties. It gives an account of prominent Asuras, their expeditions and destruction.

Section II contains legends on the glorification of Liṅga, a detailed account of the form, concept and attributes of Liṅga and the vratas, gifts and mantras related to his worship. Finally, it explains in detail the procedure of the Pāśupata Yoga as the means of attaining the ultimate goal viz., the absorption of the personal soul into the supreme soul—Lord Śiva.

The Title—Liṅgapurāṇa

The *Liṅgapurāṇa* is a Śaiva Purāṇa. It derives its name from the fact that it reveals the supreme lord Śiva in his *niṣkala* (attributeless) and *sakala* (qualified) forms, recounts his emblems, qualities, exploits and incarnations, narrates legends on the origin and importance of Liṅga—his phallic idol, dwells upon the merit of installing and consecrating it, describes the ritual and philosophical principles of the Liṅga cult and embodies sermons and dissertations on the glory of Liṅga image.

The author of the purāṇa

The authorship of the Purāṇas is attributed to the sage Kṛṣṇa Dvaipāyana but *Bhaviṣya*[3] speaks of separate authorship for different Purāṇas. According to this authority the *Liṅga* was composed by the sage Taṇḍi. But this statement of *Bhaviṣya* is not supported by the internal evidence, although the Purāṇa suggests the theory of separate authorship. For instance, when *Bhaviṣya* states that *Viṣṇu* was composed by Parāśara, we find that *Liṅga* had already stated this fact.[4] Besides, this voluminous set of Purāṇas beset with differing strata of society of different times cannot be ascribed to a single author.

Authenticity of the text

The extant *Liṅgapurāṇa* is not the same as the original which was recited by Śiva in the Agnikalpa to Brahmā and was, later

3. *Bhaviṣya*. III. 28. 10-15.
4. *Liṅga*. I. 64. 120-121.

on, divided by Vyāsa into two parts. For the Agnikalpa text, according to the Nāradīya,[5] contained 11,000 verses—a fact acknowledged by the author of the extant *Liṅgapurāṇa*—while actually the present Veṅkaṭeśvara edition has only 9, 185 verses. Furthermore, contrary to the statement of the Nāradīya, the present text deals with the matters of the Īśānakalpa[6] and not with those of the Agnikalpa. It can, therefore, be presumed that there was an old *Liṅgapurāṇa* text based upon the Agnikalpa on which the Nāradīya description is based.

The above statement is supported by the internal evidence. *Liṅga* (II. 55. 36-37) states that it is divided into two sections. Section I contains one hundred and eight chapters while Section II is comprised of fortysix. But as a matter of fact, the extant second section has fiftyfive chapters. The author of Śivatoṣiṇī,[7] a commentary on this Purāṇa, dissolves the compound ṣaṭ-catvāriṁśat as ṣaṭ ca nava ca catvāriṁśac ca (*madhyamapada-lopi-karmadhāraya*) and by this grammatical device arrives at the required number 55. But would it not be a forced and far-fetched interpretation? Conversely, would it not be rational to suppose that the original text of this section contained fortysix chapters to which nine chapters were added later on ?

Date of Composition

The *Liṅgapurāṇa* was abridged by Kṛṣṇa Dvaipāyana Vyāsa in the beginning of Dvāpara age.[8] Originally it was composed by Brahmā with the material derived from Īśāna kalpa.[9] The abridgement was a natural course, for the old contents ceased to appeal to the later generations. At the same, fresh material was available which the new compilers inserted in the old corpus. The process continued till the beginning of the fifth century A.D. when the bulk of this Purāṇa was settled to its present form.

5. *Nāradīya*. I 102. 1-4.
6. *Liṅga*. I. 2. 1.
7. His name was Gaṇeśa Nātu. He was the son of Ballāla and Yaśodā and the disciple of Nīlakaṇṭha. He lived in 1760 (or 1769) Śaka era, at Poona. Vide the introductory verses of *ST*.
8. *Liṅga* 1.2.3.
9. *Ibid.*, 1.2.1.

There are references in the *Liṅgapurāṇa* in support of this argument. Chapter 40 refers to king Pramati in the line of king Candramas who organized extensive military expeditions against the Mlecchas. In this inset of twentythree verses[10] we find a powerful and historically true description of the achievements of Candragupta Vikramāditya II. The description tallies with a similar account in the *Matsyapurāṇa* and seems to have been given by a person who was an eye-witness or who had heard from a direct source. Moreover, in II. 3.36 there is a reference to the Mlecchas having seized the idol of Viṣṇu.[11] We learn from history that Mlecchas were wild ferocious tribes, such as Huns, whose violent activities caused vast devastations and struck terror in the social life of the country. Like the cattle-lifting Paṇis of the Ṛgvedic age, these Mlecchas were the breakers or stealers of idols. The Purāṇa is also aware of the foreign tribes Kirātas (Burmese) in the east and Mlecchas in the west[12] As the destroyer of Mlecchas King Pramati of this Purāṇa can only be identical with King Candragupta Vikramāditya who destroyed the Mlecchas during his reign of twenty years by engaging his army drawn mostly from Licchavis—a kṣatra-brahmin tribe.[13] The reign of Candragupta Vikramāditya II (380-412 A.D.) is the lowest limit by which the bulk of this Purāṇa had assumed its present shape.

General Characteristics of the Liṅgapurāṇa

1. *Creation*

The supreme lord Śiva is represented by the half-male and half-female form. At the advent of Creation, the male form enters into the womb of the female form and lays the golden seed therein. The seed is of the nature of fire, the creative force and is permeated by a creative potency. According to the *Liṅgapurāṇa*[14] this creative energy is personified as Brahmā ; the recipient of the seed, the foetus, is named Viṣṇu while the sower

10. *Liṅga* I. 40. 50-72.
11. *Ibid.*, pratimāṁ ca hareś caiva mlecchā hṛtvā yayuḥ punaḥ II. 3. 36.
12. *Ibid.*, I. 52. 29; *Matsya* 50. 75-76; Mark. 57. 8.
13. Cf. *Liṅga* I. 40. 53.
14. *Liṅga* I. 20. 73 ff.

of the seed is lord Śiva himself. Thus, the half-man and half-woman form of the lord is both the efficient and the material cause of the universe.

The seed is sentient. When it enters into the womb it activates and gives impetus to the insentient Prakṛti. The Cosmic Egg is born, out of which is evolved the entire universe. In fact, both the insentient Prakṛti and the sentient principle belong to lord Śiva himself who out of sheer will and sportively too creates, dissolves and then re-creates and re-dissolves the universe. In this eternal process everything created in the feminine form is Prakṛti and everything masculine is Puruṣa. The half-man and half-woman body (ardhanārīśvara) of Śiva is responsible for the origin of creation by copulation. As stated above, the creative force is of the nature of agni (fire) and its fortynine forms[15] constitute the different forms of the supreme lord who in his qualified (*sakala*) state is characterized by three functions viz. creation, sustenance and dissolution.

According to the Purāṇic account of creation, in the beginning the insentient Prakṛti in the form of the Cosmic Egg remained in the Cosmic waters for thousands of years, until it was activated by the sentient principle which entering divided it into two halves. One of the two became the celestial and the other the terrestrial sphere both constituting the fourteen worlds.

The constituents of Prakṛti, the material cause of the universe, are twentythree in number. They are : (1) intellect, (2) ego, (3-7) five subtle elements, (8-12) five senses of action, (13-17) five senses of knowledge, (18-22) five gross elements and (23) the mind. The unevolved Prakṛti is called (24) Pradhāna. This set of twentyfour principles is insentient and to this is added a threefold set of sentient beings viz. (25) Jīva (the individual soul), (26) Puruṣa (the cosmic soul) and (27) the Supreme soul, Śiva. In this formulation, Pradhāna, the twentyfourth category, is the source of twentythree principles (mentioned above); Jīva, the twenyfifth, is the knower of Pradhāna; Puruṣa, the twentysixth, has the perception of the two lower categories viz. Jīva and Pradhāna but he cannot

15. *Liṅga* I. 6. 4; 1.7.105.

bestow grace.[16] Lord Maheśvara, the twentyseventh,[17] alone is omnipotent and is capable of bestowing grace. In this context, Prakṛti is apratibuddha, Jīva is buddhimān, Puruṣa is buddha and Maheśvara is prabuddha. The twentysix principles emanate from the saptaviṁśaka (the twentyseventh) principle viz, lord Maheśvara.

The twenty-sixth principle Puruṣa is represented as passive and a spectator of the working of Prakṛti. He is distinguished from the personal soul, Jīva, as the latter is the enjoyer of the fruits of the world-tree. Lord Maheśvara is beyond Pradhāna and Puruṣa. In his one half, i.e. the masculine form, he is devoid of qualities (*niṣkala*) but his other half (*sakala*) is characterized by the three attributes : sattva, rajas and tamas which are personified as Brahmā, Viṣṇu and Rudra.

The entire phenomenon of creation is symbolised by the phallic image[18] (*liṅga*) of lord Śiva.

According to the *Liṅgapurāṇa*[19] Pradhāna, the primary unevolved matter, the cause of the universe is Liṅga itself. At the root of Liṅga the creator Brahmā is stationed; Viṣṇu the sustainer of the world is stationed in the middle; Rudra the annihilator is stationed above; lord Śiva is its substratum. He permeates and imparts impetus to Liṅga and effects the work of creation in this way.

The Purāṇic cosmology divides creation into nine classes arranged in three groups : (1) Primary, (2) Secondary and Primary-Secondary as follows :

I Primary	II Secondary	II Primary-Secondary
1. Intellect and Ego	4. Insentient objects	9. Mind-born sons of Brahmā
2. Subtle elements	5. Animals	
3. Gross elements	6. Divine beings	
	7. Human beings	
	8. Sentient Feeling	

16. Saḍviṁśakam anīśvaram I. 17. 109.

17. yaḥ saptaviṁśako nityaḥ parāt parataraḥ prabhuḥ I. 71.51.
tasmād abhedabuddhyaiva saptaviṁśatprabhedataḥ I. 75. 34.

18. A Liṅga in the form of a column, arising out of a yoni (vaginal passage) is set up in temples dedicated to Śiva. Formerly 12 principal Liṅgas existed, of which the best known are Somanātha in Gujarat, Mahākāla at Ujjayinī and Viśveśvara at Vārāṇasī.

19. *Liṅga*. I. 74. 19-20.

According to the *Liṅgapurāṇa* this set of threefold creation—Primary, Secondary and Primary-Secondary—was unable to create. The mind-born sons of Brahmā remained celibate. Then out of his body Brahmā produced eleven sons; still the creation made no progress. Then Brahmā divided himself into two forms—one half a woman and the other half a man. In that half form of a woman he created a couple—Manu and Śatarūpā who obeyed the creator and began the work of creation.

2. *Dissolution and Re-creation* (*Pratisarga*)

The creation of the universe is not a permanent feature, for all creations end in dissolutions which in turn give place to re-creation. Thus, there are several dissolutions—minor and major.

As the Purāṇas relate, a creation lasts for a day of Brahmā equal to a kalpa, a period of four hundred thirtytwo million years of mortals. A kalpa consists of fourteen Manvantaras. Thus, a day of Brahmā, equal to a kalpa contains fourteen dissolutions. But these are partial dissolutions. At the end of fourteen manvantaras, equal to a day of Brahmā that lasts for a kalpa, there occurs a great dissolution. There is also a complete dissolution when Brahmā has completed his life-time. At the advent of this dissolution (Prākṛta pralaya), the mobile and immobile beings, Devas, Asuras, serpents, Rākṣasas etc. are all destroyed. Everything dissolves itself into Prakṛti which remains hidden in the supreme lord Śiva. The lord alone survives; there is no second being anywhere.[20]

At the advent of re-creation after dissolution, Lord Śiva is present in two forms: Prakṛti and Ātman. Lord Viṣṇu adopts the body of Prakṛti and lies on the yogic couch in the midst of waters. Then Brahmā is born of his umbilical lotus. Brahmā asks Śiva to grant him power to re-create.[21]

3. *The ages of Manus* (*Manvantara-s*)

The creation is divided into time-units—kalpas, manvantaras, yugas, saṁvatsaras and other relatively bigger and smaller units. When creation ceases to exist these time-units disappear as a matter of course.

20. *Ibid.*, I. 85. 7-8.
21. *Ibid.*, I. 85. 10-11ff.

The description of the time-unit, manvantara, is one of the many characteristics of a Mahāpurāṇa. A manvantara comprises about seventyone caturyugas equal to 1200 years of the gods or 1/14th day of Brahmā. The fourteen manvantaras make up one whole day of Brahmā, equal to a kalpa. After each manvantara there is a minor dissolution. Thus, a day of Brahmā has fourteen dissolutions and re-creations. The scheme of fourteen dissolutions repeats itself from one age of Manu to another.

The purāṇas mention fourteen manvantaras. These derive their names from fourteen successive progenitors and sovereigns of the earth. The present Purāṇa mentions fourteen Manus by name. They are (i) Svāyambhuva, (ii) Svārociṣa, (iii) Uttama, (iv) Tāmasa, (v) Raivata, (vi) Cākṣuṣa, (vii) Vaivasvata, (vii) Sāvarṇi, (ix) Dharma, (x) Sāvarṇika, (xi) Piśaṅga, (xii) Apiśaṅgābha, (xiii) Śabala, (xiv) Varṇaka. On their nomenclature the Purāṇas are not unanimous.

4-5. *Genealogy and history of Royal Houses* (*Vaṁśa and Vaṁśānucarita*)

Genealogy and history of kings and illustrious personages play an important role in the Mahāpurāṇas. The sūtas were the custodians of genealogical records which they learnt by rote and which they recited at sessional sacrifices. But in the course of oral transmission from one generation to another some variations entered in these records. Moreover, there were traditional variations too, for different versions existed in different families of sūtas. When the records were incorporated in the Purāṇas, the interpolations and the traditional variations also settled therein. This explains the difference that exists in the genealogical records of the Purāṇic literature.[22]

The *Liṅgapurāṇa* is not interested in recording the genealogies of ancient royal houses and illustrious personages. Still it

22. For instance, (1) according to *Liṅga* Āgnīdhra was the eldest son of Priyavrata. But according to a Vāyu version he was the son of Priyavrata's daughter. (ii) *Liṅga* ascribes the origin of the name Bhārata to king Bharata, the eldest of the 100 sons of Ṛṣabha and grandson of Nābhi (cf. *Vāyu* 33, 51-52; *Mārkaṇḍeya* 53. 39-40; *Bhāgavata* 11. 2. 15-17; *Sk.* 1.11.37. 55-57). But according to *Matsya* 114. 5-6, Bharata is the name of Manu himself who creates and supports the people here.

contains, in five chapters (I. 65-69), lists of the solar and lunar dynasties of Ayodhyā and Prayāga. Chapters 65-66 deal with the solar dynasty of Ayodhyā from Vaivasvata Manu to Satyavrata, from Satyavrata to Sagara and from Sagara to Bṛhadbala. Chapters 67-69 recount the lunar dynasty of Prayāga from Aila Purūravas to Yayāti, from Yayāti to Jyāmagha and from Jyāmagha to Śrīkṛṣṇa. As for the history of reigning monarchs (*vaṁśānucarita*) it is interested mainly in the records of the solar and lunar dynasties. It recounts the deeds of some monarchs of these houses. Amongst these Sagara, Yayāti, Jyāmagha and Śrī Kṛṣṇa figure prominently, while Dhundhumāra, Babhru, Satrājit, Akrūra and others occupy a secondary place.

Monism of Śiva and the means of the soul's release

The above analysis demonstrates that the *Liṅgapurāṇa* possesses the conventional character of a Mahāpurāṇa. But its real greatness lies in expounding the monistic background of Śaiva philosophy especially in the context of the Liṅga cult.

The Liṅga is described as twofold: gross and subtle. The subtle liṅga is the fourth state of the soul and beyond in which the other three states merge, losing their identity. The gross Liṅga, made of clay, wood, stone, crystal etc. is meant just to create a feeling of devotion in the gross-minded people. In fact lord Śiva, like the ether, is an indivisible centre whose division into *sakala* and *niṣkala* forms as of the ether into ghaṭākāśa and maṭhākāśa is illusory.[23] Even the state of being one (*ekatva*) is not present there as a distinct attribute. Similarly, in relation to the tattvas, he is placed in the twentyseventh category; but the tattvas too emanate from him; they are the products of his power of projection (Prakṛti or Māyā).[24] He is related to them as the gold is related to the ornaments or the ocean to the waves. Their group of twentyfour forms a noose which binds the individual and cosmic souls, categorized as the twentyfifth and twentysixth principles.

A major portion of this Purāṇa is concerned with the suppression of illusion through the attainment of knowledge by

23. *Liṅga* I. 75 ff.
24. *Ibid.*, I. 16. 32-34; II. 20.52

means of Pāśupata yoga, accompanied by purificatory and expiatory rites and acts of physical and mental worship with the Tantra, Mantra and Yantra appliances. A particular emphasis is laid upon selfpurification. Along with the purification of the three *guṇas*, viz. *sattva*, *rajas* and *tamas*, the Purāṇa enjoins the purification of the fivefold set of tattvas[25] viz. *Yauvana* (five gross elements), *Pada* (five subtle elements), *Varṇa* (five organs of knowledge), *Mātrā* (five organs of action) and *Kālādhvara* (the fourfold group consisting of intellect, ego, consciousness and mind). These practices, accompanied by mental concentration, are said to help the aspirant achieve spiritual enlightenment and attain release from the entanglement of the senses and his absorption into the supreme soul.

25. *Ibid.*, II. 20. 44-47

CHAPTER ONE

Introductory

1. Obeisance to the Supreme Soul, Rudra, Viṣṇu and Brahmā,[1] the lord of Pradhāna and Puruṣa[2] and the cause of creation, sustenance and dissolution.

2-4. The sage Nārada[3] went to Naimiṣa[4] after worshipping Śiva, in all the holy centres,[5] viz. Śaileśa, Saṅgameśvara, Hiraṇyagarbha, Svarlīna, Avimukta, Mahālaya, Raudra, Goprekṣaka, the excellent Pāśupata, Vighneśvara, Kedāra, Gomāyukeśvara, Hiraṇyagarbha, Candreśa, Īśānya, Triviṣṭapa and Śukreśvara.

5. On seeing Nārada, the residents of Naimiṣa were delighted in their minds. After honouring him they offered him a befitting seat.

1. The Śaiva Purāṇas trace the origin of Brahmā, Viṣṇu and Rudra to the Supreme Spirit (Maheśvara) and assign the functions of creation existence and dissolution of the universe to each respectively. In fact, the three gods represent the three attributes—sattva, rajas and tamas which together form Pradhāna—the original source of the universe. Thus, the trinitarian pattern of the Cosmos is a single whole at its base. Cf. *Devī Bhāga*. 1.8. 2-4.

2. Pradhāna—the primary or unevolved matter, the original source of the material world.

Puruṣa—the twenty-sixth principle represented as passive and a spectator of the working of Prakṛti—the creative force. He is distinguished from the personal soul (jīva) as the latter is the enjoyer of the fruits of the World-Tree. Cf. I. 28.7; II. 17. 26-27.

3. Nārada—the mind-born son of Brahmā and a divine sage who acts as a messenger between gods and men.

4. Naimiṣa or Naimiśa, mod. Nimsar. It is situated in the Sītāpur district in the Uttara Pradeśa, on the left bank of the Gomatī river. The place is so called because the rim (nimi) of the revolving wheel of virtue was shattered here and virtue had to make a permanent abode in this region (*Vāyu* 2.7). Or the place is so called because here an army of asuras was destroyed by the sage Gauramukha in a twinkling of eye. (Cf. *Varāha* quoted in *ST*.) On the authority of the *Matsya Purāṇa*, A Borooah (*Ancient Geography of India*) places it about the confluence of the Gomatī and the Ganges. It was sacred in the Kṛta age, as Puṣkara in the Tretā, Kurukṣetra in the Dvāpara, the Ganges in the Kali age.

5. For detail about the holy centres, see part I. Ch. 92.

6-17. He too being pleased accepted the seat offered by the excellent sages. Seating himself comfortably on the excellent seat and duly worshipped by the sages he discussed with them the holy narrative of the Liṅgas, the narrative consisting of wonderful anecdotes. At the very same time, the intelligent Sūta who was well-versed in the Purāṇas came to Naimiṣa for offering homage to the sages. The residents of Naimiṣa greeted him duly with holy songs and adorations, (since) he was the disciple of Kṛṣṇa Dvaipāyana.[6] On seeing the truly trustworthy and scholarly Sūta Romaharṣana[7] there arose in them the desire to hear the Purāṇa. They, thereafter, asked him about the meritorious Purāṇa that contained the glory and greatness of the Liṅgas.

The residents of Naimiṣa said :

"O Sūta, of great intellect, after adoring the sage Kṛṣṇa Dvaipāyana for the knowledge of the Purāṇas you have obtained the Purāṇic lore from him. Hence, O Sūta, the best among the Paurāṇikas, we desire to hear from you that Purāṇic lore illustrating the glory of the Liṅgas. Nārada, the glorious son of Brahmā, after completing his pilgrimage to the holy centres of the supreme lord Rudra and worshipping the Liṅgas therein, has arrived here. You are a devotee of lord Rudra. So also are we and Nārada. It behoves you to recount the meritorious Purāṇa containing the glory and greatness of the Liṅgas[8] in the presence of this sage. Since, everything (relating to Dharma) has been successfully achieved by you, it should all be well known to you."

Thus told, Sūta, the most gifted among the Paurāṇikas was delighted in his mind. He, the meritorious one, made obeisance

6. Kṛṣṇa Dvaipāyana Vyāsa was the son of Parāśara by Satyavatī who later on married king Śantanu. He composed the Mahābhārata and the Purāṇas and arranged the Vedas into four compendiums (*Vāyu* 1.60. 11ff)

7. Romaharṣaṇa or Lomaharṣaṇa was one of the five disciples of Vyāsa (*Vāyu*. 1.60. 13; *ŚP. Vidyeśvara-Saṁhitā*, 4.7). He was assigned the duty of preserving Purāṇic tradition while the other four Paila, Vaiśampāyana, Jaimini and Sumanta were entrusted with the task of preserving the Vedas. He is called Sūta but he is a brahmin. He should not be confused with the Sūta of mixed caste who was the offspring of a kṣatriya father and brahmin woman as described in Manu (*Manusmṛti* X. 11.17)

8. Repeated in verse 10 of this Chapter.

first to Nārada, the son of Brahmā and then to the ascetics of Naimiṣa and began narrating the Purāṇa.

Sūta said :—

18. After bowing to Śiva, Brahmā and Viṣṇu, I remember the leading sage Vyāsa in order to recount the Liṅga Purāṇa.

19-24. I bow down to the supreme lord whose body is Śabda-Brahman, who is the revealer of the Śabda-Brahman, whose limbs are the letters whose characteristics are unmanifest, but who menifests himself in diverse ways, who is constituted by the letters a, u, m, who is gross as well as subtle, who is greater than the greatest, who has the form of *Om*, whose face is the Ṛgveda, tongue the Sāmaveda, throat the Yajurveda, and heart the Atharvaveda, who is the lord beyond Pradhāna and Puruṣa, who is devoid of birth and death and who is called Kālarudra when he assumes tamoguṇa and Brahmā when he assumes rajoguṇa and the all-pervading Viṣṇu when he assumes sattvaguṇa, who is Maheśvara when devoid of all the guṇas[9], who manifests first in seven[10] forms by enveloping the body of Pradhāna, then in sixteen[11] forms, and finally in twentysix[12] forms, who is the source of origin of Brahmā, and who assumes the form of the Liṅga merely for the sport of creation, sustenance and annihilation (of the universe). After bowing down faithfully to that supreme lord, I begin recounting the auspicious narrative of the Liṅgapurāṇa.

9. Repeated in I.6.30.

10. saptadhā—a group of seven tattvas consisting of intellect (buddhi), ego (ahaṁkāra) and five subtle elements (tanmātras).

11. ṣoḍaśadhā—five senses of action (Karmendriyas), five senses of knowledge (jñānendriyas), five gross elements (mahābhūtas) and mind.

12. To the twentythree categories (supra Nos. 10, 11) are added Pradhāna (twentyfourth), Jīva (twentyfifth) and Puruṣa (twentysixth). To this group of twentysix is added another (the twentyseventh) namely the supreme lord (maheśvara).

CHAPTER TWO

Index of Content

Sūta said :—

1-3. Formerly the excellent Liṅgapurāṇa was composed by Brahmā, the great soul. It was based on the events that happened in the Īśāna kalpa, and originally it contained a crore of verses among a hundred crore that comprised all the Purāṇas. The Purāṇas were abridged into four hundred thousand verses by Vyāsas in the different manvantaras. Later in the beginning of Dvāpara, they were classified into eighteen parts, beginning with Brahmāṇda among which this Liṅgapurāṇa ranks as the eleventh. Thus I have heard from Vyāsa.

4. O brahmins, the number of verses in this Purāṇa is eleven thousand. I shall succinctly narrate it now, as it has not been heard by me in detail.

5. When the Purāṇas were abridged into four hundred thousand verses by Kṛṣṇa Dvaipāyana, the Liṅga was abridged in eleven thousand verses.

6. At the outset the creation of Pradhāna is mentioned, then the primary and secondary creation and then the origin of the cosmic egg, enveloped by eight sheaths.[13]

7. Then, the evolution of Brahmā through the cosmic egg, by the force of rajoguṇa, the evolution of Viṣṇu and Rudra, and Viṣṇu's lying down in the waters.

8. The creation of the Prajāpatis; the uplifting of the earth, the duration of Brahmā's day and night, the reckoning of his whole span of life.

9-10. The savana of Brahmā; his yuga and kalpa; the divine and human years; the years of sages, Dhruva and Pitṛs; the nativity of Pitṛs; the duties of the people in their respective stages of life; the decrease of population in the Universe; the manifestation of the creative energy.

11. The male and female nature of energy; the creation of Brahmā; the birth of twins; the eight names of Rudra in the course of weeping.

13. But in I. 3.33 the Purāṇa refers to the seven sheaths of the Cosmic Egg.

12. The dispute between Brahmā and Viṣṇu ; the manifestation of the Liṅga once again; the penance of Śilāda; the vision of Indra, the slayer of Vṛtra.

13-14. His request for a son not born through a womb ; the impossibility of getting such a son, the dialogue between Śilāda and Indra; the birth of Brahmā from a lotus ; the manifestation of Bhava in the Kali age; the preceptor and the disciple ; the incarnations of Vyāsa ; the kalpas and the manvantaras.

15-18. The nature of the kalpas and their different names ; Viṣṇu in the form of Varāha in the Vārāha kalpa—meghavāhana; the grandeur and majesty of Rudra ; the manifestation once again of Liṅga in the midst of sages ; the propitiation of Liṅga; the injunctions regarding ablution ; the nature of purity ; the glory of Vārāṇasī and of the holy centres ; the shrines of Rudra and Viṣṇu on the earth as well as in the firmament.

19. Tha fall of Dakṣa on to the earth in the Svārociṣa manvantara; the curse on Dakṣa and his release from the curse.

20. The description of Kailāsa ; the yoga pertaining to Paśupati (Śiva) ; the extent of the four yugas ; the detail of the duties assigned to each yuga.

21-22. The magnitude of the interval between the yugas ; the activities of Rudra during these intervals ; his residence in the cremation ground ; the origin of the digit of the moon on his forehead ; his marriage ; birth of his sons ; the fear of the people in anticipation of destruction due to excessive indulgence in sexual intercourse.

23-24. The curse pronounced by Satī on the Devas and on Viṣṇu who was, later on, absolved by Rudra ; Rudra's discharge of semen; the birth of Kārttikeya; the merit of performing ablution to the Liṅgas during the eclipse ; the dispute between Kṣupa and Dadhīca as also between Dadhīca and Viṣṇu.

25-27. The incarnation of the trident-bearing lord Nandi ; the narrative of the chaste lady ; the discussion about the individual soul and avidyā or ignorance ; the nature of worldly activities and of perfect knowledge ; the characteristics of those entitled to liberation ; the birth of Vasiṣṭha's sons; the description of the families of the great sages in the spiritual lineage of

Vasiṣṭha ; the devouring of Śakti by a demon-king due to the wickedness of Viśvāmitra ; the capture of the divine cow Surabhi.

28-29. Vasiṣṭha's grief over the loss of his son ; lamentations of Arundhatī; the course of their daughter-in-law ; the words of the child in the womb ; the birth of Parāśara, Vyāsa and Śuka ; the destruction of the Rākṣasas by Śakti's son Parāśara.

30-31. The truth about the deities ; the perfect knowledge as the grace of the lord ; the composition of the Purāṇas at the behest of the preceptor Pulastya ; the magnitude of the worlds ; the movement of the planets and luminaries ; rules of procedure about Śrāddha for living ones ; those who deserve Śrāddhas ; the description of Śrāddha.

32. Rules of procedure about Nāndīśrāddha ; the method of studying the Vedas ; the efficacy of the five yajñas and the rules of their performance.

33. The conduct and behaviour of women during their menstrual period; the birth of excellent sons due to that conduct; the rules about sexual intercourse in regard to persons of different castes in due order.

34. The injunctions regarding what should and what should not be eaten in respect of the people of all castes ; the expiatory rites for the general as well as for the particular sins severally and in detail.

35. The form and features of the hells ; crime and punishment; signs of men destined to be heavenly or hellish in later births.

36. Kinds of charitable gifts ; the city of the King of the Dead ; ritualistic detail of the five-syllabled mantra ; the greatness of Rudra.

37. The fight between Vṛtra and Indra ; the suppression of Vṛtra in his universal form; the dialogue between Śveta and Mṛtyu; the destruction of Kāla on behalf of Śveta.

38-41. The arrival of Śiva in the forest of cider trees; the narrative of Sudarśana; the characteristics of Krama-sannyāsa; the statement of Brahmā that Rudra could be propitiated by devotion and faith; the incident of Brahmā seized by Madhu and Kaiṭabha; then in order to impart the highest perfect knowledge to Brahmā, the story of Viṣṇu assuming the form of a fish; in all conditions the incarnation of Viṣṇu just as a matter of sport; the birth of Śrīkṛṣṇa's son Pradyumna by the grace of Rudra; Viṣṇu as a tortoise for holding the churning rod.

42. The birth of Saṁkarṣaṇa; the rebirth of Caṇḍikā; the birth of Kṛṣṇa among the Yadus.

43. The wickedness of Kaṁsa, the uncle of Kṛṣṇa; Kṛṣṇa's sporting activity during infancy; his worship of Śiva for obtaining sons.

44. The origin of water from the skull of Śiva in the form of Viṣṇu; Viṣṇu's propitiation of Rudra for lessening the burden of the earth.

45. The milking of the earth, at the outset, by Pṛthu the son of Vena; the curse of Bhṛgu incurred by Viṣṇu in the course of conflict between Devas and Asuras.

46-47. In his incarnation as Kṛṣṇa his residence in Dvārakā; the curse of Durvāsas as conducive to his welfare; the curse on Yādavas for their destruction; the growth of reeds and javelins.

48. The annihilation of the Yādavas in mutual quarrel by using reeds and Kṛṣṇa annihilating his tribe sportively through that very reed.

49. Kṛṣṇa's voluntary departure from this world; the perfect knowledge of Brahman and salvation in detail.

50-51. The subjugation of Andhaka, Agni and Dakṣa who had assumed the forms of Indra, elephant and the deer; the description of the primordial Brahman; subjugation of Kāma by Śiva, and of the enemies of devas, of the daitya Halāhala in particular; the destruction of Jālandhara and the origin of Sudarśana discus.

52-53. The acquisition of that excellent weapon by Viṣṇu; Rudra's activities; thousands of his adventures; the activities and the powers of Viṣṇu, Brahmā and Indra; the description of the world of Śiva.

54-56. Rudra's world on the earth; Hāṭakeśvara in the nether worlds; the nature of austerities; the power of brahmins; Liṅga's excellence over all other images of deities—all these are recorded in their proper order and in detail[14] in this Purāṇa. He who after knowing the gist recites it, is liberated from sins. He goes to the world of Brahmā.

CHAPTER THREE

Primary Creation

Sūta said :

1. The non-characterized is the root of the characterized. The manifest Prakṛti is the characterized, while Śiva is the non-characterized, but the characterized (Prakṛti) is said to be related to Śiva.

2-4. They call the characterized by the name Pradhāna or Prakṛti. But the non-characterized, devoid of smell, colour, taste, sound, touch and attributes, is Śiva who is stable and everlasting. [On the contrary] the characterized Pradhāna or Prakṛti is endowed with smell, colour, taste, sound and touch; it is the source of origin of the universe; it is elemental both in subtle and gross forms, O excellent brahmins; it is the non-physical body of the worlds; it has originated from the non-characterized, of its own accord.

5. [Formerly] it split itself into seven as well as eight and then into eleven.[15] The non-characterized, thus, becomes characterized through māyā.

14. *ST.* adds another interpretation. 'The order of contents (as stated in this chapter is not observed here (i.e. in this purāṇa) nor are the contents described in detail'. यद्वा अत्र उक्तकथानाम् आनुपूर्व्या अभावात् तथा कथानां प्रायशः संक्षेपात् न आनुपूर्व्येण न विस्तरेण च इत्यन्वयो बोध्यः ।

15. The twentysix principles emanate from the Saptaviṁśaka tattva: यः सप्तविंशको नित्यः पदात्परतरः प्रभुः (1. 71.51). In this formulation, Pradhāna (the twentyfourth), the source of twentythree principles is insentient; Jīva (the twentyfifth) is the knower of Pradhāna; Puruṣa (the twentysixth) has the perception of the two lower categories— Jīva and Pradhāna, but he cannot bestow grace (षड्विंशकमनीश्वरम् 1.17.109). Maheśvara (the

6-9. From them took shape, the trio of the important deities. From one of the three the universe arose; it is protected by another; by one (i.e. the third) it is destroyed.[16] In this manner, the universe is pervaded by Śiva. Thus the three mūrties have been classified as aliṅga, liṅga and liṅgāliṅga. Brahman itself is the universe. The non-characterized lord is the source of the seed. He, the Supreme lord, is both the seed and the womb as well as the seedless. Being seedless he becomes seed, i.e. the cause of the universe. The term Ātman applies to the seed (bīja), womb (yoni) and the unmanifest matter (pradhāna).

10. He who is Rudra, Brahmā and Viṣṇu is called Śiva in the Purāṇas by virtue of his eternally and intrinsically enlightened and pure nature.

11. Prakṛti, when observed by Śiva became Śaivī. O brahmins, formerly it was unmanifest, but being intrinsically endowed with the attributes it became manifest at the beginning of the creation.

12. The entire universe beginning with the unmanifest and ending with the gross elements originated from it. That Śaivī Prakṛti, the creator of the universe is known as ajā (the unborn).

13-14. The individual soul is devotedly attached to that ajā (the unborn Prakṛti) of red, white and black colour—the ajā that is single, though the mother of many. He resorts to her in her manifest form, and having enjoyed eschews her when he becomes unattached. This Prakṛti is the creator of worlds when she is presided over by Puruṣa.

15. At the time of the creation, mahat was evolved, at the behest of Puruṣa, out of Pradhāna consisting of the three guṇas and presided over by Puruṣa.

16. Being urged by the desire to create, the mahat when

twenty-seventh) alone is capable of extending grace to his devotees. In this context, Pradhāna or Prakṛtī is apratibuddha, Jīva is buddhimān, Puruṣa is buddha and Maheśvara is prabuddha.

16. Brahmā, Viṣṇu and Rudra—the personified entities of the three guṇas—rajas, sattva and tamas that constitute Pradhāna or Prakṛti, the material cause of the universe—are responsible for the creation, sustenance and destruction of the universe. The three emanate from the transcendent reality Maheśvara. (Cf. *Devī Bhāga*. 1.8.4; Brahmāṇḍa 1.4.6; Viṣṇu 1.2.66) For detail see V.S. Agrawal : *MP—A Study*, pp. 37-41.

presided over by Puruṣa enters the unchanging, unmanifest Pradhāna and effects the creation of the manifest.

17-18. Out of mahat evolved (1) sāttvika ahaṁkāra characterized by conception and determination, (also) (2) rājasa ahaṁkāra consisting of three guṇas but with rajas as prominent, (also) (3) tāmasa ahaṁkāra with tamas as prominent. The subtle elements evolved out of mahat and became the nucleus for all creation.

19. The subtle element-sound evolved out of ego and from it the unchanging ether. Thereafter the ego, the cause of sound enveloped the ether.

20. O brahmins, the creation of the gross elements from the subtle elements is expounded in this manner. O great sages, the subtle element 'touch' evolved from the ether and the air evolved from that.

21. From the air evolved the subtle element colour and therefrom agni (fire), whence evolved the subtle element taste, whence the waters. From these evolved the subtle element smell and from it the earth.

22-23. O excellent brahmins, the ether enveloped the subtle element touch. The air with the activity of blowing enveloped the subtle element colour. The fire enveloped the subtle element taste. The waters having the nature of taste enveloped the subtle element smell.

24-25. Hence the earth has five qualities; the waters have four; the fire has three; the air has two, the ether has one quality. Thus the creation of the elements originated from the subtle elements through their mutual interaction.

26. The Vaikārika as well as Sāttvika creation takes place simultaneously, yet, here, it is explained as evolved gradually in the manner described above.

27. For the purpose of perceiving sound and the rest there are five organs of sense and five organs of action. Mind (which is also a sense) belongs to both categories. (These eleven senses evolve out of ego.)

28. The constituents of creation beginning with mahat (intellect) and ending with Viśeṣa[17] (earth) generate the cosmic

17. The group of seven beginning with mahat (intellect), and ending with viśeṣa (bhūtas) constitutes the Cosmic Egg which is material, though it derives its potency of consciousness (cetanatā) from Puruṣa.

egg, whence Brahmā arose like a water-bubble.

29. He alone is Rudra and Viṣṇu pervading the universe. These worlds are within that cosmic egg and this universe is within it.

30-33. The cosmic egg is externally enveloped by water ten times its magnitude. The water is externally enveloped by fire ten times its mass. The fire is externally enveloped by air ten times its mass. The air is externally enveloped by the ether ten times its magnitude. The ether is enveloped by ego the cause of sound. The ego is enveloped by intellect and intellect is enveloped by Pradhāna. They say that the coverings of the cosmic egg are seven[18]. There within is Brahmā seated on the lotus. There are crores and crores of such eggs in existence.

34. In all these cosmic eggs there are four-faced Brahmās, Viṣṇus and Rudras. They are all created by Pradhāna after coming into contact with Śiva.

35. The dissolution is also mutual but it begins from the end and goes up to the beginning. The great lord is the sole agent for this creation, sustenance and dissolution.

36. In creation he is endowed with rajas, in sustenance with sattva and with tamas in dissolution. He alone possesses this subtle nature in due order.

37-39. He is the first creator of all beings, their protector and annihilator. So lord Maheśvara is the overlord of Brahmā. He is also known as Śiva, Sadāśiva, Bhava, Viṣṇu and Brahmā since he is all. All these worlds are in this egg, so is the creator Brahmā. Thus the elemental creation of Prakṛti has been described by me. It is presided over by Puruṣa; O brahmins, this auspicious creation with intellect (mahat) at top is primordial.

18. The Seven sheaths of the Cosmic Egg consist of intellect (mahat), ego (ahaṁkāra), and five subtle elements (tanmātras). (*Vāyu.* 4.87. *Kūrma* 1.4.46).

CHAPTER FOUR

Inauguration of Creation

Sūta said :

1-2. The period of the duration of the Prākrita creation is said to be a day of Brahmā. There is a similar period constituting the night. The lord effects creation during day time and dissolution during the night. He has neither a day nor a night (as we understand the terms). The time-duration by day and night is used in a secondary sense.

3-6. During the (so-called) day all the Vikṛtis—the Viśvedevas, the Prajāpatis and the sages stay by. During the night all of them are dissolved. They are produced (again) at the end of the night. A day of His constitutes our kalpa, His night too similarly another kalpa. There are fourteen Manus by the time a thousand sets of four yugas come to a close. O brahmins, the Kṛta yuga consists of four thousand years. Four hundred, three hundred, two hundred and hundred years respectively constitute the period of transition both at the beginning and end of a yuga.[19]

7-9. The aṁśaka, therefore, is one-sixth of the duration of each yuga. The period of duration of Tretā, Dvāpara and Kali is respectively three thousand, two thousand and one thousand years without their aṁśaka parts. That of Kṛta has been mentioned above. O men of holy rites, fifteen winks in the eyes of a man of normal health in normal condition constitute a kāṣṭhā. Thirty such kāṣṭhās make one kalā. Thirty such kalās make one muhūrta.

10-12. The night contains fifteen such muhūrtas and the day another fifteen muhūrtas. A (lunar) month according to human

19. Each yuga is prefixed and suffixed by a sandhyā which specifies the advent and culmination of a yuga. The two sandhyās of a yuga are of equal length though their period of duration differs from yuga to yuga. Thus Kṛtayuga lasts for four thousand divine years and its sandhyās for eight hundred such years; Tretā lasts for three thousand divine years and its sandhyās for six hundred such years; Dvāpara lasts for two thousand and its sandhyās for four hundred; Kali lasts for one thousand and its sandhyās for two hundred such years. The total period of duration for the four yugas is ten thousand divine years and that for their sandhyās is two thousand divine years.

reckoning constitutes the night and day of the pitṛs. Divided further, the dark half constitutes the day and the bright half constitutes their night when they go to sleep. Thirty human months make one month of the Pitṛs. The period of three hundred and sixty months calculated according to human reckoning makes one year of the Pitṛs.

13. A hundred years calculated according to human reckoning make three years of the Pitṛs.

14. Twelve months according to human calculation make one year (of the mortals); twelve months of the manes (according to their own calculation) constitute their one year.

15. According to Liṅgapurāṇa one human year constitutes the period of day and night for the manes. Their days, nights and years and their further divisions are as follows:

16. The period of Uttarāyaṇa (northern transit of the sun) is the day for the manes; the period of Dakṣiṇāyana (southern transit of the sun) constitutes their night. These days and nights are calculated in accordance with the reckoning of the devas.

17-23. Thirty human years constitute a divine month. O brahmins, a hundred human years constitute three divine months and ten days. Three hundred and sixty human years constitute a divine year. Three thousand and thirty human years constitute a year of the seven sages. Nine thousand and ninety years, according to human calculation make a year of Dhruva. Thirty six thousand human years make a century of divine years. The people who know arithmetic say that the three hundred and sixty thousand human years constitute the period of a thousand divine years.

24-35. The duration of a yuga is calculated according to the divine reckoning. The first yuga is named Kṛta; thereafter comes Tretā and then Dvāpara and Kali. O men of holy rites, these are the (names of the four) yugas. Henceforth the number of years of each yuga which have been mentioned earlier in divine reckoning are now being counted according to human reckoning. The Kṛta consists of one million four hundred and forty thousand human years; Tretā of one million eight hundred thousand years; Dvāpara of seven hundred twenty thousand years and Kali of three hundred and sixty thousand human years. Thus the duration of the four yugas, without the period of junction and transition totals to three million six hundred thousand human years. If Sandhyā periods are included, the set of four ages will consist of four million three hundred and twenty thousand years. A little over seventy one sets of four yugas—Kṛta, Tretā, Dvāpara and Kali—constitute a manvantara.[20] The number of human years in a manvantara are thirty crores six million and seven hundred and twenty thousand, O excellent brahmins. The period of a manvantara, according to this Purāṇa, is not more than this.

36. The number of years in one set of four yugas have been mentioned earlier. O excellent brahmins, a thousand such sets of four yugas constitute a kalpa (of Brahmā).

37. During Brahmā's night the creatures perish; at the end of the night they are created again. There are twenty-eight crores of gods who move in aerial chariots.

38. During the manvantaras and the intermediary periods their number increased to three hundred and ninety two crores.

39-40. O brahmins, during the last kalpa their number came to seventy-eight thousand. In all kalpas this is the position in brief. When the dissolution is imminent people abandon the persons surviving the last day of the kalpa and go to Janaloka from the world Mahar.

41-42. The number of years in half a kalpa by divine calculation is two thousand eight hundred and sixty two crores and seven millions. The kalpa too shall be similarly calculated. A thousand such kalpas make a year of Brahmā.

43. Eight thousand years of Brahmā make his yuga. A thousand yugas of Brahmā constitute a savana.

44. Nine thousand such savanas constitute a day of Rudra.

45-49. O great sages, the following are the names of some kalpas of Brahmā, viz—bhavodbhava, tapas, bhavya, rambha,

20. A manvantara comprises about seventyone mahāyugas which are equal to 12,000 years of the gods. The Purāṇas mention fourteen manvantaras. These derive their names from fourteen successive mythical progenitors and sovereigns of the earth.

kratu, ṛtu, vahni, havyavāha, sāvitra, śuddha, majjālīya, madhyama, vairāja, niṣāda, mukhya, meghavāhana, pañcama, citraka, ākṛti, jñāna, manas, sudarśa, bṛṁha, śvetalohita, rakta, pītavāsas, asita, and sarvarūpaka. O excellent sages, thousands and crores of such kalpas have already elapsed.

50. At the dissolution of a kalpa, whatever remains of creation produced during day and night is destroyed.

51-53. The destruction is subject to the behest of lord Śiva. When the creation is annihilated and the Pradhāna is stationed in itself, both Pradhāna and Puruṣa come to a standstill or remain inactive. O brahmins, it is only when the three guṇas are not in equilibrium that creation takes place. When they are in equilibrium the creation is dissolved. The great lord is the cause of both. The creation is effected by him sportively in this manner.

54-56. Such creations, effected through the agency of Pradhāna are innumerable. The kalpas together with their Brahmās and Viṣṇus are innumerable. But lord Śiva is only one. The activities of Prakṛti emerging from Pradhāna are due to His sport. The activities as characterized by the guṇas are threefold and destructible but the (uncreated) ātman has neither a beginning nor a middle nor an end.[21]

57. The life-time of Brahmā consists of two halves called parārdhas.[22] What is created during His day time is destroyed during His night.

58-61. The worlds bhūr, bhuvaḥ, svar and mahar perish; only the worlds above remain intact. At night, when the mobile and immobile perish and a vast sheet of water[23] spreads like a single ocean, Brahmā goes to sleep in the water. He is there-

21. Creation is the result of stimulation (kṣobha) of the guṇas. When there is no stimulation, creation does not exist; consequently, the time-units—kalpas, manvantaras, yugas, saṁvatsaras and other relatively bigger and smaller units disappear as a matter of course.

22. A kalpa (a period of four thousand cycles of four yugas) constitutes a day of Brahmā. It is divided into two halves : 2 parārdhas. A half kalpa covers a cycle of two thousand caturyugas. At the end of a full kalpa a great fire consumes the world.

23. Ekārṇava symbolises the state of the universe during the period of dissolution when the divided units are drawn together forming a single watery mass. For detail see *MP—A Study*. PP. 9-10.

fore known as Nārāyaṇa. At the end of the night he wakes up and beholds a void what used to be the world of mobile and immobile beings. Then he, the most excellent among the knowers of Brahman decides to create. He assumes the form of a boar[24] and lifts the earth submerged in the waters. He lifts it up and places it as before, together with all the rivers, rivulets and oceans.

62-63. With great effort he makes the earth even. He gathers together all the mountains burned by fire on the earth. He establishes the four worlds, bhuḥ, etc. as before. He, the lord creator, then decides to create everything afresh.

CHAPTER FIVE

Creation

Sūta said :

1. O brahmins, while Brahmā of unknown origin pondered on creation he became manifested as delusion enveloped in darkness.

2. Ignorance originated from the self-born Brahmā in five[25] forms:—darkness (tamas), infatuation (moha), the great infatuation (mahāmoha), gloominess (tāmisra), and blinding gloominess (andhatāmisra).

3-4. This creation of Brahmā which is enveloped by ignorance is declared to be primary. From this creation emerged the immovables (plants, mountains etc.). He considered this creation incapable of causation. He thought of creating yet. While he thus meditated, his neck turned horizontally.

5-8. At first the horizontal creation named tiryaksrotas emerged from him; the next was urdhvasrotas chiefly characte-

24. The Purāṇas often mention Varāha (Boar incarnation of Viṣṇu) lifting the earth from the depth of the Ekārṇava ocean.

25. Avidyā, also designated as viparyaya is fivefold. Cf. II.9.30. Its five kinds are defined in the *Devī Bhāga*. These are subdivided into sixty-two kinds. Cf. II. 9. 34-35.

rized by goodness. Then came arvāksrotas, after that anugraha, and lastly bhūtādi. The first creation of Brahmā is known mahat; the second of tanmātrās as bhautika; the third of the sense-organs as aindriya; the fourth of the immovables as mukhya; the fifth of animals as tiryagyoni; the sixth of gods as daivika; the seventh of mankind as mānuṣa; the eighth (of emotions) as anugraha; the ninth of Kumāras as Kaumārya.[26] These are Prākṛta and Vaikṛta creations.

9-11. Formerly, O excellent sages, Brahmā created Sananda, Sanaka and Sanātana. By refraining from worldly activities they attained the Supreme Being. By his yogic accomplishment he created Marīci, Bhṛgu, Aṅgiras, Pulastya, Pulaha, Kratu, Dakṣa, Atri and Vasiṣṭha. These nine sons of Brahmā were the knowers of Brahman and excellent brahmins. They are known as expounders of brahman and were equal to Brahmā himself.

12. [He had three more sons] Saṅkalpa, Dharma and Adharma. Adharma is always present near Dharma. Thus there were twelve progenies of Brahmā of unknown origin.

13-14. The eternal lord had at the outset created Ṛbhu and Sanatkumāra. These two eldest sons became the divine expounders of Brahman. Being free from sexual desire they remained bachelors and rose equal in wisdom to Brahmā. They were omniscient and possessed of all merits. I shall now state succinctly the names of the wives of the brahmanical sages and the birth of their progenies, O excellent sages.

15-17. The lord created Virāja (Manu) and Vairājñī Śatarūpā who was not born of womb. She bore two sons and two daughters to Manu. The elder was the intelligent Priyavrata and the younger Uttānapāda. The elder daughter was Ākūti and the younger was Prasūti.

18-26. Prajāpati Ruci married Ākūti and lord Dakṣa married Prasūti the mother of the worlds and a great Yoginī. Ākūti gave birth to a son Yajña and a daughter Dakṣiṇā. Dakṣiṇā gave birth to twelve illustrious sons. Prasūti of great penance bore twentyfour daughters to Dakṣa viz.,—Śraddhā (faith),

26. **Ninefold creation : The Purāṇic cosmology divides the cosmic creation into nine classes. For detail, see *ŚP*. (English trans. p. 248 note 214).**

Lakṣmī (good fortune), Dhṛti, Puṣṭi, Tuṣṭi, Medhā, Kriyā, Buddhi (constancy), Lajjā (Modesty), Vapus (beauty), Śānti (tranquillity), Siddhi (perfection), Kīrti (fame), Khyāti (celebrity), Satī (truth), Sambhūti (fitness), Smṛti (memory), Prīti (affection), Kṣamā (patience), Sannati (humility), Anasūyā (sincerity), Ūrjā (strength), Svāhā (oblation to the gods), Araṇi and the blessed Svadhā (oblation to the pitṛs). He gave them duly in marriage. The first thirteen daughters Śraddhā to Kīrti married the patriarch Dharma. The wise Bhṛgu married Khyāti; Bhārgava (Śukra) married Araṇi; Marīci (married) Sambhūti ; Aṅgiras (married) Smṛti. The other married pairs were : Prīti and Pulastya, Kṣamā and Pulaha, Sannati and Kratu, Atri and Anasūyā, Ūrjā and Vasiṣṭha, Svāhā and Vibhāvasu, Svadhā and the Pitṛs.

27-28. Satī the mental creation of the lord was adopted as his daughter by Dakṣa. She the mother of the worlds attained Rudra as her husband. At the beginning of the creation Brahmā had created a Being (Rudra) possessed of a body half man's and half women's[27] and then the Creator said, "Divide thyself." And he being accosted thus, divided himself into two. It was then that she was born.

29. All the women in three worlds are born of the female part. Similarly, all the eleven Rudras[28] originated from his male part.

30-33. Everything feminine in gender is she herself and everything masculine is Rudra himself. Keeping Rudra in view, lord Brahmā looked at Dakṣa and said, "Worship her, she is of good holy rites, the mother of all the worlds, of mine as well as yours. If the word putrī (daughter) is interpreted as 'one who

27. This half-male and half-female form of lord Śiva is most popular in ancient sculpture. The concept has its basis in the Puruṣa-Prakṛti doctrine of the Sāṁkhya philosophers.

28. Eleven Rudras. For the names of eleven Rudras, see I. 82. 40-41. Their names are variously mentioned in the Purāṇas. For instance, Matsya has two lists (5. 29-30; 153. 19) which differ from each other. Vāyu agrees with Matsya only in three names. Bhaviṣya (125.7) gives a different list. For the interpretation of these names and other detail, see *MP. A Study* PP. 65-67.

saves from the hell "put" she will become the excellent wife of Rudra and the mother of the Universe. She shall be your daughter and known as Satī.

Thus urged by Brahmā Dakṣa obtained her as his daughter and respectfully gave her to Rudra (in marriage).

34. The thirteen wives of Dharma, Śraddhā and others have already been mentioned. I shall now mention the progeny of Dharma from those wives, in due order.

35-36. They are Kāma (love), Darpa (pride), Niyama (restraint), Santoṣa (contentment), Lobha (covetousness), Śruta (learning), Daṇḍa (punishment), Samaya (agreement), Bodha (wisdom), Apramāda (non-erring), Vinaya (humility), Vyavasāya (industry), Kṣema (welfare), Sukha (happiness) and Yaśas (fame). These are the offspring of Dharma.

37-40. Dharma begot of Kriyā (activity) and Buddhi (intelligence) two sons each viz.,—Daṇḍa (punishment) and Samaya (agreement) of the former, Apramāda (non-erring) and Bodha (wisdom) of the latter. Hence the sons of Dharma and Adharma are fifteen in all. Bhṛgu's wife Khyāti gave birth to Śrī, (who became) the wife of Viṣṇu and to two sons Dhātṛ and Vidhātṛ who later became the sons-in-law of Meru. Prabhūti, wife of Marīci, gave birth to two sons: Pūrṇamāsa and Mārīca and four daughters: Tuṣṭi, Dṛṣṭi, Kṛṣi and Apaciti.

41-45. O great sages, Kṣamā bore to Pulaha three sons: Kardama, Varīyas and Sahiṣṇu and one daughter Pīvarī, golden in colour and stout as the earth. Pulastya begot of Prīti two sons Dattorṇa and Vedabāhu and a daughter Dṛṣadvatī. Sannati, wife of Kratu gave birth to sixty thousand sons who are known as Bālakhilyas. Smṛti, wife of sage Aṅgiras, gave birth to four daughters: Sinīvālī, Kuhu, Rākā and Anumati after obtaining three sons: Anubhāva, Agni and Kīrtimān, O sages of holy rites.

46-50. Anasūyā, the wife of Atri, gave birth to six children, a daughter Śruti and five sons: Satyanetra, Bhavyamūrti, Āpa, Śanaiścara and Soma; the sixth was Śruti (mentioned above). The affectionate mother Ūrjā bore to Vasiṣṭha seven handsome sons: Rajas, Suhotra, Bāhu, Savana, Anagha, Sutapas and Śukra. To the god of fire who identifies himself with Rudra and is the eldest son of Brahmā and also the very life of the people, Svāhā bore three sons, for the welfare of the three worlds.

CHAPTER SIX

Glory of Śiva

Sūta said :

1-3. The three sons of Agni[29] are Pavamāna, Pāvaka and Śuci. The fire produced by attrition is called Pavamāna; that from lightning is named Pāvaka; that from the sun is known as Śuci. The three were the sons of Svāhā. Together with their sons and grandsons their number goes upto fortynine (= 7 × 7). The fires are produced in sacrifices.

4. All these are ascetics and observers of holy rites. All of them are prajāpatis identical with Rudra.

5. The Pitṛs are of two categories: yajvans and non-yajvans. Yajvans are also called Agniṣvāttas, the non-yajvans as Barhiṣadas.

6. Śraddhā gave birth to the mental daughter Menā. This mental daughter is well known in the world.

7-8. Menā gave birth to Maināka Krauñca, his (Maināka's) younger sisters Umā and Gaṅgā. The latter became the holiest by virtue of her contact with the body of lord Śiva. Svadhā gave birth to a mental daughter Dharaṇī (earth) who became the support of sacrifices. That lady (Dharaṇī) of lotus-face became the wife of Meru, the king of mountains.

9-10. The Pitṛs are amṛtapas (imbibers of nectar). Their account in detail, together with that of the sages and their families I shall narrate in a separate chapter, later on.

29. For agnivaṁśa see *Vāyu* I. 29; *Brahmāṇḍa* I. 1.10; *Mārkaṇḍeya* 52. 20-21, *Viṣṇu* 1.10. 14-17. According to *Liṅga* (11.12.33) agni is the creative force that permeates the Cosmic Egg and effects the work of creation.

There are fotynine agnis (II.12.35) which are the different forms of Rudra (I.6.4), while according to *Harivaṁśa* they are the attendants of Rudra (2.122. 17-40). Though there is a general agreement in the Purāṇas in regard to the number of agnis there is a wide disagreement about their names.

Satī, the (adopted) child of Dakṣa, the future daughter of Himavat, married Rudra.

11. Later, she cursed her father Dakṣa [and immolated herself] Rudra who thought on her created many Rudras.

12. He created them in the form of his own person and they were honoured by all the worlds. O leading sages, it was at the behest of Brahmā that lord Rudra created them. The lord had laughed and they were created immediately.

13-16. The fourteen worlds[30] were completely covered by them. They were of different sort, devoid of impurities, deathless and ageless. On seeing these Rudras in front Brahmā spoke to them :

"O Rudras, obeisance to you. O three-eyed gods, you are omniscient, omnipresent and splendid. Some of you are long, some short and dwarfish. Your hair are golden. You dazzle our eyes by your splendour. You are eternal, enlightened, devoid of impurities and dvandvas. You are passionless sons of Rudra. You are the universal souls. Thus, after eulogising Rudras, lord Brahmā circumambulated them and spoke to Rudra.

17. "O lord, obeisance be to you; O great Rudra, it does not behove you to create subjects devoid of death. O lord, you should create mortal subjects."

18. Then the great lord Rudra replied thus, "My position is not of such a nature. O Brahmā, you should create such subjects endowed with death."

19. Thus, at the will of Rudra, the four-faced Brahmā created the Universe, of the mobile and immobile beings, endowed with death and old age.

20-24. Thus, as Rudra desisted from creating mortal subjects he obtained the title 'sthāṇu'. O Brahmins, Rudra alone is capable of that. He is the supreme and unsullied soul who can assume physical bodies when he wills. The lord bestows happiness on all living beings mercifully and without strain. He has, therefore, acquired the title Śaṅkara. He is the all-pervading

30. The universe is comprised of fourteen worlds, seven rising above the earth and seven lying below. The seven upper regions are (i) bhūr, (ii) bhuvaḥ, (iii) svar, (iv) mahar, (v) janaḥ (vi) tapas, (vii) satyam and the seven lower are (i) atala,. (ii) vitala, (iii) sutala, (iv) rasātala, (v) tala, (vi) talātala, (vii) pātāla.

soul who bestows blessings upon the person who out of the fear of worldly existence has resorted to yoga whereby he has become detached eschewing worldly activities and pleasures. [It is enjoined that] detachment can be produced by perfect knowledge as well. The indiscriminate eschewal of this knowledge is meaningless and is contrary to the purpose. It is through his grace that the confluence of knowledge and detachment takes place.

25-26. Virtue, knowledge, detachment and prosperity are the result of his blessing. By taking recourse to him one can be easily liberated. Even if he is engrossed in sin he does not fall into hell.

27-31. Hence, by resorting to him, people can attain eternal release from worldly existence.

The Sages said :

There are twenty-eight crores of hells from ghora to māyā where the sinners are tortured, if they do not seek refuge in Him. He is the support of all living beings. He is unchanging. He is the lord of the worlds. He is Puruṣa, the great Ātman. He is often invoked and often eulogised. He is named Kāla Rudra when he assumes tamoguṇa, and Brahmā when he assumes rajoguṇa and Viṣṇu when he assumes sattvaguṇa. When devoid of attributes he is called Maheśvara. O intelligent Sūta, now tell us, by doing what or by neglecting what do men go to hell. We are eager to hear it.

CHAPTER SEVEN

The esoteric secret of Śiva

Sūta said :

1. I shall recount to you, at the outset, the esoteric secret, in brief, of the all-knowing Śiva of unmeasured splendour.

2-3. The yogins who are conversant with the tenets, who have adopted great detachment, who are constantly associated with the eight[31]means of Yoga, such as the control of breath and who are endowed with the attributes of mercy[32] etc., go either to hell or to heaven according to their deeds.

4. By virtue of his grace, knowledge arises and yoga functions through knowledge. By dint of yoga, liberation is effected, and everything is achieved through his grace.

The sages said :

5. O best of yogins, if perfect knowledge comes through grace, you shall tell us about the form and feature as well as the divine yoga of lord Śiva (through which that grace is attained).

6. How does the lord devoid of anxiety bestow his grace on men by means of the yogic path and at what time.

Sūta said :

7. May you all hear what had been formerly mentioned by Nandin to Sanat kumāra, the son of Brahmā, in the presence of devas, sages and pitṛs.

8. O sages of good holy rites, listen to the incarnations of Vyāsas, at the end of Dvāpara and the incarnations of lord Śiva as Yogācāryas in the kali age.

9. In different areas, the four disciples of the lord, fully endowed with mental control spread the doctrines of Śiva. There grew up many disciples of disciples and the lord was pleased at this.

10. The perfect knowledge of the lord had been traditionally and gradually transmitted orally to men of the first three castes from brahmins to vaiśyas in the manner befitting them. It was done so out of mercy.

The sages said :—

11. It behoves you to tell us who those Vyāsas were who

31. The eight ancillaries of yoga constitute (1) yama, (2) niyama, (3) āsana, (4) prāṇāyāma, (5) pratyāhāra, (6) dhāraṇā, (7) dhyāna, (8) samādhi. Cf *ŚP. Vāyavīya saṁhitā*, ch. 37.

32. For the eight virtues of the soul, compare *Agnipurāṇa* as quoted in *ST*. दया क्षमानसूया च अनायासोऽथ मङ्गलम् । अकार्पण्यास्पृहे शौचं यस्यैते स परं व्रजेत् ।

incarnated during every Dvāpara age and furthermore, in which manvantara and kalpa they incarnated.

Sūta said :

12-13. O brahmins, may you be pleased to listen. I shall duly recount the Vyāsas in the Vārāha kalpa of the Vaivasvata manvantara which is still current. I shall recount the Rudras in all the manvantaras. They had been the guides and instructors of perfect knowledge of the Vedas and Purāṇas in all the circles of yugas.

14-18. O brahmins, these are the Vyāsas: (1) Kratu,[33] (2) Satya, (3) Bhārgava, (4) Aṅgiras, (5) Savitṛ, (6) Mṛtyu, (7) Śatakratu, (8) Vasiṣṭha, (9) Sārasvata, (10) Tridhāman, (11) Trivṛta, (12) Śatatejas, (13) Dharma who is known as Nārāyaṇa, (14) Tarakṣu, (15) Aruṇi, (16) Kṛtañjaya, (17) Ṛtañjaya, (18) Bharadvāja, (19) Gautama, (20) Vācaśravas, (21) Suṣmāyaṇi, (22) Śuci, (23) Tṛṇavindu, (24) Rukṣa, (25) Śakti, (26) Parāśara the son of Śakti, (27) Jātukarṇya, (28) Kṛṣṇa Dvaipāyana who was Viṣṇu himself.

Now listen to the yogeśvaras in due order in the Kali age.

19-20. They are innumerable in the various kalpas and the manvantaras. Since the incarnations of Rudras and Vyāsas in the Kali age are too many, I shall recount the incarnations in the Vaivasvata manvantara, in the Vārāha kalpa and in all the other manvantaras falling therein.

The sages said :

21. O Sūta, it behoves you now to recount the manvantaras in the Vārāha kalpa and in all the later kalpas as also recount the Siddhas in the Vaivasvata manvantara.

Sūta said :

22-28. The first Manu was (1) Svāyambhuva son of Brahmā. Then, O brahmins, was the Manu (2) Svārociṣa. The subsequent Manus were: (3) Uttama, (4) Tāmasa, (5) Raivata, (6) Cākṣuṣa, (7) Vaivasvata, (8) Sāvarṇi, (9) Dharma, (10) Sāvarṇika, (11) Piśaṅga, (12) Apiśaṅgābha, (13) Śabala, and

33. identical with 'Prabhu'. Cf. *ST*. अयमेव चतुर्विशे प्रभुरित्युक्तः ।

(14) Varṇaka. The Manus are also designated according to the vowels beginning with 'a' and ending with 'au'. O excellent brāhmins, they are also classified according to their colours as (1) śveta (white), (2) pāṇḍu (grey), (3) rakta (reddish), (4) tāmra (copper-hued), (5) pīta (yellow), (6) kapila (tawny), (7) kṛṣṇa (black), (8) śyāma (dark), (9) dhūmra (light-smoke-coloured), (10) sudhūmra (deep smoke-coloured), (11) apiśaṅga (non-tawny) (12) piśaṅga (tawny), (13) trivarṇa śabala (three-coloured) and (14) kālandhura (extreme black). Thus all the holy Manus have been mentioned by (1) name, (2) letters, and (3) colour. Those identical with the vowels are, in brief, mentioned as the leaders of the manvantaras. Among them, the seventh Manu is Vaivasvata represented by the vowel 'ṛ' and colour black. This seventh Manu is also a leader among devas. I shall mention the yogins in this repeated cycle of yugas in the kalpas that have passed by and those that are yet to come.

29-35. The current kalpa in the seventh manvantara is known as Vārāha. Now listen to the yogic incarnations of the lord and their line of disciples in due order, in all the kalpas and manvantaras. In the first Kali of Svāyambhuva Manu they were (1) Śveta, (2) Sutāra, (3) Madana, (4) Suhotra, (5) Kaṅkaṇa, (6) Logākṣi, (7) Jaigīṣavya, (8) Dadhivāhana, (9) Ṛṣabha, (10) Ugra, (11) Atri, (12) Subālaka, (13) Gautama, (14) Vedaśīrṣa. (15) Gokarṇa, (16) Guhāvāsin, (17) Śikhaṇḍabhṛt, (18) Jaṭāmālin, (19) Aṭṭahāsa, (20) Dāruka, (21) Lāṅguli. (22) Mahākāvya, (23) Śūlin, (24) Daṇḍin, (25) Muṇḍīśvara, (26) Sahiṣṇu, (27) Somaśarmā, (28) Lakulīśa. O men of holy rites, the incarnations as Yogācāryas of the lord in all the cycles of four ages in the Vaivasvata manvantara have been recounted (as twentyeight).

36. O excellent sages, in every Dvāpara age, there are Vyāsas in the same manner. The following are the recurring disciples of these Yogeśvaras, each of whom had four disciples.

37-51. They are;—(1) Śveta, (2) Śvetaśikhaṇḍin (3) Śvetāśva, (4) Śvetalohita, (5) Dundubhi, (6) Śatarūpa, (7) Ṛcīka, (8) Ketumān, (9) Viśoka, (10) Vikeśa, (11) Vipāśa, (12) Pāśanāśana, (13) Sumukha, (14) Durmukha, (15) Durdama, (16) Duratikrama, (17) Sanaka, (18) Sananda, (19) Sanātana, (20) Ṛbhu, (21) Sanat, (22) Sudāman, (23) Virajas, (24) Śaṅkhapāda,

(25) Vairajas, (26) Megha, (27) Sārasvata, (28) Suvāhana, (29) Meghavāha, (30) Kapila, (31) Āsuri, (32) Pañcaśikha, (33) Vālkala, (34) Parāśara, (35) Garga, (36) Bhārgava (37) Aṅgiras, (38) Balabandhu, (39) Nirāmitra, (40) Ketuśṛṅga (41) Lambodara, (42) Lamba, (43) Lambākṣa, (44) Lambakeśaka, (45) Sarvajña, (46) Samabuddhi, (47) Sādhya, (48) Sarva, (49) Sudhāman, (50) Kāśyapa, (51) Vāsiṣṭha, (52) Virajas, (53) Atri, (54), Devasada, (55) Śravaṇa, (56) Śraviṣṭhaka, (57) Kuṇi, (58) Kuṇibāhu, (59) Kuśarīra, (60) Kunetraka, (61) Kaśyapa, (62) Uśanas, (63) Cyavana, (64) Bṛhaspati, (65) Utathya, (66) Vāmadeva, (67) Mahāyoga, (68) Mahābala, (69) Vācaśravas, (70) Sudhīka, (71) Śyāvāśva, (72) Yatīśvara, (73) Hiraṇyanābha, (74) Kauśalya, (75) Logākṣi, (76), Kuthumi, (77) Sumantu, (78) Barbarī, (79) Kabandha, (80) Kuśikandhara, (81) Plakṣa, (82) Dālbhyāyani, (83) Ketumān, (84) Gopana, (85), Bhallāvin, (86) Madhupiṅga, (87) Śvetaketu, (88) Taponidhi, (89) Uśika, (90) Bṛhadaśva, (91) Devala, (92) Kavi, (93) Śālihotra, (94) Agniveśa, (95) Yuvanāśva, (96) Śaradvasu, (97) Chagala, (98) Kuṇḍakarṇa, (99) Kumbha, (100) Pravāhaka, (101), Ulūka, (102) Vidyuta, (103) Maṇḍūka, (104) Āśvalāyana, (105) Akṣapāda, (106) Kumāra, (107) Ulūka, (108) Vatsa, (109) Kuśika, (110) Garbha, (111) Mitra, (112) Kauruṣya. These noble souls are the disciples of the yogins in all cycles of four yugas.

52-55. They are all devoid of impurities, almost identical with Brahman, and engaged in the path of knowledge. They are devotees of Paśupati, great Siddhas and have ashes smeared on their bodies. There are hundreds and thousands of disciples and their disciples. They attain the Pāśupata yoga and Rudra's world. All beings from Devas to Piśācas are said to be Paśus. Since Lord Rudra is their overlord he is called Paśupati. O Brahmins, the yoga evolved by Rudra, the overlord of the Paśus is known as Pāśupata yoga, which leads all persons to their blissful prosperity.

CHAPTER EIGHT

Yogic zones

Sūta said :

1. I shall succinctly mention the yogic zones now. They have been established by Śiva himself, O brahmins, for the welfare of men.

2. The portion covered by a vitasti beneath the throat and above the umbilicus is the excellent zone of yoga; so also the curling lock of hair below the umbilicus and middle portion between the eye-brows.

3. The knowledge of all topics that arises in the soul is called yoga.[34] The concentration of the mind is possible only through his grace.

4. O excellent brahmins, the form of his grace can be realized by the individual alone. It cannot be imported by Brahmā or any other. It arises itself in the individual gradually.

5. Yoga indicates the region where the Supreme Lord dwells.[35] For the attainment of that region, knowledge is the cause, and this knowledge comes through his grace alone.

6. One should abstain from sensual activities and burn sins by means of perfect knowledge. The achievement of yoga shall be possible only to one who has restrained the activities of his sense-organs.

7. O excellent brahmins, yoga is restraining the functioning of the mind.[36] Eight means have been mentioned for the achievement of yoga.

8-9. They are (1) yama (restraint), (2) niyama (observances), (3) āsana (a particular posture), (4) prāṇāyāma (restraint of breath) (5) pratyāhāra (withdrawal of the senses), (6) dhāraṇā (retention), (7) dhyāna (meditation) and (8) samādhi (ecstatic trance).

10-11. Abstention by way of austerity is called restraint (yama); O foremost among those who have restraint, the first

34. Yoga is defined as the achievement of knowledge of all objects by the personal soul (jīva).

35. K. reads निर्वाणं for निर्माणम् ।

36. Cf. *Pātañjala Yogasūtra* योगश्चित्तवृत्तिनिरोधः । 1. 1.

contributory cause of restraint is non-violence (ahiṁsā), truthfulness, non-stealing, celibacy and non-acceptance of gifts are the other causes The root of niyama (observances of vows) is undoubtedly yama alone.

12. Considering all living beings as one's own self and working for the welfare of all living beings is called non-violence. It helps in achieving the knowledge of self.

13. Retelling precisely what has been seen, heard, inferred or experienced is called truthfulness (satya). It is devoid of injury or infliction of pain on others.

14. The Vedas declare. "One should not utter what is obscene in the presence of the brāhmins". "Even after knowing the defects of others one should not proclaim them to others"—this is another passage in the śruti.

15. Not stealing the possessions of others purposefully, even in emergency, mentally, physically and verbally is non-stealing in brief.

16. Not indulging is sexual intercouse,[37] mentally, verbally or physically is the vow of celibacy, with reference to the ascetics and the religious students.

17. This holds good in regard to the anchorites, forest-dwellers and widowers. I shall now tell you about the vow of celibacy of the householders who live with their wives.

18. In their case, as prescribed, indulgence in sexual intercourse with their own wives and abstention from it with other women mentally, physically and verbally should be understood as brahmacarya.

19. The householder shall take ablution after indulging in sexual intercourse with his own wife. If he is in yogic communion with his self he is undoubtedly a celibate.

20. In the case of non-violence (ahiṁsā) too, the same rule is applicable. Violence sanctioned by Śruti, in regard to the brāhmaṇas, preceptors and sacrifice comes under ahiṁsā.

21. Women are always to be avoided. One should stay

37. For eight kinds of maithuna, cf. *ST*. स्मरण कीर्तनं केलिः प्रेक्षणं गुह्यभाषणम् । संकल्पोऽध्यवसायश्च क्रियानिर्वृतिरेव च । एतन्मैथुनमष्टाङ्गं प्रवदन्ति मनीषिणः ।। विपरीतं ब्रह्मचर्यमेतदेवाष्टलक्षणम् ।। Brahmacarya (celibacy) is defined as the reverse of maithuna (sexual indulgence) and it imparts vigour and force : Cf. *Yogasūtra* : ब्रह्मचर्यप्रतिष्ठायां वीर्यलाभः ।

far off from them. A shrewd person views them as he views the corpses.

22. He should have the same attitude in the sexual intercourse with his own wife, as when discharging the faeces and urine on the ground. There should be no attitude other than this.

23. Woman is like a burning coal; man is like a vessel of ghee. He should always avoid contact with women therefore.

24. If we ponder over this, we shall know that there is no satiety in sexual pleasures. Hence, one should practise detached attitude mentally, physically and verbally.

25. Lust is never suppressed by indulging in sexual pleasures. Just as fire burns vigorously if ghee is poured in, so also lust is increased by means of indulgence.[38]

26. Hence the yogin should always practise renunciation for achieving immortality, since he who is not detached is born and re-born in different wombs.

27. The Vedas[39] declare that it is only through renunciation that immortality is attained. O brahmins, the most excellent among the knowers of Śruti and Smṛti, it is not possible through rites, through progeny or through offerings of materials of worship.

28. Hence one should practise detachment, mentally, verbally and physically. Abstention from sexual intercourse, except during the prescribed period, after menstruation is stated as celibacy in the case of householders.

29-31. Thus the restraints (yamas) are succinctly mentioned. I shall now tell you the observances (niyamas). They are ten in number : (1) cleanliness (śauca), (2) sacrifice (ijyā), (3) penance (tapas), (4) charitable gift (dāna), (5) study of the Vedas (svādhyāya) (6) restraint on the organs of generation (upasthanigraha), (7) holy rites (vrata), (8) fast (upavāsa), silence (mauna), and holy bath (snāna). According to some, observances (niyama) mean (1) absence of craving (anīhā), (2) cleanliness (śauca), (3) satisfaction (tuṣṭi), (4) penance (tapas), (5) muttering of Śiva's mantra

38. *Pañcadaśī*. 7. 47.

39. Na karmaṇā na prajayā dhanena, *TA*. 10.10.3; *Mahān*. *U*. 10.5

(japa), (6) meditation on Śiva and (7) postures such as padmaka. Of these cleanliness is twofold : (1) external and (2) internal. Of the two the internal is superior to the external.

32-35. One who has external cleanliness should practise internal cleanliness too. The holy bath should be conducted in accordance with the injunctions. It is threefold : (1) Āgneya (fiery), (2) Vāruṇa (watery) and (3) Brāhma (consisting of Brahman). It is only after he has practised the external bath that he should practise the internal. If he is devoid of internal purity, he is still dirty even if he applies clay over his body and plunges into the waters of the tīrthas. O excellent brahmins, the moss, the fishes, the sharks and the animals that prey upon fishes remain ever in water. But are they pure ? Internal cleanliness should always be pursued in accordance with the injunctions.

36. Internal cleanliness is mentioned as follows. One should apply the holy ashes of detachment with a feeling of devotion. One should take a holy dip into the waters of knowledge of the soul. This is how one can attain purification.

37-39. Siddhis are accomplished only in a pure and not in an impure person. A person of holy rites who is satisfied with the sustenance he gets by justifiable means has the characteristics of satiety (tuṣṭi). He is not worried about his needs. Austerity is the right observance of the holy rites Cāndrāyaṇa, etc. Svādhyāya is the threefold repetition of Oṁkāra mantra, i.e. (1) Vācika—oral utterance which is the basest of the three; (2) Upāṁśu—slow muttering which is better than Vācika; (3) Mānasa—when the sound does not come out of the throat which is the best of all. This is stated in detail in the ritualistic text on the five-syllabled mantra.

40-43. Śiva-praṇidhāna (contemplation of Śiva) mentally, physically and verbally, unflinching devotion to the preceptor, withdrawal of the organs of sense from the objects of worldly pleasures—this in brief is called pratyāhāra (withdrawal). Dhāraṇā (retention) is the fixation of the mind in the proper place. Dhyāna (meditation) comes through the normalcy of Dhāraṇā (retention). If it is coupled with thought, it is samādhi (ecstatic trance). In samādhi there is concentration of the mind and meditation; herein the perception of object is entirely excluded.

44. In samādhi[40] the supreme consciousness alone shines, as though it were devoid of physical body. Prāṇāyāma (control of breath) is the root of dhyāna, samādhi, etc.

45. The wind within the body is prāṇa. Its restraint is yama. As stated by the brahmins it is threefold: (1) slow (manda), (2) middling (madhya) and (3) uttama (superior).

46. The restraint of the prāṇa and apāna is called prāṇāyāma. The magnitude of the restraint of breath is stated to be twelve moments.

47-50. The slow (manda)[41] consists of twelve moments which form one stroke or blow (udghāta). The middling consists of two strokes. The superior has three strokes, i.e. thirty moments. The three respectively generate sweating, shivering and rising up. When the following symptoms are seen the prāṇāyāma[42] is excellent, for it denotes the onset of bliss. The symptoms are: reeling due to drowsiness, horripilation, sensation of hearing some sound, pressing of one's own limbs, shivering,

40. Samādhi is a fixation of the mind on the personal soul (jīva), and further, of the personal soul on the supreme soul, so as to identify the contemplator with the object meditated upon. This is the eighth and last stage of yoga. Cf. *Haṭhayogapradīpikā* :

सलिले सैन्धवं यद्वत्साम्यं भवति योगतः ।
तथात्ममनसोरैक्यं समाधिरभिधीयते ॥
तत्समञ्च द्वयोरैक्यं जीवात्मपरमात्मयोः ।
प्रनष्टसर्वसङ्कल्पं समाधिः सोऽभिधीयते ॥

With Buddhists it is the fourth and last stage of dhyāna.

41. The time of mātrā is that of a winking and opening the eye-lids once, or that of a prosodial instant. The udghāta prāṇāyāma extends during twelve mātrās or twelve prosodial instants. It is defined in the *Mārkaṇḍeya* thus :

निमिषोन्मेषणे मात्रा ततो लध्वक्षरे तथा ।
प्राणायामस्य संख्यार्थः स्मृतो द्वादशमात्रकः ॥

ŚP. defines mātrā as a unit of time required for the snapping of the fingers after moving them round the knees neither speedily nor slowly. (*Vāyavīya* 37.31).

42. For the kinds and characteristics of Kumbhaka prāṇāyāma, see *Haṭhayogapradīpikā*.

vertigo born of sweating, fixation, absence of knowledge and unconsciousness.

51-54. Prāṇāyāma is of two types: sagarbha and agarbha.[43] If it is pursued with japa, it is sagarbha; if without japa, it is agarbha. It is like an elephant, or an eight-footed animal śarabha or a formidable lion. When caught and tamed properly it becomes submissive. Similarly, for the yogins, the wind which is by nature unstable and uncontrollable becomes normal and subservient by proper practice. Just as the lion or the elephant or the Śarabha, though ferocious, is tamed after a while with a proper training, so also the wind attains normalcy and equanimity due to constant acquaintance and practice.

55-57. He who practises yoga never suffers calamity. When the prāṇa is properly trained it turns the defects of the mind, speech or body, preserving the body of the practiser. Thus, if the devotee perfects himself by taking recourse to the prāṇāyāma his defects perish; the very breath is conquered by him, and the divine quiescence etc. are achieved.

58-62. The attributes of the prāṇāyāma are four, viz, śānti, praśānti, dīpti and prasāda. They are explained in order: O brahmins, the first of these four is śānti. It means the suppression of sins congenital or adventitious. Praśānti is a perfect restraint in speech.[44] All round, all time brilliance, O brahmins, is called dīpti. Prasāda is the clarity of the mind which is of four types. It is the clarity of the sense-organs, of the intellect and the organic winds. The organic winds—prāṇa, apāna, samāna, udāna and vyāna have their functional names : Nāga, Kūrma, Kṛkala, Devadatta and Dhanañjaya respectively. The clarity of these winds is called prasāda.

43. According to *ST*. sagarbha is a variety of Kumbhaka that includes pūraka (inhaling) and recaka (exhaling) varieties of prāṇāyāma. सगर्भः पूरकरेचकसहितः, अगर्भः केवलः । *ŚP*. defines agarbha as the kind of Prāṇāyāma wherein the breath is restrained without meditation and japa, and sagarbha as that wherein meditation and japa are allowed. (*Vāyavīya* 37. 33, 34).

44. Praśāntiḥ—restrained or restricted speech. *ST*. quotes from the Mahābhārata :

अव्याहृतं व्याहृताच्छ्रेष्ठमाहुः सत्य वदेद् व्याहृतं तद्द्वितीयम् ।
धर्मं वदेद् व्याहृतं तत्तृतीयं प्रिय वदेद् व्याहृत तच्चतुर्थम् ॥

63-67. The wind which traverses through the body is called prāṇa; that which brings down food and drink is called apāna; that which enables the limbs of the body to bend is called vyāna which incites the ailments too; that which excites and afflicts the vulnerable points (in the body) is called udāna. That which normalizes the functions of the organs is called samāna. Thus the first set of five winds has been explained to you. The wind Nāga functions in the act of belching; the Kūrma in the opening of eyes; Kṛkala in sneezing; Devadatta in yawning and Dhanañjaya in making a loud report. It is present even in the dead body. By restraining these winds, one can attain prasāda. O brahmins, in the fourfold set of attributes, prasāda figures as the fourth.

68-69. O brahmins, the intellect has these synonyms—viz., visvara, mahat, prajñā, manas, brahmā, citi, smṛti, khyāti, saṁvit, Īśvara and mati. It is through prāṇāyāma that the clarity of intellect is achieved.

70-74. O excellent sages, Visvara is so called because it compromises between two conflicting opposites. Since it is the first and the greatest of all the tattvas arising out of Prakṛti it is called mahat. It is called prajñā because it is the repository of all means of knowledge. It is manas because it thinks. It is Brahmā because it is big and swells up. O most excellent among the knowers of Brahman, it is called citi because it gathers together all activities for the sake of enjoyment. It is called smṛti because it enables one to remember things. Since it obtains everything it is called Saṁvit. Because it is known everywhere by means of knowledge it is called khyāti.[45] It is called Īśvara because it is the overlord of all elements and comprehends everything. O sages, most excellent among the intelligent, it is called Mati because it is the instrument of thought subjectively and objectively. It is called Buddhi because it enlightens things and is itself the instrument of enlightenment.

75. The perspicuity of this Buddhi is achieved through

45. khyāti—a category of intellect (MP. 3.17). It is so called because it is the source of the perceived creation or the cosmos which becomes visible or the object of perception by the mind and the senses.

Prāṇāyāma. By restraining himself one shall burn all defects by taking recourse to prāṇāyāma.

76. By means of pratyāhāra (withdrawal of sense-organs) and Dhāraṇās (retentions) one shall destroy sins. By meditating on the mundane objects as if they were poisonous one destroys all ungodly qualities.

77. O excellent ascetics, one should increase the power of intellect by means of samādhi. The eight ancillaries of yoga should be practised only after securing the proper place for yogic practice.

78. The knower of the Ātman shall then duly secure Āsanas (correct postures) for achieving yogic results. If the place and time are not suitable he cannot have even a glimpse of yoga.

79-86. The yogic exercises should not be practised in the the following places or circumstances—near the fire, within water, on a heap of dry leaves, in a place infested with creatures, in the cremation ground, in a dilapidated cowpen, in the four crossroads, in a place full of noises, in a place generating fear, in a monastery, or the anthill, in an inauspicious place, in a place inhabited by wicked men and in a place infested with mosquitoes. One should not practise yogic exercises when there is some ailment in the body or when the mind is in dejection.

The devotee shall delightedly practise the ancillaries of yoga in the following places. It should be a well protected place, auspicious and pleasing; or a cave in a mountain or shrine of Śiva, or a well-guarded park or a forest, or a corner in one's own house devoid of people and animals. It should be scrupulously clean, well scrubbed, smeared with cowdung and rendered beautiful in diverse ways. It shall be spotlessly clean like the surface of a mirror. It shall be fumigated with black agallocum. Different kinds of flowers should be strewn all round. A canopy should adorn the whole place. It should be endowed with roots, fruits, tender sprouts, kuśa grass and variegated flowers. The practitioner of yoga should sit in a balanced posture. He should practise the ancillaries of the yogic exercises with delight in his mind. He should pay reverence to the preceptor Lord Śiva, Goddess Umā, Vināyaka, the leading yogins and their disciples. He should practise the posture of svastika[46] padma[47] or ardhāsana.[48]

87-90. He should sit with the knees on a level or kneel on one of the knees. Whatever the posture may be he shall sit steadily withdrawing his feet. He shall keep his mouth shut, eyes closed, chest projected in front. With his heels he should cover the testicles and the penis. With his head somewhat lifted up and the rows of teeth not touching each other, he should observe the tip of his nose. He shall not look at the quarters. He shall cover up his tamas by means of rajas and the rajas by means of sattva. Then stationing himself in the sattva he shall practise meditation of Śiva.

91. With great concentration, he shall meditate in the pericarp of the lotus, on the Supreme Being which is symbolised by Oṁkāra and is as pure as the candle flame.

92-95. He should meditate within three aṅgulas below the umbilicus, on the excellent lotus having (at its centre) an octagon, a pentagon or a triangle. He should also meditate on the fire, moon and sun together with their consorts; or the order may be : first the sun, then the moon, and then the fire. Or the order may be first the fire, then the sun and then the moon as prescribed in the Śāstras. He should conceive the four[49] aims—Virtue etc. beneath the fire and ponder over

46. svastika—a posture of sitting practised by a yogin in which the toes are placed in the inner hollow of the knees. *ŚP.* lists eight types of the yogic pose : (i) svastika, (ii) padma, (iii) ardhendu (iv) vīra, (v) yoga, (vi) prasādhita, (vii) paryaṅka, (viii) yatheṣṭa.

47. padmāsana—a particular posture of the body in religious meditation. Cf.

ऊरुमूले वामपाद पुनस्तु दक्षिणं पदम् ।
वामोरौ स्थापयित्वा तु पद्मासनमिति स्मृतम् ।।

ST. quotes from *HYP. pp.* 25-26 :

ऊरुमध्ये तथोत्तानौ पाणी कृत्वा ततो दृशौ ।
नासाग्रे विन्यसेद्राजदन्तमूले तु जिह्वया ।।
उत्तभ्म्य चुबुकं वक्षस्युत्थाप्य पवनं शनैः ।
इद पद्मासनं प्रोक्तं सर्वव्याधिप्रणाशनम् ।।

48. Construe 'ardhāsanam' with 'padmam' i.e. the lotus half seat. It is also called siddhāsana.

49. This group of four consists of (i) dharma, (ii) jñāna, (iii) vairāgya and (iv) aiśvarya.

the three guṇas over the zone. He should then think of Rudra stationed in sattva and adorned by Umā.

96. He should perform the rite of meditation in the umbilicus or the throat, or the middle of the eye-brows or on the forehead or on the crest of the head in accordance with the injunctions.

97. He should meditate on Śiva (sitting in the lotus with two, sixteen, twelve, ten, six or four petals in due order).

98-100. He should meditate on Him in a spot as lustrous as gold or as splendid as burning coal or very white or as refulgent as twelve suns or as brilliant as the disc of the moon or as flashing as millions of lightning streaks or as lustrous as fire or as glittering as a circle of lightning or as refulgent as a crore of diamond pieces or as brilliant as a ruby. He should practise meditation on the image of blue and red coloured lord (Śiva).

101. He shall meditate on Maheśvara in the heart; on Sadāśiva in the lotus-like umbilicus ; on Candracūḍa on the forehead and on Śaṅkara in the middle of eyebrows.

102-108. He shall meditate on Śiva on his forehead; on Mahādeva (the great lord) in his lotus-like heart and in the mind. The great lord is of the following description : He is devoid of impurities. He is unsullied. He is the quiescent Brahman in the form of knowledge. He has no specific characteristics. He cannot be particularly pointed out. He is minuter than the atom. He is splendid and supportless. He cannot be reflected upon. He is devoid of death and birth. He is liberation itself. He is ambrosial, imperishable and unborn. He is miraculous, the greatest and the largest bliss. He is devoid of defects and qualities. He is subtler than the subtlest, auspicious, self-cognizable, incomprehensible. He is the greatest lord identical with perfect knowledge. He is beyond the scope of sense-organs. He has no semblance. He is the greatest principle, greater than the greatest, devoid of conditioning adjuncts, comprehensible through meditation, non-dualistic, beyond all darkness and the greatest Being. The devotee should meditate in the umbilicus on Sadāśiva, the lord identical with devas.

109-111. He shall meditate on lord Śiva identical with

pure knowledge, in the middle of the body through suṣumnā[50] pass or through the Kumbhaka. He shall then perform thirty two recakas (respirations) concentrating on the heart and umbilicus. O excellent brahmins, then eschewing Recaka and Pūraka[51] respirations and taking recourse only to Kumbhaka he shall meditate on Śiva in the middle of the body with normal elegance.

112-116. After identifying with the lord he will comprehend the bliss of Brahman emerging from elegance and the state of perfect equanimity.

Twelve prāṇāyāmas make one dhāraṇā; twelve dhāraṇās make one meditation and twelve meditations make one Samādhi. O brahmins, one may attain yogic realization by contact with wise men or by his own efforts, gradually. Of course, even as he practises yoga, there may be obstacles in this path. But they perish through constant practice by the direction of the preceptor.

CHAPTER NINE

Obstacles and Portents

Sūta said :

1-3. Obstacles to yogic practice take shape in ten different ways. They are (1) lethargy, (2) ailment, (3) negligence, (4) doubt, (5) unsteady mind, (6) lack of faith, (7) illusion, (8) misery, (9) dejection and (10) indulgence in sensual

50. कन्यसमार्ग:=सुषुम्नानाडीरूपो मार्ग: । Cf. Śivagītā as quoted in ST. : अनन्तैकोर्ध्वगा नाडी मूर्धपर्यन्तमञ्जसा । सुषुम्नेति समादिष्टा तया गच्छन् विमुच्यते ।। It is a vein of the body lying between those called iḍā and piṅgalā and supposed to be one of the passages for the breath or spirit.

51. recakam pūrakaṁ tyaktvā. Kumbhaka alone is recommended for the attainment of spiritual goal; recaka and pūraka are excluded. Cf. *Haṭhayogapradīpikā* p. 70

कुम्भके केवले सिद्धे रेचपूरकवर्जिते ।
न तस्य मानुष किञ्चित् त्रिषु लोकेषु विद्यते ।।

pleasures. Of these lethargy means abstention from work due to the bulkiness of the body and mind.

4. Ailments originate from the imbalance of the constituent elements. They are the outcome of the defective previous schemes as well as of bad habits. Negligence constitutes omission to secure the means of yoga.

5-6. Doubt is a double perception—"this or that". Unsteadiness is the instability to stabilize the mind. The mind remains unsteady due to its engrossment in mundane affairs even when the ground is achieved. Lack of faith is the unemotional attitude towards the means of yoga.

7-9. Illusion is misconception of the mind as regards one's aim, the preceptor, right knowledge, good conduct and lord Śiva as also in the apprehension of self in non-self even when it is nearby. Misery is threefold : spiritual,[52] material[53] and divine[54]. There is also a natural misery due to the agitation of the mind through the frustration of desires.

10-12. When the mind is affected by tamas or rajas it is afflicted. The state of the mind at that time is called dejection. Dejection should be eschewed by strict detachment from the material objects. When one can discriminate between what is worthy and what is not worthy but still stubbornly clings to the unworthy, engrossed in diverse mundane affairs his mind becomes fickle then. These are the impediments in the realization of yoga for a yogin.

13-15. To the devotee who practises yoga excessively endowed with zeal the obstacles subside but other impediments in the form of siddhis begin to appear.[55] The siddhis are six :

52. ādhyātmika—this misery proceeds from bodily and mental causes within one's self. Cf. *Viṣṇu* आध्यात्मिको वै द्विविधः शारीरो मानसस्तथा । quoted in *ST*.

53. ādhibhautika—this misery is produced from external causes: अन्यप्राणिकृतम् *ST*.

54. ādhidaivika—this misery proceeds from the influence of the atmosphere or planets, from divine or supernatural agencies: शीतोष्णादिजन्यम् *ST*.

55. Upasarga—It is an ailment in the soul of a yogī and, if unchecked, it will hinder his progress in the path of self-realization. Liṅga records sixtyfour upasargas.

(1) pratibhā, (2) śravaṇā, (3) vārtā, (4) darśanā, (5) āsvāda, and (6) vedanā.

16. These siddhis if avoided initially when their potency is very little, lead to better results. Pratibhā (keen intellect) is the disposition (of the mind), resting on one's power of understanding.

17-20. Buddhi (intellect) is the faculty of discrimination by which anything knowable is known. If one has knowledge of things subtle or hidden far or near, past or future, at all times and places, that knowledge is called pratibhā. If the yogin is able to grasp without effort, the import of all words by merely hearing a concealed or indistinct syllable, whether short, long or prolated that ability is called śravaṇā. The perception of touch without actual contact is called Vedanā (awareness). The ability to see divine forms without effort is called darśanā. Āsvāda (appreciation) is the ability to taste divine delicacies without strain.

21. Vārtā is the intellectual perception of divine smells and subtle elements. O brahmins, through yoga, the yogins attain the knowledge of everything about the embodied beings.

22-25. In this world there are sixty four qualities present in the body. O brahmins, among these, the aupasargika qualities should be eschewed. In the region of piśācas, O brahmins, the qualities of earth (should be eschewed); in the region of rākṣasas the qualities of water; in the region of Yakṣa the qualities of fire; in the region of Gandharvas the qualities of breath; in the region of Indra the qualities of ether; in the region of Soma the qualities of the mind; in the region of prajāpati the qualities of ego; in the region of brahman the qualities of intellect should be eschewed.

26-29. In the first region (earth) there are eight qualities; in the second (water) sixteen; in the third (fire) twenty four; in the fourth (gandharva) twentytwo; in the fifth (Indra) forty. Each of the five subtle elements—smell, taste, colour, touch and sound is evolved eightfold. O excellent brahmins, there are fortyeight qualities in the region of the moon, fifty-six in the region of Prajāpati, and sixtyfour in the region of Brahman. In all the regions ending with that of Brahman, the yogin should discern obstacles through yoga and eschew them. He can realize the supreme brahman thus.

30-31. The yogic siddhi pārthiva (pertaining to the earth) is eight: (1) bulkiness, (2) leanness, (3) infancy (4) youthfulness, (5) old age, (6) ability to assume different shapes, (7) ability to hold body by means of (only) four elements without the part of the earth and (8) having perpetual sweet scent.

32-35. The yogic siddhi āpya (pertaining to the water) is sixteen : (1) He can stay under water as long as he wills; (2) he can come out of water whenever he wills; (3) he can drink up even the ocean and be none the worse for it; (4) he can let the water spring up wherever he wills; (5) whatever he wishes to eat he can transform it into tasty substance; (6) he can hold body with only three elements, viz. fire, air and ether; (7) He can hold a mass of water by the bare hands without any container; (8) he can have a body free from cuts and wounds. These eight powers together with the eight qualities of the earth constitute aiśvarya pertaining to the water.

36-38. The yogic siddhi taijasa (pertaining to the fire) is twentyfour : (1) ability to create fire from the body; (2) absence of fear from being scorched by it; (3) ability to arrange something unburnt even when the whole world is burnt; (4) ability to keep fire in the water or (5) hold it in palms, (6) ability to create fire by merely remembering it; (7) ability to re-create at will what is reduced to ashes; and (8) ability to have the body with two elements—air and ether, to the exclusion of the other three.

39-41. The yogic siddhis pertaining to the air are : (1) ability to move as fast as the mind; (2) ability to enter the bodies of living beings; (3) ability to hold weighty things like mountains on shoulders; (4) lightness, (5) weightiness, (6) holding the air with palms; (7) ability to shake the earth with the tip of the finger and (8) to create bodies with the air.

42-43. Ability (1) to have no shadow of oneself; (2) to see the subtle elements; (3) to walk over the ether; (4) to have the objects of desire at will; (5) to hear sound from a distance, (6) to comprehend all types of sounds; (7) to have a body composed only of subtle elements and (8) to see all living being—these are the powers pertaining to Indra who is so called because he creates bodies by means of these powers.

44-45. Ability (to acquire whatever he desires), (2) to wander wherever he pleases, (3) to overpower all, (4) to perceive all secret things, (5) to create according to desire, (6) to bring others under control, (7) to see things at will, (8) to perceive the whole world—these are the powers pertaining to the mind in the region of the moon.

46-47. Ability to cut, (2) strike, (3) bind, (4) create and (5) destroy, (6) bless, (7) conquer time and (8) death—these are the qualities pertaining to the ego in these regions of Prajāpati.

48-49. The following powers pertain to Brahmā—(1) creation of the world by mere conception, (2) protection, (3) dissolution, (4) exercise of authority, (5) functioning the world at will, (6) dissimilarity with all, (7) creating separately all visible things and (8) the creatorship of the universe.

50. The power greater than and beyond this is the one pertaining to Viṣṇu. It is the source of the power of Brahmā. It can be understood by Brahmā alone and not by others.

51. There is another greater power pertaining to Śiva. It is not understood even by Viṣṇu. Who else can know lord Śiva—the pure entity possessed of many qualities.[56]

52. In the course of practising yogic exercises[57] these impediments in the form of attainments do often take place. The impediments should be checked assiduously by complete detachment.

53. Knowing that worldly pleasures are highly ruinous, the detached yogin should eschew everything without the least sense of fear.

54. Absence of desire is, indeed, commendable. It is through the absence of yearning for the attainment of powers

56. It refers to the eternal transcendent spirit placed in the twenty-seventh category beyond the influence of sattva, rajas and tamas, and regarded as higher than the highest. Cf. यः सप्तविंशको नित्यः परात्परतरः प्रभुः । 1.71.51

57. व्युत्थाने—व्यवहारकाले *ST*. The sixtyfour attainments (siddhayaḥ) are useful from the materialistic point of view but they are obstacles (upasargas) to yoga.

and it is by complete detachment that the calamities can be eschewed.

55. In all the worlds, upto the world of Brahmā, one should avoid obstacles. Checking up all desires one should totally abandon them. The great lord is delighted thereby.

56-61. When the lord is delighted liberation becomes easy to attain, by virtue of complete detachment. In some cases, a sage (after getting His grace) may roam about without eschewing the Siddhis for the sake of blessing others or for mere sport. Then also he can be happy.

In some places leaving the Earth he may sport in the sky with splendour; in some places he may utter the Vedas or their subtle meanings succinctly; in some places he may compose verses based on the meaning of the vedic passage;. in some places he may compose poems in the Daṇḍaka or other meters in thousand ways. He may obtain knowledge of the cries of beasts and birds. Everything beginning with Brahmā and ending with the immobile beings may become perceptible to him like myrobalan fruit in the palm.

O excellent sages, of what avail is much talk? Knowledge in many ways and forms will rise up within that sage of great soul. It is only by practice that perfect knowledge becomes pure and stable.

62. The knower of the yoga can perceive thousands of images of devas and their splendid aerial chariots. Everything can come within the range of his ken.

63. He can see Brahmā, Viṣṇu, Indra, Yama, Agni, Varuṇa and other deities. He can see thousands of planets, stars and luminaries as well as their regions.

64-65. Entering the state of ecstatic trance he can see the dwellers of nether regions. He can dispel darkness (=ignorance) by the steady influx of his inmost spiritual light—glowing with divine grace and characterized by goodness—which he can see within himself.

66-67. No doubt need be entertained that by virtue of His grace, one can attain Dharma, riches, knowledge, detachment and salvation. The details of his grace, one cannot describe even in ten thousands of years. O leading sages, one should steadily adhere to the yoga pertaining to lord Śiva.

CHAPTER TEN

Means of Direct Perception

Sūta said :

1-9. O great brahmins, lord Śiva becomes delighted with all these persons : those who desire to be liberated, who have conquered self, the twice-born, the virtuous, who have attained sādhanās, the noble-souled, kind and merciful, the ascetics, who have renounced the world, who are detached and endowed with perfect knowledge, who have self-control, the three kinds of donors, who have subdued senses, who speak truth, who are liberal, endowed with yogic practice, conversant with śrutis and smṛtis and who do not come into clash with the śāstric injunctions. The word 'sat' refers to the Brahman. Those who are likely to attain Brahma in the end are called liberated. They who are neither angry nor delighted in regard to the ten types of sensuous objects[58] and eight types of means[59] are called self-conquerors. The brahmins, kṣatriyas and vaiśyas are called twice-born because they have special consecratory rites. The virtuous is the one who has acquired the knowledge of dharma explained in śruti and smṛti which is proper for different castes and stages of life and which brings about happiness in heaven and other worlds. One who acquires learning by serving his preceptor is a sādhu (among the religious students). The householder is also a sādhu when he performs holy rites (ordained for him). The forest-dweller becomes a sādhu when he achieves penances.

10. The striving ascetic is called a sādhu when he achieves yogic power. Thus the persons who achieve Dharma relating to ashramas or the various stages of life are called sādhus.

11-13. The persons in the different stages of life are: the religious student, the householder, the forest dweller and the ascetic. The two words Dharma and Adharma mentioned here

58. daśātmake viṣaye—objects that can be accomplished through ten organs of sense, i.e. five organs of action and five organs of knowledge.

59. This group of eight is explained in the preceding chapter.

denote activities. Auspicious activities constitute Dharma and inauspicious activities Adharma. The word Dharma is explained as that which is great in the task of Dhāraṇa (holding up, or uplifting) and Adharma (its opposite) as not holding up. In this context Dharma is instructed by the preceptors as one that takes to what is desired.

14-16. Adharma, as taught by the preceptors, is one that has as its fruit what is not desired. They call those persons Ācāryas (preceptors) who are elderly, not greedy and self-possessed; devoid of arrogance, well disciplined, and straight forward. He who practises (Dharma) himself who establishes others in dharma and who gathers together the meanings of the scriptural texts is called ācārya. What should be known or what is worthy of knowledge is śrauta if it is heard and smārta if it is remembered.

17-21. A sacrifice when it pertains to Vedas is called śrauta, and when it pertains to the varṇāśramas is called smārta. One who has found truth and does not hide it when asked for, is called an ācārya. Truth, as defined in this purāṇa, is the statement of facts exactly in the manner seen. Tapas (penance) constitutes celibacy, silence, observance of fast, abstention from injury of all sorts and quiescence. When a person behaves towards all living beings like unto himself[60] both for welfare or otherwise that attitude is called kindness. Whatever one has obtained by justifiable means, whatever one likes the most, should be given to a meritorious person. This is the characteristic feature of the charitable gift of the donor. Charitable gift is of three types viz.—the lowliest, the highest and the middling.

22-27. The sharing (of possessions) with all living beings, out of sympathy is the charitable gift of the middling order. The rites laid down by Śrutis and Smṛtis in regard to persons of different stages in life and castes constitute dharma. Dharma that does not come into clash with the conduct of the persons of disciplined life is held to be righteous.

That person is glorified as one of auspicious soul who eschews the fruits of his illusive activities.

One who has refrained from all attachments is glorified as a

60. This ethical code places this cult at par with universal religion.

Yogin. He who ponders over the risks involved in sensual pleasures and remains unattached to them even though pressed importunately from all round is called self-controlled.

The characteristic feature of perfect control constitutes the fact that sense organs do not function falsely or improperly whether for one's sake or for others.

The following is the detached state:—The person is not excited when calamities occur nor is he overjoyed when he has pleasant results. Absolute cessation of joyousness, affliction and despondency is detachment.

Renunciation of the fruits of all activities committed or omitted is called Sannyāsa.

28-31. The eschewal of both joy and misery is called Nyāsa. All created things from the unmanifest to the manifest gross elements are insentient. Perfect Knowledge is the discrimination between the sentient and the insentient. Lord Śiva, no doubt, bestows his grace on him who is endowed with such perfect knowledge. So also dharma bestows grace. Yet I shall tell you a great secret. One who is endowed with devotion to the lord is undoubtedly liberated. It is certain that lord Śiva checks the different sorts of delusion of the devotee and is delighted with him even if he (the devotee) lacks full accomplishments for yoga.

32-37. Perfect knowledge, teaching of the Vedas, offerings to the gods, meditation, sacrifices, penance, charitable gifts, study of the Vedas, all these undoubtedly contribute to the devotion of Lord Śiva. O excellent sages, devotion results from thousands of Cāndrāyaṇas,[61] hundreds of Prājāpatyas,[62] monthly fasts and other holy rites. Those who lack in devotion to the lord fall into a mountain cave and undergo the results

61. Cāndrāyaṇa : Cf. Yājñavalkya 3. 324 et seq; Manu 11.217. It is a religious observance or expiatory penance regulated by the period of the moon's waxing and waning. Herein the daily quantity of food consisting of fifteen mouthfuls at the full moon is diminished by one mouthful every day during the dark fortnight till it is increased in like manner during the bright fortnight.

62. Prājāpatya : It is a religious fast or penance. Herein one shall take food for three days in the morning, for three days in the evening, and thereafter shall abstain from food for three days.

of their karman.[63] A devotee is liberated through his devotional emotion. O brahmins, there is no doubt in this that heavenly pleasures are not difficult of access even to ordinary men, by the mere sight of the devotee; what doubt then in regard to the devotee. It is only through devotion that Brahmā, Viṣṇu, gods, sages, and others stabilise themselves and attain strength and fortune. This has been stated by the lord himself while addressing Umā.

38-41. O brahmins, these words were spoken by the lord to the goddess Umā at Vārāṇasī, in the Avimuktaka[64] region While the lord was sitting with her, she addressed him thus: "O great lord how can you be realised and worshipped. O Lord, tell me, is it by penance, or learning, or yoga ?

Sūta said:

On hearing her words and looking at her with a face resembling the full moon the lord with the crescent moon for his ornament laughed boisterously and recollected what had been formerly mentioned by Menā, the consort of the Himālaya when she saw that her daughter had overstayed there.

42-47 The lord said: "O gentle lady, O sportful one, now that you have obtained a beautiful city for your abode, do you forget what was mentioned by your mother in regard to the selection of a site for abode. O foremost among those who ask questions, formerly I was asked by Brahmā in the same manner as I have been asked by you. O splendid lady, in the Śveta kalpa, Brahmā saw me in the white colour as Sadyojāta; in the Rakta kalpa in the red colour as Vāmadeva; in the Pītakalpa in the yellow colour as Tatpuruṣa; in the Aghora-kalpa in the black colour as Īśvara; in the Viśvarūpa kalpa as the multi-coloured Īśāna. Then he said to me: O Vāma, O

63. आत्मभोगार्थम्—भोगप्राप्त्य शया ST. in expectation of enjoying the objects of senses.

64. Avimukta—same as Kāśī (Mbh. III. Ch. 84. 79-8; Viṣṇu 5.34. 30, 54; Matsya 180.54, 94 ff; Vāyu. 106. 69). For detail, vide P. V. Kane, History of Dharmaśāstra (Vol. iv. pp. 618-642). But in the Kali age it has lost its original form. Cf. Brahmāṇḍa 2.3.67, 60-64. It is called Avimukta or Avimuktaka, for it is the permanent abode of Śiva (1.92.45-46) :

विमुक्तं न मया यस्मान्मोक्ष्यते वा कदाचन ।
मम क्षेत्रमिदं तस्मादविमुक्तमिति स्मृतम् ।।

Tatpuruṣa, O, Aghora, O Sadyojātā, O Maheśvara, O lord of Devas,O great lord, you have been seen by me along with Gāyatrī. O great lord, by what means and by whom can you be controlled ? O storehouse of mercy, wherein are you to be meditated upon ?"

48-53 "O lord, how can we see you along with the goddess ? How can we worship you. It behoves you to recount it."

The lord said to the goddess :

I said (then to Brahmā), 'O lotus-born one, I can be controlled by faith alone. I am to be meditated upon in the Liṅga which both you and Viṣṇu beheld in the ocean. I am to be adored by the twice-born in the form of the five-faced deity with the five-syllabled mantra. O preceptor of the universe, born of the cosmic egg, I have been seen by you to day by virtue of your devotion to me.' He (Brahmā) then asked me to create in him a feeling of further devotion which I readily granted. O goddess, with that increased devotion he saw me clearly in his heart. I declare that I am subject to control by means of devotion alone. I can indeed be seen thereby, O daughter of the Himālaya ! And, indeed, I am always to be worshipped in the liṅga by the brahmins full of faith. Faith is the greatest and the subtlest virtue. It is perfect knowledge and sacrifice; it is penance, heaven and liberation. I am always seen through faith.

CHAPTER ELEVEN

Sadyojāta

The sages said :

1-2 How did Brahmā see the great lord as Sadyojāta, Vāmadeva, Tatpuruṣa, Aghora and Īśāna ? It behoves you to recount it precisely.

Sūta said :

The twentyninth kalpa should be known as śvetalohita.

3. In that (kalpa) when Brahmā was pursuing intense meditation a son with tuft was born unto him. He was called Śvetalohita

4-5. On seeing that Puruṣa, the glorious lord Brahmā with faces all round, thought of the noble-souled lord in the form of Brahman. Brahmā retained Sadyojāta in the heart and became engaged in meditation. After realising the greatest being through meditation Brahmā, the lord of Devas, saluted him.

6-7. Brahmā contemplated again over Sadyojāta. Thereupon from his sides were born Śvetas (white ones) of great fame, viz. Sunanda, Nandana, Viśvananda and Upanandana; these noble-souled ones were the disciples of Brahmā by whom he was always surrounded.

8. In front of him the sage Śveta, glittering in his white colour, was born. Then there was born Hara of great splendour.

9-11. There all the sages resorted to the great lord Sadyojāta with perfect devotion. They praised the eternal Brahman. Hence all those persons O brahmins, who resort to lord Viśvevara after being engrossed in breath-control and mentally devoted to Brahman, become liberated from sins. They will have the splendour of brahman and be free from impulses. They will go beyond Viṣṇu's abode and enter Rudra's world.

CHAPTER TWELVE

Glory of Vāmadeva

Sūta said:

1. Thereafter the thirtieth kalpa is called Rakta. In this kalpa, Brahmā of great splendour had the red colour.

2-5. Even as Brahmā desirous of a son was meditating, a boy of great splendour menifested himself : He was adorned in red ornaments. He wore red garlands and clothes. His eyes were red. He was valorous. On seeing that noble boy in red clothes, Brahmā resorted to great meditation and understood him to be great Lord. Brahmā, of self control bowed to Vāmadeva. and contemplated on him. Thus eulogised by Brahmā, the supreme lord Śiva was delighted at heart. He addressed Brahmā thus.

6-9. "Since, O Brahmā, I have been seen by you meditating on me with the desire for a son, with great devotion, and since I was eulogized with the mantra beginning with "brahmaṇe Vāmadevāya" you will attain the strength of meditation and will realize me as Īśvara, the assiduous creator of the worlds, in every kalpa. Thereafter four sons were born to him who were as pure and splendid as brahman. They were named as Virajas, Vibāhu, Viśoka and Viśvabhāvana.

10. They were pious and on a par with Brahmā. They were heroic and enterprising. They wore red garments and red garlands and applied red unguents.

11-13. Their bodies were smeared with red saffron; they had applied red ashes over their bodies. At the end of a thousand years they re-entered the great eternal lord. In the meantime they attempted to realize brahman. For blessing the worlds and with a desire for the welfare of their disciples they imparted instructions in dharma and became favourites of Brahmā. Ultimately, at the end of a thousand years, they re-entered the great lord.

14-15. All other brahmins who practise yoga and repeat the sacred formula 'namo brahmaṇe Vāmadevāya'[65] and who are devoted to him as their greatest resort are liberated from sins. They become devoid of impurities and they attain the strength of Brahman. They achieve the blessed region (rudraloka) whence there is no return to this (mortal) world.

65. Vāmadeva form is represented by the back-face of Śiva. In Hindu Mythology God Śiva has five faces named Īśāna, Tatpuruṣa, Aghora, Vāmadeva and Sadyojāta, representing the five elements: ether, air, fire, water and earth. Cf. part II. ch. 14. A statue of Śiva in the Elephanta caves represents this form in which the frontal view depicts three heads only, the fourth one on the back is concealed from view and the fifth one on the top is dropped out as the symbol of invisible ether.

CHAPTER THIRTEEN

Glory of Tatpuruṣa

Sūta said:

1. The thirty first kalpa is known as Pītavāsas. Therein, the blessed Brahmā was clad in yellow garbs.

2. Even as Brahmā desirous of a son was meditating, a boy of great splendour, wearing yellow robes, appeared before.

3. He was a youth with the body smeared with yellow scents. He wore yellow garlands and dress. He had long arms, a golden sacred thread and yellow turban.

4. On seeing him, Brahmā, endowed with meditation mentally resorted to and sought refuge in the overlord, the creator of the worlds.

5. Thereafter Brahmā went on meditation. He saw the excellent cow of the great lord. In her universal form it had come out of his mouth.

6. It had four feet, four faces, four hands, four udders, four eyes, four horns, four teeth and four mouths.

7-10. The cow was goddess herself who had faces all round and who possessed thirtytwo qualities. On seeing the great goddess in the form of the cow, the great lord who is worshipped by all devas said again repeating the words : 'O great goddess, symbol of intellect and memory, come on, come on.' [Thus addressed] she joined her palms in reverence to the lord and stood there. Then the lord of devas spoke to her. [O goddess,] enveloping the universe by your yogic power you should keep it under your control. You will be Umā for the welfare of the brahmins and for the attainment of their goal (of liberation).

11. The lord of devas, the preceptor of the universe gave her to Brahmā who was meditating on the lord for obtaining a son.

12. By practising meditation Brahmā realized that she was the great goddess and he accepted her from the preceptor of the worlds.

13-14. After meditating on Gāyatrī pertaining to Rudra, Brahmā became self-controlled. By performing the japa of Rudra-Gāyatrī as instructed by the lord and realizing that it was Vedic knowledge, Brahmā who is worshipped by the whole world, resorted to the great lord with his mind fixed in meditation.

15. The lord then granted him a divine yoga, great learning, riches and glory, wealth of knowledge and detachment.

16-21. Thereafter from his sides there emerged divine sons who wore yellow garlands, yellow garbs, yellow necklaces. They had yellow unguents on their bodies and yellow turbans on their heads. Their faces and hair were all yellow. For a period of thousand years, these persons of great power and splendour who were devoid of impurities spent their time for the welfare of brahmins. They were yogic souls delighting in penances. They were endowed with virtue and power of yoga. They instructed the sages engaged in long sacrifices in the system of great yoga and (finally) entered the body of the lord. Thus others too who seek refuge in him in this manner, who have restrained their souls, who have conquered the sense organs and who are engaged in meditation will become sinless. They will have the splendour of Brahman and be free from impurities. They will enter Rudra the great lord and be released from re-birth.

CHAPTER FOURTEEN

Origin of Aghora

Sūta said:

1-2. When the kalpa of yellow colour passed by and another of the self-born lord was ushered in by the name of Asita and when the universe became a vast sheet of water[66] and a thousand years by the divine reckoning passed by, Brahmā became desirous of creating the subjects. He was dejected and began to ponder.

3. Even as he was meditating with the desire for a son, his colour was changed into black.

66. See note 23 on p. 15.

4-6. Thereupon he, the lord of great splendour, saw a boy in front of him. He had black colour but he was refulgent with his brilliance. He had great prowess. He wore black garments, black turban, black sacred thread, black crown and black garlands. He had black unguents on his body. On seeing this noble-souled Aghora of terrible exploits, Brahmā saluted the miraculous lord who had the black and tawny colour.

7-10. Then the glorious lord Brahmā became engaged in Prāṇāyāma. He thought of the supreme lord Śiva within his heart. With his mind engaged in meditation he resorted to lord Aghora. He contemplated on him in the form of Brahman. When Brahmā was meditating thus, lord Aghora of terrible exploits granted him vision. Thereupon four noble sons appeared from his sides. They were black in colour and they wore black garlands and unguents. They were Kṛṣṇa, Kṛṣṇaśikha, Kṛṣṇāsya, and Kṛṣṇavastradhṛk.

11-13. By resorting to yoga they adored the great lord for a thousand years. They imparted instruction in supreme yoga to their disciples. By resorting to yoga these persons, endowed with yogic powers, thought on Śiva. They entered the region of lord Śiva, the region devoid of impurities and free from attributes. Those others too, who contemplate on him by resorting to yoga can go unto the region of that eternal lord.

CHAPTER FIFTEEN

Glory of Aghoreśa

Sūta said :

1. When the terrible kalpa of black colour passed by, Brahmā eulogised the supreme lord in the form of Aghora.

2-6. Thereafter the delighted lord Aghora blessed Brahmā and said to him: "Do not doubt that I, assuming this form, destroy all kinds of sin, including the terrible sin of brahmin slaughter. O blessed one, O deity of virtuous sacred rites, I destroy all minor and major sins of small or great power and poignancy. O Brahmā, I destroy verbal, physical, mixed and incidental sins committed wantonly and consciously. I dispel the natural and adventitious sins inherited from either parent. O lord, do not doubt that I destroy all miseries originating from sins.

7-13. O lord, by repeating one hundred thousand times the mantras of Aghora, even a brahmin-slayer is liberated from sins. O dear, for verbal sins half of this number is recommended. For mental sins, half of the previous number. If the sin is committed consciously the japa shall be four times that number. If the sin is committed out of fury, eight times that number. A slayer of a hero shall repeat the mantra a hundred thousand times; the destroyer of a child in the womb a crore times; a matricide a hundred thousand times; a destroyer of cows and women or an ungrateful wretch by repeating ten thousand times; a willing or unwilling drinker of liquor by repeating a hundred thousand times or half that number and the partaker of meals before taking bath a thousand times. The brahmin who abstains from japa or who takes meals before performing the daily sacrifice or abstains from giving charity should repeat this mantra a thousand times. The base man who steals the property of a brahmin or who steals gold is released from sin by repeating this mantra mentally a hundred thousand times. A person defiling the preceptor's bed or slaying his own mother or a brahmin shall repeat this mantra mentally the same number of times, O Brahmā.

14-17. The sin resulting from contact with the sinner is equal to the sin of the original sinner. Still by repeating the mantra ten thousand times he is liberated from sin. The person imbibing sin by the contact with the sinner shall repeat the mantra a hundred thousand times if done mentally; if done in low tones four times that number ; if in high tones eight times that number. It is enjoined that persons guilty of subsidiary sins need repeat the mantra only half the number enjoined for the main sinner; half that number if the sin is committed unconsciously. O brahmins, if a brahmin sinner commits the sin of brahmin slaughter, liquor drinking, theft of gold or defiling the preceptor's bed he should do as follows:

18-22. He should gather together (i) urine of a tawny coloured cow repeating Rudra-Gāyatrī,[67] (ii) freshly laid dung of the same or similar cow repeating the mantra Gandhadvāra,[68] (iii) ghee made from a similar cow repeating the mantra Tejosi śukram,[69] (iv) milk from the same or similar cow repeating the mantra 'Āpyāyasva'[70] and (5) fresh curds made from the milk of the same or similar cow repeating the mantra Dadhikrāṇā.[71] To this mixture water taken with a tuft of kuśa grass should be added by repeating the mantra Devasya tvā,[72] and the mixture should be well stirred in a vessel made of gold, silver or copper, or in a cup made of lotus or palāśa leaf, repeating the aghora mantra. In this vessel he should place (different) gems and a piece of gold along with a tuft of kuśa grass.

23-26. He should repeat the mantra of Aghora a hundred thousand times and perform homa with ghee, cooked rice, sacrificial twigs, gingelly seeds, barley grains and unhusked grains. He should perform homa, seven times separately with each one of these materials. If the materials are not available he should perform homa with ghee alone. O brahmins, he should perform homas as well as ablution for the lord with ghee while repeating the Aghora Mantra. He should bathe the lord with eight droṇa[73] measures of ghee and wipe it off. He should then observe fast for a whole day and night, take holy bath and drink kūrca before the image of Śiva. After performing the rite of ācamana he should repeat Gāyatrī.

27-32. By performing this the following sinners become liberated form sins:—an ungrateful person, a slayer of brahmin, a destroyer of a child in the womb, a murderer of a warrior, a slayer of preceptor, a betrayer of faith, a thief, a gold-stealer, a defiler of the preceptor's bed, a liquor-addict, a paramour, a low-caste woman, a ravisher of other men's wives, a destroyer of brahmin's property, a cow-killer, a matricide, a patricide, an idol-breaker

67. Rudra-Gāyatrī : TĀ I. 10.5 : 'tatpuruṣāya dhīmahi tanno rudraḥ pra codayāt.

68. TĀ. 10.1.10; Mahān. U. 4.8.

69. VS. 22.1.

70. VS. 12.114; TĀ, 3.17.1.

71. VS. 23.32; TS. 1.5.11.4

72. VS. 2.11; TS. 2.6.8.7.

73. It is a measure of four āḍhakas equal to 1024 muṣṭis.

and particularly the person who destroys liṅga images. If one who commits these sins is a brahmin, no matter if his sins are mental, verbal, physical or of any other type, even if he commits these a thousand times he is liberated from these by performing the aforesaid rites. Even if the sins are accumulated in hundreds of births he is liberated. This secret has been divulged by me in the context of lord Aghora. Hence a brahmin shall repeat the Aghora mantra perpetually for the expiation of sins.

CHAPTER SIXTEEN

Glory of Īśāna

Sūta said:

1. O leading sages, there was a kalpa of Brahmā known as Viśvarūpa. It was exceedingly wonderful.

2-7. When the period of dissolution passed by, when again the universe of mobile and immobile beings came into existence Brahmā began to meditate with a desire for sons. Then Sarasvatī of universal form and loud sound manifested herself. The universe constituted her garlands, garments, sacred thread and turban. The mother of the universe with all universal scents and long lips manifested herself. Brahmā meditated on lord Īśāna resembling pure crystal and bedecked in all ornaments. With concentrated mind, Brahmā paid homage to Īśāna, the omnipresent lord of all—Om O Īśāna, O Mahādeva, obeisance be to you. O lord of all learning, obeisance be to you. O lord, with the bull as your conveyance, obeisance be to you. O lord of living beings, obeisance be to you.

8. O overlord of Brahmā, obeisance be to you. Obeisance to Brahman in the form of Brahma. Obeisance to the overlord of Brahmā. O Sadāśiva, may auspiciousness befall me.

9. O lord representing oṁkāra in a physical form, O lord of devas, O Sadyojāta, obeisance be to you. I resort to you. I have resorted to Sadyojāta. Obeisance to Sadyojāta.

10. Obeisance to you, the unborn, the source of birth and who are not beyond the worldly existence. O Bhava, O Īśāna, O source of the worlds, O deity of great lustre, bless me.

11. O Vāmadeva, obeisance to you, the eldest being, the granter of boons. Obeisance to Rudra, Kāla the reckoner of time.

12. Obeisance to the lord as the mind, to the lord black in colour, to the lord as a religious student, to the lord as the strength of the strong and to the lord devoid of organs and their function.

13. Obeisance to the suppressor of Bala, to the strong, of the form of Brahman. Obeisance to the overlord, the suppressor of living beings.

14. Obeisance to the lord the impeller of the mind, obeisance to the lord of great lustre, obeisance to the refulgent Vāmadeva and to the supreme soul.

15. Obeisance to the eldest and the greatest ; obeisance to Rudra the bestower of boons. Obeisance to you the slayer of Kāla. Obeisance to you possessed of the noble soul.

16. With this prayer he bowed to the lord of Devas, to the God with the Bull as his emblem. He who reads this narrative even once becomes entitled to the world of Brahmā.

17-23. He who narrates this to the brahmins at the time of Śrāddha attains the greatest goal. When Brahmā thus paid homage to him, lord Śiva spoke: "I am delighted with you. What favour do you seek from me ?"

Then Brahmā who bowed to the delighted Rudra said with a delighted mind in clear words: know O lord, I wish to see this universal form of yours. Here is the universal cow[74] Goddess of welfare. Who is she possessed of four feet, four faces, four horns, four mouths, four curved fangs, four udders, four hands and four eyes ? How is she known as Viśvarūpā (of universal forms) ? What is her name? What is her lineage ? To whom does she belong ? What is her power of action ?" On hearing his words the bull-bannered lord Īśāna addressed Brahmā the best of Devas, born of himself, in words full of

74. Viśvagauḥ : She is identical with Prakṛti or Pradhāna. Comprising thirty two qualities she is described as the source of this universe. See below, verses 29-35.

the secret of all mantras which being pious are conducive to prosperity.

24-25. Listen to a great secret. As in the first creation, the kalpa that is current now is known as Viśvarūpa. O lord (Brahmā) there is the region of Brahmā which you have attained. O lord ! beyond that region there is an auspicious region occupied by Viṣṇu born of my left limb. Since that time, this the thirtythird kalpa has begun.

27. O lord of Devas possessed of great intellect, before you, hundreds and hundred thousands of Brahmās have passed away. Now listen.

28. You who are a devotee of the spiritual lineage of Maṇḍavya have attained the state of my son by practising penance. Stabilised in bliss you can realize the supreme bliss.

29-31. O lord, you are characterized by the following qualities: (1) Yoga, (2) Sāṅkhya, (3) penance, (4) learning (5) Śāstric injunctions, (6) holy rites (7) pleasant speech, (8) truth, (9) mercifulness, (10) Vedic knowledge, (11) non-violence, (12) wisdom, (13) forbearance, (14) meditation, (15) proximity with the lord, (16)control of the senses, (17) quiescence, (18) intelligence, (19) illusion, (20) intellect, (21) fortitude, (22) splendour, (23) ethics, (24) fame, (25) intelligence, (26) modesty, (27) vision, (28) auspicious speech, (29) satisfaction, (30) skill in the exercise of sense-organs, (31) performance of Vedic rites, and (32) pleasure. While she, the goddess, has these thirtytwo qualities recognizable in her appellation of thirtytwo syllables.

32-34. O Brahmā, the goddess Prakṛti, the source of your origin has been created by me. She is the overlord of Viṣṇu and other gods. She is my progeny. Philosophers call her by various names, the four-faced deity, the origin of the universe, primordial nature, cow or speech, Gaurī, Māyā, Vidyā, Kṛṣṇā, Haimavatī, Pradhāna or Prakṛti.

35-39. She alone is unborn.[75] She is red, white and black in colour; She creates subjects in the universe that are of the form as she herself. I am unborn, know me to be omnipresent and know her to be Gāyatrī of universal form.

75. TĀ.10.1; Mahān. U. 9.2, Śvet. U 4.5.

After saying this, the lord created four sons. They were boys of all forms, who stood beside the Goddess. They were known Jaṭī Muṇḍī, Śikhaṇḍī Ardhamuṇḍa. Resorting to the yaugic practices they of great splendour worshipped the lord. They carried out their task of instruction in dharma. They followed the path of yogic practice. These controlled souls of good conduct entered lord Rudra at the end of a thousand divine years.

CHAPTER SEVENTEEN

Origin of the Liṅga

Sūta said :—

1-5. Thus the origin of Sadyojāta has been succinctly narrated. He who reads or listens to or narrates this to excellent brahmins attains identity with brahman by the grace of the supreme lord.

The sages said :

How did Liṅga originate ? How should lord be propitiated in Liṅga ? What is this Liṅga ? What its substratum ? O Sūta, you should narrate all this to us.

Romaharṣaṇa said:

Formerly, Devas and Sages had, in reverence, asked Brahmā thus : "O lord, how did Liṅga originate by itself ? How should lord Rudra be worshipped in the Liṅga. What is Liṅga? What its substratum ?

Brahmā said :

Pradhāna is Liṅga and lord Śiva is its substratum.

6-13. O excellent Devas, it was for us both—Viṣṇu and myself that Liṅga manifested itself in the ocean. It was when the aerial charioteers had gone to the Janaloka together with the Sages and when the period of sustenance being over the creation was withdrawn and when at the end of a thousand sets of four yugas, they had gone to Satyaloka and in the end, except their overlords, had attained identity with me, then all immobile beings had dried up due to all-round drought and other beings like men, animals, Piśācas, Rākṣasas, Gandharvas including plant life were scorched to death by the rays of the Sun. Everything was a single vast sheet of water. It was terribly dark all round. In that vast sheet of water, the lord devoid of impurities and free from calamities had gone to sleep. He had a thousand heads,[76] a thousand eyes, a thousand feet and a thousand arms. He, the universal soul, omniscient, the source of origin of all, was characterized by the qualities of rajas, tamas and sattva in the form of Brahmā, Rudra and Viṣṇu. He was omnipresent and the supreme lord in view of his being the soul of all. He was in the form of Kāla with Kāla in his umbilicus. He was white, black, pure, of huge arms, the soul of all and identical with Being and non-*B*eing.

14. On seeing the lotus-eyed deity lying thus, I was deluded by his *māyā*. I asked him angrily :

15-16. Who are you ? Tell me. Then with my hand I raised up the eternal lord. Due to the severe and firm blow of my hands he woke up from sleep and sat in his serpent couch.[77] Within a moment he regained control of himself and with his lotus-like bleary eyes he looked at me.

17. Enveloped that he was by a halo of brilliance he spoke to me as I stood before him. He got up from bed and laughing awhile addressed me sweetly.

18-32. "I welcome you, O dear Brahmā of great brilliance." O leading Devas, when I heard his words uttered smilingly my arrogance was provoked by rajas and I spoke to him thus: "With smiles within, you call me by the appellation 'Dear' (as if I were inferior to you). But know that I am the cause of creation and annihilation of the universe. O sinless one, you address me as a preceptor would address his disciple. But I am the creator of the universe, the promptor of Prakṛti, the eternal, unborn Brahmā, the origin and soul of the universe. I am the lotus-eyed lord. Now tell me quickly why you speak thus in utter delusion.

76. ṚV. X. 90. 1.

77. In Hindu Mythology Viṣṇu is represented as reclining on the serpent Śeṣa. A vivid picture of Śeṣaśāyī Viṣṇu is depicted on the outer wall of the Daśāvatāra temple at Deogarh.

He then replied to me—"See for yourself that I am the creator, sustainer and destroyer of the universe. You are born of my eternal body. You forget that I am the lord of Universe, the Supreme soul invoked and eulogised. I am Viṣṇu, Acyuta, Īśāna, the origin of the universe. It is not your fault that you have forgotten me. This has been effected by me through my māyā. Listen to the truth, O four-faced[78] deity. Indeed, I am the lord of all devas. I am the creator, leader and destroyer. There is no other lord like me. I alone am the Supreme Brahman. O Brahmā, I am the greatest principle, the greatest luminary, the supreme soul. O four-faced lord, whatever is seen or heard in this universe—the mobile and immobile, is identical with me and permeated by me. Formerly the unmanifest pradhāna the twenty-fourth principle[79] from the gross to the indestructible atom was created by me. Out of fury were Rudra and others created. Out of joy and sport you were born as also the Cosmos: Intellect, the threefold[80] ego, subtle elements sense-organs including the mind; and gross elements were also created by me.

As he finished his speech, a terrible, thrilling fight ensued between us. In the middle of that ocean of dissolution we were engaged in fight, instigated by rajas.

33. In the meantime a brilliant Liṅga appeared in front of us in order to suppress our dispute and enlighten us.

34. It had thousands of clusters of flames. It was comparable to hundreds of (all-consuming fires). It was stable, with no decline or increase. It had neither a beginning nor an end nor a middle.

35. It was incomparable, inexplicable, and indistinct. It was

78. Brahmā is four-faced (Caturmukha). It is stated that originally he had five heads but one was cut off by Śiva for telling a lie. According to another version, the fifth head was burnt off by the fire of Śiva's eye for speaking disrespectfully of Śiva. We read in the Śatarudra saṁhitā that it was Kālabhairava, a terrible form of Śiva who cut off the fifth head. Viṣṇu Purāṇa (ch.8) however gives a different version. It states that Bhairava attempted to cut off the fifth head of Brahmā at the instance of Śiva but gave up the attempt when Śiva intervened at the behest of Viṣṇu.

79. It refers to the invisible (avyakta) Pradhāna, the twentyfourth category in Sāṁkhya philosophy.

80. Ahaṁkāra (ego) is threefold : sāttvika, rājasa and tāmasa.

the source of the universe. Lord Viṣṇu was deluded by its thousand flames.

36. I too was deluded. Then Viṣṇu said to me—"Let us test this fiery Being. I shall go to the root of this incomparable column of fire.

37-38. You should go up assiduously". After saying this, Viṣṇu assumed the form of a boar. O Devas, I assumed the form of a swan. Ever since they call me haṁsa (swan) or Virāṭ haṁsa (cosmic swan).

39-43. He who repeatedly calls me swan, shall himself become a swan of bright and white colour, with fiery eyes and feathers. O gods ! I assumed the speed of the wind and the mind and went higher and higher. Viṣṇu the all-pervading soul assumed the form of a black boar and went lower and lower. The boar looked like a heap of blue collyrium. It was a hundred Yojanas in length, ten Yojanas in girth. Its body was huge as the mount Meru. It had white and curved teeth. It had the refulgence of all-consuming sun with long snout and loud grunt. Its legs were short and its body of diverse colours. It was victorious, firm and incomparable. Assuming this form of a black boar, Viṣṇu went lower and lower, hurriedly, for a period of one thousand years.

44. Still he could not reach the root of the Liṅga. O destroyer of enemies, throughout that period of time I was going higher and higher.

45. I hurried up my efforts to see the end of that Liṅga. I was tired. Arrogant that I was I could not see the end and returned to the place of my start.

46. Similarly, Lord Viṣṇu was also tired. His fear was evident in his eyes. He, the origin of all Devas, immediately came up there.

47. We bowed to lord Śiva. The noble-minded Viṣṇu was deluded by Śiva's Māyā and he stood there in mental dejection.

48. We bowed to lord Śiva at the sides, behind and in front and wondered what that was.

49. O great Devas ! then a loud sound Om[81] issued (out of the column). It was clearly a prolated sound.

81. Om is a mystic syllable consisting of three sounds a, u, m. It is the object of profound religious meditation. The highest spiritual efficacy is attributed not only to the whole word but also to each sound separately.

50-51. Thinking what it could be, Viṣṇu stood there together with me. Then he saw the eternal first letter 'a' on the right hand side of the Liṅga; then on the left the letter 'u'; thereafter, the letter 'm' in the middle and the vibratory tone in the end. That tone was 'Om'.

52-55. Viṣṇu saw the first syllable 'a' in the south, like the disc of the sun, the second syllable 'u' as refulgent as fire in the north, the third 'm' in the middle as refulgent as the sphere of the moon; above it, he saw the lord like the pure crystal. It was the fourth entity, devoid of attributes, nectarine, unsullied, undisturbed, devoid of mutually clashing opposites, unique, void, without an exterior or interior but still endowed with exterior and interior, as it was stationed both without and within. It was devoid of beginning, middle and end, it was the cause of bliss.

56-62. The three mātrās and half a mātrā called nāda, together constitute Brahman. The three Vedas Ṛk, Yajus and Sāman are in the form of the three mātrās. Viṣṇu contemplated on Śiva, the universal soul, through the words of the Vedas. The Vedas became a sage. Viṣṇu understood the glorious essence of the Vedas—the supreme lord through that sage alone.

Brahmā said :

Rudra is free from anxieties and worries. Speech recedes along with the mind being unable to attain him. He is expressible through the single syllable (om)[82], which is the Divine order, the supreme cause, truth, bliss, nectar, the supreme Brahman, greater than the greatest. Out of that single syllable 'om', the syllable 'a' is Brahmā; 'u' Viṣṇu, and 'm' is Rudra 'a' is the cause of creation, 'u' of illusion and 'm' of bliss.

63-65. The syllable 'm' is the sower, 'a' is the seed and 'u' is the womb. The three symbolise the lord, Pradhāna and Puruṣa. Thus the sower, the seed and the womb, together with nāda,

82. Om is a symbol of Brahma : Cf. *Yogasūtra* : 'tasya vācakaḥ praṇavaḥ'. In later times it came to represent the Hindu triad, viz., a (Viṣṇu), u (Śiva), m (Brahmā). But this order is not followed in some Purāṇas. For instance, according to Liṅga 'a' represents Brahmā, 'u' Viṣṇu and 'm' Rudra.

constitute lord Śiva. The sower divided itself out of his own free will. Out of the liṅga of the lord the sower created the seed 'a' which he discharged into the womb 'u' where it increased all round.

66. It turned into a golden egg enveloping the first letter 'a'. This divine egg was ensconced in the water for many years.

67-68. Then at the end of a thousand years the egg that had evolved out of the unborn and stationed in the waters was split into two by the primeval lord himself. The splendid golden skull of the egg became heaven and the base became the earth.

69. From the egg the four-faced Brahmā was born. He is the creator of the universe, the lord of three forms.

70-72. The wise exponents of Yajus say that Om is Brahman. The Ṛk and Sāman śrutis too have declared similarly. On the lord of Devas precisely we meditated and we eulogised him by reciting the Vedic mantras. Delighted by our eulogy the unsullied lord delightfully stationed himself into the divine Liṅga after assuming the form of sound.

73-82. The letter 'a' was his head; 'ā' the forehead; 'i' the right eye; 'ī' the left eye; 'u' the right ear; ū the left ear; 'ṛ' the right cheek; ṝ the left cheek, 'lṛ' and 'lṝ' the pairs of his nostrils; 'e' the upper lip, 'ai' the lower lip; 'o' and 'au' the two rows of teeth; 'aṁ' and 'aḥ' the palates; the five letters beginning with 'k' his five hands on the right side; the five letters beginning with "c" his five hands on the left side; the five letters beginning with 'ṭ' his right leg; the five letters beginning with 't' his left leg; the letter 'p' his belly; 'ph' his right side, 'b' his left side; 'bh' his shoulder, 'm' his heart; the letters 'y' to 's' the seven dhātus; 'h' his soul and 'kṣ' his anger. On seeing the great lord along with Umā, Viṣṇu bowed and then looked up at him. He saw a mantra emerging from 'Om' with five digits. Resembling pure crystal it contained thirty eight syllables. It was conducive to the increase of knowledge, and it was the means of achievement of all righteous matters. He saw the Ṛk of twenty four syllables and four digits in Gāyatrī metre and in green colour, with the efficacy for gaining control. He saw the Atharvan mantra of thirty three syllables, eight digits, black in colour and with its efficacy of black magic. He saw the Yajus mantra of thirty five syllables, eight digits, white in colour, with the efficacy for peace. He saw the Sāman mantra of sixtysix syllables, of thirteen digits, in the jagatī metre, in the coral-red colour, with the efficacy for creation and dissolution of the universe.

Having obtained these five mantras, lord Viṣṇu performed japa. He saw lord Śiva in all digits and syllables (constituting the limbs) with body consisting of Ṛk, yajus, and sāman, with Iśāna for his coronet, Tatpuruṣa for his face, Aghora for his heart, Vāmadeva for his private parts, sadyojāta for his feet, serpents for his ornaments, with eyes and hands all round. On seeing the great lord (of above description) the overlord of Brahmā, the cause of creation, sustenance and dissolution and the granter of boons, Viṣṇu eulogized him with pleasing words.

CHAPTER EIGHTEEN

Viṣṇu's praise of Śiva

Viṣṇu said :

1. Obeisance to the single-syllabled Rudra, 'a' in the form of Ātman; obeisance to the primordial deity whose physical body is learning.

2. Obeisance to lord Śiva, the supreme soul in the form of the third syllable 'm'. Obeisance to the lord who is as lustrous as the sun or the fire or the moon. Obeisance to him in the form of yajamāna who performs sacrifice.

3. Obeisance to fire in the form of Rudra. Obeisance to the lord of Rudras. Obeisance to Śiva of auspicious mantra. Obeisance to Sadyojāta. Obeisance to Vedhas, the creator.

4. Obeisance to the illustrious Vāmadeva, the granter of boons and the immortal lord. Obeisance to Aghora, Atighora, Sadyojāta and the deity of vehemence and impetuosity.

5. Obeisance to Iśāna, Śmaśāna (i.e. the lord of cremation ground); obeisance to one of high velocity. Obeisance to the speedy lord whose foot is the Vedas, who has an upward Liṅga and who is Liṅga himself.

6. Obeisance to him who has a golden Liṅga or who is gold himself or who is of watery Liṅga or who is water himself. Obeisance to Śiva, the Liṅga of Śiva. Obeisance to one who pervades all, including the firmament itself.

7. Obeisance to the wind or to one who has the velocity of the wind, and who pervades the wind. Obeisance to the fire, the lord of all fiery articles and who pervades the fire.

8. Obeisance to the water and to one who has become water. Obeisance to one who pervades water. Obeisance to the earth or the atmosphere. Obeisance to one who pervades the earth.

9. Obeisance to one, of the form of sound and touch, taste and smell and to one who has smell. Obeisance to the lord of Gaṇas, and to one who is the most secretive.

10. Obeisance to the infinite. devoid of forms, obeisance to the infinite, devoid of ailments; obeisance to the permanent, the most excellent, who is in the womb of waters, and who is the Yogin.

11. Obeisance to one who is stationed in between Brahmā and Viṣṇu in the midst of waters; obeisance to the splendour, the protector, the destroyer, the perpetual maker and the Death. Obeisance to lord Śiva.

12. Obeisance to the insentient, worthy of contemplation who removes the stress and strain of the sentient, who is formless or of good forms, who has no limbs or who is attractive with limbs.

13. Obeisance to one who has smeared ashes all over the body; obeisance to the cause of the sun, moon and fire; obeisance to the white, of white colour; and to one moving about on the mountain of snows.

14. Obeisance to one of excessively white complexion, white face, white tuft, and white blood.

15. Obeisance to one who facilitates easy crossing (of the ocean of mundane existence), obeisance to the splendid one, obeisance to one having two forms, to one of hundred forms, to one devoid of forms and to one holding a banner.

16. Obeisance to one who has prosperity, grief and absence of grief; obeisance to the Pināka-bearing lord, with matted hairs, devoid of noose, holding a noose, the destroyer of noose.

17. Obeisance to one of good sacrifice, to one having sacrificial offering, to one favourably disposed to the Brahmins. Obeisance to one who is a poet. Obeisance to one having good face and good mouth; who is difficult to be suppressed and who is of good mental control.

18. Obeisance to one who assumed the form of a Brahmin,[83] who is Yama[84] and who has made serpent his bangle. Obeisance to one who is Sanaka, Sanātana, Sanandana and Sanat.

19. Obeisance to one who hunts the deer,[85] who is the great ātman, and the eye of the world. Obeisance to one who has three abodes and to one who is devoid of rajas.

20. Obeisance to Śaṅkhapāla, Śaṅkha, rajas and tamas. Obeisance to Sārasvata, the cloud and the cloud-vehicled. Obeisance be to you.

21. Obeisance to one of good vehicle, devoid of vehicle, the bestower of boons to the devotee, to Śiva, Rudra and pradhāna.

22. Obeisance to you, possessed of three guṇas, having the nature of the four vyūhas, the cause of existence and dissolution.

23. Obeisance to you of the form of salvation, the granter of liberation, the supreme soul, the sage and the all-pervader.

24. Obeisance to you the holy lord, the lord of serpents, of the form of 'Om' and the omnipresent lord.

25. Obeisance to you identical with all,[86] all-pervader, and the primordial lord.

26. Obeisance to the unborn, the lord of subjects, the cause of vyūhas and the great lord of Devas.

27. Obeisance to Śarva, Satya, (truth) and Śamana (the subduer) and Brahmā. Obeisance to the omniscient deity of living beings.

28-29. Obeisance to you, the supreme soul. Obeisance to one invested with the form of intellect, consciousness, memory and knowledge. Obeisance to one comprehensible through knowledge. Obeisance to one in the form of concord and summit. Obeisance to one whose neck is blue.

83. It refers to Śiva disguised as a Brāhmaṇa. ST.
84. i.e. Yama, the god of death and destruction. ST.
85. as a hunter kills the birds and animals. ST.
86. The epithet is applied to Viṣṇu because the waters (nāra) were his first place of motion (ayana). (Cf. Manu : āpo nārā iti praktā*ḥ*), but here, as applied to Śiva it means 'one who lives among the people : नराणां समूहो नारं तदयनं स्थानं यस्य तस्मै ST.

30. Obeisance to one whose half body is female[87], who though unmanifest has eleven forms. Obeisance to one who is immovable.

31. Obeisance to the sun, the moon, who establishes and destroys the universe. Obeisance to one who is the cause of fame, who brings on peace and is the lord of all.

32. Obeisance to the lord of Ambikā, and the lord of Umā. Obeisance to one of golden arms and of golden semen.

33. Obeisance to the blue-tressed one who is wealth. Obeisance to the black-necked deity with matted hairs Obeisance to one with the serpent for his ornament.

34. Obeisance to one riding the bull; obeisance to the creator and destroyer of all; obeisance to one who excelled even the heroic Rāma in prowess; obeisance to you, the lord of Rāma.

35. Obeisance to the Emperor of kings, to one attained by kings, to the overlord of protectors; obeisance to you, O Destroyer of demons.

36. Obeisance to one bedecked in keyūras (armlets). O lord of cows, obeisance be to you. Obeisance to lord Śrīkaṇṭha holding a likuca fruit in the hand.

37. Obeisance to the lord, the chief of the worlds; and to one whose Scripture is the Veda; obeisance to you, to Sāraṅga the Royal Swan.

38. Obeisance to one with golden necklaces and shoulder-lets; to one with serpents for sacred thread, ear-rings and garlands; obeisance to one who has made a serpent his waist-band.

39-42. O Śiva, obeisance to you, having the Vedas in the womb. Obeisance to the foetus containing the entire universe.

Brahmā said :

After having eulogised thus, Viṣṇu ceased along with Brahmā. This excellent hymn is holy, it is destructive of all sins. He who reads this himself or narrates this to the brahmins well versed in the Vedas goes to Brahmā's region though he might have incurred sins. Hence one should perform the Japa of this, read this or narrate this to splendid brahmins for washing off his sins. It has been so ordained by Viṣṇu.

87. Cf. note 27. on p. 18.

CHAPTER NINETEEN

Enlightenment of Viṣṇu

Sūta said :

1. The Supreme Lord said : O excellent among the Devas, I am delighted with you. On beholding me, the great lord, you should cast off all fear.

2-3. Both of you very powerful were born of me formerly. Brahmā, the grandfather of the universe was born from my right side; Viṣṇu, the soul of the universe, sprang from my left side. I am extremely pleased with both of you. I shall grant you the boon of your choice.

4. After saying this, the lord, the storehouse of mercy patted Viṣṇu with his gentle and smooth hands out of compassion.

5. Then with a delightful mind, Viṣṇu bowed and spoke to the great lord who though devoid of Liṅga was stationed in the Liṅga.

6. If love has been generated in you, if boon has to be granted to us, may our devotion to you remain perpetual and unswerving.

7. O Devas. the moon-crested lord accordingly granted them an unswerving devotion and faith.

8. Then Viṣṇu knelt on the ground and bowed to the lord. With perfect control over himself he spoke to the lord in low tones.

9. O lord of the Devas, our controversy has borne splendid fruits, since you yourself have come over here to remove the same.

10. On hearing this, Lord Śiva again spoke smiling to Viṣṇu who bowed to him with his head bent down and who stood with palms joined in reverence.

Lord Śiva said :

11. O lord of earth, you are the projector of dissolution, sustenance and creation. O dear Viṣṇu, protect this world with all its mobile and immobile beings.

12. O Viṣṇu, I am lord Śiva, the unsullied, I divided my-

self into three forms[88] under the names of Brahmā, Viṣṇu and Rudra with the activities of creation, protection and dissolution.

13. O Viṣṇu, abandon your delusion. Protect this Brahmā, who in the Padmakalpa, will become your son.

14. Then you will see me thus, so will the lotus-born Brahmā too. Thus saying the lord vanished there itself.

15. Ever since then the worship of the Liṅga was well established in the world. The great goddess is the altar for the Liṅga. The Liṅga is the great lord himself.

16-17. Liṅga is so called because, O gods, everything gets dissolved in it. The brahmin who reads this narrative of Liṅga, in the presence of the Liṅga image attains Śiva-hood. No doubt need be entertained in this respect.

CHAPTER TWENTY

The enlightenment of Brahmā

The sages said :

1-6. How did Brahmā become the lotus-born (deity), formerly, in the Padmakalpa ? How did Viṣṇu and Brahmā see lord Śiva ? Please recount all this particularly now.

Sūta said :

It was one vast sheet of water, terrible, undivided and full of darkness.

In the middle of that vast sheet of water lay Lord Viṣṇu holding the conch, discus and the iron club. He had the lustre of the cloud. His eyes resembled the lotus. He wore the coronet. He was known as Hari, lord of Śrī, Nārāyaṇa and Puruṣottama. From his mouth emerged all souls, all beings. He had eight arms and a large chest. He, the source of origin of the universe, the yogic ātman, the knower of the yoga, adopted an inconceivable yoga and occupied the lofty body of

88. The supreme lord in his qualified (sakala) state is characterized by three functions : viz. creation, sustenance and destruction. The idea is often repeated in the Purāṇas.

a huge serpent that had a thousand hoods and whose splendour was incomparable. In that vast sheet of water, the lord lay on that great couch of serpent.

7-8. A tall and lofty lotus was sportively created in his umbilicus as he lay there all-powerful self-contented but unwearied in activities. It was hundred Yojanas long. It resembled the mid-day sun. It had adamantine stalk.

9-11. Even as the bountiful lord was playing (with the lotus), Brahmā, who was born of the cosmic Egg of golden womb, who had golden colour, who was beyond the pale of the sense-organs, who had four faces and large eyes came near the lord casually. On seeing Viṣṇu of splendid eyes sporting with the lotus that was glorious, divine, splendid and fragrant, Brahmā was surprised and asked in a tone filled with gentleness—

"Who are you lying (here) in the middle of the waters?"

12-16. On hearing the splendid words of Brahmā, Viṣṇu got up from his couch and with his eyes beaming with surprise replied:—

"In every kalpa this is my shelter and asylum. What had been done, whatever is being done and what would be done (everything is done here itself). The heaven, the atmosphere and the earth everything is my region."

After saying thus, lord Viṣṇu addressed him again—"Who are you? Whence do you come near me? Where do you intend to go? Where is your abode? Who are you that have the universe for your physical body? What can I do for you?"

17-24. Thereupon Brahmā replied to Viṣṇu. Being deluded by the Māyā of lord Śiva, he could not fully comprehend Viṣṇu who himself was deluded by the Māyā of Śiva and hence unknowable.

Brahmā said :

"Just like you I too am the Prajāpati, the primordial creator." On hearing with wonder the words of Brahmā the creator of the worlds and on being permitted by him, the source of origin of the universe, the great yogin, Viṣṇu entered through the mouth of Brahmā, out of curiosity. Within the belly of Brahmā he saw the eighteen continents[89] together with the oceans and mountains. On entering the belly of Brahmā, Viṣṇu of great splendour and brawny arms saw the eternal seven worlds[90] up to the column of Brahmā in which the people of the four castes[91] stayed. Then uttering repeatedly, "How powerful is his penance" he wandered through different worlds of diverse creation. Though he wandered for a thousand years, he could not reach the end. Then he (Viṣṇu) the support of the worlds who had Śeṣa the lord of snakes as his bed, came out of Brahmā's mouth, and addressed him thus:

25 "O sinless one! You are the beginning, the end and the middle of the universe. You are Time, the quarters and the ether. O sinless one, I do not perceive the limits of your belly."

26-28. After saying thus, Viṣṇu spoke to Brahmā again—"In the same manner as you, I also am a lord. O illustrious one, please enter my belly and see the wonderful worlds therein." On hearing these pleasant words of Viṣṇu, Brahmā of truthful exploits approved of them and entered his belly. Then he saw those very worlds stationed in his womb.

29-30. He roamed about therein but he could not find the end. Then on observing the movement of Brahmā, lord Viṣṇu closed the openings of the passage and slept a perfect sleep.

On seeing the openings closed Brahmā assumed a subtle form and found an opening in the umbilicus.

89. Dvīpa in the broader sense signifies a continental division of the terrestrial world. The number of such divisions varies according to different authorities being four, seven, nine, thirteen or eighteen. According to the Purāṇic tradition dvīpas are situated round the mountain Meru like the petals of a lotus flower and separated from one another by a distinct ocean. In the restricted sense dvīpa is a land enclosed between two rivers (mod. doab). The word 'dvīpa' is used in both these senses in the Purāṇas.

90. Seven regions. Cf. 1.23.53-54. The three—Bhū, Bhuva and Svar are separated from the four higher regions—Mahas, Jana, Tapas and Satya by a mountain Lokāloka. The light of the luminaries illumines the three worlds but fails to reach the four higher regions.

91. Cāturvarṇya. 'The concept of fourfold social organization is already found in the *ṚV.* (x.90.12). The idea is developed in the Purāṇas. *Vāyu* (Ch.9) speaks of the cosmic origin of society (113-114; 139-140). Śiva is the originator, Manu the founder and Bali the propagator of Varṇa (*Ibid.* 1.30.218; 59, 35-36; 61-98, 95-32).

31. Then the four-faced Brahmā came out of the stalk of the lotus and assumed his own form.

32. The Self-born Brahmā, the source of the origin of the universe sat in the lotus, resembling in lustre the interior of the lotus itself.

33-37. In the meantime, even as either of them was wholly engaged in a struggle with the other in the middle of the ocean, lord Śiva of immeasurable soul, the lord of living beings appeared there itself. Holding a trident in hand and clad in garments of pure gold he came to the place where Viṣṇu was lying on Śeṣa—the lord of serpents. As he waded through the waters quickly, big drops of water rose up in the sky, kicked up by his feet. The wind that blew was very hot and cold. On perceiving this wonderful phenomenon, Brahmā spoke to Viṣṇu "See how hot and cold waters make the lotus shake.

38-40. Clear this doubt of mine and tell me what else you wish to do now."

On hearing these words uttered by lord Viṣṇu, the destroyer of Asuras and of unequalled exploits meditated thus:—"What? Who is this great being occupying my umbilicus? He speaks pleasing words though I have been angry with him." After thinking thus, Viṣṇu spoke in reply:—

41-48. "O Sir, are you in a perplexed state inside the lotus? O lord, what is it that I have done wherefore O excellent one among men, you speak to me thus: What is it for? Tell me factually." Lord Brahmā, the storehouse of the Vedas, replied to the lotus-eyed lord of Devas who spoke thus in accordance with the activities of the world:—"It was I who formerly entered your belly in accordance with your wish. Just as all the worlds within my belly were seen by you O lord, so also all the worlds in your belly are seen by me. O sinless one after a thousand years I returned. With a spirit of rivalry and a desire to subject me to control, all the openings were closed suddenly by you. O blessed one, I pondered over it. By dint of my own splendour I gained exit through the umbilicus by the lotus stalk. Let there be no dejection in your mind: O Viṣṇu, this is the sequence of events in their gradual advancement. What should be done by me hereafter, kindly tell me: What shall I do?"

49-51. On hearing these loving, pleasing auspicious and irreproachable words of Brahmā, Viṣṇu the destroyer of Hiraṇyakaśipu and of immeasurable soul, spoke sincere and simple words. This type of adverse action was not envisaged by me. I closed all the openings sportively and casually out of a desire for enlightening you.

52. You should not mis-understand me. You deserve my respect and worship. O auspicious one, forgive if at all I have committed any offence against you.

53-58. You are borne by me, O lord, descend from this lotus. I cannot bear you. You are refulgent and weighty. Thereupon Brahmā said once again: 'Tell me, what boon you desire to have. O lord, take me down from the lotus'. Then Viṣṇu said : 'O slayer of enemies, you should be my son. You will attain splendid pleasure. Speak agreeable and loving words. O lord, descend from the lotus. You are a great yogin. You are worthy of our worship. You are the Praṇava itself. Henceforth you will be the lord of all; adorned with a white turban you will be known as 'padmayoni'[92]—one whose source of origin is a lotus. O Brahmā, O lord, as son to me, you will be the overlord of seven worlds'.

Thus the lord granted him the boon and Brahmā accepted the same cheerfully and spitelessly. Just then on seeing the miraculous, huge-faced Śiva with the lustre of the rising sun, Brahmā said to Viṣṇu.

59-62. "O Viṣṇu, who is this incomprehensible person with a huge face and curved fangs? With hairs dishavelled, with ten arms stretched and holding a trident, with all-round eyes he seems to be the lord of the universe. He has a deformed body and a girdle of Muñja grass. With huge penis lifted up, he is roaring loudly and terribly. With a mass of splendour and lustre he has enveloped the quarters and the firmament. He comes this way itself." On being addressed thus by Brahmā, lord Viṣṇu replied as follows:

92. The Purāṇas describe the golden lotus flower of one thousand petals sprung up from the navel of Viṣṇu while he lay recumbent in the ocean. Cf. *Matsya* 168.15. According to *Harivaṁśa* (Bhaviṣya-parva, chs. 7-14) the golden lotus became the seat of Brahmā and also his birth-place. Hence Brahmā is called padmayoni.

63-66. "He is wading through the ocean with great speed. When his feet press the surface of water, as he wades through the ocean with great speed, masses of water rise up even to the sky. O lotus-born one, you are being sprinkled from all sides with a heap of water. By the wind coming out of his nostrils, this great lotus emerged out of my navel is being shaken. It is lord Śiva who has no origin and who destroys the world that has come. Let us eulogise the bull-bannered lord with hymns of prayer."

67-68. Then Brahmā who was infuriated spoke to Viṣṇu whose eyes resembled the lotus:—"Indeed you do not know yourself as the lord of all the worlds. You do not know me also as Brahmā, the eternal creator of the worlds. Who is this Śiva apart from us both?"

69-73. On hearing these words of Brahmā uttered in rage Viṣṇu spoke: "O auspicious one, bestower of welfare, do not speak ill of the great soul. Here is he who has the lustre of the splendid yoga, who is the invincible bestower of boons, who is the unchanging ancient Puruṣa, the cause of this universe. He is the sower of seeds and the refulgence of seeds, shining by himself. He, the lord, plays with toys as do the childern. Pradhāna, the eternal womb, the unmanifest Prakṛti and the quality tamas—darkness—these are my names, since I perpetually give birth to creation. The person of your query is lord Śiva who is the goal of the ascetics who, being afraid of the pangs of birth and death resort to him. He is the sower of the seed; you are the seed itself and I am the eternal womb."[93] On being addressed thus, Brahmā, the soul of the universe asked again:

74. "How is it that you are the womb, I am the seed and he

93. According to the Purāṇic account of creation (sarga), in the beginning, the Cosmic Egg which arose out of the waters was insentient. It remained in this state for thousands of years until it was activated by the sentient principle which entering divided it into two parts. One of the two halves became the celestial and the other the terrestrial sphere.

The creation is traced to the seed, personified as Brahmā, deposited in the foetus personified as Viṣṇu, by Śiva the sower of the seed. In fact, both the insentient egg and the sentient principle that activates it belong to Śiva himself who out of sheer will and sportively too, creates, dissolves and then re-creates and re-dissolves the universe.

(lord Śiva) the sower. This is a puzzle which you alone can solve."

75-79. After thinking about the multiformed creation, Viṣṇu spoke in answer to this specific query of Brahmā, the creator of the worlds.

There is no other greater living being than him. He is a great mystery, the dimensional abode of intellect and the coveted goal of spiritualists. He split himself into two. His unqualitative part remained unmenifest; the qualitative one came into appearance. Of him who was aware of activities of Prakṛti and who was inaccessible and fathomless, the seed was born, formerly, at the first creation. This seed was laid into my womb which, after the lapse of some time, grew into a golden egg in the ocean.

80. For a thousand years the Egg lay in the waters. Thereafter it was split into two by the force of the wind.

81. The upper lid of the Egg became the heaven and the lower lid became the earth. The foetus became the lofty golden mountain Meru.

82. Then with the soul entering the womb, you, the lord, Hiraṇyagarbha the most excellent of the lords of Devas, and of four faces were born.

83. On seeing that the world with stars, sun and moon, was void you meditated. Then the kumāras were born to you.

84. Pleasing to look at, they became ascetics, the predecessors of yatis. Thus at the end of a thousand years they were born as your sons.

85-87. They resembled the terrestrial fire in brilliance. They had eyes large as the petals of a lotus. Sanat and Ṛbhu remained celibate having sublimated sexuality; the other three were Sanaka, Sanātana and Sanandana who were born simultaneously and who could visualize things even beyond the scope of sense-organs. They possessed great intellect; they were the cause of the sustenance of the worlds. They were devoid of the three types of miseries and they desisted from worldly activities.

88-90. Seeing that life and death in the world yield but little pleasure, that it is attended with great strain and pain, that births and deaths recur again and again, that there is little pleasure in heaven, that miseries abound in hell, knowing the Śāstraic injunctions about the inevitability of the future as also that Ṛbhu and Sanat were under your control, the three—Sanaka, Sanatana and Sanāndana of great prowess eschewed the three guṇas and took to spiritual life.

91-94. Thus in the functioning of the kalpa, when the three sons—Sanaka and others took to detachment you will become confused and deluded through the illusory power of lord Śiva. Then O sinless one, your consciousness will perish. In the present kalpa, the elements both gross and subtle will be affected by his māyā who, in fact, is the activizer of these elements. This great and glorious account of the most excellent of all Devas is as famous as the golden Meru—the mountainous abode of Devas.

95-97. Knowing him as the great lord and knowing me as the lotus-eyed Viṣṇu, knowing also that the lord is the greatest of all living beings, the bestower of boons and the preceptor of the universe, you should bow to him, uttering the praṇava (oṁkāra) mantra and the Sāman verses. If he is infuriated he will burn us both by his very breath. After realizing the lord of great strength and yoga, I shall keep you in front and eulogize him who is of fiery and dazzling splendour.

CHAPTER TWENTY ONE

Eulogy of Lord Śiva

Sūta said:

1-3 Thereafter keeping Brahmā in front, the Garuḍa-emblemed deity Viṣṇu recited the hymn to lord Śiva, containing his past, present and future names as enjoined by the Vedas.

Viṣṇu said :

Obeisance to you, O deity of holy rites, of infinite splendour, the overlord of the field (kṣetra), the sower of the seed, the trident-bearer, of excellent penis deserving worship, the staff-holder and of dry and arid semen.

4. Obeisance to the eldest, the excellent, the foremost and the first; Obeisance to one who is worthy of honour and worship. Obeisance to Sadyojāta.

5. Obeisance to the unfathomable and the lord of jīvas (personal souls). Obeisance to the naked and the lord of all created beings.

6. Obeisance to the lord of the Vedas, the Smṛtis and the lord of activities, charities and substances.

7. Obeisance to the lord of Yoga and Sāṅkhya. Obeisance to the lord of the sages who are bound together by the Polar Star.

8. Obeisance to you, the lord of stars and planets; obeisance to the lord of thundering sound of lightning, thunderbolt and clouds.

9. Obeisance to the lord of great oceans and their islands. Obeisance to the lord of mountains and continents.

10. Obeisance to the lord of the rivers and rivulets, to the lord of medicinal herbs and plantations.

11. Obeisance to the cause of Dharma, piety and righteousness, to the lord of maintenance (of all created beings), to the lord of Pārvatī and her eternal associate.

12. Obeisance to the lord of 'rasas', jewels, and the units of time.

13. Obeisance to the lord of day, night, fortnights and months; Obeisance to you, the lord of seasons and the lord of number.

14 Obeisance to the lord of 'aparārdha' (half of Brahmā's age) Obeisance to the lord of Parārdha (the other half of Brahmā's age); Obeisance to the lord of Purāṇas and to the lord of creation.

15-17. Obeisance to the lord of the Vyantaras, of yoga, and of fourfold creation. Obeisance to one of infinite vision; to the lord of all occupations that have sprung up from the beginning of kalpa (that is creation itself). Obeisance to the lord of the universe and to the overlord of Brahmā. Obeisance to the source of origin of sacred lores and to the overlord of holy rites.

18-19. Obeisance to the source of origin and the overlord of mantras, pitṛs and the individual souls. Obeisance to you, the deity of righteous speech, the ancient bull and the lord of souls. Obeisance to the deity who has Nandin, the leader of cows and bulls, as his banner.

20. Obeisance to the lord of Prajāpatis, to the lord of the Siddhas, to the lord of daityas, dānavas and rākṣasas.

21. Obeisance to the lord of gandharvas, yakṣas, garuḍa, snakes, serpents and birds.

22. Obeisance to the overlord of the guhyas and piśācas, to Gokarṇa, to the protector, to Saṅkukarṇa (one whose ears resemble the pike).

23. Obeisance to the incomprehensible varāha (boar); to the star bear, devoid of rajas, the lord of Devas and asuras and gaṇas.

24. Obeisance to the lord of the waters; the lord of refulgence; the lord of Lakṣmī (glory and splendour) and the lord of the earth.

25. Obeisance to one who unifies the strong and the weak; to the agitator who cannot be excited; to the bull (Nandi) who has a single illuminated horn; and a huge hump.

26. Obeisance to one who is stable in the body; to one enveloped in halo; to one who represents the past, future and present.

27. Obeisance to the brilliant and virile, to the heroic and the unconquered, to the bestower of boons, to the best of persons of great soul.

28. Obeisance to mahat (the first evolute of Prakṛti) in all its 3 stages, past, present and future;[94] obeisance to you representing the people; to penance, to the bestower of boons.

29. Obeisance to the minute as well as the great; to the all-pervading lord. Obeisance to bondage and liberation; to heaven and hell.

30. Obeisance to lord Śiva, who is worthy of worship. Obeisance to the sacrifice, and to the deity of effulgent brilliance. Obeisance to the principle beyond all attributes.

31-32. Obeisance to the noose, to the weapon, to one equipped with missiles as ornaments; to one who is the material for sacrifice; to one invoked; to one who partakes of what is offered in the sacrifice; to one who does desirable acts; to one who does acts of charity, such as digging wells; to the

94. The 26b, 27 and 28a are repeated in 34 and 35 of this Ch.

brahmin performing agniṣṭoma; to the member of the assembly; to one who does the sacrificial ablution after giving rewards to the sacrificers.

33. Obeisance to one refraining from violence, to one devoid of temptations, to one who is a redeemer of souls (Jivas), to one who bestows nourishment, to one who habitually represents and practises good conduct.

34-35. Obeisance to one who represents the past, future and present. Obeisance to the brilliant and virile, to the heroic and the unconquered, to the bestower of boons and to the best of persons of great soul. Obeisance to 'mahat' the first evolute of Prakṛti in all its three stages: past, present and future. Obeisance to one without a fear.

36. Obeisance to the ever young, of golden form, the bestower of boons, the lower, the upper and the lord of the sleepers-on.

37-38. Obeisance to the wearer of garlands, to the enjoyer of objects through the vehicle of sense-organs. Obeisance to one representing the universe, to one who is universe-formed and to one with heads, hands and feet all round. Obeisance to Rudra the unsurpassed. Obeisance to one who receives offerings poured into the fire. Obeisance to one who represents fire that carries oblations to the gods.

39. Obeisance to the holy one who has all attainments. Obeisance to the sacrifice and to one devoted to the sacrifice, to one who is a good warrior, to one of terrible aspect and to one who agitates persons who cannot be easily excited.

40. Obeisance to one of good progeny, to one of good intellect and to one who is the brilliant sun. Obeisance to the enlightened, pure and all-pervasive and to one who is contemplated on by all.

41. Obeisance to one who is both gross and subtle, to one who is both visible as well as invisible. Obeisance to one who showers and blazes, and who is both the wind and the winter.

42. Obeisance to you, of curly hairs, of great chest and tuft, of golden colour, or resembling gold.

43. Obeisance to one who has odd eyes, to one assuming the form of Liṅga, to one of tawny colour, to one of great prowess and to the destroyer of rain, to one of gentle eyes.

44. Obeisance to one of brown, white, black, red, tawny and yellow colours. Obeisance to one who is possessed of a quiver.

45. Obeisance to you, marked and not marked by special traits; Obeisance to one worthy of worship and adornment, Obeisance to one who is a suitable patron.

46. Obeisance to one befitting welfare. Obeisance to the elderly one. Obeisance to one favourably disposed. Obeisance to one representing the past, to the truthful one. Obeisance to one who is both true and untrue.

47-48. Obeisance to one of lotus colour, to the destroyer of death, the lord of death, to one of white, dark, tawny and red colours and to one having the colour of a charmingly brilliant cloud at dusk, to one initiated, to one having lotus-like hands; to one without garments and to one with matted hair.

49-50. Obeisance to one without magnitude; to one identical with all; to the unchanging and immortal one; to one who represents colour and smell; to the eternal and to the uninjured one; to the huge one in front; to one without illusions; to one full and satisfied; to one difficult of access; to one representing anger and to the tawny coloured one.

51. Obeisance to one whose physical body is capable of being known and (at the same time) not known; obeisance to the powerful, to the brave; and the speedy one; obeisance to the deity behind sandy soil and behind current of water; to one stationed, extended and stretched.

52. Obeisance to you the intelligent potter; obeisance to you, with the crescent Moon on the forehead. Obeisance to the wonderful one of variegated dress and colours and of the form of intellect.

53. Obeisance to one, of great consciousness and alertness; obeisance to you, the most satisfied one and the best bestower of favours; obeisance to the forbearing one, to one having self-control; and to one of adamantine body.

54-55. Obeisance to the destroyer of the Rākṣasas, to the dispeller of poisons, to the bright-necked one and to one who is above anger. Obeisance to the all consuming God of Death; and to one holding sharp weapons, to one endowed with great joy, to one with great gaiety, to one comprehensible only to the ascetics; to one devoid of ailments, to one identical with all and to the great god of Death.

56. Obeisance to Praṇava; to the lord of Praṇava; to the destroyer of Bhaganetra; to the hunter of deer; to the diligent one and to the destroyer of Dakṣa's sacrifice.

57. Obeisance to one, the soul of all creatures, to one who excels all lords, to the destroyer of the Puras, to one having good weapons and to one having bow and axe.

58. Obeisance to one who destroyed Pūṣadanta and Bhaganetra; to the bestower of desires; to the excellent one; to one who burnt the body of Kāma.

59. Obeisance to one of terrible face in the battlefield; to one having face of a great elephant; obeisance to the lord who destroyed the Daityas and to one who caused distress to the Daityas.

60. Obeisance to the destroyer of snow; to the severe one; to one wearing wet hide; to one having perpetual interest in the cremation ground; to one holding the fire-brand.

61. Obeisance to you the protector of lives; to the wearer of skulls and to one surrounded by care-free goblins of different classes.

62. Obeisance to one having male-cum-female body; to one who pleases the Goddess; to one having matted hair; to one having tonsured head and to one having the serpent for sacred thread.

63. Obeisance to one the habitual dancer, to one fond of dance and music, to the lord of anger, to one practising music and to one who is sung about by the sages.

64. Obeisance to one in the form of a lion, to one of sharp nature, to one both pleasing and not pleasing, to the horrifying and the terrible one, to the suppressor of Bhaga demon.

65. Obeisance to one praised and sung about by the enlightened souls. Obeisance to the highly blessed, to one who laughs boisterously, who roars like a lion and who flaps and blows.

66. Obeisance to one who roars and jumps; obeisance to the joyous soul, to the benevolent, to one who breathes, runs and controls all.

67. Obeisance to one who meditates, yawns, cries, runs, gallops and sports about; to one who has a protruding belly.

68. Obeisance to one who has functions and no functions to perform, to one who has a thousand heads, to one who is poor or miserly, to one who has an impassioned body, to one who has small anklet-bells.

69. Obeisance to one of deformed dress; to the ruthless and unforgiving; to one who cannot be measured; to the protector; to the illuminated and devoid of attributes.

70. Obeisance to one fond of the elegant, to the beautiful, to one adorned with a crest-jewel, to the minutest of the minute and to one who cannot be measured or known by qualities.

71-74. Obeisance to one possessed of good qualities; to the secret one, to one who goes to impassable places. This earth is the mother of worlds. Your feet are resorted to by good men. Your belly, the support of all Siddhis, contains the wide firmament bedecked in clusters of stars. Just like the galaxy of stars the glorious necklace shines on your chest. To you, the ten quarters are the ten arms bedecked in shoulderlets and bracelets. Your neck has great girth and extent; it is comparable to the blue collyrium; it is adorned with golden threads.

75. Your face is irrepressible; it is terrible due to the curved fangs; it is incomparable. Your head which is heaven itself shines all the more with its turban of lotus garlands.

76-81. Refulgence in the sun, brilliance in the moon, firmness in the mountains, strength in the wind, heat in the fire, chilliness in the waters and sound in the firmament—the wise know these qualities to be due to the internal throbbing of the imperishable lord.

The following names of lord Śiva are to be used for Japa, viz.—Mahādeva, Mahāyoga, Maheśvara, Puriśaya (lying in the city of mind), Guhāvāsin (dweller in the cave), Khecara (moving about in the sky), Rajanicara (walking at night), Taponidhi (storehouse of penance), Guhaguru (Sire of Guha), Nandana (delighter), Nandavardhana (the increaser of delight), Hayaśīrṣa- (horse-necked), Payodhātā (yielder of milk), Vidhātā (dispenser of justice), Bhūtabhāvana (activiser of living beings), Boddhavya (the object of knowledge), Bodhitā (the subject of knowledge) Netā (leader), Durdharṣa (invincible), Duṣprakampana (unshakeable), Bṛhadratha (having a great chariot), Bhīmakarman (of terrible activities) Bṛhatkīrti (of great fame), Dhanañjaya (conqueror of wealth), Ghaṇṭāpriya (fond of bells), Dhvajin (one with a banner), Chatrin (one with an umbrella), Pinākin (bearer of the bow Pināka), Dhvajanīpati (Lord of the army) Kavacin, (having armour), Paṭṭiśin (having the iron club), Khaḍgin (having sword),. Dhanurhasta (having the bow in the hand), Paraśvadhin (having the axe), Aghasmara (non-destroyer), Anagha (sinless), Śūra (heroic), Devarāja (king of Devas), Arimardana (Supressor of enemies).

82-83. Formerly, after propitiating you the enemies were slain by us in the battle. You are a submarine fire. Not satiated by drinking all the waters of the ocean, you are infuriated in form, but delighted within. You are the bestower of desires; you can go as you wish; you are fond (of us); you are the celibate religious student. You are unfathomable and favourably disposed towards the Brahmins; you are adored by the society.

84. You have made sacrifice the everlasting treasure of the Devas. The fire-god bears to you the offering, as mentioned in the Vedas O supreme lord, if you are pleased we too become pleased.

85. You are the lord of Pārvatī, you are beginningless. At the time of first creation you are Brahmā, the maker of worlds. The followers of the Sāṁkhya system realise you as one beyond prakṛti and at the close of meditation they enter you, devoid of death.

86. Those who meditate on you, understand you as perpetual siddha through yoga and then eschew those yogas. Those enlightened persons who resort to you through their actions enjoy divine bliss.

87. The greatness of yours has been glorified in accordance with what we know according to our capacity. Your reality and principles cannot be enumerated; you are the supreme soul who cannot be easily crossed.

88-91. Be auspicious towards us everywhere. As you are so you are; obeisance be to you.

Sūta said:

He who recites this prayer by Brahmā and Viṣṇu, he who narrates this to the brahmins, or he who listens to this with concentration shall obtain that benefit which one attains after performing ten thousand horse sacrifices. Even a man of sinful activity who listens to this in the temple of Śiva or respects this will be liberated and will live in Brahmā's world. He who recites this at the time of śrāddha or a divine rite or during sacrifice or during the sacred ablution or in the midst of good men reaches the proximity of Brahmā.

CHAPTER TWENTY TWO

Creation of Rudras

Sūta said:

1-2. On seeing both of them extremely humble, the lord of Umā with eyes tawny as honey, was much delighted, thanks to the exposition of truth. The three-eyed, the pināka-bearing, and the trident-holder lord Śiva, the destroyer of Dakṣa's sacrifice became very glad.

3. On hearing their nectar like words lord Śiva sportingly asked them though he knew their intentions.

4-7. "Who are you noble souls eagerly yearning for each other's welfare? You lotus-eyed ones have somehow met together in this terribly extensive flood."

Glancing at each other, the noble souls replied: "O lord, what is there that remains unknown to you? O lord Rudra of great 'Māyā', we two have been created by you willingly."

On hearing their words and having honoured and greeted them the glorious lord spoke sweetly in smooth words :—

"O Brahmā ! O Viṣṇu ! I am speaking to you.

8. I am delighted by your devotion couched in words of perpetual value. Both of you are endearing to my heart.

9. What shall I give you now? Which is sweeter boon you desire?" Then the blessed lord Viṣṇu spoke to lord Śiva :

10. O lord ! everything has been granted by you. If you are so pleased with me, O lord ! grant that my devotion for you remains stable.

11. On being requested thus lord Śiva realised it. He honoured Viṣṇu and granted him devotion to his lotus-feet.

12. "You are the creator of this world. You are its presiding deity. Hail unto you, O dear, O lotus-eyed lord, I shall go (now)."

13-15. After saying this the lord blessed Brahmā too. Greatly delighted he patted Brahmā with his auspicious hands and said:—"O dear, surely you are equal to me. You are my devotee too. Hail unto you. I shall leave now, O deity of good rites, may there be perfect awareness in you."

16-17. After saying this, the lord of the Gaṇas bowed to by all Devas, vanished there itself. After attaining perfect knowledge from Viṣṇu, Brahmā whose source of origin was the lotus, performed terrible penance with a desire to create. Even as he performed this penance, nothing resulted.

18. After a great deal of time his misery turned into anger. From the eyes overwhelmed with anger drops of tears fell down.

19-20. From those drops of tears, huge poisonous snakes appeared. They had all the three humours, the wind, bile and phlegm. They were highly blessed; they were adorned with Svastika marks. Their hairs were dishevelled and scattered. On seeing the snakes born at the outset Brahmā censured himself.

21. O fie upon the fruit of my penance of this sort, if it were to be like this. Even in the beginning, my progeny has become the destroyer of the world.

22. Originating from anger and fury a severe loss of sense overwhelmed him. Out of the distress resulting from his loss of sense, he lost his life.

23. From the body of Brahmā of unequalled valour, the eleven Rudras[95] sprang up crying, out of sympathy and mercy.

95. The word Rudra is derivable from √ru to cry and √dru to move. The Purāṇas make frequent reference to the crying of Rudras. *ŚP.* (*Vāyavīya* 12. 25-30) identifies Rudras with the life principles, i.e. the prāṇas that activate the insentient matter for creation. As soon as Rudra or Prāṇa becomes

24. They became known as Rudras due to their crying. The Rudras and the prāṇas are identical with each other.

25-28. The prāṇas are stationed in all living beings. The trident-bearing lord Śiva who enforces strict discipline granted him life again. After obtaining life, lord Brahmā saluted lord Śiva, the lord of Devas. By means of Gāyatrī he perceived him as identical with the universe. On seeing and eulogizing him as such, Brahmā was struck with wonder. Bowing to him again and again, he proclaimed : "O lord ! how is it that you have assumed such forms as Sadyojāta and others."

CHAPTER TWENTY THREE

Various Kalpas

Sūta said:

1. On hearing the words of Brahmā, lord Śiva in the form of Brahman spoke to him smilingly, in order to enlighten him.

2-3. When the Śveta kalpa was current, it was I who existed then. I had white turban, white garlands and white garments. I was white myself with white bones, white hairs, white blood and white complexion[96] So the kalpa too was known as Śvetakalpa.

4. Gāyatrī, the goddess of Devas, born of me, had white limbs, white colour, white blood. She was known as Brahmāṇī.

5. O lord of Devas, that was why I had been understood by you as the secret deity. By my penance I had assumed the form of Sadyojāta.

manifest in the organism it cries for food. Cf. *Harivaṁśa* 2.74.22; 3.14.39. Another characteristic of the Rudras is their rhythmic movement (dravaṇa, from √dru to move) which is responsible for the incessant flow of creation represented by the Śatarudrīya or Koṭirudrīya concept. Cf. असङ्ख्याता सहस्राणि ये रुद्रा अधि भूम्याम् *YV*. 16.4; *Vāyu* 10.58.

96. Śvetalohitaḥ—nūtana-śveta-rūpaḥ *ST*., of new white complexion. For "lohita" as a synonym of 'new' see *Viśva*: 'lohitaḥ syān nave bhaume'.

6. The title Sadyojāta is a secret Brahma ; the twice-born who know me, who have assumed secret nature, shall attain nearness to me whence there is no return.

7-12. When the next kalpa known as lohita, as a result of my colour, came, Gāyatrī glorified as a cow, born with red flesh, red bone, red blood, red milk, red eyes and red udders was known as Brahmāṇī. Since the colour was changed into red and since the lord was Vāma, I was known as Vāmadeva. O deity of great strength, then also I, who was in a different colour, was recognised by you who had practised self-control by resorting to yoga. I was then known as Vāmadeva. The twice-born who realise my Vāmadeva form shall go to Rudra's world whence there is no return.

13. When the yuga gradually changed and I became yellow in colour, the kalpa was known as Pīta—the name assigned by me.

14. Gāyatrī, the goddess of Devas born of me was named Brahmāṇī. She was yellow in body, yellow in blood and yellow in colour.

15-17. O deity of great strength, there too, I was realized by yogins devoted to the practice of yoga, through your yogic mind. I was realized by you in the form of Tatpuruṣa. Hence, it was, O deity born of the golden egg, I got the Tatpuruṣa form. Persons endowed with penance, devoid of impurities, who are in contact with Brahman and who know me as Rudra, and Rudrāṇī as Gāyatrī—the mother of the Vedas go to Rudra's world whence there is no return.

18-21. When I became terrible and black in colour the kalpa was known as Kṛṣṇa after the colour assumed by me. There I resemble Kāla (god of death). I am Kāla (Time), the reckoner of the worlds. O Brahmā, I was then known by you as Ghora (the terrible) with terrible exploits. O lord of Devas, Gāyatrī, born of me, was black in body, black in blood, black in form and was named Brahmāṇī. Hence to those who know me that I have assumed the ghora form, I, the changeless one, shall be Aghora (non-terrible) and Śānta (quiescent).

22-25. O Brahmā, when I assumed the universal form I was realized by you by means of the yogic trance. Gāyatrī, the sustainer of the worlds[97], also assumed the universal form. To those who know me as having assumed this universal form, I shall always become auspicious and gentle. That Kalpa too will be known as Viśvarūpa (= of universal form).

26-29. These four who are of all kinds of forms will become popular as my sons. Since they are of different colours, their subjects too will be of different colours or castes (Varṇas), and allowed the use of Gāyatrī. Man's aim of life will be fourfold: virtue, wealth, desire and liberation. All living beings will come under four groups[98], four stages of life. The feet of Dharma will be four[99] since my sons are four in number.

30. Hence the universe consisting of the mobile and immobile beings is stationed in the four yugas. Since it is stationed in the four yugas it shall have four feet.

31-32. There are eight worlds: Bhūḥ, Bhuvaḥ, Svar, Mahar, Janar, Tapas, Satya and Viṣṇu. These are established in the eight substratums each of which is imperishable. Bhuḥ, Bhuvaḥ, Svar and Mahaḥ constitute the four substratums.

33. The first is Bhūḥ, the second Bhuvaḥ, the third Svar and Mahar is the fourth.

34-35. The fifth is Janaḥ, the sixth Tapas, the seventh Satya whence people do not return to this world. The world of Viṣṇu is the eighth. It is also the spot whence a return to this world is difficult. Beyond that is the world of Skandha and Umā endowed with all attainments.

36-39. Beyond that is the world of Rudra—the splendid region of yogins. The twice-born who are devoid of ego, who have neither lust nor anger and whose minds are devoted to yoga alone can enter it. Since Gāyatrī was seen by you as four-footed, the worlds are also four, viz. the world of Umā, Kumāra, Maheśvara and Viṣṇu.[100] Again, since Gāyatrī was

97. Sarvabhakṣā—"resorted to by all". *ST.* interprets differently: sarvam pātālajātam bhakṣayati nāśayati sā—one who consumes all the products of the nether regions.

98. catvāraḥ—four classes of living beings as mentioned by *ST*: jarāyuja-aṇḍaja-svedaja-udbhijjarūpāḥ.

99. The four feet of righteousness, according to *ST.* comprise dayā (compassion), dānam (charity), tapaḥ (penance), satyam (truth).

100. *pādānta*—the ultimate region, i.e. the world of Viṣṇu.

seen as four-footed, the animals shall also be four-footed. Their udders too will be four.

40-41. Since the Soma-juice, which is the life of living beings, accompanied by Vedic chants, fell off from my mouth, the cows came to be known as those whose udders are sucked. Hence the nectar in the form of the Soma-juice is known as the life of living beings. Hence too, the animals became quadrupeds; the whiteness of their milk is also due to that.

42-44. Since the great Goddess was seen as biped in the course of the rites, Gāyatrī the creator of the worlds is also of the same nature. Hence all human beings are bipeds, endowed with two breasts. Since the great goddess, the unborn deity of great strength, was seen by you as supporting all living beings, therefore, the subjects will have all kinds of form.

45-51. The unborn deity shall have great splendour and universal form and from his face there will come out the fire-God whose energy will be unfailing. Hence, the pure and all-pervading fire-god has the form of living body. The pure-souled men of two births who see me as endowed with the faculties of overlordship, sense-control and omnipresence become liberated from rajas and tamas. Eschewing physical body they attain my vicinity and never return to this earth.

O brahmins, lord Brahmā who was thus addressed by Rudra bowed to him. Becoming purified in the mind he spoke to him again. "O lord, you are aware of the greatness of Gāyatrī as well as the glory of the Supreme lord (Maheśvara). O lord, may you kindly grant me the highest abode of Gāyatrī and that of yourself". The lord then granted the boon to him, Hence, he who knows the multiformity or the universality of the supreme lord as also of Gāyatrī attains identity with Brahman, as stated to Brahmā by the lord himself.

CHAPTER TWENTY FOUR

Incarnations of Śiva

Sūta said :

1. On hearing everything uttered by Rudra, Brahmā the Prajāpati bowed to Rudra, lord of Devas and spoke thus :

2. "O lord, lord of the chiefs of Devas, O multiformed, O Maheśvara, O husband of Umā, O great god, honoured by all, obeisance to you.

3-4. O multiformed, O highly blessed god, when and in which age (yuga) will these bodies honoured by all be seen by the brahmins and by what penance or meditation of yoga? Obeisance to you, O lord Mahādeva".

5. On hearing his words and seeing him in front, the great lord Rudra revealed by Ṛk, Yajus and Sāman smiled and said:—

6-9. Except through meditation, neither through penance nor by conduct nor through gifts and holy rites nor by visits to pilgrim centres nor through sacrifices with ample monetary gifts nor through the study of the Vedas[101] nor through wealth nor through knowledge of various kinds is it possible for men to see me.

O Brahmā, in the Varāha kalpa—the seventh in number, Varāha, will be the illuminator of the kalpa and your grandson, Vaivasvata, will be the Manu.

10-13. In the course of that kalpa containing the four yugas, towards the end of Kali, I will be born to bless the worlds and for the welfare of the brahmins, O Brahmā. As the yuga proceeds further, when the great lord himself becomes Vyāsa, during the first Dvāpara age I will be born at the end of Dvāpara[102] as sage Śveta. I will be endowed with a tuft and will stay on the excellent mountain Chāgala[103] a beautiful peak of the Himālaya mountain.

101. Vedanaiḥ—śāstraiḥ *ST.* by sacred books.

102. Yugāntike—dvāpara-samāptau *ST.*—at the end of Dvāpara age.

103. Chāgala: This peak of the Himālayas has not been identified so far.

14-18. Then my disciples will be four noble brahmins, the masters of the Vedas and having tufts. They will be Śveta, Śvetaśikha, Śvetāsya and Śveta-lohita. After attaining Brahman's goal, they will approach me and will be devoted to the path of meditation and yoga. O Brahmā, in the second Dvāpara age lord Prajāpati will become Vyāsa, known as Sadya. Then, in the Kali age, I will be born by the name Sutāra for the welfare of the world, with a desire for blessing the disciples. My disciples then will be known by these names:

19-24. Dundhubhi, Śatarūpa, Ṛcīka and Ketumān. After attaining yoga and meditation and after establishing the Brahma[104] on the earth they will attain the region and companionship of Rudra. In the third age, Dvāpara, Bhārgava will be the Vyāsa. Then, at the end of Dvāpara I will be born as Damana. There too four boys will be born to me, namely, Vikeśa, Vikośa, Vipāśa and Śāpanāśana. These four of great prowess will go to the world of Rudra through the same yogic path and will never return. In the fourth Dvāpara yuga, Aṅgiras will become Vyāsa. At that time I shall be born by the name Suhotra. There too, four ascetics will be born as my sons.

25. They will be excellent brahmins of steadfast rites and yogic souls. They will be known as Sumukha, Durmukha, Dardura and Dhṛtikrama.

26-28. By performing subtle yogic practices they will become pure and shall wash off their sins by taking recourse to the subtle yogic practice. Endowed with yoga and through the same path (as described above) these courageous souls will go to the world of Rudra and never return. In the fifth Dvāpara age Savitṛ will be the Vyāsa. At that time, I shall be born as a person of great penance with the name Kaṅka for blessing the worlds and propagating yoga among the people.

29-30. Four blessed persons of pure origin shall be my disciples. They will be yogic souls with steadfast rites. They will be known as Sanaka, Sanandana, Sanātana and Sanat. They will be devoid of ego, altogether.

31-38. In the end they will come to my abode and never return. In the sixth yuga, Mṛtyu will be the Vyāsa and I shall

104. **Brahma-jñānam** *ST*.—**knowledge of Brahma, the impersonal spirit, the supreme soul.**

be known as Laugākṣi. Then also my disciples will be four, all yogic souls with steadfast rites, all blessed and popular. They will be known as Sudhāmā, Virajas, Śaṅkhapāda and Rajas. They all will be yogic, noble souls, pious and sinless, and endowed with yogic practices. Through the path of meditation they will come near me and never return.

In the seventh cycle of yugas, Śatakratu, who was famous in the previous birth as Vibhu the shining one, becomes the Vyāsa. Then at the end of Dvāpara and the advent of Kali I shall be born as Jaigīṣavya, the omnipresent, renowned, and the best of yogins. There too four sons will be born to me. They will be known as Sārasvata, Megha, Meghavāhana and Suvāhana. Devoted to the path of meditation those noble souls will, through the very same path, go to Rudraloka devoid of misery.

39-42. In the eighth cycle, Vasiṣṭha will become the Vyāsa. I will be born by the name Dadhivāhana. There too my sons will be yogic souls of steadfast rites and great yogic practice. There will be none equal to them. They will be known as Kapila, Āsuri, Pañcaśikha[105] and Bāṣkala. These will be righteous souls of great prowess. After attaining the yoga of the lord they will burn their sins and come near me, never to return.

43-47. In the ninth cycle when Sārasvata will be the Vyāsa I will be born by the name Ṛṣabha. There too, my sons will be persons of great prowess. They will be Parāśara, Garga, Bhārgava and Aṅgiras—all brahmins well versed in the Vedas, exalted with the strength of their penance, and capable of cursing and blessing. Attaining the path of meditation in the the manner prescribed in the yogic system those ascetics will go to Rudraloka never to return.

48-51. In the tenth Dvāpara age, the sage Tripāda will be the Vyāsa. Then I will be born as a brahmin sage on the excellent

105 **Kapila is considered as the founder of the Sāṁkhya system of philosophy. Āsuri and his pupil Pañcaśikha, like the founder-teacher Kapila, are known only by their names. Perhaps they preached their cult by oral transmission. Their works, if any, are lost to us.**

hill Bhṛgutuṅga,[106] a beautiful peak of the Himālayas. That peak adored by Devas is well known through the name of sage Bhṛgu. There too my sons will be steadfast in their holy rites. They will be known Balabandhu, Nirāmitra, Ketubhṛṅga and Tapodhana. They will be yogic and noble souls, endowed with penance and yoga. With their sins burned through penance they will go to Rudraloka.

52-54. In the eleventh Dvāpara age, Trivrata will become Vyāsa. Then I will be born at Gaṅgādvāra in[107] the Kali age as a person of great splendour named Ugra, famous in all the worlds. There too I will have four sons of great prowess, viz.—Lambodara, Lambākṣa, Lambakeśa and Pralambaka. After attaining the yoga of Maheśvara they will go to Rudra's world.

55-58. In the twelfth cycle the sage Śatatejas of great splendour, the best among the wise, will become Vyāsạ. At that time, when Dvāpara ends, and Kaliyuga starts, I shall be known by the name Atri in the forest Haituka[108]. There too will be born my sons who will have ashes for ablution and unguent, who will be such yogins, and who will be devoted to Rudra's world. They will be known as Sarvajña Samabuddhi, Sādhya and Sarva. After attaining the yoga of Mahe vara they will go to Rudraloka.

59-62. When the thirteenth cycle sets in due order, Dharma under the name Nārāyaṇa will be the Vyāsa. At that time, I will be born as the sage Vāli in the holy penance grove of Vāla-

106. Bhṛgutuṅga is one of the peaks of the Himālayas. According to *Varāha* (ch. 146, 45-46) it is a mountain in Nepal on the eastern bank of the Gaṇḍaka river where the celebrated sage Bhṛgu had a hermitage. The *Vā.* (81. 33) locates it near the Vitastā (Jhelum) and Himavat. See *GEAMI* part 1. p.70.

107. Gaṅgādvāra represents modern Haradvara. It is also known by other names like Haridvāra, Mokṣadvāra, Māyādvāra. Cf. *SK* iv. 1.7.114:

But according to *ŚP. KRS.* (25.3) Gaṅgā is said to have descended from Brahmagiri situated in the south (*Ibid.* 24. 3) in the proximity of Nasik near Tryambaka. This place of Gaṅga's descent is said to be Gaṅgādvāra (*Ibid.* 27. 6).

108. Haituka vana. It is not identifiable.

khilya on the mountain Gandhamādana[109]. There too those ascetics will be born as my sons. They will be known as Sudhāmā, Kāśyapa, Vāsiṣṭha and Virajas. They will all be endowed with the power of great yogas, be devoid of impurities and will remain celibate. After attaining the yoga of Maheśvara they will go to the world of Rudra.

63-66. In the fourteenth cycle Tarakṣu will be the Vyāsa. There too in the final yuga, I will be born in the excellent family of Aṅgiras under the name Gautama. That penance grove[110] too will be named after Gautama. There too my sons will be born in the Kali age. They will be known as Atri, Devasada, Śravaṇa and Śraviṣṭhaka. They will be yogic noble souls, and endowed with yoga. After attaining the yoga of Maheśvara they will go to Rudraloka.

67-71. When the fifteenth cycle comes in due order, Trayyāruṇi becomes the Vyāsa.

I will be born as a brahmin by name Veda iras. Then I shall have a powerful missile known as Vedaśiras. There will be a hill named Vedaśiras[111] on the banks of the Sarasvatī[112] behind the Himālayan slopes. There also four ascetics will be my sons, viz., Kuṇi, Kuṇībāhu, Kuśarīra and Kunetra. All of them will be yogic and noble souls who will remain ascetics throughout. After attaining the yoga of Maheśvara they will go to Rudraloka.

72-75. In the sixteenth cycle of four yugas when Deva is the Vyāsa, I shall be born by the name Gokarṇa[113] in order to

109. Gandhamādana. Its location is highly controversial. According to the Pauraṇic account this mountain forms the division between Ilāvṛta and Bhadrāśva to the south of Meru and is renowned for its fragrant forests.

110. Gautamavana can be placed in the proximity of Brahmagiri near Tryambaka in which Godāvarī has its source where the sage Gautama had its hermitage.

111. Himavat or Himālaya. This most celebrated mountain forms the northern boundary of Bhārata extending from the eastern to the western sea.

112. Sarasvatī. This sacred river rises in the Sirmur hills of the Sivalika range in the Himālayas.

113. Gokarṇa. The Gokarṇa forest referred to here is located in the Western Ghat. This place is sacred to Śiva and is celebrated for a jyotirliṅga of Śiva. There is also another Gokarṇa in Nepal on the Bāgamatī river.

spread yoga among the devotees of restrained souls. That forest (where I live and preach) will become sacred and famous as Gokarṇa. There too the four yogins will be my sons viz., Kāśyapa, Uśanas, Cyavana and Bṛhaspati. They will be endowed with meditation and yoga. By following the same path and attaining the yoga of Maheśvara they will go to Rudra Himself.

76-84. When the seventeenth cycle sets in duly, O Lord Brahmā, Kṛtañjaya[114] will be the Vyāsa, and I shall be born, under the name Guhāvāsa on the lofty and beautiful peak of the Himālayas, Mahālaya[115]. I shall be known as Guhāvāsin. This Mahālaya will become a Siddhakṣetra the place of sanctity. There too my sons will be conversant with yoga and expounders of Brahman. They will be noble sons and devoid of ego. They will be known as—Utathya, Vāmadeva, Mahāyoga and Mahābala. At that time, in the practice of yogic meditation, they will have hundreds and thousands of disciples. Engaged in the practice of yoga, and meditating upon the great lord within their hearts, they after observing the footprints in the Mahālaya will attain the region of the lord. The other noble souls who engage their minds in meditation at the end of Dvāpara age and the advent of Kali will become sinless and pure in intellect. Devoid of distress they will go to Rudraloka, by my grace. By visiting the sacred Mahālaya, the region of the great lord, a devotee will cross the ocean of worldly existence and redeem his ten previous and ten future generations. Thus, including himself, he will redeem twenty one generations in Mahālaya. These being free from fever will go to Rudraloka, by my grace.

85-89. O lord, in the eighteenth cycle the sage Ṛtañjaya will become a Vyāsa. Then I shall be born in the name of Sikhaṇḍin in the most sacred region of the Siddhas which is adored by Devas as well as Dānavas. On the beautiful peak of the Himālayas there is a hill named Śikhaṇḍin,[116] wherein is situated the penance grove of the sage Śikhaṇḍin, resorted to by the Siddhas. There too four ascetics will be born

114. Deva-kṛtañjayaḥ. *ST*. takes Deva in the vocative case :
115. This peak of the Himālayas has not been identified so far.
116. Not identifiable.

to me. They will be known as Vācaśravas, Ṛcīka, Śyāvāśva and Yatīśvara. They will be yogic and noble sons and masters of the Vedas. After attaining the yoga of Maheśvara they will go to Rudraloka.

90-93. When the nineteenth cycle sets in duly, the great sage Bharadvāja will become the Vyāsa. Then I will be born by the name Jaṭāmālin on the beautiful peak of the Himālayas where the mountain Jaṭāyu[117] exists. There too four sons of great prowess will be born to me. They will be known as Hiraṇyanābha, Kauśalya, Laugākṣi and Kuthumi. Characterized by yogic virtues they will remain celibate. After attaining the yoga of Maheśvara they will go to Rudraloka.

94-99. When the twentieth cycle of yugas sets in, the sage Gautama becomes a Vyāsa. Then I shall be born by the name Aṭṭahāsa, most liked by the people. There itself on the ridge of the Himavat a great mountain Aṭṭahāsa[118] is the abode of Devas, Dānavas, Yakṣas, Siddhas and Cāraṇas. There too, powerful sons will be born to me. They will be yogic and noble souls, habitually meditating and performing the holy rites. They will be known as Sumantu, Barbari, Kabandha and Kuśikandhara. After attaining the Yoga of Maheśvara they will go to Rudraloka.

100-102. When the twenty-first cycle sets in duly, the excellent sage Vācaśravas becomes a Vyāsa. Then I shall be born by the name Dāruka. Hence there will be a splendid and sacred forest of Deodars[119]. There too my sons will be very powerful. They will be known as Plakṣa, Dārbhāyaṇi, Ketumān and Gautama. They will be yogic and great souls, well controlled and celibate. After practising the perpetual holy rites they will go to Rudra's region.

103-106. In the twenty-second cycle when Śuṣmāyaṇa becomes a Vyāsa, I shall be born as a great sage by the name

117. Not identifiable.

118. Not identifiable.

119. Devadāruvana. It is identical with Dāru or Dārukā vana and is placed close to the western ocean (*ŚP. KRS* 29. 4). Another vana of the same name also stands in the Himālayas near Badrinath (*Mbh.* XIII, 25. 27).

of Lāṅgalin the terrible, at Vārāṇasī[120]. There the Devas including lord Indra will see me in the Kali age as Bhava and Halāyudha. There too my virtuous sons will be known as Bhallavī, Madhupiṅga, Śvetaketu and Kuśa. After attaining the yoga of Maheśvara they will be engaged in meditation. Free from impurities and identical with Brahman they will enter Rudra's world.

107b-111a. In the twenty-third cycle of four yugas when the sage Tṛṇabindu becomes a Vyāsa O Brahmā, I shall be born as the virtuous son of a sage under the name Śveta with a great body. At that time I shall be spending my days (in penance) on a mountain which will therefore be named Kālañjara[121]. There too four ascetics will become my disciples. They will be known as Uśika, Bṛhadaśva, Devala and Kavi. After attaining the yoga of Maheśvara they will go to Rudraloka.

111b-114a. In the twenty-fourth cycle, O lord, when Ṛkṣa will be a Vyāsa, I will be born at the end of Dvāpara, in that Kali age as a great yogin named Śūlin in the Naimiṣa[122] forest, saluted by Devas. There too these ascetics will be my disciples viz.—Śālihotra, Agniveśa, Yuvanāśva and Śaradvasu. They too will go to Rudraloka by the same path.

114b-117a. When the twenty-fifth cycle of four yugas sets in, the son of Vasiṣtha, Śakti by name, will become a Vyāsa. At that time, I will be born as Lord Daṇḍī Muṇḍīśvara with shaven head and a staff in the hand. There too these ascetics will be my sons, viz.—Chagala, Kuṇḍakarṇa, Kumbhāṇḍa and Pravāhaka. After attaining the yoga of Maheśvara they will attain immortality.

117b-120. In the twenty-sixth cycle when Parāśara will become Vyāsa, at the end of Dvāpara and the advent of Kali age I shall be born by the name Sahiṣṇu. I shall go to the city, Bhad-

120. Vārāṇasī—ancient Kāśī. It came to be so called because it was situated between the two rivers: Barnā and Asi.

121. Kālañjara: The *Mbh.* (III. 85, 56) associates Kālañjara with Citrakūta. According to this reference, it lies in the Madhya Bhārata territory formerly known as Bundelkhaṇḍa. Cunningham (A.G. see map at the end) places it to the east of Mahoba, below Citrakūṭa.

122. See p. 1. note 4.

ravaṭa[123] where the four righteous sons will be born to me. They will be Ulūka, Vidyuta, Śambūka and Āśvalāyana. After attaining yoga of Maheśvara they will go to Rudraloka.

120-124a. When the twenty-seventh cycle of four yugas arrives duly, the ascetic Jātūkarṇya will become a Vyāsa. Then I shall be born as the brahmin Somaśarman at Prabhāsa[124] Tīrtha. I shall be known as a yogic soul by taking resort to yoga. There too four ascetics will be my disciples, viz. Akṣapāda, Kumāra, Ulūka and Vatsa. They will be great yogic souls, pure in intellect and devoid of impurities. After attaining the yoga of Maheśvara they will go to Rudraloka.

124b-133. When the twenty-eighth cycle of four yugas occurs in due order, the glorious son of Parāśara named Dvaipāyana[125] will become a Vyāsa. He is Viṣṇu himself, the grandfather of the worlds. At that time, Vāsudeva, black in colour and the best among men and exalted among the Yadus, will be born of Vasudeva. At the same time, by the power of my yogic illusion I the Yogātman will be born as Brahmacārin and inspire awe among the people. On seeing a dead body left in the cremation ground without a claimant, I shall be entering it by the yogic power for the welfare of the brahmins. Along with you and Viṣṇu[126] I will enter the divine and holy cave of the Meru.[127] O Brahmā, at that time, I will be known as Lakuli. That holy place where I entered the dead body will be known as Kāyāvatāra—a name that will last as long as the earth lasts. There too the ascetic sons will be born to me.

123. Bhadravaṭa: Cf. ŚP. SRS. 5.39. This town has not been identified so far.

124. It is a celebrated place of pilgrimage in Saurāṣṭra, the southern part of Kathiawar.

125. Dvaipāyana Vyāsa : See p. 2. note 6.

126. tvayā sārdhaṁ ca Viṣṇunā. ST. construes tvayā with Viṣṇunā (tvayā Viṣṇunā sārdham) and thus excludes Brahmā.

127. Meru : It is situated in the centre of the earth. It is described in the Purāṇas as the four-armed svastika, evolving in four directions, each with seven constituent members. It can be identified with the highland of Tartary, north of the Himālayas. It is variously called Su-meru, Hemādri (the golden mountain), Ratnasānu (jewel-peaked), Karṇikācala (lotus mountain), Amarādri, Deva-parvata, 'mountain of the Gods'. On its extent and identification with the Great Pamir knot of Asia, see *The Geography of the Purāṇas*:—S. M. ALI. Ch. III. pp. 47-52.

They will be known as Kuśika, Garga, Mitra and Kauruṣya. They will be great yogic souls and brahmins who will have mastered all the Vedas. They will remain celibate and free from impurities. After attaining the yoga of Maheśvara they will go to Rudra's world, never to return.

134-140. All these enlightened souls will be the devotees of Śiva and will have their bodies smeared with ashes. They will be perpetually engaged in worshipping Liṅga. They will be steadfast and firm in body and the mind. With devotion towards me and by means of yoga they will be established in meditation and acquire self-control. The great Pāśupata yoga can snap worldly ties and illuminate the path of knowledge. It is also conducive to Real knowledge. There are several paths of yoga and several paths of knowledge. But without taking recourse to the five-syllabled Mantra[128] one cannot attain eternal bliss. When a person performs penance eschewing Dvandvas (mutually clashing opposites) he can become a liberated soul, as one who has attained the ripe fruit. Even if a man performs Pāśupata rite for a single day he can obtain fruits, the like of which he cannot have either by Pañcarātra[129] or Sāṅkhya.

Thus I have narrated the characteristics of incarnations in the course of twenty-eight sets of four yugas in due order, beginning with Manu and ending with Kṛṣṇa. The classification of the Vedas revealing Dharma will take place in the kalpa when Kṛṣṇa Dvaipāyana becomes a Vyāsa.

Sūta said :

141-144. On hearing about the incarnations of Rudra described thus by the supreme lord, Lord Brahmā, of great splendour bowed to him and eulogised him with pleasing words. Then he spoke to lord Śiva.

Brahmā said:

All the Devas and all the Gaṇas are identical with Viṣṇu. There is no other goal equal to the goal of attaining Viṣṇu.

128. The five-syllabled mantra of Śiva : namaḥ Śivāya.

129. Pañcarātra—a name of the sacred books of the various Vaiṣṇava sects.

Thus sing the Vedas perpetually. Then how did this happen that the lord of Devas worshipped you in the Liṅga and remained ever devoted to you?

145-150. On hearing the words of Brahmā lord Śiva was delighted on account of the weighty relevancy of the question. He looked at him as if he would drink him through his eyes. Facing him, he then described the method of worship of the Liṅga. It was after worshipping the Liṅga in accordance with the instructions that you (Brahmā), Viṣṇu and Indra, the best of Devas and the sages, had attained their respective status. O lord, hence they continue to worship me further. There cannot be steadiness[130] in piety without the worship of the Liṅga; hence lord Viṣṇu worships me perpetually with due devotion and faith.

After saying this and blessing Brahmā by glancing at him once again, Śiva, the lord of Devas, vanished there itself.

After gaining enlightenment[131] from Śiva to create everything afresh, Brahmā joined his palms in reverence and bowed to Śiva in the direction where he had vanished.

CHAPTER TWENTY-FIVE

Method of Ācamana and Ablution

The sages said :

1. O Romaharṣaṇa,[132] how is the great lord to be worshipped in his Liṅga-form? Please explain this to us now.

Sūta said :

2. At Kailāśa[133] the great lord was asked the same by the Goddess Pārvatī, the daughter of the lord of the Himālaya, who was seated on his lap. The lord, then, described to her the procedure of worshipping the Liṅga.

130. niṣṭhā—niscala-sthānam *ST*. a permanent abode.

131. labdha-saṁjñaḥ—prāptānujñaḥ *ST*. sañjñā here means a direction, command or order. Ed.

132. See p. 2 note 7.

133. Mount Kailāsa is a part of the Himālayan range lying to the north of Mānasa-sarovara, not far off from the source of Ghogra (Sarayu) river. The detailed description of the mount is found in the *Matsya P*. Ch. 121.

3-5. At that time, Nandin the son of Śālaṅkāyana was standing nearby. O sages of good rites, he heard everything and mentioned it to Brahmā's son Sanat. From him Vyāsa of great refulgence received the great discourse on the worship of the Liṅga, as also the bathing and other rites, as declared in the Vedas. I shall recount the same in the manner he heard it orally from Nandin.

Nandin said :

6. Henceforth, for the welfare of the brahmins, I shall recount the rules of procedure for the sacred ablution, which is destructive of all sins. Formerly it was declared by lord Śiva himself.

7. By taking holy bath in accordance with this procedure, by worshipping lord Śiva and by observing Brahmakūrca[134] at a time, one is liberated from sins.

8. O most excellent among the sons of Brahmā, three types of ablution are enjoined by Śiva, the lord of Devas, for the welfare of the brahmins and others.

9-10. One shall at the outset perform the watery bath and then the sacred ash-bath[135] and thereafter the Mantra ablution and then the worship of the lord. One who is defiled in emotions and feelings is not purified even after taking bath in water or after applying ashes. Only one who is emotionally pure will proceed with purificatory rites and not otherwise.

11. There is no doubt that an emotionally defiled man does not become pure even if he takes bath in rivers, ponds and lakes till the dissolution of the universe.

12. The lotus-like mind of man is asleep due to Tamas. When it is wakened up by the refulgence of knowledge, man becomes pure[136].

13-14. The devotee shall take clay, cowdung[137], gingelly

134. It is a kind of penance in the observance of which the five products of the cow (pañcagavya) are eaten.

135. āgneyam—It is the bath of bhasma (ashes)—the product of fire-consumed cow-dung or wooden sticks.

136. This verse is a fine piece of poetical composition involving metaphor.

137. śakṛt—cow-dung. It is considered to be pure and used in religious rites.

seeds, flowers and ashes for bath and keep them on the bank. He shall then scatter Kuśa grass into the holy water for bath. After washing his feet, doing ācamana and removing dirt from the body with the articles placed on the bank, he shall perform the rite of ablution.

15-16. Repeating the Mantra "Uddhṛtāsi"[138] he shall clean the body again with a small quantity of clay and wearing another cloth he shall bathe. Repeating the Mantra "Gandhadvārāṁ Durādharṣām"[139] he shall smear himself with the cowdung of the tawny cow gathered even before it touches the ground.

17-20. Taking bath again he shall discard the dirty cloth; wear (fresh) white one and perform ablution again. For dispelling sins he shall invoke Varuṇa. He shall then worship the lord by meditation. He shall perform ācamana thrice. and then plunge into the holy waters (all the while) thinking about Śiva. Again doing ācamana he shall inspire the holy water with Mantras. Plunging again into the water he shall repeat the Aghamarṣaṇa[140] Mantra. With great self-control the devotee shall remember the discs of the sun, moon and fire in that water.

21-22. The knower of the Mantras shall perform Ācamana, and rise up from the waters and standing in the middle of holy waters he shall pour water over his head from cow's horn,[141] or by means of cups made of well washed Palāśa leaf. The water shall be scattered with Kuśa grass and flowers.

23-25. O brahmins, while pouring water over his head, he shall repeat these mantras remembering the forms of the respective deities (invoked therein) and the sages concerned for increase of his holiness. The mantras include Rudra,[142] Pavamāna what is called Tvarita, two Śāntimantras[143] and the mantra 'śan no devī,[144] and the five holy mantras[145] of Sadyojāta.

138. Udhṛtāsi Varāheṇa *TA*. 10. 1.8; *Mahān* u. 4.5.
139. gandhadvārāṁ durādharṣām *TA*. 10. 1; *Mahān* u. 4. 8.
140. aghamarṣaṇa : ṛtaṁ ca satyam *TA*. 10. 1. 13; *Mahān* u. 5.5.
141. śṛṅgeṇa—gośṛṅgeṇa *ST*. with the cow's horn.
142. tvarita—yo rudro *TS*. 5.5.9.3.
143. śāntidvayena—śanno mitrā *ṚV*.1.90.9.10.
144. śāntidharmeṇa—śanno devī *ṚV*. 10.9.4.
145. pañca-brahma-pavitrakaiḥ—mantras beginning with sadyojāta.

He shall then meditate in his heart on lord Tryambaka[146] having five faces.[147]

26-29. After rinsing his mouth and doing ācamana as prescribed in his own Sūtra and wearing pavitra in the hand, he shall sit comfortably in a clean spot, sprinkle kuśa water on his body with his right hand and perform ācamana again. Then artfully he shall wheel water round him and perform circumambulation. This will wipe off his sins of violence. O virtuous brahmins, this excellent procedure of ablution and ācamana has been succinctly mentioned for your welfare.

CHAPTER TWENTY SIX

Procedure of Sacred Ablution

Nandin said :

1. Thereafter he should invoke the glorious and great goddess Gāyatrī the mother of the Vedas, with the mantra : "āyātu varadā devī".[148]

2-3. He shall offer pādya, ācamanīya, and arghya. He shall then perform three prāṇāyāmas. Thereafter, either sitting or standing he shall repeat the Gāyatrī along with Praṇava *Om* adopting one of the three modes, viz., repeating it a thousand or five hundred or hundred and eight times.

4-6. He shall offer the arghya again and worship the mother Goddess. He shall bow to her and then ritualistically dismiss her by repeating the mantra "uttame śikhare devī,"[149] etc. Looking towards the east and saluting the goddess Gāyatrī, mother of the Vedas, he shall with the palms joined in reverence, pray to the Sun God repeating the Mantras "Udutyaṁ Jātavedasam", "Citram" and others. He shall then salute the sun and Brahmā in accordance with the injunctions.

146. tryambakam—three-eyed or three-mothered Śiva.
147. pañcāsyam—five-faced. See p. 49 note 65.
148. āyātu varadā devī *TA*. 10.26.1.
149. uttame śikhare devī *TA*. 10.3.1.

7-10. He shall repeat the hymns to Sūrya, from Ṛk, Yajus and Sāman. He shall thereafter circumambulate the sun[150] thrice. He shall then bow to Ātman, Antarātman and Paramātman the sun, Brahmā and fire.[151] Thereafter he shall invoke the sage, the Pitṛs and Devas with their respective names by saying "I am invoking all". Then he shall duly perform the tarpaṇa rite facing either east or north after meditating on their actual principal forms and saluting them in due order.

11. The tarpaṇa to Devas shall be performed with the water inlaid with flowers, the rites to the sages with the water mixed with Kuśa grass and the rites to the Pitṛs with water mixed with gingelly seeds. Scents should be mixed in the water in all cases.

12. O leading brahmins, the sacred thread is worn in the usual manner (i.e. over the left shoulder) when the rites to Devas are performed; it is worn like a garland when the tarpaṇa to the sages is performed; it is worn from right shoulder leftward when the tarpaṇa to Pitṛs is performed.

13-15. For procuring all achievements the wise devotee who is well versed in the Vedas shall perform tarpaṇa to Devas with waters flowing down the tips of all fingers. He shall perform tarpaṇa to the sages with waters flowing down the tip of the little finger. He shall perform tarpaṇa to the pitṛs with waters flowing down the thumb of the right hand.

Similarly, O leading sages, he shall perform the five sacrifices, viz., Brahma, Deva, Manuśya, Bhūta and Pitṛ. He shall be devotedly engaged in these rites and be pure in soul.

16-19. O brahmins, the study of the Vedic texts of one's own branch is Brahmayajña;[152] the offering of cooked rice into the sacred fire is Devayajña; the offering of oblations to Bhūtas (living beings) as prescribed in the ritual is Bhūtayajña; it bestows prosperity on all living beings. The devotee shall bow to brahmins well-versed in the Vedic rituals as well as

150. Vibhāvasu—the sun. *ST*. quotes Amara : "vibhāvasur grahapatiḥ".

151. Vibhāvasu—the fire. *Ibid* : "citrabhānu vibhāvasuḥ".

152. brahma-yajña is defined as sva-śākhādhyayanam—the study of particular recensions to which the scholar belongs. *ST*. quotes from an unknown source : "yat svādhyāyam adhīyīta ekāmapi ṛcaṁ yajuḥ sāma vā tad brahma-yajñaḥ".

feed them and their wives. This is Manuṣya Yajña. What is offered for the sake of Pitṛs (the departed souls) is Pitṛyajña. Thus he shall perform these five Yajñas[153] for achieving Siddhis.

20. Listen O Brahmins! Brahmayajña is the greatest of these Yajñas. A man engaged in Brahmayajña is honoured in the world of Brahmā.

21-24. By Brahmayajña all the Devas including Indra, Lords Brahmā, Viṣṇu and Śiva, all the Vedas and Pitṛs are pleased. No doubt need be entertained in this respect. The brahmin who is adept in Brahmayajña when he goes out of his village out of sight of hundreds of huts, shall turn towards the east, north or north-east[154] and then perform the sacred rite of Ācamana for the sake of Brahmayajña. For propitiating the Ṛks, O brahmins, he shall fill the cup of his palm and drink water thrice.

25. For propitiating the Yajus he shall wash his hands. and wipe off his face twice with water. For the propitiation of Sāmaveda he shall touch the head.

26. The brahmin shall wash the eyes, nostrils and other limbs for the propitiation of the Atharvan and Aṅgiras texts.

For the propitiation of eighteen[155] Purāṇas beginning with Brāhma, for the propitiation of eighteen Upapurāṇas beginning with Saura, and for the propitiation of holy Itihāsas beginning with Śaiva he shall touch his ears and the cardiac region. O sages, most excellent among the knowers of the Kalpa, for the propitiation of the Kalpa texts, he shall perform the Ācamana rite. After scattering bundles of Darbha grass, the devotee shall sit down and keep the right palm over the left palm. There must be a golden ring or the Kuśa loop[156] round his

153. The five daily sacrifices to be performed by a householder constitute brahma-yajña, pitṛ-yajña, deva-yajña, bhūta-yajña and nṛ-yajña. These are defined as :

अध्यापनं ब्रह्मयज्ञः पितृयज्ञस्तु तर्पणम् ।
होमो दैवो बलिर्भौतो नृयज्ञोऽतिथिपूजनम् ॥

Liṅga substitutes अध्ययनम् for अध्यापनम् ।

154. prāgudīcyām—īśānyām ST. in the north-eastern direction.

155. For the nomenclature and number of the Purāṇas, see Introduction.

156. brahma-bandha : the term is not clear.

finger. With great concentration and following his own school he shall perform the Brahmayajña duly. Though an excellent brahmin or sage but if he takes food without performing the five great Yajñas, he will be born in the womb of sows. Hence a person should assiduously perform the same seeking for auspiciousness.

33. After Brahmayajña he shall perform Ablution for the self, collect the holy water duly and enter the camp with perfect self-control.

34. Outside the house he shall wash his hands and feet with water. Thereafter, for purity's sake he shall perform the sacred bath with ashes duly.

35-36. The ashes should be perfectly cleaned by means of Praṇava . It must be taken from what remains after performing Agnihotra. When the sun has risen in the morning the Agnihotra should be performed with the Mantra "Jyotiḥ sūryaḥ."[157] In the evening the same should be performed with the Mantra "Jyotir Agniḥ".[158] If the sun has not risen fully, the performance of Agnihotra is rendered ineffective. The ashes of the sacrifice performed after the sun has risen is alone sacred and splendid.

37-41. There is nothing holy like truth and nothing sinful like untruth. Repeating the Mantra of Īśāna he shall smear ashes on the head; repeating the Mantra of Tatpuruṣa, he shall smear ashes on his face; repeating the Mantra of Aghora he shall do so over his chest; O men of holy rites ! he shall apply ashes over the secret parts by repeating the Mantra of Vāmadeva and similarly on the feet by repeating the Mantra of Sadya. By repeating the Praṇava he shall smear ashes all over the body. Thereafter he shall wash hands and feet. After wasing them off he shall take ashes with his mind set on the lord of Devas and perform Ablution repeating the Mantras viz., "Āpo hi ṣṭhā[159] and other sacred formulas taken from Ṛk, Yajus and Sāman texts. Thus for your welfare O brahmins, the mode of procedure for holy bath has been described to you succinctly. He who performs thus even for once shall attain the highest abode of God.

157. jyotiḥ sūryaḥ *TA*. 4.10.5.
158. Jyotir agniḥ *TA*. 4.10.5.
159. Āpo hi ṣṭhā *TS*. 4.1.5.1.

CHAPTER TWENTY SEVEN

Worship of Liṅga

Nandin said :

1. Listen, I shall briefly mention the rules of procedure for the worship of Liṅga. It is not possible to recount them in detail even in a hundred years.

2. After bathing thus[160] in a befitting manner the devotee shall enter the place of worship, take three prāṇāyāmas and meditate on the three-eyed lord.

3-4. He shall resort to the form of the deity as follows. He has five faces and ten arms. He shines like pure crystal. He is bedecked in all ornaments and clothes of variegated colours. By means of certain Tantric practices such as dāhana, plāvana etc., he shall transform himself into the body of lord Śiva and begin to worship him.

5. After purifying the body he shall perform the rite of Nyāsa of the mūla mantras. Everywhere the five Brahmans (Sadyojāta etc.) shall be fixed with the Praṇava in order.

6-7. In the highly splendid aphorism viz., "Namaḥ Śivāya" the Vedas are present in subtle form. Just as the holy fig tree is present in the subtle seed of the Nyagrodha so also the great Brahman is present in the great and splendid aphorism, all by Himself in a subtle form.

8. The devotee shall sprinkle the place of worship with scented sandal water, and consecrate the materials of worship either by washing or by sprinkling water.

9-10. The washing and sprinkling is performed by repeating the Praṇava . The intelligent devotee shall duly cover the vessels with a cloth; these are the Prokṣaṇī (vessel containing holy water), Arghya, Pādya and Ācamanīya vessels.

11. These shall be covered with Darbha grass and sprinkled with pure water. He shall then pour cool water in the different vessels.

12. The intelligent devotee shall pour water in them after observing the materials. He shall place Uśīra and sandal in the Pādya.

160. It refers to the threefold bath, namely vāruṇa, āgneya and māntra as specified in Ch. 25. 9.

13. He shall duly powder nutmeg (Jāti), momordica mixta (Kankola seed), the root of Bahumūla (a herb), Xanthocymus epictorius (Tamāla seed) and camphor and put the same in the Ācamanīya vessel.

14. Similarly he shall put camphor, sandal and different kinds of flowers in all the vessels.

15. He shall put tips of Kuśa grass, unbroken rice grains, barley grains, cereals, gingelly seeds, ghee, white mustard, flowers and ashes in the Arghya vessel.

16. Repeating the Praṇava he shall put Kuśa grass, flowers, barley grains, bits of Bahumūla herb and Tamāla root as well as ashes into the Prokṣanī vessel.

17. He shall perform the rite of Nyāsa of the five-syllabled Mantra, and of Rudra Gāyatrī or only of Praṇava—the excellent essence of the Vedas.

18. Thereafter he shall sprinkle the materials of worship with water from the Prokṣaṇī vessel, repeating Praṇava as well as the five Yajus beginning with Īśāna.

19-21. By the (right) side[161] the lord of Devas, Nandin, i.e. myself, shall be worshipped. I shall have the lustre of ten thousand blazing fires, three eyes, the face of a monkey, four arms, the crescent moon as coronet, wearing flower garlands, gentle, and bedecked in all ornaments. My wife Suyaśā the auspicious and holy daughter of the Maruts shall be worshipped to the north of Nandin i.e. myself.[162] She who performs holy rites shall be engaged in embellishing the feet of Ambā (Goddess Pārvatī).

22-23. After worshipping thus he shall enter the sanctum sanctorum of lord Śiva. He shall then offer handfuls of flowers on the five heads of the Lord repeating the five Mantras. With different kinds of incense and scented flowers he shall worship Śiva, Skanda, Gaṇeśa and the goddess, and then consecrate the Liṅga.

24. After repeating the Mantras beginning with Praṇava[163]

161. pārśvataḥ—dakṣiṇa-pārśve *ST*. on the right side.

162. ātmanaḥ—nandinaḥ mama *ST*. of Nandi the speaker.

163. praṇavādi-namontakam—mantras beginning with "Oṁ nidhānapataye namaḥ" and ending with "parama-liṅgāya namaḥ".

and ending with Namas he shall conceive of a lotus seat[164] for the deity, by repeating the Praṇava.

25-28. Its imperishable petal in the East shall be Aṇimā; Laghimā shall be the petal in the South; Mahimā the Western petal; Prāpti the Northern, Prākāmyam the South-eastern, Īśitva the South-western, Vaśitva the North-western, Omniscience the North-eastern petal. The moon will be the pericarp. Beneath the moon is the sun and beneath the sun the fire-god. Dharma[165] and others shall be installed in the subsidiary quarters. He shall then instal Ananta. He shall instal Avyakta etc. in the four quarters[166] in order and the three Guṇas at the extremity of Soma.

29-34. Above it he shall instal the three Ātmans[167] and in the end Śiva's pedestal. Repeating the Mantra "I resort to Sadyojāta"[168] he shall invoke the supreme lord. With the Mantra of Vāmadeva he shall instal Him over the seat. With Rudragāyatrī he shall establish His presense and with Aghora Mantra he shall stabilise the presence of deity. He shall then worship with the Mantra "Īśānaḥ Sarvavidyānām.[169] He shall then offer Pādya, Ācamanīya and Arghya to the lord. In accordance with the injunctions he shall be the Rudra with scented sandal paste water. After gathering Pañca Gavya in a vessel and after inspiring it with Praṇava he shall bathe the deity with Pañcagavya. Repeating the Praṇava he shall perform the rite of ablution to the deity (successively) with ghee, honey, sugar-cane juice and other holy materials of worship. With holy Mantras, using pure vessels he shall pour water over the deity.

35-39. The aspirant shall wipe it off with a white cloth.

164. padmāsana : see p. 35 note 47.

165. dharmādayaḥ—a group of four, viz., dharma (virtue), jñāna (knowledge), vairāgya (detachment) and aiśvarya (supremacy or supernatural power).

166. avyaktādi—a group of four, viz. pradhāna (invisible prakṛti), mahat (intellect), ahaṁkāra (ego), and manas (mind).

167. ātma-trayam—a trio consisting of Viśva, Taijasa and Prājña.

168. "sadyojātam prapadyāmi". Mark the use of parasmaipada in 'prapadyāmi' for the grammatically correct form 'prapadye' in ātmnepada.

169. iśānaḥ sarvavidyānām *TA*. 10.47.

He shall put Kuśa grass, Apāmārga, camphor, Jasmine, China rose, white jasmines, lotuses, lilies, white oleanders and other flowers into the water along with sandal paste. He shall inspire the water by repeating the Mantras of Sadyojāta. The water may be taken in a vessel made of gold, silver or copper. It may be in a lotus cup or a cup of palāśa. The conch or an earthern jar can be used. In the latter case it should be fresh and well washed. Repeating the requisite Mantras he shall bathe the deity in the water containing Kuśa grass[170] or flowers. For all achievements he shall repeat the Mantras. Now I shall mention the mantras to you; please listen.

40-45. A man who worships the Liṅga even once with the following Mantras will be liberated. Those who are conversant with the Mantra Śāstra use the following Mantras for the rite of Ablution : Pavamāna,[171] Vāma,[172] Rudra,[173] Nīla[174] Rudra, Śrīsūkta,[175] Rātrisūkta,[176] Camaka Hotāra, Atharvaśiras, Śānti, Bhāruṇḍa, Āruṇa, Vāruṇa, Jyeṣṭha, Vedavrata, Rathantara, Puruṣa, Tvarita, Rudra,[177] Kapi, Kapardi, the Sāman Ā vo rājānam,[178] Bṛhaccandra, Viṣṇu, Virūpākṣa Mantra, Śkanda, a group of hundred hymns, the hymns of Pañca Brahmans, Pañckṣara Mantra or Praṇava alone.

46-48. The devotee shall bathe the lord of the chiefs of Devas for the suppression of all sins. He shall then offer the following to the deity: Clothes, the sacred thread, Ācamanīya, scents and flowers, incense, light, cooked rice, scented water and Ācamanīya once again. Thereafter he shall offer a crown,

170. sakūrcena—kūrca is a handful of kuśa grass used in religious rites.

171. pavamāna—a group of mantras designated after their sanctifying efficiency.

172. Vāmīyaka—Vāma sūkta beginning with 'asya vāmasya'.

173. Rudreṇa—Rudra mantras of *Rudrādhyāya* also called śatarudrīya. *ST.* quotes from *Śiva-rahasya* : Vedeṣu śatarudrīyam devatāsu maheśvaraḥ.

174. nīlarudreṇa—Atharvavedīyaiḥ tatsaṁjñakair mantraiḥ *ST.* Rudra mantras of the *Atharvaveda-saṁhitā*.

175. Śrī sūkta *RV.*

176. Rātri sūkta *RV.*

177. tvarita, see p. 102 note. 142

178. ā vo rājānam *TS* 1.3.12.1.

an umbrella and ornaments. Repeating the Praṇava alone he shall offer the scented betel.

49-54. On the top of the Liṅga he shall worship the unsullied, imperishable Lord, shining like a crystal glass, the cause of all Devas, identical with the universe, imperceptible to the sages, Devas, Brahmā, Indra, Viṣṇu, Rudra and others. The Śruti says "He is imperceptible through even Vedāntas, to the knowers of the Vedas too". He is devoid of beginning, middle and end. He is a medicine unto those who are afflicted by the sickness of worldliness.[179] He is known as Śivatattva (Principle of Śiva) and is stationed in the Śiva Linga. He shall duly repeat the prayers and make obeisance. He shall circumambulate, offer Arghya, scatter flowers at the feet, bow to the lord of Devas and superimpose Śiva on the Ātman. This, in brief, is the procedure of worshipping Śiva in Liṅga. Now I shall describe the internal worship of Liṅga to you.

CHAPTER TWENTY EIGHT

Mental Worship of Śiva

Nandin said :

1-2. The fiery, solar and the lunar[180] disc shall be thought of within the heart. Above that the trio of the Guṇas and the Ātmans shall be conceived. Above it, the devotee shall meditate upon and worship the lord in both the aspects with and without attributes with half his body taken over by his beloved.

3-4. Since there are many objects to think upon, the thinker shall not think of anything except the following. The meditator shall conceive no distinction between the object and the means of meditation; otherwise, (i.e. if he thinks of anything other than these) knowledge does not arise in him.

179. bheṣajam bhava rogiṇām Cf. bhiṣaktamaṁ tvāṁ bhiṣajāṁ śṛṇomi. *ṚV*. 2.33.4.

180. amṛtam—somaṁ candrarūpam *ST*. lunar orb.

5-6. The word Puruṣa is derived thus : puri śete (he who lies in the body). He who worships the deity, the object of worship by means of meditation, is known as yajamāna. Dhyeya (the object of meditation) is the lord himself. Dhyāna is the act of thinking. Niruktī (bliss) the fruit of dhyāna. One who knows about this attains the ultimate reality which is the substratum of Pradhāna and Puruṣa.

7-10. Here the supreme lord, the object of meditation, is the twenty-sixth principle,—the meditator (jīva) is the twenty-fifth, the avyakta or pradhāna is the twenty-fourth. The seven principles constitute mahat, ahaṁkāra, and five tanmātras. The organs of action are five, as also the organs of sense; then there is the mind and the five elements. Thus Śiva is the twenty-sixth principle. He alone is the creator and sustainer. He is greater than Brahmā. He has created Brahmā. He is one who is above and greater than the universe, and is the universe itself.

11. Just as children are not born without their parents, so also the three worlds are not born without Śiva and his consort.

Sanatkumāra said :

12-13. If the great lord who is the supreme power and the supreme soul is himself the doer how can he be an agent who causes activity of the individual souls? But the supreme lord has been mentioned by you as eternal, enlightened and unqualitative.[182] How can he then bestow liberation? If he is without attributes how can he function?

Nandin said :

14. It is Kāla (Time) that evolves everything. Lord Śiva evolves the Kāla always. When the mind devoid of qualities

181. jīvātmā, the individual soul, the enjoyer of the fruits of the world-tree (cf. ebhiḥ sampāditam bhuṅkte puruṣaḥ pañcaviṁśakaḥ. *Matsya* 3.27), constitutes the twenty-fifth category. He is also called 'bhoktā puruṣaḥ', 'bhoktā suparṇaḥ' and he is controlled by the will of Īśvara (cf. Īśvarecchāvaśaḥ so'pi jīvātmā kathyate budhaiḥ). The latter is called ṣaḍviṁśaka Śiva—the twenty-sixth category who though transcendent is not competent to bestow grace. (Cf. ṣaḍviṁśakamanīśvaram 1.71.109).

182. niṣkalaḥ—devoid of attributes, hence passive or inactive, but who imparts impetus to Time—Kāla who creates the universe—कलयति ।

is set on lord Śiva, lord Śiva reveals His true, attributeless nature.[183]

15-17. The universe appears to be existent by his very activity. The eight[184] forms of the lord represent the empirical universe. Without the five elements—ether, earth, wind, fire and water and without the priest, the sun and the moon, the world has no existence. On consideration, it is evident that the gross world consisting of the mobile and immobile beings is the gross body of Rudra. These eight are the cosmic forms of the lord.

18-19. O excellent brahmins the sages declare that the subtle body of the lord is inexpressible. (The Vedas declare) "From him the words recede after failing to reach him along with the mind. He who realizes the bliss of the Brahman eschews fear from any quarter".[185] Hence, after realizing the bliss of the pinãka-bearing lord, no one need be afraid.

20. After perceiving through their imagination that the elegances[186] of Rudra are present everywhere, the sages who perceive the truth say, "Everything is Rudra."

21-22. By making incessant obeisance to Brahmã one's prestige is increased. All this is Brahman; everything is lord Rudra. Puruṣa is the great lord; Śiva is the supreme lord. Thus the lord has been specified. Meditation is the sole thought about him.

183. The mind too when stabilized by concentration becomes inactive (niṣkriya) as this helps in the emancipation of jīva. Cf. *ST*. :

मन एव मनुष्याणां कारणं बन्धमोक्षयोः ।
गुणेषु सक्तं बन्धाय मोक्षाय तपसि स्थितम् ।।

But, as a matter of fact, the terms—bondage and release are illusory and so are creation and dissolution. Cf. *Pañcadaśī* as quoted in *ST* : न निरोधो न चोत्पत्तिर्न बद्धो न च साधकः । न मुमुक्षुर्न वै मुक्त इत्येषा परमार्थता ।। VI. 35.

184. The eight forms of lord Śiva constitute the five gross material elements, the soul, the sun and the moon. Each stands in relation to its constituent as follows :

(i) Śarva—earth (ii) Bhava—water, (iii) Rudra—fire, (iv) Ugra—wind, (v) Bhīma—ether, (vi) Paśupati—soul, (vii) Īśāna—sun, and (viii) Mahādeva—moon.

185. Cf. TA. 8.4.1. TU 2.41, 9.1. Brahman is here identical with Śiva.

186. Rudrasya vibhūtayaḥ. The vibhūties of Rudra comprise ṛta, satya etc. Cf. ṛtaṁ satyam param brahma, quoted in *ST*.

23. O sage of good, holy rites, he should be thought upon in fourfold[187] manner and perceived. He, the cause of worldly existence, is the world itself. He is the cause of liberation. He is the greatest ecstasy.

24-27. The four-arrayed path is prescribed for a practising yogin. Thought is counted as manifold. If it is centred in one place it is called Suniṣṭhā;[188] if centred in Rudra it is called Raudrī; if centred in Indra Aindrī; if in Soma Saumyā; if in Nārāyaṇa or in the sun or in the fire it is called after those names. If the devotee fixes in his mind in both ways that he is I and I am he that thought is called Brāhmī. O brahmins, thus should a devotee think of this universe—both mobile and immobile—as identical with Brahman.

28-29. Keeping the goal in his mind, the devotee shall eschew the thought of division between the mobile and imobile,[189] as also between what should be eschewed and what should not be eschewed, as also between what is possible and what is not possible of achievement and what should be done and what should not be done. He shall also remain satiated and contented. Such a man's contemplation is the real one pertaining to Brahman and not otherwise. Thus in due order the mental worship of the lord has been recounted.

30-33. Those who carry out this sort of mental worship should also be adored by means of obeisance, etc. Even if they are hideous and deformed, these expounders of Brahman should not be censured. They should not be subjected to scrutiny by a discerning person. Those who censure them are narrow-minded persons who will become miserably unhappy as those sages of old who censured the lord in the Dārukā forest. The

187. caturvyūha : Four vyūhas constitute prāṇa, manas, vijñāna and ānanda and exclude the gross annamaya kośa. *ST.* offers an alternative explanation : yad vā dhyeya-dhyāna-yajamāna-prayojanarūpaiḥ caturvyūhaiḥ. But according to Liṅga purāṇa, the caturvyūha consists of (1) existence (saṁsāra), cause of existence (saṁsārahetu), cause of emancipation (mokṣahetu) and emancipation (nirvṛti).

188. suniṣṭhā—knowledge pertaining to Rudra (raudrī cintā) that releases jīva from the so-called bondage of birth and death.

189. carācara-vibhāgam—Jagadbrahmarūpam *ST.*—distinction between Brahma and the mundane oɹldw.

knowers of the Brahman who are beyond the bounds of castes and stages of life should always be served and bowed to by the persons devoted to the rigid discipline of castes and stages of life.

CHAPTER TWENTYNINE

Victory over Death

Sanatkumāra said :

1-3. O holy lord, now I wish to know what was committed by the dwellers of the Dāruvana, those persons who had purified their souls by means of penance. How did Rudra the naked lord of sublimated sexuality assume a hideous form and go to Dāru forest ? What did that great soul do there ? Please recount factually the activities of that lord of Devas.

Sūta said:

4. On hearing his words Nandin, the most excellent among the knowers of the Vedas, said after remembering Śiva and smiling a little.

Nandin said :

5. In order to propitiate the lord of Devas, the sages performed a terrible penance in the Dāru forest.[190] They were accompanied by their wives, sons and sacrificial fires.

6. Rudra, the lord of the universe, the bull-emblemed omniscient deity known as Nīlalohita, Dhūrjaṭi and Parameśāna was delighted.

7-9. The lord of the universe, Rudra,[191] wanted to test the sincerity of the dwellers of the Dāru forest in respect of their sacrificial rites. He wanted to turn their minds from the observance of sacrificial rites to the path of renunciation. Thus in order to test their faith, and sportively too, he assumed a

190. See p. 96 note 119.

191. Cekitānaḥ—who creates doubts by his power of creating illusion. *ST*. quotes Śivagītā : जातं वापि शिवज्ञानं न विश्वासं भजत्यलम् ।

deformed but attractive appearance. He had three eyes and two hands. He was nude, and dark in complexion.

10. Even in this form he was extremely handsome. He was smiling and singing, with seductive play of his eyebrows, thereby creating feelings of love in the hearts of women.

11. He the destroyer of cupid, the lord of extremely handsome features increased their sexual feelings.

12. On seeing a man of deformed features, black-red (in colour), even the chaste women followed him with great enthusiasm.

13. On receiving the gesture of a smile from his lotus-like face the women who had gathered at the threshold of huts in the forest or who stayed on the huts above trees, stopped all other activities and followed him not caring for their loosened garments and ornaments.

14. Some of these women, on seeing him felt their eyes reeling due to excitement. Even the old women who were beyond the age of seductive charms of the eye-brow began to display their amorous gestures.

15. On seeing him some women wore smiling faces. With their garments loosened a little, and with their waist bands dislodged they began to sing.

16. Some brahmin ladies on seeing him in the forest found that their own fresh silken garments had got loosened. They cast off their bangles of diverse colours and went to their kinsmen.

17. One of them, on seeing him did not know that her upper and lower garments had stripped off. Others in their excitement could not distinguish between their kinsmen and the multi-branched trees though they were familiar.

18-19. Some sang; some danced; some fell and rolled down on the ground. O leading brahmin, another lady sat on the ground like an elephant and began to talk aloud. Looking smilingly they began to embrace one another all round. After stopping Rudra on his way they began to show all shrewd gestures.

20. They asked, "who are you ?"

Others said, "Be seated".

Delighted in their minds some said, "Where are you going? Be pleased with us."

21. Due to the Māyā of Rudra even the chaste ladies fell down in an awkward posture with their clothes loosened and their tresses dishevelled, in the very presence of their husbands.

22. Even after hearing their words and seeing their diverse activities, the unchanging lord Rudra did not utter anything, good or bad.

23. On seeing the crowd of women and Rudra in this situation the brahmins, the leading sages began to say harsh words.

24. Their powers of austerity were ineffective against Rudra in the same manner as the lustre of the stars in the sky against the refulgence of the sun.

25. (Such had been the spiritual prowess of the sages, formerly) that the sacrifice of the great-souled Brahmā perished due to the curse of a sage,[192] even though the sacrifice was meant for general welfare.

26. Due to the curse of Bhṛgu[193], Viṣṇu of great prowess was compelled to take ten incarnations and undergo suffering in each incarnation.

27. O knower of Dharma, Indra's organ too was cut and cast off by the infuriated sage Gautama[194].

28. The Vasus had to prolong their stay in the womb by a brahmin's curse.[195] Nahuṣa was turned into a serpent by the curse of sages.[196]

29. The milk ocean was dried by the curse of brahmins though it was the perpetual abode of Viṣṇu. The watery ocean was made unfit for drinking by the brahmins' curse.

30-32. In order to atone for this Viṣṇu went to Vārāṇasī[197] and resorted to the lord of Avimukta.[198] He performed the ablution of the three-eyed lord, the lord of Devas, with milk. With unswerving devotion, he, together with Brahmā and the

192-196. The detail can be traced to the Mbh. It shows how the spiritual power possessed by the sages was misused for worldly ends.

197. See p. 97 note 120.

198. avimukteśvara, the celebrated liṅga of Śiva is placed in the holy city Vārāṇasī.

sages, sprinkled Śiva with milk which coming in contact with the body of the lord became nectarlike and filled the ocean wherein lord Viṣṇu made his residential abode.

33. Dharma had been cursed by the noble sage Māṇḍavya. The Vṛṣṇis along with Kṛṣṇa had been cursed by Durvāsas and other noble sages.

34. Rāma and his younger brother Lakṣmaṇa had been cursed by the noble sage Durvāsas. Lord Viṣṇu was even kicked by the sage Bhṛgu.

35. These and many others, except the odd-eyed lord of Umā, the overlord of Devas had been made subservient by the brahmins.

36. Thus deluded the sages of Dāruvana did not understand Rudra[199]. They spoke harsh words to Rudra who thereupon disappeared.

37-38. In the morning all those sages with perplexed minds and blurred thinking went from Dāruvana to Brahmā of noble soul who was seated in the highest seat. They informed him about what had happened in that holy Dāru forest.

39-40. Pondering over everything in his mind Brahmā understood what they did in the holy Dāru forest. He stood up with palms joined in reverence and bowed to Rudra. He then spoke hurriedly to the sages who had their abodes in Dāru forest.

41. Fie upon you all who had attained excellent treasure,[200] O brahmins, but had unluckily wasted it.

42. The man with a Liṅga who had been seen by you all without Liṅgas, the person of deformed features was the supreme lord himself.

43. O brahmins, never should the guests be dishonoured by the householder even if they happen to be deformed, dirty or illiterate.

44. Formerly, on this very same earth even Kāla the God of death was defeated by the excellent brahmin sage Sudarśana through the adoration of a guest.

45. Excepting the adoration of the guests there is no

199. Dāruvana : See p. 96 note 119.

200. prāptanidhanān i.e. though you have obtained a rich treasure in the visit of Śiva to your hermitage.

mode of self-expiation in this world, for excellent brahmin householders; there is no other way to cross the ocean of worldly existence.

46. Formerly, a householder known as Sudarśana, vowed to conquer the God of Death.[201] He said to his chaste wife.

47. "O lady of good holy rites, fine eye-brows and good fortune, listen to what I say, assiduously. Never should you dishonour the guests who visit your house.

48. Since everyone of the guests is the Pinākā-bearing lord, you should dedicate even your self to the guest and adore him.

49. That chaste lady, on being urged thus, became extremely dejected. Helpless that she was, she wept and said to her husband—"O lord ! please explain what you have just said."

50. On hearing her words Sudarśana said again—"O noble lady everything belongs to lord Śiva and since the Guest is lord Śiva himself, everything is his. Hence the guest should always be adored."

On being urged thus by her husband the chaste wife accepted this behest (wholeheartedly) just as one places on his head (reverently) the flowers offered to God. Thus she went on (attending to her duties).

O excellent brahmins, in order to test their devotion, Dharma himself assumed the form of a brahmin and came to the house of the sage. That sinless lady welcomed the guest and worshipped him with the materials of worship.

54. Thus worshipped by her, Dharma disguised as a brahmin said—"O gentle lady where has your noble husband Śudarśana gone ?

55-58. O noble lady, enough of this cooked rice and other eatables ! I say, you should dedicate yourself (to me)" Remembering what had been previously mentioned by her husband that chaste lady full of bashfulness and with closed eyes, began to move (towards him). Again she began saying. But then. . all the same, she made up her mind to dedicate herself to Dharma[202] there itself at the behest of her own husband. In the

201. jetum (mṛtyum iti śeṣaḥ) i.e. to conquer death.

202. dharme—dharmarūpe dvije *ST*. in regard to Dharma who had assumed the guise of a brahmin. Or dharme—dharmviṣaye *ST*. in regard to virtue.

meantime, Sudarśana, the husband of that lady, came to the threshold and called to her—"Come, come, O gentle lady? Where have you been?"

It was the guest himself who replied to him.

59-64. "O Sudarśana, O highly blessed one, I am now engaged in sexual intercourse with this wife of yours. What should be done here may kindly be mentioned. O leading brahmin, the sexual intercourse is concluded. O excellent brahmin, I am satisfied."

Sudarśana the noble brahmin then said in great delight:—

"O excellent brahmin, enjoy her as you please. I shall go away now."

Thereafter Dharma who was delighted (at this incident) revealed himself (in his own form). He granted him whatever he desired and told him again.—

"O leading brahmin, even mentally this splendid lady has not been enjoyed by me. Undoubtedly, it was to ascertain her devotion that I came here. O brahmin of good rites, with this single act of piety you have conquered death. O the prowess of this penance!" Saying thus he went away. Hence all guests should be worshipped in the same manner.[203]

65. O unfortunate noble brahmins, of what avail is much talk. All of you should seek refuge in the very same Rudra immediately.

66. On hearing the words of Brahmā the leading brahmins became distressed. With eyes blinded by tears they saluted Brahmā and said:

The Brahmins said :

67-69. O blessed one, we do not care even slightly for our lives or for our woman folk who have become deformed. But that irreproachable omnipresent trident-bearing and pinākaholding lord has been censured and cursed by us out of ignorance, though our power to curse was rendered ineffective by his mere looking at us. O lord of Devas, you should now tell us the procedure for renunciation in order to see the terrible lord, the chief of Devas, the god with the matted hair.

203. tathā—Sudarśanavat *ST*. just as Sudarśana did.

Brahmā said :

70-74. O excellent brahmins, the devotee shall, at first, learn the Vedas with great devotion from his preceptor. He shall always ponder over their meanings and understand Dharma. He shall remain a disciple till he completes all learning or upto twelve years.

He shall then take the sacred ablution at the conclusion of his student life. He shall marry a wife, and procreate thereafter sons of holy rites. He shall then allot befitting means of livelihood to his sons. Then he shall perform the rites of worship to the lord by performing Agniṣṭoma and other sacrifices. After going to forest he shall worship the great soul. Maintaining a diet of milk and controlling his senses he shall worship Devas in the fire, for a period of twelve years, or twelve months or twelve fortnights or twelve days.

75-76. Then he shall offer in the same fire all vessels used for the sacrifice. He shall consign all the earthen and wooden vessels to the waters and the metallic ones to his preceptor. He shall distribute all his belongings to the brahmins without hesitation. He shall prostrate on the ground and make obeisance to the preceptor. Becoming detached he shall then renounce everything and become an ascetic.

77. He shall have off his hairs along with the tuft and cast off his sacred thread. He shall perform five offerings in the waters saying "Bhūḥ svāhā".

78-80. Thereafter he shall roam about for attaining complete[204] liberation, observing the sacred rite of refraining from taking food, and maintaining himself either on water, or leaves, or milk or fruits. If living thus, the ascetic does not die within six months or a year he shall strain his body by undertaking hazardous journeys. By these activities he attains identity with Śiva.

81-83. O men of steadfast holy rites, one endowed with devotion[205] may even attain lib eration immediately—. Of what

204. Śiva-vimuktaye—Śivarūpā vimuktiḥ kaivalyarūpā ityarthaḥ *ST.* for absorption in Śiva; for the total mergence of the individual soul into the supreme soul.

205. Cf. *Bhagavadagītā* : तपस्विभ्योऽधिको योगी ज्ञानिभ्योऽपि मतोऽधिकः कर्मिभ्यश्चाधिको योगी तस्माद्योगी भवार्जुन ।। योगिनामपि सर्वेषां मद्गतेनान्तरात्मना । श्रद्धावान् भजते यो मां स मे युक्ततमो मतः ।।

avail are these to a devotee of Rudra? Neither the holy rites nor renunciation, in accordance with the injunctions, nor sacrifices, nor charitable gifts, nor the different sorts of Homas nor the acquisition of all kinds of Sāstras and Vedas are of any avail to him. By means of devotion to Rudra, death was conquered by Śveta.[206] May you too have such devotion to the great lord, the benefactor and the Supreme Soul.

CHAPTER THIRTY

The Story of Sage Śveta

Nandin said :

1. On being thus urged by Brahmā, the leading brahmins, the great sages asked him about the sacred story of Śveta.

Brahmā said :

2-6. O brahmins, there was a certain sage named Śveta in the cave of a mountain. His span of life was nearing its end. Hence he worshipped and eulogised the great lord with devotion. He repeated the Mantras of the holy hymn Rudrādhyāya beginning with "Namaste" (Obeisance so Thee).[207] Then the god of Death, of great splendour thought that the time of death had arrived[208] for the excellent brahmin. O leading brahmins, thinking of taking him away he approached the sage. Śveta saw Kāla and though the time of his death was imminent he meditated upon the three-eyed lord Rudra and worshipped him:

"I worship the three-eyed lord[209] of great fragrance, who increases prosperity. What will god of Death do for me? Since I am Death of Death."[210]

206. Śvetena—by Sage Śveta. For detail, read Ch. 30.
207. Namaste rudra manyave. *TS.* 4.5.1.1.
208. Kālaprāptam—gatāyuṣam i.e. dead.
209. Cf. tryambakaṁ yajāmahe sugandhim puṣṭivardhanam. *TS.* 1.8.6.2.
210. mṛtyor mṛtyuḥ—destroyer of death. Cf.

Having fed on death that feeds on men,
Death being dead there is no dyin gthen.

Looking at Śveta, the god of death terrifying to the worlds said smilingly:

7-11. "Come, O Śveta. What fruit do you gain by this means? O excellent brahmin, who can save one caught in my clutches even if he be Rudra, or Viṣṇu or Brahmā the lord of the universe? O brahmin, how does this procedure pertaining to Rudra affect me. I am bent upon taking you to my world O sage, since your span of life has come to an end."

On hearing these terrible words though mingled with virtuous thoughts, the leading sage cried out "Hā Rudra, Rudra, Rudra." Glancing at Kāla he spoke with eyes full of tears, excitedly, in dejected mood:

Śveta said:

12. O Kāla, what can be done by you if our bull-emblemed lord, Rudra, the source of origin of all Devas, is present in this Liṅga?

13. O lord of great arms, of what avail is this behest (of yours) to persons like me who are extremely devoted to Rudra? I ask you to go away, the way you have come.

14-15. On hearing this Kāla of sharp fangs and terrible to look at, became infuriated. The terrible god with the noose in his hands roared like a lion and clapped his hands again and again. He then bound the sage whose time of death had arrived and addressed him thus:

16. "O brahmin sage, O Śveta, you have been bound by me for being taken to my abode. What has been done now by your Rudra the lord of Devas?

17. Where is Rudra and where your devotion? Where is your worship and where the fruit thereof? Where am I and whence have I to fear? O Śveta, you have been bound by me.

18. O Śveta, is your Rudra stationed in this Liṅga? If so, he is utterly inactive. How can he be worshipped?"

19-20. Then Rudra, the destroyer of Kāma and sacrifice, the three-eyed lord came hurriedly with a laugh, accompanied by Umā, Nandin and the leading gaṇas in order to slay Yama who had come to kill the brahmin.

21. O brahmins, then on seeing Rudra, the mighty Yama[211]

211. balī—valorous (Yama).

abandoned the brahmin, out of fear and fell down near the sage.

22-23 On looking at lord Rudra, the destroyer of death, as also at Yama who fell instantaneously at the sight of the lord, Śveta roared loudly.[212] O leading brahmins, the gods too cried loudly, and bowed to the lord as well as Umā. The leading sages were delighted much.

24. Over the heads of the sage and Rudra, the sky-roving gods showered cool and splendid flowers from the firmament.

25-26. On seeing Yama dead, Nandin bowed to lord Rudra. He the leader of the gaṇas and the follower of lord Rudra, spoke to the lord in great astonishment. "This Yama of puerile intelligence[213] is dead. Now, be favourable to the sage."

27. On seeing Yama destroyed in a trice, the lord blessed the excellent brahmin and disappeared.[214]

28. Hence, O brahmins, One should devoutly worship the lord, the conqueror of the god of Death. He is the bestower of liberation as well as of worldly pleasures. He is the benefactor of all.

29. Of what avail is much talk? After renouncing and worshipping Rudra with great devotion you will all become free from grief.

Nandin said:

30-31. On being addressed thus by Brahmā, the sages, the expounders of Brahman said once again :—O lord, be pleased. By what penance or sacrifice or holy rites can devotion to Rudra, the Pināka-bearing lord, be acquired? How will the twiceborn become the devotee of Rudra?

Brahmā said :

32-34. Neither by charitable gifts, nor by learning, can, O excellent sages devotion to Śiva, the great cause (of the universe) be acquired. It cannot be acquired by long or sessional

212. uccadhīḥ—uccā dhīr yasya *ST*.—the intelligent (Śvtea).

213. Bāladhiḥ—the stupid (Yama).

214. Gūḍha-śarīram—the invisible form. Construe : kṣaṇād gūḍhaśarīraṁ viveśa.

sacrifice, holy rites, vedic texts, yogic treatises or by restraints. It is acquired only by God's grace.

On hearing these words the anxious sages bowed to Brahmā along with their wives and sons. Hence, devotion to lord Rudra bestows virtue, love and wealth. It yields victory to the sage. It grants him victory over death.

35-37. Formerly, by means of devotion, Dadhīca conquered lord Viṣṇu and his associate Devas. He killed Kṣupa with the tip of his foot. He acquired adamantine bones. By glorifying the lord, I too conquered death. Even by the great sage Śveta who had fallen into the jaws of death, death was conquered by the grace of the lord, in the manner it was conquered by me.

CHAPTER THIRTY ONE

Hymn to Śiva

Sanatkumāra said:

1. O holy lord, please now recount to us how the dwellers of Dāru forest sought refuge in the lord, thanks to his grace.

Nandin said:

2. The self-born deity (Brahmā) spoke thus to the blessed residents of Dāru forest who had the lustre of fire due to their penance.

Brahmā said:

3. This great lord should be known as Maheśvara. Greater than him there is no other protection to be sought.

4-5. He is the lord of Devas, sages and pitṛs. During the period of dissolution at the end of a thousand sets of four yugas,[215] the lord becomes Kāla and destroys all living beings. He alone creates subjects by his splendour.

215. The period of dissolution is equal to a kalpa, or a night of Brahmā, equal to a period of four hundred thirty two million years of mortals.

6. He is the thunderbolt-armed (Indra) and the discus-bearing Viṣṇu marked by Śrīvatsa. He is called Yogin in the Kṛta age, Kratu in the Tretā, Kālāgni in the Dvāpara and Dharmaketu in the Kali age. These four are the forms of Rudra which the learned men meditate upon.

8. The Liṅga should be symmetrical within and without; at the place of support of the swollen knob it should be octangular. In other places it should be cylindrical and of attractive appearance. One should worship only such a fine Liṅga.

9. Tamas is the fire god; Rajas is Brahmā and Sattva is Viṣṇu. Although there is a single deity at the base these are glorified as its forms.[216]

10-11. The leading brahmins who have conquered their anger and sense-organs, make the Liṅga endowed with all these traits. It is there that the Brahman stays along with all his yogic powers. Hence they worship (in the liṅga) lord Īśāna the lord of the chiefs of Devas, the unchanging deity.

12-17. The Liṅga should be cylindrical, splendid, of the size of a thumb, appealing to all and level in the umbilical region. It may have eight or sixteen equal angles. Its zone must be well built so that it should yield all desires. The supporting altar is twice its size or equal in size, and approved by all. The cow's hole shall have all the characteristics of the altar and shall be a third of its size. O excellent brahmins, the border all round shall be at least one yava in breadth. The Liṅga shall be made of gold, silver or copper. The altar shall extend up to thrice its size all round. It (the altar) shall be circular, triangular, quadrangular or hexagonal in shape. It shall be free from cracks, and with all characteristics clearly defined. After installing it duly in accordance with the rules governing worship, O brahmins, the Kalaśa (water-pot) shall be placed in the middle of the altar.

18. A piece of gold and cereals[217] shall be placed within it. The holy water shall then be inspired with the Mantras of

216. Cf. *Devī Bhāga*. 1.8.4; *Brahmāṇḍa*, *prakriyā*. 4.6; *Mar*. 40.18; *ŚP Vāyavīya* 10.27; *Liṅga*, 1.1.22.

217. sabījam—pañcākṣara-mantra-sahitam *ST*. including the five-syllabled mantra 'namaḥ Śivāya'.

the five auspicious Brahmans[218] (Sadyojāta etc). The devotee shall thereafter sprinkle the Liṅga with the holy water repeating the sacred five mantras.

19. If you worship with such materials as are available you will attain Siddhi. All of you joined by your sons and kinsmen shall worship him with concentration and mental purity.

20. All of you with your palms joined in reverence shall resort to the trident-bearing lord. You will then see the lord of Devas who is inaccessible to persons with no self-control.

21-22. On seeing him your ignorance and sins will perish.

Thereafter forest-dwellers circumambulated Brahmā of unmeasured prowess and returned to Dāruvana. They propitiated the lord in the manner prescribed by Brahmā.

23-27. In the different dry tracts of land, or in the caves of the mountains or in the auspicious but isolated banks of the rivers they performed penances. Some stayed in water, looking splendid with moss clinging to them, some were exposed to the rain in the course of penance and some stood on the tips of their toes. Others lived on grains crushed by teeth. Others on grains crushed with pieces of rocks. Some adopted Vīrāsana postures and others were engaged in the activities of deer. Thus these wise devotees spent time in penance and worship. When a year was completed and Spring arrived, in that Kṛta age, the lord wanted to bless them with his grace. With sympathy towards his devotees, the delighted lord came to Dāru forest on the splendid mountain Himālaya.[219]

28-32. The lord had vulgar traits. He was stark nude. He had smeared his limbs with ashes. His hands were engaged in whirling a firebrand. His eyes were red and tawny. Sometimes he laughed biosteriously, sometimes he sang surprisingly. Sometimes he danced amorously and sometimes he cried repeatedly. He roamed round the hermitages and begged for alms. He assumed forms of his choice by his māyā. When the lord thus came to the forest the sages eulogised him with devotion. By their pleasant countenance and in the company

218. brahmabhiḥ—sadyojātādimantraiḥ—with mantras beginning with 'sadyojātāya namaḥ'.

219. See p. 94 note 111.

of their wives, sons and attendants, they greeted the lord with waters, garlands of variegated colour, incense and scents. They spoke to the lord thus:

33-35. "O lord of chief of Devas, please forgive whatever fault has been committed by us mentally, verbally and physically, out of our ignorance. O Rudra, your activities wonderful and incomprehensible are secret and unintelligible even to Brahmā and other Devas. We do not understand either your progress or regress."

36. O lord of the universe, O supreme lord, you are as you are. Obeisance be to you. The sages of noble soul eulogise you as the lord of Devas, the supreme lord.

37. Obeisance to Bhava, to the splendid one, to the conceiver of all objects, to the source of their origin, to one of infinite strength and prowess and to the lord of all living beings.

38. Obeisance to the destroyer, to the tawny-coloured one, to the changing and the unchanging one, to one who bore the flow of the Gangetic waters and to the support of all. Obeisance to one who manifests in all the three Guṇas.

39. Obeisance to the Lord with three eyes, to the holder of the excellent trident, the bestower of pleasure[220] to the fire god and the great Ātman.

40. Obeisance to the bull-emblemed Śiva, to the lord of Gaṇas; to Kāla armed with a staff and a noose in his hands.

41-42. Obeisance to one who is the chief deity of the Vedic hymns, and who has hundred tongues. O lord, this entire universe is born out of your body whether it be of the past, present or future, whether it be mobile or immobile. O lord, welfare unto you. You protect and destroy everything. Hence be pleased with us.

43. Whatever man does out of ignorance or knowledge is done by the lord [221] himself through his yogic Māyā.

220. kandarpāya—kaṁ sukhaṁ tena darpayati harṣayati, mohayati vā kandarpaḥ tasmai *ST*. One who delights his devotees by giving them pleasure.

221. bhagavān—It has been defined as उत्पत्तिं च विनाशं च भूतानामागतिं गतिम् । वेत्ति विद्यामविद्यां यः स वाच्यो भगवानिति ॥ *Viṣṇu* quoted in *ST*.

44-46. After eulogising the lord with delighted inner soul, the sages endowed with austerities requested[222] him—"Let us see you in your real form." Then the delighted lord assumed his real form of three eyes. To see that form the lord granted them divine eyes. Looking at the three-eyed lord of Devas by the vision they had acquired, the dwellers of Dāruvana again eulogised the lord.

CHAPTER THIRTYTWO

Hymn to Lord Śiva

The sages said :

1. Obeisance to the lord who is naked,[223] who bears the trident, who dissolves the universe,[224] who is handsome,[225] who is an axe to the tree of the universe,[226] to one with terrifying face.[227]

2. Obeisance to formless one; to one of handome form; to one of the form of the universe. Obeisance to one who embraces the elephantine face of his son Gaṇeśa;[228] obeisance to Rudra; obeisance to one in the form of yajamāna.[229]

3. Obeisance to one bowed by all; obeisance to one who bows to his own Ātman; obeisance to one with blue tuft;[230] obeisance to one with poison in his neck.

4. Obeisance to one who is blue-necked, to one who applies the ash from the cremation ground all over the body. You are Brahmā among all Devas. You are Nīlalohita among all Rudras.

222. yācanta—an archaic form for ayācanta.
223. digvāsase—aparichinnarūpāya *ST.*—not conditioned by limit.
224. kṛtāntāya—pralayakāraṇāya *ST.*—the cause of dissolution.
225. Vikaṭāya—sundarāya *ST.*—of beautiful form.
226. karālāya—kuṭhārāya *ST.*—an axe to the world-tree.
227. karāla-vadanāya—of terrible face.
228. kaṭaṅkaṭāya—who one touches lovingly the elephantine face of Gaṇeśa.
229. svāhākārāya—one who has a form of yajamāna.
230. nīla-śikhaṇḍāya—of dark hair.

5-6. You are the soul of all living beings. You are known as Puruṣa in the Sāṅkhya system. You are Meru among mountains; moon among planets; Vasiṣṭha among sages; Indra among Devas; Om among Vedas and the excellent Sāman among Sāman verses.

7. You are lion among beasts; bull among animals and lord of all men.

8. In whatever form you are, whatever form you may assume, may we be able to see you there in the manner mentioned by Brahmā.[231]

9. Lust, anger, covetousness, despondency and arrogance —we wish to know all these; be pleased, O supreme lord.

10. When the time of great Dissolution arrived, O lord, the hand was rubbed against the forehead and fire was generated by you the self-possessed soul.

11. Then the whole world was enveloped by that fire. Hence these (lust, anger etc.) are distorted fires equal to the fire of dissolution.

12-16. Lust, fury, greediness, delusion, arrogance and harassment and all living beings mobile and immobile are burned by the fire originating from you. O lord of Devas, be our protector even as we are being burned. O highly blessed one, O supreme lord, for the welfare of the world you sprinkle the living beings. O auspicious observer, O lord, command us: we shall carry out your behest, in thousands and crores of living beings, in hundreds and crores of forms, we are unable to reach the extremities. O lord of Devas, obeisance be to you.

CHAPTER THIRTYTHREE

Statement of the Sages

Nandin said:

1. Thereafter the lord was delighted and he blessed them. On listening to their eulogy he spoke thus:

231. paśyāmaḥ—tathā kurv iti śeṣaḥ *ST*. Do so that we may see you.

2. The brahmin who reads or listens to the hymn glorified by you all or narrates this to the brahmins shall attain leadership among my attendants.

3-4. O leading sages, I shall mention what is conducive to your welfare and sacred to the devotees. Everything feminine is goddess Prakṛti born of my body. O brahmins, everything masculine is Puruṣa born of my body. O brahmins, undoubtedly my creation is through both of these.[232]

5. Hence no one shall censure the naked ascetic who is devoted to me, who expounds Brahman but who behaves like children and mad people.

6-8. Those devotees of Mahādeva who are interested in applying ashes; who burn their sins through ashes; who are engaged in meditation and carry out what has been laid down in the scriptures; who have perfect control over the sense-organs; who have sublimated their sexuality; who worship the great lord with perfect verbal, mental and physical control; reach Rudra's world and do not return therefrom. Hence this secret, sacred and divine rite of the deity of manifest Liṅga.

9. The observers of the above holy rite have all types of forms; they shave off their heads and they observe the rite of ashes. No learned man shall revile at them nor should they be transgressed.

10. No one shall laugh derisively at them nor shall he speak words displeasing to them if he desires for welfare here and hereafter. The stupid man who censures them, censures the lord himself.

11-12. He who worships them worships Śiva. Thus, with a desire for the welfare of the worlds, the great lord sports about as a great yogin in every yuga, with ashes smeared all over his body.[233]

232. The half man and half woman form of Śiva known as 'ardhanārīśvara'. It symbolises the origin of creation by copulation. Cf. Mbh. as quoted in *ST*. न पद्माङ्का न चक्राङ्का न वज्राङ्का यतः प्रजा। लिङ्गाङ्का च भगाङ्का च तस्माद् माहेश्वरी प्रजा।

233. Cf. *Bhagvadgaītā* : यद् यदाचरति श्रेष्ठस् तत्तदेवेतरो जनः। स यत् प्रमाणं कुरुते लोकस्तदनुवर्तते ॥ Quoted in *ST*.

You too shall observe all the rites. Then welfare will be yours and you will attain perfection.

13. Grasping the great knowledge imparted by Śiva, which being incomparable is the destroyer of fear, the sages bent their heads and made obeisance to Śiva with their minds cleared of fear, greed and delusion immediately.

14-15. On hearing what was recounted thus, the delighted brahmins, began the ablution of lord Śiva with pure scented waters with Kuśa grass and flowers scattered therein. They poured water out of water jars. They sang various songs of esoteric meaning and produced huṁkāras with sweet tones.

16. Obeisance to the overlord of Devas; obeisance to the great lord, obeisance to one who shares half of body with his consort;[234] obeisance to the initiator of Sāṅkhya and Yoga.

17. Obeisance to one who is black as a cluster of clouds. Obeisance to one wearing elephant's hide. Obeisance to one having deerskin for the upper garment; obeisance to one having serpent for the sacred thread.

18. Obeisance to Śiva with wonderful well-arranged ear-rings; with well knit garlands and ornaments; to one with the fine lion skin as garb; obeisance to one of extensive reputation.

19. Then the delighted lord spoke to the sages—"O ye of good rites, I am delighted with your penance. Choose your boons."

20-24. All those sages bowed to the lord. Then Bhṛgu, Aṅgiras, Vasiṣṭha, Viśvāmitra, Gautama, Atri, Sukeśa, Pulastya, Pulaha, Kratu, Marīci, Kaśyapa, Kaṇva and Saṁvarta of great penance, spoke to the lord after paying due homage: "We wish to know the mystic secret behind the smearing of ashes, nudity, indirectness (in worship) contrariety in the natural order,[235] the propriety of service or otherwise." On hearing their words the great lord looked at the excellent sages and said smilingly.

234. See p. 18. note 27.

235. Vāmatvam—savya-mārga-prakāraḥ *ST*. the left-hand ritual or doctrine of the Tantras. pratilomatā—the opposite of Vāma-mārga, i.e. a tantric ritual in which left hand practices find no place.

CHAPTER THIRTYFOUR

Praise of the Yogin

The lord said :

1. I shall recount to you the whole story in a nutshell. I am Agni (Fire god) the creator of Soma and I am Soma that resorts to Agni.

2. Agni carries what is consigned to it by way of Homa. Since it rests in the world, the universe consisting of the mobile and immobile beings is often burned by it.

3. Everything reduced to ashes becomes excellent and sacred. With ashes Soma attains power and rejuvenates living beings.

4. He who performs the rite of oblation into the fire[236] as also the rite of 'Tryāyuṣa'[237] is liberated from sins due to the virtue of ashes which constitute power.

5. The word Bhasman is derived from 'bhās' to shine, bhāsate-shines or from causal of 'bhū' to cause to reach, भावयते or from 'bhakṣ' to eat, भक्षति; since it devours all sins it is called Bhasman.

6. The Pitṛs drink fire; Devas drink Soma. The entire universe of the mobile and immobile beings is of the nature of Agni and Soma.

7. I am Agni of great splendour. This great Umā is Soma. I am Agni and Soma together. I am Puruṣa as well as Prakṛti.

8. Hence, O blessed ones ! the ashes constitute my virility. I hold my virility by my physical body. This is the fact.

9. Ever since then, protection is afforded by the ashes. At times of inauspicious events and even in lying-in chambers it is resorted to for securing protection.

10. One whose soul is purified by applying ashes over the body, one who has conquered anger and the sense-organs, never returns after coming near me.

236. agnikāryam—sacrificial rite.

237. tryāyuṣam—ash-bath by reciting the mantra 'tryāyuṣaṁ jamadagne' *VS*. 3. 62.

11. The holy Pāśupata yoga and the Sāṅkhya of Kapila[238] have been evolved by me. It was the excellent Pāśupata rite that was evolved at the outset.

12. Persons occupying different stages of life have been created by Brahmā afterwards. This creation involving bashfulness, delusion and fear has been evolved by me.

13. Devas and sages are verily born nude. The other human beings are also born nude.

14. A man may be clad in silken garments. But if his sense-organs are not in control he is naked. But if his sense-organs are subdued he himself is well covered (even if he does not put on clothes). The cloth is not regarded as the specific cause in these cases.[239]

15. Forgiveness, fortitude, non-violence, detachment, equal reaction in regard to honour and dishonour—all these constitute excellent covering for the body.

16-17. One who has taken holy bath of ashes, one who after smearing ashes over the body, mentally meditates on Śiva, even if he has committed thousands of faults gets all his sins washed by the ash-bath in the manner as the fire burns the forest. He who strenuously takes holy bath of ashes thrice a day would attain the status of the lord of Gaṇas.

18-21. Those who perform sacrifices,[240] observe holy rites and meditate on the great lord with devout feelings about the divine sports of the lord, attain immortality by passing through the noble northern path. Those who resort to the cremation ground, by means of the southern path, attain the eight perfections : Aṇimā: Garimā, Laghimā, Prāpti, Kāmāvasāyitā, Prākāmya, Īśitva Vaśitva and also immortality (in the end).[241]

238. Kāpilam—Sāṁkhya-śāstrām *ST.* a system of philosophy founded by Kapila and known after his name.

239. Mark the contribution of ethics to the Śaivite cult.

240. kratūn—five great sacrifices (mahoyajñas) described in Ch. 26, Verses 14-19 (p. 104)

241. The eight siddhis (attainments of supernatural power) comprise (i) aṇimā (the power of becoming as small as an atom), (ii) laghimā (the faculty of assuming excessive lightness at will), (iii) prāpti (the power of obtaining everything), (iv) prākāmya (irresistible will) (v) mahimā (the power of increasing one's size at will), (vi) īśitva (supremacy), (vii) vaśitva (the power of subduing all to one's own will) and (viii) kāmāvasāyitā (the

22. Indra and other Devas who had adopted the holy rite conducive to the realisation of all desires attained the greatest power and prosperity; all of them are well known for their splendour and refulgence.

23. One shall be devoid of delusion, arrogance, passion and the defects of tamas and rajas in his character. Understanding that things of the world are subject to decay and destruction one shall always be devoted to the yoga of Paśupati.[242]

24-26. He should meditate on the vrata of Paśupati (Śiva) that is destructive of all sins.

He who reads this, being pure and faithful, having conquered the sense-organs, shall become purified of all sins and shall go to Rudra's world. On hearing this all those sages, Vasiṣṭha and others and all the excellent brahmins smeared their bodies with ashes and became freed of all desires. At the end of the kalpa they started towards the world of Rudra.

27. Hence even the deformed and dirty persons are worthy of worship and should not be censured. Leading brahmins whether handsome or dirty should also be worshipped. They may be leading yogins.

28. Of what avail is much talk ? Excellent brahmin devotees of Śiva should be worshipped by all means like Śiva himself.

29-31. Even dirty leading brahmins may be devotees of Śiva and steady in their rites. By devotion to Śiva much can be achieved in the world in the manner of Dadhīca who could conquer even Viṣṇu the lord of Devas. Hence by all means, those devotees with matted hair or tonsured head, or naked anchori-

power of suppressing desire). The last one is sometimes substituted by sarvajñatva. Liṅga reads icchā-kāmāvasāyitvam for kāmāvasāyitvam.

Some other siddhis such as dūra-śravaṇa (hearing from a distance), agnistambha (checking the heat of the fire) etc. are also added to these. For detail, see Vācaspati's *Tattva-Kaumudī* on Īśvarakṛṣṇa's Sāṁkhya-Karikā.)

242. Paśupati-yoga—a concentrated devotion in lord Śiva, who is called paśupati, the lord of the paśus (jīvas) whom he binds with the pāśas (strings) of viṣayas (objects of senses). Cf. *Rudra-bhāṣya* of Ahobala cited in *ST*. "Brahmādyāḥ paśavas teṣām patiḥ paśupatiḥ smṛtaḥ". Jīvas in different strata of life from Brahmā to man are paśus, bound with the noose of viṣayas—objects of worldly pleasure. But each paśu can get release by eschewing these viṣayas and by his concentrated meditation on Śiva.

tes, who have smeared their bodies with ashes should be worshipped always like Śiva himself mentally, verbally and physically.

CHAPTER THIRTYFIVE

Defeat of Kṣupa

Sanatkumāra said:

1-2. O sage of holy rites, how did Dadhīca strike king Kṣupa with his foot after conquering Viṣṇu, the lord of Devas in battle? How did that sage of great penance attain adamantine bones from lord Śiva? O Nandin, please recount how Death was conquered by you.

Nandin said:

3. There was a king of great splendour known as Kṣupa. He was the son of Brahmā. He, the lord of the people, was the friend of Dadhīca, a leading sage.

4. In course of time, incidentally a dispute arose between Kṣupa and Dadhīca as to who was the better—a Kṣatriya or a Brahmin.

5-6. (Kṣupa said) The king holds the physical body of the eight guardians of the quarters.[243] Hence I am Indra, Agni, Yama, Nirṛti, Varuṇa, Vāyu, Soma (Moon), and Dhanada (Kubera, the lord of wealth). I am Īśvara (overlord). I should not be dishonoured.

7-9. O sage of holy rites, that deity (i. e. the king) is

243. The king embodies the essence of eight lokapālas—the guardian deities presiding over the quarters, viz. (1) Indra, east; (2) Agni, south-east; (3) Yama, south; (4) Sūrya— south-west; (5) Varuṇa, west; (6) "Vāyu, north-west; (7) Kuvera, north; (8) Soma, north-east. As such, he is a divine being. He is authorized to maintain the system of four varṇas and Āśramas. But none of the sacred texts—śrutis and smṛtis—empowers him to rule over the Brāhmaṇa varṇa. Cf. G. Dh. S. rājā sarvasyeṣṭe brāhmaṇa-varjam.

greater than the greatest.[244] Hence, O blessed one, O son of Cyavana, I must never be insulted by you. I must always be honoured.

On hearing that opinion of Kṣupa the great sage Dadhīca, son of Cyavana, struck Kṣupa on the head with his left fist, believing in his own supremacy as a brahmin. But the powerful Kṣupa hit Dadhīca with his thunderbolt.

10-12. Formerly, he was born in the world of Brahmā when Brahmā sneezed. He was urged by the thunderbolt-wielding Indra to perform a task. He obtained the thunderbolt as a reward for his task. Out of his own will, he became a human, being and afterwards a king. The powerful king then conquered the leading brahmin like the powerful Indra himself, full of tamas qualities. When struck by the thunderbolt the leading brahmin fell on the ground.

13-14. Out of sorrow he remembered sage Bhārgava. Bhārgava, the best among the embodied beings, came there and by his yogic power he stitched the body of Dadhīca who had been struck by the thunderbolt. After stitching the severed body Bhārgava said:

15-16. O highly blessed Dadhīca, worship Śiva, the unsullied lord of Devas, worthy of worship by Brahmā and others. O brahmin sage ! by the grace of the three-eyed lord, you become immortal. O brahmin, this power of resuscitating one to life has been obtained from him by me.

17. There is no fear, anywhere, from death for the devotees of Śiva. I shall now tell you Śiva's Mantra that revives one to life.

18-21a "We worship the lord, father of the three worlds,[245] the lord of the three deities, three Guṇas, three principles, three sacred fires, of three Vedas, of everything splitin to three. He is the scented one, the increaser of nourishment in all living beings in all places: in the Prakṛti having the three Guṇas, in the sense-organs and their objects, in Devas and Gaṇas. The fragrant lord is as subtle as fragrance in the flowers.

244. Cf. Manu : महती देवता ह्येषा नररूपेण तिष्ठति । 7.8.

245. triyambakam—tryambakam. Cf. *TS*. 1.8.6.2.

21b-25. O excellent brahmin of holy rites, O great sage, because puṣṭi (nourishment) is the very name of Puruṣa, He is the increaser of nourishment (puṣṭivardhana) of all the divine creations beginning with Mahat and ending with Viśeṣa, of Viṣṇu, of Brahmā, of sages, of Indra, and of Devas. Hence, we do worship that immortal nectarine lord Rudra by means of actions, by penance, by study of the Vedas, by yoga and by meditation. By this truth, Śiva himself shall liberate us from the bondage of Death. The lord is the cause of bondage and liberation like the cucumber fruit."[246] This Mantra that resuscitates life has been acquired by me from Śiva.

26. By repeating this Mantra, by doing sacrifice with this, by drinking water inspired by this mantra, by meditating on this Mantra in the presence of the Liṅga, O brahmin, one shali not have any fear of death.

27. After hearing his words Dadhīca propitiated Śiva by means of penance and attained adamantine bones, indestructibility and absence of affliction.

28-30. Having obtained indestructibility and adamantine bones Dadhīca hit the king severely on the head with the tip of his foot. King Kṣupa, in return, hit Dadhīca in his chest with his thunderbolt. But by the grace of lord Śiva the thunderbolt was rendered ineffective. It could not injure Dadhīca the great soul of adamantine body.

31. On seeing the greatness and power of Dadhīca by way of indestructibility and unafflicted state, Kṣupa propitiated the lotus-eyed lord Viṣṇu, the younger brother of Indra.

246. *TS.* 1.9.6.2. Cf. भिद्यते हृदयग्रन्थिश्छिद्यन्ते सर्वसंशयाः । क्षीयन्ते चास्य कर्माणि मयि दृष्टेऽखिलात्मनि । Śivagītā quoted in *ST.*

CHAPTER THIRTYSIX

Dialogue between Kṣupa and Dadhīca

Nandin said :

1-3. Lord Viṣṇu was pleased with his(Dadhīca's) worship. Accompanied by Śrī and Bhūmi (his consorts), holding the conch, the discus, the iron club and lotus in his hands, wearing crown, bedecked in all ornaments, clad in yellow robes, surrounded by Devas and asuras, the Garuḍa-bannered glorious lord Viṣṇu granted him divine vision. Seeing him by his divine vision, Kṣupa bowed to the Garuḍa-bannered deity and eulogised him with pleasing words.

4-8. You are the primordial deity with no origin. You are Prakṛti, you are Puruṣa, the protector of the world. You are Viṣṇu the lord of the universe. You are Brahmā, with the universe for your body. You are the first principle. O Viṣṇu, you alone are the greatest luminary. You are the supreme soul, O lord of Śrī, you are the greatest abode. O lord of the earth, Rudra enveloped by tamas originated from your fury. Brahmā, the creator of the universe enveloped by rajas was born of your grace. The lord enveloped by sattva, was born of your grace. O Viṣṇu, O Rudra, you are identical with the universe.

9. The principles of intellect, ego, the subtle elements and the sense-organs O lord, omniformed, are all presided over by you alone.

10. O great lord, O lord of the universe, O Brahmā, O preceptor of the universe, be pleased, O lord of the chiefs of Devas, be pleased.

11. O Lord of the universe, be pleased. I seek refuge in you, worthy of being sought refuge in. O omniscient lord of long arms.

12. O liberator of mankind, O highly blessed one! O lord of great strength ! O best of souls ! O unopposed ! O great Viṣṇu ! perpetual obeisance be to you.

13-14. O Viṣṇu your divine invisible seat in the midst of the ocean is the thousand-hooded Śeṣa enveloped in tamas.

O lord of Devas, O deity of holy rites, beneath this seat, virtue, knowledge, prosperity and detachment form the four feet.

15-18. The seven nether worlds are your feet; the earth constitutes your loins; the seven oceans[247] are your clothes; the four quarters are your great arms. O lord, the heaven is your head; the sky is your umbilicus; the wind is your nose; the sun and the moon are your eyes, Puṣkara and others constitute your tresses. The stars, constellations and firmament are the ornaments round your neck. How shall I eulogise you the lord of Devas? You are worthy of worship. Whatever was done, heard and glorified faithfully as divine, whatever was sacrificed by me O Lord ! you shall bear all. Obeisance be to you.

Nandin said :

19-21. This hymn of Viṣṇu is destructive of all sins. He who reads or listens to this hymn uttered by Kṣupa, he who narrates this to the brahmins with devotion, goes to the world of Viṣṇu. After worshipping thus and eulogising the invincible lord who is eulogised by the lord of Devas and others and after bowing to him with bent head, Kṣupa spoke in submission.

The King said :

22. O lord, long before, a certain Brahmin, known as Dadhīca became a friend of mine. He is the knower of Dharma and a humble soul.

23-25. He is engaged in worshipping Śiva always. He cannot be killed by anyone at all times. O lord of Devas, he struck me on the head with his left foot, in the open assembly with great contempt. O Viṣṇu, O Viśva, O lord of the Universe, arrogantly he said: "I am not afraid of any body anywhere". O lord of universe, I wish to defeat that brahmin Dadhīca. O Viṣṇu, please, help me to my welfare.

247. sapta sāgarāḥ. The purāṇas mention seven oceans, viz., of salt, sugarcane, wine, ghee, curd, milk and water which surround Jambu, Plakṣa, Śālmali, Kuśa, Krauñca, Śāka and Puṣkara continents respectively.

Nandin said:

26. Viṣṇu understood that Dadhīca was indestructible. Viṣṇu then remembered the incomparable prowess of Śiva.

27. After remembering thus, Viṣṇu said to Kṣupa, born of the sneeze of Brahmā—"O leading king, after attaining lord Śiva, brahmins have nothing to fear.

28. Particularly O king, the devotees of Rudra are free from fear always. If this be true in every respect in regard to base men what then in the case of Dadhīca ?

29. Hence, O blessed one, O king, you have no hope of victory. Of course I shall give a slight pain to the brahmin inviting a curse on me along with Devas.

30. O leading king, at Dakṣa's sacrifice due to Dadhīca's curse I and other Devas will be destroyed but revived again.

31. Hence, O king, coming into contact with the leading brahmin I shall endeavour for your victory over Dadhīca.

Nandin said :

32. On hearing these words Kṣupa said to Viṣṇu—"So be it" The lord too went to the hermitage of the brahmin Dadhīca.

33. The lord, favourably disposed to his devotees, assumed the form of a brahmin. The preceptor of the universe congratulated the brahmin sage Dadhīca and said:—

The lord said :

34. "O Dadhīca, O brahminical sage, O unchanging one engaged in the worship of Śiva, I desire to choose a boon from you. You should grant the same".

35. On being requested by Viṣṇu, the lord of Devas, Dadhīca said:—"All that you desire has been understood. I am not afraid of you.

36-37. O Viṣṇu, you have come to me in the guise of a brahmin. By the grace of Rudra, I can understand everything the past, future and present. O Viṣṇu, O lord of Devas, O deity of good rites, leave off this guise of a brahmin. O destroyer of Madhu, O lord of Devas you have been propitiated by Kṣupa.

38. O lord Viṣṇu, I know you are favourably disposed towards your devotees. O lord Viṣṇu, your favouritism to your devotees is but proper.

39. O lord, O lotus-eyed, bestower of boons, it behoves you to say frankly if you are afraid of me engaged that I am in the worship of Śiva.

40. O Viṣṇu, I do not speak in vain. I am not afraid. In this world I am not afraid of Devas, Daityes or brahmins.

Nandin said:

41. On hearing the words of Dadhīca Viṣṇu in a moment cast off his guise of a brahmin. He assumed his own form and said smilingly.

The Lord said:

42. O Dadhīca of good holy rites ! You have no fear anywhere since you are engaged in the worship of Śiva. Indeed you are omniscient.

43. O leading brahmin, at my behest you should say at least once "I am afraid". Obeisance to you. Please say to Kṣupa in the open assembly that you are afraid.

44. Even after hearing the appeasing words of Viṣṇu, the great sage did not say that he was afraid.

45. It was due to the prowess of the Pināka-bearing Śiva, the lord of Devas, the benefactor and omniscient lord that the great sage did not say he was afraid.

46. Then the infuriated lord Viṣṇu desired to burn the sage and so raised his discus.

47. By the power of Dadhīca even in the presence of Kṣupa, the discus Sudarśana became blunted.

48. On seeing the discus with blunted tip, Dadhīca said to the Discus-bearing lord, who is the cause of manifesting distinction between the existent and non-existent.

49. O lord Viṣṇu, formerly, the terrible discus, Sudarśana was assiduously got by you from Śiva.

50. That discus can never kill me. You now try with the missile of Brahmā or other similar weapons.

Nandin said.

51. On hearing his words and on seeing his own weapon powerless, lord Viṣṇu discharged all missiles from all directions towards him.

52. The powerful Devas thereafter rendered help to Viṣṇu who was engaged in fighting against a single brahmin.

53. Then Dadhīca who had adamantine bones and who had perfect all-round self control took up a handful of kuśa grass. Remembering Śiva he discharged it against Devas.

54. It became a divine trident as lustrous as fire of dissolution. Like fire at the close of a yuga it felt inclined to burn all Devas.

55. O sage, all those weapons which were discharged by Indra, and other Devas bowed to the trident.

56-57. O excellent brahmin, Devas whose strength was dissipated fled from the scene. Then lord Viṣṇu, created out of his body millions and millions of divine attendants resembling himself. The excellent sage burnt all of them immediately.

58-60. Thereafter, Viṣṇu became Universe-formed in order to instil awe in Dadhīca. The excellent brahmin saw several groups of Devas distinctly, as also crores of Rudras, crores of Gaṇas, crores of Cosmic Eggs in the body of Viṣṇu. On seeing all these therein, the son of Cyavana was surprised.

61. The great sage sprinkled the universe-formed Viṣṇu with water. He spoke to Viṣṇu, the unborn lord of the universe, identical with the universe.

62. O mighty-armed one, eschew this deception. O Visṇu, there are thousands of skills (or tricks) with me also which are difficult to comprehend, and which come handy by mere thinking.[248]

63. O uncensured one, you can see within me the entire universe along with yourself, Brahmā and Rudra. I shall give you divine vision.

64. After saying this, the sage showed everything in his own body. He spoke again to lord Viṣṇu, the source of origin of all Devas.

65. "Of what use is this deception ? O lord, of what avail is the power of magic ? O Viṣṇu, what purpose is served by the intrinsic power of objects or by the power of meditation ?

66-67. Hence, eschewing this deception you should fight against me strenuously."

248. Vijñānam—māyā.

On hearing these words and on seeing his miraculous power Devas ran away once again. The lotus-born preceptor of the universe Brahmā restrained lord Viṣṇu who had become inactive.

68. On hearing the words of Brahmā, lord Viṣṇu who was defeated bowed to the sage and went away.

69. Kṣupa was extremely afflicted and dejected. He honoured and adored Dadhīca the leading sage and prayed thus :

70. O Lord and friend Dadhīca, what has been committed by me due to ignorance may be excused. What can be affected by Viṣṇu or Devas in your case since you are a devotee of Rudra ?

71. O great Lord, be pleased. O brahmin, the most excellent among men of devotion, devotion of this type is difficult of access to wicked persons, to base Kṣatriyas like me.

72. On hearing the words of the king the brahmin Dadhīca, the most excellent of those who perform penances blessed the king . The leading sage then cursed Devas.

73-74. May you including Indra and lord Viṣṇu and all great sages be destroyed by the fire of fury of Rudra in the holy sacrifice of the patriarch Dakṣa.

After cursing thus and glancing at Kṣupa the brahmin said again.

75. O leading king, brahmins should be worshipped by Devas, kings and by the different groups of people. O leading king, the brahmins alone are strong and powerful.

76. After saying this the brahmin of great lustre entered his own hut.

After saluting Dadhīca the king too went to his own abode.[249]

77. The place of this event is known as the holy centre. Sthāṇvīśvara.[250] After reaching Sthāṇvīśvara one shall attain identity with Śiva.

249. kṣayam—gṛham *ST.* abode.

250. Sthāneśvara or Sthāṇvīśvara is mentioned by Bāṇabhaṭṭa in his historical prose kāvya Harṣacarita written in the first half of the seventh century A.D. The earliest notice of this place by a foreigner is found in the record of the Chinese pilgrim Hieun Thsang, the contemporary of Harṣavardhana, the king of Sthāneśvara and Kannauj.

The city is identified with the modern town Thanesar, near Kurukṣetra, Haryana State. It derives its name from an ancient temple dedicated to lord Śiva.

78. O great sage, the dispute between Kṣupa and Dadhīca has been briefly recounted to you, as also the power of Śiva and his protege Dadhīca.

79. He who reads this divine dispute between Kṣupa and Dadhīca will conquer premature death. After Death he will go to the region of Brahmā.

80. He who enters the battlefield after repeating this story need not be afraid of death. He will always come out victorious.

CHAPTER THIRTYSEVEN

Grant of boons to Brahmā

Sanatkumāra said:

1. How did you attain Mahādeva the lord of Umā? O holy lord, it behoves you to narrate everything. I wish to hear.

Śailādi said:

2. O great sage, my blind father Śilāda was desirous of a progeny. For a long time he performed a penance very difficult to be performed by others.

3. The thunderbolt-wielding lord Indra was pleased with his penance. He said to Śilāda—"I am pleased. Choose your boons".

4. O leading sage, he bowed down to the thousand-eyed lord of Devas along with Devas. With palms joined in reverence he spoke to him.

Śilāda said:

5. O lord of good holy rites, O destroyer of the enemies of Devas, O bestower of boons, I wish for a son devoid of death and not born of a womb.

Indra said:

6. O brahmin sage, I shall give you a son born of a

womb and liable to die. I will not give you anyone otherwise. There are no persons without death.

7. O great sage, even lord Brahmā will not grant you a son without death or not born of a womb. Then what about others ?

8. Even that lord Brahmā is not devoid of death himself. The lord himself is born of a womb. The lotus-born deity of great splendour is born of an egg.

9. The lord is born of Maheśvara. He is the son of Umā. His span of life is limited to two Parārdhas.

10. Thousands and crores of kalpas that constitute his day have passed by. So many yet remain.

11. Hence O leading brahmin, eschew your ardent desire for a son devoid of death or not born of a womb. Accept a son like yourself.

Śailādi said:

12. On hearing his words my meritorious father well-known in the world as Śilāda again spoke to the husband of Śacī (i.e. Indra).

Śilāda said:

13. O lord, I have already heard that Brahmā was born of an Egg, was born of a lotus and also was born of Maheśvara.

14-15. Formerly O Mahendra, of great arms, Nārada my elder brother, had been saying this and I have heard it from him. But tell me, how this can be ? Dākṣāyaṇī was the grand-daughter of Brahmā since Dakṣa was the son of the lotus-born deity ? How then can Brahmā be her son ?

Indra said:

16-18. O brahmin, your doubt is reasonable. I shall tell you the cause of the same that happened to Brahmā in the Tatpuruṣa kalpa. After pondering over all things the supreme lord created Brahmā. In the Meghavāhana kalpa, Viṣṇu, the lord of the universe, became a cloud and bore the supreme lord Śiva for a thousand years with ease and comfort.

19. On seeing the devotional feeling of Viṣṇu towards him-

self the great lord entrusted to him everything alongwith Brahmā with instructions to create further.

20-21. Then they call that kalpa by the name Meghavāhana. On seeing him born of His body Brahmā approached Śiva and said: "O lord, Viṣṇu was born of your left and I am born of your right side."

22-26. "Still Viṣṇu created the entire universe along with me. Taking the form of a cloud identical with the world he bore you the lord of Devas, preceptor of the universe, day and night. O lord, I am a better devotee of yours than him. Be pleased with me, O lord, grant me omniscience."

Then Brahmā attained omniscience in a trice. He then hurried out and met Viṣṇu in the vast ocean[251] enveloped by darkness. He saw Viṣṇu in an illustrious spot studded with gold and jewels which was mentally created by Viṣṇu himself. It was inaccessible to wicked persons, invisible even to the pious like Indra and others.

27-32. Brahmā saw the Puruṣa in whose heart the entire universe rested. He was lying down on the couch constituted by the body of the serpent Śeṣa.[252] He had lotus-like eyes and four arms holding the conch, dicus, iron club, and the lotus. He was wearing ornaments and in that form he resembled the orb of the moon. He bore the mark Śrīvatsa over his breast. Brahmā beheld him with pleasure evident in his face. His lotus-like feet had turned red due to the contact with the lotus-like soft hands of Lakṣmī. He was Īśāna the greatest Ātman. By tamas he was in the form of Kāla. By rajas he was the initiator of creation of the world. By sattva he was the sustainer of all. He was Parameśvara, the soul of all, the noble Ātman, the supreme soul. Brahmā saw him lying down in his yogic slumber in the milky ocean full of nectar. On seeing him he spoke to him thus:

33-35. "Just as you had swallowed me before, so also I shall swallow you now by the grace of Śiva. The lord with great arms woke up a little surprised and looking at him smiled slightly. Swallowed by that noble soul, he entered the body

251. See p. 15 note 22.
252. See p. 15 note 23.

of that deity born of the Egg. Then Brahmā created Viṣṇu through the middle of the eye-brows. Created by him Viṣṇu stood near him observing.

36-40. In the meantime Rudra, the source of origin of all Devas, who had granted boons to both, assumed an uncivil form and came to the place where Viṣṇu stood. Lord Parameśvara, the soul of the universe, wanted to bless both with great favour. Both of them simultaneously saw the lord resembling the fire of Death. They eulogised the terrible lord with matted hair. They bowed to the lord, the bestower of boons, standing far away out of respect. The great lord, the protector of the universe blessed Brahmā and Viṣṇu and vanished there itself.

CHAPTER THIRTYEIGHT

Creation of Brahmā

Śailādi said:

1. When lord Śiva had gone, lord Viṣṇu, the origin of Brahmā, bowed down in that direction and said to the lotus-born deity.

Śrī Viṣṇu said:

2. The supreme god Śiva, the lord of the universe, is omnipresent. He is the lord and refuge of us both as well as of the entire universe.

3. O Brahmā, I am born of the left side of Śiva the supreme soul. You are born of his right side.

4. The sages observe me and say that I am Pradhāna, the Prakṛti, the Avyakta (unmanifest) and the Aja (unborn). They call you Puruṣa.

5. They call the supreme lord the cause of us both, as lord of the universe. He is the unchanging lord Īśvara.

6. At the instance of the lord of the immortals, the lotus-born deity eulogised and bowed to Rudra the most excellent one and the bestower of boons.

7. Then Viṣṇu assumed the form of a Boar and lifted up the earth submerged under the water. He re-established it as it was originally.

8. With great effort he made the earth even, without ups and downs. The lord created the rivulets, rivers and the oceans as before.

9. The lord having the form of a boar[253] the uplifter of the earth, gathered all the mountains together. As before he created the four worlds beginning with Bhūḥ.

10. The lord who was the most excellent of all intelligent persons became inclined to create the chief creation, the animal creation, and then the divine and human creations.

11-16. With the intellect free from wretchedness the lord at the outset created Sananda, Sanaka and Sanātana the most excellent among the good. All these practised Naiṣkarmya and attained the greatest being. By his yogic learning he created Marīci, Bhṛgu, Aṅgiras, Pulastya, Pulaha, Kratu, Dakṣa, Atri, Vasiṣṭha, Saṅkalpa, Dharma and Adharma. Thus there are twelve sons to Brahmā born of the unmanifest.

At the outset the eternal lord had created Ṛbhu and Sanatkumāra. These two fresh born sons had sublimated their sexuality, and were divine expounders of Brahman. They were bachelors, omniscient, conceivers of everything and equal to Brahmā himself. After creating the sargas—Mukhya etc. O Śilāśana, the lotus-born deity, the creator of the universe, evolved all the special characteristics of the different ages.

253. bhūdharākṛti—in the person of King Pṛthu, son of Vena. *Bhāg*. ascribes the levelling of the earth to King Pṛthu. चूर्णयन् स्वधनुष्कोटया गिरिकूटानि राजराट् । भूमण्डलमिदं वैन्यः प्रायश्चक्रे समं विभुः—cited in *ST*. which offers also another interpretation : यद्वा भूधरा आकृतिर्यस्यासौ महावराहस्वरूप इत्यर्थः in the form of boar, uplifting the earth submerged in waters.

CHAPTER THIRTYNINE

Specific Dharmas of Four Yugas

Śailādi said:

1. On hearing the narration of Indra, my father, the great sage, bowed to the lord of Devas, and with the palms joined in reverence he asked him again.

Śilāda said:

2-3. O lord Indra, O omniscient one, bowed down by the chiefs of Devas O lord of Śacī, O thousand-eyed lord of the universe, O Maheśvara, how did the lotus-born deity Brahmā evolve the specific dharmas of the yugas? It behoves you now to recount it to me who have bowed down to you.

Śailādi said:

4. On hearing the words of Śilāda, the noble-souled Indra recounted the dharmas of the yugas in detail in the manner seen by him.

Indra said:

5. Know that first comes Kṛtayuga. O sage, Tretā comes next. Thereafter Dvāpara and Tiṣya (Kali) yugas. These are the four yugas in brief.

6. Sattvaguṇa signifies Kṛta yuga; rajas signifies Tretā; rajas-cum-tamas signifies Dvāpara. Tamas signifies Kali. These should be known as the special characteristics in each of the different yugas.

7. Meditation is the greatest activity in Kṛta yuga; yajña (sacrifice) in Tretā; worship is the main activity in Dvāpara and pure charitable gift in the Kali age.

8. Four thousand divine years constitute Kṛta yuga. So many hundred years (i.e four hundred) constitute the preceding transition period (sandhyā). The following transition period (sandhyāṁśa) is also of the same duration.

9. O Śilāśana, O man of good holy rites, know that the longevity of the subjects in Kṛta is four thousand human years.

10. When the Kṛtayuga together with its sandhyāṁśa passes off, the yuga dharma becomes reduced by a quarter all round.

11. The excellent Tretā yuga extends to a period one fourth less than Kṛta. Know that Dvāpara extends to half of the duration of Kṛta. Kaliyuga is still half of it.

12. O sage, the Sandhyā periods are respectively three hundred, two hundred and one hundred years. The sandhyāṁśa periods are also the same. The same thing holds good in all the kalpas, and yugas.

13-14. In Kṛta, the eternal dharma has all the four feet; in Tretā it has three feet; it stays on two feet in Dvāpara; in Kali, it is devoid of three feet and is stationed by its mere existence. In Kṛta, the subjects are born in twins; their avocation abounds in taste and happiness.

15. They are always satisfied. They enjoy all pleasures and bliss. There is no inferiority or superiority among them; there are no special characteristics among subjects; they are all auspicious.

16. Longevity, happiness and features among the people in Kṛta are the same for all; they have no special liking; they have no Dvandvas (mutually opposing pairs), no hatred, no fatigue.

17-19. Those who have no abodes live on mountains and in the oceans. Even then they are devoid of misery. They have mostly sattva guṇas and are mostly isolated. They move about without specific desires; they are perpetually delighted in their minds. They refrain from virtuous and sinful activities.

At that time there was a well-defined arrangement of castes and stages of life; but there was no intermingling of castes. O brahmin, by efflux of time, in Tretā yuga their tastes and happiness perish.

20-22. When that Siddhi has perished another is generated. When water attains subtlety it gets transformed into clouds. From the thundering clouds rainfall proceeds. As soon as the surface of the earth comes into contact with rain, trees appear. These trees form their abodes. The subjects have their sustenance and pleasures out of these trees.

23-26. In the beginning of Tretā the subjects sustained themselves through them. Then after the lapse of a great deal of time, when there was a change, the feeling of lust and covetousness was sudden. The trees which formed their abodes began to perish. When they perished the twin-born subjects at that time were bewildered. Thereafter they began to ponder over the matter. Since they were truthful in their thought the trees reappeared.

27-28. They used to produce clothes, fruits and ornaments. On the very same trees honey of great potency but not generated by bees, got evolved in every leafy cup. This honey had great fragrance, good colour and sweet taste The subjects always sustained themselves thereby and passed their days comfortably at all times.

29. They were delighted and well-nourished. Through this achievement they were free from ailments. Then after the lapse of some time, they became greedy.

30-32. They began to chop off the trees and take the honey forcibly. Due to their misdemeanour as well as their greed the kalpa trees perished in certain places along with honey. As time rolled on only a little of this perfection survived. As Tretā was repeated in every cycle the Dvandvas (mutually conflicting pairs) cropped up. Then the subjects became very miserable due to the chilly rain and scorching sun.

33. When they were harassed by Dvandvas they began to make clothes and garments for covering themselves. They made abodes on the mountains in order to ward off Dvandvas.

34. Formerly they roamed about as they pleased. They had no fixed abodes. Now they began to stay in houses in accordance with their availability and pleasure.

35-36. After taking preventive measures against the Dvandvas they began to think about their means of sustenance. When the kalpa trees had perished along with honey, the subjects became confounded and agitated due to disputes. They were harassed by thirst and hunger. Then, again in Tretā, new perfections came in sight.

37. They had more rains than they desired or needed for production. Heavy downpour of waters flowed down the slopes.

38. Due to continuous rain sources of water currents arose. Thus in the course of second creation of rains, streams and rivers began to function.

39. Small collection of those waters fell on the earth. Due to the mingling of waters and the earth, plants and herbs came into being.

40-41. Then trees and hedges grew up. Very few of them were cultivated. They were not sown. Fourteen[254] types of trees and grasses grew up in the rural and forest areas. They put forth flowers and fruits in accordance with the season. Different types of trees and medicinal herbs also appeared. The subjects sustained themselves with these at that time of Tretā.

42. Thereafter the subjects became lustful and greedy in every respect on account of what is destined to happen inevitably in Tretā age.

43. Then the subjects forcibly occupied the fields near the rivers and on the mountains. They seized the trees, hedges and herbs as much as they could.

44-45. On account of this perversity the fourteen types of medicinal herbs perished. Thinking that these plants and herbs have entered the earth, Brahmā milked the earth assiduously for the welfare of living beings. Ever since, the plants are ploughed by ploughshares here and there.

46. Those who were desirous of sustaining themselves assiduously took to agriculture. The word Vārtā means avocation and the avocation in this context is the endeavour and desire for agriculture.

47. Otherwise, towards the close of Tretā, the subjects have no means of livelihood. Then water has to be lifted by hand in general.

48. In that Tretā the subjects in their fury seized one another, even their sons, wives, riches etc., forcibly. Such was the characteristic of that yuga.

254. The Purāṇas divide the vegetation life into three classes, viz. (1) grāmya, (2) grāmāraṇya, (3) yajñīya (cf. Vāyu) but this classification is very obscure.

Manu classifies the plant-world into (1) Vanaspati (trees not having flowers, (2) Vānaspatya trees bearing fruits and flowers), (3) Oṣadhi (plants such as grass) and (4) latā, valli (creepers). Further, Viṣṇu (cited in ST.) mentions fourteen oṣadhis by name. They are vrīhi, yava, māṣa, godhūma, aṇu, tila, priyaṅgu, kulittha, śyāmāka, nīvāra, jartila, gavedhuka, Veṇuyava, and markaṭaka.

49. Knowing all this, the lotus-born lord created Kṣatriyas, to protect people from wounds and injuries and also for establishing the rules of conduct.

50. Characterised by his own splendour the lord established castes and stages of life. The lord of the universe then created avocation and conduct of life for respective castes of people.

51. The avocation of sacrifices was evolved in Tretā gradually. But persons of good holy rites did not resort to animal sacrifice even then.

52. It was then that the seer Viṣṇu performed sacrifices forcefully. That is why the brahmins praise a non-violent sacrifice.

53. In the Dvāpara too, men have different inclinations mentally, verbally and physically. It is with great difficulty that agriculture proceeds in that age.

54-55. Then all living beings exert gradually and strain their bodies. Covetousness, service on wage basis, business, fighting, indecision about principles, division of Vedas, confusion of dharmas, destruction of discipline among the four castes and stages of life, lust and hatred—these are the specifics pertaining to that age.

56. It is in this Dvāpara that the following begin to function, viz—passion, covetousness, arrogance, etc. In the beginnings of Dvāpara the Vedas are classified into four by Vyāsa.

57. It is laid down that during Tretā the Vedas constituted one single whole with four sections. Since the span of life becomes less and less the Vedas are classified in Dvāpara.

58-59. They are further differentiated through the whims of the sons of sages, when the order of Mantra and Brāhmaṇa texts is altered and the accents and letters are changed. The compendiums of Ṛk Yajus and Sāmans are compiled by the learned men. Although the texts are common, they are differentiated due to different view-points.

60. The different sections to the Vedas are evolved, viz.,—

Brāhmaṇas[255] Kalpasūtras[256] and Mantrapravacanas.[257] Some departed from them and some abided by them.

61-63. The Itihāsas and Purāṇas[258] differ from time to time. They are Brāhma, Pādma, Vaiṣṇava, Śaiva, Bhāgavata, Bhaviṣya, Nāradīya, Mārkaṇḍeya, Āgneya, Brahmavaivarta, Laiṅga, Vārāha, Vāmana, Kūrma, Mātsya, Gāruḍa, Skānda and Brahmāṇḍa—these are the eighteen Purāṇas.

64-65. The eleventh Liṅga Purāṇa was classified in Dvāpara. The following sages, thousands in number, wrote Smṛtis etc.—Manu, Atri, Viṣṇu, Hārīta, Yājñavalkya, Uśanas, Aṅgiras, Yama, Āpastamba, Saṁvarta, Kātyāyana Bṛhaspati, Parāśara, Vyāsa, Śaṅkha, Likhita, Dakṣa, Gautama, Śātātapa, Vasiṣṭha and others.

66-70. Absence of rain, death, the harassments of pestilence etc. occur. Indifference to worldly affairs results from various miseries, mental, verbal and physical. From this indifference they begin to think about their liberation from pain and misery. This process of thinking leads to detachment and from detachment they begin to realize the deformities and defects in the world. Thanks to this perception, perfect knowledge becomes possible in Dvāpara. This is due to the behaviour of mixed rajas and tamas. In the first yuga viz. Kṛta yuga dharma originates. In Tretā it begins to function. In Dvāpara it becomes distracted gradually and in Kali it perishes altogether.

255. Brāhmaṇam. Brāhmaṇa literature comprises treatises such as Aitareya, Taittirīya, Gopatha, Śatapatha, etc, and their ancillaries Āraṇyakas and Upaniṣads which together with the mantra portion, called Saṁhitā constitute the Vedas. Cf. mantra-brāhmaṇayor Veda-nāmadheyam.

256. Kalpasūtras—kriyā-pratipādakasūtrāṇi ST. ritual treatises—Arṣeya, etc.

257. Mantra-pravacanāni—mīmāṁsā-nyāyasūtrāṇi ST., philosophical treatises such as mīmāṁsā and nyāya.

258. On the authenticity, extent and number of the Purāṇas, see Introduction.

CHAPTER FORTY

Extent of four Yugas

Indra said:

1. In Kali age men excited by tamoguṇa adopt Māyā (deception) and jealousy. They do not hesitate to kill ascetics. They are always tormented by jealousy.

2. In Kali age there is always carelessness, illness, hunger, fear, and terrible suffering from drought. There is also opposition from and among the different parts of the country.

3. Śruti (i. e. Vedas) is not considered an authority. Men resort to sinful activity. People are sinful, irritable and narrow-minded. They misbehave.

4. Greedy and wicked subjects, born in Kali utter falsehood. They are engaged in evil desires, evil study, misbehaviour and misleading scriptural texts.

5. Due to defects in the activities of the brahmins fear arises in the subjects. The twice-born neglect the study of Vedas and do not sacrifice as prescribed.

6-7. Men perish. Kṣatriyas and Vaiśyas decline gradually. In Kali Śūdras claim kinship with brahmins through their learning through interdining and sharing seats and beds. Kings become mostly. Śūdras and they harass brahmins.

8. Killing of foetus and murder of heroes become prevalent. Śūdras adopt the conduct of life prescribed for the brahmins and the brahmins adopt the ways of Śūdras.

9. Thieves function as kings and kings function as thieves. The chaste ladies cease to exist and wanton sluts increase in number.

10. Stability and discipline of four castes and stages of life disappear from all places. At that time the earth yields very little fruit in one place and great fruits in another.

11. O Śilāśana, the kings confiscate and misappropriate public property. They cease to be protectors. Śūdras acquire knowledge and are honoured by the brahmins.

12. Non-kṣatriyas become rulers. Brahmins depend on Śūdras. Śūdras proud of their intellect remain sitting in their seats and do not stir on seeing brahmins.

13-18 Petty-minded Śūdras strike the leading brahmins. Out of humility, brahmins keep their hand over their mouth and whisper into the ears of base Śūdras. O noble Brahmins, knowing that Śūdras are seated on lofty seats amidst brahmins, the king does not punish them. People of meagre learning, fortune and strength worship Śūdras with flowers, scents and other auspicious things. O brahmin, arrogant Śūdras do not even glance at the excellent brahmins. Waiting for their opportunity to serve them, the brahmins stand at their thresholds: The brahmins depending upon Śūdras serve them when they return seated in their vehicles and eulogise them by means of eulogies and prayers. In Kali, even the excellent brahmins demean themselves by selling the fruits of their austerities and sacrifices.

19-25. In Kali there will be many ascetics. As the yuga draws to a close, men become reduced in number while women increase in proportion. In Kali even the brahmins censure Vedic learning and holy rites. In Kali lord Mahādeva, Śaṅkara, Nīlalohita reveals himself as one of deformed features, for the establishment of righteousness. The brahmins who resort to him by any means conquer the evils of Kali and attain the highest abode.

It should be known that towards the close of yuga, the beasts of prey will be very violent. Cows will decline and good men will recede from active spheres. Their Dharma which is subtle, conducive to good results and difficult of access, which has its roots in charitable gifts, becomes shaky due to instability in the four stages of life. The kings misappropriate shares from the oblations offered to God. They do not protect the people. Towards the close of yuga, they will be more interested in protecting themselves. In Kali cooked food will be kept for sale in living places. The selling of Vedas and other sacred literature will occur in cross streets; young women will sell even their honour.[259]

259. aṭṭaśūlāḥ—aṭṭaṁ kanyādravyaṁ śūlo yeṣāṃ ST.—those who indulge in the barter of girls. Or aṭṭa—cooked food. Śivasūlāḥ—those who indulge in the sale of Vedas. Catuṣpathāḥ—brāhmaṇas (Medini cited in ST.) Keśaśūlāḥ—tyaktalajjāḥ ST. Or those who have bartered their chastity. * mukta-keśāḥ—apagatahrīkāḥ. Cf. Viśva cited in ST.

26-31. The lord of rain will be wayward in making showers at the close of yuga. Merchants will resort to malpractices. They will be surrounded by heretics indulging in vain outward show. There will be many beggars and petitioners among the people soliciting one another. There will be no one not indulging in harsh words; there will not be any straightforward man; there will hardly be anyone who is not jealous; when the yuga comes to a close, there will scarcely be any man readily willing to return the help rendered. Fallen people and censurers characterise this closing period of yuga. The earth will be devoid of kings, riches and foodgrains will not flourish; groups of conspirators will be formed in the cities and countries. The earth will have short supply of water and will be deficient in fruits. Those assigned to be protectors will not be so. They will not be subject to discipline.

32-33. Men will rob others of their wealth and violate the chastity of other men's wives. They will be lustful, wicked at heart, base and foolhardy. They will lose proper perspective of things. Suffering from colic they will have their hairs dishevelled. Towards the close of the yuga people will be born whose age will be only sixteen years.

34. When the end of the yuga is imminent Śūdras will begin the practice of dharma with white teeth, deerskin and Rudrākṣa beads, with shaven heads and ochre-coloured robes.

35. Men will steal plants and grains. They will covet the clothes they see; thieves will rob other thieves of their wealth; one robber will rob another.

36-37. When noble and befitting holy rites are no longer performed; when all the people become inactive and lethargic, germs, mice and serpents will torment men. Prosperity, welfare, health and efficiency will be difficult to attain. People afflicted by hunger and fear will resort to the lands near the Kauśikī[260] river.

260. Kauśikī. It is the modern Kosi that issues from the Himālayas, flows through Nepal and Tirhut and joins the Ganges below Patna. But originally the river passed through North Bengal and fell into the Brahmaputra. See Sircar, GAMI p. 42.

38-39. People overwhelmed by misery will never see the maximum span of life of hundred years. In Kali all the Vedas will not be available. Yajñas perish afflicted by people of no virtue. Ochre-robed and naked anchorites will be wandering and many Kāpālikas (ascetics holding skulls as their begging bowls) will infest the territories.

40-41. Some sell Vedas and others sell Tīrthas (holy waters). i.e. make illegal gain out of these. When Kali yuga begins heretics will be born who will be opposed to the system of four castes and stages of life. Śūdras will learn the Vedas and will become experts in the meaning of dharma.

42-44. Kings born of Śūdra wombs will perform horse-sacrifice. People begin to harass one another by killing women, children, cows and one another.

Since people are inclined towards evil, their behaviour will be wrought by tamoguṇa. At that time the crimes such as the slaughter of a brahmin begin to appear.

45. Hence during Kali, longevity strength and features become less and less. Men attain perfection within a short while.

46-47. Excellent brahmins of blessed nature will still practise dharma without malice towards the end of yuga as laid down in the Śrutis and Smṛtis. What is gained by the practice of dharma for a year in Tretā is attained by the practice of it for a month in Dvāpara. In Kali an intelligent devotee attains the same in a day by practising Dharma strenuously.[261]

48. This is the state of affairs in the Kali yuga. Understand the situation in the period of ending junction (sandhyāṁśa) from me. In every yuga the Siddhis are reduced to three-fourths of what they were in the beginning.

49. Only a quarter of the features of the yugas remains in their sandhyās (preceding transition periods). Similarly only a quarter of the features of the sandhyās abides in the sandhyāṁśas (succeeding transition periods) (i.e. during the sandhyāṁśa period only 1/6th of the yug a Dharma will prevail).

261. Cf. Viṣṇu as cited in ST. यत्कृते दशभिर्वर्षैस्त्रेतायां हायनेन तत् । द्वापरे यज्ञमासेन अहोरात्रेण तत्कलौ ॥ तपसो ब्रह्मचर्यस्य जपादेश्च फलं द्विजाः । प्राप्नोति पुरुषस्तेन कलिः साध्विति भाषितम् ॥

50-53. When the yuga has come to a close and the period of junction too has arrived, the chastiser of the wicked people will rise up in order to kill all the bad living beings. He will be born in the family of the Moon. He will be called Pramiti by name. Previously in the Svāyambhuva manvantara, he had been born of the parts of Manu (i.e. in the family of then Manu); for full twenty years he will be roaming about on the earth. He will be taking along with him a big army consisting of horses, chariots and elephants. He will be surrounded by hundreds and thousands of brahmins wielding weapons. He will kill the Mlecchas (alien outcaste people) in thousands.

54-55. After killing the kings of Śūdrā wombs he will exterminate the heretics completely. He will kill those who are not pious and virtuous. He will kill those who are born of different castes and those who depend upon them.

56. Thus making himself powerful with an active army under his control, he the destroyer of the Mlecchas, invincible to all living beings, will roam about the world.

57-58. In the previous birth he was born in the family of Manu who himself was a part incarnation of Viṣṇu. When the Kali yuga is complete (i.e. coming to an end) he will be born in the line of the Moon as the powerful Pramiti.[262] He will start his campaign in his thirty second year and continue it for twenty years.

59. He will be killing hundreds and thousands of living beings. By means of this cruel act be will reduce the entire earth to the seeds.

60-69. Getting infuriated mutually (the people will attack one another). Pramiti will defeat all those alien outcastes and all unrighteous persons and ultimately rest in the middle land between the Gaṅgā and Yamunā along with his ministers and followers, after killing all the kings and alien outcastes in thousands. When the sandhyāṁśa period sets in at the end of the yuga there will be groups of people among the subjects left behind here and there. Getting unrestrained and covetous they will be attacking and killing one another. When anarchy

262. Pramiti—Candragupta Vikramāditya II, son of Samudragupta. A similar account is found in *Matsya*, Ch. 144. For detail, see *MP*—A Study, by V.S. Agrawal, pp. 228-231.

spreads in view of the series of affairs in the yuga, when people begin to suspect one another, all those people will be afflicted by fear. Agitated and bewildered they will leave off their wives and houses. They will not care even for their own lives. Though themselves miserable yet they will be worthless. When the holy rites laid down in the Śrutis and Smṛtis perish, these people will attack and kill one another. When Dharma is destroyed they will become mannerless, unbounded, shameless and unloving. They will not hesitate to attack one another. They will be stunted in growth and live as far as twentyfive years.[263] Getting involved in disputes they will abandon wives and sons. When lack of rain affects them they will. abandon agriculture. They will leave off their land and resort to frontiers.[264] They will resort to rivers, oceans, mountains and wells.

70. In their misery they will sustain themselves on wine, meat, roots and fruits. They will wear barks of trees, leaves or deer skin. They will not perform holy rites or accept monetary gifts.

71. They will fall off from the rigid discipline of four castes and stages of life. They will be involved in a terrible calamity. Thus the few remaining subjects at the end of Kaliyuga will be in miserable circumstances.

72-73. They will be afflicted by old age, sickness and hunger. Due to sorrow their minds will become dejected. Through dejection thinking sets in. An even attitude of the mind is what is called vicāraṇā (thinking). This attitude leads to knowledge. Through true knowledge arises pious nature. The subjects who survive the concluding years of Kaliyuga will be devoid of physical features and mental peace.

74-78. At that time, the yuga changes for them overnight, after creating illusion in their minds as in the case of a sleeping or mad man. Thanks to the inevitability and force of future events Kṛtayuga will set in. When thus the Kṛtayuga is ushered in, the subjects surviving from the Kaliyuga, become those

263. pañcaviṁśakāḥ i.e. with their span of life extending only to twentyfive years or whose gross and subtle bodies constitute twentyfive tattvas.

264. pratyantān—mlecchadeśān *ST*. Cf. pratyanto mlecchadeśaḥ syāt—*Amara*.

belonging to the Kṛtayuga. Those Siddhas[265] (enlightened souls) who still remain and move about invisibly, will be made manifest then alongwith the sleeping Saptarṣis. (seven sages).[266] There will be some brahmins, kṣatriyas, vaiśyas and śūdras for the purpose of seeds [i.e. as nucleus for the subsequent generation. They will get mixed with the people surviving from the Kaliyuga. The seven sages and others will teach these people their Dharma.

79. They will teach them the two-fold Dharma of the Śruti and Smṛti[266a] alongwith the conduct of life peculiar to the four castes and stages of life.

Thereafter when they begin to perform holy rites, the subjects flourish in the Kṛtayuga.

80-83. When the Dharmas have been propounded by the seven sages, other sages promulgate them (among the people) by differentiating them between those pertaining to Śruti and Smṛti. Some of these sages stay even at the time of dissolution for the purpose of establishing Dharma. The sages indeed stay in office throughout the manvantara, just as trees remain (unaffected) when the forest fire consumes the grass. But when rain falls this grows up again. In the same manner, after the people of Kali die the people of Kṛta yuga come up. The continuity from one yuga to another goes on without break in this manner till the manvantara comes to a close.

84. Happiness, longevity, strength, beauty (or physical features), virtue, wealth and love become reduced to three-fourths from yuga to yuga gradually.

85. The Siddhis of Dharma become (proportionately)

265. Siddhas—a class of human beings of great purity, holiness and divine power. They are said to be seven. Cf. mantrajño mantravit prājño mantrarāṭ siddhapūjitaḥ siddhavat paramaḥ siddhaḥ sarvasiddhipradāyinaḥ —cited in *ST*.

266. seven sages, viz. Marīci, Atri, Aṅgiras, Pulastya, Pulaha, Kratu and Vasiṣṭha. They are represented by a group of seven stars called Ursa Major. ST. cites a verse with a few variations in names : Kaśyapo' trir bharadvājo Viśvāmitro' tha Gautamaḥ Vasiṣṭho Jamadagniś ca saptarṣaya udāhṛtāḥ

266a. Śrauta and Smārta dharma : norms of righteousness derived from the authority of Śruti (Vedas) and Smṛtis (legal treatises).

reduced in the parts of the junctions of yugas. Thus the mode of achievement in order has been recounted.

86-92. In the same manner all the four yugas must be understood. A thousand such cycles of four yugas are said to constitute one day of Brahmā. The night too consists of as many yugas. By the time the yuga comes to a close the living beings lose their straightforward and sentient feelings. This is the characteristic feature of all the yugas. Seventyone cycles of four yugas constitute a manvantara. What happens in one set of four yugas is repeated in the other cycles of four yugas in the same manner and at the same time as well as in the same order. The differences that occur from creation to creation are limited to twentyfive, neither more nor less. The kalpas too have the same characteristics as the yugas. The same characteristics mark all the manvantaras also.

93. Just as the changes and alterations in the yugas have happened from early days (and have continued for a long time) in view of the nature of the yugas, so also the world of living beings goes round and round alternating between death and birth.

94. Thus the characteristic feature of the yugas of the past and future in all the manvantaras has been recorded in brief.

95. With the explanation of one manvantara all the manvantaras have been undoubtedly explained; similarly with one kalpa and other kalpas too.

96-100. In regard to the future kalpas the same argument should be continued by one who knows. In all the manvantaras past and future, the eight[267] classes of Devas, the ruling lords of manvantaras, Manus and sages will have the same status through their names and forms, as also the same purpose and intention. The same is the case with the division of castes and stages of life in every yuga. It is the lord who lays down the nature and characteristics of the yugas, the divisions of castes and stages of life, the yugas and the Siddhis of the yugas. Incidentally, the magnitude of the yugas was mentioned to you. I shall now recount to you how the lotus-born deity became Brahmā the son of the goddess.

267. Eight classes of Devas : Cf. Āditya-viśva-vasavas-tuṣita-bhāsvarānilāḥ mahārakṣika-sādhyās ca rudrās ca gaṇadevatāḥ—cited in *ST*.

CHAPTER FORTYONE

Nativity of Brahmā

1. When the period of a thousand yugas lapsed and it was morning for him, lord Brahmā created once again the subjects who had fallen off, in the same manner as they were before.

2-6. O leading brahmin, when thus the period of twice Parārdha lapsed, the earth merged into the water, the water into the fire, the fire into the wind, the wind into the ether along with the tanmātras. O excellent brahmin, eleven sense-organs and the tanmātras merged into the ego lo ! in a trice. Ego merged into intellect (mahat) in a moment. O brahmin, the intellect also attained the unmanifest (avyakta) and merged into it. The unmanifest became merged into the lord along with its Guṇas. Thereafter creation took place as before from Puruṣa Śiva.[268] Then the mental sons were created by him by mere thinking.

7-9. The subjects thus created by the lotus-born deity did not flourish in this world. For the purpose of increase, lord Brahmā performed a penance with the supreme lord in view, in the company of his mental sons. The great lord was pleased by their penance. Realising Brahmā's desire, the lord pierced through the middle of Brahmā's forehead. Saying "I am your son" he then became male-cum- female in his form.

10-14. The lord with half-female body became his son. Then the lord burnt Brahmā, the preceptor of the universe. Thereafter for the purpose of the flourishing incrcase of the worlds the lord adopted the yogic path and enjoyed his own prosperous semi-Mātrā, Parameśvarī. He created Viṣṇu and Brahmā in her. The lord of the universe, the soul of the universe, created the Pāśupata missile too. Hence Viṣṇu and Brahmā were born of the part of Mahādevī. Thus Brahmā who was the Egg-born, and the lotus-born was born also of the body of the lord.[269] Thus, in brief, the

268. At first there was nothing except Prakṛti and Puruṣa (i.e. Śiva and Māyā). Then Śiva created twentyfive tattvas out of himself. Cf. तत्त्वानि शिवजातानि पञ्चविंशन्मनीषिभिः । *Liṅga,* part II; and *ŚP* cited in *ST.*: नान्यत्किञ्चित्तदा ह्यासीत्प्रकृतिं पुरुषं विना । एतस्मिन्नन्तरे ब्रह्मंस्तत्त्वान्यासन्महात्मनः ।।

269. Brahmā is born of (i) the Cosmic Egg, (ii) the lotus, as well as (iii) the body of Śiva.

entire anecdote has been mentioned to you, as also what happened during the first Parārdha of Brahmā.

15-21. I shall now briefly mention the detachment of Brahmā born of tamoguṇa. Lord Viṣṇu split his body into two and created universe consisting of the mobile and immobile beings. He then created Brahmā who in turn created Rudra. O sage, in another kalpa, Rudra created Brahmā. Then O sage, in another kalpa, Viṣṇu created Brahmā, then Brahmā created Viṣṇu, then the lord created Brahmā. Then Brahmā thought that the world was full of misery and he abandoned the activity of creation. He engaged his soul in the higher soul. He restrained the movement of the vital breaths and remained motionless like a rock. He remained in Samādhi (ecstasy) for ten thousand years. The splendid lotus that faced downwards and was stationed in the heart was filled with inhalation. It became blossomed out. When by means of retention of breath it was restrained that lotus became ūrdhva-vaktra (with face lifted upwards).

22-27. In the middle of its pericarp he installed the lord. Then Brahmā, the self-controlled who had purified his soul by perfect restraint of his senses installed the great lord Śiva in his heart. The lord was situated there in a space as small as the hundred part of the thread of the lotus stalk[270] by repeating 'om' in a series of half measures of time. He who was worthy of worship himself,[271] then propitiated the unchanging lord (i.e. Śiva) by means of flowers of restraint etc.[272] Then at the behest of the Īśvara situated in the heart-lotus (of Brahmā) the all-pervading lord born of the body of Bhava came out of Brahmā by piercing through his forehead.

That lord born from Śiva's heart was blue originally but became red by contact with fire. Because that Puruṣa was both Nīla (blue) and Lohita (red) just like the form of Kāla, the God

270. mṛṇāla-tanu-bhāga : Cf. nīvāraśūkavat tanvī pītā bhāsvatyaṇūpamā tasyāḥ śikhāyā madhye hi paramātmā vyavasthitaḥ; also Bālāgramātraṁ hṛdayasya madhye...cited in *ST*.

271. yājyaḥ—yajanayogyaḥ *ST*. worthy of worship.

272. yama-puṣpādibhiḥ : in the form of observances such as yama, niyama, āsana, prāṇāyāma, pratyāhāra, dhāraṇā, dhyāna and samādhi.

of Death, he was named Nīlalohita by Īśvara and lord Kāla by Brahmā. The all-pervading one (i.e. Kāla) became pleased thereby.

28. O great sage, Brahmā, the soul of the universe eulogised the lord who was delighted in his mind and who had the universe as his form by means of the Nāmāṣṭaka—the set of eight names.[273]

Brahmā said :

29-32. O lord *Rudra*, obeisance to you of unmeasured splendour like the sun. Obeisance to you lord *Bhava* identical with water and taste. Perpetual obeisance to *Śarva* who has the form of earth and smell. Obeisance to you, *Īśa*, identical with air and the quality of touch. Obeisance to *Paśupati* the lord of individual souls, identical with fire of excessive splendour. Obeisance to you, *Bhīma*, identical with ether having the quality of sound. Obeisance to *Mahādeva*, identical with the moon—the abode of nectar. Obeisance to you, *Ugra*, the Yajamāna (one who performs sacrifice) who is the agent for all actions.[274]

33-34. He who reads this hymn sung by Brahmā unto Rudra, he who listens to this or he who narrates this to brahmins with great concentration will attain identity with the lord of eight cosmic bodies, within a year. After eulogising thus, Brahmā looked at the great lord.

35-36. The great lord stood with the eight forms spread all round. The sun shone. So also the fire and the moon. There were earth, wind, water, ether and yajamāna—the sacrificer. Ever since that time they call Īśvara, Aṣṭamūrti.

37-38. Thanks to the grace of Aṣṭamūrti, Brahmā created again. After creating the world of mobile and immobile beings, he fell asleep for the period of a thousand yugas. In the next kalpa when he woke up he became desirous of creating the subjects, and so he performed great and severe penance.

273. Eight names of Śiva. *ŚP. Vidyeśvara-saṁhitā* (Ch. 20. 47) mentions eight names as Hara, Maheśvara, Śambhu, Śūlapāṇi, Pinākadhṛk, Śiva, Paśupati and Mahādeva. But Liṅga has a different list, represented by the the eight forms of Śiva.

274. karma-yogine : karma-yogin is the eighth form of Śiva called yajamāna (a sacrificer) and Ugra. According to *ST.* karmayogine=karmaphala-bhoktre—one who enjoys the fruits of his actions i.e. Jīva.

39. Even when he performed the penance thus, nothing happened. After a great deal of time he became miserable and his sorrow turned into anger.

40. When he was overwhelmed with anger, drops of tears fell from his eyes. From those drops of tears goblins and ghosts originated.

41. On seeing this first-born creation consisting of goblins, ghosts and demons, the unborn deity lord Brahmā censured himself.

42. Thereupon, the infuriated lord Brahmā, abandoned his life. Thereafter, Rudra in the form of Prāṇa (vital breath) appeared through the mouth of lord Brahmā.

43. The lord, having a lustre resembling that of the rising sun became Ardhanārīśvara (male-cum-female form). He divided himself into eleven[275] parts and settled down there.

44. With half a portion of himself Ardhanārīśvara, the soul of all, created Umā. She created Lakṣmī, Durgā and Sarasvatī.

45-48. (She further created) Vāmā, Raudrī, Mahāmāyā, Vaiṣṇavī the lotus-eyed goddess, Kalavikariṇī, Kālī residing in the lotus, goddess Balavikariṇī, Balapramathinī, Sarvabhūatadamanī, (the suppressor of all living beings) and Manonmanī. Similarly thousands of other women were created by her. Accompanied by those ladies and the Rudras, Mahādeva, Parameśvara the lord of the three worlds stood in front of lord Brahmā, Parameṣṭhin who was the soul of all but was now lying dead.

49. Lord Maheśvara, the sympathetic son of Brahmā, granted him vital airs.

50. Then Rudra the lord of Devas was delighted and he spoke these pleasant words to Brahmā who regained his life a little.

51. O highly blessed lord Brahmā, O preceptor of the worlds, do not be afraid; the vital airs have been established here iu your heart. Hence, O lord get up.

275. ekādaśadhā : in eleven forms, as stated in Viṣṇu (cited in *ST*). They are named Aja-ekapād, Ahirbudhnya, Tvaṣṭṛ, Rudra, Hara, Tryambaka, Aparājita, Vṛṣākapi, Śambhu, Kapardin and Raivata. Other Purāṇas give different lists. For detail, see *Matsyapurāṇa—A study*, pp. 65-67.

52-54. On hearing his words as though in dreams passing through his mind, Brahmā became delighted in his heart. With the vital airs coming back to him, he looked at Maheśvara with his eyes that had the lustre of full blown lotus. After glancing up at him for a long time, lord Brahmā got up and said with palms joined in reverence in a tone affectionate and majestic.

"O highly blessed one, tell me. You are delighting my mind: Who are you standing with eight cosmic bodies and in eleven forms?"

Indra said:

55-58. On hearing his words, Maheśvara the slayer of the enemies of Devas spoke through all his mouths.

The lord said:

"Know me the great soul and know her the birthless Māyā. These standing by are the Rudras, who have come here to protect you".

Thereafter Brahmā bowed down to the lord of Devas and said with palms joined in reverence. His words were choked with delight.

"O lord, O lord of the chiefs of Devas, I am agitated and excited due to miseries.

59-60. O Īśāna, O Śaṅkara, it behoves you to release me from the bondage of worldly existence.

Thereupon the lord of Umā laughed at Brahmā. Then the lord of the universe vanished from there along with Umā and the Rudras.

Indra said:

61-64. Hence O Śilāda, understand that in all the worlds it is difficult to get a person who is not born of a womb and who is deathless. Even the lotus-born deity has death. But if Rudra the lord of Devas is pleased, a son not born of a womb and devoid of death is not difficult for you to get. It is not possible for me, for Viṣṇu and for Brahmā to offer you a son not born of a womb and devoid of death.

Śailādi said:

After speaking thus to the leading brahmin and blessing him, the kind lord accompanied by Devas went away riding on his white elephant.

CHAPTER FORTYTWO

The origin of Nandīśvara

Sūta said:

1. When the thousand-eyed meritorious bestower of boons had gone, Śilāda propitiated Mahādeva. He delighted the lord by means of penance.

2. Even as the brahmin pursued the penance eagerly and perpetually, a thousand divine years surprisingly passed off like a moment.

3. The sage was completely enveloped by an anthill. He became the victim of torture by groups of worms and blood-sucking insects with their mouths pointed like diamond needles.

4. With skin alone, devoid of flesh and blood he stood there like a wall unaffected. He was a mere skeleton then. The auspicious lord thought of him then.

5. When the sage was touched with hand by the lord, the enemy of the Cupid, the leading Brahmin sage eschewed all his fatigue and strain.

6. Lord Śiva was delighted at the penance of the sage. (Approaching him) along with his Gaṇas and Umā he said to him, "I am delighted with your penance".

7. "O highly intelligent one, what with this penance? I shall give you an omniscient son who has mastered all the Scriptural topics".

8. Thereafter bowing down to the lord of Devas and eulogising him Śilāda spoke to the moon-bedecked lord, accompanied by Umā,[276] with words choked with great pleasure.

276. somam—Umayā saha, accompanied by Umā.

Śilāda said:

9. "O lord, O Śaṅkara the most excellent among the good, O lord of the chiefs of Devas, O destroyer of Tripuras, I wish for a son not born of a womb and devoid of death".

Sūta said:

10. Rudra, Parameśvara who had already been propitiated by his penance by Brahmā spoke thus again to Śilāda with very great pleasure.

The lord said:

11. O brahmin, O ascetic, formerly I had been propitiated by Brahmā, sages and Devas by penance, for the sake of my incarnation.

12. I shall become your son, not born of a womb, by the name Nandin. O sage, I am the father of worlds and you will become my father.

13. After saying thus to the sage who was standing there after bowing to him and looking up to him, the delighted merciful lord who was accompanied by Umā and who was comparable to the Moon vanished there itself.

14-15. O great sage, having obtained the assurance of a son from Rudra, my father was delighted. He was the most excellent among the knowers of sacrifice. For the purpose of sacrifice he came to the courtyard of a great sacrificial chamber. Formerly I was born in that courtyard as his son, at the behest of lord Śiva. I had the lustre of fire at the closing of a yuga.

16. When I was born as the son of Śilāda, the clouds Puṣkara, Āvartaka and others showered rain. The heaven-walkers—Kinnaras, Sādhyas and Siddhas sang songs. Viṣṇu showered fragrant flowers.

17-19. I had then the lustre of Kālasūrya (sun at the time of pralaya or dissolution). I was having matted hair and coronet. In the form of an infant I had three eyes, four arms holding the trident, axe, iron club and thunderbolt. My curved fangs were adamantine. I was the infant adored by the thunderbolt-wielding Indra. I was terrible in appearance with diamond ear-rings. My voice was comparable to the thundering sound of the clouds. On seeing me Brahmā, Indra and all other gods and leading sages eulogised me. The groups of celestial damsels shouted and danced all round.

20. O leading sage, with mantras pertaining to Maheśvara as well as those taken from Ṛk, Yajus and Sāman, the overjoyed sages eulogised and bowed down to me.

21-25. The following stood all around me:—Brahmā, Viṣṇu, Rudra, Indra, Śivā, Ambikā herself, Jupiter, the moon, the sun of great splendour, wind god, fire god, Īśāna, Nirṛti, Yakṣa, Yama, Varuṇa, Viśve Devas, Rudras, Vasus of great strength, Lakṣmī herself, Śacī, Jyeṣṭhā, goddess Sarasvatī, Aditi, Diti, Śraddhā, Lajjā, Dhṛti, Nandā, Bhadrā, Surabhi, Suśīlā, Sumanas, the lord of bulls, Dharma of great splendour and the sons of Dharma. They surrounded me, embraced me and eulogised me. O excellent sage, even Śilāda my father, the sage, on seeing me like that bowed to me with love. The meritorious soul eulogised his son who gave him what he liked.

Śilāda said:

26-31. O lord, O lord of the chief of Devas, O three-eyed one, O unchanging one, you are my son since you are my protector and the protector of worlds from misery. Since you are the protector of worlds, O son, you are my father. You are omnipresent. O son, not born of a womb, obeisance to you, O source of origin of the universe, O grand father, O father, O son, O Maheśāna, O preceptor of the universe, O dear one, O highly blessed one, O Parameśvara protect me. O lord of Devas, since I am delighted by you, you are to be known by the name Nandin. Hence O Nandin, delight me. I bow down to you, the lord of the universe. O lord, delight my parents who have gone to Rudra's world. O lord, my grandfather too has gone to the world of Rudra. O Nandin, when Maheśvara has incarnated my birth in the world is fruitful. O lord, the birth of the worlds too is fruitful.

32. When you have incarnated as my son for my protection O Īśvara, O Nandin, O lord of Devas, obeisance to you. O Nandīśvara, obeisance to you.

33-38. O son of mighty arms, protect me. O lord of Devas,

O preceptor of the worlds, O dear one, please forgive what was said by me considering you as my son. You are worthy of being eulogised by means of hymns by Devas and Asuras.

Whoever reads or listens to this speech addressed to my son, whoever narrates this to brahmins with devotion, rejoices along with me. After eulogising the boy his son, after bowing down to him with respect and looking at the leading sages Śilāda of good holy rites said:—

"O ye sages, see my great fortune, since the unchanging lord has incarnated as Nandin in the courtyard of the sacrificial hall. Which man is like me in this world? Neither Devas nor Dānavas are equal to me since this Nandin is born in the sacrificial ground for the sake of my welfare.

CHAPTER FORTYTHREE

Coronation of Nandīśvara

Nandīśvara said:

1. After bowing down to Maheśvara, my delighted father immediately went back to his hut along with me like an indigent man after obtaining a treasure-trove.

2. O great sage, when I went to the hut of Śilāda I eschewed my divine form and assumed a human shape.

3-4. My divine memory was obliterated for some unknown reason. On seeing that I had assumed human form, my father, worshipped by all the worlds, became extremely miserable and he lamented. Surrounded by his kinsmen, he, the knower of everything, performed my postnatal and other holy rites.

5-8. Śilāda son of Śālaṅkāyana was highly fond of me his son. It was he who taught me all these:—viz, the recensions of Ṛgveda, Yajurveda and the thousand branches of Sāmaveda with their ancillaries and subdivisions. He taught me Āyurveda (science of medicine), Dhanurveda (science of archery), Gāndharva (musicology), Aśvalakṣaṇa (characteristics of horses), the details of elephants and also the characteristics of men. When I completed my seventh year two excellent divine sages Mitra and Varuṇa, who were equipped with penance, and yogic power came to his hermitage to see me. It was at the behest of the lord that they had come there.

9-11. On seeing me repeatedly the two noble sages said: "O dear one, though this Nandin has mastered all the scriptural topics, he is shortlived. This type of wonder has not been seen before. His life does not extend beyond a year.

When they said thus Śilāda the leading brahmin, extremely fond of his son, embraced me. Excessively dejected he lamented with a highly discordant voice, "alas my son! my son, my son" He then fell down flat.

12-13. He was sad and he said—"Alas! the power of the adverse fate and of the creator !" On hearing his lamentation the residents of the hermitage gathered there in great bewilderment. They evolved amulets and observed auspicious rites to ward off the evil. They eulogised Mahādeva, the three-eyed lord of Umā.

14. They performed homa repeating the mantra of Triyambaka, offering ten thousand times Dūrvā (Darbha grass) soaked in honey, and accompanied by other materials of worship.

15. My father and grandfather lost consciousness. With all their activities ceased, they lamented, fell down as though dead.

16-19. I was afraid of death. Ere long I bowed down to my father and grandfather who were lying down as though they were dead. I circumambulated them. I was then engaged in the repetition of Rudra mantra. I meditated on the three-eyed lord in the lotus cavity of my heart, the quiescent lord Sadāśiva with ten arms and five faces. Even as I was standing in the middle of the holy river the delighted lord Mahādeva accompanied by Umā, and adorned by the crescent moon appeared and said—O dear Nandin of great arms, whence is fear from death for you?

20-24. Those two brahmins had been sent by me alone. There is no doubt that you are like myself. O dear, this body of yours is factually worldly. It is not divine. O dear, what was formerly seen and worshipped by Śilāda, Devas, sages, Siddhas, Gandharvas and Dānavas was divine. O Nandīśvara.

this is the nature of the world that happiness and misery befall repeatedly one after the other. It is the duty of the discriminating man to avoid birth through the womb.[277] After saying thus to me, Parameśvara, lord Rudra, Hara, the great lord of all Devas, the destroyer of distress touched me with his splendid hands.

25-28. After glancing at the goddess, Umā the daughter of the Himavat, and at the chieftains of the Gaṇas, the bull-emblemed Mahādeva, Lord of Devas, said with satisfaction in his heart, "Along with your father and friends you will be unageing and deathless. You will be devoid of pain and misery. You will be imperishable and unchanging. You will have my virility and exploit. You will be my favourite chief of Gaṇas. I will be always fond of you. You will be at my side for ever. You will have my strength. You will be endowed with great yogic power."

29-31. After saying this to me the lord accompanied by his attendants, took off his lotus garland. The bull-emblemed lord of great splendour tied it on me. With that splendid garland clinging to my neck I became as though a second Śaṅkara with three eyes and ten arms. Then Parameśvara took me by the hand and said—"Tell me. What excellent boon shall I give you now?"

32-35. The bull-emblemed lord then took the pure water embedded in his matted hairs. Saying "Be a river" he cast it down. Then it began to flow as a great river full of splendid, divine, white (shining) water with lots of lotuses and lilies in it. Mahādeva said to that extremely splendid river—"Since you began to flow as a great river from the waters of my matted hairs you will be an excellent holy river named Jaṭodakā."

36-39. "Any man will be liberated from all sins by taking bath in you." Then lord Mahādeva said to the goddess "This is your son" and made me the son of Śilāda, fall at her feet. She kissed me on the head and stroked me with her hands. With three pourings of water as white as the conch, with three sons she bathed me with the affection due to a son all the while glancing at the lord of Devas. These three pour-

277. Nṛṇāṁ yoniparityāgaḥ : release from the bondage of Birth and Death, which is the goal of man's life. According to *ST*. yoni-parityāgaḥ= strī-samāgama-tyāgaḥ. *ST*. cites Bhāgavata in support of this meaning.

ings flowed down to become a river with three branches. The lord Bhava therefore called it Trisrotas (river with three tributaries).

40-43. On seeing the river Trisrotas the bull (vehicle of Śiva) was extremely delighted. It bellowed. From that bellowing sound another river originated. That river was called "Vṛṣadhvani" by the lord of Devas. The bull-emblemed lord placed on my head his divine golden crown that was made by Viśvakarman, studded with all jewels, and that was variegated auspicious and wonderful. Mahādeva, Maheśvara himself fitted in my ears his splendid divine ear-rings bedecked with diamonds and Lapis Lazuli.

44-47. O sage, on seeing me honoured thus, the sun in the sky showered Śilādana with waters from the clouds. When he was thus showered, those waters flowed as a stream. Since this river originated from gold, the three-eyed lord of Devas called her Svarṇodakā. Since another splendid river originated from the crown made of gold they call that river Jāmbūnadī. Thus the set of five rivers flowed near the lord Japyeśvara.

48. He who visits Pañcanada,[278] takes the holy dip there and worships Lord Japyeśvara shall undoubtedly attain identity with Śiva.

49. Then lord Mahādeva, Bhava, the lord of all living beings said to goddess Śarvāṇī, Umā, the unborn, and daughter of the mountain.

50. O goddess, I am going to crown lord Nandīśvara as the lord of goblins. I shall call him the leader of the Ganas. O unchanging goddess, what do you think ?

51-53. On hearing his words the delight of Bhavānī was evident in her face. Smilingly she said to Bhava her lord, the lord of goblins, and the bestower of boons, "O lord of Devas, it behoves you to grant him the overlordship of the worlds as also the leadership of the Gaṇas, Śailādi is my own son."

Thereafter lord Śarva, the lord of the chiefs of the world, the bull-emblemed lord, remembered all the divine chiefs of the Gaṇas.

278. pañcanadam : a confluence of five rivers, viz. Jaṭodakā, Trisrotas, Vṛṣadhvani, Svarṇodakā, and Jāmbūnadī.

CHAPTER FORTYFOUR

Coronation of Nandiśvara

Śailādi said:

1. As soon as Rudra remembered them, the leaders of Gaṇas came there. All of them had a thousand arms with weapons in all their thousand hands.

2. They had three eyes. These noble gaṇas were saluted even by Devas. They resembled crores of fires that burn at the time of dissolution. They had matted hairs and crowns.

3. Innumerable lords of Gaṇas of noble souls came there with jubilation. They were accompanied by crores and crores of Gaṇas all equal in exploits to the chief. Their faces were terrible due to the curved fangs. They were eternal, enlightened and devoid of impurities.

4. Those strong ones were singing, running, dancing and playing on various instruments with facial gestures.

5. These Gaṇas rode in chariots, on elephants, horses, lions and monkeys. They were seated in aerial chariots decorated in gold.

6-8. The Gaṇas of great yogic power came to the assembly of the lord, playing on drums and other musical instruments such as Bherī, Mṛdaṅgaka, Paṇava, Ānaka, Gomukha, Paṭaha, Ekapuṣkara, Ādambaraka, Muraja, Ḍiṇḍima, Mardala, Veṇu (flute), Vīṇā (lute), different kinds of cymbals, Dardura, Talaghāta, Kacchapa and Paṇava.

9. Those lords of Gaṇas of great strength and stamina, the lords of the chiefs of Devas bowed down to the lord and the goddess and spoke these words:

10. O blessed lord, O lord of the chiefs of Devas, O three-eyed lord, O bull-emblemed lord, why are we summoned? O lord of great splendour, command us.

11. Shall we dry up the oceans? Shall we kill Yama along with his servants? Shall we kill Mṛtyu, the daughter of God of Death? Shall we kill the lotus-born deity as an insignificant animal?

12. Infuriated that we are, shall we bind up Indra along with Devas or Viṣṇu along with Vāyu or Daityas along with Dānavas and bring them here?

13. O lord, at your behest, to whom shall we bring about destruction and distress today? Who has great festivities today for the prosperity and increase of his desires?"

14. The lord honoured crores and hundred crores of those chieftains of Gaṇas. Even as they earnestly spoke to him thus, he replied as follows:

15. "You are all persons striving for the welfare of the universe. Listen why you have been called. O noble ones of pure souls, on hearing it do accordingly without hesitation.

16. This Nandīśvara is our son. He is the lord of all chiefs. He is a prosperous brahmin, your leader and commander-in-chief.

17. Hence at my bidding, you all, highly respected ones, crown him as your lord and commander-in-chief, as the great lord of yogas"

18. Thus directed by the lord, the chieftains of the Gaṇas agreed to the same, by saying "so be it" and thereafter began to gather all the requisites.

19-23. They brought the usual divine seat of Śarva, the splendid seat made of gold, the beautiful one resembling Meru to be offered as seat for him (Nandin). They made a Maṇḍapa with many pillars shining with golden lustre. Pearl pendants were suspended and they were studded with gems and jewels. There were columns of Lapis Lazuli covered with small tinkling bells. The Maṇḍapa had doors on all sides bedecked in beautiful gems and jewels. After making the Maṇḍapa they placed a splendid seat in the middle. In front of it was the foot-stool shining with blue stones. For the installation of the pedestal they kept two water jars nearby. They were filled with sweet waters and covered with lotus flowers.

24. There were a thousand jars of gold, silver, copper and clay. They were filled with waters from all Tīrthas.

25-26. Brahmā, Parameṣṭhin the noble soul, offered these things, viz:—a pair of cloths, divine scents, shoulderlets, ear-rings, crown, necklace, hundred-ribbed umbrella and the chowries.

27. There was a fine Cāmara (bushy tail of deer used as a flyflap or fan) with gold shaft. The fan was as pure as the moon. It shone with its back as white as conch or pearl necklace.

28. The divine elephants Airāvata and Supratīka were fully caparisoned. A gold crown was made by Viśvakarman.

29-30. There were two pure and divine ear-rings. The excellent weapon thunderbolt was kept there. There was a golden thread and two bracelets. The unexcited leaders of Gaṇas highly honoured by Devas brought many requisite materials from all round.

31-34. Then all these assembled there joyously: – Devas along with Indra, Viṣṇu and others, the sages, Brahmā and nine Brahmās[279]. When all of them had come, lord Parameśvara directed Brahmā to perform the rite. At the behest of the lord, Brahmā performed the rite of ablution with great attention. After worshipping him Brahmā himself poured the water.

35. At the behest of Śiva, Viṣṇu, Indra and the guardians of quarters bathed the leaders of Gaṇas in succession.

36-37 The sages with Brahmā at their head eulogised him. While they eulogised, Viṣṇu the lord of the universe kept his joined palms over the head and eulogised with great attention. With palms joined in reverence he bowed down and cried out shouts of victory.

38-39. Then the commandants of Gaṇas, Devas and Asuras one after the other, eulogised and bathed him. Thus after being eulogised and bathed by Devas along with Brahmā, his marriage too was performed at the behest of Parameṣṭhin. His wife was the gentle lady named Suyaśā, the daughter of the Maruts.

40-41. A well-decorated umbrella having the lustre of the moon was offered to her. She had Cāmaras also and she was accompanied by groups of women holding Cāmara in their hands. Along with me, the most excellent throne was occupied by her. She was adorned by Mahālakṣmī with coronet and other ornaments.

42-43. The excellent necklace from the neck of the goddess was gifted to her. The leading bull, the white elephant, the lion, the lion-emblem, the chariot, the golden umbrella with

279. *Cf. Liṅga*. Ch. 70, 81-82. They are called Marīci, Bhṛgu. Aṅgiras, Pulaha, Pulastya, Kratu, Dakṣa, Atri and Vasiṣṭha.

the lustre like that of the disc of the moon—all these were there. Till now no other lord was equal to me.

44-45. The great lord mounted the bull after taking me on, along with all the members of my family, kinsmen and relatives. He set off with the goddess. On seeing the goddess and the lord along with me, the sages, Devas, Siddhas and brahmins requested for the lord's order.

46-49. At the behest of the lord, the husband of the daughter of the mountain, Nandī granted those who deserved the splendid behest of the lord. On receiving the order from the leading sage they became great devotees of Śiva. Hence one should worship the lord.

If a person utters the name of the lord without obeisance he will incur great sin on a par with that of ten brahmin-slayers. Hence by all means, one shall utter words of obeisance. At the outset one shall make obeisance and at the end utter the name Śiva.[280]

CHAPTER FORTYFIVE

Description of Nether Worlds

The sages said:

1. O Sūta, everything pertaining to Lord Śiva has been clearly stated. It behoves you to narrate the form of the lord as the soul of all.

Sūta said :

2-3. Bhūḥ, Bhuvaḥ, Svaḥ, Mahaḥ, Jana, Tapas, Satya, Pātāla, the crores of hellish seas, stars, planets, the sun, the moon, the polar star, the seven sages (Great Bear) and those going about in aerial chariots—all these abide by his grace.

4. All these are created by him. O excellent brahmins,

280. It refers to the five-syllabled mantra of Śiva—"namaḥ śivāya."

they have him as their soul. Śiva is always stationed in the form of samaṣṭi (the collective whole). He is the soul of all.

5. Those who are confounded, those who are deluded by his Māyā do not know the great lord Maheśvara the noble soul, the Ātman of all.

6. Indeed the three worlds constitute his body. Hence after bowing to him I shall recount the splendid detail of the worlds.

7. Formerly, I had mentioned to you about the shape and features of the Cosmic Egg. I shall now describe the features of the worlds in the cosmic Egg.

8. The Earth, the firmament, Svaḥ, Mahaḥ, Jana, Tapas and Satya—these seven are the splendid worlds originating from the Cosmic Egg.

9. O brahmins, beneath these are the seven worlds beginning with Mahātala. Beneath them are the hells one by one.

10. Mahātala has the golden ground surface, which is rendered splendid by jewels, mansions and shrines dedicated to lord Śiva.

11. It is occupied by Ananta, Mucukunda and king Bali who is the resident of Pātāla and Svarga.

12. O brāhmins, Rasātala is rocky, Talātala is full of gravels, Sutala is yellow and Vitala has the lustre of coral.

13-15. Atala is white. Tala is black. O men of good holy rites, the extent of all the Talas below is as much as that of the earth, viz., 1000 yojanas each. The sky above each Tala extends to ten thousand yojanas. The magnitude of all the seven along with the clouds is seven thousand lakhs of yojanas. The root (i.e. the space below the last world Pātāla) is thirty thousand yojanas.

16. O excellent sages, the splendid Rasātala is frequented by Suvarṇa, Vāsuki and by others as well.

17. What is famous as Talātala is endowed with all splendours and is frequented by Virocana, Hiraṇyākṣa, Naraka and others.

18. Sutala is occupied by Vaināyaka and others, by Pūrvadevas (demons) with Kālanemi at the head and by others too.

19. Vitala is occupied by Dānavas and others beginning

with Tārakāgni, serpents Mahāntaka and others and by the Asura Prahlāda.

20. Atala is occupied by Kambalāśva, by the heroic Mahākumbha and the intelligent Hayagrīva.

21. Tala (i.e. Mahātala) is rendered splendid and occupied by Śaṅkukarṇa and other heroes beginning with Namuci.

22-23. In all these nether worlds the great lord is present along with Umā, Skanda, Nandin and all the chieftains of Gaṇas. O excellent ones, above all these seven Talas are the earth and other worlds. The earth too is of seven divisions about which I shall tell you now.

CHAPTER FORTYSIX

Dvīpas and their lords

Sūta said:

1. The Earth consists of seven continents.[281] It is full of rivers and mountains. It is surrounded by seven oceans[282] all round and embellished by them.

2. The seven continents beginning with the inner one are Jambū, Plakṣa, Śālmali, Kuśa, Krauñca, Śāka and Puṣkara.

3. Lord Śiva is present in all the seven continents, accompanied by Umā (his consort), surrounded by the Gaṇas, and assuming different guises.

4-5. The seven oceans in order are those having, (1) briny water, (2) sugercane juice, (3) wine, (4) ghee, (5) curds, (6) milk and (7) sweet water. In all these oceans the glorious lord Śiva assumes the form of water and sports with the waves along with the Gaṇas.

281. seven continents: p. 71, note 89. The verse 2 of this ch. mentions their names. On the identification of these dvīpas on the basis of climatic and vegetation data available in the Purāṇas, see S. M. Ali. op. cit. Ch. II.

282. samudraiḥ saptabhiḥ—by seven seas. According to S. M. Ali, "*samudra* does not necessarily mean 'a watery sea'. The Purāṇic sea can be a large expanse of sand as well as water. The sea of sand and that of water as barriers to human settlement and movement are synonymous when considering the geography of the inhabited world."

6. Lord Viṣṇu always sleeps in yogic slumber in the milky ocean as though he were the nectar from that, with his intellect concentrated on the knowledge of Śiva.

7. When the lord wakes up, the entire universe wakes up; when he is asleep it is also asleep; the mobile and immobile beings are identical with him.

8. With the favour of Parameṣṭhin lord of Devas, everything was created, held, protected and annihilated by him alone.

9. O excellent sages, those who are well known as suṣeṇas worship Aniruddha the leading Puruṣa holding conch, discus and iron club.

10-14. O sages, most excellent among the knowers of Ātman ! those who meditate on Aniruddha Puruṣa are all similar to Viṣṇu and become endowed with all riches. Sanandana, Sanaka, Sanātana, Vālakhilyas, Siddhas, Mitra and Varuṇa these all worship Viṣṇu who is the origin of the universe. In all the seven continents there are lofty mountains, some rising to great heights, some extending as far as the oceans, others having many peaks and caves. There were many kings in these continents who were overlords and who ruled with efficiency according to the demands of the period. They were powerful, thanks to the lord (Śiva), the father of the enemy of Krauñca[283] (i. e. Kārttikeya).

15-18. I shall mention the kings in all the manvantaras past and future, beginning with those in the Svāyambhuva manvantara. The grandsons of Svāyambhuva Manu were all very strong, with similar status, honour and identical purposes. They were the heroic sons of Priyavrata[284] and they are reputed to be ten,[285] viz., Āgnīdhra, Agnibāhu, Medhā, Medhātithi, Vasu, Jyotiṣmān, Dyutimān, Havya, Savana and Putra. Priyavrata crowned seven of them as kings over the seven continents.

283. Krauñcāriḥ : the enemy of Krauñca, i.e. Kārttikeya, so called because he split the Himālaya range Krauñca, situated in the eastern part of the chain on the north of Assam.

284. Priyavrata, son of Svāyambhuva Manu and Śatarūpā.

285. Though the number is the same, their names differ in the Purāṇas.

19-24. He made Āgnīdhra the lord of Jambūdvīpa and Medhātithi the king of Plakṣadvīpa. He crowned Vapuṣmān the king of Śālmali, Jyotiṣmān the king of Kuśadvīpa, Dyutimān the king of Krauñcadvīpa, Havya the lord of Śākadvīpa. O sages of good holy rites, he made Savana the overlord of Puṣkara. Savana had two sons Mahāvīra and Dhātakī. They were most excellent that men could have. The kingdom of Mahāvīra is known as Mahāvīra Varṣa after the name of that noble soul. The kingdom of Dhātakī is called Dhātakīkhaṇḍa.[286] Havya the lord of Śākadvīpa procreated seven sons.

25. They were Jalada, Kumāra, Sukumāra, Maṇīcaka, Kusumottara, Modāki and Mahādruma.

26-29. The Varṣa continent of Talada is called (1) Talada; the Varṣa of Kumāra is called (2) Kaumāra; that of Sukumāra is glorified as (3) Sukumāra; the Varṣa of Maṇīcaka is called (4) Māṇīcaka; the Varṣa of Kusumottara is (5) Kusumottara, the Varṣa of Modāki is glorified as (6) Modaka; after the name of Mahādruma, the next Varṣa is (7) Mahādruma; all the seven Varṣas are thus named after their rulers.

30-34. Dyutimān, the lord of Krauñca Dvīpa had seven sons named Kuśala, Manuga, Uṣṇa, Pīvara, Andhakāraka, Muni and Dundubhi who had splendid sub-continents named after them, in the Krauñca Dvīpa. The sub-continent of Kusala is Kuśala; that of Manuga is Manonuga; that of Uṣṇa is Uṣṇa; that of Pīvara is Pīvara; the land of Andhakāra is Andhakāraka; the land of Muni is called Muni and that of Dundubhi is Dundubhi. These seven shining countries are in Krauñca Dvīpa.

In the Kuśadvīpa, Jyotiṣmān had seven powerful sons.

35. They were Udbhida, Veṇumān, Dvairatha, Lavaṇa, Dhṛti, Prabhākara and Kapila.

36-37. The first Varṣa is Udbhida; the second is Veṇumaṇḍala; the third is Dvairatha; the fourth is Lavaṇa; the fifth is Dhṛtimat; the sixth is Prabhākara, and the seventh is Kāpila.

38-41. The seven sons of Vapuṣmān were the rulers of

286. Dhātakī Khaṇḍa. Prof. Ali identifies this with the Gobi desert on the west of Khingan range in the Japanese Highlands. See *The Geography of the Purāṇas*, p. 287.

various countries of Śālmali Dvīpa. They were Śveta, Harita, Jīmūta, Rohita, Vaidyuta, Mānasa and Suprabha; The land of Śveta is Śveta; that of Harita, Hārita; that of Jīmūta is Jīmūta; that of Rohita is Rohita; that of Vaidyuta is Vaidyuta; that of Mānasa is Mānasa and that of Suprabha is Suprabha; thus there are seven countries marked after the names of their rulers. I shall mention the divisions in the Plaksadvīpa that is beyond Jambūdvīpa.

42-45. Medhātithi had seven sons; they were the kings of Plakṣa Dvīpa which consists of seven Varṣas. The eldest among the sons was Śāntabhaya. After him were Śiśira; Sukhodaya, Ānanda; Śiva, Kṣemaka and Dhruva. The continent was divided into seven Varṣas and named after these sons. Formerly in the Svāyambhuva manvantara these Varṣas were colonised by them. Subjects endowed with the discipline of four castes and four stages of life were colonised in the Varṣas by those sons of Medhātithi, the residents of Plakṣadvīpa.

46-47. In the five continents beginning with Plakṣadvīpa and ending with Śākadvīpa, the Dharma, was promulgated in accordance with the division of four castes and four stages of life. O excellent brahmins, in these five Dvīpas, happiness, span of life, handsome features, strength and Dharma were their individual characteristics respectively.

48-49. The characteristic common to all the five continents was that the subjects there were all perpetually engaged in the worship of Rudra and devoted to Maheśvara. The kings born in the Puṣkaradvīpa enjoy the nectar of their devout feelings towards Prajāpati and Rudra.

CHAPTER FORTYSEVEN

Bhārata sub-continent

Sūta Said :

1. King Priyavrata crowned his eldest son Āgnīdhra who was the eldest inheritor and who was a loveable son of great strength, as the king of Jambūdvīpa.[287]

287. For detail, *Ibid*. p. 64 ff.

2. O leading brahmins, he was an ascetic and a great devotee of Śiva. He was a young man engaged in the worship of Śiva. He was prosperous and intelligent and he possessed many cows.

3. He had nine sons at par with Prajāpatis. All of them were followers of Maheśvara and devoted to Mahādeva.

4. His eldest son was known as Nābhi. Kimpuruṣa was his (Nābhi's) younger brother. The third son was Harivarṣa. The fourth son was Ilāvṛta.

5. Ramya was the fifth; the sixth was Hiraṇmān. Kuru was the seventh. Bhadrāśva was the eighth.

6. The ninth was Ketumāla. Understand their lands now. The subcontinent of Nābhi inherited from his father is called Hema which lies in the south.

7. He gave Kimpuruṣa the subcontinent Hemakūṭa. He gave the subcontinent called Naiṣadha to Hari.

8. To Ilāvṛta he gave the midlands encircling the mountain Meru. He gave Ramya the subcontinent around Nīlācala.

9. The subcontinent Śveta to the north of it was given to Hiraṇmān. He gave Kuru the subcontinent Śṛṅga Varṣa which is to the north of it.

10. He gave the subcontinent round about Mālyavān to Bhadrāśva. He gave Gandhamādana to Ketumāla.

11-12. These are the nine great subcontinents in brief. After crowning his sons as the kings in those subcontinents, Āgnīdhra[288] the virtuous became engaged in penance. After purifying himself by penance he became engaged in the study of the Vedas.

13-15. After being engaged in the study of the Vedas he became engaged in meditation on Śiva. There is natural perfection in all the eight excellent subcontinents beginning with Kimpuruṣa. Without any strain the subjects are always happy. The opposite of joy is not seen in them. They have no fear from death or old age. They have neither Dharma nor Adharma. There is no distinction such as the excellent, the middling and the base. In all these eight subcontinents there are no subdivisions of yugas.

288. According to *Liṅga*, Āgnīdhra was the eldest son of Priyavrata. But according to a Vāyu version he was the son of Priyavrata's daughter.

16. Those who die in a holy centre of Rudra whether mobile or immobile whether devotees or casual visitors are reborn there.

17. For their benefit eight holy centres were created by Rudra. In all those places Mahādeva was always present.

18. By seeing Mahādeva in their hearts the residents of the eight holy centres were always happy. He alone was the greatest goal unto them all.

19-20. I shall now recount the country of Nābhi marked by 'hima' (snow; i.e. Bhāratavarṣa as mentioned below). The intelligent Nābhi begot a son of Merudevī, Ṛṣabha by name who was a great king adored by all kṣatriyas. A heroic son Bharata was born to Ṛṣabha. He was the eldest among his hundred sons.

21-25. Ṛṣabha who was fond of his son Bharata crowned him as king. By adopting the path of knowledge and detachment he conquered the serpents of his sense-organs; by all means he stabilised Īśvara, the supreme Ātman, within his own heart; he was immersed in devout feelings; he observed fasts; he wore bark garments and matted hair. He retired into darkness (i.e. solitary place). Devoid of all desires and his doubts all cleared, (in the end) he attained the great region of Śiva. He gave the subcontinent to the south of the mountain Himavat to Bharata. Hence learned men call that subcontinent as Bhārata Varṣa[289] after his name. Bharata's son was the virtuous Sumati. Bharata entrusted the kingdom to his care. After transferring the royal glory to his son the king entered the forest for penance.

289. Bhārata. *Liṅga* ascribes the origin of the name to King Bharata, the eldest of the hundred sons of Ṛṣabha and grandson of Nābhi. Cf. Vāyu 33. 51-52; Marka 53. 39-40. For detail see *Bhāga* 11.2. 15-17 and Sk I. 11. 37. 55-57. But according to Matsya 114-5-6, Bharata is the name of Manu himself who creates and supports the people here. For further detail, see Avasthi : *Studies in Skandapurāṇa*, pp. 17-23. Formerly Bhārata was known as Hima-varṣa or Haimavata Varṣa.

CHAPTER FORTYEIGHT

The Mountain Meru

Sūta said:

1. In the middle of this Jambu Dvīpa is the great mountain Meru[290]. It is the most excellent among the mountains, having many peaks full of jewels.

2. It is reputed to be eightyfour thousand yojanas in height. It has entered sixteen thousand yojanas beneath the ground and it extends to sixteen thousand yojanas.

3. Since it is stationed like a shallow plate the extent on the top is thirty-two thousand yojanas. Three times its width is its girth at the ridges.

4. It is rendered golden due to the auspicious contact with the body of Maheśa. It resembles the flower of the Dhattūra plant (thorn apple). It is the abode of all Devas.

5. It is the sporting ground for Devas. It is full of miracles. The total width and extent of this mountain is a hundred thousand yojanas.

6-7. O leading brahmins, beneath the earth its extent is sixteen thousand yojanas. The remaining part of that mountain is above the earth. The extent at the root is thus sixteen thousand yojanas and the extent above, they say, is twice the extent at the root.

8. In the east it has the lustre of the ruby; in the south it resembles gold; in the west it shines like the blue stone and in the north it has the coral lustre.

9. In the eastern side of this mountain is Amarāvatī (the city of Indra). It is full of mansions of different kinds. It is thronged by different groups of Devas. It is surrounded by clusters of jewels.

10-14. It has many ornamental gateways of different shapes bedecked in gold and jewels. The arches at the gateways are rendered wonderful with gold, with jewels set in. Thousands of women throng the roadways. They are clever in conversation and elocution. They are bedecked in all ornaments. They stoop down due to the weight of their heavy breasts and their eyes

290. P. 98, note 127.

roll to and fro due to intoxication. The Apsaras (water nymphs) move about all round. There are wonderful lakes, tanks, and rivers, all clustered with full blown lotuses. They have golden lines of steps. Even the sands on their banks are golden. Blue and fragrant golden lotuses abound in them. Thus the whole city shines splendidly. With that city the mountain is considered auspicious.

15. In the south-eastern side of the mountain is Tejasvinī the city of the fire god. It is divine and similar to Amarāvatī. It is endowed with all means of pleasures.

16. O sages, most excellent among those who have self-control, in the southern side of the mountain is the city of Yama Vaivasvata. It is full of many divine abodes built in gold and very splendid.

17-18. In the south-west is the splendid dark-coloured city Śuddhavatī.[291] Similarly in the north-west is the splendid city Gandhavatī. The city in the north is Mahodayā and that in the north-east is Yaśovatī. Thus cities in all the quarters always shine.

19. There are the abodes of Brahmā, Viṣṇu and Maheśa as well as of others on it. Thus the mountain endowed with all means of pleasures and containing many lakes, is the most excellent among the mountains.

20. It is full of Siddhas, Yakṣas, Gandharvas, sages and the four kinds of living beings.

21-22. O leading brahmins, on the mountain towards the left, stands a palace of seven storeys that is as clear as pure crystal. It is as extensive as though it has a thousand landing grounds. There stays lord Śiva of great arms, whose eyes are the sun, moon and fire. He is seated in a gemset throne along with the goddess and the six-faced deity Kārttikeya.

23-27. The palace of Viṣṇu is also there. It extends to half of that of lord Śiva and he (Viṣṇu) stays there. In the south is the divine palace of the lotus-born deity Brahmā. It is full of rubies. There is the city of Indra which is very large. There is the beautiful city of Yama. There are the cities of

291. Since no city in the west is mentioned, Kṛṣṇavarṇā and Śuddhavatī in the first half of V-17 may also mean two cities, i.e. Kṛṣṇavarṇā in the south-east and Śuddhavatī in the west.

Soma, Varuṇa, Nirṛti, Pāvaka (fire-god), Vāyu (wind) and Rudra. In their different respective palaces there are the abodes of all people. In the north-east in the holy centre of the lord, perpetual worship is maintained. The holy Nandī stays there alongwith his disciples and the leading Siddhas. Sanat is comfortably lodged there alongwith the Siddhas. The lord of Devas is there alongwith Sanaka, Sananda and others.

28. Some part of it, is the ground for the practice of yoga. In some places are the grounds for enjoyment of pleasures. There is a splendid palace with seven storeys resembling the rising sun.

29-35. It is the splendid palace of Nandī and the chieftain of the Gaṇas is seated there in the midst of six-faced deity, Gaṇeśa, thousands of Gaṇas, Suyaśā of beautiful eyes, the mothers and Madana. The river Jambū[292] flows round the base of this mountain.

To its right there is a splendid Jambū (Rose Apple) tree. It is very tall with extensive growth all round. It yields fruits at all times. The Ilāvṛta sub-continent is splendid and extensive all round the Meru. Some subsist there on the fruits of Jambū and some on nectar. Some have the lustre of gold and others are of various colours. They enjoy all kinds of pleasures. O brahmins, this is the splendid mid-land of the Dvīpa, which extends all round the foot of the Meru. There are nine sub-continents in Jambūdvīpa.[292a] I shall recount all of them with their rivers, streams, and mountain ranges. Understand their extent in yojanas.

292. Jambū : According to *Marka.* (55. 28-30) this river springs from the juice of the fruits which the Jambu tree produces on the Gandhamādana. The river passes around Meru and then enters Jambūmūla.

292a. Jambūdvīpa represents the geographical conception of the territory ruled over by the Aryan people. The territory was divided into nine units (varṣas), of which Bhārata was one. St. Epiphanius (the end of the fourth century A.D.) has recorded that India was formerly divided into nine kingdoms (vide S.B. Chaudhuri, *JIH.* Vol. XXVII part III, 1949, pp. 241).

CHAPTER FORTYNINE

Ilāvṛta sub-continent

Sūta said:

1. The first Dvīpa, it is said, extends to a thousand yojanas. The other Dvīpas successively extend to twice the previous one.

2-3. The earth along with all the oceans is stated as extending to fifty crores of yojanas. It consists of seven Dvīpas. It is splendid and is surrounded by the Lokāloka mountain.[293] The mountain Nīla is to the north of the Meru. The Śveta is to the north of this and the Śṛṅgī is still further north of Śveta. O brahmins, these three are the mountains of the sub-continents in the north.

4. The Jaṭhara[294] and the Devakūṭa[295] are the mountains in the eastern quarter. The Niṣadha[296] is to the south of the Meru. Still south of it is the mountain Hemakūṭa.[297] The Himavat is to its south.

5. To the west of the Meru there are two mountains: Mālyavān[298] and Gandhamādana.[299] These two extend towards the north.

293. Lokāloka—a belt of mountains bounding the outer-most of the seven seas and dividing the visible world from the regions of darkness.

294-295. On the eastern side of Meru there are two mountains, namely the Jaṭhara and the Devakūta which run north to south and stretch up to the Nila (Tien Shan) and Niṣadha mountains (*Vāyu* 35.8). Jaṭhara is identified with Kuruk-Tagh and Devakūṭa with Altin Tagh—Nan Shan Tsing-Ling of Sinkiang and Northern China. *The Geography of the Purāṇas*, pp. 99-100.

296. Niṣadha: Śp. places it to the south of the Meru, along with the Himavat and Hemakūṭa. It represents Hindukush Kunlun chain.

297. Hemakūṭa : a sacred hill situated to the north of Mānasarovara It represents Ladakh-Kailash-Trans-Himalayan chain.

298. Mālyavān : This mountain bounds Ilāvṛta Varṣa on the east.

299. Gandhamādana : It is placed to the south of Meru.

6. All these leading mountains are frequented by the Siddhas and Cāraṇas. The inter-space between two mountains is nine thousand yojanas in each case.

7-10. This sub-continent south of the Himavat is known as Bhārata. Hemakūṭa is beyond that. The sub-continent within it is Kimpuruṣa. Niṣadha is beyond Hemakūṭa. Its sub-continent is called Harivarṣa. Beyond Harivarṣa and Meru is the splendid Ilāvṛta. Beyond Ilāvṛta is Nīla and the sub-continent Ramyaka. Beyond Ramyaka is Śveta and the sub-continent known as Hiraṇmaya. The mountain beyond Hiraṇmaya is known as Śṛṅgī and sub-continent beyond it is Kuru. The two Varṣas one in the south and one in the north (i.e. Himavarsa and Ramyaka) are stationed like an arch.

11. The other four are horizontal in shape. Ilāvṛta is in the middle; to the west and east of the Meru there are two sub-continents and they are smaller (than the four mentioned before).

12. The area above Niṣadha is known as the northern Vedyardha (half of the whole Dvīpa which is conceived as a sacrificial altar). Thus there are three Varṣas in the southern half and three Varṣas in the northern half.

13. Ilāvṛta with the Meru in the middle is in the midst of the two halves.

14-15 The great mountain Mālyavān extends towards the north. Its width above is two thousand yojanas. Its length is stated to be thirtyfour thousand yojanas. The mountain Gandhamādana is to the west of it.

16-17. Its length and width is similar to that of Mālyavān. These six Varṣa mountains of good ridges extend to the east and are bounded on both sides by the Eastern and Western seas.

18. Himavat is full of snow. The Hemakūṭa contains gold. The Niṣadha is also golden resembling the morning sun.

19. The golden Meru which extends upwards has four colours. Its girth is symmetrical and cylindrical. It rises high.

20. The mountain Nīla is full of Lapis Lazuli stones. The Śveta is white in colour and full of gold. The three-peaked mountain Śṛṅgī has the colour of the feathers of the peacock and contains gold.

21-25a. Thus the mountains have been succinctly recounted. Again listen to the description of the leading hills or peaks.

Mandara and Devakūṭa are the mountains in the eastern quarter. Kailāsa and golden Gandhamādana extend from the east towards south and end within the ocean. The excellent mountains Niṣadha and Pāriyātra are stationed in the west, like those in the east. Triśṛṅga and Jārudhi are the excellent mountains in the north. They are embedded within the ocean and they also extend towards the East. Learned men call these mountains "Maryādāparvatas" (mountains of the boundary).

25b-27. O excellent brahmins there are foot ranges to the lofty golden mountain Meru, extending to the four quarters. Supported by these, the earth consisting of the seven Dvīpas, does not move. Their length is mentioned to be ten thousand yojanas. In the east it is Mandara; in the south it is Gandhamādana, in the west it is Vipula and in the north it is Supārśva.

28-34. Four lofty trees grow on these as though they are the flagstaffs of the Dvīpas. The great tree on the peak of the mountain Mandara is the Kadamba, the king of flagstaffs. It has long hanging branches. It acts as a caityapādapa (holy big tree in a sacred temple).

On the peak of the mountain in south (i.e. Gandhamādana) there is a Jambū tree (Rose Apple) with holy fruits and flowers hanging in garlands. The Jambū tree is known in all the worlds as the flagstaff in the southern region.

On the peak of the lofty mountain Vipula, in the west, a great Aśvattha tree (holy fig tree) grows like a great Caityapādapa (a sacred tree in a holy temple). On the peak of the mountain Supārśva in the north grows the big Nyagrodha (Indian fig tree), with a huge trunk extending to many yojanas in circumference.

I shall now mention the four sporting grounds of Devas on the leading mountains. They are devoid of human beings and have trees and plants that bloom in all the seasons.

35-57. There are groves in the four directions. Understand them by their names. The forest grove in the east is Caitraratha; in the south it is Gandhamādana; it is Vaibhrāja in the west; in the north it is the garden of Savitṛ (sun).

(The holy shrine) in the east is Mitreśvara. Thereafter

(i.e. in the south) it is Ṣaṣṭheśvara. In the west it is Varyeśvara and in the north it is Āmrakeśvara.

Similarly, O leading sages, there are four great lakes also.

38-40. The sages sport about there on the mountains and in the gardens.

The lake in the east is Aruṇoda;[300] that in the south is Mānasa; in the west Sitoda and in the north Mahābhadra.

In the south there is the holy centre of Śākha, in the west it is of Viśākha; in the north of Naigameya and in the east of Kumāra. I shall mention briefly the leading peaks beginning from the eastern lake Aruṇoda only by their names. It is not possible to describe them in detail.

41-45a. These are the great mountains, viz:—Sītānta, Kuraṇḍa, Kurara, Vikara, Maṇiśaila, Vṛkṣavān, Mahānīla, Rucaka, Savindu, Dardura, Veṇumān, Samegha, Niṣadha and Devaparvata. These and other mountains are the abodes of Siddhas in the east of Mandara. There are divine shrines of Rudra, Viṣṇu and Nārāyaṇa on all these hills, their caves and forests.

45b-49. I shall now mention the great hills to the south of the lake Mānasa in brief. Śaila, Viśiras, Śikhara, Ekaśṛṅga, Mahāśūla, Gajaśaila, Piśācaka, Pañcaśaila, Kailāsa, and Himavat. These are all lofty excellent hills frequented by Devas. On all these different mountains and forests divine shrines of Rudra have been installed by Devas. The mountains in the southern direction are thus mentioned to you. I shall now tell you about the hills in the west.

50-52. To the west of the lake Sitoda there stand Surapa, Mahābala, Kumuda, Madhumān, Añjana, Mukuṭa. Kṛṣṇa, Pāṇḍura, Sahasraśikhara, the leading hills Pārijāta and Śrīśṛṅga. These are the prominent excellent mountains frequented by Devas in the western quarter and they contain shrines of Rudra.

53. The extremely powerful mountains to the north of the lake Mahābhadra are being stated now succinctly.

300. Aruṇoda. It lies to the east of Meru.

54-56. They are:—Śaṅkhakūṭa, Mahāśaila, Vṛṣabha, Haṁsaparvata, Nāga, Kapila, Indraśaila, Sānumān, Nīla, Kaṇṭakaśṛṅga, Śataśṛṅga, Puṣpakośa, Praśaila, Virajas, Varāhaparvata, Mayūra and Jārudhi.[301] All these are stationed in the north.

57. There are thousands of divine palaces of the trident-bearing lord on those divine hills.

58. In the interstices of these leading hills there are many internal water reservoirs, lakes and parks.

59. Thanks to the favour of Parameṣṭhin, Devas, sages, Siddhas purified by their devotional thoughts of Śiva reside here along with their families in their respective abodes.

60-69. The different deities reside in the various forests as follows:—

The residence of Lakṣmī is in the Bilva grove; Kaśyapa and others stay in the Kakubha grove; the residence of Indra, Upendra and of the snake gods is in the Tālavana (forest of palm trees); the residence of Kardama and his tribe is in the Udumbara grove; the residence of the Vidyādharas and Siddhas is in the holy and splendid mango-grove; the abode of the Nāgas and Siddhas is in the forest of Nimba (Margosa), that of the sun and Rudra is in the Kiṁśuka; the preceptor of Devas is stationed in the holy forest of Bījapūra; the abode of the noble lords beginning with Viṣṇu is in the forest of lilies; the serpents stay on the Nyagrodha within the clusters of Sthalapadma (land lotuses). It is here that Śeṣa the lord of the nether worlds stays. He alone is the god of Death unto all. The ploughshare-armed lord is only a form of Viṣṇu himself, the preceptor of the universe; he is the leaning couch of Viṣṇu; he is the bangle of the lord (Śiva). Dānavas including their preceptor Śukra stay in the forest of jack trees. The serpents are stationed in the Viśākhaka forest along with the Kinnaras; there are innumerable trees of all kinds in this beautiful forest. Nandīśvara is also stationed there and is being eulogised by the leading Gaṇas. Goddess Sarasvatī stays in the middle of the region full of Santānaka (wish-yielding) trees.

301. Jārudhi : This range is identified with the Kirghiz-Zailai Al-Tau, Ketmen chain. GP. p. 82.

The abodes of Devas

Thus are the residents of these forests recounted in brief. It is not possible to describe them in detail.

CHAPTER FIFTY

The abodes of Devas

Sūta said:

1a. Indra stays in the auspicious forest of Pārijāta[302] (wish-yielding tree) on the peak called Śītānta.[303]

1b-2a. To the east of it is the extensive peak of Kumuda[304] mountain. O excellent brahmins, on it are the eight cities of Dānavas.

2b-3a. In the holy Suvarṇakoṭara, O excellent brahmins, they say, are the sixty-eight cities of the noble-souled Rākṣasas called Nīlakas.

3b-4a. There are fifteen cities on the leading mountain Mahānīla which are the abodes of the horse-faced Kinnaras.

4b. O men of good holy rites, there are three cities of the Vidyādharas on Veṇusaudha, the great mountain.

5. The glorious Garuḍa stays in Vaikuṇṭha. The prosperous Nīlalohita stays in Karañja.[305] The Vasus live in Vasudhāra.

302. Pārijāta-vana—forest of coral trees (Erythrina Indica) which lose their leaves in June and are then covered with large crimson flowers.

303. Śītānta : It means 'end of cold'. i.e. "a range which marks the dividing line between the cold and hot regions. If the river Kizil-Su represents the head waters of the Purāṇic river Sītā, Śītānta is obviously the Kashghar range, i.e. the last longitudinal range of the Pāmir region facing the Tarim basin, on the east. It is a range which, to a traveller coming from the east across the hot and sandy Tarim Basin, stands athwart the route towards the west and promises a cool climate beyond. It is an effective climatic barrier which separates a hot and dry desert on the east from the cold plateau on the west. Coming from the west it literally marks the 'end of cold' and is therefore rightly qualified for its name, Śītānta". GP. pp. 100-101.

304. Kumuda : Peak Barzengi (16,456 feet) beyond the Pakshif Pass.

305. Most of the mountains mentioned in this chapter are not identifiable.

6. There are seven holy spots on the mountain Ratnadhāra, belonging to the noble seven sages. They contain the abodes of the Siddhas as well.

7. The great abode of Prajāpati is on the mountain ekaśṛṅga. Durgā and others stay on the Gajaśaila and the Vasus on the Sumedha.

8. The Ādityas, Rudras and Aśvins have their abodes in eighty divine cities on the mountain Hemakakṣa.

9. There are five hundred crores of abodes of the Rākṣasas on the Sunīla mountain which has five peaks with five crores of cities in each.

10. The hundred cities of the Yakṣas of unmeasured prowess are on the Śataśṛṅga; the cities of Kādraveyas are on the mountain Tāmrābha; the city of Guha is on the Viśākha hill.

11. O excellent sages, the abode of Suparṇa is on the Śvetodara; the abode of Kubera is on the Piśācaka and that of Viṣṇu is on the Harikūṭa.

12-14a. The residence of the Kinnaras is on the Kumuda; that of Cāraṇas is on the Añjana; Kṛṣṇa has the abode in the mansions of the Gandharvas; there are seven cities of Vidyādharas on the Paṇḍura and they contain all the means of pleasures, O Brahmins. There are seven thousand cities of the Daityas of terrible activities, the enemies of Indra, on the mountain Sahasraśikhara.

14b-16. The residence of the Pannagas (serpents) O Leading sages, is on the Mukuṭa, full of flowers. The residences of Vaivasvata, Soma, Vāyu and the overlord of serpents are in four abodes on the Takṣaka mountain. The abodes of Brahmā, Indra, Viṣṇu, Rudra, Guha, Kubera, Soma and other noble persons are on the Boundary mountains.

17-19. The residence of lord Śiva[306] along with Umā is in the cave of mountain Śrīkaṇṭha. Śrīkaṇṭha is the overlord of all the chiefs of Devas. Undoubtedly the Cosmic Egg functions by the grace of Śrīkaṇṭha. Ananta, Īśa and others are severally the protectors of the Cosmic Egg. They are called Vidyeśvaras as well as Cakravartins (Emperors).

306. Sarvāvāsaḥ—i.e. Śiva. sarvaṁ viśvam āvāso yasya saḥ. ST.

20-21. Now, I shall briefly describe all the abodes presided over by Śrīkaṇṭha on the border mountains. The universe consisting of the mobile and immobile beings is presided over by Śrīkaṇṭha. How can I recount all in detail upto Kālāgni—Śiva ?

CHAPTER FIFTYONE

Various Continents

Sūta said:

1-7. The beautiful forest Bhūtavana, the residence of the different groups of Bhūtas (goblins), is on the highly splendid mountain Devakūṭa. This mountain has great peaks. It is splendid and devoid of impurities. It is made up by gold, Lapis Lazuli, rubies, emeralds, lustrous Gomeda (onyx) and other precious stones. It ranges in a number of branches on all sides. It is adorned with all kinds of trees such as Campaka, Aśoka, Punnāga, Bakula, Asana and Pārijāta. It contains many flocks of birds and herds of elephants. It is variegated in colour with hundreds of minerals. It abounds in wonderful specimens of flowers. Its ridges are covered with bunches of flowers hanging down. Various kinds of animals live therein. It contains many springs and fountains with pure and sweet water. It is adorned with many waterfalls and cascades strewn with flowers. It is beautified by running streams with rafts of flowers floating on them. This Bhūtavana[307] has pleasing colours. It contains many trees with great roots and stems. The thick shade of these trees spreads to ten yojanas all-round.

8. The bright and well-lit abode of lord Mahādeva, the noble-souled Śaṅkara, is there. It is beautified by means of great jewels.

9-10. It has ornamental gateways made of crystal and shaped in different wonderful forms. It has golden rampart walls. It is well adorned with festoons of jewels. There are

307. **Bhūtavana : Bhūta is a name of Śiva; Bhūta-vana—Śiva's forest.**

many splendid gem-set thrones covered with five cloths placed here and there on the ground and occupied by Lord Śiva now and then.

11-16. In that mansion of Śiva there are many apartments decorated with garlands of never-fading flowers of different colours. There are many raised platforms (Maṇḍapas) of different shapes and sizes with crystal columns. The leading goblins (Bhūtas) adored by Brahmā, Indra and Upendra stay there. There are many Pramathas with their faces resembling those of boars, elephants, lions, bears, tigers, camels, vultures, owls, deer, humped bulls and goats. They are stout and huge like great mountain peaks. They are terrible with having huge arms. Some have green hairs on their heads. They are of different shapes and sizes. They are seated in all possible postures and positions. There are splendid Gaṇas such as Nandīśvara, with bright beaming faces and spotless character. They possess supernatural qualities and they resemble Brahmā, Indra and Viṣṇu. The place is never devoid of crowds of immortal beings, (i.e. Devas) who worship the lord of Bhūtas (i.e. Śiva) there, always.

17-19. Śaṅkara, Mahādeva, the lord of Pramhathas is worshipped by the Siddhas, Devas, Gandharvas, Brahmā, and others such as Upendra. They use these musical instruments (drums, etc.) in the course of their worship—Jharjharas (cymbals) conches, Paṭahas, Bherīs, Diṇḍimas, Gomukhas. During their worship they sing in low, middle and high pitches; they also jump, dance and shout in joy. Śaṅkara when being worshipped thus appears as though he has divided into two the beautiful peak (Kailāsa) having the lustre of the conch.

20. Kailāsa[308] is the abode of Kubera, the king of Yakṣas as well as other noble beings.

21. There too, Śiva the lord of Devas has a great abode. He stays there always accompanied by Umā and the chiefs of Gaṇas.

22-25. The holy river Mandākinī with plenty of water and abounding in lotuses flows over the splendid peak Kubera Śikhara; the steps leading to its waters are built of gold and set

308. Kailāsa : p. 100 note 133

with gems. There are golden lotuses with fragrance, very soft to the touch. There are great lilies with sweet smells and leaves resembling blue lapis lazuli. The river is beautifully adorned with big lotuses and lilies. It is frequented by the womenfolk of the Yakṣas and Gandharvas. The waters of the holy and splendid river Mandākinī[309] are used by Devas, Dānavas, Gandharvas, Yakṣas, Rākṣasas and Kinnaras for bathing and drinking purposes.

26. On its northern bank is the splendid abode of Lord Śiva, finished with lapis lazuli and other gems. He, the unchanging lord, stays there.

27. O brahmins, on the eastern and southern banks of the river Kanakanandā there is a forest with thousands of Brāhmins,[310] animals and birds.

28-31. There also the lord sports in a mansion similar to the one on the mountain (Kailāsa) along with Umā and chief Gaṇas. On the western bank of the Nandā[311], a little towards the South there is the city Rudrapurī. It is full of many mansions. In these also Lord Śiva assuming hundreds of forms sports about along with Umā and the Gaṇas. It is called Śivālaya (abode of Śiva). Thus there are hundreds and thousands of shrines of Śiva in every Dvīpa, O excellent sages, on the mountains, in the forests, on the banks of rivers, lakes and on the junctions of waters.

309. Mandākinī : identical with Svargaṅgā. For detail, see Gaṅgāvatāra-varṇana (Vāyu, ch. 47; Matsya ch. 124). According to this description "cold and fresh water from the springs of the Kailāsa mountain flows into a lake from which issues river Mandākinī around which stands the picturesque Nandana forest of vast dimensions." S.M. Ali holds that the river Mandākinī probably refers to the river Umā and the Zhong Chhu, which flow through Gaurī Kuṇḍa (lying on the eastern flank of Mount Kailāsa) in the Rākṣasa Tal (the twin lake of Mānasarovar)".

310. dvija here means 'ascetic brāhmaṇas'.

311. Nandā : Nandā, Alakanandā and Bhāgīrathī are three famous branches of Gaṅgā in the upper course in the Pauri-Garhwal region. According to Pargiter (Mark. p. 383), the nrivers andā and Apara-nandā are often mentioned as situated in the north between the Ganges and Kauśikī or Kosi, and near the river Bāhudā and mount Hemakūṭa.

CHAPTER FIFTYTWO

Geography of the World

Sūta said :

1-2. O best of Brahmins, on every sub-continent there are many holy rivers always full of water and originating from great lakes. They flow in all four directions : east, south, north and west.

3. The storehouse of water in the sky which is called Soma (moon) is the support of all living beings. To Devas, it is the receptacle of nectar.

4-8. From this has originated the river of auspicious waters and it flows in the firmament. With nectarine waters it functions through the seventh path of the wind. This river follows the path of the luminaries. It is frequented by groups of luminaries, and by thousands and crores of stars of the sky.[312] Just like the moon it also goes round and round every day.

Mahāmeru, the tender sporting ground of Śrīkaṇṭha is eighty four thousand yojanas high. Lord Śiva is seated there together with Umā and the chiefs of his Gaṇas and also sports[313] about there for a long time. This auspicious river of holy waters circumambulates the mountain Meru.

9. With its waters agitated by the wind and by its own velocity, the river flows down on all the four inner peaks of the Meru.

312. The Purāṇas describe the three stages in the evolution of Gaṅgā: (i) It is a starry river (i.e. ākāśa-Gaṅgā the Milky Way) in the form of snow. (ii) As the snow falls on the high plateau of the Pamīr (Meru) (v.7) and also on the high ridges and ranges which surround and radiate from the Pāmīr region, it is still 'snowy Gaṅgā' (=hima-Gaṅgā). (iii) As snow melts, it divides into the four main rivers (v. 9) of Asia which radiate in different directions. The Gaṅgā at this stage becomes a stream, or rather streams of water. After passing through thousands of mountains, valleys, forests and caves, it falls into the southern sea (v. 10)

313. Mark the archaic form 'krīḍate' in the ātmanepada for 'krīḍati' in the parasmaipada.

10. After going beyond all the mountains partially it enters the great sea at the behest of lord Śiva.

11. There are hundreds and thousands of rivers branching out from this, which flow through all the sub-continents and continents as well as the mountains therein.

12a. Since the Gaṅgā has gone to the earth from the firmament, there are innumerable small rivers.

12b-13a. In the Ketumāla subcontinent men are dark-coloured.[314] They subsist on jack fruits. Their women have the lustre of blue lotuses. Their life span is ten thousand years.

13b-15a. In the Bhadrāśva sub-continent women are white-coloured, resembling the rays of the moon. They have their staple diet of black mangoes. They are devoid of anguish and agony and fond of sexual pleasures. Mentally meditating on Śiva they live upto ten thousand years. Like the Hiraṇmayas[315] they have freely dedicated their minds to Īśvara.

15b-18. In the sub-continent Ramaṇaka, the living beings subsist on the fruits of the Nyagrodha (the holy fig tree). They live up to eleven thousand five hundred years. They are all white-complexioned and engrossed in the meditation on Śiva. The highly blessed Hairaṇamayas are those dwelling in the forest of Hiraṇmaya. They live upto twelve thousand five hundred years mainly subsisting on the Aśvattha (holy fig tree) fruits. They have also dedicated their minds freely to the lord like the Hiraṇmayas.

19. The Kurus in Kuruvarṣa are those who have fallen down there from the heavenly world. All of them are born by copulation. They are fond of milk[316] and live on milk diet.

20. They love one another and have qualities similar to those of the Cakravāka birds. They are devoid of ailments and sorrow and perpetually seek happiness.

21. They live up to fourteen thousand five hundred years. They have great virility, but do not associate with other women.

314. **kālāḥ=kṛṣṇavarṇāḥ ST. of dark complexion.**

315. **Hairaṇmayāḥ—residents of Hiraṇmaya Varṣa.**

316. **Kṣīriṇaḥ—of milk-white complexion. Contrast with Kālāḥ V. 12.**

22. All the residents of the Kuruvarṣa like the heaven-dwellers die simultaneously. They are delighted and flourishing. They take in all kinds of cooked rice and nectar.

23. They shine always like the moon; they have perpetual youth; they are dark in colour in their bodies and always wear ornaments.

24. Among all the sub-continents in the Jambūdvīpa the sub-continent of Kuruvarṣa is extremely splendid. There is a magnificent palace of the moon-crested lord Śiva. It has the lustre of the moon.

25. In the sub-continent Bhāratavarṣa[317] men are auspicious and their longevity depends on their Karmans. They are said to live for a hundred years. They are of different colours and their bodies are small.

26. They are engaged in the worship of different Devas; they experience the fruits of different kinds of Karmans; they are richly endowed with knowledge and with different materials. They are weak and have very little pleasures.

27-28. Some of them have gone to Indradvīpa[318] and some to Kaseruka. Others have gone to Tāmradvīpa and some to the country Gabhastimat. Some have gone to Nāgadvīpa, some to Saumyadvīpa, and others to the Dvīpa of Gandharvas as well as of Varuṇa. Some of them are Mlecchas and Pulindas born of different castes.

29. In the Eastern parts of the Dvīpa are the Kirātas; in the western extremities the Yavanas; in the middle the Brahmins Kṣatriyas and Vaiśyas. The Śūdras are everywhere.[319]

317. The glorification of Bhārata is one of the common topics in the Purāṇas.

318. Bhārata is one of the nine khaṇḍas of Jambūdvīpa; the other eight being Indradvīpa, Kaśerumān, Tāmra-varṇa, Gabhastimān, Nāga, Saumya, Gandharva, and Varuṇa.

319. The Purāṇas are conscious of the foreign tribes that surrounded Bhārata (cf. *Matsya*. 50. 75-76; *Mark*. 57,8.). The Kirātas mentioned along the eastern limits are probably the uncivilized tribes of the forests and mountains with the Burmese type of features. The Yavanas in the west are Greeks originally and afterwards the Mohammedans.

30-31. They are established there maintaining themselves by worship, warfare and business dealings (respectively). Mutual dealings in connection with the activities of the different castes are related only to virtue, wealth and love. They are interested in their own duties. The conception and pride in performing the duties of the various stages of life are maintained properly.

32. It is only here that human beings endeavour for heavenly pleasures and salvation. O leading sages, only here they pursue the duties specified for each yuga,[320] not elsewhere.

33. In the sub-continent Kimpuruṣa men live up to ten thousand years. Men are golden-complexioned and women resemble the celestial damsels.

34. They are devoid of ailments and sorrow. They are all purified by meditations on Śiva. They have Sattva qualities and the lustre of gold. They live on Plakṣa fruits along with their wives.

35-37a. Men in the sub-continent Harivarṣa have complexion resembling gold. They are persons fallen from the world of Devas. They have divine forms and features in every respect. They worship lord Śiva. They imbibe the auspicious sugarcane-juice. Hence old age does not afflict them and they do not decay. They live upto ten thousand years.

37b-38. In the sub-continent Ilāvṛta that was mentioned by me as situated in the middle of the Dvīpa, the sun does not dlaze and men do not become old. There is no light in Ilāvṛta, neither the sun nor the moon nor the stars.

39. The people there have the lustre of lotuses. Their faces resemble the lotus. Their eyes are like the petals of the lotus. They have the fragrance of the petals of the lotus. They are purified by their meditation on Śiva.

40. The juice of the Jambū fruits constitutes their diet. They are sweet-scented. They have no duties to perform.[321] They have come there from the world of Devas and have neither death nor old age.

320. Since Bhārata alone is Karma-Bhūmi (land for performing action), the yuga-dharmas (duties pertaining to yugas) prevail only here. Cf. *Viṣṇu* cited in *ST*.

321. agnispandāḥ. N.S. reads aniṣpandāḥ (=dharmādiśūnyāḥ *ST*).

41. In the divine sub-continent Ilāvṛta, the excellent men live their full span of life which is thirteen thousand years.

42. By drinking the juice of the Jambū fruits they are not afflicted by old age. They have neither hunger nor fatigue. They do not die a premature death.

43. The gold found there is called Jāmbūnada. It is the divine metal. It shines and resembles a glow-worm.

44. Thus the persons occupying the nine sub-continents have been recounted by me. Their colour, span of life, diet and other things have been succinctly mentioned and not in detail.

45-46. It should be known that the Gandharvas, and celestial nymphs reside in Hemakūṭa. Śeṣa, Vāsuki, Takṣaka and all others live in Niṣadha. The very strong Brāhmaṇas called Yājñikas live on sacrifices. They number thirty three thousands and they live happily on the mountain Nīla, full of lapis lazuli, the Siddhas and Brahmarṣis devoid of impurities.

47-51. The mountain Śveta is the homeland of the Daityas and Dānavas. The mountain Śṛṅgavān (Śṛṅgī) is the abode of Pitṛs. The Himavat is the abode of Yakṣas, goblins and lord Śiva. The lord is seen in all the mountains and forests. He is accompanied by Viṣṇu, Brahmā, Umā, Nandin and Gaṇas. In particular, lord Nīlalohita is seen on the mountains Nīla, Śveta, and Triśṛṅga[322] perpetually together with the Siddhas, Devas and Pitṛs.

The Nīla is of the colour of lapis lazuli. The Śveta is white. The Hiraṇmaya has the colour of the feather of the peacock. The Triśṛṅga is golden in colour. All these lofty mountains are in the Jambūdvīpa.

322. Nīla-Śveta-Triśṛṅge: i.e. on the mountains of Jambū, viz., Nīla Śveta and Triśṛṅga.

CHAPTER FIFTYTHREE

Geography of the World

Sūta said :—

1. There are seven important mountains in each of the seven Dvīpas beginning with Plakṣa. They extend straight in all directions and form the boundaries of the great continents.

2-4. I shall mention the seven great mountains in the Plakṣadvīpa. The first mountain is Gomedaka; the second is Cāndra; the third is Nārada; the fourth is Dundubhi; the fifth is Somaka; the sixth Sūmanas, the same is called Vaibhava; the seventh is Vaibhrāja. These are the seven important mountains in the Plakṣa Dvīpa.

5-9. There are only seven important mountains in the Śālmalīdvīpa. I shall mention them in order. They are Kumuda, Uttama, Balāhaka Droṇa, Kaṅka, Mahiṣa and Kakudmān.

In the Kuśadvīpa there are seven sub-continents and seven Kulaparvatas. I shall mention them by name, in brief. The first mountain is Vidruma, the second is Hemaparvata the third is Dyutimān, the fourth is Puṣpita, the fifth is Kuśeśaya, the sixth Harigiri, the seventh is the glorious mountain Mandara. It is the abode of the great lord. The word Manda denotes the waters. Since the mountain holds the waters, it is called Mandara.

10. The bull-emblemed lord of the universe Śiva, the deity without impurities, stays there in person in an excellent golden palace accompanied by Umā and Nandin.

11-13a Formerly the lord was propitiated in the great holy centre, Avimukta, by the mountain Mandara. He then obtained a great boon. Mahādeva was requested by him for his stay there along with Umā. The lord left Avimukta and stayed on the Mandara along with his Gaṇas, Nandin and Umā. Therefore, he does not leave this mountain.

13b-16. The Kula Parvatas in the Krauñca Dvīpa are seven. They are Krauñca, Vāmanaka, Andhakāraka Divāvṛt, Vivinda, Puṇḍarīka. and Dundubhisvana. These seven mountains in the Krauñca Dvīpa are full of gems.

17-19a. There are seven mountains in the Śākadvīpa. They are Udaya, Raivata, Śyāmaka Rājata, Āmbikeya, Ramya containing all medicinal herbs and Kesarī. It is from this Kesarī that wind is generated.

19b-24. In the Puṣkara Dvīpa there is only one glorious mountain named Mahāśaila. It has wonderful peaks full of jewels. The rocky ridges are lofty. In the eastern half of the Dvīpa it rises very high with ridges of variegated colours. Above the ground level it is fifty thousand yojanas high. The great mountain goes deep below the ground level thirty four thousand yojanas. This mountain stretches over half of the Dvīpa with the Mānasa range to the north of it. Situated near the sea shore it appears like the newly rising moon.

Above the ground level it rises fifty thousand yojanas high. Its total width and girth is also that much. The same is called Mānasa in the western portion of the Dvīpa. The same mountain of great ridges appears split into two due to its position.

25-26. There are two meritorious and splendid Janapadas on either side of the Mānasa mountain, and shining like silver. The sub-continent Mahāvīta[323] is on the exterior of the Mānasa. The Janapada in the interior is called Dhātakīkhaṇḍa.[324]

27-28. The Puṣkara Dvīpa is surrounded by the ocean of sweet water. All round this ocean extends to as much area as the Puṣkara Dvīpa. In girth and extent it is equal to Puṣkara.

In the same manner all the seven Dvīpas are surrounded by oceans severally and there are seven oceans in all.

29. The seventh ocean is beyond all Dvīpas. Thus the comparative sizes of dvīpas and oceans are stated.

30. The great ocean of sweet waters is stationed enveloping the Puṣkara.

31. Beyond that is the situation of the world. The earth is golden and twice in extent. The entire thing is comparable to a single rock.

32. Beyond it is the globular mountain of delimitation.

323-324. Mahāvīta and Dhātakīkhaṇḍa. These are the two provinces of Puṣkara-dvīpa (identified with Japan, Manchuria and SE Siberia). The mountain Mānasa runs in a circle like a full moon and divides the two provinces. The exterior province is Mahāvīta and the interior is Dhātakī.

It is partially dim and partially bright. It is called Lokāloka.

33. O brahmins, this earth abides, as long as this visible-cum-invisible mountain exists. Its height is stated to be ten thousand yojanas.

34. The extent of the great mountain Lokāloka is also that much. The rays of the sun pass over its inner and nether half.

35. In its other half there is perpetual darkness. Hence it is called Lokāloka. Thus, the world Bhūr is explained succinctly.

36-39. The Bhuvarloka is upto the sun. O excellent sages, the Svarloka is upto Dhruva (pole star). There are seven wheels of the wind,[325] viz., Āvaha, Pravaha, Anuvaha, Saṁvaha, Vivaha, Parāvaha and Parivaha, O brahmins, these are the seven wheels of the wind.

O brahmins, the clouds, sun, moon, stars, planets, seven sages (Great Bear) are one above the other. The distance from the surface of the earth up to pole star is fifteen hundred thousand yojanas.

40-43. The solar sphere is one hundred thousand yojanas above the surface of the earth. Above it the chariot of the sun is sixteen thousand yojanas. The Meru is eighty-four thousand yojanas above the surface of the earth. The Maharloka extends to a crore of yojanas above Dhruva. O brahmins, the Janaloka extends to two crores of yojanas beyond Maharloka. Tapoloka extends to four crores of yojanas beyond Janaloka. Beyond that the Brahmaloka extends to six crores of yojanas. O brahmins, the holy worlds in this Cosmic Egg are thus seven.

44. Beneath the seven nether worlds are the crores of hells. They are twentyeight in number beginning with Ghora and ending with Māyā.

45-46a. The sinners are cooked in them in accordance with their past activities. They say that in each of them there are five hells beginning with Raurava and ending with Avīci.

46b-47. The Cosmic Egg has been mentioned by me at the outset. So also the sheaths of the Cosmic Egg. Incidentally the creation of Brahmā too was mentioned in great detail. It should

325. All the Purāṇas mention seven divisions of the strato-sphere.

be known that there are thousands and crores of Eggs like these.

48-52. Since Pradhāna is present everywhere within each of these Cosmic Eggs there are fourteen worlds in all sides as well as above and below. O leading brahmins, the cause of their creation is lord Śiva himself. The eight-bodied Śiva is present in all the Eggs, in the exterior of the Eggs, in the coverings of the Eggs, in the extremities of the darkness and beyond darkness. Wonderful it is, every thing in the universe is the body of the unembodied great Ātman, of Maheśa, of the intelligent Mahādeva.

The mistress of the eight-bodied Śiva is the divine Prakṛti. Mahat etc. are his progeny; all the Paśus (Individual Souls) who identify themselves with their bodies are His servants.[326]

53. The lord Śiva is infinite. He is devoid of beginning and end. He is the Puruṣa. He is identical with the seven principles[327] beginning from Pradhāna. His body is Pradhāna itself, having sixteen limbs.[328] (i.e. the organs of knowledge, organs of action, elements and mind). He himself is Maheśvara and Aṣṭatanu (eight-bodied).

54. It is due to the power of His command that the earth is held steady. So also the mountains, clouds, oceans, luminaries, Devas beginning with Indra, those who go about in the aerial chariots as well as the mobile and immobile beings.

55. Devas including Indra saw the lord devoid of specific characteristics in the guise of a Yakṣa.[329] On seeing him they wondered "What is this?" They went to the Yakṣa. Unable to come to any conclusion, fire and others exerted themselves but became weak and inefficient.

56. O brahmins, in front of that Yakṣa the fire-god could not burn even a blade of grass; the wind-God could not shake a blade of grass; all the leading immortal beings failed to exercise their respective powers over him.

57. At that time, the enemy of Vṛtra (i.e. Indra), the lord

326-328. The aṣṭamūrti (eight-formed, p. 166) Śiva is the householder whose mistress is Prakṛti, whose subjects are intellect, ego and five subtle elements. His eight-formed body has sixteen parts, viz., five gross elements, five organs of action, five organs of knowledge and the mind.

329. Yakṣa—Śiva in the form of Yakṣa—a semidivine being, cf. Brahma-Gītā cited in *ST.*: स्वस्य दर्शयितुं तेषां दुर्ज्ञेयत्वं तथैव च ।। आविर्बभूव सर्वज्ञो यक्षरूपेण हे सुराः ।।

of Devas, the cause of all prosperity, approached him along with the leading Devas. He said to the Yakṣa, the lord of Devas, with great curiosity in his mind, "Who are you, Sir ?"

58. At that time the Yakṣa vanished. Then the splendid-faced daughter of Himavat, Umā, shining gloriously with many auspicious ornaments appeared in front of him.

59. Indra and others asked that unborn daughter of Himavat, Umā, the intensely bright one;—"O Goddess, O excessively refulgent, what is this ? O Umā, who was this shining one in the body of Yakṣa ?"

60. On hearing it, Umā said : "the Yakṣa is invisible." Devas including Indra bowed down to that deity having the gait of a lion, and to Umā unborn and of red, white and black colour.

61. On being honoured by all the leading immortal beings, the deity, the cause of the activity of Devas and Asuras, said:— Formerly I was Prakṛti subservient to the behests of the Puruṣa the Yakṣa.

62. Hence, O brahmins, the entire Egg originated from the unborn at his behest and from the Egg originated Brahmā. The entire world originated from him along with the luminaries. Thus the universe is identical with the Unborn (aja).

CHAPTER FIFTYFOUR

Movements of Luminaries

Sūta said :

1. In order to comprehend the movements of the planets[330] after observing the holy centres of the lord I shall mention the movements of luminaries within the Cosmic Egg succinctly.

330. The system of stars, planets and constellations known as Śiṁśumāra-cakra is conceived as rotating like the potter's wheel. In the vast space the stars are arranged like the body of an alligator. They move around Dhruva (i.e. the fixed centre). But it should be known that Dhruva is relatively fixed, for, in fact, it itself moves in the heavens. (Cf. *Liṅga*. 55. 10; Matsya 125.6) For detail, Matsya. Chs. 124-128.

2-3. In the east of the Meru, the city of Mahendra is situated on the mountain Mānasa; in the south the city of the son of the sun (i.e. Yama); in the west is the city of Varuṇa and in the north the city of Soma (Moon). In all these directions, the deities of the quarters are stationed. They are the cities of Amarāvatī, Saṁyamanī, Sukhā and Vibhā in order.

4. Understand the movement of the sun when he has reached quarter over and above the guardians of the quarters in the course of his southern transit.

5. In his southern transit the sun rushes on like an arrow that is shot. Taking the multitude of luminaries with him he revolves perpetually.

6. O brahmins, when the lordly sun comes to the extremity of the city of Indra the sunrise is seen by all the people in Saṁyamanī.

7. At the same time in Sukhāvatī the sun is seen as at the close of the night. But in Vibhā, the lord, the eye of the universe, i.e. the Sun sets.

8. It has been mentioned by me that just as he absorbs waters in Amarāvatī so also he, the traverser of the firmament, after reaching Saṁyamanī, Sukhā[331] and Vibhā, absorbs waters.

9-11. When there is afternoon in Āgneyī (i.e. south-east), O brahmins, it is forenoon in the south-west. When it is terrible latter half of the night in the north-west, it is the earlier part of the night in the north-east. Similarly, when the sucker of waters (i.e. the sun) moves about in the middle of Puṣkara[332] the mountain to the north of Mānasa, he traverses a thirtieth part of the earth in a Muhūrta (48 mts). Understand this number in yojanas travelled in a Muhūrta.

12-17. The speed of the noble-souled sun per Muhūrta is three million one hundred and fifty thousand yojanas. When the sun moves to the southern quarter with this speed from the north through the middle of Puṣkara during his northern transit and when he moves into the northern direction (from

331. Sukhā or Suṣā. It is the capital of Varuṇa in the western direction and is the same as Susā of the ancient Achemenian empire in Iran.

332. Puṣkara *or* sky, atmospheric region. Cf. Viśva cited in ST. "Puṣkaram paṅkaje vyomni".

the south) through the Mānasa hill in the course of his southern transit, he, of great splendour, passes over one hundred and eighty maṇḍalas (degrees of space). The northern and southern transits are called the exterior and interior (parts of the celestial sphere). The sun traverses through these (180) maṇḍalas everyday (both ways). Just as the end of the potters' wheel whirls, more quickly (than its middle part), the lord (sun) traverses quickly in his southern transit.[333]

18-19 Hence he traverses a greater area in a short time. In the course of Dakṣiṇāyana (southern transit) the sun traverses to the extent of thirteen and a half stars (i.e. star spaces) during the day time in only twelve muhūrtas; while during the night time of eighteen muhūrtas he covers as many stars (star spaces).[334]

20. Just as the middle of the potter's wheel moves more slowly (than the end part) so also in the Uttarāyaṇa (northern transit) the sun moves slowly.

21-25. Hence he traverses a smaller area in the course of a longer time. That chariot of the sun is occupied by Ādityas, sages, Gandharvas, Apsarases, Grāmaṇīs, Serpents, and Rākṣasas. The thousand-rayed sun emits his rays in front, behind, below and above. Thereby he illuminates the excellent assembly of Brahmā. During the sandhyās (dawn and dusk) the brahmins and sages offer water-libations. With these waters, the sun kills the demons as and when they come near him and then goes ahead.

333. The text here appears highly defective. Uttarāyaṇa or northern transit is the period from 22nd Dec. to 21st June and Dakṣiṇāyana or southern transit is from 22nd June to 21st Dec. During the former, the sun appears to travel from Capricorn to Cancer (through Aquanus, Pisces etc.) and during the latter from Cancer to Capricorn. But as the earth revolves round all the signs of the Zodiac once a day, the sun is said to travel over these, every day. The word maṇḍala is used in the peculiar sense of degree as no other meaning will suit the context.

334. A star space is 360°27 or $13\frac{1}{3}$° $13\frac{1}{2}$ Star space is thus equal to 180°. In other words the whole consists of 360° which is the space of the 27 constellations Aśvinī etc. The sun is visible at any time only on half of the sphere (called day). Hence half of the sphere is 180° or $13\frac{1}{2}$ star spaces. The reference here is to that day when the day time is shortest (i.e. 9 hours 36 minutes) and night longest (14 hours 24 minutes) which occurs in India in Kashmir.

During the latter part of the uttarāyaṇa the day extends to eighteen muhūrtas, during which the sun moves slowly. He covers the extent of thirteen and a half stars during the night consisting of twelve muhūrtas and as many stars during the day consisting of eighteen muhūrtas.

26. Just as the wheel whirls slowly at the nave, so also Dhruva whirls like the lump of clay in the middle.

27-28. Those who know the ancient lore, say that thirty muhūrtas constitute a day and a night during which the sun traverses the space in between the two limits (i.e. the solstitial points). Just as the nave of the wheel of the porter remains there alone (i.e. without moving) so also Auttānapāda (i.e. Dhruva) rotates (without moving) as the leader of the luminaries along with the planets.

29-33. The group of the sages and the luminaries moves in accordance with his will (mind). Presided over by him the sun, along with the wind, takes up water from everywhere.

The son of Uttānapāda attained the state of Dhruva, thanks to the favour of Viṣṇu. It was obtained by Auttānapāda on account of his father.

The waters drunk by the sun penetrate the moon gradually and from the moon they drip down to the clouds. On being tossed about by the wind, the cluster of clouds causes shower on the earth. The word bhāskara (sun) is derived as follows:— Bhāsayet tena bhāskaraḥ—(He who illuminates is bhāskara). There is no destruction of water. The same water revolves.

34-38. For the welfare of creatures, the waters have been evolved by lord Śiva as their ultimate resort. The waters alone constitute Bhū, Bhuvaḥ, Svaḥ, anna (cooked rice) as well as nectar. The waters are the vital breaths of the worlds, the living beings, the worlds themselves. Of what avail is much talk? The world of mobile and immobile beings is constituted by the waters.

Lord Śiva is the overlord of the waters. He is glorified as such. The universe is identical with him. What is there to wonder at in this? The designation Nārāyaṇa was acquired by Viṣṇu by the grace of the waters. Viṣṇu is the abode of worlds and the waters constitute his abode. When the mobile and immobile beings are being burned by the fire and tossed up as smoke by the wind, the vapours that go up urged by the wind form the clouds.

39-40. Hence the mixture of smoke, fire and wind is called cloud. The word abhra (cloud) is derived as follows: "that which showers water." The lord of the clouds is the thousand-eyed Indra. The cloud originating from sacrificial smoke is conducive to the welfare of the twice-born. The cloud originating from the smoke of the forest fires, is conducive to the welfare of the forests.

41. O brahmins, the cloud originating from the smoke of the dead bodies brings about evil. The cloud originating from the smoke of the fire during magic rites brings about the destruction of living beings.

42. Thus there is weal or woe unto the worlds due to different kinds of smokes. Hence a man shall stifle the smoke arising from the black magic rites.

43. If a brahmin were to perform black magic rites without covering up the smoke thereof, he will wantonly become the cause of destruction of the world.

44. O men of holy rites, the clouds that are receptacles of waters shower waters at the behest of the wind for six months for the welfare of the worlds.

45. The thunder pertains to the wind; the lightning arises from fire. O leading sages, the origin of snow from those clouds is in three ways.

46-48. The word abhra is derived thus:— na bhraśyanti yataḥ (since they do not become destroyed).

The word megha is derived as mehanāt meghah—It is called megha because it makes waters.

The clouds are of different kinds, viz.,—Kāṣṭhāvāhas, Vairiñcyas and Pākṣas.

When kāṣṭhās (sacrificial wigs) soaked in ghee come into contact with fire, smoke is generated (and this smoke forms the clouds). The origin of the second type of clouds is from the exhaled breath of Brahmā. The origin of the third type of clouds is from the wings of mountains chopped off by Indra.

The clouds arising from fires are auspicious and their place of resort is Āvaha (a particular region of wind).

49-53a. All those clouds arising from the breath of Brahmā

are in the layer of the wind Pravaha, while the clouds originating from Pakṣa (wings)[335] —Puṣkara and others —shower water. They are respectively silent, noisy and destructive[336]. The different clouds behave differently—Some rain in showers; some have cool winds blowing for a long time, some are enliveners; some are weak being devoid of lightning and thunder. Some stay here and there in the sky within a krośa (3 kms) from the surface of the earth. All the clouds clinging to the mountains are within half a krośa. The clouds (called) meghas stay within a yojana from the surface of the earth. They shower much water on the earth because it is possible for them to do so. They are equipped with lightning.

53b-56. Their way of making downpours of three types has thus been narrated to you. The clouds of the Pakṣaja type originate from the clipped wings of the mountains. They are called kalpajas (born in the kalpas). These autumnal clouds shower at night towards the close of the kalpa bringing about destruction.

When the Pakṣaja, Puṣkara and other clouds shower water, everything becomes a vast sea of water. During the night, the lord lies down there.

O leading brahmins, the smoke of the clouds arising from fire, from the exhaled breath and from the clipped wings, is refreshingly enlivening.

57. The showers of the clouds Pauṇḍras, (i.e., those falling in the land of Puṇḍra) are accompanied by lightning, are cool and hence conducive to plant (growth). They are ice-cool and look like the spray of waters from elephants' trunks.

58. The clouds called Gāṅgas originate from the waters of Gaṅgā. Through the wind in the Parāvaha region these agitate the mountains, rivers and elephants of the quarters.

59. The water separated from the clouds goes from one mountain to another. The wind Parāvaha takes the cloud to the Himavat mountain.

60. O brahmins, the remaining shower after crossing the

335. Puṣkarādyāḥ : Puṣkara, Āvarta, etc. comprise a class of clouds that rain in torrents at the dissolution of the world.

336. duṣṭāśāḥ-duṣṭā āśā yeṣām, pralayakarāḥ ST. of wicked intention since they cause destruction of the world.

Himavat approaches the sub-continent Bhārata in order to make the other side flourish.

61. The showers have been recounted now. They are of two types being conducive to the increase of two types of vegetation. I shall mention them briefly according to my knowledge.

62. The sun of great splendour, the lord with the eye of the universe is the creator of rains. O excellent brahmins, he is the great Īśāna, Śiva himself.

63-64. He alone is the splendour, power and strength, O brahmins. He is fame himself. He is the eye, ear, mind, Mṛtyu, soul, Manyu, the quarters and the interstices, truth, order, discipline, wind, firmament, planets, the guardians of the quarters, Viṣṇu, Brahmā, Rudra and Maheśvara himself.

65-68. This glorious thousand-rayed deity lord Śiva is very auspicious. He has eight hands, a body semi-female and three eyes. He is the overlord of Devas. O brahmins, it is due to his favour alone that rain of various kinds occurs. The sun takes up water by his rays in order to give it back thousandfold. There is neither increase nor decrease of water, if we consider it duly. The wind presided over by Dhruva withdraws the rain. It falls off the planet sun and spreads through the sphere of the stars. At the close of the movement, it re-enters the sun and is presided over by Dhruva.

CHAPTER FIFTYFIVE

The sun's chariot[337]

1-2. I shall briefly describe the chariot of the sun, moon and other planets as also how the sun traverses drinking up the waters.

337. The solar car. Cf. *Matsya*, Ch. 125. For the 12 Heptads of the solar system Cf. *MP.—A Study* pp. 211-212. The solar system with the sun as the central point is conceived as a chariot which moves upto 180 degrees both north and south of the equator (V. 14; also *Matsya*, 125.57).

The chariot of the sun has been created by Brahmā for a specific purpose. O leading brahmins, it is conceived through the parts of the year.

3. The golden chariot of the sun is the abode of all Devas. It has a single wheel with five spokes and three naves.

4. Its length and breadth is nine thousand yojanas. Twice that length is the distance between the driver's box and the poleshaft.

5. The horses are stationed on the side where the wheel is. They are unattached[338] but appear to be yoked. There are seven horses. They are evolved out of the vedic passages and metres.[339]

6. The horses are bound to the side of the wheel. The axle is fitted to the poleshaft. The chariot revolves along with the wheel and the horses, and the poleshaft revolves along with the axle.

7. The axle prompted by the poleshaft whirls along with the single wheel. It is the intelligent Dhruva (Pole star) that urges the luminaries by means of the wind and the rays (or by the wind which acts as reins).

8. There are two reins in the chariot. They are united to the extremities of the yoke and the axle. The chariot tied by means of the reins to the yoke and the axle revolves by the grace of Dhruva.

9. As the chariot whirls and moves along the firmament there shall be circles of bright lustre. The extremities of the yoke and the axle are to the right of the chariot.

10. When the horses beyond the wheel[340] are pulled by Dhruva by means of reins, both of them (the yoke and axle) as also the reins follow the poleshaft that whirls.

11-13. The extremity of the yoke and the axle of this chariot which has the steed of wind whirls in all directions like a rope fixed to a nail. In the course of Uttarāyaṇa as the chariot moves about in the maṇḍalas the reins increase in size (i.e.

338. asaṅgaiḥ=antarikṣagaiḥ ST. those that move in the void.

339. The seven horses of the solar car are the seven metres, viz., gāyatrī, uṣṇik, anuṣṭup, bṛhatī, paṅkti, triṣṭup and jagatī.

340. Vicakrāśve—when the horses, wheel and Aruṇa the driver (are secured by Dhruva).

are let loose). In the course of the Dakṣiṇāyana, when the chariot moves about in the maṇḍalas the reins are pulled inwards. In either case, the reins are operated by Dhruva and then the sun seated within, moves about in the maṇḍalas.

14-15. The distance between the two solstices consists of one hundred and eighty degrees. The sun moves about the maṇḍalas externally as the reins are being released by Dhruva. He then encircles the maṇḍalas and moves quickly.

16. Devas and sages perpetually worship lord Bhāskara, who is himself Bhava and Īśvara day and night.

17. That chariot is occupied by Devas, Ādityas sages, Gandharvas, Apsarases as well as serpents, Rākṣasas, and Grāmaṇīs.

18. These reside within the sun for two months in succession and develop and nourish the auspicious sun by means of their splendour.

19. The sages eulogise the sun by means of hymns. The Gandharvas and Apsarases worship him by music and dance.

20. The Grāmaṇīs, Yakṣas and Bhūtas hold the reins. The serpents bear the sun and Yātudhānas (Rākṣasas) follow him.

21. The Vālakhilyas surround the sun from his rise to his setting and accompany him. In this manner these reside in the sun for two months in succession.

22-23. O leading brahmins, the following twelve months constitute the human year:—Madhu (Caitra), Mādhava (Vaiśākha), Śukra (Jyeṣṭha), Śuci (Āṣāḍha), Nabhas (Śrāvaṇa), Nabhasya (Bhādrapada), Iṣa (Āśvina) Ūrja (Kārttika), Sahas (Mārgaśirṣa) Sahasya (Pauṣa), Tapas (Māgha) and Tapasya (Phālguna).

24. The (six) Ṛtus (seasons) are Vāsantika (Spring), Graiṣma, (summer) Vārṣika (rainy season) Śarad (autumn), Hima (early Winter) and Śiśira (late Winter)

25.44

The seven groups accompany and abide in the sun, as follows:—

1. Devas are twelve in number. They nourish the sun by means of lustre. They are:—Dhātṛ, Aryaman, Mitra, Varuṇa,

Indra, Vivasvān, Pūṣan, Parjanya, Aṁśu, Bhaga, Tvaṣṭṛ and Viṣṇu.

2. The sages are twelve in number. They eulogise the sun by means of hymns. They are:— Pulastya, Pulaha, Atri, Vasiṣṭha, Aṅgiras, Bhṛgu, Bharadvāja, Gautama, Kaśyapa, Kratu, Jamadagni and Visvāmitra.

3. The serpents are twelve in number. They bear the great lord Sun. They are :— Vāsuki, Kaṅkaṇīkara, Takṣaka, Nāga, Elāpatra, Śaṅkhapāla, Airāvata (Irāvān), Dhanañjaya Mahāpadma, Karkoṭaka, Kambala and Aśvatara.

4. The twelve excellent Gandharvas worship the sun that takes in water by means of Songs. They are:—Tumburu, Nārada, Hāhā, Hūhū, Viśvāvasu, Ugrasena, Surugi, Parāvasu Citrasena, Ūrṇāyu, Dhṛtarāṣṭra and Sūryavarcas.

5. The twelve Apsarases worship the sun by their charming Tāṇḍava dance. They are:—Kṛtasthalā of splendid face, the divine lady Puñjikasthalī of splendid hips, Menakā, Sahajanyā, Pramlocā of sweet smiles, Anumlocā, Ghṛtācī, Viśvācī, Urvaśī also known as Pūrvacitti, the gentle lady Tilottamā and Rambhā of lotus-like face.

6. The twelve Grāmaṇīs hold the reins. They are:— Rathakṛt, Rathaujas, Rathacitra, Subāhu, Rathasvana, Varuṇa, Suṣeṇa, Senajit, Tārkṣya, Ariṣṭanemi, Kṣatajit and Satyajit.

7. Then there are twelve Yātudhānas. Wielding their weapons they accompany the sun. They are:—Rakṣoheti, Praheti, Pauruṣeya, Badha, Sarpa, Vyāghra, Apa, Vāta, Vidyut, Divākara, Brahmopeta the leading Rākṣasa and Yajñopeta.

These seven groups of twelve members in each are proud of their position.

Two from each of these seven groups occupy the sun for two months. The details are given below:

45-48.

During the Months of Caitra-Vaiśākha

1.	*Twelve Devas*	Dhātṛ and Aryaman
2.	*Twelve Sages*	Pulastya and Pulaha
3.	*Twelve Serpents*	Vāsuki and Kaṅkaṇīkara

4. Twelve Gandharvas	Tumburu and Nārada
5. Twelve Apsarases	Kṛtasthalā and Puñjikasthalā
6. Twelve Grāmaṇīs	Rathakṛt and Rathaujas
7. Twelve Yātudhānas	Rakṣoheti and Praheti

49-51.

During the Months of Jyeṣṭha and Aṣāḍha

1. Devas	Mitra and Varuṇa
2. Sages	Atri and Vasiṣṭha
3. Serpents	Takṣaka and Nāga
4. Gandharvas	Hāhā and Hūhū
5. Apsarases	Menakā and Sahajanyā
6. Grāmaṇīs	Subāhu and Rathacitra
7. Yātudhānas	Pauruṣeya and Badha

52-54.

During Śrāvaṇa and Bhādrapada

1. Devas	Indra and Vivasvān
2. Sages	Aṅgiras and Bhṛgu
3. Serpents	Elāpatra and Śaṅkhapāla
4. Gandharvas	Viśvāvasu and Ugrasena
5. Apsarases	Pramlocā and Anumlocā.
6. Grāmaṇīs	Rathasvana and Varuṇa
7. Yātudhānas	Sarpa and Vyāghra

55-57.

During Āśvina and Kārttika

1. Devas	Pūṣā and Parjanya
2. Sages	Bhāradvāja and Gautama
3. Serpents	Irāvān and Dhanañjaya
4. Gandharvas	Suruci and Parāvasu
5. Apsarases	Ghṛtācī and Viśvācī
6. Grāmaṇīs	Suṣeṇa and Senajit
7. Yātudhānas	Āpa and Vāta

58-61.

During Mārgaśīrṣa and Pauṣa

1. Devas	Aṁśu and Bhaga
2. Sages	Kaśyapa and Kratu

3. Serpents	Mahāpadma and Karkoṭaka
4. Gandharvas	Citrasena and Urṇāyu
5. Apsarases	Urvaśī and Pūrvacitti
6. Grāmaṇīs	Tārkṣya and Ariṣṭanemi
7. Yātudhānas	Vidyut and Divākara.

62-65

During Māgha and Phālguna

1. Devas	Tvaṣṭṛ and Viṣṇu
2. Sages	Jamadagni and Viśvāmitra
3. Serpents	Kambala and Aśvatara
4. Gandharvas	Dhṛtarāṣṭra and Sūryavarcas
5. Apsarases	Tilottamā and Rambhā
6. Grāmaṇīs	Rathajit and Satyajit
7. Yātudhānas	Brahmopeta and Yajñopeta

66. These deities occupy the sun for two months (in different groups as mentioned above). These twelve Heptads are the governing forces during the twelve months of the solar year.

67-69. The deities nourish and develop the sun by their splendour. The sages eulogise the sun by the hymns of the Vedas. The Gandharvas and the Apsarases worship him by their music and dance. The Grāmaṇīs, Yakṣas and Bhūtas hold the reins; the serpents bear the sun, and Yātudhānas follow him; Vālakhilyas lead the sun to his setting place after surrounding him at the time of his rise.

70-71. The sun is nourished by the splendour of all these. The sun blazes in accordance with their splendour, penance, yogic power, Mantras, Dharmas and strength. These stay in the sun in groups, for two months each.

72-73. The sages, Devas, Gandharvas, Serpents, groups of Apsarases, Grāmaṇīs, Yakṣas, and Yātudhānas mainly—these blaze, shower rain, illuminate, blow, create and remove the evil activities of living beings. They are glorified as such.

74. They destroy the merits of the wicked and the sins of good persons in certain cases.

75. They are seated in an aerial chariot that is divine, that has the speed of the wind and that can go wherever it wills. These move ahead along with the sun throughout the day.

76. They shower rain. They blaze, they delight. O Sages, they protect all the living beings and firmament from destruction.

77. They take pride and identify themselves with their positions in all the manvantaras of the past, present and future.

78. These seven groups live in the sun in groups of fourteen in all the fourteen manvantaras.

79. O leading sages, the activities of the intelligent lord of Devas have been recounted, some in brief and some in detail, in accordance with what I have heard and how they had happened.

80. These seven groups of twelve deities in each are those who take pride in their positions and identify themselves with them. They reside in the sun for two months in the above order.

81. Thus the sun, the harbinger of the day moves ahead quickly in a single-wheeled chariot[341] drawn by seven green imperishable horses.

82. He whirls day and night in his chariot which has a single wheel. He traverses in heaven over the seven continents and oceans with the help of seven groups.

CHAPTER FIFTYSIX

Description of the Moon

Sūta said :—

1. The Moon traverses the stars stationed in its orbit. His chariot has three wheels and the horses are on either side.

2. The chariot is fitted with three wheels, each with hundred spokes. The horses are white in colour and ten in number. They are divine and stout. They are not connected with the yoke. They have the speed of the mind.

3. The moon traverses in this chariot along with Devas

341. ekacakra—The single wheel of the solar chariot is represented by the year (saṁvatsara).

and Pitṛs. It has white rays in the form of sparkling water particles.

4-6. The moon increases in force in the beginning of the bright half and is stationed in the way of the sun. Day by day it gets refilled till the end of that half. The sun develops and nourishes it. It is drunk up by Devas during the dark half.[342] It is being drunk in continuity for fifteen days by Devas. The sun refills it part by part by his single ray Suṣumnā : Thus the physical body of the moon is developed and nourished by the vigour of the sun.

7-10a. On the full moon day it appears with its full white disc. Beginning with the second and ending with the fourteenth day in the dark half, Devas drink up the moon that was nourished and developed day by day during the bright half. They drink the watery honey and nectar that had been accumulated in the course of half a month, thanks to the splendour of the sun. They sit near the moon for a single night on the full moon day for drinking up the nectar from the moon, along with the sages and Pitṛs.

10b-13. The digits of the moon facing the sun get diminished daily, being drunk up from the beginning to the end of the dark half. Thirtysix thousand three hundred and thirty three Devas drink the moon. After the moon has been drunk for half a month, day by day by them, those excellent Devas go away on the new moon day. On the new moon day the Pitṛs occupy the Moon.

14-18. When the fifteenth part remains as the last digit, the groups of Pitṛs occupy this in the afternoon. For the duration of two kalās (units of time) they drink up the remaining digit—the nectar of svadhā that has oozed out of the rays on the Amāvāsyā day. After drinking the nectar they attain full satiety for the whole of month and then go away. By the time the remaining digit of the moon drunk by the Pitṛs gets dissolved, a fifteenth part is replenished. The increase and the decrease of the moon in the beginning of each fortnight is on the sixteenth day.[343] The increase in the moon is thus due to the sun.

342. Cf. suṣumṇaḥ sūryaraśmiś candramā gandharvaḥy .TS 3.4.7.1.
343. ṣoḍaśyām=on the sixteenth, i.e. on the new-moon day.

CHAPTER FIFTYSEVEN

Movements of the Planets[344]

Sūta said : —

1-5. The chariot of the son of the Moon (i.e. Budha—Mercury) is fitted with eight horses, tawny-coloured and very splendid. It has the characteristics of water and fire.

The chariot of Śukra (Venus) the preceptor of Daityas is fitted with ten stout horses of different colours. It is earthen in nature.

The chariot of Bhauma (Mars) is golden, splendid and fitted with eight horses.

The horse of Jīva (Jupiter) is also golden and fitted with eight horses.

The chariot of Manda[345] (Saturn) is made of iron. It is fitted with ten black horses and is watery in nature.

The chariots of Rāhu and Ketu are fitted with eight horses each. All these planets are bound to Dhruva (Pole Star) by reins which are of the form of wind. Made to whirl by the Pole star they move ahead.

6. There are as many rays as there are stars. All of them are bound to the Pole star. While revolving (round it) they make it revolve also.

7. The stars and the luminaries, urged by the circular gusts of wind, move like fire brands. Since the wind bears the luminaries, it is called Pravaha.

8. Along with the planets and constellations, the sun and stars occupy the firmament in a circle looking upwards and sideways.

9. Presided over (i.e. controlled) by Dhruva they circumambulate Dhruva. They move on in the firmament to see Lord Dhruva that acts like the pivot.

344. Chapters 56-57 describe the movement of the planets—Soma, Budha, Maṅgala, Bṛhaspati, Śukra, Śani and Rāhu.

345. alāta-cakra-vat : The imagery of the wheel implies a fixed centre (meḍhībhūtaṁ dhruvaṁ divi, ch. 57.9) to which the whole system of moving stars is secured by certain pulls, spoken of as winds. (vāta-raśmibhiḥ, ibid, V. 5; Matsya 125.7; vātānīkamayair bandhaiḥ.)

10. The diameter of the sun is nine thousand Yojanas. Its circular area is three times this.

11. The extent of the moon is twice that of the Sun. Rāhu assumes a size equal to them and moves ahead beneath them.

12. The abode of Rāhu is full of darkness and is the third (one in size) because it is evolved out of the circular shadow of the earth.

13. The diameter, the circumference and the distance in yojanas of Bhārgava (Venus) is a sixteenth part of that of the moon.

14-18. Bṛhaspati (Jupiter) is of three-fourths of the size of Venus. Mars and Saturn are three-fourths of the size of Bṛhaspati. Budha (Mercury) is three-fourths of their size in extent and circumference. The stars and constellations, that have a body are equal to Budha in extent and circumference. The knower of truth must note that the stars that are in conjunction with the moon are ordinarily known as Ṛkṣas. The spheres of the comparatively smaller stars extend to five, four, three or two yojanas. Over all these there are still clusters of smaller stars which extend only to two hundred yojanas. There is none smaller than this.

19-20. Over and above these starry spheres are the three planets viz., Saturn, Jupiter and Mars, which travel at a great distance from them. They should be known as slow-moving ones.

There are four other great planets beneath them, viz. the Sun, Moon, Mercury and Venus. They traverse quickly.

21. Altogether there are as many crores of stars as there are constellations. They too are stationed in the orbit of constellations due to the restraining force of Dhruva.

22-26. The sun that has seven horses has an upper and a lower position by turns. When the sun is in his northern transit and when the moon on the full moon nights, appears quickly because its position is above, but the rays are not very clear, the moon (?) then is in the southern orbit that is lower. The sun covered by the line of the earth on Full moon and New Moon days is seen at the usual time, but it sets quickly. Hence on the New-Moon day the moon is in the northern orbit. It is invariably not seen in the southern path on account of the movement of the planets and because it is enveloped by the shadow of the sun. On the equinotical days the sun and the moon rise and set simultaneously.[346]

27-28. In the northern orbits they rise and set without any difference in time on new moon and full moon days. They should then be known as following the groups of luminaries. When the sun is in the southern transit, it moves ahead beneath all other planets.

29. Keeping his sphere wider the moon revolves above it (the sun). All the groups of constellations move above the moon.

30. Mercury is above all constellations; Venus is above Mercury. Mars is above Venus and Jupiter is above Mars.

31. Saturn is above it. Above Saturn is the sphere of seven sages (Great Bear) and Dhruva (Pole Star) is stationed above the seven sages.

32-39. By knowing the region of Viṣṇu, beyond all these, one is liberated from sin. Two hundred thousand Yojanas above constellations, stars, the planets—Sun and Moon which are united with divine refulgence, move ahead day and night in due order. They come into contact with the constellations everyday. Hence they are sometimes stationed below, sometimes above and sometimes in a straight line. They glance at the subjects (below) simultaneously when in conjunction or when separated.

There are six seasons but of five distinct features. They overlap one another and their combination should be understood by learned men without overlapping. O brahmins, thus the movement of planets has been succinctly mentioned in the case of the sun and other planets as I have heard and observed. The thousand-rayed lord Sun was crowned as the overlord of planets by the lotus-born Brahmā, like Guha who was crowned by Rudra.

Hence, for the realization of purpose and (to ward off evils) at the time of harassment of the planets and the sun, the worship of the planets should be pursued by good men, Offerings should be made to fire in accordance with the injunctions of the Śāstras.

346. Cf. Viṣṇu, cited in ST. मेषादौ च तुलादौ च मैत्रेयविषुवत्स्थितः ।
तदा तुल्यमहोरात्रं करोति तिमिरापहः ॥

CHAPTER FIFTYEIGHT

Coronation of the Sun and others

The sages said :

1. Tell us now how Brahmā Prajāpati, who is the soul of all, crowned as overlords, Devas, Daityas and others.

Sūta said:

2. Lord Brahmā crowned the Sun as the overlord of planets. Brahmā, Prajāpati, crowned Soma (Moon) as the lord of constellations and medicinal herbs.

3. (He crowned) Varuṇa as the lord of the Waters; the leading Yakṣa[347] (Kubera) as the lord of riches; Viṣṇu as the lord of Ādityas; and Pāvaka (fire) as the lord of Vasus.

4. (He crowned) Dakṣa as the lord of Prajāpatis; Indra as the lord of Maruts; Prahlāda, the leading Daitya as the overlord of Daityas and Dānavas.

5. (He crowned) Dharma as the overlord of the Pitṛs; Nirṛti as the overlord of Rākṣasas; Rudra as the overlord of Paśus (Individual Souls) and Nandin, the leader of Gaṇas,[348] as the overlord of Bhūtas (goblins).

6. (He crowned) Vīrabhadra as the overlord of heroes; Bhayaṅkara (the terrible one) as the overlord of Piśācas (ghosts); Cāmuṇḍā who is bowed to by Devas as the sovereign of Mothers.

7. (He crowned) lord Nīlalohita, lord of the chiefs of Devas, as the overlord of Rudras; the elephant-faced lord Vināyaka, born of Vyoman[349] as the overlord of obstacles.

8. (He crowned) goddess Umā as the sovereign of women; goddess Sarasvatī as the sovereign of speech; Viṣṇu as the overlord of the wielders of Māyā and himself[350] as the overlord of the worlds.

9. (He crowned) Himavat as the overlord of the mountains; the Ganges (born of sage Jahnu) as the sovereign of the rivers; and ocean the storehouse of the waters as the lord of all seas.

347. yakṣa-puṅgavam : chief of the Yakṣas, i.e. Kubera.
348. gaṇa-nāyakam : read nandinaṁ gaṇa for nandināṁ gaṇa.
349. vyomajam : son of Śiva, i.e. Gaṇeśa.
350. svātmānam : his own self, i.e. Brahmā.

10-12. Brahmā crowned the Plakṣa and Aśvattha as the lords of trees; he made Citraratha the lord of Gandharvas, Vidyādharas and Kinnaras; Vāsuki of terrible vigour as the lord of Serpents and Takṣaka of terrible vigour as the lord of Sarpas (Cobras). He made the leading elephant Airāvata of terrible valour the lord of elephants. He made Garuḍa the lord of birds. He made Uccaiśśravas (the horse of Indra) the king of horses.

13. He made the lion the lord of animals; the bull the lord of the kine and Śarabha (the fabulous eight-footed beast) the lord of lions; the incomprehensible Guha the lord of all commanders-in-chief and Lakulīśa the lord of Śrutis and Smṛtis.

14. He made Sudharman, Śaṅkhapāla, Ketumān and Hemaroman the overlords of all quarters in order.[351]

15. (He crowned) Pṛthu as the lord of the earth; Maheśvara as the lord of all; the bull-bannered omniscient lord Śaṅkara as the overlord among the four deities.[352]

16. By the grace of Śiva, the lord crowned these in due order. After crowning them at first the lord of the worlds felt fully satisfied.

17. O leading sages, this has been mentioned to you in detail: These persons of special characteristics were all crowned by Lord Brahmā the source of origin of the universe.

CHAPTER FIFTYNINE

The form of solar rays

Sūta said :

1. On hearing this, the sages became overwhelmed with doubts and again asked Romaharṣaṇa.

351. The four guardian deities, viz. Sudharman, Śaṅkhapāla, Ketumān ,Hemaroman were consecrated in their respective quarters. Cf. Viṣṇu सुधर्मा शङ्खपालश्च कर्दमस्यात्मजौ द्विज । हिरण्यरोमा चैवान्यश्चतुर्थः केतुमानपि । निर्द्वन्द्वा निरभिमाना विस्रस्ता निष्परिग्रहाः । लोकपालाः स्थिता ह्येते लोकालोके चतुर्दिशम् ॥ cited in *ST*.

352. caturmūrtiṣu : in four forms, viz. Viśva, Prājña, Taijasa, and Turīya.

The sages said :

2. O Sūta, most excellent among the speakers, kindly tell us in detail the exact nature of the luminaries briefly.

3. On hearing their words, Sūta of great concentration and purity spoke these weighty words in order to clear their doubts.

4. In this matter I shall tell you what has already been stated by highly intelligent persons[353] with tranquil wisdom. I shall recount the movement of the sun and the moon.

5. I shall tell you how the sun, the moon and other planets are the abodes of Devas. Thereafter, I shall mention the three[354] types of fires and their origin.

6-9. The three types of fire are : the divine fire, the elemental fire and the terrestrial fire.

When the night of Brahmā born of the unmanifest reached the stage of dawn, this visible universe was one that had not been analyzed. It was still enveloped in the nocturnal darkness. When the worlds were still in the state of destruction, when a fourth of the period still remained, the self-born lord, he who achieves all the affairs of the worlds, moved about like a glow-worm, with a desire to manifest. At the beginning of the world, he created Agni (heat) in combination with earth and water. The Lord gathered these together to make it shine and then divided it into three.

10-11. The fire in the world of mankind is called Pārthiva. The fire that blazes in the sun is called Śuci. The fire born of lightning is known as Abja (i.e. originating from the water portion). I shall now mention their characteristics. There are three types of fires with water within, viz., Vaidyuta, Jāṭhara (gastric) and Saura (Solar).

12-13. Hence, imbibing water through his rays the sun blazes (further). The Abja (waterborn—lightning) fire even when immersed in water is not quenched by it. The fire that is

353. mahāprājñaiḥ : by the most intelligent men, i.e. by Vyāsa and others.

354. Threefold fire : (i) celestial, as represented by the sun, (ii) atmospheric, as symbolized by the lightning, (iii) terrestrial, which is used for the sacrificial and household purpose. Fire is called Pāvaka on earth, Śuci in heaven and Vaidyuta in firmament.

within the stomach of men is not put out by water. The gastric fire emits flames (i.e. heat), but is devoid of lustre.[355]

14-19. When the sun is setting, the solar lustre becomes a circular mass without heat and enters the fire at night through his rays. Hence the light of fire is seen even from a distance at night. The heat is transmitted to the sun from fire, when the sun rises. Only partially does the terrestrial fire enter the sun. Hence the fire continues to blaze. Thus the fire element in both terrestrial and solar fires contains heat and light. They penetrate mutually and develop each other. In the northern and southern hemispheres of the earth, the fire and the sun thus develop each other. The sun rises up from the waters and re-enters them. Therefore, due to this exit (from and into waters) by day and by night, the waters become copper-coloured. Again when the sun sets, the day (i.e. daylight) enters the waters. Hence at night. the waters are seen shining white.

20. By means of this activity he enters waters perpetually, during day and night at the time of rising and setting both in the southern and northern hemispheres.

21. The sun who blazes, imbibing the waters through his rays has the mixture of earthly and fiery particles within it. It is called divine fire.

22-23. This fire (i.e. sun) has a thousand feet (i.e. rays). It is like a circular pot. It takes up waters from various water-resorts through the thousand tubular rays. It takes waters from the rivers, seas, wells, clouds etc. It takes up both mobile and immobile waters i.e. those of the canals and tanks.

24-25. He has a thousand rays emitting snow, rain and heat. Of them four hundred tubular rays have forms of variegated colours. They shower rain. Their collective name is Amṛta and the several individual names are Bhajanas, Mālyas, Ketanas and Patanas.

26-27a. The tubular rays carrying and emitting snow are three hundred in number. The several names of these rays emitting snow are Reśas, Meghas, Vātsyas and Hlādinīs. Their collective name is Candrabhā and they are yellow in lustre.

355. Fire on earth is the symbol of heat and fire in heaven is the symbol of light and both are interdependent. Cf. Matsya. 128.12. प्राकाश्यं च तथोष्णं च सौर्याग्नेये तु तेजसी । परस्परानुप्रवेशादाप्यायेते दिवानिशम् ॥

27b-28a. Śuklaḥ, Kakubhaḥ and Viśvabhṛt are the individual names of the rays emitting heat; their collective name is also Śukla.

28b-29. The moon sustains human beings, Pitṛs and Devas through them (the above rays).[356]

He propitiates human beings through the medicinal herbs; the Pitṛs with Svadhā and Devas through nectar.

30-31a. During spring and summer the sun blazes by his three hundred rays. During the rainy season and Autumn he showers rains through the four hundred tubular rays. During the early and the late winter he discharges snow through his three hundred rays.

31b-35a. The twelve suns are Indra, Dhātṛ, Bhaga, Pūṣan, Mitra , Varuṇa, Aryaman, Aṁśu, Vivasvān, Tvaṣṭṛ, Parjanya and Viṣṇu.

Varuṇa is the sun in Māgha; Pūṣan in the Phālguna. In the month of Caitra, Aṁśu is the sun. Dhātṛ is the sun in Vaiśākha. In Jyeṣṭha Indra is the sun. In Āṣāḍha, the sun is Aryaman. Vivasvan is the sun in Śrāvaṇa. In Bhādra the sun is Bhaga. Parjanya is the sun in Āśvina. Tvaṣṭṛ is the sun in Kārttika. In Mārgasīrṣa Mitra is the sun and Viṣṇu is the sun in Pauṣa.

35b-38. While performing the duty of the sun, Varuṇa has five thousand rays; Pūṣan six thousand rays; Aṁśu seven thousand rays; Dhātṛ eight thousand rays; Indra nine thousand rays; Vivasvān ten thousand rays; Bhaga eleven thousand rays; Mitra seven thousand rays; Tvaṣṭṛ eight thousand rays; Aryaman ten thousand rays; Parjanya nine thousand rays; Viṣṇu scorches the earth with six thousand rays.

39-40. In the spring the sun is tawny coloured; in the summer he has the lustre of gold. During the rainy season the colour of the sun is white. In the autumn the sun is grey-coloured. In the early winter the sun is copper-coloured and in the late winter he is red in colour.

356. The numerous solar rays have their functional division. For instance, four hundred of them function for creating rain (V.24-26), three hundred for heat (V.28) and three hundred for cold (V.26). These rays are distributed over the seasons and bring about the changes of cold, heat and rain.

41-45. The sun infuses strength into the medicinal herbs; he propitiates the Pitṛs by means of Svadhā rays; he instils nectar into the immortal beings. Thus, he imparts three things to the three groups.

The thousand rays of the sun serve the purpose of the world. Reaching the earth they assume different forms by emitting snow, rain and heat. Thus the sphere of the sun is white and is named after him. He is the support and source of origin of the stars, planets and the moon.

It should be known that the moon, stars and planets are all born of the sun. The moon is the lord of constellations and the left eye of the lord. The right eye of the lord is the sun himself. The word nayana (eye) is derived from √ni—"that which leads (nayati) the people to this world."

CHAPTER SIXTY

The Solar Sphere

Sūta said:

1. It is cited[357] that the sun is fire and the moon is water. The other five planets are known as lords who move about as they please.

2. Understand the source of origin of the remaining planets which is clearly being recounted now. It is cited that the planet Mars is Skanda (Karttikeya) the commander-in-chief of the army of Devas.

3-5. People of perfect knowledge say that Mercury is lord Nārāyaṇa. O excellent brahmins, the great planet Śanaiścara, the slow-moving Saturn is Yama, the lord of the worlds. The preceptors of Devas and Asuras are the great planets Venus and Jupiter with (refulgent) rays. They are mentioned as the sons of Prajāpati.[358]

357. For the celestial fire as identical with the sun, cf. अयं वै स्वर्ग्योऽग्नि: पारयिष्णुरमृतात्सम्भूत: cited in ST.

358. Śukra (Venus) and Bṛhaspati (Jupiter), the preceptors of Dānavas and Devas are respectively the sons of patriarchs Bhṛgu and Aṅgiras.

There is no doubt that the three worlds have their source in the sun.

6-8. The entire universe including Devas, Asuras and human beings originates from him. He is the lustre of all luminaries and the universal refulgence. The refulgence of Rudra, Indra, Upendra, the moon, the leading brahmins, the fire and the heaven-dwellers comes from the sun. He is the soul of all. He is the lord of all worlds. He alone is Mahādeva, Prajāpati and the lord of the three worlds. He is the original great deity. Everything originates from him and dissolves in him.

9. The existence and non-existence of the worlds originated from the sun formerly. O brahmins, this refulgent sun of great lustre is an incomprehensible planet.

10-11. All these units of time begin from him and end in him again and again, viz., kṣaṇas (moments), muhūrtas (a unit of 48 mts.), days, nights, fortnights, months, years, seasons and yugas. Hence without the sun there is no reckoning of time.

12-15. Without Kāla (time) there is no order, no initiation, no daily ritual. How can there be the division of the seasons? Whence are these flowers, roots and fruits? Whence is the outcome of plants? How can there be the different kinds of grass and medicinal plants? The dealings of the creatures in heaven and here too will be non-existent without the sun who is the form of Rudra, the scorcher of the universe. He alone is time, fire, Dvādaśātman (one having twelve forms) and Prajāpati. O excellent brahmins, he scorches the three worlds including the mobile and immobile beings. He is the mine of splendour. He is all in all, the whole set of worlds.

16. Adopting the excellent path, he scorches the entire universe from the sides, from above and from below in the course of nights and days.

17. If a bright lamp is hung in the middle of the house, it dispels darkness from the sides, the portion above and the portion below, at the same time.

18. In the same manner the thousand-rayed sun, the king of planets, the lord of the universe, illuminates the entire universe by means of his rays.

19. Seven rays, that are the source of origin of the planets

are the most excellent ones among the thousand rays mentioned by me before.[359]

20-21. They are Suṣumna, Harikeśa, Viśvakarman, Viśvavyacas, Sannaddha, Sarvāvasu and Svarāṭ.

The sun's ray Suṣumna makes the southern region flourish.[360] Suṣumna is glorified as the ray that moves about above, below and on the sides.

22-26. Harikeśa which is in front (in the east) is glorified as the source of origin of constellations.[360a] In the south, the ray Viśvakarmā develops Budha (Mercury). The ray Viśvavyacas which is in the west (behind) is the source of origin of Śukra (Venus). The ray Sannaddha is the source of origin of Mars. The ray Sarvāvasu is the source of origin of Bṛhaspati (Jupiter). The ray Svarāṭ nourishes Śanaiścara (Saturn). Thus it is due to the power of the sun that the constellations, planets and stars are seen in the heaven. This entire universe is sustained by him. The constellations are called Nakṣatras. The word is derived from √kṣi with the prohibitive particle 'na' i.e. na kṣīyante (i.e. those which do not perish).

CHAPTER SIXTYONE

The situation of the planets

1-2. All these are the abodes which blaze by means of solar rays. The constellations and stars are the abodes to be attained by merits. They are called Tārakas because they enable people to cross the ocean of worldly existence and also because they are white.

3. The sun is called Āditya because he takes up the divine and terrestrial splendours as well as the nocturnal darkness.

359. The principal seven rays, Suṣumna etc., of the thousand-rayed sun are the source of energy and movement of stars, planets and constellations. For instance, the solar ray, called Suṣumna, causes the movement of the moon.

360. dakṣiṇāṁ rāśim i.e. the moon. The Liṅgapurāṇa describes vividly the respective functions of the seven solar rays.

360a. Each planet or star has its respective sphere (deva-sthāna) in which its influence reigns supreme. These spheres are established by the Creator in the beginning of a kalpa and they last till the dissolution of that kalpa.

4. The root 'su' is used in two meanings to extract juice or to flow. Since the sun extracts refulgence and makes water flow, it is called Savitṛ.

5. The root 'cadi' from which the word Candra is derived means 'to delight'. It implies whiteness, chillness, and nectarine nature of the moon (Candra).

6. The divine discs of the sun and the moon are refulgent. They move in the sky. They are white and are of the nature of fire and water. They are splendid and they resemble a circular pot.

7. The disc of the moon is of the nature of dense water. The disc of the sun is white and is of the nature of dense fire.

8. Devas reside in constellations, sun and planets. They live everywhere in these abodes in all the manvantaras.

9. Hence the planets are abodes named after their respective planets. The Sun entered the abode Saura. The Moon entered the abode Saumya.

10. Venus entered the abode Śaukra. Jupiter, the valorous, with sixteen rays entered the abode Bṛhad (big). The Mars entered the abode Lohita pertaining to Mars.

11. The Saturn entered the abode Śanaiścara. The Mercury entered the abode Baudha. The evil planet Rāhu entered the abode Svarbhānu (named after him).

12. The deities of constellations entered all these abodes. These luminaries are the abodes of meritorious souls.

13. These abodes have been created by the selfborn deity. They began to function at the beginning of kalpa and they stay until all the living beings are dissolved.

14. In all the manvantaras they alone are the abodes of Devas. These deities who have identified themselves with the abodes occupy these divine abodes again and again.

15-20. They occupy these abodes along with Devas of the past, present and future. In this current manvantara the planets are moving about in aerial chariots.

In the Vaivasvata manvantara the sun is Vivasvān the son of Aditi; the lustrous lord Moon the son of sage Atri; lord Śukra, Bhārgava, is known as the priest of Asuras.

The preceptor of Devas, the shining one of massive splendour, is the son of Aṅgiras (Bṛhaspati). Budha (Mercury) is the charming son of a sage. Saturn is the ugly son of Vivasvān born of Saṁjñā. Agni was born of Vikeśī[361] as the youthful son of Lohitārchis. The constellations named Nakṣatra and Ṛkṣa are Dākṣāyaṇīs (daughters of Dakṣa). Rāhu is the son of Siṁhikā. He is an Asura causing distress to living beings.

21. Thus the constellations and planets in the sun and the moon as also their abodes and the various deities occupying them have all been mentioned.

22. The fiery abode Saura belongs to the thousand-rayed Vivasvān. The abode of the snow-rayed moon is watery and white.

23. The abode of Budha (mercury) is watery, dark-coloured and charming. The region of Śukra (Venus) is also watery but white with sixteen rays.

24. The abode of Bhauma (Mars) is reddish and it has nine rays. The abode of Bṛhaspati (Jupiter) is yellow with sixteen rays and is very large.

25. The abode Śani (Saturn) is black with eight rays. The abode of Svarbhānu (Rāhu) is gloomy and is a place of great distress to living beings.

26. All the stars should be known as the abodes of sages with one ray each. They are the resorts of men of meritorious renown and are white in colour.

27. They are of the nature of dense water (snow). They were created in the beginning of the kalpa. Thanks to the contact with the rays of the sun they have a shining appearance.

28. The diameter of the sun is nine thousand yojanas. The extent of its circular surface is three times that.

29. The extent of the moon is twice that of the sun. Rāhu assumes a form equal to both of them and moves about beneath them.

30. The third massive abode of Rāhu is dark and dreary. It is created in the form of a circle out of the shadow of the earth.

361. Vikeśī: The graha Bhauma (Maṅgala) born of Vikeśī is here called agni (fire). Cf. agnir mūrdhā(RV. 8.44.16) wherein Bhauma is called agni. Vikeśī is one of the eight wives of the eight-formed (aṣṭamurti) Rudra, others becalā, Svavarcalā 'Umā, Śivā, Svāhā, Dik, Dīkṣā and Rohiṇī.

31-32a. Setting out from the sun during the parvan days it goes to the moon.[362] Again during the solar parvan days it goes to the sun from the moon. Since Rāhu pushes and prompts the sun in the heaven it is called Svarbhānu.

32b-33. The diameter, circumference and distance in terms of yojanas of Venus is a sixteenth part of that of the moon. Jupiter is three-fourths of the size of Venus.

34. Mars and Saturn are a fourth less than Jupiter. In extent and width Mercury is a fourth less than these two.

35. The forms of those constellations and stars that are embodied are equal to Mercury in width and circular area.

36-39. The constellations that are in conjunction with the moon are ordinarily known as Ṛkṣas. The spheres of the comparatively smaller stars are five, four, three or two yojanas. Over all these there are clusters of still smaller stars which extend to only half a yojana in width. There is none smaller than this. Over and above these starry spheres are the three planets which move at a great distance from them. They should be known as slow moving ones. The speed of these has already been mentioned in due order.

40-45. All the planets are born of constellations. O excellent sages, the sun, the son of Aditi, the first among the planets, is born of the constellation Viśākhā. The lustrous son of Dharma, lord Vasu, Soma (moon), the cool-rayed lord of the night, is born of the constellation Kṛttikā. The sixteen-rayed son of Bhṛgu, Śukra (Venus) who is the most excellent among the stars and planets after the sun, is born of the constellation Tiṣya. The planet Bṛhaspati (Jupiter), the twelve-rayed son of Aṅgiras, the preceptor of the universe, is born of the constellation Pūrvaphālgunī.

The planet (Mars) son of Prajāpati, the nine-rayed red bodied planet is born of the constellation Pūrvāṣāḍhā.

The son of sun, the seven-rayed Saturn, was born of the constellation Revatī.

46-47. The five-rayed planet Budha (Mercury) the son of the moon is born of the constellation Dhaniṣṭhā.

Śikhī (Ketu) the great planet that destroys all, who is dark in nature, who is the son of Mṛtyu the god of Death and who is

362. Read Somam for samam.

the cause of destruction of the subjects, is born of the constellation Āsleṣā. Dakṣa's daughters were born of the constellations which have their own names.

48. Dark-sphered Rāhu who is full of Tāmasaic vigour, is the planet that suppresses the moon and the sun. He is born of the constellation Bharaṇī

49-50. It should be noted that the planets beginning with Bhārgava (Venus) are known as star-planets (i.e planets resembling stars). Persons who are affected by afflictions from their birthday stars are liberated from that defect by devotion to their respective planets. Among all the planets the first one, it is said, is Āditya (Sun).

51-54. Among all the star-planets Śukra is the first. Among all the Ketus (flaglike Meteors) the smoky one is the first. (It is usually called Dhūmaketu). Dhruva is the first among the planets distributed in all the four quarters. Among constellations the first is Śraviṣṭhā[363]. Among the Ayanas (transits) the Uttarāyaṇa (northern transit) is the first. Among the five[364] years the first is Saṁvatsara. Among the seasons it is the late winter (śiśira). Among the months it is Māgha. Among the fortnights it is the bright half and among Tithis it is Pratipat (first day). Among the division of days and nights, the day is the first. The first of the muhūrtas is that the deity of which is Rudra.

55-58. Kṣaṇa has the nimeṣa as its first unit of time, O excellent ones among the knowers of time. Beginning with the constellation Dhaniṣṭhā and ending with Śravaṇa shall be a yuga comprising of five years. The universe whirls like a wheel due to the movement of the sun. Hence the sun is the lord and deity delimiting time. He is the instigator and castigator of the four types of living beings. Rudra, the lord himself, is the inducer

363. Śraviṣṭhā=Dhaniṣṭhā.

364. A group of five years constitutes a yuga which should not be confused with the cycle of four yugas. This five-yearly cycle forming a yuga corresponds to the Vedic doctrine of pañca-devatā or five deities who have entered the Puruṣa. Cf. TB 1.4.10.1. The five years with their presiding deities are named (i) saṁvatsara—agni; (ii) parivatsara—sūrya; (iii) iḍāvatsara—soma; (iv) anuvatsara—vāyu; (v) vatsara—rudra. Cf. Matsya. 141. 17-18.

of that sun[365]. Thus the specific and fixed establishment of the luminaries and planets has been evolved by the great lord for the working of the world.

59-63. It has been made to function intelligently by the lord at the beginning of the kalpa. The lord is the support of all luminaries and he identifies himself with them. This is a wonderful phenomenon that is caused by the unique Pradhāna and is incomprehensible. The movement of the luminaries cannot be understood by the man with his physical eye. It can be understood by the learned man only through Vedic treatises, by inference and direct perception, by cogent arrangements and careful analysis in his mind.

O excellent sages, the causes for the decision in regard to the validity concerning the luminaries are five viz :—the eye, scripture, water, the written document and calculation.

CHAPTER SIXTYTWO

Situation of Dhruva

Sages said :

1. O foremost among the intelligent, it behoves you now to recount how, due to the grace of Viṣṇu, Dhruva became the central pivot of the planets.[366]

Sūta said :

2. O brahmins, when he was asked about this matter by me in former time, Mārkaṇḍeya who is an expert in different sciences said to me as I was desirous of hearing.

Mārkaṇḍeya said :

3. An emperor of great splendour, the best among all those who wield weapons, king Uttānapāda, ruled over the earth.

365. For Rudra as the life-principle of the sun compare : 'bhīṣodeti sūryaḥ.'—cited in *ST*.

366. The Sūta narrates the legend of Dhruva, son of Uttānapāda and Sunīti, how Dhruva became the pole star, the pivot of the solar system. Here, the astronomical phenomenon is sought to be explained on the basis of a legend.

4-5. He had two wives, Sunīti and Suruci. A highly intelligent son of great renown, named Dhruva was born of Sunīti the elder wife. He had great understanding and was the light of the family. When he was seven years old, once he sat in the lap of his father.

6. O leading brahmins, Suruci who was proud of her beauty pushed him away. Delighted in her mind she placed her own son on the lap of his father.

7. The intelligent boy Dhruva became dejected in his mind because he was unable to occupy the lap of his father. He went to his mother and lamented.

8. Overwhelmed by her grief the mother said to her weeping son :—"Suruci is the most beloved of her husband. Her son too is likewise.

9. You, a son born of me, a very unfortunate woman, are also equally unfortunate. Why do you bewail ? What for do you weep again and again ?

10. If you are distressed in heart you will increase my sorrow. My dear son, you shall by your own power attain a more comfortable and stable abode."

11-12. On being advised thus by his mother he set out towards the forest. On meeting Viśvāmitra, he bowed to him duly and spoke with his palms joined in reverence:—

"O holy sir, foremost among the pious sages, it behoves you to tell me how I shall obtain a place above everyone.

13. O sage, I was seated on the lap of my father. My step-mother Suruci pushed me aside. My father, the king, did not protest.

14-16. For this very reason, O brahmin, I went to my mother in fright. My mother said to me :—"O son, do not be sorry. You deserve to attain a far greater abode by your own endeavour". On hearing her words, O great sage, I have come to you for shelter in this forest. O holy sir, O brahmin, I have now met you. By your grace I shall attain the wonderful and excellent abode.

17-18. On being requested thus, the glorious sage said laughingly "O Prince, listen to this. You will attain an excellent abode by propitiating Keśava the lord of the worlds, and the destroyer of distress. He is born of the right limb of Śiva the intelligent great lord.[367]

19. O highly intelligent one, repeat the Mantra of the lord continuously. It is great, pure and holy, it destroys all sins and yields all desires.

20. Repeat this divine Mantra controlling your sense, with the Praṇava :—"Namostu Vāsudevāya" [Obeisance be to Vāsudeva]. Meditate on the eternal Viṣṇu. Be interested in japa and homa.

21-24. On being advised thus, the boy of great renown bowed to Viśvāmitra and began his japa facing the east He restrained himself and was delighted in his mind. Alertfully he repeated the mantra continuously without break for a year, sustaining himself on vegetables, roots and fruits. Terrible vampires and demons, large fierce beasts like lions rushed at him in order to confound his wits. But, repeating the name Vāsudeva he did not take notice of anything else.

25. A female ghost assuming the form of his mother Sunīti came near him and wept bitterly and miserably.

26-27. "O you are my only son. Why do you torture yourself? Leaving me helpless, you have taken to penance".

The boy continued his great penance and did not even glance at the lady who spoke thus. With delight in his heart he repeated the name Hari.

28-29. Then all the forms of impediment and harassment subsided from all sides. Seated on Garuḍa lord Viṣṇu who resembled the black cloud in lustre, who is the destroyer of enemies, who was surrounded by Devas and who was being eulogised by great sages, came there before Dhruva.

30-31. On seeing the lord come near, he simply thought within his mind "who is this?" Drinking as it were Hṛṣikeśa the lord of the Universe, by his eyes the boy of great lustre, seated himself and repeated "Vāsudeva". With the tip of his conch the lord touched his face.

32. Thereupon he attained the highest knowledge. With his palms joined in reverence he eulogised the lord the most excellent of all divine beings.

367. Viṣṇu is born of the right side of Śiva, while Brahmā is born of the left.

33. Be favourable, O lord of the chiefs of Devas, O wielder of conch, discus and iron club ! O soul of the worlds ! O soul of all, O soul of all secrets of the Vedas, O Keśava, I have sought refuge in you.

34. Even the great sages Sanaka and others have not comprehended you, the great Ātman. Then how can I know you ? O lord of the worlds, obeisance to you.

35. Then Viṣṇu said to him smiling :—"O dear one, come on. You are Dhruva (steady). Attaining a fixed and steady abode be the first among all luminaries.

36. You along with your mother shall attain the abode of luminaries. This abode is mine, the greatest, the steady splendid abode.

37-38. It was acquired by me from lord Śiva formerly after propitiating him by penance. The devotee who repeats continuously the name Vāsudeva along with the Praṇava 'om' the word 'Bhagavat' and the word 'namas' denoting obeisance attains the fixed abode of Dhruva."

39-42. Then all Devas, Siddhas, sages and Gandharvas installed Dhruva in that abode along with his mother. Thus, at the behest of Viṣṇu he attained the abode of luminaries. By means of the twelve-syllabled mantra[368], Dhruva of great splendour attained the highest perfection.

Sūta said:

Hence, the man who makes obeisance to Vāsudeva attains the world of Dhruva and achieves steadiness.

CHAPTER SIXTYTHREE

Origin of Devas and others

The sages said:

1. O Sūta, recount the origin of Devas, Dānavas, Gandharvas, Serpents and Rākṣasas, in an excellent way and in due order.

368. The twelve-syllabled mantra of Viṣṇu is : Oṁ namo bhagavate Vāsudevāya.

Sūta said :

2. The creation of ancient people was by means of mental conception, direct perception or touch. Subsequent to Dakṣa the son of Pracetas, creation is by means of sexual intercourse.

3-6. When he began to create the group of Devas, sages and serpents, the world did not increase. Thereupon, by means of sexual intercourse, Dakṣa begot of Sūti, five thousand sons.

On seeing those blessed ones who were desirous of creating different kinds of progeny, Nārada spoke to Haryaśvas, the sons of Dakṣa who had assembled together.

"Understand the extent of the earth[369] from above and below, O excellent sages, and then proceed ahead with your special creation."

On hearing his words they went away in all directions.

7-10. Even today they have not returned like the rivers after joining the ocean.

When Haryaśvas vanished, lord Dakṣa Prajāpati begot of Sūti herself another thousand sons. O brahmins, they were named Śabalas and they assembled together for the purpose of creation.

Nārada spoke to those persons of solar splendour, who had assembled before him—"You should proceed with your special creation after understanding the full extent of the earth, or on return after finding out what has happened to your brothers.

They too followed their brothers and attained the same goal as their brothers before.

11 When they too vanished the Prajāpati Dakṣa the son of Pracetas, begot sixty daughters of Vīriṇī.

12-15. He gave ten of them in marriage to Dharma, thirteen to Kaśyapa, twentyseven to the moon, four to Ariṣṭanemi, two to the son of Bhṛgu, two to the intelligent Kṛśāśva and two to Aṅgiras. Now listen to the names of the mothers of Devas and the details of their progeny from the very beginning.

The ten wives of Dharma were :—Marutvatī, Vasū,

369. or after knowing the extent of the field (i.e. the subtle body) as also its capacity for creating the living beings. ST. cites Bhāga. in support of this interpretation : भूक्षेत्रं जीवसंज्ञं यदनादि निजबन्धनम् । अदृष्ट्वा तस्य निर्वाणं किमसत्कर्मभिर्भवेत् ॥

Yāmi, Lambā, Bhānu, Arundhatī, Saṅkalpā, Muhūrtā, Sādhyā and Viśvā.

I shall tell you the names of their sons.

16-20a. The Viśvedevas were born to Viśvā. Sādhyā bore the Sādhyas. Marutvats were born of Marutvatī. Vasus were born of Vasū. The Bhānus were born of Bhānu; the Muhūrtakas were born of Muhūrta; the Ghoṣas were born of Lambā. Nāgavīthī was born of Yāmi. Saṅkalpa was born of Saṅkalpā. I shall tell you the creation of the Vasus. Devas who are luminous and who pervade all the quarters are called Vasus.[370] They are the well wishers of all living beings. They are reputed to be eight, viz.—Āpa, Dhruva, Soma, Dharā, Anila, Anala, Pratyūṣa and Prabhāsa.

20b-22a. The eleven Rudras,[371] the leaders of the Gaṇas are :—Ajaikapād, Ahirbudhnya, Virūpākṣa, Bhairava, Hara, Bahurūpa, Tryambaka the lord of Devas, Sāvitra, Jayanta, Pinākin and Aparājita.

22b-26. I shall mention the sons and grandsons of Kaśyapa from his thirteen wives :—Aditi, Diti,, Ariṣṭā, Surasā, Muni, Surabhi, Vinatā, Tāmrā, Krodhavaśā, Ilā, Kadrū, Tviṣā and Danu.

I shall tell you the names of the sons of these.

Devas who were known as Tuṣitas in the Cākṣuṣa manvantara are spoken of as the twelve Ādityas in the Vaivasvata manvantara. The following twelve are the thousand-rayed Ādityas :—

Indra, Dhātṛ, Bhaga, Tvaṣṭṛ, Mitra, Varuṇa, Aryaman, Vivasvān, Savitṛ, Pūṣan, Aṁśumat and Viṣṇu.

27. We have heard that Diti had two sons from Kaśyapa viz. Hiraṇyakaśipu and Hiraṇyākṣa

28. Danu bore a hundred sons to Kaśyapa. They were mighty and arrogant. O excellent brahmins, among them Vipracitti was the chief.

370. Vasus are a class of deities, eight in number. They seem to have been personifications of natural phenomena. They are Āpa (water), Dhruva (Pole star), Soma (moon), Dharā (earth), Anila (wind), Anala (fire), Prabhāsa (dawn) and Pratyūṣa (light).

371. In regard to the names of the eleven Rudras the Purāṇas are not unanimous.

29. O leading brahmins, Tāmrā bore six daughters[372] viz.—Śukī, Śyenī, Bhāsī, Sugrīvī, Gṛdhrikā and Śuci.

30-31. Śukī duly gave birth to parrots and owls. Śyenī gave birth to hawks (falcons), etc. Bhāsī gave birth to deers. Gṛdhrī bore the vultures, doves, pigeons and other birds. Śuci gave birth to swans, cranes and other aquatic birds such as Kāraṇḍa, Plava.

32-34. Sugrīvī gave birth to goats, horses, sheep, camels and donkeys. Vinatā gave birth to Garuḍa and Aruṇa, (two sons) and then a daughter Saudāminī (lightning) terrible unto all the worlds.

A thousand cobras were born to Surasā. Kadru gave birth to a thousand thousand-hooded serpents. Twenty-six excellent ones among them are well known as their chiefs.

35-37. They are :—Śeṣa, Vāsuki, Karkoṭa, Śaṅkha, Airāvata, Kambala, Dhanañjaya, Mahānīla, Padma, Aśvatara, Takṣaka, Elāpatra, Mahāpadma, Dhṛtarāṣṭra, Balāhaka, Śaṅkhapāla, Mahāśaṅkha, Puṣpadaṁṣṭra, Śubhānana, Śaṅkhaloman, Nahuṣa, Vāmana, Phaṇita, Kapila, Durmukha and Patañjali.

38-41. Krodhavaśā gave birth to the Rākṣasas wielding great power of deception and also the group of Rudras. The excellent lady Surabhi, gave birth to cows and buffaloes as the children of Kaśyapa. Muni gave birth to the group of sages and Apsaras. Ariṣṭā gave birth to Kinnaras and Gandharvas. Ilā gave birth to grasses, trees, creepers and hedges. Tviṣā gave birth to crores and crores of Yakṣas and Rākṣasas

These are the immediate descendants of Kaśyapa, narrated succinctly.

42-45. These had their own numerous sons, grandsons etc. Their races are many. After the children had been procreated by the noble Kaśyapa, after all the mobile and immobile beings had been well established, Prajapati crowned the chief ones among each of them as overlords. He made Vaivasvata Manu the overlord of human beings. Those who were crowned by Brahmā in the Svāyambhuva manvantara, even

372. Kaśyapa's wives and children are given differently in other authorities, e.g. Mbh. Ādi p. xvi. lxv and lxvi; Kūrma xviii; Agni xix; Bd. V. 143-146.

now protect and rule over the earth with its seven continents and mountains. They rule virtuously in accordance with the instructions of the lord.

46. Only those who had been crowned formerly in the Svāyambhuva manvantara by Brahmā are crowned now. They become the Manus.

47-49. In the past manvantaras these had been the kings. Others are being crowned when a new manvantara arrives. All the kings of the past and future manvantaras are mentioned in detail.

After procreating these sons for the continuity of the race Kaśyapa performed penance once again with the desire to have a son who will preserve the spiritual line.

50-51. Even as Kaśyapa was meditating thus, two son's of great prowess manifested themselves by the grace of Brahman. Those two Vatsara and Asita were expounders of Brahman. Naidhruva and Raibhya were born of Vatsara.

52-54. The sons of Raibhya are known as Raibhyas. I shall mention those of Naidhruva. Sumedhas was born of the daughter of Cyavana. She became the wife of Naidhruva and the mother of Kuṇḍapāyins.

The glorious son Devala was born of Ekaparṇā and Asita. He was a knower of Brahman, the best of all the Śāṇḍilyas and one possessing great penance. Thus the descendants of Kaśyapa became three branches; Śāṇḍilyas, Naidhruvas and Raibhyas.

55-58. Devas had nine sources of origin. I shall mention the line of Pulastya.

After eleven cycles of four yugas have practically passed by when Manu was the lord and half the period of Dvāpara had passed by, Dama was born as the son of Nariṣyanta, a descendant of Manu. Dama's descendant known as Tṛṇabindu became king in the third quarter of Tretāyuga. His daughter Ilavilā was unrivalled in beauty and the king gave her in marriage to Pulastya.

59. Viśravas the great sage was born of Ilavilā. His four wives are the progenitors of the famity of Pulastya.

60-65. The first wife Devavarṇinī was the splendid daughter of Bṛhaspati. The second and third wives were the two daughters of Mālyavān, viz. Puṣpotkaṭā and Balākā and the fourth wife Kaikasī was the daughter of Mālin.

Now listen to the children of these ladies. Devavarṇinī bore the eldest son Vaiśravaṇa to him. Kaikasī gave birth to Rāvaṇa, the king of Rākṣasas, Kumbhakarṇa, Śūrpaṇakhā and Vibhīṣaṇa. O excellent brahmins, Puṣpotkaṭā bore him Mahodara, Prahasta, Mahāpārśva, Khara and the daughter Kumbhīnasī. Now listen to the childern of Balā [i. e. Balākā]. They were Triśiras, Dūṣana, Vidyujjihva and the daughter Mālikā. Thus the Rākṣasas of ruthless activities belonging to the family of Pulastya are nine.

66-68. Vibhīṣaṇa is glorified as the knower of Dharma. He was a highly pure soul.

The deer, the fanged animals, tigers, goblins, ghosts, serpents, boars, elephants, monkeys, Kinnaras and Kimpuruṣas were the sons of Pulastya.

In the Vaivasvata manvantara Kratu is said to be issueless. Atri had ten beautiful and chaste wives.

69-70. Bhadrāśva begot of the celestial damsel Ghṛtāci ten children viz Bhadrā, Abhadrā, Jaladā, Mandā, Ānandā (or Nandā), Balā, Abalā, Gopābalā, Tāmarasā and Varakrīḍā

71-73. These are the progenitors of the family of Ātreya. Their husband is Prabhākara. When the sun was swallowed by Rāhu and he fell down towards the earth from the heavens the whole world was enveloped in darkness. At that time Atri spread lustre everywhere. He said "Hail to Thee" and then the falling sun ceased to fall at the instance of the brahmi n sage. Then Atri was called Prabhākara by the great sages.

74. He begot of Bhadrā the renowned son Soma (Moon). The sage procreated more sons of those wives.

75. They are well known as Svastyātreyas. They were sages and masters of the Vedas. Two of them became well renowned. They had realised Brahman. They were very powerful.

76. Datta was the eldest son of Atri. Durvāsas was his younger brother. The youngest sister was Amalā, an expounder of the Brahman.

77. Four of them born of two Gotras are well known in the world, viz. Śyāva, Pratvasa, Vavalgu and Gahvara.

78. Four lines of the spiritual family of Ātreyas of noble souls are known as Kāśyapa, Nārada, Parvata and Anuddhata.

79. These were born as mental sons. Now understand the children of Arundhatī. It was Nārada who gave Arundhatī to Vasiṣṭha.

80-82. Due to a curse of Dakṣa, Nārada of great splendour became a bachelor by compulsion.

Formerly, when a terrible war between Devas and Asuras, on account of the demon Tāraka, took place, the world was oppressed due to drought. Along with the guardians of the quarters, the intelligent sage Vasiṣṭha sustained the subjects by means of his penance. He made water, cooked rice, roots, fruits and medicinal herbs and out of mercy he enlivened the people with medicines.

83. Vasiṣṭha begot hundred sons of Arundhatī. Adṛśyantī bore to Śakti, the eldest of those hundred, the son Parāśara.

84-88. Śakti was swallowed by the demon Rudhira (along with his brothers). Kālī bore to Parāśara the son Kṛṣṇa Dvaipāyana.

Dvaipāyana begot of Araṇī the son Śuka and the son Upamanyu of Pīvarī.

Know that the following are the sons of Śuka viz. Bhūriśravas, Prabhu, Śambhu, Kṛṣṇa and Gaura. There was a daughter Kīrtimatī. She was a yogic mother, performing holy rites. She was the wife of Aṇuha and mother of Brahmadatta. The following are the descendants of Parāśara viz Śveta, Kṛṣṇa, Gaura, Śyāma, Dhūmra, Aruṇa, Nīla and Bādarika. Thus there are eight lines of these noble-souled Parāśaras.

89-91. Henceforth understand the descendants of Indrapramiti. Vasiṣṭha begot of Ghṛtācī the son Kapiñjalya. He who is known as Trimūtri is called Indrapramiti. Bhadra was born of Pṛthu's daughter. His son was Vasu whose son was Upamanyu. There are many descendants of Upamanyu, Mitra and Varuṇa. Those who are known as Kauṇḍinyas are the descendants of Mitra and Varuṇa.[373]

373. Kauṇḍinyas and Vāsiṣṭhas have a common ancestry in Mitrā-Varuṇa. Hence the matrimonial alliances do not take place between them.

92-95. There are others of single sage-head, who are well known as Vāsiṣṭhas. There are ten lines of the noble descendants of Vasiṣṭha.

Thus these mental sons of Brahmā are known on the earth. These blessed ones are the supporters of the spiritual legacy. Their descendants are well known. They are competent to support even the three worlds. They are born of the families of divine sages. Their sons and grandsons are hundreds and thousands. The three worlds are pervaded by them in the same manner as by the rays of the sun.

CHAPTER SIXTYFOUR

Grant of boons by Pulastya

The sages said:

1. O Sūta, O best speaker, it behoves you to recount how Śakti the son of Vasiṣṭha was devoured by a demon along with his younger brothers.

Sūta said:

2-3. The demon Rudhira[374] devoured Śakti the son of Vasiṣṭha along with his younger brothers due to a curse by Śakti on king Kalmāṣapāda. O leading brahmins, urged by Viśvāmitra, Rudhira haunted the king Kalmāṣapāda for whom

374. There are different versions of this legend in the Rāmāyaṇa, Mahābhārata and Viṣṇupurāṇa. According to Mbh. Kalmāṣapāda, king of the solar race, was the son of Sudās and a descendant of Ikṣvāku. While he was out hunting in the forest he met Śakti, the eldest son of Vasiṣṭha. Since Śakti refused to get out of his way, Kalmāṣapāda was enraged. He then struck Śakti with the whip. Thereupon, Śakti cursed him to become a rākṣasa. Thus, Kalmāṣapāda was turned into a rākṣasa Rudhira by name and he devoured Śakti together with his brothers. But according to Liṅga, the rākṣasa Rudhira entered the body of King Kalmāṣapāda when the latter was engaged in sacrifice, under the leadership of Vasiṣṭha. Instigated by Viśvāmitra, who was a rival priest, Rudhira devoured Śakti as well as his ninety-nine brothers.

Liṅga refers to the legend of Viśvāmitra. According to Vālmīki's Rāmāyaṇa, Śakti was cursed by Viśvāmitra in the context of king Triśaṅku's sacrifice.

a sacrifice was being performed by Vasiṣṭha and swallowed Śakti.

4-5. On hearing that the most powerful Śakti had been devoured by that demon along with his brothers, Vasiṣṭha repeatedly lamented "hā (my) son, hā (my) son". The wailing sage fell down on the ground along with Arundhatī.

6-10. Remembering his hundred sons, the eldest of whom was Śakti, and knowing that the family was extinct, the powerful sage decided to die. Coming to this conclusion that he will not remain alive without his sons, he felt all the more miserable. Vasiṣṭha the son of Brahmā, the knower of everything, the self-possessed sage who had realized the Ātman, climbed to the top of a mountain along with his wife. With tears welling up in the eyes he suddenly fell down on the ground. As he fell down on the ground, the earth (assuming the form of a lady) who had a wonderful necklace and the sportive gait of an elephant, caught him up with her lotus-like hands and as he cried she too bewailed with him. At that time, his daughter-in-law, the wife of Śakti, cried in great fright and spoke thus to Vasiṣṭha, the great sage and the best among the eloquent sages.

11. "O lord, O excellent brahmin, O powerful sage, preserve this excellent body of yours to see your grandson, that is my son.

12. O leading brahmin, this splendid body should not be discarded by you, since the child that is born of Śakti and that is bound to be one who realises all objects, is within my womb."

13-14. After saying thus, that lady who was conversant with Dharma and whose eyes resembled lotus flowers lifted up her father-in-law by her hands and wiped his eyes with water. Although she was herself miserable she requested the dejected Arundhatī to save her father-in-law.

15-16. On hearing the words of his daughter-in-law Vasiṣṭha got up from the ground after regaining consciousness. Arundhatī embraced him in great distress and fell down. The leading sage touched Arundhatī, in whose eyes tears had welled up and cried along with her.

17-18. Thereafter the son seated in the couch of the womb of his mother, like the four-faced lord Brahmā in the umbilical lotus of Viṣṇu repeated a sacred verse. The holy sage Vasiṣṭha listened enthusiastically to the sacred verse wondering, by whom could it have been repeated. He then meditated with great concentration.

19. Thereupon Viṣṇu whose eyes resemble the lotus petals, who had been stationed in the courtyard of the firmament, who is the soul of the universe and who is the storehouse of mercy spoke to Vasiṣṭha mercifully.

20. O dear one, O dear one, O Vasiṣṭha the leading brahmin, fond of his son, this sacred verse has emanated from the lotuslike face of your grandson.

21. O sage, this grandson of yours, the powerful one born of Śakti is on a par with me. Hence, O most excellent sage and son of Brahmā, discard your grief and rise up.

22. The child in the womb is a devotee of Rudra. He is engaged in the worship of Rudra. Thanks to the power of Rudra he will redeem your family.

23. After saying thus to Vasiṣṭha, the leading Brahmin sage, the merciful lord vanished there itself.

24. Vasiṣṭha of great splendour bowed his head to the lotus-eyed lord and then stroked the belly of Adṛśyantī with great respect.

25-27. O brahmins, he cried out "hā my son, hā my son", and fell down extremely depressed. Glancing at Arundhatī who was also crying and remembering his own son he cried out in misery—"O son, come again, come again. O Śakti, after the birth of your son who will sustain this family. I shall undoubtedly come near you along with your mother".

Sūta said :

After saying this, the crying brahmin embraced Arundhatī. Beating her belly she was about to fall.

28-32. The auspicious lady Adṛśyantī who was distressed beat her belly—the abode of the child in womb. She cried out in distress and fell down. Arundhatī and Vasiṣṭha, both of them were extremely frightened. They lifted up the young woman their daughter-in-law and said thus:—

"O silly woman, tell us how you have attempted to destroy the family of Vasiṣṭha by striking at the region of womb. For seeing your son, the child born to Śakti and for tasting the nectar of the boyish face of the noble son, the leading sage has decided to preserve his body. Hence protect your body".

Sūta said:

33-34. After pulling up her daughter-in-law and the sage, Arundhatī the wife of Vasiṣṭha stood up and said though highly distressed and agitated.

"O lady of good holy rites, since the life of this sage, and that of mine depend on you, you should preserve your life. As a nurse do what is beneficial to us."

Adṛśyantī said:

35. "If the excellent sage has decided to preserve his life I shall somehow preserve my body pure or impure.

36-37. It is because of my sin that I have to bear the sorrow of separation from my husband. O sage, I am burnt with grief, even though I am your daughter-in-law, O sage. Alas, a miracle has been seen by me. O lord, I am the victim of grief. O brahmin, be my saviour from misery, O son of Brahmā, O preceptor of the universe.

38. Still, a woman without a husband shall be miserable. O noble lord (sage), save me from that situation.

39. The father, mother, sons, grandsons, even the father-in-law, all are helpless to such a woman. None of them can be a real kinsman unto women. It is the husband alone who is her real kinsman, her greatest salvation.

40. What has been mentioned by the learned men ! viz. the wife is half of the husband, has turned out to be not true in my case. Śakti has gone. But I still survive.

41. O leading sage, alas ! the hardness of my mind ! even after leaving off my husband who is like my own vital breath, I could live for even a moment.

42. O Vasiṣṭha, just as a creeper climbing on the holy fig tree, survives even after being cut off from its roots, I too survive

even after I have become miserable on being abandoned by my husband".

43. On hearing these words of his daughter-in-law, the intelligent Vasiṣṭha who observed the duties of his stage of life decided to go to his hermitage along with his wife.

44. The meritorious-souled holy lord Vasiṣṭha though suffering badly, entered his hermitage quickly, accompanied by his wife and Adṛśyantī, and began to ponder.

45. O leading sages, that chaste wife of Śakti preserved the child in the womb with great difficulty for the continuity of the family line.

46. In the tenth month the wife of Śakti gave birth to a lustrous son in the same manner as Arundhatī had previously given birth to Śakti.

47. Śakti's wife gave birth to Parāśara like Aditi who gave birth to Viṣṇu, like Svāhā who gave birth to Guha and like Araṇi who gave birth to Agni.

48. When the son of Śakti incarnated on the earth, Śakti, abandoned his sorrow and attained equality with the Pitṛs.

49. O leading sages, that meritorious son of Vasiṣṭha, stationed in the world of the Pitṛs along with his brothers shone like the sun along with the Ādityas.

50. O leading brahmins, when Parāśara incarnated, the departed father sang, the grand-fathers and great-grand-fathers danced.

51. The Pitṛs who previously expounded the Brahman on the earth and the deities in heaven danced. Puṣkara and others moved about in the firmament showering flowers.

52. O brahmins, in the cities of the Rākṣasas there were odd and painful shouts. The sages in their hermitage applauded continuously with delightful experiences.

53. Just as the four-faced lord incarnated from the Cosmic Egg, just as the sun emerges from the clusters of clouds, so also Parāśara was born of Adṛśyantī.

54. On seeing the son and remembering her husband, O brahmins, even Adṛśyantī felt both joy and grief. So was the case with Arundhatī and sage Vasiṣṭha.

55. On seeing her son, the highly refulgent Parāśara, the agitated lady lamented. With her throat choked she fell down.

56. Even as her sinless son adored by the groups of Devas and Dānavas, was born the mother realized that he was highly intelligent. With tears in her eyes she lamented.

57. "Hā, son of Vasiṣṭha, you have gone somewhere after abandoning me whose wretchedness is visible in the face. You have left me in the middle of the forest as one desirous of seeing her son. O lord, you too, see your bosom-born, sinless son.

58. O Śakti, with his delight evident in his face Maheśvara saw his six-faced son along with his Gaṇas. Similarly, you too see your son in the company of your brothers".

59. On hearing her lamentation, the excellent sage Vasiṣṭha became miserable and said to his daughter-in-law, "Do not cry."

60. At the behest of Vasiṣṭha, that noble lady eschewed her sorrow. That lady with roving eyes like the fawn nursed and nurtured her son.

61. On seeing his chaste mother as a weak lady, devoid of ornaments, sitting down dejectedly, with tears agitating the eyes, the boy said to her.

Śakti's son said :

62. "O mother, O sinless one, your slender body does not appear to be splendid without ornaments. It is like the night bereft of the disc of the moon.

63. O my mother, O my mother, O splendid lady, it behoves you to recount to me why you are sitting here setting aside your auspicious marks as a woman without her husband."

64. On hearing the words of her son, Adṛśyantī did not tell her son anything, good or bad.

65. The son of Śakti said to Adṛśyantī again, "O mother where is my holy father of great refulgence? Tell me, tell me."

66. On hearing the words of her son, she became extremely agitated and wept. Saying "your father was devoured by a Rākṣasa" she fell down unconscious.

67. On hearing the words of his grandson, the kind-hearted

Vasiṣṭha cried and fell down. So also Arundhatī and the leading sages, the residents of the hermitage.

68. On hearing directly from his mother—"Your father was devoured by a demon", the intelligent Parāśara spoke thus with his eyes dimmed and darkened by tears.

Parāśara said :

69. O mother, I think I will be able to show my father in a moment by worshipping the lord of the chiefs of Devas and of the three worlds including the mobile and immobile beings.[375]

70. On hearing these splendid words she was surprised. Smilingly she looked at him and said :—"O son, this is true. Worship the lord."

71. On understanding the proposal and decision of the son of Śakti, Vasiṣṭha the holy lord, the intelligent leading sage, and the storehouse of mercy, spoke to his grandson as follows :—

72-74. "O my grandson, O excellent sage of good holy rites, your proposal is proper and suitable. Still, listen, it does not behove you to destroy the world. You can worship the lord for exterminating Rākṣasas. But, O son of Śakti, what is the harm done to you by the world that you need destroy it?"

Thereafter at the behest of the Vasiṣṭha the extremely intelligent son of Śakti directed his mind towards the extermination of Rākṣasas.

75-78. Parāśara bowed down to Adṛśyantī, Vasiṣṭha and Arundhatī. In the presence of the sage he made a single Liṅga, in a trice, out of dust. Repeating the following Mantras from the Vedas he worshipped it. The mantras were Śivasūkta, Tryambakasūkta, Tvaritarudra, Śiva Saṅkalpa, Nīlarudra, Rudra, Vāmīya, Pavamāna, Pañca Brahman, Hotṛsūkta, Liṅgasūkta and Atharvaśiras. After worshipping duly he offered the eightfold Arghya to Rudra.

375. trailokyaṁ sacarācaram: Change the accusative case into the genitive case and supply 'īśam' to obtain the required meaning. The expression 'trailokyasya sacarācarasya īśam' would mean 'lord of the three worlds including the mobile and immobile beings'. ST. is not in favour of this change. It supplies 'dagdhvā' which it construes with 'trailokyam sacarācaram; i.e. 'having burnt the three worlds including the mobile and immobile beings'.

Parāśara said :—

79. "O lord Rudra, O Śaṅkara, my father of great refulgence was swallowed by the demon Rudhira along with his brothers.

80-81. O lord, I wish to see my father along with his brothers."

Submitting thus he bowed down to the Liṅga again and again, cried "ha Rudra, ha Rudra" and prostrated before him.

On seeing him, lord Rudra said to the goddess.

82. "O highly blessed lady, see this boy whose eyes are dimmed and darkened with tears. He is engaged in propitiating me."

83-84. The spotless great goddess saw Parāśara, his eyes dimmed and his body drenched by tears due to misery. He was interested only in the act of worshipping the Liṅga. He repeated the names "Hara", "Rudra" etc. Umā then spoke to Śiva her husband and the lord of the worlds.

85-86. O supreme lord, be pleased, grant him all his desires. On hearing her words, Śaṅkara Parameśvara, the swallower of halāhala poison, spoke to his noble consort Umā—" I shall save this brahmin boy whose eyes resemble full blown blue lotus.

87-88. I shall give him divine vision and enable him to see my form." After saying this, lord Nīlalohita, Parameśvara, surrounded by the divine Gaṇas—Brahmā, Indra, Viṣṇu, Rudra, and others granted vision to that intelligent son of the sage.

89. On seeing Mahādeva, his eyes became dimmed with tears of delight. Delighted in his heart he fell at his feet with great respect.

90 Thereafter he grasped the feet of Umā and the noble Nandı and then spoke to Brahmā, and others—"My life is fruitful today.

91. Today the crescent moon-bedecked diety has come for my protection. Who else can compare with me in this world, whether a Deva or a Dānava ?"

92. Thereafter in a moment, Parāśara the son of Śakti saw his father standing in heaven along with his brothers.

93. On seeing him accompanied by his brothers in an

aerial chariot that resembled the solar sphere and was open on all sides, he was delighted. He bowed down to his father.

94. Then the bull-bannered lord who was accompanied by his wife and the leading Gaṇas spoke thus to Śakti, the son of Vasiṣṭha who was eager to see his son.

The glorious lord said:—

95-96. O Śakti, see your son, the boy whose eyes are dimmed with tears of delight. O leading brahmin, see Adṛśyantī, Vasiṣṭha your father, Arundhatī your mother, the highly blessed auspicious lady comparable to goddess. O highly intelligent one, make obeisance to both your father and your mother.

97-98. At the behest of Śaṅkara, Śakti immediately, at first, bowed down to the lord of Devas and to Umā. He then bowed to the excellent Vasiṣṭha and to Arundhatī his highly blessed mother, the auspicious lady who considered her husband her god. At the behest of the lord of the Universe the powerful Śakti said :—

The son of Vasiṣṭha said :—

99. O dear son, O leading brahmin, Parāśara of great refulgence, I have been saved by you who had been in the womb when I died and who are a noble soul.

100-101. O dear son, Parāśara the attributes and the prosperities Aṇimā[376] etc. have been attained by me, on seeing your face today. O dear one, of great intellect, at my behest[377] protect Adṛśyantī the highly blessed lady and Arundhatī, as also my father Vasiṣṭha.

102. O dear son, our entire family has been redeemed by you. This has always[378] been said by the learned that one conquers the worlds through one's son.

103. Choose the desired[379] boon from the lord who is source of origin of the worlds. After bowing down to the lord I shall go along with my brothers.

376. See P 134 note 241

377. Construe 'mamājñayā' (v-100) with 'Adṛśyantīṁ rakṣa' (v-101), i.e. 'at my behest you shall take care of Adṛśyantī.'

378. sadaiva—always. or read sadeva—ucitam eva ST: 'it is proper or truthful that...........'

379. īpsitaṁ varay eśānam: take recourse to Śiva for obtaining your desire, viz, the destruction of Rākṣasas.

104-106. Thus taking leave of his son after bowing down to Maheśvara and after seeing his wife in the assembly, the sage of perfect control over the senses went away to his fatherland. On seeing his father gone after worshipping the lord, the son of Śakti eulogised him with pleasing words. Thereafter the delighted Mahādeva, the suppressor of the Cupid and of Andhaka, blessed the son of Śakti and vanished there itself.

107. After Maheśvara had gone away accompanied by Umā, the son of Śakti, the knower of charms, burned the race of Rākṣasas by means of Mantras.

108. Then Vasiṣṭha the knower of Dharma, surrounded by the sages, said to his grandson, "O dear son, stop this excess of fury. Eschew your anger.

109. The Rākṣasas are not guilty. It had been so ordained[380] in your father's case. Anger provokes only the fools and not the intelligent people.

110-111. O dear son, who is killed by whom? Man is but the partaker of fruits of his own activities.

O dear son, fury is but the destroyer of fame and penance which men accumulate after a great deal of stress and strain. Enough of these Rājasaic activities of burning innocent people.

112-113. Let your sacrifice cease. Indeed, good men have forbearance as their strong point." Thus at the instance of Vasiṣṭha, the leading sage, the son of Śakti wound up his sacrifice immediately after giving due deference to his words. Therefore holy lord Vasiṣṭha, the excellent sage was delighted.

114-117. Pulastya the son of Brahmā had attended the Satra. Vasiṣṭha duly offered him worship and the sage Pulastya was duly honoured. He then spoke to Parāśara who was standing by after due obeisance.

"In the course of this great enmity you have adopted forbearance at the instance of your preceptor. Hence you will understand all the scriptural texts. My line of descendants has not been broken by you even though you were infuriated. Hence, O blessed one, I am giving you another great boon. O

380. **vihitam—destined.**

dear one, you will be the compiler of the Purāṇa Saṁhitā (the compendium of ancient lore).

118-119a. You will understand precisely the real nature of the deities.[381] Due to my blessing your intellect will be devoid of impurities of activities, whether of active or absentious type and free from doubts."

119b-120a. Thereafter the holy sage Vasiṣṭha the most excellent of all eloquent ones said:—"Whatever has been said by Pulastya will take place wholly."

120b-121. Then by the grace of Pulastya and the intelligent Vasiṣṭha, Parāśara composed the Vaiṣṇava Purāṇa. By means of six modes[382] (i.e.parts) it expounds all the topics. It is a mine of knowledge.

122-123. It extends to six thousand verses, and contains Vedic topics. It is the fourth[383] among the Purāṇa collections and a splendid one. Thus O leading sages, the origin of the descendants of Vasiṣṭha and the prowess of the son of Śakti has been succinctly recounted to you.

CHAPTER SIXTYFIVE

Thousand names of Śiva

The sages said:

1. O Romaharṣaṇa, the best among the knowers of races, it behoves you to recount succinctly to us the solar race and the lunar race.

Sūta said:

2. O brahmins, Aditi bore to Kaśyapa the son Āditya. Āditya had a chief wife and three others.

3-5. They were Queen Saṁjñā, Rājñī, Prabhā and Chāyā. I shall mention their sons to you. Queen Saṁjñā the daughter

381. devatā-paramārtham—vāstava-svarūpam ST. i.e. facts.

382. ṣaḍ-prakāram—ṣaḍ-aṁśarūpam 'consisting of six parts'.

383. caturtham. But according to the serial order (of. *Liṅga* 39. 61—63) Śiva, and not Viṣṇu, is the fourth.

of Tvaṣṭṛ bore to the Sun the excellent Manu. Rājñī gave birth to Yama, Yamunā and Revata. Prabhā bore to the sun the son Prabhāta. Saṁjñā gave birth to Chāyā. O brahmins, Chāyā bore to Sāvarṇi, Śani, Tapatī and Viṣṭi in due order.

6-7. More than her own sons Chāyā loved Manu.[384] Yama could not brook this. He became exceedingly infuriated. Lifting up his right foot he kicked her furiously. Assaulted by Yama, Chāyā became very miserable.

8. Due to the curse of Chāyā one healthy foot of Yama became watery i.e. covered with eczematic eruptions and full of foetid blood and swarms of germs.

9. He went to Gokarṇa travelling on a plank, and propitiated Mahādeva there for millions of years living only on air.

10-11a. By the grace of Bhava he attained the excellent guardianship of the Southern quarter, the overlordship of the Pitṛs and freedom from the curse. He attained these by the power of the trident-armed lord of Devas.

11b-12. Formerly the spotless daughter of Tvaṣṭṛ, unable to bear the excess of refulgence of the sun, created out of her own body another lady called Chāyā.

The lady of good holy rites assumed the form of a mare and performed penance.

13. In course of time lord sun the husband of Chāyā realised after a great effort that she was only a shadow. Assuming the form of a horse he indulged in sexual intercourse with Saṁjñā who had adopted the form of a mare.

14. Thus Saṁjñā the daughter of Tvaṣṭṛ who was in the guise of a mare bore to him the twin lords Aśvins, the excellent physicians of Devas.

15-16a. Later, the sun was ground down[385] by the noble-souled father of Saṁjñā. It was from the disc of the sun (i. e. the ground portion) that the terrible discus of Viṣṇu his chief divine weapon was evolved by lord Tvaṣṭṛ.

16b-17a. Lord Kṛṣṇa obtained this famous Sudarśana discus that shone like the fire at the time of dissolution, thanks to the grace of Rudra.

384. Pūrvo Manu: i.e. Vaivasvata. Construe: pūrvo Manu cakṣāma, Manus tu na (Cakṣāma).

385. For detail about the paring of glory of the sun, see *Mārka*. Ch. 108.

17b-19a. The first Manu (i. e. born of Saṁjñā) had nine sons all equal to him. They were:—Ikṣvāku, Nabhaga, Dhṛṣṇu, Śaryāti, Nariṣyanta, Nābhāga, Ariṣṭa, Karūṣa and Pṛṣadhra. These nine are known as Mānavas (sons of Manu).

19b-21. Ilā his eldest daughter and the most excellent one had formerly attained the state of a man. O leading sages, it was due to the grace of Mitra and Varuṇa that she attained the state of a man when she was known as Sudyumna. Again she went to Śaravaṇa[386] and regained the state of a woman at the behest of Bhava. Sudyumna the glorious son of Manu became a woman for the increase of the lunar race.

22. It was at the time of the horse-sacrifice of Ikṣvāku that Ilā became a Kimpuruṣa. During the state of Kimpuruṣa, also Ilā is called Sudyumna.

23-24. Then it chanced she was a woman for one month and a man for another. Ilā resorted to the house of Budha, the son of Soma. Finding an opportunity she was made to indulge in sexual intercourse by Budha. Purūravas was born as the son of Ilā and Budha.

25. He was intelligent and the first-born in the line of Soma. He was a devotee of Śiva and very valorous. O ascetics, I shall dilate later on the extent of expansion of Ikṣvāku race.

26. O excellent brahmins, Sudyumna had three sons viz. :—Utkala, Gaya and Vinatāśva.

27. The land of Utkala was assigned to Utkala, the western land was given to Vinatāśva. Gayā is said to be the excellent city of Gaya.

28. In Gayā Devas and the Pitṛs are stationed always.

The eldest of brothers, viz. Ikṣvāku obtained the Madhya deśa (Middle land)

29-32. In view of his feminine nature Sudyumna did not get his share but at the instance of Vasiṣṭha, Sudyumna was installed in Pratiṣṭhāna, as its glorious and righteous king. After attaining kingdom, the highly blessed son of Manu equipped with the characteristics of both man and woman, the king of great renown gave that kingdom to Purūravas.

386. Śaravaṇa: a Himālayan forest where Kārttikeya, the eldest son of Śiva, was born. Lord Śiva had pronounced a curse that a man entering this forest would turn into a woman.

The heroic son of Ikṣvāku was Vikukṣi who was the best among the knowers of Dharma as also the eldest of Ikṣvāku's hundred sons. He had fifteen sons. The eldest was Kakutstha. From Kakutstha was born Suyodhana.

33. O excellent sages, thereafter were born Pṛthu, Viśvaka and Pārthiva. Viśvaka's son was Ārdraka ; Yuvanāśva was his son.

34. Thereafter were born Śrāvastī[386a] of great splendour and then Vaṁśaka. O excellent brahmins, it was by the former that Śrāvastī city was built in the Gauḍa Deśa.

35. Vaṁśa's son was Bṛhadaśva. Kuvalāśva was his son. By killing Dhundhu of great strength he acquired the name of Dhundhumāra.

36. Dhundhumāra had three sons well known in the three worlds. They were Dṛḍhāśva, Caṇḍāśva and Kapilāśva.

37. Pramoda was the son of Dṛḍhāśva. Haryaśva was his son. Nikumbhā was the son of Haryaśva. Samhatāśva was his son.

38. Kṛśāśva and Raṇāśva were the two sons of Saṁhatāśva. Yuvanāśva was the son of Raṇāśva and his son was Māndhātā.

39. Māndhātā had three sons well known in the three worlds. They were Purukutsa, Ambarīṣa and Mucukunda.

40-42. Yuvanāśva the second is said to be the heir to Ambarīṣa. Harita was the son of Yuvanāśva and from him began the line of Hāritas. These were brahmins in the line of Aṅgiras, but Kṣatriyas in temperament.

Purukutsa's successor was Trasadasyu of great renown. Sambhūti born of Narmadā was his son. Viṣṇuvṛddhā was his son and after him his descendants are known as Viṣṇuvṛddhas.

43. These also resorted to the line of Aṅgiras and were equipped with the characteristics of Kṣatriyas. Sambhūti procreated another son named Anaraṇya.

44. O brahmins, in the course of his conquest of the three worlds, Anaraṇya was killed by Rāvaṇa. Bṛhadaśva was the son of Anaraṇya and Haryaśva was his son.

45. King Vasumanas was born of Dṛṣadvatī and Haryaśva. His son was the king Tridhanvan a great devotee of Śiva.

46-51 a. He became the disciple of Taṇḍin, the son of Brahmā. By his grace he attained the fruit of a thousand

386a. a city in ancient Oudh.

horse-sacrifices. At his behest he became a valorous devotee of Śiva and attained the lordship of Gaṇas.

At the outset he had no money with him. The righteous soul pondered over this :—How shall I perform the horse-sacrifice ?" O excellent brahmins, it was then that he met the son of Brahmā, the brahmin Taṇḍin and acquired from him the thousand names of Rudra, formerly mentioned by Brahmā. Taṇḍin eulogised the great lord Śiva by means of these thousand names. The excellent brahmin born of Brahmā thereby acquired the lordship of Gaṇas. Thereafter the king too obtained the thousand names mentioned by Taṇḍin formerly. By repeating them he too acquired the lordship of Gaṇas.

The sages said :—

51b-52a. O Sūta, of good holy rites, the thousand names[387] of Rudra had been repeated by Taṇḍin born of Brahmā. They contain a good lot of the meanings of all Vedic texts. It behoves you to mention those splendid names to us.

Sūta said:—

52b-54a O sages of good holy rites, listen to the thousand and eight names of Śiva who is the soul of all living beings and whose splendour is unmeasured. It was by repeating these that he attained the lordship of Gaṇas.

387. In fact, the text records less than one thousand names, unless we include 'mataḥ' (repeated thrice, cf. verses 61, 75, 87) etc. as proper names. It may also be observed that some names are identical in form: Nīlaḥ (105, 116), Aninditaḥ (121, 124), Guhāvāsī (131, 138), Viṣṇu (126, 162), Jaṭī (55, 81), Dhātā (126, 141), Balaḥ (99, 122), Muniḥ (91, 91), Lambitoṣṭhaḥ (109, 123), Mahākaṇṭhaḥ (108, 147), Vṛkṣaḥ (85, 132); others are repetitive in sense: Śmaśānavāsī (57), Śmaśānavān (108); Naraḥ (59), Nara, Vigrahaḥ (105); Mahāromā (110), Mahākeśaḥ (110); Candraḥ (61) Induḥ (150); Others are the names of gods and sages: Vāsudevaḥ (92), Adhokṣajaḥ (101), Viṣṇu (126, 162) (of Viṣṇu); Dhātā (126) (of Brahmā); Devendra (155), Śakra (126), Amareśa (122), Vajrī (154) (of Indra); Vāmadeva (92), Kapila (119) (of sages).

ST. explains these anomalies in the following way: (1) Identical forms are interpretable differently. (2) Śiva is omni-formed and hence can be identical with Viṣṇu, Brahmā, Indra, fire, air, etc. (3) Originally, there were ten thousand names whose authorship was assigned to Brahmā. They were reduced to one thousand and eight numbers by Brahmā himself and handed down to Taṇḍin for propagation among the worshippers.

54b-60. *Rudra's thousand names*: (1) Sthira (steady) (2) Sthāṇu[388] (fixed as a stump) (3) Prabhu (lord) (4) Bhānu[389] (sun) (5) Pravara (very good one) (6) Varada[390] (one who grants boons) (7) Vara (excellent) (8) Sarvātman (soul of all) (9) Sarvavikhyāta (well known to all) (10) Sarva (identical with all) (11) Sarvakara[391] (doing everything) (12) Bhava (source of all) (13) Jaṭin (having matted hair) (14) Daṇḍin (having the staff) (15) Śikhaṇḍin[392] (having the tuft) (16) Sarvaga (reaching everything) (17) Sarvabhāvana (conceiver and creator of all) (18) Hari (identical with Hari) (19) Hariṇākṣa (deer-eyed) (20) Sarvabhūtahara (destroyer of all living beings) (21) Smṛta (remembered) (22) Pravṛtti (activity) (23) Nivṛtti (withdrawal of worldly activity) (24) Śāntātman[393] (of quiescent soul) (25) Śāśvata (permanent) (26) Dhruva (steady) (27) Śmaśānavāsin[394] (residing in the cremation ground) (28) Bhagavān[395] (lord) (29) Khecara (one walking over the sky) (30) Gocara (one walking over the earth) (31) Ardana[396] (one who harasses) (32) Abhivādya (one who is worthy of being saluted) (33) Mahākarman (one of great tasks) (34) Tapasvin (ascetic) (35) Bhūtadhāraṇa (one

388. Sthāṇuḥ—tiṣṭhanty asmin ST.: the abode of the universe. Cf. 'saṁsāramaṇḍapasyāsya mūlastambhāya śambhave'—cited in ST.

389. Bhānu—the sun or the illuminator of the universe. Cf. 'yasya bhāsā sarvam idaṁ vibhāti'—cited in ST.

390. Varadaḥ—one who grants boons or one who destroys the covering of illusion (māyā-vilāsān dyati khaṇḍayati) ST.

391. Sarvakaraḥ—the material cause of the universe. Cf. 'yato vā imāni bhūtāni jāyante'—cited in ST.

392. Śikhaṇḍī—in the form of a hunter adorned with the peacock feathers.

393. Śāntātmā—identical with the persons devoid of desires. Cf. yaccāsya santato bhāvas tasmādātmeti gīyate—cited in ST.

394. Śmaśāna-vāsī—one who abides in suṣumnā artery. For this meaning suṣumnā ST. quotes Haṭha-yoga-pradīpikā: "suṣumnā śūnyapadavī brahmarandhram mahāpathaḥ / śmaśānaṁ śāmbhavī madhyamārgascetyekavācakāḥ.

395. bhagavān—ṣaḍguṇaiśvarya-viśiṣṭhaḥ ST. Cf. Viṣṇu. 'utpattim pralayaṁ caiva bhūtānām āgatiṁ gatiṁ vetti vidyām avidyāṁ ca sa vācyo bhagavān iti.

396. Ardanaḥ—one who causes distress to the sinner (ardayati=pīḍayati) or one who lives on alms (bhaikṣya-caryayā carati) ST.

who sustains the living beings) (36) Unmattaveṣa[397] (one who appears in the guise of a mad man) (37) Pracchanna (one who is in disguise) (38) Sarvaloka (omni-seer), (39) Prajāpati (lord of subjects) (40) Mahārūpa[398] (one having great forms) (41) Mahākāya (one of great body) (42) Śivarūpa[399] (one of auspicious forms) (43) Mahāyaśas (one whose fame is great) (44) Mahātman (Great soul) (45) Sarvabhūta (one who has become all) (46) Virūpa[400] (deformed) (47) Vāmana (dwarf) (48) Nara[401] (man) (49) Lokapāla (the protector of the worlds) (50) Antarhitātman (one whose soul is hidden) (51) Prasāda (pleasure) (52) Abhayada[402] (bestower of fearlessness) (53) Vibhu[403] (all-pervading) (54)) Pavitra (holy) (55) Mahān (great) (56) Niyata (restrained) (57) Niyatāśraya (invariable support). (58) Svayambhū (self-born) (59) Sarvakarman (one performing all holy rites) (60) Ādi[404] (the first one) (61) Ādikara[405] (one who creates the first) (62) Nidhi (treasure for all).

61-70 (63) Sahasrākṣa (thousand-eyed) (64) Viśālākṣa (wide-eyed) (65) Soma (accompanied by Umā) (66) Nakṣatra Śādhaka (the creator of stars) (67) Candra (identical with the moon) (68) Sūrya (identical with the sun) (69) Śani (identical with saturn) (70) Ketu (identical with Ketu) (71) Graha[306] (planet) (72) Grahapati[407] (the lord

397. Unmatta-Veśaḥ—this refers to his abnormal behaviour in Daru forest (Ch.).

398. Mahārūpaḥ—of great dimension. Cf 'mahato mahīyān'—cited in ST.

399. N.S. Text reads sarvarūpaḥ for Śivarūpaḥ or Śavarupaḥ.

400. Virūpaḥ—śarabha-pakṣirūpaḥ ST. one who has the form of a bird (=vi). See ch. 31.

401. Naraḥ—one who assumed a human shape.

402. Abhayadaḥ—abhayaṁ svātmaikyaṁ dadāti ST. one who identifies himself with his devotees and thus makes them fearless. Cf. 'bhayaṁ dvitīyābhiniveśataḥ syāt—cited in ST.

403. Vibhuḥ—omnipresent. Cf 'tenedam pūrṇam puruṣeṇa sarvam' cited in ST.

404. Ādiḥ—primeval being. Cf. 'yo devānām prathamam purastāt—cited in ST.

405. Ādikaraḥ—the creator of the creator. Cf. 'yo brahmāṇam vidadhāti pūrvam'—cited in ST.

406. Grahaḥ—Vṛṣṭyavagrahakārako bhaumaḥ ST. Mars who withholds rains.

407. Grahapatiḥ—lord of planets (grahas), i.e. Jupiter (Bṛhaspati).

of planets) (73) Mata[408] (identical with Budha (74) Rājan[409] (king) (75) Rājyodaya[410] (cause of the rise of kingdoms) (76) Kartā (the doer) (77) Mṛgabāṇārpaṇa[411] (one who discharges arrows on the deer) (78) Ghana (solid, cloud) (79) Mahātapas (of great penance) (80) Dīrghatapas (of long penance) (81) Adṛśya (invisible) (82) Dhanasādhaka (realiser of riches) (83) Saṁvatsara (vear) (84) Kṛtī[412] (one who has fulfilled duties) (85) Mantra (identical with mantra) (86) Prāṇāyāma, (87) Parantapa (one who scorches enemies) (88) Yogin (89) Yoga (90) Mahābīja (having great seed) (91) Mahāretas (one whose semen virile is great) (92) Mahābala (one of great strength) (93) Suvarṇaretas (having golden semen) (94) Sarvajña (omniscient) (95) Subīja[413] (having good seed) (96) Vṛṣavāhana (bull-vehicled) (97) Daśabāhu (having ten arms) (98) Animiṣa (winkless) (99) Nīlakaṇṭha (blue-necked) (100) Umāpati[414] (lord of Umā) (101) Viśvarūpa (universal formed) (102) Svayaṁśreṣṭha (one who is the most excellent oneself) (103) Balavīra (strong and heroic) (104) Balāgraṇī (leader of the army) (105) Gaṇakartā (creator of gaṇas) (106) Gaṇapati (lord of the gaṇas) (107) Digvāsas (naked) (108) Kāmya (one worthy of being loved) (109) Mantravit (knower of the mantras) (110) Parama (greatest) (111) Mantra (112) Sarvabhāvakara (inducer of all emotions) (113) Hara (destroyer) (114) Kamaṇḍaludhara (holding the water-pot) (115) Dhanvin (holding the bow) (116) Bāṇahasta (having arrows in the hand) (117) Kapālavān (having the skull) (118) Śarī (having the arrows) (119) Śataghnī (having the hundred-killer weapon) (120) Khaḍgin (having the sword) (121) Paṭṭiśin (having the iron club) (122) Āyudhin (having

408. Mataḥ—the planet mercury (budha).

409. Rājā—the planet Venus.

410. Rājyodayaḥ—Rāhu ST.

411. Mṛgabāṇārpaṇaḥ. ST. cites *Mahimna stotra* to explain the legend of Brahmā becoming a deer and of Śiva, an arrow.

412. Kṛtī=N.S. text reads kṛtaḥ=kṛta-yugarūpaḥ ST.

413. Subījaḥ—whose semen virile is infallibly productive. It refers to the birth of Kārttikeya, the son of Śiva, out of the fire. The fire could not destroy the semen of Śiva.

414. Umā-patiḥ—lord of Energy in the form of Om, or the master of Brahma-vidyā. Cf. *Kena*—'Brahma-vidyaiva om—cited in ST.

weapons) (123) Mahān (great) (124) Aja (Unborn) (125) Mṛgarūpa (having the form of the deer) (126) Tejas (splendour) (127) Tejaskara (creator of splendour) (128) Vidhi (precept) (129) Uṣṇīṣin (having turban) (130) Suvaktra (having good face) (131) Udagra (exalted) (132) Vinata (humble) (133) Dīrgha (long) (134) Harikeśa[415] (green-haired) (135) Sutīrtha (having good holy centres) (136) Kṛṣṇa[416] (black or identical with Kṛṣṇa, the son of Vasudeva) (137) Śṛgālarūpa[417] (one having the form of a jackal) (138) Sarvārtha (having all riches) (139) Muṇḍa (one with tonsured head) (140) Sarvaśubhaṁkara (one who does good to all) (141) Siṁhaśārdūlarūpa (one having the forms of lion and tiger) (142) Gandhakāri (one causing fragrance) (143) Kapardin (one having matted hair) (144) Ūrdhvaretas (one of sublimated sexuality) (145) Urdhvaliṅgin (one having the penis lifted up) (146) Urdhvaśāyin[418] (one lying upwards) (147) Nabhas (one abiding in the sky) (148) Tala (of the form of pātāla—nether world), (149) Trijaṭin[119] (one having three locks of matted hair) (150) Cīravāsas (one wearing bark garments) (151) Rudra (of tearful form) (152) Senā (in the form of army of Devas) (153) Patī (sustainer of the people) (154) Vibhu (lord).

71-80. (155) Ahorātram (of the form of day and night) (156) Naktam (of the form of night) (157) Tigmamanyu (of fierce anger) (158) Suvarcas (having good refulgence) (159) Gajahā (slayer of the elephant) (160) Daityahā (slayer of the daityas) (161) Kāla (death, time) (162) Lokadhātā[420] (creator of the worlds) (163) Guṇākara[421] (mine of good qualities) (164) Siṁhaśārdūlarūpāṇām ārdra-carmāmbara-dhara (one who wears the fresh hide of the lion and tiger as his cloth) (165) Kālayogin (one who connects everything with

415. Harikeśaḥ—lord of Viṣṇu (Hari) and Brahmā (k).
416. Kṛṣṇa—in the form of Aghora.
417. Śṛgālarūpaḥ—See ch. 92.
418. Urdhvaśāyī—one who sleeps in the firmament ST.
419. Tri-jaṭi—having Prakṛti of three guṇas as his consort.
420. Loka-dhātā—support of the fourteen worlds.
421. Guṇākaraḥ—mine or the receptacle of yogic guṇas (ch. 16) or of the 24 guṇas admitted by the Nyāya philosophy.

time or death) (166) Mahānāda (having great sound) (167) Sarvāvāsa (abode of all) (168) Catuṣpatha[422] (one who goes in all four ways at the same time) (169) Niśācara (one walking at night) (170) Pretacārin[423] (walking among the ghosts) (171) Sarvadarśin (seeing all) (172) Maheśvara (great lord) (173) Bahu (omni-formed) (174) Bhūta (of the form of the past) (175) Bahudhana (one having much wealth) (176) Sarvasāra (essence of all) (177) Mṛteśvara (lord of the dead) (178) Nṛtyapriya (one who is fond of dances (179) Nityanṛtya (one who dances perpetually) (180) Nartana[424] (one who makes others dance) (181) Sarvasādhaka (achiever of all) (182) Sakārmuka (one who has a bow) (183) Mahābāhu (large-armed) (184) Mahāghora (extremely terrible) (185) Mahātapas (of great penance) (186) Mahāśara[425] (of great arrows) (187) Mahāpāśa (having a great noose) (188) Nitya (permanent) (189) Giricara (walking over the mountains) (190) Amataḥ (not recognizable)[426] (191) Sahasrahasta (thousand-armed) (192) Vijaya (victorious) (193) Vyavasāya (enterprise) (194) Anindita (uncensured) (195) Amarṣaṇa (angry) (196) Marṣaṇātmā (one who endures and excuses) (197) Yajñahā[427] Destroyer of the sacrifice) (198) Kāmanāśana (destroyer of Kāma) (199) Daksahā (slayer of Dakṣa) (200) Paricārin (one who walks all round) (201)

422. Catuṣpathaḥ—the path of the four goals of life, viz. (i) dharma, (ii) artha, (iii) kāma, (iv) mokṣa. Or the originator of four stages of life, viz. (i) brahma-carya (stage of celibacy) (iii) gṛhastha (stage of a householder), (iii) Vānaprastha (stage of a forester), (iv) sannyāsa (stage of a renouncer).

423. Preta-vāhanaḥ—one who has a preta (a departed being) as his vehicle. Cf. Cāmuṇḍā śava-vāhanā—cited in ST.

424. Nartanaḥ—sarva-prerakaḥ. ST. one who instigates all to activity.

425. Mahāśaraḥ—one who has a powerful missile. ST. refers to Śiva's destruction of Tripuri.

426. ST. dissolves 'giricaro mataḥ' as 'giricaraḥ amataḥ'; amataḥ —unknown or unrecognized. ST refers to the event of Dāru forest when the sages could not recognize him dressed in strange guise.

427. Yajñahā—destroyer of sacrifice. It refers to the legend of Śiva who destroyed Dakṣa's sacrifice.

(201) Prahasa[428] (one who laughs aloud) (202) Madhyama[429] (Middling) (203) Tejsas[430] (of the form of fire) (204) apahārin (destroyer of the universe) (205) Balavān (strong) (206) Vidita[431] (known) (207) Abhyudita (one who has risen up) (208) Bahu[432] (many) (209) Gambhīraghoṣa (one whose voice is profound) (210) Yogātman of yogic soul (211) Yajñahā (i.e. destroyer of the sacrifice) (212) Kāmanā (of the form of desire for release) (213) Aśana (Destroyer) (214) Gambhīraroṣa (one whose fury is profound) (215) Gambhīra (majestic) (216) Gambhīra Balavāhana (one whose strength and vehicle are profound) (217) Nyagrodharupa (one who has the form of the holy fig tree) (218) Nyagrodha (identical with the holy fig tree) (219) Viśvakarman (one of universal activities) (220) Viśvabhuk (swallower of the universe) (221) Tīkṣṇa (one having fierce form) (222) Apāya (one who does not take the riches of his devotees) (223) Haryaśva[433] (having green horses) (224) Sahāya (help) (225) Karma[434] (of the form of sacrificial ritual) (226) Kālavid[435] (one who knows the time) (227) Visṇu (pevading all) (228) Prasādita (one who has been propitiated) (229) Yajña (230) Samudra (ocean) (231) Baḍavāmukha (mouth of the submarine fire) (232) Hutāśanasahāya (one who is helped (assisted) by fire) (233) Praśāntātman (quiescent soul) (234) Hutāśana (fire) (235) Ugratejas (one whose refulgence is fierce) (236) Mahātejas (of great splendour) (237) Jaya (victory) (238) Vijayakālavid (one who knows the time of victory).

428. Prahasaḥ—who is prone to laughter. Cf. 'sphuṭāṭṭahāso-ccalitāṇḍakośaḥ'—*Śiva Kavaca* as cited in ST.

429. Madhyamaḥ the middling. It refers to the Rudra form of Śiva. Cf. "madhyato Rudram īśānam"—cited in ST.

430. Tejas—in the form of fire. Cf. "Rudro vā eṣa yad agniḥ"—cited in ST.

431. Viditaḥ—brahmavid-rūpaḥ. *ST.* one who has identified himself who those with have realized Brahman. "brahma-vid brahmaiva bhavati"—cited in *ST.*

432. Bahuḥ—*ST.* dissolves as 'a-bahuḥ'—one, not many. "ekaṁ sad viprā bahudhā Vadanti" -cited in *ST.*

433. Haryaśvaḥ—one who has Viṣṇu for his vehicle *ST.*

434. Karma—one who symbolises pious or charitable deeds.

435. Kālavid—one who knows auspicious or inauspicious times *ST.*

81-100. (239) Jyotiṣāmayanam (the cause of the transit of the luminaries) (240) Siddhi (Achievement) (241) Sandhi (alliance) (242) Vigraha (clash) (243) Khaḍgin (one who has a sword) (244) Śaṇkhin (one who has a conch) (245) Jaṭin[436] (one who has matted hair) (246) Jvālin (one who has flames) (247) Khecara (one moving about in the firmament) (248) Dyucara (one moving about in the heaven) (249) Balin (strong) (250) Vaiṇavin (one having the lute) (251) Paṇavin (one having the Paṇava drum) (252) Kāla (Death, Time) (253) Kālakaṇṭha (dark-necked) (254) Kaṭaṅkaṭa (one who lovingly touches the elephantine face of his son Gaṇeśa) (255) Nakṣatravigraha[437] (one having the stellar body) (256) Bhāva (emotion) (257) Vibhāva (friend) (258) Sarvatomukha[438] (having faces all round) (259) Vimochana[439] (one who releases (260) Śaraṇa (refuge) (261) Hiraṇyakavacodbhava (born of golden armour) (262) Mekhalā (one in the form of yoni—womb) (263) Kṛtirūpa (one in the form of effort) (264) Jalācāra[440] (one having actions similar to those of senseless persons) (265) Stuta (one who is eulogised) (266) Vīṇi (one having the lute Vīṇā) (267) Paṇavin (one having the drum Paṇava) (268) Tālin[441] (one having the Tāla (beating of the time) (269) Nālin[442] (one having the tube) (270) Kalikaṭu (one who is harsh to Kali) (271) Sarvatūryaninādin (one who sounds his instruments) (272) Sarvavyāpyāparigraha[443] (one who is omnipresent and does not accept gifts) (273) Vyālarūpin (one having the form of a tiger) (274) Bilāvāsa (one residing in a hollow) (275) Guhāvāsa[444] (one whose residence is

436. Jaṭī—one who is the base of the universe *ST*.

437. Nakṣatravigrahaḥ—one who is the abode (vigraha) of constellations.

438. Sarvatomukhaḥ—having face in all directions. "Viśvataś cakṣur uta viśvatomukhaḥ"—cited in *ST*.

439. Vimocanaḥ—one who releases jīvas from the net of twentyfour tattvas.

440. Jalācāraḥ or Jalādhāraḥ—one who is the support or the cause of movement for watery reservoirs, rivers, streams and oceans.

441. Tālī—one who has a tāla—a musical instrument.

442. Nālī—one who holds a lotus in his hand or is born of a lotus. *ST*.

443. Sarva-vyāpī—one who has an all-pervasive subtle body.

444. Guhā-vāsaḥ—one who abides in guhā (intellect)

cave) (276) Tarangavid (one who knows the innermost idea) (277) Vṛkṣa (kalpavṛkṣa) (278) Śrimālakarmin[445] (one who has Śrīkṣetra as the sphere of his worship) (279) Sarvabandhavimocana (one who releases (devotees from all bondages) (280) Bandhana (one who binds the non-devotees) (281) Surendrāṇām yudhi śatruvināśana (one who destroys the enemies of Devas in the battle) (282) Sakhā[446] (friend) (283) Pravāsa[447] (shelter for all) (284) Durāpa (unattainable) (285) Sarvasādhuniṣevita (one who is resorted to by all good men) (286) Praskanda (one who is drying up and moving ahead) (287) Avibhāva (one who is not comprehended) (288) Tulya (equal)[448] (289) Yajñavibhāgavid (one who knows the divisions of yajñas) (290) Sarvavāsa[449] (one who abides in all) (291) Sarvacārin (one who goes everywhere) (292) Durvāsas Identical with the sage of that name) (293) Vāsava (Indra) (294) Mata[450] (non-dual) (295) Haima (pertaining to gold or snow) (296) Hemakara (one who has gold in his hands) (297) Yajña (sacrifice) (298) Sarvadhāri (holding all) (299) Dharottama (best among the supporters) (300) Ākāśa[451] (firmament) (301) Nirvirūpa[452] (having no form) (302) Vivāsas[453] (one who has no clothes) (303) Uraga (serpent) (304) Khaga (going in the sky) (305) Bhikṣu (beggar, mendicant) (306) Bhikṣurūpin (one who is in the guise of a mendicant) (307) Raudrarūpa (one who has a terrible form)(308) Surūpavān[454]

445. Śrīmālakarmin—one who resorts to the abode of Lakṣmī (Śrīmāla) for yogic trance.

446. One who is the friend of Jīva (i.e. the individual soul) "suparṇav aitau sadṛṣau sakhāyau". –cited in *ST*.

447. Pravāsaḥ—one who is the eternal abode of all mobile and immobile beings.

448. Tulyaḥ—unprejudiced.

449. Sarva-vāsaḥ –one who is the sheath of all. "īśāvāsyam idaṁ sarvam" cited in *ST*.

450. Mataḥ—advaita-mata-rūpaḥ *ST*. of non-dual form

451. Ākāśaḥ—one who shines splendidly.

452. Nirvirūpaḥ— nirgataṁ virūpaṁ śarabha-pakṣirūpaṁ yasmāt *ST*. the source of origin of Śarabha. It refers to the narrative of Śarabha occurring in this purāṇa.

453. Vivāsā—one who has no covering over his body. i.e. naked.

454. Surūpavān—of auspicious form: "tasyaite tanuvau ghorā anyā śivarūpā"—cited in *ST*.

(one who has good forms) (309) Vasuretas (one whose semen virile causes riches) (310) Suvarcasvin (having good refulgence) (311) Vasuvega (one who has the velocity of the Vasus) (312) Mahābala (one who has great strength) (313) Manas (mind) (314) Vega (one who has velocity) (315) Niśā (night) (316) Cara (a spy) (317) Sarvalokaśubhaprada (one who grants auspicious things to all the worlds) (318) Sarvāvāsin[455] (one whose residence is in everything) (319) Trayīvāsin[456] (one who resides in the three Vedas) (320) Upadeśakara (one who gives instructions) (321) Adhara (one having no support) (322) Muni[457] (sage) (323) Ātman (soul) (324) Muni (sagacious) (325) Loka (world) (326) Sabhāgya (Fortunate) (327) Sahasrabhuk[458] (one who enjoys thousand things) (328) Pakṣin[459] (bird) (329) Pakṣarūpa[460] (having the form of the wing) (330) Atidīpta (highly illuminated) (331) Niśākara (moon) (332) Samīra (wind) (333) Damanākāra (one who has the form of a suppressor) (334) Artha (wealth, meaning purpose) (335) Arthakara (serving the purpose) (336) Avaśa[461] (uncontrolled by another) (337) Vāsudeva[462] (identical with that god) (338) Deva (lord) (339) Vāmadeva (lord of opposites) (340) Vāmana (Dwarf) (341) Siddhiyogāpahārin (one who removes Siddhi and Yoga) (342) Siddha[463] (self proved) (343) Sarvārthasādhaka (one who realises all purposes) (344) Akṣuṇṇa (undefeated) (345) Kṣuṇṇarūpa (one who has the form of the defeated) (346) Vṛṣaṇa (one who extends

455. Sarvāvāsī—all-pervasive.

456. Trayīvāsī—one who abides in the three Vedas.

457. Muniḥ—in the form of sacred tree agasti. *ST.* cites Viśva in support of this meaning.

458. Sahasrabhuk—one who destroys (bhuṅkte) or protects (bhunakti) people.

459. Pakṣī—one who has two wings: Ṛk and Sāman. "Ṛk dakṣiṇaḥ pakṣaḥ samottaraḥ pakṣaḥ". ST.

460. Pakṣarūpaḥ—in the form of two fortnights: white and dark.

461. Vaśaḥ—amenable to the wishes of his devotees. Or dissolve 'avaśaḥ'—free.

462. Vāsudevaḥ—*ST.* offers a far-fetched explanation: one who sports in disguise.

463. Siddhaḥ—Kapila: "siddhānāṁ Kapilo muniḥ" Bhagavad-Gītā cited in *ST.*

morality) (347) Mṛdu[464] (soft) (348) Avyaya (unchanging) (349) Mahāsena (one who has a big army) (350) Viśākha[465] (Kārttikeya) (351) Śaṣṭibhaga[466] (one-sixtieth part) (352) Gavām pati[467] (lord of the line) (353) Cakrahasta (having discus in the hands) (354) Viṣṭambhi[468] (impending) (355) Mūlastambhana[469] (one who steadies the root) (356) Ṛtu (season) (357) Ṛtukara (one who causes the seasons) (358) Tāla (palmyra tree) (359) Madhu (honey) (360) Madhukara (bee) (361) Vara (excellent one) (362) Vānaspatya (belonging to a tree) (363) Vājasana[470] (one loving clarified butter) (364) Nitya (eternal) (365) Āśramapūjita (worshipped by people in all stages of life) (366) Brahmacārin (religious student) (367) Lokacārin (one who walks over the world) (368) Sarvacārin (moving about on everything) (369) Sucāravit (one who knows good conduct) (370) Īśāna[471] (371) Īśvara[472] (lord) (372) Kāla (time, death) (373) Niśācārin (one moving about at night) (374) Anekadṛk[473] (having many eyes) (375) Nimittastha (one stationed in the cause) (376) Nimittam (cause) (377) Nandi (delighted and delighter) (378) Nandikara (one causing others to be delighted) (379) Hara (destroyer) (380) Nandi (Nandin) (381) Īśvara[474] (382) Sunandin (383) Nandana (delightful) (384) Viṣamardana (one suppressing poison)

464. Mṛduḥ—of soft nature. "ākrānta-sapta-pātāla-kuharopi mahā balaḥ prāpte Kaliyuge ghore mṛdutām upayāsyati"—cited in *ST*.

465. Viśākhaḥ—of the form of Kārttikeya.

466. Saṣṭibhāgaḥ—one who has sixty tattvas at his command. See *Māṇḍūkyopaniṣad*.

467 Gavām patiḥ—lord of the sacred hymns. *ST*. quotes Śiva Gītā: "Chandasām yastu dhenūnām ṛṣabhatvena Kīrtitaḥ".

468. Viṣṭambhī—one who makes others motionless.

469. Mūlastambhanaḥ—Controller of Prakṛti (mūla).

470. Vājasanaḥ—of the form of Vājasaneyi śākhā of the Śukla Yajurveda.

471. Īśānaḥ -lord of all knowledge: "Īśānaḥ sarva-vidyānām".

472. Īśvaraḥ—controller of all beings. "iśvaraḥ sarva-bhūtānam"—cited in *ST*.

473. Aneka lṛk -multi-eyed. Cf. "namo astu nīlagrvāya sahasrākṣāya mīḍhuṣe"—cited in *ST*.

474. Iśvaraḥ—abounding in wealth or prosperity. Cf "iśvaro vibhavair āḍhyaḥ"—Viśva cited in *ST*.

(385) Bhagahārin (remover of Bhaga) (386) Niyantṛ[475] (one who restrains, a charioteer) (387) Kāla (388) Lokapitāmaha (grandfather of the worlds) (389) Caturmukha[476] (four-faced) (390) Mahāliṅga (having great liṅga) (391) Cāruliṅga (having charming liṅga) (392) Liṅgādhyakṣa[477] (presiding deity of the liṅgas) (393) Surādhyakṣa (presiding deity of Devas) (394) Kālādhyakṣa (presiding deity of time) (395) Yugāvaha (bringing about the yuga) (396) Bījādhyakṣa[478] (presiding deity of the seeds or corns) (397) Bījakartā (the maker of the seeds) (398) Adhyātma (self-centred) (399) Anugata (one with the followers in spiritual line) (400) Bala[479] (strength) (401) Itihāsa[480] (Mythological text) (402) Kalpa (ritualistic text) (403) Damana (suppressor) (404) Jagadīśvara (lord of the universe) (405) Dambha (arrogance) (406) Dambhakara (one causing arrogance) (407) Dātṛ (donor) (408) Vaṁśa (race) (409) Vaṁśakara (one who maintains the family) (410) Kali (identical with the yuga Kali).

101-110. (411) Lokakartā (maker of the worlds) (412) Paśupati (lord of the Paśus or individual souls) (413) Mahākartā (the great maker) (414) Adhokṣaja[481] (Viṣṇu, identical with Viṣṇu) (415) Akṣaram (imperishable) (416) Paramam (great) (417) Brahman (brahman) (418) Balavān (strong) (419) Śukra (Venus) (420) Nitya (permanent) (421) Anīśa (having no lord above him) (422) Śuddhātmā[482] (Pure soul) (423) Śuddha (pure) (424) Māna (measure) (425) Gati (goal) (426) Havis (rice and ghee offering) (427) Prāsāda (mansion) (428) Bala[483] (strength) (429) Darpa (arrogance) (430)

475. Niyantā—charioteer. "jagad-yantra-svarūpasya rathasya śrī-maheśvaraḥ/niyantā tata eveśaḥ sūta ityabhidhiyate"—Ahobala cited in *ST*.

476. Caturmukhaḥ—of the form of four-faced Brahmā.

477. Liṅgādhyakṣaḥ—lord of unmanifest Prakṛti (liṅga).

478. Bījādhyakṣaḥ—dispenser of the fruits of dharma and adharma.

479. Balaḥ—strong one. Cf. "balāya namaḥ" -cited in *ST*.

480. Itihāsaḥ- of the form of tradition.

481. Adhokṣajaḥ—not realizable by the organs of sense.

482. Śuddhātmā—of pure mind. For 'ātman' in the sense of 'mind', see Viśva: 'ātmā deha-mano-buddhiṣu'—cited in *ST*.

483. Bala—one who has an abode in the form of Kailāsa). *ST*. cites Viśva: 'balaṁ sthane'.

Darpaṇa (mirror) (431) Havya (offering consigned to the fire) (432) Indrajit (conqueror of Indra) (433) Vedakāra (maker of the Vedas) (434) Sūtrakāra (compiler of the Aphorisms) (435) Vidvān (scholar) (436) Paramardana (suppressor of enemies) (437) Mahāmeghanivāsin[484] (resident of the great cloud) (438) Mahāghora (extremely terrible) (439) Vaśin[485] (one who keeps persons under control) (440) Kara (the destroyer of the universe) (441) Agnijvāla (flame of the fire) (442) Mahājvāla (having great flame) (443) Paridhūmrāvṛta (one surrounded by smoke) (444) Ravi (sun) (445) Dhiṣaṇa (intelligent one) (446) Śaṅkara (447) Anitya (non-eternal in the form of the universe) (448) Varcasvin (refulgent) (449) Dhūmralocana (having smoke-coloured eyes) (450) Nīla[486] (blue-coloured) (451) Aṅgalupta[487] (one deficient in a limb) (452) Śobhana (splendid one) (453) Naravigraha[488] (one having human body) (454) Svasti (hail) (455) Svastisvabhāva (naturally faring well) (456) Bhogin (enjoying pleasures) (457) Bhogakara (causing pleasures) (458) Laghu (light) (459) Utsaṅga (lap, devoid of attachment) (460) Mahāṅga (having great limbs) (461) Mahāgarbha (having great womb) (462) Pratāpavān (valorous) (463) Kṛṣṇavarṇa (black in colour) (464) Suvarṇa (having good colour) (465) Indriya (sense-organ) (466) Sarvavarṇika [of all castes (colours)] (467) Mahāpāda (having big feet) (468) Mahāhasta (having big hands) (469) Mahākāya (of great body) (470) Mahāyaśas (having great fame) (471) Mahāmūrdhā (having great head) (472) Mahāmātra[489] (having great Mātrās (units of time) (473) Mahāmitra (Great friend (474) Nagālaya[490] (having mountain as residence) (475) Mahāskandha (having great shoulder) (476) Mahākarṇa (having great ears) (477) Mahoṣṭha (having

484. Mahāmegha-nivāsin—one who has Viṣṇu (mahāmegha) for his abode.

485. Vaśī—controller.

486. Nīlaḥ—blue or dark. It refers to his aghora form.

487. Aṅga-luptaḥ—part of whose body is possessed by Umā.

488. Nara-vigrahaḥ—one who had a battle with Arjuna.

489. Mahāmātraḥ—controller of elephants in the form of death.

490. Nagālayaḥ—one who lives on mountains.

490a. Śmaśānavān—śmanāṁ śarīrāṇām śānaṁ tanū-karaṇam punarjanma-nivāraṇaṁ Kāśīpuraṁ yasya—one who saves men who live in Kāśī from the circle of birth and death.

great lips) (478) Mahāhanu (having great jaws) (479) Mahānāsa (having great nose) (480) Mahākaṇṭha (having great neck) (481) Mahāgrīva (having great cervix) (482) Śmaśānavān[490a] (having the cremation ground) (483) Mahābala (having great strength) (484) Mahātejas (having great splendour) (485) Antar (omnipresent)[491] (486) Ātman (immanent soul) (487) Mṛgālaya (abode of the deer) (488) Lambitoṣṭha[492] (having suspended lips) (489) Niṣṭha (steady) (490) Mahāmāya (having or wielding great Māyā) (491) Payonidhi (storehouse of water, milk) (492) Mahādanta (having great teeth) (493) Mahādaṁṣṭra (having great curved fangs) (494) Mahājihva (having great tongue) (495) Mahāmukha (having great face) (496) Mahānakha (having great nail) (497) Mahāroman (having great hairs) (498) Mahākeśa (having great tresses of hair) (499) Mahājaṭa (having great matted hair).

111-120. (500) Asapatna[493] (having no rivals or enemies) (501) Prasāda[494] (grace) (502) Pratyaya (belief) (503) Gīta-sādhaka (one who practises music) (504) Prasvedana (one who sweats) (505) Asvedana[495] (one who does not perspire) (506) Ādika[496] (one who is the first of all) (507) Mahāmuni[497] (great sage) (508) Vṛṣaka[498] (dharma) (509) Vṛṣaketu[499] (the bull-bannered) (510) Anala (fire) (511) Vāyuvāhana[500] (wind-vehicled) (512) Maṇḍalin (one having halo) (513) Meruvāsa (one having the Meru as residence) (514) Devavāhana (deva-vehicled) (515) Atharvaśīrṣa (the name of the Vedic Text; having that as the head) (516) Sāmāsya (having Sāman as the face) (517) Ṛksahasrorjitekṣaṇa (having

491. Antar—one who abides in all.

492. Lambitoṣṭhaḥ—It refers to Gaṇeśa.

493. Asapatnaḥ—without a foe or a co-wife.

494. Prasādaḥ—one who destroys (prakarṣeṇa sādayati) asuras.

495. Asvahenaḥ (a-su-aha-inaḥ)—lord of Viṣṇu. *ST*.

496. Ādikaḥ—the primeval (patriarch). "prajāpatīnām prathamam" Mbh. (Droṇa parva)—cited in ST.

497. Mahāmuniḥ—in the form of Nārada.

498. Vṛṣakaḥ—in the form of Dharma.

499. Vṛṣaketuḥ—one who has Vṛṣa (Nandikeśvara) on his flagstaff.

500. Vāyu-vāhanaḥ—one who has wind as his Vehicle. Cf. "Marunmaya-rathaḥ śambhuḥ".—Śiva-rahasya cited in *ST*.

the thousand Ṛk verses as eyes of great power) (518) Yajuḥpādabhuja (having the Yajur mantras as feet and arms) (519) Guhya (worthy to be secret) (520) Prakāśaujas (of manifest power) (521) Amoghārthaprasāda (one whose grace is never futile) (522) Antarbhāvya (one who should be meditated upon, within the heart) (523) Sudarśana (good to look at) (524) Upahāra[501] (one to whom gifts are presented) (525) Priya (loving (526) Sarva (All-in all) (527) Kanaka (gold) (528) Kāñcanasthita (one stationed in gold) (529) Nābhi (the nave) (530) Nandikara (one who causes delight) (531) Harmya[502] (having a mansion) (532) Puṣkara[503] (having a lotus as [residence]) (533) Sthapati (monarch, architect) (534) Sthita (stationed) (535) Sarvaśāstra (having all sacred scriptures) (536) Sarva-dhana (having all riches) (537) Sarvādya (first among all) (538) Sarvayajña (having all Yajñas) (539) Yajvā (performer of sacrifices) (540) Samāhita (one who has concentration and mental purity) (541) Naga (having mountain as home) (542) Nīla[504] (blue) (543) Kavi (poet) (544) Kāla (time, death) (545) Makara (crocodile) (546) Kālapūjita (one who is worshipped by kāla) (547) Sagaṇa (having attendants) (548) Gaṇakāra (Maker of the gaṇas) (549) Bhūtabhāvanasārathi (one who has Brahmā as his charioteer) (550) Bhasmaśāyin (one who lies in Bhasma) (551) Bhasmagoptṛ[505] (protector of bhasman) (552) Bhasmabhūtatanu[506] (one whose body is fully covered with ash) (553) Gaṇa (attendant) (554) Āgama (sacred literature) (555) Vilopa (one who dissolves) (556) Mahātman (noble soul) (557) Sarvapūjita (adored by all), (558) Śukla (white) (559) Strīrūpasampanna

501. Upahāraḥ—one to whom offerings are made. Cf. "sarve asmai balim āharanti"—cited in *ST*.

502. Harmyaḥ—one who has got a palace for his abode.

503. Puṣkaraḥ—one who abides in Puṣkara. Puṣkara is a sacred place where Brahmā is stated to have set up Nīlalohita (Śiva-liṅga) (Sk. I. ii. 45. 105). It lies near Ajmer.

504. Nilaḥ—one who has some peculiar marks on his body. Cf. Viśva as cited in *ST*.

505. Bhasma-goptā—one who protects through ashes. *ST*. quotes Mbh. : "rakṣārthaṁ maṅgalārthaṁ ca pavitrārthaṁ ca bhāmini lāñchanārthaṁ ca bhaktānāṁ bhasma dattaṁ mayā purā //

506. Bhasma-bhūta-tanuḥ—who is the source of the origin of ashes. *ST*. refers to a *Mbh*. legend in this context.

(equipped with the form of a lady) (560) Śuci (pure) (561) Bhūtanisevita (resorted to by the goblins) (562) Āśramastha (one stationed in the hermitage) (563) Kapotastha[507] (one stationed in the dove) (564) Viśvakarmā (doing everything) (565) Pati (lord) (566) Virāt (huge massive one) (567) Viśāla-śākha[508] (having wide branches) (568) Tāmroṣṭha (having copper-coloured lips) (569) Ambujāla (having collection of waters) (570) Suniścita (well decided) (571) Kapila (tawny-coloured) (572) Kalaśa (water pot) (573) Sthūla (stout) (574) Āyudha (weapon) (575) Romaśa (hairy) (576) Gandharva (577) Aditi (578) Tārkṣya (579) Avijñeya (incomprehensible) (580) Suśārada (very young and fresh) (581) Paraśvadhāyudha (axe-armed) (582) Deva (illustrious deity) (583) Arthakārin (creator of wealth) (584) Subāndhava (good kinsman).

121-140. (585) Tumbavīṇa (having the lute made of Tumba (a kind of gourd) (586) Mahākopa[509] (having great wrath) (587) Ūrdhvaretas (one who has sublimated sexuality) (588) Jaleśaya (one lying down in the waters) (589) Ugra (fierce) (590) Vaṁśakara (sustainer of the families) (591) Vaṁśa (race, bamboo) (592) Vaṁśavādin (one who expounds races) (593) Anindita[510] (uncensured) (594) Sarvāṅgarūpin (one who assumes the form of the part of all) (595) Māyāvin (wielding Māyā) (596) Suhṛda (friend, having good heart) (597) Anila[511] (wind) (598) Bala (strength) (598) Bandhana (binding) (600) Bandhakartā (cause of bondage) (601) Subandhanavimocana (one who liberates people from bondages easily) (602) Rākṣasaghna (slayer of Rākṣasas) (603) Kāmāri (enemy of kāma) (604) Mahādaṁṣṭra[512] (one

507. Kapotasthaḥ—one who assumed the form of a pigeon. *ST*. refers to the legend of Śibi in the *Mahābhārata*.

508. Viśāla-śākhaḥ –Veda-drumarūpaḥ in the form of the tree of knowledge.

509. Mahākopaḥ—mahān pūjyaḥ kopo yasya—one whose wrath is worshipped. Cf. "namaste rudra manyave" cited in *ST*.

510. Aninditaḥ—aḥ Viṣṇu nindito yasmāt, through whom Viṣṇu was humiliated. It refers to the legend of Dadhīci.

511. Anilaḥ—one who is distinct from Jīva (=nila), the latter being attached to the objects of senses.

512. Mahādaṁṣṭraḥ—one who has projected tusks. This refers to his boar-form.

who has large curved fangs) (605) Mahāyudha (having great weapons) (606) Lambita (one who is suspended down) (607) Lambitoṣṭha (one whose lips hang down suspended) (608) Lambahaṣta (one whose hands hang down) (609) Varaprada (one who grants the boon) (610) Bāhu (arm) (611) Anindita[513] (uncensured) (612) Sarva (all) (613) Śaṅkara (614) Akopana (having no work) (615) Amareśa (lord of the immortal beings) (616) Mahāghora (extremely terrible) (617) Viśvedeva (lord of the universe) (618) Surārihā (destroyer of the enemies of Devas) (619) Ahirbudhnyad[514] (620) Nirṛti (621) Cekitāna (knowing and conversant) (622) Halin (balarāma with the ploughshare) (623) Ajaikapād[515] (the single-footed unborn) (624) Kāpālin[516] (having the skull for rituals) (625) Śam (one who renders joy) (626) Kumāra (one who kills with spikes) (627) Mahāgiri[517] (great mountain) (628) Dhanvantari[518] (629) Dhūmaketu (comet) (630) Sūrya (sun) (631) Vaiśravaṇa[519] (632) Dhātṛ (633) Viṣṇu (634) Śakra (635) Mitra (636) Tvaṣṭṛ (637) Dhara (mountain) (638) Dhruva (steady) (639) Prabhāsa (640) Parvata (641) Vāyu (642) Aryaman (643) Savitṛ (644) Ravi (645) Dhṛti (courage) (646) Vidhātṛ (Creator) (647) Māndhātṛ (648) Bhūtabhāvana (purifier of the living beings) (649) Nīra (water) (650) Tīrtha (holy centre) (651) Bhīma (terrible) (652) Sarvakarman (performing all duties) (653) Guṇodvaha (one who lifts up the good attributes) (654)

513. Aninditaḥ—nāstī inditaṁ paramaiśvaryaṁ yasmāt *ST*. the most prosperous lord.

514. Ahirbudhnyaḥ—Śeṣa-rūpaḥ *ST*. the Dragon of the Deep, one who has monopolized all powers and forms within himself and lies concealed in the region of primeval darkness.

515. Aja-ekapād—one-footed goat, one who is devoid of motion prior to creation. According to *ST*. it refers to his half man and half woman (ardhanārīśvara) form.

516. Kāpāli—one who has created this universe consisting of heaven and earth *ST*.

517. Mahāgiriḥ, i.e. Himālaya. Cf. *Bhagavad-Gītā*. 'sthāvarāṇāṁ mahāgiriḥ"—cited in *ST*.

518. Dhanvantari : the physician. Cf. "bhiṣaktamaṁ tvā bhiṣajāṁ śṛṇomi"—cited in *ST*.

519. Vaiśravaṇa—son of Viśravaṇa, i.e. Kubera.

Padmagarbha (one who has lotus within) (655) Mahāgarbha (having a large womb) (656) Candravaktra (moon-faced) (657) Nabhas (sky) (658) Anagha (sinless) (659) Balavān (powerful) (660) Upaśānta (quiescent) (661) Purāṇa (ancient one (662) Puṇyakṛt) (meritorious) (663) Tamas (characterized by tamas quality) (664) Krūrakartṛ (Ruthless maker) (665) Krūravāsin (ruthless dweller) (666) Tanu (slender) (667) Ātman (668) Mahauṣadha (great medicine) (669) Sarvāśaya[520] (Asylum of all) (670) Sarvacārin (moving in everything) (671) Prāṇeśa (lord of the vital breaths) (672) Prāṇinām pati (lord of the living beings) (673) Devadeva (lord of Devas) (674) Sukhotsikta[521] (proud due to happiness) (675) Sat (existent) (676) Asat (non-existent) (677) Sarvaratnavid (knower of all jewels) (678) Kailāsastha (stationed in Kailāsa) (679) Guhāvāsin[522] (residing in a cave) (680) Himavad (snowy) (681) Girisaṁśraya (one who has resorted to the mountain Himālaya) (682) Kulahārin (one who removes the families) (683) Kulākartā (one who does not shape the race) (684) Bahuvitta (one having much wealth) (685) Bahupraja (one who has many children) (686) Prāṇeśa (lord of the vital breaths) (687) Bandhakī[523] (of the form of māyā) (688) Vṛkṣa[524] (the destroyer of māyā (689) Nakula (mangoose) (690) Adrika (mountaineer) (691) Hrasvagrīva (one with a short neck) (692) Mahāsānu (one with large knees) (693) Alola (not fickle) (694) Mahauṣadhi (great medicine) (695) Siddhāntakārin (one who gets according to principles) (696) Siddhārtha (one who has achieved the purpose) (697) Chandas (of the form of chhandas, Gāyatrī etc.) (698) Vyākaraṇodbhava (one originating from prosody and grammar) (699) Siṁhanāda (one whose sound is like the roaring sound of the lion) (700) Siṁhadaṁṣṭra (one having the curved fangs of a lion) (701) Siṁhāsya (leonine faced) (702) Siṁhāvāhana (lion vehicled) (703) Prabhāvātman (one who has prowess

520. Sarvāśayaḥ—the resting place for all. *ST*.

521. Sukhotsiktaḥ—the source of pleasure. Cf. "tasyaiva ānandasya mātrām upajīvanti"—cited in *ST*.

522. Guhāvāsi—one who abides in Meru-guhā (the cavity of the heart).

523. Bandhakī—in the form of allusion (māyā).

524. Vṛkṣaḥ—destroyer of Māyā.

in the Ātman) (704) Jagatkāla (death unto the Universe) (705) Kāla (706) Kampin (shaking) (707) Taru[525] (tree) (708) Tanu (slender) (709) Sāraṅga (Deer) (710) Bhūtacakrāṅka[526] (one marked with the multitudes of goblins) (711) Ketumālin (one having garlands of banners) (712) Suvedhaka (one who pierces well) (713 Bhūtālaya (one who is the abode of living beings) (714) Bhūtapati (lord of the goblins) (715) Ahorātra (day and night) (716) Mala[527] (dirt) 717) Amala[528] (devoid of dirt) (718) Vasubhṛt (one holding riches) (719) Sarvabhūtātman (the Ātman, soul of all living beings) (720) Niścala (non-moving) (721) Subudha (good scholar) (722) Vibudha (deva) (723) Durbudha (very difficult to comprehend) (724) Sarva bhūtānām asuhṛt (he who takes away the life of all living beings) (725) Niścala (unmoving) (726) Calavid (one who knows the mobile beings (727) Budha (scholar) (728) Amoghasaṁyama (one whose restraint is never futile) (729) Hṛṣta (delighted) 730) Bhojana (of the form of food) (731) Prāṇadhāraṇa (one who sustains life) (732) Dhṛtimān (courageous) (733) Matimān (intelligent) (734) Tryakṣa[529] (three-eyed) (735) Sukṛta (well conducted) (736) Yudhāmpati (lord of battles) (737) Gopāla (protector of the kine) (738) Gopati (lord of the kine) (739) Grāma (village) (740) Gocarmavasana (one wearing the leather of the bull) (741) Hara[530] (742) Hiraṇyabāhu (one who has gloden arms) (743) Guhāvāsa[531] (resident of the cave) (744) Praveśana (one who enters the cavity) (745) Mahā-

525. Taruḥ—in the form of tree, i.e. creation.

526. Bhūta-cakrāṅkaḥ -one is the source of the origin of beings. Cf. "yato vā imāni bhūtāni jāyante"—cited in *ST*.

527. Malaḥ—not benevolent towards the heretics.

528. Amalaḥ—sinless.

529. Tryakṣaḥ—three-eyed, so called because a third eye burst from his forehead with a great flame when Umā, playfully placed her hands over his eyes after he had been engaged in austerities in the Himālayas. This eye has been very destructive. It rendered Kāma, the God of Love, to ashes; Dowson, *H. M.* See under Trilocana.

530. Haraḥ -one who destroys all at the time of dissolution. Cf. "brahmāṇam indraṁ varuṇaṁ yamaṁ dhanadaṁ eva ca / nigṛhya harate yasmāt tasmād dhara iti smṛtaḥ" *Mbh.* (Droṇa p.) cited in *ST*.

531. Guhāvāsaḥ -one who has an abode in intellect.

manas (lofty-minded) (746) Mahākāma (one who has great love) (747) Cittakāma (one who has kept Kāma within the mind) (748) Jitendriya (one who has conquered the sense-organs) (749) Gāndhāra (750) Surāpa[532] (one who drinks wine) (751) Tāpakarmarata (one who is engaged in beating activity) (752) Hita (Beneficent) (753) Mahābhūta[533] (great goblin) (754) Bhūtavṛta (surrounded by goblins) (755) Apsaras[533a] (having a watery pond in the form of the moon) (756) Gaṇasevita (one who is resorted to by the Gaṇas) (757) Mahāketu (big-bannered) (758) Dharāḍhātā (creator of the earth) (759) Naikatānarata (one who does not concentrate on a single note) (760) Svara (one in the form of Tone) (761) Avedanīya (one who cannot be understood) (762) Āvedya (one who cannot be informed) (763) Sarvaga[534] (omnipresent) (764) Sukhāvaha (one who causes happiness).

141-150. (765) Tāraṇa (redeemer) (766) Caraṇa (walking) (767) Dhātṛ (creator) (768) Paridhā[535] (in the form of earth) (769) Paripūjita (one who is worshipped all round) (770) Saṁyogin[536] (united) (771) Vardhana (one who increases) (772) Vṛddha (old) (773) Gaṇika (A member of the Gaṇas) (774) Gaṇādhipa (overlord of the Gaṇas) (775) Nitya (eternal) (776) Dhātṛ (creator) (777) Sahāya (assistant) (778) Devāsurapati (lord of Devas and asuras) (779) Pati (lord) (780) Yukta[537] (united) (781) Yuktabāhu (of united arms) (782) Sudeva (good deva) (783) Suparvaṇa (of good joints) (784) Suṣāḍha (785) (one who helps to calmly bear pain) (786) Skandhada[539] (one who pacifies Kārttikeya) (787) Harita (green) (788) Hara (789) Vapus[540] (sower of seed) (790)

532. Surāpaḥ—one who drinks Surā (a kind of wine). Cf. "Jivhvāpraveśa-sambhūta-vahninotpāditaḥ khalu / candrāt sravati yaḥ sāraḥ sā syād amara-vāruṇi // *HyP*—cited in *ST*.

533. Mahābhūtaḥ—designated as a great being. Cf. "Jyeṣṭhaṁ bhūtaṁ vadanty enam". *Mbh.* (Droṇa p.) cited in *ST*.

533a. Apsaraḥ—a reservoir of water.

534. Sarvagaḥ—sung by all.

535. Paridhā—in the form of earth *ST*.

536. Saṁyogī—united with Prakṛti.

537. Yuktaḥ—united with Umā.

538. Suṣāḍhaḥ—one who makes pains bearable.

539. Skandhadaḥ—one who removes the anger of Kārttikeya.

540. Vapuḥ—the sower of seeds.

Āvartamāna (one who turns round and round) (791) Anya[541] (Another) (792) Vapuḥśreṣṭha (one who has excellent body) (793) Mahāvapuḥ (one who has great body) (794) Śiras[542] (in the form of Yajus) (795) Vimarśana (one who examines the head) (796) Sarvalakṣyalakṣaṇabhūṣita (one who is adorned by all examples and characteristics (797) Akṣaya (one who is imperishable) (798) Rathagīta (one who has music in the chariot) (799) Sarvabhogin (one who enjoys all pleasures) (800) Mahābala (one who has great strength) (801) Sāmnāya (one who has the Vedas) (802) Mahāmnāya (one whose Vedas are great) (803) Tīrthadeva (lord of the holy centres) (804) Mahāyaśas (having great fame) (805) Nirjīva (one from whom emanates all life) (806) Jīvana (one who enlivens) (807) Mantra (808) Subhaga (fortunate) (809) Bahukarkaśa (excessively hard) (810) Ratnabhūta (one who has become precious) (811) Ratnāṅga (one who is part of a jewel) (812) Mahārṇavanipātavid (one who knows the fall into a great sea) (813) Mūlam (root) (814) Viśāla (wide) (815) Amṛtam (nectar) (816) Vyaktāvyakta (one who is clear and not clear) (817) Taponidhi (storehouse of austerities) (818) Ārohaṇa (one that ascends) (819) Adhiroha (one who rides) (820) Śīladhārin (one who holds good conduct) (821) Mahātapas (one of great penance) (822) Mahākaṇṭha (one who has a great neck) (823) Mahāyogin (great Yogin) (824) Yuga (825) Yugakara (creator of yugas) (826) Hari (827) Yugarūpa (having the form of the yuga) (828) Mahārūpa (one who has great forms) (829) Vahana (bearing) (830) Gahana (inaccessible) (831) Naga (mountain) (832) Nyāya (logic, justice) (833) Nirvāpaṇa[543] (alleviating, pacifying) (834) Apāda (footless) (835) Paṇḍita (scholar) (836) Acalopama (comparable to a mountain) (837) Bahumāla (having many garlands) (838) Mahāmāla (having great garland) (839) Śipiviṣṭa[544] (one who has penetrated the rays) (840) Sulocana (having good eyes) (841) Vistāra (extension)

541. Anyaḥ—distinct from Prakṛti.

542. Yajuḥ—in the form of Yajur-veda, Cf. "tasya yajur eva śiraḥ"—cited in *ST*.

543. Nirvāpaṇaḥ—the eternal sower of seeds.

544. Śipiviṣṭaḥ—in the form of Viṣṇu. Cf. Viṣṇuḥ Śipiviṣṭaḥ—cited in *ST*.

(842) Lavaṇa (salty ocean) (843) Kūpa (well) (844) Kusumāṅga (one whose limbs are flower-like) (845) Phalodaya (one who acts well till the fruit is reaped) (846) Ṛṣabha (bull) (847) Vṛṣabha (taurus) (848) Bhaṅga (breaking) (849) Maṇibimbajaṭādhara (one who holds jewelled image and matted hair) (850) Indu (moon) (851) Visarga (discharge) (852) Sumukha (having good face) (853) Śūra (heroic) (854) Sarvāyudha (one who has all weapons) (855) Saha (one who endures).

151-168. (856) Nivedana (one who informs) (857) Sudhājāta (one born of nectar) (858) Svargadvāra[545] (one who is the gateway to the heaven) (859) Mahādhanus (one who has great bow) (860) Girāvāsa (one who resides in speech) (861) Visarga (subsidiary creation) (862) Sarvalakṣaṇalakṣyavid (knower of all characteristics and examples) (863) Gandhamālin (one who has sweet smelling garlands) (864) Bhagavān[546] (lord) (865) Ananta (endless) (866) Sarvalakṣaṇa (one who has all characteristics) (867) Santāna (series) (868) Bahula (a bestower of riches) (869) Bāhu (one having long arms) (870) Sakala (having the digits) (871) Sarvapāvana (sanctifier of all) (872) Karasthālī[547] (having the pot in the hand) (873) Kapālin[548] (having the skull) (874) Urdhvasaṁhanana (having the body lifted up) (875) Yuvan (youthful) (876) Yantra-tantra-suvikhyāta (one who is well known for his yantras and tantras) (877) Loka (world) (878) Sarvāśraya (one who is the support of all) (879) Mṛdu (soft) (880) Muṇḍa (one with shaven head) (881) Virūpa (deformed) (882) Vikṛta (spoiled) (883) Daṇḍin (one having the staff) (884) Kuṇḍin[549] (one having the sacrificial pit) (885) Vikurvaṇa[550] (one who alters and affects) (886) Vāryakṣa (one who has the eyes in

545. Svarga-dvāraḥ—the door to happiness. For the definition of Svarga compare: "yan na duḥkhena sambhinnaṁ na ca grastam anantaram abhilāṣopanītaṁ ca tat sukhaṁ svaḥpadāspadam.

546. Bhagavān—aiśvaryavān *ST*. glorious or prosperous.

547. Karasthāli –one who eats in the palm of his hands. Cf. "tataḥ karatalīkṛtya vyāpi hālāhalaṁ Viṣam", Bhāg.–cited in *ST*.

548. Kapāli—one who sustains or nourishes Brahmā (ka).

549. Kuṇḍī—one who carries Ganges over his forehead.

550. Vikurvaṇaḥ—one who is not accessible through activities.

water ?) (887) Kakubha[551] (prominent) (888) Vajrin (having the thunderbolt) (889) Dīptatejas (one of illuminated splendour) (890) Sahasrapād (thousand-footed) (891) Sahasramūrdhan (thousand-headed) (892) Devendra (lord of Devas) (893) Sarvadevamaya (identical with all Devas) (894) Guru (preceptor) (895) Sahasrabāhu (thousand-armed) (896) Sarvāṅga (having all limbs) (897) Śaraṇya (worthy of being sought refuge in) (898) Sarvalokakṛt (maker of all the worlds) (899) Pavitra (holy) (900) Trimadhu (having threefold honey) (901) Mantra (in the form of the sacred hymns of the Vedas (902) Kaniṣṭha[552] (youngest) (903) Kṛṣṇapiṅgala (dark and tawny-coloured) (904) Brahmadaṇḍa-vinirmātṛ (maker of the staff of Brahmā) (905) Śataghna (one who kills a hundred) (906) Śatapāśadhṛk (one who wears a hundred nooses) (907) (identical with the units of time[553] such as Kalā (908) Kāṣṭhā (909) Lava (910) Mātrā (911) Muhūrta (912) Ahaḥ (day) (913) Kṣapā (night) (914) Kṣaṇa (915) Viśvakṣetraprada (one who grants the holy centres of the universe) (916) Bīja (seed) (917) Liṅgam (918 Ādya (primeval being) (919) Nirmukha (one whose face has vanished) (920) Sadasad (existent-cum-non-existent) (921) Vyakta (visible) (922) Avyakta (invisible) (923) Pitṛ (father) (924) Mātṛ (mother) (925) Pitāmaha (grandfather) (926) Svargadvāram (the gateway of the heaven) (927) Mokṣadvāram (gateway of the salvation) (928) Prajādvāra (one who is the arch-door for his devotee) (929) Triviṣṭapa (heaven) (930) Nirvāṇam (salvation) (931) Hṛdaya (heart) (932) Brahmaloka (the world of Brahmā) (933) Parāgati (the greatest goal) (934) Devāsuravinirmātṛ (one who creates Devas and the Asuras) (935) Devāsuraparāyaṇa (one who is interested in Devas and Asuras) (936) Devāsuraguru (the preceptor of Devas and Asuras) (937) Deva (the lord) (938) Devāsuranamaskṛta (one who is bowed to by Devas and the Asuras) (939) Devāsuramahāmātra (high official and minister unto Devas and Asuras) (940) Devāsuragaṇāśraya (one who

551. Kakubhaḥ—one who carries triśūla in his lap *ST*.

552. Kaniṣṭhaḥ—ever youthful or of unmanifest form. Cf. "nityayūne kaniṣṭhāya yadvā 'vijñeya-mūrtaye".—Ahobala cited in *ST*.

553. Kalā —who symbolises units of time, such as Kalā, etc.

is the support of the groups of all Devas and Asuras (941) Devāsuragaṇādhyakṣa (the presiding officer of the groups of all Devas and Asuras) (942) Devāsuragaṇāgraṇī (the leader of the groups of all Devas and Asuras) (943) Devādhideva (the overlord of all Devas) (944) Devarṣi (the divine sage) (945) Devāsuravarapradа (one who grants boons to all Devas and Asuras) (946) Devāsureśvara (lord of all Devas and the Asuras) (947) Viṣṇu (948) Devāsuramaheśvara (great lord of all Devas and Asuras) (949) Sarvadevamaya (identical with all Devas) (950) Acintya (unthinkable) (951) Devatātman (the Ātman of the deities) (952) Svayambhava (the self-born) (953) Udgata (one who has come up) (954) Trikrama (one who has taken three steps) (955) Vaidya (physician) (956) Varada (granter of boons) (957) Varaja[554] (born of Viṣṇu) (958) Ambara (in the form of firmament) (959) Ijya (worthy of being worshipped) (960) Hastin (elephant) (961) Vyāghra (tiger) (962) Devasiṁha (lion among Devas) (963) Maharṣabha (great bull) (964) Vibudhāgrya (leader among Devas) (965) Sura (god) (966) Śreṣtha (excellent) (967) Svargadeva (lord of the heaven) (968) Uttama[555] (the most excellent one) (969) Saṁyukta (united) (970) Śobhana (splendid) (971) Vaktā[556] (eloquent speaker) (972) Āśāprabhava (source of all hopes) (973) Avyaya (the unchanging one) (974) Guru (preceptor) (975) Kānta (splendid) (976) Nija (one's own) (977) Sarga (creation) (978) Pavitra (holy) (979) Sarvavāhana (having all vehicles) (980) Śṛṅgin (having born) (981) Śṛṅgapriya (fond of horn peaks) (982) Babhru (tawny coloured) (983) Rājarāja (king of kings) (984) Nirāmaya] (free from ailments) (985) Abhirāma (beautiful) (986) Suśaraṇa (a good refuge) (987) Nirāma (devoid of unripe things) (988) Sarvasādhana (having all means) (989) Lalāṭākṣa (having an eye in the forehead) (990) Viśvadeha (hāving the universe as the body) (991) Hariṇa

554. Varajaḥ—born in the form of 'sāmba-Śiva' at the behest of Viṣṇu. Or dissolve 'avara-jaḥ' born in the form of fire at the time of dissolution.

555. Uttamaḥ—the supreme soul. Cf. "uttamaḥ puruṣas tvanyaḥ paramātmetyudāhṛtaḥ // *Bhagavad-Gītā* cited in *ST*.

556. Vaktā—the best speaker. Cf. "adhivaktā"—cited in *ST*.

(deer) (992) Brahmavarcasa (having the refulgence of the brahman) (993) Sthāvara pati (lord of the immobile things) (994) Niyatendriyavartana (one who remains with restraints on the sense-organs) (995) Siddhārtha (one who has achieved the purpose) (996) Sarvabhūtārtha (one who has all realities) (997) Acintya (unthinkable) (998) Satya (true) (999) Śuci-vrata (one of pure holy rites) (1000) Vratādhipa (the lord of holy rites) (1001) Param (the highest being) (1002) Brahma (the brahman) (1003) Muktānām paramā gati (the greatest goal of the liberated souls) (1004) Vimukta (the liberated one) (1005) Muktakeśa[557] (one whose tresses are loosened) (1006) Śrīmān (glorious) (1007) Śrīvardhana (one who increases prosperity and glory) (1008) Jagat (universe).

169. In accordance with the importance of the name,[558] the lord of sacrifices was eulogized by me with devotion and attention.

170-171. Then the king who was well known in the three worlds obtained the hymn of Śiva from Taṇḍin. He eulogized the lord, the goal of the devotees, after the approval of Taṇḍin. By the grace of holy lord—Taṇḍin, the king Tridhanvā of great fame attained the merit of a thousand horse-sacrifices and also the overlordship of Gaṇas.

172-175. O Brahmins, he who reads this or listens to it or narrates this to the Brahmins, attains the merit of a thousand horse-sacrifices. In order to obtain release, the following sinners should repeat for a year these names, during the three Sandhyās (morning, midday and dusk) in the temple of Śiva or in the region sacred to Śiva and they should also worship the lord. They are :—the slayer of a Brahmin, the wine addict, the thief, the defiler of the preceptor's bed, the murderer of a refugee, and the one who commits breach of faith with his friends. So also the slayer of mother, father, warrior and the child in the womb.

557. Muktakeśaḥ—lord of the released souls.

558. Yathā-pradhānam—the principal name Śiva (not mentioned in the above list), with the ending in the dative case, is to be added to each of the names which are also to be put in the dative case. e.g. Oṁ muktakeśāya Śivāya namaḥ.

CHAPTER SIXTYSIX

The narrative of Yayāti

Sūta said:

1-2. By the grace of the lord of Devas as well as of Taṇḍin, Tridhanvan attained assiduously the benefit of a thousand horse-sacrifices. Thereafter he gained the lordship of Śiva's attendants. He was bowed to by all Devas. The scholarly king Trayyāruṇa was the successor to Tridhanvan.

3-4. He had an extremely powerful son named Satyavrata. He killed the king of Vidarbha[658a] of unmeasured prowess[559] and abducted his wife before the mantras of the wedding celebrations were brought to a close. The king Trayyāruṇa abandoned him because he was defiled by that evil.

5. When abandoned, he said to his father "Where shall I go ?" O brahmins, the father replied to him "Go and live among the Cāṇḍālas.

6-11. On being ordered thus, he went out of the city. At the instance of his father, the intelligent Satyavrata went to the Cāṇḍāla colony. On being abandoned by his father thus he stayed near the slum while his father went to the forest. The valiant (son) and meritorious king Satyavrata became famous in all the worlds under the name Triśaṅku. Once Vasiṣṭha pronounced on him a curse. Viśvāmitra of great splendour granted him boons and crowned him king in the hereditary kingdom. The sage performed a sacrifice on his behalf. Even as Devas and Vasiṣṭha were watching, the holy lord Viśvāmitrā raised him up to heaven in his human form.[560] His wife, Satyavratā born of the Kekaya family[561] gave birth to a spotless son Hariścandra. Hariścandra's son Rohita was very powerful.

12. Harita was the son of Rohita. Dhundhu was the son of Harita. Vijaya and Sutejas were the sons of Dhundhu.

558a. Vidarbha—i.e. the king of Vidarbha, mod. Berar, now placed under the administration of Mahārāṣṭra province.

559. Amitaujas—according to *ST*. it is the name of a king.

560. For detail, Dawson : *Hindu Mythology*, pp. 288-289.

561. Kekaya—Kekayas lived between the Jhelum and the Beas and had their capital at Girivraja (Girijak modern Jalālpur) on the Jhelum river.

13. Vijaya was so called because he conquered the kings of the Kṣatriyavarṇa. His son Rucaka was a righteous king.

14. Vṛka was the son of Rucaka. From him was born Bāhu. Sagara, an extremely virtuous king was his son.

15. Sagara had two wives, Prabhā and Bhānumatī. The fiery sage Aurva[562] was propitiated by both of them, with a desire for sons.

16-17. The delighted Aurva asked them to choose a boon of their liking out of the two, viz. one would have sixty thousand sons and the other a single son, who would continue the family line. Prabhā chose to have many sons and Bhānumatī one son who was Asamañjasa.

18. Thereafter Prabhā gave birth to sixty thousand sons. While digging the earth, they were burned by the angry outbursts of Viṣṇu[563] in the guise of Kapila as if through arrows.

19-20. Asamañjasa's son is well known as Aṁśumān. His son was Dilīpa. From Dilīpa was born Bhagīratha who performed penance and brought the Ganges to the earth. So it is called Bhāgīrathi. Bhagīratha's son was Śruta.

21. Nābhāga was his successor. He was a valorous devotee of Śiva. His son was Ambarīṣa, from whom was born Sindhudvīpa.

22. The earth, ruled over by Nābhāga Ambarīṣa with the power of his arms became entirely devoid of the three-fold distress.

23. The valorous son of Sindhudvīpa was Ayutāyus. Ṛtuparṇa of great fame was the son of Ayutāyus.

24-25. This powerful king was a friend of Nala. He was conversant with the secret of dice. In the Purāṇas, two Nalas of stable holy rites are well known. One was the son of Vīrasena and the other born in the family of Ikṣvāku. Sārvabhauma the lord of the subjects was the son of Ṛtuparṇa.

26. King Sudās was his son. He was equal to Indra. King Saudāsa was the son of Sudās.

562. Aurvo agniḥ—agnisadṛśaḥ Aurvo ṛṣiḥ *ST*. the fiery sage Aurva, the son of Urva and the grandson of the famous sage Bhṛgu.

563. Viṣṇu—i.e. the sage Kapila who destroyed the sons of king Sagara by uttering "hum". For detail, see *Śp*. (Umāsamhitā, p. 1610). Also *H.M.* pp. 271-272.

27-28. His actual name was Mitrasaha but he was more famous as Kalmāṣapāda.[564] Vasiṣṭha of great splendour begot of the wife of Kalmāṣapāda the son Aśmaka who continued the line of Ikṣvāku. Mūlaka was the son of Aśmaka and Uttarā (his wife).

29-30. That king was always surrounded by women due to his fear of Paraśurāma. Desirous of protection he had recourse to the excellent shield in the form of women. The virtuous king Śataratha was the son of Mūlaka. The powerful king Ilabila was born of Śataratha.

31. The valorous Vṛddha Śarmā was the son of Ilabila. The daughter of the Pitṛs bore him the son Viśvasaha.

32-33. Dilīpa was his son. He was famous by the name Khaṭvāṅga. He obtained a life for the duration of a Muhūrta. From heaven he came to this world for this period and conquered the three fires and the three worlds by means of his intellect and truthfulness. His son was Dīrghabāhu and Raghu was born of him.

34. The powerful and valiant Aja was born of Raghu. From him was born the glorious Daśaratha, the sustainer of the family of Ikṣvāku.

35. The heroic Rāma who was conversant with Dharma and who was well known in all the worlds was born of Daśaratha. So also were Bharata, Lakṣmaṇa and Śatrughna.

36-38. Rāma, the best among them, had great splendour and excellent valour. After killing Rāvaṇa in battle and performing sacrifices Rāma who was conversant with Dharma ruled over the kingdom for ten thousand years. A son well known as Kuśa was born to Rāma. His other son Lava was highly blessed, truthful and intelligent. Atithi was born to Kuśa and his son was Niṣadha.

39. Nala was born of Niṣadha and Nabhas was his son. A son called Puṇḍarīka was born to Nabhas, and Kṣema Dhanvan was his son.

40-41. His son was the heroic and valorous Devānīka. Ahīnara was his son and thereafter was Sahasrāśva. From him were born Candrāvaloka and Tārāpīḍa. His son was Chandragiri. Bhānucandra was his son.

564. **Kalmāṣapādaḥ—the same as Mitrasaha, a king of Ikṣvāku dynasty. For detail, Dawson *H.M.* pp. 144-145.**

42. His son was Śrutāyu who was also known as Bṛhadbala. This powerful king was killed by Saubhadra (son of Subhadrā i. e. Abhimanyu) in the Bhārata war.

43. These are the successor kings of Ikṣvāku. In general only the more important ones in the dynasty are mentioned here in order of their importance.

44-45. All of them had realized Śiva. In accordance with their knowledge[565] they had worshipped the lord and performed sacrifices according to the rules. The noble souls had all attained heaven. Some of them were liberated souls and yogins. As the result of the curse of a brahmin, Nṛga attained the state of a chameleon.

46. Dhṛṣṭa had three virtuous sons, viz., Dhṛṣṭaketu, Yamabāla and Raṇadhṛṣṭa.

47. Śaryāti had a son Ānarta and a daughter Sukanyā. Ānarta's son was Rocamāna.

48-49a. Rocamāna had a son Reva. From Reva were born Raivata and Kakudmin. Reva was the eldest of a hundred sons. His daughter Revatī was the wife of Balarāma.

49b Nariṣyanta's son was Jitātman.

50-51a From Nābhāga was born Ambarīṣa, the devotee of Viṣṇu. Ṛta was his glorious son. He was the best among those conversant with Dharma. Kṛta was his virtuous son also known as Pṛṣita.

51a. The sons of Karūṣa were known as Kārūṣas.

52. Pṛṣita incurred great sin by killing the cow of his preceptor.[566] It is well known that he was degraded as a Śūdra due to the curse of Cyavana, his preceptor.

53. Diṣṭa's son was Nābhāga and from him was born Bhalandana. His son Ajavāhana was a king of great exploits.

54. Thus (the successors of) the mighty sons of Manu are told briefly and the dynasty of Ikṣvāku (in some detail). Now I shall recount to you the dynasty of Aila.

565. pāśupataṁ jñānam—yogic practices as enjoined in Śaiva cult. Cf. p. 135 note 242.

566. Pṛṣata killed, in ignorance, the cow of his preceptor: Cyavana, mistaking it for a tiger in the darkness of night.

Sūta said:

55-56. O brahmins, Purūravas a valorous son of Ilā and a devotee of Rudra, held an unhindered sway in the holy land Prayāga[567] which is situated on the northern bank of the Yamunā[568] frequented by sages. He was the glorious lord of Pratiṣṭhāna[569] (Prayāga), and well established there.

57-58. He had six powerful glorious sons, well known in the region of the Gandharvas and devoted to Śiva. All of them were divine, being the sons of Urvaśī.[570] They were:—Āyu, Māyu, Amāyu, Viśvāyu, Śrutāyu and Śatāyu.

59. Āyu had five sons of great power. They were kings born of Prabhā the daughter of Svarbhānu.

60. Nahuṣa the first among them was known in all the worlds and conversant with Dharma. Nahuṣa's successors were six and they were comparable to Indra in splendour.

61-62. Those (kings) of great power were born of Virajā the daughter of the Pitṛs. They were Yati, Yayāti, Saṁyāti, Āyati, Andhaka and Vijāti. All these six were well renowned. Yati was the eldest of them and Yayāti was junior to him.

63. The eldest royal son Yati seeking salvation, was united with Brahman. Among the other five Yayāti was the strongest and most valorous.

64. He married Devayānī the daughter of Śukra. She became the demoness Śarmiṣṭhā the daughter of Vṛṣaparvan.

65. Devayānī gave birth to two sons Yadu and Turvasu. Both of them performed sacrificial rites. They were highly spoken and were experts in all lores.

567. Prayāga—this is a celebrated place of pilgrimage at the confluence of the Ganges and Jumnā in the Naimiṣa forest (*Sp.* Vs.1.4). It is situated on the northern bank of the Ganges (*Sk* II. 11.12.36). The name Prayāga is recorded by Huen Tsang in the seventh century and is as old as the reign of Aśoka who set up the stone pillar about 235 B.C. The Gupta emperors regarded the place as the capital of Madhyadeśa.

568. Yamunā—this river rises in the Himālaya mountains among the Jumnotri peaks, flows for 860 miles on the plains before it joins the Ganges at Prayāga.

569. **Pratiṣṭhāna**—The Purāṇas are not agreed upon its locus. Some place it on the north and some on the east side of the Ganges. Others place it on the north bank of the Yamunā.

570. Urvaśī—a celebrated celstial nymph.

66-67. Śarmiṣṭhā the daughter of Vṛṣaparvan gave birth to Druhyu, Anu and Pūru. Propitiated by Yayāti, Śukra, the leading brahmin gave him a shining well-built golden car and two everlasting great quivers.

68. The chariot was yoked to horses as quick as the mind. It was in this chariot that he brought home his bride. With that excellent chariot he conquered the earth within six months.

69-71. Yayāti was invincible to Devas, Dānavas and mortals. He was a devotee of Śiva, a meritorious soul abiding by Dharma. He performed sacrifices. He conquered anger. He was sympathetic to all living beings. That excellent chariot was inherited by all the descendants of Kuru until Janamejaya the son of Parīkṣit the king in the line of Pūru. As a result of the curse of the sage Garga[571] that chariot was destroyed.

72-76. The king Janamejaya harassed the son of Garga, the boy Akrūra, and hence attained the sin of brahmin slaughter. The king began to emit the odour of rusting iron. He ran about helterskelter. Since he was boycotted by the citizens and the people of the land he did not obtain happiness. Dejected, he did not even have perfect knowledge anywhere. In his anguish he went to sage Śaunaka and sought refuge in him. The liberal-minded sage who was known as Indreti performed sacrifice on his behalf. O excellent brahmins, for the sake of purification he made the king Janamejaya perform a horse sacrifice.

77-79. That king of great renown was relieved of the bad odour of iron as well as of his sin. In the middle of the Avabhṛtha ablution the divine and splendid chariot vanished. Lost from that family it was given to Vasu king of Cedi[572] by the delighted Indra. From him Bṛhadratha acquired the chariot. Thereafter, killing Jarāsandha (a successor of Bṛhadratha) Bhīma, the scion of the family of Kurus, gave that excellent chariot to Śrīkṛṣṇa out of love.

571. śāpād gargasya—by the curse of the sage Garga. The legend is not traceable.

572. Cedi-pateḥ—of the king of Cedi tribe or clan. Haimakoṣa identifies Cedi-nagarī with Tripurī (modern Tewar), situated on the Narmadā river near Jabalpur.

Sūta said:

80-83. King Yayāti son of Nahuṣa crowned his son Pūru (as king). O excellent brahmins, it was by that Pūru alone that he had been helped before. People of all castes including the leading brahmins spoke to the king who was desirous of crowning his youngest son:— O lord, how does the youngest son deserve the kingdom after overlooking the claims of the eldest son Yadu, the son of Devayānī and the grandson of Śukra? We are addressing you to keep up the traditional Dharma."

CHAPTER SIXTYSEVEN

The Narrative of Yayāti

Yayāti said:

1. Let the members of all castes beginning with the brahmins listen to my words in regard to this why I have decided that the kingdom should in no way be given to the eldest son Yadu.

2. My behest was not carried out by Yadu my eldest son. The son who is mentally opposed to his father is not approved of by good men.

3. The son who acts according to the instructions of his parents is praised by good men. He is the real son who behaves towards his parents in a manner befitting a son.

4. I have been treated with disrespect by Yadu, Turvasu, Druhyu and Anu.

5. My instructions were particularly honoured and carried out by Pūru. He is my youngest son by whom my old age had been taken over.

6. Because of Devayāni, Śukra had ordained that I would be attacked by old age. When he was requested, my old age was made transferable by him.

7-10. This boon was given by Śukra himself—"The son who favours you shall be your heir to the kingdom." May ye all, O sires, approve of it. Pūru shall then be crowned king."

The Sages said:

"The son who is endowed with good qualities and who is always beneficent to his parentsdeserves all welfare, although he may be the younger son. Lord Pūru deserves this kingdom since he is the son who has carried out your instructions. Because of the boon granted by Śukra this cannot be made otherwise."

Sūta said:

The son of Nahuṣa was told thus by the delighted people of the land.

11. After crowning his son Pūru in his own kingdom he directed Turvasu his son to be the southern border chief.

12. Similarly the king employed the eldest son Yadu in the southern frontier and Druhyu and Anu in the west and in the north respectively.

13. After conquering the earth including the seven islands and seven oceans, the son of Nahuṣa divided the kingdom into three parts among his sons.

14. With the royal glory transferred to his sons and with the burden placed on his kins, the king became pleased. His mind was filled with delight.

15-24. In this context the following song was formerly sung by the great king Yayāti :—

A man shall be glorious if only he withdraws all his desires like the tortoise withdrawing all its limbs; otherwise not, even if he performs a crore of holy rites.

Lust is never quelled by the enjoyment of desires. Just as the fire becomes all the more blazing with oil poured into it so also it is heightened by the same.[573]

Whatever grain or barley the earth contains, the entire gold it has, and all the animals and women of the earth are not enough for the insatiable desire of even a single individual. Considering this fact, man should remain tranquil (i.e. free from desires).

When man has no sinful motives towards any living being mentally, verbally or physically he attains Brahman.

573. This verse is repeated (I. 8.25). It is the same as *Pañcadaśī* (7.47).

When man is not afraid of others, when others are not afraid of him, when he neither despises nor hates, he attains Brahman.

Happiness is attained by one who eschews covetousness which is difficult to avoid by wicked men, which does not age even if he ages and which is an ailment that ends only with his life.

When one ages, his hairs, his teeth, his eyes, his ears all do age. But greed alone remains free from old age[574]

Everything in respect of a person does age of its own accord, not otherwise. But the yearning for life and the craving for riches do not age even if the person ages.

The happiness arising from the fulfilment of desires in the world, and the great divine happiness of heaven do not merit even a sixteenth part of that happiness which one has when thirst for objects is dispelled.[575]

After saying this that saintly king entered the forest accompanied by his wives.

25-28. He performed penance on the peak Bhṛgutuṅga.[576] There the renowned king practised fast and attained heaven along with his wives. His line of successors consisted of five holy kings who were honoured even by divine sages. The entire earth is pervaded by these descendants like the rays of the sun. By reading or listening to the holy narrative of Yayāti a man becomes intelligent, rich, long lived, famous and blessed with issues. Liberated from all sins he shall be honoured in the world of Śiva.

574. This is an oft-quoted verse.

575. This is an oft-quoted verse.

576. Bhṛgu-tuṅga—this is a peak of the Himālayas. *Varāha* (ch.146. 45-46) places it in Nepal on the eastern bank of the Gaṇḍaka where the sage Bhṛgu had a hermitage. *Vāmana*. (31-33) locates it near Vitastā and Himavat. *GEAMI*. part I. p.70.

CHAPTER SIXTYEIGHT

The race of Jyāmagha

Sūta Said :

1. I shall enumerate the members of the family of the glorious Yadu, the eldest son of Yayāti. Even as I narrate them succinctly and in the proper order listen to it and understand.

2. Yadu had five sons comparable to the sons of Devas. Sahasrajit was the eldest. The others were Kroṣṭu, Nīla, Ajaka and Laghu.

3. The king Śatajit was the son of Sahasrajit. Śatajit had three renowned sons.

4. They were Haihaya, Haya and the king Veṇuhaya. The successor of Haihaya was the well known Dharma.

5. O brahmins, his son was Dharmanetra. Kīrti was the son of Dharmanetra and his son was Sañjaya.

6. The virtuous Mahiṣmān was the heir and successor of Sañjaya. The valorous Bhadraśreṇya was the son of Mahiṣmān.

7. Bhadraśreṇya's legal heir was the king named Durdama who had an intelligent son known as Dhanaka.

8-9. The sons of Dhanaka were four and they were very popular. They were—Kṛtavīrya, Kṛtāgni, Kṛtavarmā and Kṛtaujas. Arjuna was the son of Kṛtavīrya. He was born with thousand arms and became the best of the lords of the seven islands.

10-12. Rāma who was identical with Nārāyaṇa was the cause of his death. He had a hundred sons. Five of them were great heroes. They were strong, heroic, virtuous and learned. They had good practice in the use of all missiles. They were Śūra, Śūrsena, Dhṛṣṭa, Kṛṣṇa and Jayadhvaja the king of Avanti. Jayadhvaja's son Tālajaṅgha was very powerful.

13. He had a hundred sons. They were known as Tālajaṅghas. The eldest of them the powerful Vītihotra was the ruler.

14. Vṛṣa and others too were his sons of meritorious deeds. Vṛṣa was the founder of a dynasty. His son was Madhu.

15-18. Madhu had hundred sons and Vṛṣṇi the eldest was the founder of a dynasty. Vṛṣṇi's descendants were also called Vṛṣṇis and those of Madhu are known as Mādhavas.

Since the Haihayas belonged to the family of Yadu they are also designated as Yādavas. There were five groups or families of the Haihayas of noble souls. They were—Vītihotras, Haryātas, Bhojas, Āvantis and Śūrasenas. The last were known as Tālajaṅghas also. The most famous kings among the Haihayas were Śūra, Śurasena, Vṛṣa, Kṛṣṇa, and Jayadhvaja.

19. Śūra and Śūravīra were the pious descendants of Śūrasena. The land of these noble souls is known as Śūrasenas.

20. The son of Vītihotra was the well known Narta. Durjaya the son of Kṛṣṇa was a destroyer of his enemies.

21. Listen to the race of the saintly king Kroṣṭu. It consisted of excellent men. Viṣṇu the scion of the family of Vṛṣṇi was born of this race.

22. Kroṣṭu had a son of great renown named Vṛjinīvān. His son was Svāti and Kuśaṅku was his son.

23. Desirous of progeny, the extremely powerful king Kusaṅku performed great sacrifices of various kinds with the requisite gifts.

24-25. Citraratha his son did glorious deeds. The heroic son of Citraratha was king Śaśabindu who performed sacrifices giving large sums as gifts. He observed excellent holy rites, and was an Emperor of great strength and valour over a large number of subjects.

26. Śaśabindu had twenty thousand sons. They specifically praise Anantaka as the most excellent of all of them.

27-28. The son Yajña was born to Anantaka. Yajña's son was Dhṛti. His son was Uśanas. That most virtuous king after obtaining the kingdom, performed a hundred horse sacrifices. The king named Siteṣu is known as the son of Uśanas.

29. Marutta, the saintly king who made his family flourish, was his son. The heroic Kambalabarhis was the son of Marutta.

30-31. Rukmakavaca, a learned king was the son of Kambalabarhis. This Rukmakavaca had killed in battle many heroic archers wearing coats of mail with sharp arrows and attained great glory. The pious soul gave land to the Ṛtviks (Brahmins officiating) in the Horse-sacrifice.

32. Parāvṛt, the slayer of heroic enemies, was born of Rukmakavaca. Five sons of great strength were born to Parāvṛt.

33. They were Rukmeṣu, Pṛthurukma, Jyāmagha, Parigha and Hari. The father fixed Parigha and Hari in Videha.

34. Rukmeṣu became the king and Pṛthurukma was dependent on him. Compelled by them, king Jyāmagha abdicated the throne and stayed in the hermitage.

35-36. He remained quiescent while he stayed in the forest. He received enlightenment from the brahmins. Then he took up his bow and went to another land in his chariot decorated with flags. He went to the Narmadā[577] river accompanied by his wife. He went to the mountain Ṛkṣavān[578] and passed his days.

37-39. Śaibyā the chaste woman of good conduct was the wife of Jyāmagha. After observing severe penance that fortunate lady, in her advanced age, gave birth to Śruta and Vidarbha. King Śruta had no son. Two scholarly sons Kratha and Kaiśika were born to Vidarbha. They were heroic and very efficient in battle. A third son was Romapāda and Babhru was his son.

40. Sudhṛti a learned and very pious king was his son. His son was Kuśika who was the originator of the family of Caidya.

41-42. Kratha was the son of Vidarbha. His son was Kunti. Kunti's son was Vṛta and from him was born the valorous Raṇadhṛṣṭa. His son Nidhṛti was a slayer of enemies. The son of Nidhṛti was Dāśārha, the destroyer of his foes.

43. Vyāpta was the son of Dāśārha, and Jīmūta his son. Vikṛti was the son of Jīmūta. His son was Bhīmaratha.

44. Navaratha was the son of Bhimaratha. He was perpetually engaged in charitable gifts and holy rites. He was devoted to truthfulness and good conduct.

45. His son was Dṛḍharatha. Śakuni was his son. Karambha was born of him. Devarāta was his son.

46. From Devarāta was born king Devarāti of great renown. He was equal to the son of Devas. From him was born Devakṣatra.

577. Narmadā—this river rises in the Vindhya mountain and falls into the gulf of Cambay. It flows in a wide flood-plain and is fairly deep. It forms a suitable boundary between the political units north and south of it.

578. Ṛkṣavān—Rāmāyaṇa places it on the Narmadā river. "ṛkṣavantaṁ giriśreṣṭham adhyāste Narmadām piban—*Rāma*.

47. Devakṣatra's son was Madhu of great renown. He was the founder of the line of Madhus. From Madhu was born Kuruvaṁśaka.

48. After Kuruvaṁśa was Anu and from him was born Purutvān, the best among men. From him Aṁśu was born to queen Bhadravatī of Vidarbha.

49-51. Aṁśu married Aikṣvākī and Sattva was born of him. From Sattva was born Sāttvata, endowed with good qualities who enabled the family to flourish. The dynasty of Jyāmagha has thus been narrated to you in detail. He who reads or listens to this lineage of Jyāmagha lives for a long time and attains heavenly kingdom and happiness.

CHAPTER SIXTYNINE

Śrīkṛṣṇa, his birth and life.

Sūta said :

1-2. Sāttvata endowed with the sattva guṇa begot four sons: Bhajana the brilliant, the divine king Devāvṛdha, Andhaka the highly blessed one and Vṛṣṇi the delighter of all the descendants of Yadu. Hear in detail the families of these four.

3. Ayutāyus, Śatāyus and the powerful Harṣakṛt were born to Sṛñjayī and Bhajana the brilliant.

4. Among the four sons of Sāttvata, king Devāvṛdha performed a great penance desiring, "I shall have a son endowed with good qualities."

5. It is heard that those who are conversant with the mythology of the race of Anu sing that his son was known as Babhru. He was an excellent king of meritorious renown.

6. Noble men glorify the qualities of Devāvṛdha the great soul. Just as we hear about them from far we see them from near.

7-9. Babhru is the best among men and Devāvṛdha was equal to Devas. Fourteen thousand and sixty five persons had attained immortality, thanks to Babhru and Devāvṛdha. He performed sacrifices. He was charitably inclined. He was a hero favourably disposed towards brahmins. He was steady in holy rites. He was famous. He had great splendour. Among the Sāttvatas he was a great hero. It was in his family that the Bhojas equal to Devas were born.

10. Gāndhārī and Mādrī were the wives of Vṛṣṇi. Gāndhārī gave birth to Sumitra and Mitranandana.

11. Mādrī obtained from him the son Devamīḍhuṣa at first and then two excellent heroes Anamitra and Śini.

12. Anamitra's son was Nighna. Nighna had two sons the highly blessed Prasena and Satrājit.

13. The sun was an intimate friend of Satrājit. He gave him the jewel Syamantaka.[579]

14-16. This jewel was the best among all the jewels in the world. Once he went for hunting along with Prasena. He was killed there by a terrible lion as he was helpless. From Śini the youngest son of Vṛṣṇi a son Satyaka was born. He was faithful in words and was richly endowed with truthfulness. His son was the valorous Yuyudhāna, the grandson of Śini.

17. Asaṅga was the son of Yuyudhāna. Kuṇi was his son. The son of Kuṇi was Yugandhara. Thus the descendants of Śini (Śaineyas) have been described.

18. A son was born to Yudhājit the son of Vṛṣṇi and Mādri. He was known as Śvaphalka. He was the benefactor of the three worlds.

19. Wherever the pious king Śvaphalka was present, there was no fear of either ailment or of drought.

20. Śvaphalka took as his wife, Gāndinī the daughter of the king of Kāśī, who gave him his daughter.

21-24. For many years she remained in the womb of her mother without being born. The father spoke to her even as she was within the womb. "Be born quickly. Welfare unto thee. Why dost thou tarry." Then the girl Gāndinī stationed within the womb replied to him—"O father, everyday you must give a cow to a brahmin. If you give thus for three years I will come out of the womb of my mother."

The father said, "So be it" and he fulfilled her desire. Her son from Śvaphalka is said to be Akrūra. He was charitable,

579. Syamantaka. *See H.M.* p.167.

heroic, a performer of sacrifices, learned, and fond of guests. During sacrifices he distributed wealth as gift.

25-29. Akrūra married Ratnā the daughter of Śaiva. He begot of her Upamanyu, Māṅgu, Vṛta, Janamejaya, Girirakṣa, Upekṣa, Śatrughna, Arimardana, Dharmabhṛt, Vṛṣṭadharmā, Godhana, Vara, Āvāha and Prativāha. He had also an excellent daughter Sudhārā. Two sons who delighted the family were born of Ugrasenī (daughter of Ugrasena) to Akrūra. They were Devavān and Upadeva equal to Devas.

The renowned Citraka was born as the son of Sumitra.

30-31. The following were the sons of Citraka—Viprthu, Pṛthu, Aśvagrīva. Subāhu, Sudhāsūka, Gavekṣaṇa, Ariṣṭanemi, Aśva, Dharma, Adharmabhṛt, Subhūmi and Bahubhūmi. He had two daughters Śraviṣṭhā and Śravaṇā.

32. To Andhaka the daughter of the king of Kāśī bore four sons viz:—Kukura, Bhajamāna, Śuci and Kambalabarhis.

33. Vṛṣṇi was the son of Kukura. Śūra was the son of Vṛṣṇi. The highly powerful Kapotaromā was his son and his son was Vilomaka.

34. He had a scholarly son Nala who was a comrade of Tumburu. He is known by the name Candanānaka Dundubhi.

35. From him was born the son Abhijit. His son was Punarvasu. That king performed a horse sacrifice for obtaining a son.

36. In the course of that sacrifice when Atirātra mantras were being chanted in the middle of the assembly of priests the child Punarvasu was born. Later on he became a scholar, omniscient, charitable and a performer of sacrifices.

37. Twins were born to Abhijit also. They were well known as Āhuka and Āhukī. They were the best among renowned people.

38. Two sons were born to the daughter of the king of Kāśī and Āhuka:—viz. Devaka and Ugrasena. Both of them were equal to the sons of Devas.

39. Childern equal to Devas were born to Devaka. They were Devavān, Upadeva, Sudeva and Devarakṣita.

40-41. They had seven sisters. The king gave them to Vasudeva. They were Vṛṣadevā, Upadevā, Devarakṣitā, Śrīdevā

Śāntidevā, Sahadevā and Devakī of slender waist and the best among them.

42. Ugrasena had nine sons. Kaṁsa was the eldest among them. Their sons and grandsons were hundreds and thousands.

43. The daughter of Devaka and the wife of Vasudeva was worthy of being honoured and worshipped even by Devas.

44. The other two wives of Ānakadundubhi, (Vasudeva) viz. the blessed Rohiṇī and Pauravī the daughter of Bāhlika were also worthy of being worshipped by Devas.

45. Rohiṇī gave birth to Rāma who wielded the plough-share as his weapon and had great strength. Due to the fear of Kaṁsa he had resorted to his own tranquil self.

46. After the six innocent childern had been killed, and after Balarāma had been born the intelligent Vasudeva, begot Kṛṣṇa of Devakī.

47. He alone is the supreme soul. He is Viṣṇu the lord of Devas. Balarāma was the lord Śeṣa with silver lustre.

48. Under the pretext of the curse of Bhṛgu, Viṣṇu agreed to take a human body and was born of Devakī as the son of Vasudeva.

49. At the same time the Yogicslumber Kauśikī originating from the body of Umā became the daughter of Yaśodā at the behest of the lord of Devas.

50. She alone is the Prakṛti bowed to by all Devas. Lord Kṛṣṇa is Puruṣa the bestower of the fruit of virtue and salvation.

51-52. Saving his own son from Kaṁsa, Vasudeva took the daughter of Yaśodā and instead gave her his own four-armed, wide-eyed son who was marked by the scar Śrīvatsa and who held the conch, discus, iron club and lotus.

53. After giving to Nanda (the husband of Yaśodā) his son Viṣṇu the protector of the worlds who had taken up a physical form out of his own will, he said to Nanda—"May he be protected."

54-55. It was due to the grace of Śiva the lord of Devas of immense splendour that Viṣṇu assumed the physical body. Along with Rāma he handed over the lord the bestower of boons, the great Īśvara, the preceptor of the universe, who had incarnated for dispelling the burden of the earth, saying "Hereby the Yādavas will attain all auspicious results. This child of Devakī will remove all our distresses."

56-59. Ānakadundubhi then intimated to Kaṁsa the son of Ugrasena that a daughter endowed with good signs had been born. There had been an aerial announcement—"O Kaṁsa of good holy rites the eighth child of Devakī will no doubt be the cause of your death." Hence, Kaṁsa attempted to kill the child. But that child (of Nanda) the goddess of eight arms slipped from his hands and crossed to the sky. She said in a voice as majestic as the rumbling sound of the cloud. "Save your own skin. Your death has come.

60. O foolish Kaṁsa, even as you were guarding your own body you have committed sins. Indeed your destroyer is already born."

61. It is said that due to his fear of Devakī, Kaṁsa killed the eighth child. But the eighth son of Devakī was really the cause of his death.

62. O leading sages, all attempts of Bhoja to take revenge on him became futile due to Kṛṣṇa's power. Moreover he was rendered insentient by the Māyā Kauśikī.

63. Thus Kaṁsa was killed by Kṛṣṇa of unimpeded activity. Many other destroyers of Devas and brahmins too were killed.

64. Kṛṣṇa's sons Pradyumna and others have already been enumerated. They were many and all of them were experts in battle.

65-69. Kṛṣṇa's sons were equal to Kṛṣṇa. Among all these sons Cārudeṣṇa and his brothers are of special importance. They were the sons of Rukmiṇī. They were the destroyers of their enemies. Kṛṣṇa had sixteen thousand and one hundred wives. The most beloved and the eldest of them all was Rukmiṇī.

Lord Śiva was worshipped for twelve years by her and Kṛṣṇa of unimpaired activity, for the sake of sons, living only on air (all those years).

By the grace of the trident-bearing lord the following sons were born to Kṛṣṇa viz:—Cārudeṣṇa, Sucāru, Cāruveṣa, Yaśodhara, Cāruśravas, Cāruyaśas, Pradyumna and Sāmba.

70. On seeing those heroic sons of Rukmiṇī as well as Rukmiṇī, Jāmbavatī the wife of Kṛṣṇa once spoke to him thus.

71. O lotus-eyed one, it behoves you, if you are delighted, to give me a son equal to Devas, a son endowed with superior qualities.

72. On hearing the words of Jāmbavatī, Kṛṣṇa the lord of the universe and a real storehouse of penance began to perform penance.

73-75. Kṛṣṇa Nārāyaṇa, the wielder of the conch, discus and iron club, went to the excellent hermitage of the sage Vyāghrapāda. After bowing to the sage, Kṛṣṇa obtained the divine Pāśupata Yoga. At his behest he shaved off the beard, moustache and the hair on the head, applied ghee all over the body and wore the girdle of the Muñja grass. Thus initiated, lord Kṛṣṇa the scorcher of foes performed a great penance.

76. He performed the penance in various poses. He stood with arms raised up and without support, he stood on the tips of his toes. He spent three seasons sustaining himself on fruits, water and air.

77. Satisfied with his penance, lord Śiva granted him boons. He gave Sāmba the son of Jāmbavatī to Kṛṣṇa the noble soul.

78. On getting the son Sāmba from Kṛṣṇa, his wife Jāmbavatī became highly delighted in the same way as Aditi when she obtained Āditya.

79. O leading sages, by the curse[580] of Lord Śiva the thousand hands of Bāṇa were cut off by Kṛṣṇa.

80. Then with Balarāma to assist him he carried out the destruction of Daityas. He sportively killed several wicked kings in the battlefield.

81. He killed the leading Daitya Naraka born of Devas.

580. **Rudrasya śāpāt—Sāmba, son of Śrīkṛṣṇa, cut off a thousand arms of Bāṇa. For a slightly different version, see H.M. p.42.**

thanks to a boon granted by the noble brahmin Ūrdhvacakra.[581]

82. The excessively strong one, of unequalled exploit, Kṛṣṇa took up sixteen thousand one hundred girls for his own pleasure.

Under the pretext of a curse from the brahmins he destroyed the family of Vṛṣṇis. After that he, the lord, remained in Prabhāsa.[582]

84-85. More than hundred years elapsed thus even as Kṛṣṇa ruled over Dvārakā* removing the distress due to old age. He acceded to the curses of Viśvāmitra,[583] Kaṇva[584] and Nārada,[585] as also the words of Durvāsas (and stayed) in Piṇḍāraka.[586]

86. Kṛṣṇa abandoned the human form under the pretext of the arrow of the hunter Jaraka, and after blessing that hunter he returned to heaven.

87. Due to the curse of Aṣṭāvakra[587] as also due to his own Māyā (power) the wives of lord Kṛṣṇa were abducted by thieves.

88-91. Balarāma abandoned his human form and assuming that of Śeṣa went to his heavenly abode. The auspicious queens of Kṛṣṇa—Rukmiṇī and others—entered fire along with the body of their lord. O brahmins, the gentle lady Revatī too entered the pyre along with her husband Balarāma and followed his path. The extremely powerful Arjuna performed the obsequies of Kṛṣṇa, Rāma and also of other Vṛṣṇis. O men

581. It refers to the legend narrated in *Harivaṁśa* :

सत्यं बत पुरा वायुरिहास्मान्वाक्यमब्रवीत् ।
सर्वभूतमतज्ञश्च देवर्षिरपि नारदः ।।
विष्णुर्नारायणो देवः शङ्खचक्रगदासिभृत् ।
स भौमं नरकं हत्वा भर्ता च भविता शुचा ।।

582. Prabhāsa—it is a celebrated place of pilgrimage in Saurāṣṭra the southern part of Kāthiawar. *a city near Okha in Kathiawar.

583-585. For detail, *Bhāga*. Janayiṣyati vo mandā musalaṁ kulanāśanam –cited in *ST*.

586. Piṇḍāraka—a sacred bathing pond, somewhere in the country of the Yādavas, not identifiable.

587. The curse of Aṣṭāvakra. Cf यस्माद्विरूपरूपं मां मत्वा हासावमानना। भवतीभिः कृता तस्मादेष शापं ददाम्यहम् ।। मत्प्रसादेन भर्तारं लब्ध्वा तु पुरुषोत्तमम् । मच्छापोपहताः सर्वा दस्युहस्तं गमिष्यथ ।। *Viṣṇu* cited in *ST*.

of good holy rites, with bulbous roots, fruits and roots he performed the rites of oblation, for want of wealth.

92-94. Then Arjuna too went to heaven together with his brothers. Thus, the exploits and end of the noble Kṛṣṇa of unimpaired activity, who adopted human form out of his own free will, has been succinctly mentioned to you. O brahmins, he who reads this narrative of the kings of lunar race or listens to it or narrates it to others undoubtedly goes to the world of Viṣṇu.

CHAPTER SEVENTY

Various Creations

The sages said:

1. O Sūta, the primordial creation had been indicated by you but not clarified. O person of good holy rites, it behoves you to recount it in detail now.

Sūta said:

2. O leading sages, the great lord Śiva is stationed beyond Prakṛti and Puruṣa.[588] He is the greatest soul.

3. The unmanifest originated from that lord as the greatest cause. Thinkers on metaphysical reality call it Pradhāna or Prakṛti.

4. It is devoid of smell, colour and taste. It has neither sound nor touch. It is unageing, stable, imperishable and perpetually stationed in the soul.

5. It is the source of origin of the universe. It is the eternal great Brahman, the massive being. It is the physical body of all living beings. It is induced by the command of the lord.

6. At the outset the Pradhāna existed in the form of Brahman.[589] It had neither beginning nor end. It was unborn and subtle consisting of the three Guṇas. It was the source of

588. The transcendent God Maheśvara is higher than Prakṛti and Puruṣa. (See p. 41 note 56). Cf. *ŚP*. Prakṛteś ca paraṁ Brahma yat tac chivaṁ udāhṛtam—cited in *ST*.

589. Brahma. Cf. "sad eva saumy edam agra āsīt"—cited in *ST*.

origin of the universe as well as eternal. It was neither mani-, fest nor comprehensible.

7. When the Guṇas were in equilibrium, when it had not been differentiated, when it was identical with darkness,[590] all this visible universe had been pervaded by its existence due to Śiva's will.

8. At the time of creation, as the Pradhāna was presided over by the individual soul—Puruṣa, the principle Mahat menifested revealing itself as subsidiary to Prakṛti.

9. It was enveloped by the subtle and great Avyakta (unmanifest). At the outset, when the principle of Mahat had the predominance of Sattva, then only it revealed existence.

10. The Mahat should be known as the Cosmic Mind. It is said to be the sole cause of creation. It originated as presided over by the individual soul and only as a beneficent symbol.

11. Its forms Dharma etc., are the causes of the principles and objects of the world. Induced by the desire to create the Mahat carries on the activity of creation.

12. It is named variously as Manas (mind), Mahat (great), Mati (intellect), Brahman, Pūḥ (city), Buddhi (intellect), Khyāti (faculty of discriminatory knowledge), Īśvara (lord), Prajñā (perfect knowledge), Citi (consciousness), Smṛti (memory), Saṁvid (cognition), and Viśveśa (lord of the universe).

13. It is called Manas because it ponders over the fruit of the activity of all living beings [from the root man to think] Subtle as it is, the fruits of its activities appear to be divided i. e. many and different.

14. It is called Mahat because it originated at the outset prior to all other principles as well as due to its magnitude. It is greater than Viśeṣas[591] and Guṇas.[592]

15. It possesses magnitude [Mānaṁ Bibharti]. It ponders and causes differentiation. It is also greatly related to the enjoyment (i. e. experience) of Puruṣa. Hence, it is known as Mati.

16. It is defined as Brahman because of its bṛhatva (massiveness) and bṛṁhaṇatva (state of becoming swollen)

590. tamomaye. Cf. "tamā āsīt tamasā gūḍham agre"—cited in *ST*.
591. viśeṣebhyaḥ—sattvādibhyaḥ *ST*. from the attributes, sattva, etc.
592. guṇebhyaḥ—śabdādibhyaḥ *ST*. from the subtle elements, (tanmātras—sounds, etc

and also because it contains (within itself) all experiences which are dependent on all external objects.

17. It is called Pūḥ because it fills Devas with blessings and leads men to the state of awareness [from the root pṝ].

18. Since the Puruṣa is known through it and since it makes known all objects, what is wholesome, from what is not it is called Buddhi.

19. Since enjoyment of pleasures is based on the knowledge thereof, and also since each item of enjoyment is dependent on knowledge, it is known by the word khyāti.

20. The principle of Mahat is called by the term "Khyāti" also because objects in many instances are named (khyāyante) through its qualities such as knowledge, etc.

21. It is a great soul and it directly perceives everything. Hence, it is called Īśvara. Since it follows up knowledge it is called Prajñā.

22. Since it collects such forms as Jñāna (knowledge) etc., and the fruits of many holy rites, for the sake of enjoyment, it is called citi (from the root ci).

23. Since it remembers all affairs of the present, past and future it is called Smṛti (from the root smṛ).

24. It is called Saṁvid because it obtains the entire knowledge and knows the greatness of everything [from the roots vid to know and vind to obtain].

25. O excellent sages, (for another reason also) it is called Saṁvid by great men. It exists [from root vid to exist] everywhere and within it one obtains everything [vindati].

26. From the root Jñā (to know) they call it Jñānam. For the lord is the fountainhead of all knowledge. Since it repudiates bondage etc., [the Mahat] is called Īśvara by learned men.

27. This first excellent tattva—Mahat—has been thus explained by many synonymous words by those who are conversant with the nature of tattvas and who always think about the existence of the lord.

28. The Mahat carries out the work of creation when it is induced by the desire to create. Saṁkalpa (volition) and Adhyavasāya (effort) are its two traits.

29. (From this Mahat) having three Guṇas but with Rajas prevailing, the Ahaṁkāra (ego) originated. All the

creation was thus enveloped by Mahat. It is exterior to Bhūtādi (ego, the cause of the elements).

30. From the same ahaṁkāra with tamas predominating over the other two came about the creation of Bhūtatanmātras (the essence of sound, etc). It is called Bhūtādi (cause of the elements) and it is tāmasa in nature.

31. The Bhūtādi on disintegration created Śabdatanmātra (the essence of sound). From this was born Ākāśa (ether) (also called) Suṣira (hole), that is marked by sound.

32-34. Ākāśa characterised by sound enveloped Sparśatanmātra which on disintegration created Vāyu characterised by touch. Vāyu on disintegration created Rūpatanmātra. Therefore, it is said that Jyotis originated out of vāyu, with colour as its quality. Jyotis on disintegration created Rasatanmātra. Āpaḥ (waters) originated from it with taste as their main quality.

35. Agni (i. e. the fiery element) with the Rūpa-tanmātra enveloped Rasatanmātras. Waters on disintegration created Gandhatanmātra.

36. From it the saṅghāta (solid earth) originated. Its special attribute is smell when each of the elements remains within its specific quality(sound, etc) it is called tanmātra and this exclusive nature is called tanmātratā.

37. The Tanmātras are also called Aviśeṣas, because in that stage they do not define anything in particular (as distinct from others. They are Aviśeṣas for another reason also—they are Praśāntas (quiescent) or Ghoras (terrible) or Mūḍhas (confused).

38. This creation by the tanmātras of the Bhūtas should be known as one that is mutual. The other creations are from the Vaikārika (that which has undergone alteration) i.e. the Ahaṁkāra (ego) or from the Sāttvika wherein sattva guṇa predominates.

39-40. The Vaikārika creation functions simultaneously. There are five senses of knowledge and five senses of activity. These ten senses are the means of achievement. The eleventh is mind. By its very nature the mind has both qualities i. e. of the organ of sense and of the organ of function.

41. The five organs of sense are, ear, skin, eye, tongue,

palate and nose. They are endowed with the power of perceiving their respective qualities (i.e. ear receiving sound, skin receiving touch, etc).

42. The legs, rectum, private parts, hands and the organ of speech (the tenth Indriya) are the organs of function or activity. Their activities are respectively gait (movement), evacuation, pleasure, arts, crafts and speech.

43. Both ether and the element of sound penetrated the element of touch. Hence wind has both the attributes —sound and touch.

44. Similarly both sound and touch entered colour. Hence, the fire has three attributes, viz, sound, touch and colour.

45. The attributes of sound, touch, and colour penetrated the element of taste. Hence, waters have four attributes including taste as their special attribute.

46. Sound, touch, colour and taste penetrated smell. Combined with the element of smell they pervaded the earth.

47. Hence, the earth contains all the five attributes and is considered the grossest of all elements. They are quiescent, terrible or confused. Hence, they are called Viśeṣas.

48. Since they have penetrated mutually they sustain one another.[593]

Everything within the earth is enveloped by the mountain Lokāloka.

49. They are called Viśeṣas because they can be perceived by means of the sense-organs invariably. The latter ones have all the qualities of the previous creation.[594]

50-52. Each of these qualities is a distinct characteristic of each element. (Any other quality found in an element should be known to be due to the contact of the other element; (for example) experiencing smell in water some may say that it is the quality of water, yet, it should be known that it

593. Parasparānupraveśa : Each preceding element enters into each succeeding element. Each new life-centre is a link in the chain. The seed is permeated by its creative potency. The seed in the form of the father is reborn as the son in endless generations. This principle of anupraveśa, i.e. the ancestor transmitting its whole potency to the successor is a biological law.

594. See verses 43-47 of this chapter.

is the quality of earth alone. It is because the particles of earth have got mixed with water and wind that the smell appears to be present in them.

These seven massive beings beginning with intellect (Mahat) and ending with Viśesas (gross elements) create the cosmic egg[595] because they depend upon one another, because they are presided over by Puruṣa and because they are blessed by the unmanifest.

53. Like the bubbles in the water the big cosmic egg is born at once from the Viśeṣas. The whole egg is embedded in water.

54. The cosmic egg is encircled by waters ten times in extent. The waters are externally encircled by the fire ten times in extent.

55. The fire is externally encircled by the wind ten times in extent and the wind is externally encircled by the ether ten times in extent.

56. The wind is encircled by the ether. The ether is encircled by the ego. The ego is encircled by intellect and intellect is encircled by the unmanifest.

57-59. Śarva is stationed in the covering lid of the cosmic egg. O persons of good holy rites, Bhava is stationed in waters; Rudra is stationed in the middle of fire. Ugra is stationed in the wind. Bhīma is stationed in the middle of the earth. Maheśvara is stationed in ego. Lord Īśa is stationed in intellect. Parameśvara is stationed everywhere. The egg is encircled by the seven coverings originating from Prakṛtis. These eight Prakṛtis are thus stationed encircling one another.[596]

60. Stationing themselves thus at the time of creation they attract one another. Thus mutually interdependent they uphold one another.

595. Read mahadādi for mahādayo (Liṅga. 1.3.18). The principle of intellect and mind and the five gross elements constitute each Egg. These seven constituents of the Egg are also known as the seven sages, seven Aṅgirases (Cf. Liṅga. 1.70.51).

596. The Egg constitutes the unmanifest Prakṛti (avyakta) and its manifestations—intellect (mahat,) ego (ahaṁkāra) and the five gross elements (bhūtas). (Cf. Vāyu.1.4.76). These seven comprise the shells of the life-principle in the egg. Cf. Bhāg. 6.16.37 : "kṣityādibhir eṣa kilāvṛtaḥ saptabhir doṣa-guṇottarair aṇḍakośaḥ".

61-63. The vikāras (effects) exist in the vikārins (cause) by means of the relationship of the support and the supported. Maheśvara is beyond Avyakta. The egg is born of Avyakta. The same lord is born of the egg as Puruṣa with solar lustre. In it the generating of the effect is achieved by his own free will. He alone is the primordial embodied being, called Puruṣa. Viṣṇu who is bowed to by all Devas is born of his left limb.

Thanks to the wish of parameṣṭhin, the lord Viṣṇu originated together with goddess Lakṣmī. Brahmā the preceptor of the universe is born of the right limb of the lord along with Sarasvatī.

65-67. These worlds are in that Cosmic egg. This universe is within the Cosmos. The moon and the sun along with the stars, planets, wind and the Lokāloka mountains are stationed within Cosmic Egg. O Brahmins, whatever time interval is necessary for the creation I have enumerated above, that period is the day time of Parameśvara. His night also extends over the same duration.

68-70. The period of his creation is his day and the period of dissolution his night.

Really, it should be known that he has neither day nor night [as we conceive of it]. It is used metaphorically for the facility of the people.

The objects stay during the day of the lord, viz.—the sense-organs, the objects of the senses, the five great elements, all living beings, intellect and the deities.

71-73. At the end of the day they get dissolved. At the end of the night they originate again.

When the unmanifest is stationed in His soul, when the effects are dissolved, both Pradhāna and Puruṣa remain quiescent i.e. with their common characteristics, tamas, sattva and rajas in equilibrium. They remain interlinked like threads woven together in the same warp and woof.

It should be known that there is dissolution when the guṇas are in equilibrium and when they are upset there is creation.

74. Just as there is oil latent in the gingelly seed, just as the ghee is present in the milk, so also the universe is present in tamas, sattva and rajas.

75. After enjoying the goddess throughout the night the creator begins to function in the beginning of the day when Prakṛti originates from Him.

76. The great lord penetrates Pradhāna and Puruṣa agitating[597] them by means of yoga.

77. The three deities originate from the great lord, the lord of the Universe. They are permanent, extremely worthy of concealment and protection, embodied ones, and the souls of all.

78. These alone are the three devas, the three Guṇas, the three worlds, and the three fires.[598]

79. They are mutually supported and they devotedly follow one another. They exist on mutual help and they hold one another.

80. They are paired together and mutually interdependent. There is not even a moment's separation among them. They do not eschew one another.[599]

81. Śiva is the greatest lord. Viṣṇu is beyond or above intellect. Brahmā is endowed with rajas. He functions at the beginning of Creation.

82-87. That Puruṣa is known as Parà and Prakṛti as Parā.

The Prakṛti which is presided over by the great lord begins to function when it is induced from all sides. The principle of intellect functions following this. Since it is permanent and stable, it resorts to the object of the sense, by itself. When there is disturbance in the Guṇas (qualities) of Pradhāna the period of creation functions from that which is of Existent-cum-nonexistent nature and presided over by Īśvara.

Rudra became fully equipped for evolving the effects at the very outset. He is unequalled in brillance, intelligent and illuminating. He indeed is the first embodied soul and is called

597. When the life-principle enters into Prakṛti, there occurs an agitation (kṣobha) in the form of contraction and expansion. Out of this agitation which is a process of Coming and Going, the universal seed is created, which has both the characteristics of the male and female. For detail, see *MP. A study*, pp. 36-37.

598. Out of this egg agitated thus, there come into existence the triadic principles known as Brahmā, Viṣṇu and Śiva identical with three guṇas—rajas, sattva and tamas.

599. The Purāṇas refer to the joint birth and joint activity of the triad.

Puruṣa. Lord Brahmā, the four-faced[600] Prajāpati was born of Him. He also became fully equipped for evolving the effects (i.e. creation). So, the same lord is stationed in three forms.

88. He is endowed with positive knowledge and lordship. They, (i.e. the three devas) are also endowed with positive virtue and detachment.

89. Whatever has been mentally conceived or uttered by them is born out of the unmanifest, since it has been made to be subservient, and since the activities are dependent on the three Guṇas by nature.

90. The self-born deity has three conditions: in the capacity of Brahmā he is the four-faced one; in the capacity of Kāla (i.e. Rudra) he is the destroyer; he is the thousand-headed Puruṣa (i.e. Viṣṇu) also.

91. In the capacity of Brahmā, he creates the worlds; in the capacity of Kāla, he destroys the world; in the capacity of Puruṣa, he is indifferent. Prajāpati has three stages.

92. Brahmā has the lustre of the interior of a lotus; Rudra is like the fire at the time of dissolution; Puruṣa is lotus-eyed. This is the form of the great soul.

93. The lord takes up a single body, two bodies, three bodies, and then many bodies. He creates and destroys these bodies, and dispels them too.

94. The great lord creates and destroys bodies of different shapes, activities, forms and names.

95. Since he assumes three different forms, he is called Triguṇa. When divided into four, he is called Caturvyūha. (having four arrays).

96. He is defined as ātman (soul) because he attains the sense objects (√āp to attain), because he takes up (ā + √dā to take up) the sense objects and because he swallows up (√ad to eat) the sense objects. Moreover, he has perpetual existence.

97. He is called Ṛṣi because he goes everywhere. He is Śarīrin because he is its (body's) lord. He is (called) Svāmin because he possesses everything. He is called Viṣṇu because he enters everything.

98. He is called Bhagavān because he possesses Bhaga

600. See p. 60 note. 78

(loveliness, excellence, fortune, glory). He is called Śiva because he is devoid of impurities. He is called Parama because he is distinguished and eminent. Since he protects he is called Om.

99. He is called Sarvajña because he knows everything perfectly. He is Sarva because he is identical with all. He divides himself into three and functions in the three worlds.

100. By means of three forms he creates, swallows and protects. Since he is primordial he is called "Ādideva". He is called Aja because he is not born.

101. Since he protects people he is known as Prajāpati. Since he is the greatest among Devas he is called Mahādeva.

102. He is Omnipresent and not subservient to Devas. Hence, he is Īśvara. He is Brahmā because he is massive. He is called Bhūta because of his existence.

103. He is called the knower of the field (i.e. body); he comprehends the inner organs, mind, etc. Since he is single he is called Kevala. Since he lies down in the soul he is called Puruṣa.

104. He is known as self-born because he has no beginning and he is prior to all. Since he is worthy of worship he is called Yajña. He is Kavi because he can see what is beyond the sense organs..

105. He is Kramaṇa because he has access to all (or is accessible to all). He is Pālaka because he protects all. He is Āditya because he is tan-coloured. Being born at the outset he is Agni (fire).

106. Because he is the cause of origin of all golden things and also because he is born of the golden Egg, he is called Hiraṇyagarbha.

107. The time that has gone by after the self-born has been in existence cannot be reckoned even in hundreds of years.

108. The first half Parārdha in the age of the present Brahmā has already elapsed and another period of equal duration i.e. second half still remains. At its end begins the dissolution of the worlds.

109. Crores and thousands of crores of these days of kalpas

have come and gone. As many yet remain. The kalpa that is current now is known as Vārāha kalpa.

110-112. O brahmins, this is the first kalpa (Brahmā's day) within that Vārāha kalpa (age). In this there are fourteen Manus beginning with Svāyambhuva. This entire earth consisting of the seven continents and mountains are to be protected by those great lords (i.e. the fourteen Manus) past, present and future by means of their penance and through the subjests. Listen to their detailed account.

113. If one manvantara is recounted, the other manvantaras are also recounted. If one kalpa is explained, all the other kalpas too are explained.

114. The past kalpas are such that they leave their consequences on the future ones along with (or including) the dynasties of Kings etc. and the same reasoning should be applied to future kalpas by the knowing man (i.e., the past has left its marks on the present and in the same way the future will carry the marks of the present.

115-117. The waters were in existence at the outset when the whole surface of the earth had been destroyed. In the vast quiet and sparkling waters nothing else was known. When the mobile and immobile beings are destroyed in that vast, sealike expanse of water, Brahmā assumes a form with thousand eyes, thousand feet, thousand heads.[601] He is then called Nārāyaṇa. He is the golden-coloured Puruṣa beyond the sense organs. He had his slumber in that expanse of water.

118. When sattva guṇa was prevalent he woke up and found the world a void. They cite this verse about Nārāyaṇa.

119-125. We hear that the word Nāra means waters or sons of waters. He filled the void with waters and made it his resort. Since he lies down in the waters he is known as Nārāyaṇa.[602] After spending the night consisting of a thousand cycles of four yugas in the water, at the end of the night he assumed the form of Brahmā for the purpose of creation. Brahmā adopted a gaseous form and moved about over those waters like the glowworm at night during the rainy season. He knew that the

601. Cf. *RV*. 10.90.1. *VS*. 31. 1.

602. See p. 66. note. 86.

earth had gone under the water by means of inference. But he did not get disillusioned over the lifting up of the earth (from the waters). In previous eras in the beginning of the kalpas he had assumed another body. Then the lord of great soul pondered over that divine form. Seeing the earth submerged in water all round he thought "What form shall I adopt to lift up this Earth ?" He adopted the form of a boar as befitting the sport in water. The form was unassailable to all living beings. It had speech and was actually "Brahman" itself. He entered the nether worlds in that form for lifting up the earth.

127. In that boar form he approached the earth enveloped by water and quickly lifted it up.

128-132. The waters immediately filled up the oceans, and the rivers. For the welfare of the worlds, the lord lifted up the earth by means of his curved fangs, the earth, that had submerged and got embedded in the nether worlds. The holder of the earth, Lord Viṣṇu, the lifter of the earth held it, brought it to its original place and left it there as it was before. The earth stood like a great ship above that vast collection of water and on a par with it. Because of its massive body the earth did not sink and get submerged. After lifting it up the lotus-eyed lord with the desire to fit the world firmly turned his attention towards the demarcation of the earth. He made the earth level and then collected the mountains.

133-134. When everything of the previous creation was burnt by the fire at the time of dissolution the mountains got scattered over an extensive area. Due to chilliness in that vast sea-like expanse of water the scattered pieces of mountains were heaped up by the wind. Wherever they were deposited they became the stable mountains.

135. Mountains are called acalas because they never move, they are called parvatas because they have knots (parvans). They are giris because they are absorbed and hidden. They are called śiloccayas because they keep lying down.

136. Thereafter when crores of mountains were scattered about, Viśvakarman the architect of the gods, divided and classified them again and again at the beginning of every kalpa.

137. He then divided the earth into seven continents,

oceans and mountains. Thereafter he evolved the four worlds beginning with Bhūḥ.

138. After evolving the worlds, the self-born Brahmā, the lord who was desirous of creating different subjects, began creating them.

139-141a. He created everything at the beginning of the kalpa in the same manner as it was before. While he meditated on creation beginning with intellect and simultaneous with it, Illusion, ignorance identical with darkness, originated from the great soul in five stages[603] viz.—tamas (darkness) moha (delusion), mahāmoha (great delusion), tāmisra (murkiness) and andhatāmisra (blinding gloominess).

141b-143. This first creation of the meditating and self-confident lord came to stay as a fivefold one; viz. (1) those enveloped by darkness; (2) half open and half covered like the sprout from a seed; (3) those that have no light inside or outside; (4) those that are stiff and rigid and (5) senseless. Because their intellect, miseries and senses were all enshrouded, they are called important immobiles with covered souls.

144. On seeing this first creation in that situation as well as useless for any action (being immobile) he became dissatisfied in mind, and thought about another.

145. Even as he meditated over it the Tiryaksrotas creation (moving sideways) was developed. Since it functioned sideways it is called Tiryaksrotas.

146. The animals etc. (i.e. birds and reptiles) constitute this well-known creation. O brahmins, they are those who adopt wrong paths. So he meditated on another creation and the Sāttvika creation was evolved.

147-148. This third creation is Ūrdhvasrotas which is directed upwards. Since it functions upwards it is called Ūrdhvasrotas. The beings created under this category are mostly happy and delighted. They are enshrouded within and without as well as illuminated on both sides.

603. Avidyā—the scheme of ninefold creation is mentioned in all the Purāṇas. It is said that the creation arose out of ignorance (avidyā) classified into five heads, viz., tamas (darkness), moha (confusion), mahāmoha (obsession), tāmisra (gloominess), and andhatāmisra (blind gloominess). *Linga* (2. 9. 30, 35) divides these into sixtyfour categories.

149. Because they have been created with the union of Sattvaguṇa, they are known as originating from Sattva. This third creation of Ūrdhvasrotas is that of Devas.

150. The creations originating in the category of Ūrdhvasrotas are brilliant within and without. The Ūrdhvasrotas creations are stated by the learned to be satisfied souls.

151. When Devas, the creations in the category of Ūrdhvasrotas were created Brahmā, the lord who grants boons, became delighted, but he still meditated on another creation.

152-153. He pondered over the creation that will be Sādhaka[604] (active and fit for action). Even as he was meditating truthfully, the active Arvāksrotas creation manifested itself from the unmanifest Prakṛti. Since it functions downwards it is called Arvāksrotas.

154. The beings created thus are mostly brilliant; rajas predominates in them and there is a mixture of tamas also. Hence, there is a predominance of misery and they do their tasks again and again.

155. They are human beings enshrouded within and without, and active. They are classified into eight categories through their redeeming feature.

156. They are men who have realized souls with attributes similar to those of Gandharvas. Thus, the creation of Arvāksrotas is called Taijasa (luminous, fiery).

157-158. The fifth creation is Anugraha (the creation of blessings). It is fourfold according to the distinctive feature of contrariety, power, achievement and satisfaction. The contrariety inheres the beings that are immobile; the power is the element that characterizes the Tiryak yonis (animals); men are characterized by their realized souls. Of Devas and sages satisfaction is the distinctive feature.

159. This group is called Prākṛta (pertaining to Prakṛti). This fifth (fourfold) Vaikārika creation is the best (anavamaḥ) among all. The creation of the origins of gross elements and the gross elements, siddhas, sages, etc., is the sixth. The creation of

604. **sādhakaḥ—sakala-kāraṇaḥ *ST.*, the cause of all creation. Cf. nṛdeham ādyam—*Bhāg.* cited in *ST.***

(ordinary) human beings (as distinct from the sages, etc.) out of the subtle and gross elements is the seventh.

160-161. They (of the sixth group represented by the sages) know what has taken place in the past, what is taking place at present, and what will take place in future.[605] These (sages, etc.) remain detached though they enjoy and share the fruits of their activities.

162-164. This creation is characterized by contrariety and imperfection. The first (1) creation of Brahmā is that of Mahat; the next (2) that of tanmātras; the third (3) is Vaikārika (i.e. of the nature of transformation and ramification); this three-fold creation was evolved prior to intelligence. (4) The primary (mukhya) creation (of insentient beings) is the fourth. The immobile beings are the mukhyas.

165. Then there are (5) tiryak (horizontal); (6) ūrdhva (upward) and (7) arvāksrotas (downward) creations. (8) Then comes the anugraha creation, the eighth in the serial order. It is both Sāttvika and Tāmasa.

166. Thus with the five vaikṛta types and three prākṛtas there are eight types of creation. (9) The ninth creation, i.e., of Kumāras is both prākṛta and vaikṛta.

167. The three prākṛta creations are prior to the creation of intellect. But the other six creations (Nos. 4-9) are posterior to intellect.

168. I shall now give the detail of Anugraha sarga which you will understand properly. It stands in four ways[606] among all living beings.

605. The text is corrupted. The commentator's interpretation is far-fetched. He explains prākṛtaḥ (V-159) as prakṛta-nirūpaṇa-viṣayaḥ—the subject of present discourse. He dissolves vaikṛto navamaḥ as vaikṛtaḥ anavamaḥ and explains anavamaḥ as śreṣṭhaḥ, superior.

606. The anugraha creation is characterized by contrariety (viparyaya), power (śakti), satisfaction (tuṣṭi) and perfection (siddhi).

The scheme of ninefold creation as outlined in the Purāṇas can be summarised as follows :

(i) Mahat : (creation of the great principle : intellect). (ii) Tanmātra: (creation of subtle elements). (iii) Bhūta : (creation of gross elements). (This set of three-fold creation is primary and originates from avidyā—ignorance). (iv) Mukhya (the principal creation comprising the immobile world of insentient beings such as mountains). (v Tiryak (the animal)

169. The Prākṛta and Vaikṛta creations together are nine. The learned consider them interconnected through causes.

170. At the outset, Brahmā created the mental sons equal to himself. Among them Ṛbhu and Sanat were sages of sublimated sexuality.

171-173a. They were born at the outset. They were senior to all others. After the eighth kalpa was over, these two ancient ones, the witnesses of the worlds constricted their splendour and settled themselves in the terrestrial world in the Vārāhakalpa. They performed such actions leading to salvation after steadying their mind in their soul. Eschewing progeny, ritualistic activities and affection they adopted detachment. Sanat continued to have the same child-like form as at the time of his birth. Hence, his name is celebrated as Sanatkumāra.

173b-177. Brahmā created Sananda, Sanaka and Sanātana. By means of their perfect knowledge those sages of great power abstained from worldly acts. These yogins were enlightened in the diversity of the world and so refrained from worldly activities. Without creating progenies they passed away at the time of dissolution. After they had gone away, Brahmā created other mental sons who were fit for action and who took pride in their positions. These sages by whom this earth was sustained remained until the final dissolution of all living beings.

178-182. Brahmā created the waters, fire, earth, firmament, heaven, oceans, rivers, mountains, herbs, creepers, trees and plants, the units of time such as lavas, kāṣṭhās, kalās, muhūrtas, junctions, nights, days, fortnights, months, ayanas (half-yearly transit of the sun), years and yugas. All these who identified themselves with these abodes are known by the names of their abodes. He created Devas and sages too. They

creation wherein the stream of life is horizontal) (tiryaksrotas). (vi) Deva° (creation of Devas in which the stream of life moves upwards) (ūrdhva-srotas). (vii) Mānuṣa° (creation of mankind in which the stream of life moves downwards (arvāk-srotas). (viii) creation of Feeling such as contrariety, power, satisfaction and perfection found respectively in the immobile, mobile, human and divine beings. This set of creation (Nos iv-viii), born of intelligence is said to be secondary; but *Vāyu* includes anugraha in the primary creation. (ix) Kumāra° creation of the mental sons of Brahmā—Sanat etc. This ninth creation is said to be both primary and secondary.

were Marīci, Bhṛgu, Aṅgiras, Pulastya, Pulaha, Kratu, Dakṣa, Atri and Vasiṣṭha. Brahmā created these nine sons mentally. They are stipulated in the Purāṇas as the Nine Brahmās.

183. As before, the lotus-born deity assigned abodes to all the expounders of Brahman, who were equal to Brahmā himself.

184-185. Then the lord created Saṁkalpa and Dharma: Dharma through enterprise and Saṁkalpa out of determination. Then another mental son Ruci was born of lord Brahmā.

186. Brahmā created Dakṣa from his vital breath and Marīci from his eyes. Bhṛgu was born of the heart of Brahmā.

187. He created Aṅgiras from his head and Atri from his ears. He created Pulastya from the organic wind Udāna and Pulaha from the wind Vyāna.

188. Vasiṣṭha was born of Samāna. He created Kratu from Apāna. Thus these divine sons of Brahmā are eleven altogether.

189-191a. Dharma etc. are the first born sons of Brahmā. The nine sons, Bhṛgu and others, were created as expounders of Brahman. They were ancient householders who propagated Dharma. Among them, twelve were the lords of Devas. Their dynasties were divine, endowed with sāttvic qualities. They were active, had good progenies and were adorned among the sages.

191b-195a. Ṛbhu and Sanatkumāra were sages of sublimated sexuality. They were first born and therefore senior to all others. When the eighth kalpa had elapsed these ancient sages, the cosmic witnesses, shone in the world after constricting their splendour. Both of them did abide, by performing yogic rites after super-imposing the individual soul over the supreme soul. Eschewing progeny, worldly rites and affection they adopted detachment. Sanat continued to have the child-like form. Hence his name has been stabilised as Sanat.

195b. Thereafter, as he (Brahmā) continued his meditation, mental sons were born to him.

196. Individual souls were born out of the body of that intelligent lord through the cause and effect process.

197-199. Thereafter he was desirous of creating the four groups, viz. Devas, Asuras, Pitṛs and human beings. He infused himself in the waters. Even as he did so, even as he assiduously meditated on creation, the particles of darkness grew up in excess. Then out of his buttocks were produced the Asuras. O brahmins, the word 'asu' means vital breath. Those born of the vital breath are called Asuras.

200. And he then eschewed that body whereby the Asuras were created and cast it off. It then became Night.

201. Since Night is mostly constituted of darkness it is something that restricts movement. The subjects enveloped in darkness, sleep at night.

202-203. After creating the Asuras he took up another body. It was unmanifest and it mostly consisted of the quality of goodness. So he adored it. Even as he united that body in yogic activities he was pleased. Then from his shining mouth were born Devas.

204-205. Since they were born of him even as he was shining they are called Devas (shining ones). The root 'Div' means 'to play'. Therefore, Devas were born sportingly. After creating them the lord of Devas took another body.

206. That body was cast off by him and when cast off it became day. Hence, Devas adore the day that consists of Dharma.

207-209. Then he took up another body characterized by the quality of goodness. The lord considered himself like a father meditating on sons. Hence, the Pitṛs were born in between the night and day from his two sides. Hence, Devas are the Pitṛs and their state of being Pitṛs is due to that. He cast off that body too. That body cast off by him, immediately became the Twilight.

210-211. The day pertains to Devas and the night to Asuras. In between the two is stationed the body that belongs to the Pitṛs. Hence, all Devas, Asuras, sages and men adore the body that lies in between night and day.

212-213. Then Brahmā adopted another body characterized by the particle of passion. The lord created with his mind the mental sons of passionate activities. Thereby, the passionate sons were born of him.

214-215a. After creating them he cast off that body. That body cast off by him, immediately became moonlight. That is why the people become delighted when moonlight spreads.

215b-216. Thus the bodies cast off by that noble soul became immediately night, day, the morning twilight and evening twilight and moonlight. The moonlight, the twilight and the day, these three consist of the quality of goodness.

217-218a. The night is characterized by the quality of darkness. Hence it is called Niśā. Because Devas were created by day, through pleasure and out of Brahmā's mouth, they are said to be dayborn and powerful by day.

218b-220. The lord created Asuras by night from his loins. That body of the lord became night. Since they were born at night the Asuras are powerful by night. These times become the causes for all (past and) future Devas, Asuras, Pitṛs and human beings in all past and future manvantaras.

221-224. The morning twilight, night, day and evening twilight, these four are the bodies of Brahmā. They are called 'Āmbhāṁsi'. The root bhā means to 'shine'. The word Ambhāṁsi is traced by the learned to this root. After creating these, Prajāpati created Devas, human beings, Dānavas and Pitṛs from his body. Thereafter he foresook that body which turned into moonlight and assumed another form characterized by passion and darkness. The lord created other beings during the night; these beings were overwhelmed with hunger.

225-228. These hungry beings created by him attempted to seize the bodies of the lord. Some of them who said, "We will protect these bodies" were known as Rākṣasas. They were night-walkers who were overcome by hunger. Those who said, 'We will eat them up,' were called yakṣas as also guhyakas because of their secret activity. The root 'rakṣ' means 'to protect and the root 'yakṣ' means 'to eat.' On observing this creation, the hair of the intelligent lord Brahmā became withered due to displeasure.

229-233a. Those of the withered hair that slipped off his head and glided downward became snakes. Since they were defective they are known as Ahis. Since they fell from his head they are known as Pannagas and they are Sarpas because they creep. The fire of his terrible anger turned into poison and entered the serpents; that is why they are born alongwith poison. After creating the serpents the angry lord created other irate souls, who looked savage in their tawny colour.

They were fierce and flesh-eating goblins. Since they came into being they are known as Bhūtas, and as Piśācas because they ate flesh.

233b-234. From him then were born the Gandharvas singing joyously. The root Dhai means to imbibe. They were born even as they were imbibing speech. Hence they are known as Gandharvas.

235. After these eight divine beings had been created that lord created birds from his own youthful stage out of his own inclination.

236. Since they are able to move as they please they are known as such. They are named Vayas (birds) because they were created from his youth. After creating the animals the lord of Devas created the flocks of winged animals.

237-239. He created goats from his mouth; he created sheep from his chest; he created cows and bulls from his belly and sides. From his feet he created horses, elephants, donkeys, deer, camels, mules and other kinds and classes of beasts. Plants and fruit trees were produced from the hair of his body. After creating the cattle and plants, he engaged himself in a sacrifice.

240. They call these the domesticated animals, viz.—the cow, the bull, the man, the ram, the horse, the mule, the donkey. Understand the wild animals.

241-242. They call these the wild animals, viz.—the beasts of prey, the cloven hoofed elephants, monkeys, fifthly, birds, sixthly, aquatic beasts and seventhly, the reptiles. The following seven are forest animals, viz.—buffaloes, gavayas (a species of ox), bears, monkeys, śarabhas (the fabulous animal of eight feet), wolves, and lions.

243. From his front face he created Gāyatrī and ṛc Mantras, Trivṛt Sāman, Rathantara and Agniṣṭoma verses.

244. From his southern face he created Yajur hymns, Triṣṭubh metre, Pañcadaśama Stoman, bṛhat Sāman and Ukthya verses.

245. From his western face he created Sāman, the metre Jagatī, Saptadaśama Stoman, Vairūpa Sāman and Atirātra verses.

246. From his northern face he created the set of twenty

one Atharvan hymns, Āptoryāma, Anuṣṭubh metre and the Vairāja metre.

247. At the beginning of the kalpa the lord created the lightning, the thunderbolts, the clouds, the reddy rainbows and the luminaries.

248. The high and the low living beings were born from his limbs.

249-250. After creating the four groups, viz. Devas, Asuras, human beings and Pitṛs he created beings, mobile and immobile, Yakṣas, Piśācas, Gandharvas, Apsarases, Naras, Kinnaras, Rākṣasas, birds, cattle, wild animals and snakes.

251-261. There are mobile and immobile as well as changing and unchanging created beings. Whatever activities they had in a previous creation they resume the same activities in succeeding creations. They have the same nature, etc. whether savage or timid, kind or cruel, righteous or evil, true or false. Urged by their attributes they adopt and take pleasure in their respective qualities.

When the great elements—the objects of the senses and their forms—were created, the creator himself settled the application of the elements as objects of the sense organs.[607] Some men say that human effort is the cause of various activities; others say that it is divine fate. The materialists say that it is Nature. But really manly effort, working of fate and nature all depend on the nature of the fruit or result. They know that none of these by itself is superior to the other nor can one be separated from the other. This is their nature. They cannot be all one nor are they two together, because they have separate entities.

Those who abide by activities may call that result contrary, those who abide by the quality of goodness observe impartial outlook.

The names and forms of the elements and the further development of the created ones were evolved by the great lord at the beginning itself through the words of the Vedas. The unborn

607. The Purāṇas assign the division of society and the distribution of functions to the primeval being—Maheśvara, Cf. yajño janturanīśoyam ātmanaḥ sukhaduḥkhayoḥ / īśvara-prerito gacchet svargaṁ narakam eva vā //—cited in *ST*.

lord assigns names and activities in regard to the Vedas, to the sages born at the end of the night of dissolution in the same manner as before. Such are the creations of Brahmā of unmanifest origin. The mobile and immobile beings created through his mental perfection are seen at the end of his night. They resort to the mental perfection. When these excellent subjects created by him did not prosper, Brahmā who had been enveloped by the quality of darkness became miserable with grief.

262-263a. Thereupon, he applied his intellect to come to a fixed decision. Then he saw within his mind that the particles of darkness were the sole controlling factors eschewing both the particles of goodness and passion.

263b-264. Therefore, the lord of the universe was miserable due to that sorrow. Then he prodded the tamas, and rajas and covered both with sattva. The tamas thus prodded became a twin.

265-267. Adharma (sin) was born of tamas and Hiṁsā (violence) was born of grief. When this pair of terrible nature originated, the life (vital breaths) left the lord and pleasure resorted to him. Then Brahmā eschewed his shining body and bifurcated it. With one half of his body he became a man. With the other half he created a woman Śatarūpā.

268. With love the lord created Prakṛti, the mother of the elements. With her greatness she stood pervading heaven and earth.

269-270. The first half of body of Brahmā envelopes heaven and stays there. The woman Śatarūpā.[608] born out of the other half performed difficult penance for hundred thousand years and obtained a man of brilliant renown as her husband.

271. That man is at the outset called Manu the self-born. Seventy sets of four yugas constitute his manvantara.

272. That man obtained as his wife Śatarūpā who was not born of a womb. He sported with her. Hence, she is called Rati (pleasure).

608. The Purāṇa speaks of Brahmā splitting his body into two parts : the male and female, viz. Manu and Śatarūpā. Cf. *Matsya* 3.31. Thus Manu and Śatarūpā are said to be ayonija—not born of a womb.

273. The first mutual relation of two souls took place at the beginning of the kalpa when Brahmā created Virāṭ. He became the Virāṭ (massive) Puruṣa.

274. Śatarūpā was the empress. The son of Virāṭ, i.e. Svāyambhuva was known as Manu. Manu Vairāja created the subjects.

275. From the heroic son of Virāṭ (i.e. Vairāja) Śatarūpā gave birth to two sons : Priyavrata and Uttānapāda who were honoured by the worlds.

276. She gave birth to two blessed daughters also from whom the subjects of the world were born. They were the gentle ladies Ākūti and Prasūti.

277. The lord Svāyambhuva Manu gave Prasūti to Dakṣa. Dakṣa should be known as Prāṇa (vital breath); Manu is Saṅkalpa (Idea).

278-279. He gave Ākūti to Ruci the Prajāpati. Ruci the mental son of Brahmā begot auspicious twins of Ākūti. Yajña and Dakṣiṇā were born as twins: Yajña begot of Dakṣiṇā twelve sons.

280. The devas called yāmas were born as his sons in the Svāyambhuva manvantara. Hence, they too are known as Yāmas.

281. Two groups, the Ajitas and the Śukras were created by Brahmā. The Yāmas who were born at the outset became heaven-dwellers.

282. Lord Dakṣa begot of Prasūti, the daughter of Svāyambhuva, twentyfour daughters who became the mothers of the worlds.

283. All of them were highly blessed, lotus-eyed, pleasure-seeking and yogic mothers.

284-285. All of them were expounders of the Brahman as well as mothers of the universe: Lord Dharma took as his wives thirteen of the daughters of Dakṣa, viz:—Śraddhā (faith); Lakṣmī (fortune), Dhṛti (fortitude), Tuṣṭi (satisfaction), Puṣṭi (nourishment), Medhā (intellect), Kriyā (rituals), Buddhi (wisdom), Lajjā (bashfulness), Vapuḥ (beauty), Śānti (peace), Siddhi (achievement) and Kīrti (renown) the thirteenth.

286-292. The lord Dharma took these daughters of Dakṣa

as his wives. Their younger sisters were the eleven splendid-eyed ladies, viz.—Satī, Khyāti, Sambhūti, Smṛti, Prīti, Kṣamā, Sannati, Anasūyā, Ūrjā, Svāhā and Svadhā. Other great sages took them as their wives—they were Rudra, Bhṛgu, Marici, Aṅgiras, Pulaha, Kratu, Pulastya, Atri, Vasiṣṭha, Vahni and the Pitṛs. He gave Satī to Bhava; Khyāti to Bhṛgu; Sambhūti to Marīci; Smṛti to Aṅgiras, Prīti to Pulastya; Kṣamā to Pulaha, Sannati to Kratu, Anasūyā to Atri, Ūrjā to Vasiṣṭha, Svāhā to Agni and Svadhā to the Pitṛs. All these ladies were highly blessed; they closely followed their progeny in all the manvantaras until the dissolution of all living beings. Now listen to their progeny.

293-298. Śraddhā gave birth to Kāma. Darpa was the son of Lakṣmī; Niyama of Dhṛti; Santoṣa of Tuṣṭi; Lobha of Puṣṭi; Śruta of Medhā; Daṇḍa and Samaya were born as the sons of Kriyā; Bodha and Pramāda of Buddhi; Vinaya (Humility) was born of Lajjā; Vyavasāya (Enterprise) of Vapus; Kṣema of Śānti; Sukha of Siddhi; and Yaśaḥ of Kīrti—these were the offspring of Dharma. Harṣa was Kāma's son born of the gentle lady Prīti. Thus, the creation of Dharma has been recounted. Hiṁsā bore to Adharma, Nikṛti and Anṛta.

299-302. Pairs of twins were born of Nikṛti : Bhaya and Naraka; Māyā and Vedanā. Māyā gave birth to Mṛtyu, the dispeller of living beings. Raurava got a son of Vedanā called Duḥkha. From Mṛtyu were born Vyādhi, Jarā, Śoka, Krodha and Asūyā. All these ending with Duḥkha had the characteristics of Adharma. These had no wives nor sons. They live in perpetual chastity. Thus, the Tāmasa creation was evolved with Adharma as the controlling factor.

303-304. Nīlalohita was given the direction by Brahmā to create the subjects. Meditating on his wife Satī he created thousands of hide-clad beings as his mental sons who were neither superior nor inferior but equal to him.

305-313. They were all equal to him in form, splendour, strength and learning. They were tawny-coloured. They were equipped with quivers. They had their matted hairs of reddish hue. They were having special features. Their hairs were greenish. They held skulls. They could kill with their eyes. They had massive figures. They were deformed. They had universal forms. They had his own forms. They had chariots, shields, coats of mail, and protective front-fenders in their chariots. They had hundreds and thousands of arms. They could go to heaven, firmament as well as walk over the earth. They had stout heads, eight curved fangs, two tongues and three eyes. They were eaters of cooked food. Some were eaters of flesh, some imbibers of ghee and some drinkers of Soma juice. Some were bountiful; some had great skulls; some were blue-necked. They had sublimated their sexuality. They were partakers of offerings; they were conversant with Dharma. They were virtuous and adorned with peacock feathers fixed to their clubs. They were seated, they were running in groups of five and there were thousands (of such groups); some were teachers and some students; others performed japas and yogic practices some emitted smoke and blazed; some lived on rivers; some were very bright; others were aged and intelligent; they were engrossed in meditation on Brahman; they were of auspicious visions; they were blue-necked; they had thousand eyes; they were mines of mercifulness and patience; they were invisible to living beings; they had great yogic practices; they had great powers and splendour. Thousands of them roamed about, rushed on and jumped up here and there. He created these excellent beings, the Rudras, even before a Yāma (a period of 3 hours) had elapsed.

314-317. On seeing him (i.e. Rudra) Brahmā spoke to him—"Do not create subjects like these. O lord, do not create subjects equal to yourself. Obeisance be to you! Welfare unto you. Create subjects endowed with death. Subjects devoid of death will not start holy rites."

On being urged thus, he told him—"I will not create the subjects equipped with death and old ege. Welfare unto you. I am standing by; you create the subjects yourself. These beings of great strength will be known by the name 'Rudras'. They will resort to the earth, firmament and all quarters.

318. A hundred Rudras will be devoted to sacrifice. They will partake offerings in sacrifices along with the groups of Devas.

319. They will stay till the end of a yuga. They will be worshipped along with Devas in different manvantaras."

320. Thus addressed by the intelligent lord, Brahmā the delighted patriarch bowed down to him and replied.

321. "O lord, welfare unto you. Let it be even as it had been mentioned by you." When it was approved by Brahmā, everything happened in that manner.

322-324. Ever since that day, the lord of Devas (i. e., Rudra) did not procreate progeny. He remained as Sthāṇu with sublimated sexuality till the time of Dissolution. Since lord Mahādeva, the Puruṣa shining like the sun said "I am staying"; he is known as Sthāṇu (motionless).

325. He has the female form in one half of his body. In splendour he is comparable to the fire. By his own will he divided himself into two, a separate woman, and a separate man.

326-327. The same lord stationed himself in eleven halves.[609] The great goddess mentioned before as the highly blessed lady sharing half the body of the lord became Satī for the welfare of the worlds. The goddess had been formerly propitiated by Dakṣa.

328-329. "For the sake of creation, divide yourself into two, right half being white and the left black."—On being asked thus by lord Śiva, O brahmins, she bifurcated herself into white and black. I shall mention her names; listen attentively.

330-335. They are:—Svāhā, Svadhā, Mahāvidyā, Medhā, Lakṣmī, Sarasvatī, Satī, Dākṣāyaṇī, Vidyā, Icchā Śakti, Kriyātmikā, Aparṇā, Ekaparṇā, Ekapāṭalā, Umā, Haimavatī, Kalyāṇī, Ekamātṛkā, Khyāti, Prajñā Mahābhāgā, Gaurī, Gaṇāmbikā, Mahādevī, Nandinī, and Jātavedasī. These are some of the names when she was one (i.e. before division). After she had divided into two, her names are:—Sāvitrī, Varadā, Puṇyā, Pāvanī, Lokaviśrutā, Ājñā, Āveśanī, Kṛṣṇā, Tāmasī, Sāttvikī, Śivā, Prakṛti, Vikṛtā, Raudrī, Durgā, Bhadrā, Pramāthinī, Kālarātrī, Mahāmāyā, Revatī, Bhūtanāyikā. At the end of Dvāpara yuga, O sages of good holy rites, her names are as follows:—

609. Lord Śiva has a body half man and half woman. Thus when we speak of eleven Rudras we mean eleven half males and eleven half females. Both the male and female forms, divided into hundreds and thousands, have their distinct names and activities.

336-339. Gautamī, Kauśikī, Āryā, Caṇḍī, Kātyāyinī, Satī, Kumārī, Yādavī, Varadā, Kṛṣṇapiṅgalā, Bahirdhvajā or Barhirdhvajā, Śūladharā, Paramā, Brahmacāriṇī, Mahendropendrabhāginī, Dṛṣaḍvatī, Ekaśūladhṛk, Aparājitā, Bahubhujā, Pragalbhā, Siṁhavāhinī, the slayer of the Daityas such as Śumbha and others, the suppressor of the great demon Mahiṣa, Amoghā, Vindhyanilayā, Vikrāntā and Gaṇanāyikā. These are the various names of the goddess in order.

340. The names of Bhadrakālī mentioned by me yield the best results. Those men who read these become devoid of sons.

341-342. In the forest, on the mountain, in the city or in the house, in the water or on dry land these names are used as saving remedy. One shall repeat them when there is danger from tigers, elephants, kings or thieves—nay in all adversities.

343. One shall repeat these names as protective measure in the case of children afflicted by evil eye, evil planets, goblins as well as mothers.

344. The following two are the parts of the great goddess. They are Prajñā and Śrī. From these two were born thousands of goddesses by whom the entire universe is pervaded.

345-347. Rudra, Maheśvara the lord of Devas stationed himself along with his consort Satī, for the benefit of the worlds. He is Parameśvara, Rudra and Paśupati. Formerly the three cities were burned by him. By his brilliance, Devas became Paśus (Individual Souls). He who reads or listens to the splendid order of the primordial creation attains the world of Brahmā. He who narrates the same to the excellent brahmins also attains Brahmā's world.

CHAPTER SEVENTYONE

The statement of Nandikeśvara

The sages said:

1. The splendid process of creation has been mentioned succinctly and in detail by you. How did Paśupati, Maheśvara happen to burn the three cities of Asuras ?

2-4. O holy lord, how did Devas including Brahmā become Paśus? The set of cities was formerly built by Maya by performing penance. It was an excellent set of three cities of divine nature, made of gold, silver and iron. We have heard that these along with their forts were burned by the lord of Devas. How did the lord who struck down the eyes of Bhaga burn these cities by discharging a single arrow even though it was divine.

5. That set of three cities was not burned by the goblins created by Viṣṇu. The entire details of the origin of the cities and the acquisition of boons have been heard formerly.

6-9. O sage of good holy rites, it behoves you to narrate the burning of the cities wholly.

On hearing their words, Sūta, the most excellent among the knowers of the Purāṇas, said what he had heard from Vyāsa in the manner as he had indicated all the necessary topics.

Sūta said:—

Due to the curse of the three worlds originating from mind, speech and body, the asura Tāraka, the son of Tāra, was killed along with his kinsmen by Skanda assiduously. His sons, all of noble soul, great strength and exploits, viz:—Vidyunmālin, Tārakākṣa and Kamalākṣa, performed penance.

10-12. Those excellent Dānavas, while performing fierce penance, observed great restraints. By means of penance they emaciated their bodies. The delighted Brahmā, the bestower of boons granted them the boon of their choice.

The Daityas said:—

"We want not to be killed by any living being at any time."

Thus they jointly requested the grandfather of all worlds. Then the eternal lord of the worlds spoke to them thus :

13. "O Asuras, there is no universal immortality. Desist from this desire. Choose another boon that may appeal to you."

14. Then the Daityas after consulting one another bowed to Brahmā, the preceptor of the universe and said to him:—

15. "By your grace, O lord of worlds, O preceptor of the universe, we shall roam over this earth and live in three cities.

16. Once in a thousand years we shall meet together. O sinless one, these cities shall then fuse into one city.

17. The lord who strikes at these when they have fused into one with a single arrow shall be death unto us.

18. Replying—"Let it be so", the lord entered the heaven. Thereafter the heroic Maya built the cities by means of his penance.

19. The cities of those noble asuras were stationed as follows:—the golden one was in the heaven; the silver city was in the firmament and the iron city was on the earth.

20-22. Each of these cities was a hundred yojanas in length and in breadth. The city of Tārakākṣa was made of gold; the city of Kamalākṣa was made of silver; that of Vidyunmāli was made of iron; they had three types of excellent forts. Maya was worshipped by the Daityas and Dānavas there. This powerful architect built his own abode in everyone of them and lived there.

23. Thus, O men of good holy rites, came into existence the well-fortified three cities. O leading brahmins, they were like the three worlds.

24. When the trio of cities grew up, the Daityas in the three worlds entered the three cities and became superior in strength.

25. The cities were full of kalpa trees.[610] They abounded in elephants and horses. There were innumerable mansions richly decorated with clusters of jewels.

26-27. There were aerial chariots that resembled the solar

610. kalpa-druma—one of the five trees of Indra's paradise fabled to fulfil all desires, the other being Mandāra, Pārijātaka, Santāna and Haricandana.

disc and that had faces on every side. The palaces were splendid with rubies studded. They were as refulgent as the moon. Their ornamental gateways were divine and resembled the peaks of Kailāsa. Their three cities shone with the excellent mansions built separately.

28. O excellent brahmins, it was filled with divine ladies (i.e. ladies of divine beauty and excellence), Gandharvas, Siddhas and Cāraṇas. There were shrines of Rudra in every house and Agnihotra was performed every day.

29-37. They were filled with wells, tanks, large oblong lakes all round. Herds of elephants in their rut, splendid horses, chariots of every shape, wonderfully made with faces on all sides—all these abounded there. There were drinking sheds, assemblies, playgrounds, etc. Different kinds of halls and chambers for the study of the Vedas were found all round. The cities were well fortified and made unassailable even mentally by others, due to the illusionary power of Maya. O leading sages, the cities were frequented by chaste ladies everywhere. There were many Daityas. Although they committed great sins they got rid of them through their worship of Śaṅkara. O brahmins, the leading Daityas were highly blessed. They were accompanied by their wives and sons. They were conversant with the holy rites laid down in the Śrutis and Smṛtis. They were engaged in those virtuous rites always. They abandoned all lords other than Mahādeva and were engaged in the worship of that lord alone. They had broad chests and shoulders like those of bulls. They used to hold all weapons. They were always hungry. Their eyes shone like the forest fire. Some of them were quiescent; some were infuriated. Some were dwarfish and some were hump-backed; they had the lustre of blue lotuses; their hairs were darkcoloured and curly. They resembled the blue mountain and the Meru; their voice was comparable to the sound of the rumbling cloud. All of them were protected by Maya. They were well-trained and were desirous of fighting. That trio of cities was well frequented by the firm and steadfast suppressors of Devas (i.e. Daityas) who were interested in fighting always and all round, who had perfectly achieved prowess and virility by the worship of Śiva and who resembled the sun, wind and king of immortal beings.

38. O excellent brahmins, thanks to the prowess of the Daityas, Devas including Indra were burned by the fire of the set of three cities like the trees consumed by the forest fire.

39. Devas who were thus scorched saluted lord Viṣṇu of unrivalled splendour and said to him.

40-41. The glorious lord, Nārāyaṇa thought within his mind as to what should be done in the affairs of Devas. Janārdana, whose form is sacrifice, who was himself the performer of sacrifices, who was the partaker of the fruit of sacrifices and who is the lord and bestower of benefits unto those who perform sacrifices, remembered the sacrifice.

42. The sacrifice remembered by him for the achievement of the objects of Devas bowed down to that lord and eulogised him.

43. Seeing the smiling sacrifice, the eternal lord Viṣṇu observed Devas including Indra and said:—

Śrī Viṣṇu said:—

44. For the destruction of the three cities and for the prosperity of the three worlds, O Devas, worship the lord with ths Upasad sacrifice.

Sūta said:—

45. On hearing the words of the intelligent lord of Devas, Devas made great leonine roaring sound and eulogised the lord of sacrifices.

46. Thereafter, lord Viṣṇu himself thought once again. The lord of Devas again spoke to all Devas.

47. Even after killing and burning all living beings and even after enjoying pleasures without the basic justice, if one worships Mahādeva, one is undoubtedly sinless.

48-49. There is no doubt that sinless persons should not be killed and only sinners should be killed assiduously. O excellent Devas, how could the wicked Asuras be killed by Devas although they are sinners and Devas are very strong? Hence they should not be killed due to the power of Rudra Parameṣṭhin.

50. Without the grace of the lord who am I? O Devas,

who is Brahmā ? Who are the Daityas ? Who are the slayers of the enemies of Devas ? Who are the noble-souled sages ?

51. He is the lord, greater than the greatest. He is perpetual; he is the twentyseventh principle;[611] who is worthy of being saluted, who is the lord of all the immortal beings in the universe and who is Maheśvara the support of the universe.

52. He alone is the lord of all Devas. He is the benefactor of all. He has made a distinction between Devas and Daityas sportingly.

53. It is by worshipping a part of his[612] that Devas attained immortality; Brahmā attained his status as Brahmā and I attained my status as Viṣṇu.

54. Without worshipping him, which man attains perfection in this world ? Thanks to the worship of Liṅga, they could be killed by him alone.

55-56. Moreover, all of them abide by their Dharmas. They adhere to the injunctions of Śruti and Smṛti. Still we shall worship Rudra by performing the rite of Upasad pertaining to that lord and become victorious over the excellent Daityas. Excepting the sole lord, the three-eyed deity, who else is competent to destroy the Tripuras ? They are well protected by Maya along with Tārakākṣa. They have the sole lustre of crystals and they are well stationed in themselves.

Sūta said:—

57. After saying this Viṣṇu performed the worship of the lord by means of Upasad sacrifice. Sitting there he saw thousands of goblins.

58-59. They were armed with spears, javelins and iron clubs. They had various weapons; they were in various guises. They resembled Rudra fierce as the fire at the time of dissolution; they were comparable to Rudra the destroyer. They bowed to him and halted. Lord Viṣṇu then spoke to them.

611. See p. 8 note 15 Cf. 1.75.34: 'tasmād abheda-buddhyaiva saptaviṁśatprabhedataḥ.

612. Śiva in his sakala form of liṅga.

Viṣṇu said:—

60. "O heroic ones, go to the three cities of Daityas, burn them, split them and swallow them. Then return to the surface of the earth in the manner you had gone."

61. Thereafter, the groups of goblins bowed down to the lord of Devas and entered the three cities. Like the moths in fire, they became destroyed.

62-63a. At the behest of the lord of Daityas, all the goblins were destroyed. Thousands of Daityas rejoiced, danced and sang. They eulogised Rudra the lord of Devas, the great soul.

63b-64. Devas including Indra, who had been defeated in a trice and whose prowess had been destroyed, came unto Viṣṇu, the lord of Devas and resorted to his support out of fear. On seeing them the lord Viṣṇu thought thus.

65-66. "What is to be done?" After thinking thus he became distressed as he looked at the distresed Devas including Indra. After a while he thought again "How shall I destroy the army of Daityas assiduously and carry out the tasks of Devas without the grace of the supreme lord. If one ponders over it, there is no doubt about this that those who are virtuous have no sin at all.

67-71. Hence, know that the Daityas cannot be killed by those Bhūtas originating from the Upasad sacrifice. They dispel sin by means of Dharma. Everything is founded on Dharma. The eternal Śruti says that prosperity originates from Dharma. All these Daityas, the residents of the three cities, are virtuous. Hence, O leading brahmins, they have attained immortality and not otherwise. Even after committing a very great sin, people are liberated from all the sins if they worship Rudra. They are not affected by sins like the lotus leaves which are not affected by water. O brahmins, the achievement of worldly pleasures definitely takes place through his worship. Hence, those Daityas who are devoted to the worship of the Liṅga do enjoy worldly pleasures. Hence, O Devas, for your purpose I shall create obstacles in the holy rites of Daityas by means of my Māyā and so shall conquer the three cities instantaneously"

Sūta said:—

72. After thinking thus, the lord Viṣṇu decided to bring about impediments in the holy rituals of asuras.

73. Viṣṇu of great splendour, wielding Māyā generated an illusory Puruṣa[613] born of himself to create obstacles to the holy rites of Daityas.

74. Viṣṇu the ruler of all, the person who could assume any form he liked, the wielder of Māyā, evolved a holy treatise that could fascinate everyone and that had within its basic principles the belief in what is seen.

75. This sacred treatise contained one million six hundred thousand verses.[614] Lord Viṣṇu taught this scripture to the Puruṣa born of his own limbs.

76-77. It was against those treatises that followed the Śrutis and the Smṛtis. It was devoid of the discipline pertaining to the four castes and four stages of life. It was taught in it that heaven and hell are here itself.[615] There was no belief otherwise. Viṣṇu himself taught this scripture to that Puruṣa. For the destruction of the three cities he said to that Puruṣa:

78. "O, undoubtedly it behoves you to go there for the quick destruction of the residents of the three cities. May their Dharmas in pursuit of the Śrutis and Smṛtis be destroyed."

79. The wielder of Māyā[616], the expert in the deceptive scripture, bowed to him. After entering those cities the sage immediately created his Māyā.

80. On account of his Māyā, those Daityas who were the residents of the three cities, eschewed their holy rites based on the Śrutis and Smṛtis and became his disciples.

81-82. They left off Śaṅkara, Mahādeva, the great Īśvara.

613. According to the present context Viṣṇu created a delusive teacher called Māyāmoha who created a Māyāśāstra of sixteen lakhs of verses preaching *a-dharma* for misguiding the Asuras. Māyāmoha created disciples for the propagation of *a-dharma*. He preached non-violence, forbade Śrauta and Smārta rituals, discarded Varṇāśrama system, created an order for women that resulted in leaving their home and leading the life of nuns. In some versions, the role is assigned to Bṛhaspati, the preceptor of Gods who in the guise of the preceptor Śukra deludes the Asuras. For detail, see Māyāmoha prakaraṇa in *Padma*, *Viṣṇu*, *Matsya* and *Śiva* purāṇas.

614. This is not clear which text is meant.

615. On the heretic doctrines compare :

इहैव स्वर्गनरकौ प्राणिनां नान्यतः क्वचित्। सुखं स्वर्गः समाख्यातो दुःखं नरक एव हि। सुखेषु भुज्यमानेषु यत्स्याद्देहविसर्जनम्। अयमेव परो मोक्षः न मोक्षोऽन्यः क्वचित्पुनः ॥ cited in *ST*.

616. Muniḥ—Bauddha-bhikṣuḥ *ST*.

At the behest of the lord, the wielder of Māyā, Nārada, the practitioner of deception, also entered the trio of cities and associated himself with the wielder of Māyā. That sage was himself surrounded on all sides by his disciples and their disciples.

83-88. He ordained rules of conduct for women that would give them the benefit of licentious activities. They followed those rules and achieved the result immediately. These women began to censure the ladies faithful to their husbands and themselves became enamoured of other people. Even today in the Kali age, base women give due honour to the sage Nārada[617], abandon their husbands and move about unfettered. Really it is the husband who is mother, father, kinsman, comrade, friend and relative unto the women. There is no doubt about this. Still he said thus through his Māyā. Really the woman who has love towards her husband shall attain the greatest heaven even after committing a great sin. She who does contrary to this attains hell. O leading sages, formerly, chaste ladies forsook all Dharmas, all Devas and other preceptors of the universe and worshipped their husbands always. After attaining the heavenly world they became free from ailments and rejoiced. But those who were the followers of Māyā attained hell. Hence, it is the husband who is the greatest goal.

89-91. Yet on account of the Māyā of the lord of Devas and at the behest of lord Viṣṇu, the women abandoned their husbands and became self-willed and unrestrained in their conducts. Misfortune went to the three cities at the behest of that lord himself. The glory and prosperity that they had obtained from Brahmā, the unborn lord, the lord of Devas, abandoned them and went out of the cities.

92-97. The lord thus preached delusion of the intellect as evolved by the Māyā of Viṣṇu. The Puruṣa deluded the Daityas and Nārada the wielder of Māyā deluded the ladies. In order to create obstacles in Dharmas these two were comfortably seated there. They were unexcited and unchanging,

617. **The preaching in regard to sexual freedom is attributed to Nārada, the disciple of Māyāmoha.**

when the splendid Dharma pertaining to the Śrutis and the Smṛtis, perished; when heresy was proclaimed by Viṣṇu, the source of origin of the universe; when Maheśvara and the worship of his Liṅga were abandoned by Daityas; when the virtuous activities of the women were entirely destroyed and wicked conduct was stabilised; the lord of Devas Viṣṇu appeared contented. After practising penance he approached the consort of Umā along with Devas and eulogised him. Lord Viṣṇu said :—

Obeisance to you, to Lord Maheśvara, to the great Ātman, obeisance to Nārāyaṇa, to Śarva, to Brahmā, to one having the form of Brahman; obeisance to the permanent one, to the infinite one, to the unmanifest one.

Sūta said:

98-99. After eulogising the great lord and after bowing down like a long staff, the lord Viṣṇu stationed himself in water and performed the japa of the Rudra Mantra ten million times. All Devas including Indra, Sādhyas, Yama, Rudras and Maruts eulogised lord Śiva.

Devas said :

100. Obeisance to you the Ātman of all; obeisance to Śaṅkara the dispeller of affliction, to Rudra, to Nīla Rudra, to Kadrudra and to Pracetas.

101. You are our perpetual goal; the suppressor of the enemies of Devas should be always worshipped and honoured by us. You are the primordial one; you are the endless one; you are the infinite imperishable lord.

102. O preceptor of the universe, you are Prakṛti and Puruṣa himself; you are the creator, the destroyer; the protector; the leader of the brahmins in this universe, O deity, favourably disposed towards the brahmins.

103-104. You are the granter of boons; you are identical with speech. You are worthy of being directly expressed; you are devoid of the expressed and expression. For the sake of salvation, you are worshipped by the yogins and by those who whirl in the yogic practice. You are stationed in the cavity of the lotus-like heart. The wise call you *Sat* (the existent), the greatest one in the form of Brahman.

105. O lord, the noble sages say that you are reality, the mass of splendour, greater than the greatest and the greatest Ātman in this world.

106. O preceptor of the universe, you are everything that is seen, heard, stationed or born. They call you minuter than the minutest and greater than the greatest.

107. They call you one with hands and feet everywhere, one with eyes, heads and mouths everywhere. You have ears all round and you stand enveloping everything in the world.

108-110. They call you Mahādeva, the omniscient, one without ailment, one who cannot be specifically pointed out, one having a universal form, one with deformed eyes, Sadāśiva without ailment, one who makes others in the world function, one who makes Prakṛti work, the great-grandfather, the lord who bestows boons, the self-born deity, the abode of all and the lord of twentysix principles. You resemble ten million suns in refulgence; you are similar to ten million moons in brightness, you are on a par with ten million fires that blaze at the time of dissolution and you have no other lord to control you.

111-114. The Śrutis and the people who are conversant with the essence of Śrutis call you the essence of the Śrutis. O deity with many forms, that which is evolved in the world without you has not been seen by us. You alone protect the Daityas, Devas, Bhūtas, the mobile and immobile beings, O Śambhu, we have no other goal. Protect us by killng all the Asuras.

O Parameśvara, all are deluded by your Māyā. Just as the waves and billows in the ocean come into clash with one another and ultimately become water, so also Devas and Asuras and all creations of Brahmā (fighting one another) are rendered insentient by the lord [a pun on the word jala (water) which is also pronounced as jaḍa when it means insentient, inactive].

Sūta said :

115. The man who gets up early in the morning, purifies

himself and repeats this holy hymn or listens to this shall attain all desires.

116-119a. Maheśvara, who was thus eulogised by Devas, was pleased by it as well as by the Japa performed by Viṣṇu. Accompanied by Umā, he embraced Umā and smilingly kept his hand on Nandin. Glancing at Devas, he said in a majestic tone :—"O leading Devas, this task has been understood by me now. I know the power of the Māyā of Viṣṇu and the intelligent Nārada; O excellent Devas, I shall cause the destruction of all those Daityas engaged in evil activities. I shall destroy the three cities as well."

Sūta said :—

119b-121a. Then Devas came there along with Brahmā, Indra and Viṣṇu. On hearing the words of the lord they bowed to him and eulogised him. In the meanwhile the goddess glanced at the lord with surprise. She hit the bull-bannered deity with her toy lotus and said.

The Goddess said :—

121b-125. O lord, see our son, the six-faced Kārttikeya, resembling the sun in refulgence. He is playing. O excellent one among those blessed with sons, he is adorned with excellent ornaments such as coronets, bangles, ear-rings, bracelets, anklets, belly-bands, tinkling bells, golden fig leaves, etc. His forelocks are bedecked with the flowers of the kalpa tree. His necklace is studded with rubies and other precious gems. He is adorned with shoulderlets and pearl necklaces having the lustre of the full moon. He has the caste-marks on his foreheads. O Mahādeva, see our splendid son.

126-129. He is marked with saffron. A round mark has been made with Bhasma. O lord, see the row of faces like the cluster of lotuses. O lord, see his splendid eyes. See the splendid marks of collyrium applied by his mothers Gaṅgā, Kṛttikā and Svāhā[618] as an auspicious benediction."

Śiva who was thus addressed by Umā, the mother of the worlds, began imbibing the nectar from the faces of Skanda.

618. **Mothers of Kārttikeya. See *ŚP. Rudra Saṁhitā*, ch.2.**

He was not satiated thereby. He even forgot Devas who harassed by the Daityas had assembled there.

130. He embraced Skanda, kissed him, smelling the head and said—"Dance, dear son". The great boy, dispelling the anguish of all danced gently and sportingly.

131. The other leading Gaṇas danced along with him. At the bidding of the lord, the entire universe, danced for a moment.

132. All the Nāgas (serpents) and Devas with Indra at their forefront danced. The chiefs of the Gaṇas eulogised Skanda. Umā and the mothers rejoiced.

133. The Gandharvas and Kinnaras showered flowers and sang. On drinking the nectar of the fine dance Pārvatī and Parameśvara attained satisfaction along with Nandin and the leading Gaṇas.

134. Then along with Nandin, Kārttikeya, and the daughter of the king of mountains, Śiva entered the divine abode, like the cloud entering other clouds. He too had the lustre of the clouds.[619]

135. Devas stood by the door of the abode. Slightly distressed in their minds they eulogised the lord.

136. They told one another: "What is this? What is this?" and they looked at one another in their excited dejection. Some said, "we are sinners", still others said, "we are unfortunate".

137. The leading Devas said :—Daityas are lucky. Others said, "This is the fruit of their worship." Still others said—"No."

138. In the meantime, on hearing their grim voices Kumbhodara[620] of great splendour struck them with his staff.

139. Devas were frightened. Crying "Hā, Hā" they fled. The sages and Devas fell on the ground.

140-141. The sages Kaśyapa and others said—"O our adverse fate!" The brahmins said "Even after seeing the lord, the task of Devas has not been accomplished due to the ill luck of Devas. Still others said, "Obeisance to Śiva" after worshipping him slightly in their hearts.

619. ambudābhaḥ—*ST.* interprets differently : ambudavat sūryavad ābhā kāntir yasya—who resembles the sun in brilliance.

620. Kumbhodaraḥ—a gaṇa of lord Śiva.

142-146. At the behest of Mahādeva Nandīśa, the favourite sage of the lord came there riding on a white bull. He had matted hair and held the trident and the iron club. He wore garlands, necklaces, ear-rings and bangles. On seeing Nandin, the Kumbhodara bowed to Nandin with his lowered head and hastened along with him. Nandin of great splendour was seated on the back of a bull. He had the bull banner. He was the commander-in-chief of the Gaṇas and was accompanied by the Gaṇas like the great lord himself, riding on the back of the cloud.[621] The white umbrella of Nandin stretched to ten Yojanas. It was bedecked in clusters of pearls. It shone like the firmament. The splendid pearl necklace suspended from it from within appeared like the Gaṅgā falling from the sky over the head of the lord.

147-153. O leading sages, at the behest of Indra, the wielder of the thunderbolt, the splendid divine drums were sounded in honour of the presiding officer of the Gaṇas. They eulogised him with pleasing words, just as they eulogised Śiva with thrilling joy and loving devotion. At the bidding of the thunderbolt-wielding lord, the sky-walkers showered fragrant flowers from the firmament over the head of Nandin. Satisfied with that shower he shone with real and sincere satisfaction. Nandin was drenched in fragrant water dropping from the moon on the forehead of the lord. The back of the bull shone with different kinds of flowers. O sages of good holy rites, just as the firmament is scattered with stars so also the back of the bull was covered with flowers. Covered by them Nandin shone on the back of the bull, like the moon on the back of the firmament. O sages of holy rites, on seeing Nandin that way Devas including Indra and Viṣṇu eulogised the chieftain of the Gaṇas as if he was another lord of Devas.

Devas said :

154-160. Obeisance to you the devotee of Rudra, to one engaged in the japa of Rudra mantras; obeisance to one who

621. **meghapṛṣṭhe—megha-rūpa-Viṣṇu-pṛṣṭhe** *ST*. **This refers to Viṣṇu in the form of cloud which lord Śiva made his vehicle. Hence, Śiva is called 'megha-vāhana.'**

destroys the agony of the devotees of Rudra; obeisance to you engaged in rites pleasing to Rudra; obeisance to the leader of Kūṣmāṇḍa; obeisance to the lord of yogins; to the bestower of everything; to one worthy of being sought refuge in; to the omniscient one; to the dispeller of agony; to the lord of the Vedas; obeisance to one comprehensible only through the Vedas; obeisance to one wielding thunderbolt; to one whose curved fangs are adamantine; to one who renders the thunderbolt of Indra ineffective; to one whose body is bedecked in diamonds; to one propitiated by Indra, the wielder of thunderbolt; obeisance to the Rakta (red coloured) ;to one with red eyes; to the wearer of red garments; obeisance to one who bestows the world of Rudra to those who are devoted to his lotus-like feet. Obeisance to the commander of the armies; to the lord of Rudras; to the lord of goblins and to the lord of the worlds; obeisance to the dispeller of sins; obeisance to Rudra, to Rudrapati (Lord of the Rudras) ; obeisance to Śiva; obeisance to the gentle one; obeisance to you who are the devotee of Rudra.

Sūta said:

161-163. Thus eulogised, the delighted presiding officer of the Gaṇas, the son of Śilāda said to Devas:—

"It behoves you all to prepare a chariot, a charioteer, a bow and an arrow for Śambhu with assiduity thinking that the trio of the cities was as good as destroyed." Then the Devas strenuously made the chariot through their artificer Viśvakarman assisted by Brahmā, for the use of Śiva the intelligent lord of Devas.

CHAPTER SEVENTYTWO

Construction of Rudra's chariot

1. With great assiduity and eagerness the divine and cosmic chariot[622] of lord Rudra was made by Viśvakarman.

2. It was identical with all living beings;[623] it was bowed to by all Devas; it was identical with all Devas;[624] it was golden and it was honoured by all.

3. The sun was the right wheel and the moon was the left wheel. The right wheel had twelve spokes and the left wheel had sixteen spokes.

4. O leading brahmins, the twelve Ādityas were in those twelve spokes on the right. O sages of good holy rites, in the sixteen spokes of the left wheel were the sixteen digits of the moon.

5. The constellations were the ornaments of the left wheel[625] alone. The six seasons were the rims of those two wheels, O leading brahmins.

6. The firmament was the roof[626] of the chariot and the interior[627] of the chariot was the Mandara. The mountain of rising sun and the mountain of the setting sun were the poles to which the yoke was fixed.

7. Mahāmeru was the pedestal and the mountain Kesara was the supporting seat. The year was its velocity and the two transits of the sun were the joints of the wheels.

8. The Muhūrtas were holes to fix the nails or pins and

622. In the Purāṇas Viśvakarman is invested with the powers and offices of the Vedic Tvaṣṭṛ. He is the great architect, executor of handicrafts and the builder of great cities. He is the son of Prabhāsa, the eighth Vasu, by his wife Yogasiddhā.

623-624. The cosmic chariot represents the cosmic powers with seven worlds as wheels, with five gross elements and all-gods as its constituents.

625. Vāma i.e the moon, the left side of the cosmic car.

626. puṣkara—vacuum, it stands in apposition to antarīkṣa—the atmospheric region, the sky.

627. ratha-nīḍaḥ—sārathi-sthānam ST., the sitting place for the charioteer.

Kalās were the pins of the yoke. The Kāṣṭhās were its nostrils and the Kṣaṇas were its axles.

9. The Nimeṣaṣ were its Axle-tree and the Lavas constituted its shafts. The sky was the fender of that chariot. The heaven and salvation were its flags.

10. Virtue and detachment were its staffs and sacrifices were the supports of the staffs. The monetary gifts were the joints and the fifty fires were the iron pieces or bolts.

11. Dharma and Kāma (love) were the tips of the two yokes; the unmanifest principle was the poleshaft; the cosmic intellect was its connecting shaft.

12. The ego was its angular points; the elements were its strength; the sense organs its ornamental fittings all round.

13. Śraddhā (faith) was its movement; the Vedas were its horses; the Padas (words) of the Vedas its ornaments and the six ancillaries were its trinkets.

14. O sages of good holy rites, the Purāṇas, Nyāya(science of logic), Mīmāṁsā (treatise on holy rites), the Dharmaśāstras (ethical literature) were its perfect screen cloths and supports of the tails. It was equipped with all characteristics.

15. The mantras, syllables, feet and the four stages in life were its bells. Ananta the serpent adorned by his thousand hoods formed its bounding limit.

16. The quarters and the interstices were the pillars of this chariot. The Puṣkara and other clouds were its golden banners studded with jewels.

17-18. The four oceans formed the blankets spread on its surface. The Gaṅgā and other rivers appeared splendid in female forms, bedecked in all ornaments and holding the chowries in their hands. They occupied different parts in the chariot and rendered it beautiful.

19. The seven layers of winds, Āvaha etc. were the seven excellent golden steps. The charioteer was lord Brahmā and he held the reins.

20-21. Praṇava with Brahman for its deity was the whip. The mountain Lokāloka was its landing ground with stairs all round. The splendid Mānasa mountain was its external precipice. The other mountains constituted its noses all round [the upper timbers].

22. The Tala and the residents thereof constituted its pigeon holes, and the pigeons. The mountain Meru was the great umbrella and the Mandara constituted the side drum.

23. The king of mountains (Himavān) was his bow and the bowstring was the lord of serpents (Vāsuki) himself, along with Kālarātri (the night of nightmares) and Indradhanus (rainbow).

24. The bell of the bow was goddess Sarasvatī of the form of the Śrutis (Vedas). Viṣṇu of great splendour was the arrow and Soma (moon) was the spike-head of the arrow.

25. The Kālāgni fire at the end of kalpa was the sharp and terrible point of that arrow. The army originated from the waters. The winds were feathers fixed to the arrow.

26-27. After making the divine chariot, bow and arrows with Brahmā the lord of the worlds as his charioteer, Śiva mounted the divine chariot wearing martial decorations. He was accompanied by the groups of Devas and he shook heaven and earth by his movements.

28-31. Eulogised by the sages and saluted by the bards the shining splendid lord, the bestower of boons occupied the chariot glancing at the charioteer. The groups of Apsarases, skilled in dancing, danced in his presence (to honour him). When he got into the chariot, evolved out of the different material, the horse originating from the Vedas fell headlong over the earth. The lord Dharaṇīdhara (uplifter of the earth i.e., Viṣṇu), assuming the form of a leading bull lifted up the chariot for a while and tried to stabilise it. But at the next moment even that leading bull slipped down to the earth on his knees.

32. At the instance of the lord Śiva, lord Brahmā who held the reins in his hands lifted up the horses and steadied the splendid chariot.

33. Then he drove the horses that had the speed of the wind, towards the cities of the swift and courageous Dānavas. The cities till then had peace and comfort.

34. Thereafter looking at Devas, lord Rudra said:—

"Give unto me the lordship of Paśus.[628] Then I shall kill the Asuras.

35. O excellent Devas, only after assigning you a status of animal souls distinct from that of Devas and others, can they be killed, not otherwise, O excellent ones."

36. After hearing these words of the intelligent lord, all of them became suspicious and uneasy over this change and felt great distress.

37. On realising their mental reaction, the lord spoke to them thus:—"O excellent Devas, let there be no fear or misgiving in you in regard to your becoming Paśus.

38-41. Now listen and try to pursue the means of liberation from the state of Paśu. He who performs the divine holy rite "Pāśupata" will be liberated from the state of Paśu. O pure ones, I solemnly promise this to you. O excellent Devas, there is no doubt in this that those others too who perform the Pāśupata rite will be liberated from the state of a Paśu. He who renders service steadily for twelve years or even half that period or even three years can be liberated from that state. Hence, O excellent Devas, perform this great and divine rite".

42-50. "So be it", said Devas to Śiva, who is bowed to by all the worlds. That is why Devas, Asuras and human beings are called Paśus. Rudra is the lord of Paśus[629] and the liberator of Paśus from their bondage. He who is Paśu, shall eschew that state through this holy rite. The scriptures declare that even by committing sins he does not become a sinner.

628. paśūnām ādhipatyam—lordship of the individual souls (jīvas); Cf. "so 'bravīd varaṁ vṛṇā ahameva paśūnām adhipatir asāni"—cited in *ST*.

629. Śiva is named Paśupati, the lord of animals. According to the legend, recorded in the present chapter, every deity was asked by Śiva to declare himself a mere Paśu or animal before Tripuras could be slain in the battle. The Gods accepted the proposal, declared themselves as animals and fought brutally. Lord Śiva won them the battle but Gods were still distressed. The lord then enjoined the observance of Pāśupata vrata for the attainment of their release from animal nature.

This legend forms the basis for the formulation of Pāśupata sect which aims at the release of Paśu (the individual soul) from the bondage of re-birth.

Then Vināyaka himself, the boy with the exploit of an adult, forbade Devas as he had not been duly worshipped by Devas and said thus—

Śrī Vināyaka said:—

Which man, may he be a Deva or a Dānava, attains perfection in this world without worshipping me by means of splendid foodstuffs, edibles, etc. Hence, O leading Devas, I will cause impediments in a trice in your tasks. O leading Devas, how is it that you had attempted to perform this without worshipping me.

Thereafter all Devas including Indra became frightened. After worshipping that lord and propitiating him with all kinds of edibles and foodstuffs, with loaves and sweet-meats they spoke to lord Gaṇeśa—"Let now our task be achieved without impediments."

Lord Rudra, the chief of all leading Devas, embraced his son and kissed him on the head. He worshipped and propitiated Gaṇeśa with flowers of sweet fragrance and juicy edibles and foodstuffs.

After worshipping Vināyaka the leader of chieftains, worthy of being worshipped, lord Rudra who had the lord of mountains for his bow started along with the groups of Devas and the chiefs of the Gaṇas, in order to burn the three cities.

51. The groups of Devas, Siddhas, Bhūtas, Gaṇas and their lords beginning with Nandin followed Īśa, Maheśvara, the lord of Devas, with their respective vehicles.

52. Mounted on a chariot as huge as the lord of mountains, Nandin went ahead of Devas and the chiefs of Gaṇas, in order to strike at the trio of the cities, like the great lord Īśa going ahead to strike the god of Death.

53. Mounting on lordly elephants, huge bulls and stately horses, Devas, the lords of Gaṇas, and the Gaṇas, with thier respective weapons and symbols in their hands followed their leader Nandin.

54. Mounting on the lord of the birds (i.e. Garuḍa) as huge as the lord of mountains the bird-bannered lord Viṣṇu of great prowess hurriedly went ahead, on the left side of Rudra in order to burn the three cities for the welfare of the worlds.

55. All Devas followed that lord of the world, the lord of Devas and Asuras, the incomprehensible deity, with their excellent weapons such as the sharp lances, axes, iron clubs, tridents and swords.

56. In the middle of Devas, lord Viṣṇu whose vehicle was a bird and whose complexion was like that of the lotus leaf (petal) shone in the same manner as the thousand-rayed fierce sun when he ascends the peak of Sumeru.

57. In order to destroy the cities, like Garuḍa who destroyed the serpents, the thousand-eyed Indra, the first among Devas, went ahead on the right side of Rudra. He was seated on his lordly elephant.

58. The heroes of the Siddhas, Gandharvas and leading Devas all round, eulogised Indra who was the bestower of desired objects and who was the overlord of the leading Devas by saying "Be victorious." They honoured him with the excellent shower of flowers.

59. At that time those who were stationed in the heaven bowed to the thousand-eyed Indra, who was the paramour of Ahalyā, who was the overlord of the universe and who was the leader of Devas after seeing him sporting like the son of Umā i.e. Kārttikeya.

60. Yama, Fire, Kubera, Vāyu, Nirṛti, Varuṇa and Īśāna followed Rudra.

61-64. Vīrabhadra who was very efficient in battle, followed at the south west side of the chariot. He was mounted on a huge bull and surrounded by the beings born of his hairs. He thus served the three-eyed lord of Devas in order to destroy the Asura cities. Mahākāla of great splendour who appeared like another Mahādeva, served the chariot on its north-western side.

The six-faced deity Karttikeya who resembled the king of mountains, who was born of the fire god, and who was surrounded by the army of Devas, served the chariot along with the Siddhas, Cāraṇas, warriors and elephants.

65. After creating impediments unto the leading Asuras and after removing obstacles in the case of Devas, lord Gaṇeśa Vighneśvara went to the camp of Īśāna, accompanied by the groups of Vighnas (his followers).

66-67. At that time, Kālī went ahead of Gaṇeśa along with the intoxicated Piśācas and Gaṇas. She had skulls for her ornaments. She was whirling in her hand a trident that shone like Kālarātri. She was intoxicated by drinking the blood of Asuras which tasted like wine (unto her). She made the leading Asuras tremble. She had the gait of the elephant in rut. Her eyes were tremulous due to inebriation. Her body was covered with the hide of the elephant.

68. Saying "Be victorious", the chiefs of the Siddhas, Gandharvas, Piśācas, Yakṣas, Vidyādharas, lordly serpents and leading Devas bowed to the goddess, the daughter of the mountain of snow and eulogised her loudly.

69. The mothers (Brāhmī, Māhesvarī, etc.) who were respectfully adored by the groups of Devas and who were bent on killing the Rākṣasas went to the great Mother (Ambā, Gaurī) on their vehicles, along with their followers who held banners all round.

70. Riding on a lion, the goddess Durgā went forth to chastise Daityas. The auspicious deity was one whose orders could not be transgressed. In her mighty arms she held weapons of different kinds such as the trident, axe, goad, noose, discus, sword and conch. She burned and scorched the pathway with her eyes as dazzling as thousands of midday suns and fires. Though a woman, her exploits were uncommon among women.

71. The leading chiefs of the Gaṇas who shone like the lord of Devas and the sun, followed lord Īśa on elephants, horses, lions, chariots and bulls in order to destroy the three cities.

72. Equipped with ploughs, ploughshares, iron clubs, missiles, Bhuśuṇḍas and peaks of lofty mountains, the lords of Devas and the chiefs of goblins as huge as mountains went ahead of Maheśvara.

73. Devas, the chiefs of whom were Indra, the lotus-born Brahmā, Viṣṇu, and the lords of Gaṇas, surrounding lord Gaṇeśa on all sides, spoke the words, "Be victorious" with palms joined in reverence over their coronets.

74. With staffs in their hands the sages with matted hairs danced. Siddhas, Cāraṇas and other heaven-walkers showered

flowers. The three cities echoed and reverberated on all sides, O leading brahmins.

75. Bhṛṅgi, the most excellent among all the leading Gaṇas, was surrounded by lords of Gaṇas and Devas. A Yogin, he got into an aerial and went forth like Mahendra, to destroy the three cities.

76-84. The following leaders of Gaṇas surrounded Īśa and went forth to chastise the Tripuras:—Keśa, Vigatavāsas, Mahākeśa, Mahājvara, Somavallī, Savarṇa, Somapa, Senaka, Somadhṛk, Sūryavāca, Sūryapeṣaṇaka, Sūryākṣa, Sūrināma, Sura, Sundara, Prakuda, Kakudanta, Kampana, Prakampana, Indra, Indrajaya, Mahābhī, Bhīmaka, Śatākṣa, Pañcākṣa, Sahasrākṣa, Mahodara, Yamajihva, Śatāśva, Kuṇṭhana, Kaṇṭhapūjana, Dviśikha, Triśikha, Pañcaśikha, Muṇḍa, Ardhamuṇḍa, Dīrgha, Piśācāsya, Pinākadhṛk, Pippalāyatana, Aṅgārakāśana, Śithila, Śithilāsya, Akṣapāda, Aja, Kuja, Ajavaktra, Hayavaktra, Gajavaktra, Ūrdhvavaktra and others. They surrounded lord Soma in groups and went ahead. There were thousands and thousands of Rudras of sublimated sexuality. Surrounded by crores and crores of Gaṇas they rallied round Mahādeva, Maheśvara, the lord of Devas and went forth to burn the three cities.

85. The thirtythree, the three hundred and three and three thousand and three Devas went forth on all sides.

86. The mothers of the world, the mothers of Gaṇas, and the mothers of the Bhūtas followed the lord.

87. Seated in the middle of the chariot amongst Gaṇas the lord of the Gaṇas shone like the moon amongst stars and constellations.

88. Goddess Gaurī, the daughter of the Himalaya, identical with the worlds, was seated on the left side of the lord. She shone forth as though due to the splendour of lord Śiva.

89. The goddess, of auspicious marks, on the left side of the lord, shone with the tips of her hands holding the chowries. She had the lustre and colour of the golden lotus.

90. The pure white body of the supreme lord, the lord of Devas, was shining with Bhasman. In the company of Ambikā it shone like the white cloud in the sky with the streaks of lightning.

91. The gentle body of lord Śiva, having the lustre of the moon shone with the golden bow like the sky that shines with the rainbow or the universe that shines with the Meru mountain.

92. His white umbrella interspersed with the rays of jewels shone like the full disc of the moon at the time of its rising.

93. The gem-set necklace round the neck of Śiva suspended along with his silken upper cloth near the extremity of the umbrella shone like the excellent river Gaṅgā falling from the sky.

94. Then the lord whose lotus-like feet were bowed to by Indra, Brahmā, fire-god and others, went to the three cities along with Ambā for the welfare of the world.

95. The trident-bearing lord is competent to burn mentally, within a trice, the entire universe including the mobile and immobile beings. Why should then the Pināka-bearing lord go there himself along with the Gaṇas in order to burn the three cities ?

96. Devas, Viṣṇu, Brahmā and Indra said:—"Of what avail is the chariot to Śambhu ? Of what avail is the excellent arrow to him ? What has he to do with the groups of Devas ? He is never wanting in power to burn the three cities. Then what is this ?

97. We think that just for his pastime the Pinākabearing lord set about doing all these things. Otherwise, what other benefit has he to derive from this elaborate show ?

98. Delighted in the company of leading Devas and Gaṇas headed by lord Nandin, and with the universe for his chariot he shone along with the goddess, like the mountain Meru with its eight peaks. He shone thus as he neared the three cities.

99. On seeing Īśvara, the lord of Devas seated in the arena of the three cities along with Gaṇas and the daughter of Himavat, the group of Devas followed him.

100. O leading sages, the three cities appeared like another set of the three worlds (because it was occupied) by leading men, the Gaṇas, Devas and the three kinds of Asuras.

101. Then Śarva tied up the string of the bow, fitted the

arrow, joined it with the miraculous missile pertaining to Paśupati and thought of the three cities.

102. When the great lord stood ready with the bow well-drawn, the three cities merged into one.

103. When the three cities had attained fusion into one, the delight of the noble-souled deities was tumultuous and excited.

104. Eulogising the deity with eight cosmic bodies, all the groups of Devas, Siddhas and sages shouted the words, "Be victorious".

105. Even when the auspicious Puṣyayoga was attained, the lord, the husband of Umā, who had destroyed the eye of Bhaga indulged in sportive pastime. Then lord Brahmā spoke to him:—

106. O Mahādeva, Parameśvara, this gesture on your part is but proper, since, O lord, Asuras and Devas are equal to you.

107. Still, in view of the fact that Devas are virtuous and asuras are sinful, it behoves you, O lord of the universe, to eschew your sportive pastime.

108. O Īśa, O lord, of what avail is the chariot, or the banner or the arrow, or Viṣṇu, or I or even these goblins unto you for burning the three cities ?

109-113. It behoves you to burn the trio of the cities even as the Puṣya conjunction still prevails. O lord of Devas, it behoves you to burn the three cities quickly lest they should get separated. Then the great lord Virūpākṣa, glanced at the three cities. Instantaneously they were reduced to ashes. All those deities, viz., Soma (Moon), lord Viṣṇu, Kālāgni (Black fire) and Vāyu who were stationed in the arrow bowed down to the lord and said:—"O lord of Devas, although the trio of the cities has been burned by your glance it behoves you to discharge the arrow for our welfare." Thereupon O leading brahmins, Īśvara, Tripurārdana, laughingly brushed the string of the bow, pulled it as far as his ear and discharged the arrow.

114-121. After burning the three cities in a moment the arrow that brought about the destruction of the Tripuras came back to the lord of Devas, bowed to him and stood by. The three cities that contained hundreds of crores of Daityas, on being burned by that arrow, shone like the three worlds burned by Rudra at the end of the kalpa. Those Daityas who had been worshipping Rudra even at that stage along with their kinsmen, attained the chieftainship of the Gaṇas, thanks to the power of the duly performed worship. Devas including Indra and Viṣṇu and the lords of Gaṇas, looked at the lord and the goddess, the daughter of the Himavat with awe and fear. They did not say anything. On seeing Devas thus frightened, the leading Deva, i.e., Rudra asked them, "What next?" But they merely bowed to him from all sides. They saluted Nandin who had the moon for his ornament. They saluted the daughter of the king of mountains. They saluted the son of the daughter of the mountain, viz., Gaṇeśa. They saluted Maheśvara. With due attention, Brahmā eulogised lord Bhava, Īśvara the enemy of Tripuras, along with Devas and Viṣṇu.

Brahmā said:

122. Be pleased, O lord of the chiefs of Devas; be pleased, O Parameśvara; be pleased, O lord of the worlds; be pleased, O eternal lord, the bestower of bliss.

123. O Rudra of five faces, obeisance to you; obeisance to one who has fifty crores of physical forms; obeisance to the principle of learning, seated on the threefold Ātman.

124. Obeisance to Śiva, to the principle of Śiva; obeisance to Aghora; obeisance to the principle of the set of eight forms[630] Aghora and others; obeisance to one of the form of twelve[631] Ātmans.

125. Obeisance to the Ātman of Śiva stationed in this world after adopting the splendid form that resembles crores of lightnings and that has sway over the eight quarters.

126. Obeisance to the fierce one of fiery complexion; obeisance to one with Ambikā occupying half of his body; obeisance to the immortal being; to the bestower of salvation unto those of white, black and red colour.

630. **aghorāṣṭaka-tattvāya**—the set of eight forms beginning with Aghora.

631. **dvādaśātmā**—the sun ST.

127. Obeisance to the Eldest one in the form of Rudra; to the deity accompanied by Umā; to the bestower of boons; obeisance to the deity of the three worlds; obeisance to the Trinity; obeisance to Vaṣaṭkāra.

128. Obeisance to the one of the form of firmament in the middle; obeisance to you stationed in the firmament; obeisance to the deity with eight forms[632] in the eight shrines;[633] obeisance to one having eight principles.[634]

129. Obeisance to one stationed in three different sets of four [635] and two different sets of five;[636] obeisance to one having five mantras as his physical form.

130. Obeisance to the letter "A", of sixtyfour[637] types; obeisance to the letter "U" of the form of thirty two[638] principles.

131. Obeisance to the letter "M", having the sixteen forms[639] of the Ātman; obeisance to the deity in the eight forms[640] of half a Mātrā.

132. Obeisance to you, to the Oṁkāra stationed in four[641] ways; obeisance to the lord of the firmament, to the lord of heaven.

133. Obeisance to the lord having the seven worlds (as his form); obeisance to the lord of the Pātāla (Nether-worlds) and Naraka (hell); obeisance to the deity having eight forms in the eight[642] holy shrines; obeisance to the deity greater than the greatest.

134. Obeisance to you having a thousand heads; obeisance to you who stays in thousands (i.e., in many forms); obeisance

632. aṣṭa-kṣetra—eight stations, sun, etc.

633. eight shrines—Rudra, etc.

634. eight tattvas, eight elements, earth, etc.

635. It refers to four Vedas, four āśramas and four vyūhas.

636. It refers to five mahābhūtas, five forms, Sadyojāta, etc., and five mantras.

637. It refers to the syllable 'a' and its sixtyfour divisions.

638. It refers to the 'u' and its thirtytwo kinds.

639. It refers to the syllable 'm' and its sixteen divisions.

640. It refers to the eight-formed Śiva.

641. It refers to the syllables 'a', 'u', 'm' and nāda sound.

642. It refers to the eight forms of Śiva, such as consist of earth, water, fire, etc.

to Śarva possessing a thousand feet; obeisance to Parameṣṭhin.

135. Obeisance to one with the form of nine[643] principles of the Ātman; obeisance to one having nine times eight[644] Ātmans and Ātmaśaktis; obeisance to one having eight[645] modes of revelation; obeisance to one having eight times eight[646] physical forms.

136. Obeisance to one possessing sixtyfour[647] principles of the Ātman, obeisance to one (stationed) in eight[648] different forms; obeisance to one encompassed by the eight Guṇas;[649] obeisance to one the Saguṇa as well as Nirguṇa.

137. Obeisance to you stationed at the root; obeisance to the resident of the eternal abode; obeisance to one stationed in the umbilical regions; obeisance to one who causes sounds in the heart.

138. Obeisance to one stationed in the neck; to one who is stationed in the aperture of the cymbals; to one stationed in the middle of the eyebrows; to one stationed in the middle of sounds.

139. Obeisance to Śiva stationed in the disc of the moon; to one of auspicious forms; to one, having the forms of fire, moon and the sun; obeisance to one having the form of the thirtysix[650] Śaktis.

140. Obeisance to one who is the Ātman of the Serpent that is asleep after encircling the worlds three times; obeisance to one stationed in three different forms; obeisance to one with the forms of threefold (sacrificial) fires.

141. Obeisance to Sadāśiva; to the Pināka-bearing quiescent Maheśa; obeisance to the omniscient one; worthy of being sought refuge in; obeisance to Sadyojāta.

142. Obeisance to Aghora; to Vāmadeva; to Tatpuruṣa; and to Īśāna.

643. It refers to his nine forms. Cf. Mbh : puruṣaḥ prakṛtir vyaktam ahaṁkāro nabho' nilaḥ / jyotir āpokṣitir iti tattvānyuktāni te nava.

644. It refers to the seventytwo forms not mentioned by name.

645. i.e., manifesting in syllables through the eight organs of speech.

646. aṣṭāṣṭaka-mūrtaye, i.e., of the form of 64 syllables.

647. i.e. the life-principle of sixtyfour yoginīs.

648. aṣṭavidhāya—of eight forms or names, Bhava, etc.

649. guṇāṣṭaka-vṛtāya—invested with eight guṇas. Cf. "saṁkhyādikāḥ pañca buddhir icchāyatno'pi ceśvaraḥ"—*Nyāyasiddhānta-muktāvali* cited in *ST*.

650. The text does not mention the names of the thirty-six śaktis.

143. Obeisance to one having thirty[651] modes of revelation; obeisance to one beyond Śāntā (the digit of that name); obeisance to the lord Ananta to the subtle and the excellent one.

144. Obeisance to you, the single-eyed; obeisance to you, the Ekarudra; obeisance to you, the trinity;[652] to Śrīkaṇṭha; to Śikhaṇḍin (the tufted one).

145. Obeisance to the Infinite one; to one stationed in the seat of the Infinite; obeisance to the cause of destruction; obeisance to one devoid of impurities; obeisance to the large one; obeisance to you of pure body.

146. Obeisance to one stationed in the seat devoid of impurities;[653] obeisance to one of the form of wealth for the pure purpose; obeisance to the yogin stationed in yogapīṭhas; obeisance to the bestower of yoga.

147. Obeisance to one stationed in the heart of yogins like the awn of the wild rice Nīvāra; obeisance to you the Pratyāhāra, to you engaged in Pratyāhāra.

148-149. Obeisance to one stationed in the heart of those who are engaged in Pratyāhāra, and Dhāraṇā (retention) and Dhyāna (meditation); of the form of Dhāraṇā and Dhyāna; and to one who is comprehensible through Dhyāna.

150. Obeisance to one worthy of meditation. Obeisance to one approachable through meditation; obeisance to you of laudable meditation; obeisance to one worthy of meditation even by those who themselves are worthy of meditation; obeisance to you the worthiest of those who are worthy of meditation by others.

151. Obeisance to one worthy of approach through contemplation; obeisance to you, who are contemplation itself; obeisance to one in the form of Nirvikalpa object unto those who are engaged in meditation.

152. O Rudra, by burning the three cities this entire set of the three worlds has been redeemed by you today. Who will

651. **triṁśatprakāśāya—one who shines throughout the thirty muhūrtas, i.e. ever shining.**

652. **i.e. in the form of Brahmā, Viṣṇu and Rudra.**

653. **Verses 145-149 speak of his yogic postures, viz. āsana, pratyāhāra, dhāraṇā, dhyāna and samādhi.**

dare to eulogise you (befittingly) ? How shall I eulogise you who are of this extraordinary nature ? Obeisance to you O delightful Śiva.

153. O lord of Devas, thanks to their devotion, contentment and vision of miracle, that the mortals, immortals, Gaṇas, and Siddhas, make obeisance to you. O lord of Gaṇas, obeisance to you.

154. O lord, you are competent to burn the three cities, nay even the three worlds by a single glance of yours. Leisurely sporting with Ambikā, you have burned them in a trice; and the arrow too was discharged.

155. For your work of annihilating the Tripuras, I made with great deal of effort the excellent chariot, the speedy arrow and the splendid bow; but the benefit thereof was not seen by Devas as well as Siddhas.

156. O lord, you are all these combined:—the chariot, the charioteer, Viṣṇu the excellent Deva Rudra himself, Śakti and Pitāmaha. How shall I adequately eulogise you? I bow down my head to you, who cannot be adequately propitiated.[654]

157. O lord, you have infinite number of feet, infinite number of arms, infinite number of heads and infinite number of forms. You are the annihilator as well as the auspicious one. Shall I propitiate you of this nature? How shall I please you, who are of this nature?

158. Obeisance to you, the knower of everything; obeisance to you Rudra, Śarva and Bhava; obeisance to the gross, to the subtle, to the subtler than the subtlest; to the creator and to one conversant with the subtle meaning.

159. Obeisance to the creator, sustainer and the annihilator of all Devas and Asuras; obeisance to the creator of the worlds, to the leader of Devas and the lord of Asuras. Obeisance to the giver, to the ruler, to the chastiser of all.

160. Obeisance to the purest one comprehensible only through Vedānta; obeisance to one continuously eulogised by those who know the meanings of Vedas; obeisance to Bhava in

654. atoṣyam—toṣayitum aśakyam. According to *ST*. 'one who cannot be described by speech or conceived by the mind.' Cf. "yato vāco nivartante aprāpya manasā saha"—cited in *ST*.

the form of the Ātman of the Vedas; obeisance to you, to the last one, to the middle one, to the upper one.

161. Obeisance to one who is devoid of a beginning or an end; to one who exists; to one devoid of expressibility; to the Liṅgin (one having a Liṅga form); obeisance to you who have no symbols and yet are identical with the Liṅga; to Liṅga identical with Veda, etc.

162. Obeisance to Rudra who had severed my head—I am the primordial lord and yajñamūrti (one whose form is yajña). O lord, it was for dispelling my darkness that you had severed my head* by the tip of your finger on observing my crime which deserved that punishment.

163. O lord of Devas, O lord of Asuras, wonderful indeed are your activities. O deity devoid of attributes and forms, like an embodied soul you will carry out the task of Devas along with them.

164. Among your tattvas one is gross;[655] one is subtle; one is very subtle; one is both embodied and unembodied; one is embodied; one is unembodied; one is visible; and one is invisible and one is worthy of being meditated upon, the wonderful Īśa.

165. O lord, what is seen in a dream is an uncharacterised objeet; I think that it certainly appears as well as does not appear; Your divine form cannot be perceived even by Devas, in spite of their efforts. Yet it appears in the visible liṅga form.

166. O lord of Devas, where is your divine prowess? Where are we? Where is devotion? Where is your eulogy? Still, O lord, forgive me who though a primeval being am lamenting, inspired by devotion.

Sūta said:—

167. O excellent brahmins, he who listens to this hymn of the chastiser of Puras, or he who reads it after bowing to the lord on the ground eschews the bondage of sins.

* This is contradicted in *ŚP*. p. 58.

655. The verse explains the characteristics of each of the eight forms of Śiva, viz., gross (earth), subtle (water), subtler (fire), manifest-unmanifest (moon), manifest (sun), unmanifest (wind), having the quality of sound (ether), and the object of meditation (dhyeyam īśam) on the part of the mind.

168. On hearing this hymn, the mighty-armed resident of the peak of Mandara who was eulogised devotedly by the four-faced deity looked laughingly at the daughter of the mountain and said to Brahmā of great exalted dignity.

Śiva said:—

169. O lotus-born one, I am delighted by this hymn as well as by your devotion. Welfare unto you. Choose the boons in accordance with the desire of Devas.

Sūta said :

170. Thereupon, after bowing to the lord of Devas, the lotus-born deity became delighted in his mind and spoke with palms joined in reverence.

Brahmā said :

171. O lord Śaṅkara, O lord of the chiefs of Devas, O destroyer of Tripuras, O Parameśvara, be pleased to confer on me the greatest devotion towards you.

172. O lord, the bestower of all riches on all Devas. Be pleased with our devotion towards you always as well as with my charioteership.

173. Lord Viṣṇu also bowed down to Maheśvara. Joining his palms together in reverence he said thus to the three-eyed lord accompanied by Umā.

174-175. "O lord, be pleased with me. O lord of Devas, obeisance be to you. I perpetually desire to be your vehicle. I wish for your devotion as well as my efficiency to bear you. O Śaṅkara, the bestower of boons, I wish for omniscience and all-pervasiveness.

Sūta said :

176. On hearing their submission Parameśvara, Mahādeva, Bhava engaged them respectively in charioteership and the position of vehicle.

177. After burning Daityas, and after giving boons to Brahmā and Viṣṇu, Śiva, the noble-souled lord of Devas, vanished along with the goddess, Bhūtas and Nandin.

178-179. When the lord had gone away from the battle-field along with his Gaṇas, the awe-struck lords of Devas bowed down to Bhava and Pārvatī. They became devoid of misery and returned to heaven on their vehicles. The lords of Devas, the chiefs of sages, the lords of Gaṇas and Bhāskaras went to heaven.

180-184. O brahmins, he who reads this chapter on the exploits of the destroyer of Tripuras, originally composed by Brahmā formerly or he who narrates this devotedly to the brahmins at the time of Śrāddha or during the rites of Devas goes to the world of Brahmā. O excellent brahmins, the individual soul is liberated from all kinds of sins mental, physical or verbal. He is liberated from the principal as well as subsidiary sins, gross, subtle or subtlest on hearing this splendid chapter. His enemies will perish and he will be victorious in battle. He will never be harassed by any sickness. Adversities will not afflict him. He shall attain wealth, longevity, renown, learning and incomparable prowess.

CHAPTER SEVENTYTHREE

Glory of worshipping Śiva

Sūta said :

1. When lord Maheśvara departed thence after burning the three cities in a trice the lotus-born deity (Brahmā) spoke thus in the assembly of the leading Devas.

Brahmā said :

2-6. Due to the Māyā of Lord Viṣṇu the following Daityas forsook Mahādeva and perished along with their cities and citizens. They were the grandson of Tāra of great brilliance, the powerful son of Tāraka, the asura Tārakākṣa, the powerful Kamalākṣa, Vidyunmālin, the lord of Daityas and many others along with kith and kin. They left the worship of the lord Maheśvara and so they perished. Hence Sadāśiva in the Liṅga form should always be worshipped since Devas have stability only as long as they worship the lord. Śiva should always be adored by the leading Devas with faith. The entire world is based on the Liṅga. Everything is founded in the Liṅga.

7-9. Hence, he who wishes for perfection of the soul shall worship the Liṅga. It is only through the worship of the Liṅga that Devas, Daityas, Dānavas, Yakṣas, Vidyādharas, Siddhas, Piśitāśanas, Pitṛs, Sages, Piśācas, Kinnaras and others have undoubtedly achieved Siddhi. Hence, O Devas, by any means whatsoever one should always worship the Liṅga.

10-21. *The holy rite Pāśupata.*

We are all Paśus of that intelligent lord of Devas. Eschewing Paśutva and adopting the holy rite Pāśupata, the eternal Mahādeva in the Liṅga form should be worshipped. The five elements should be cleansed simultaneously by means of five[656] Praṇavas along with five Prāṇāyāmas (control of breath), O leading Devas. Then the process should be repeated with four Praṇavas; then with three; and then with two, always accompanied with an equal number of Prāṇāyāmas. He shall then utter Oṁkāra and control the Prāṇa and Apāna. He shall fill all the limbs with the nectar of perfect knowledge as well as Praṇava. He shall then purify the three Guṇas, the fourth called Ahaṁkāra (ego)[657] and the tanmātras, O Devas of good holy rites. Then he shall cleanse the elements, the organs of sense and the organs of action. After cleansing the two,[658] viz., the Puruṣa and the Cidātman he shall repeat "Agniḥ Bhasma" (the fire is the Ash) and touch the body (?) He shall then say similarly that the wind, ether, water and earth are ashes and then smear his body with ashes during the three sandhyās throughout life. (By doing so) one becomes a Yogin conversant with all tattvas (principles). This is the Pāśupata vrata) pertaining to Śiva. O excellent Devas, it was for the liberation from bondage that this has been mentioned by the lord himself. By performing the Pāśupata rite in this manner and by worshipping the great lord in the Liṅga formerly seen

656. i.e. the five prāṇāyāmas preceded by the five praṇavas (om syllables).

657. fourfold, viz., manas (mind), buddhi (intellect), ahaṁkāra (ego), and citta (consciousness).

658. the two puruṣas : taijasa (the universal) and prājña (the individual) soul.

by me and the noble-souled Viṣṇu, O Devas, people cease to be Paśus within a year. All rites should be performed assiduously by us after worshipping lord Īśvara externally and internally. O excellent Devas, this is my divine vow as well as that of Viṣṇu.

22-25. There is no doubt that it is the vow of the sages also. Hence one should worship Śiva. If one does not think about the only God Śiva, even for a moment, it is a loss, it is a great blemish, it is delusion, it is silence. Those who indulge in devotion to him, those who mentally bow down to him, and those who attempt to remember Bhava are never subjected to misery. The fruit of the worship of Śiva is as follows :—Pleasant and charming abodes, divine ornaments, women, and riches till one is satisfied. May those who wish for enjoyment of great pleasures or the kingdom of heaven, worship Maheśvara in the Liṅga form, at all times.

26-29. Even after striking and destroying all living beings, and after burning this entire universe if one should worship the only God Virūpākṣa (i.e. Śiva), one is never tarnished with sins.

After saying, "My Liṅga is made of rock, it is bowed to by all Devas," Brahmā worshipped Rudra, the lord of the three worlds at the outset and eulogised the three-eyed lord of Devas with pleasing words. Ever since then, Indra and others too worshipped the lord directly after performing the Pāśupata rite and smearing their bodies with ashes.

CHAPTER SEVENTYFOUR

Description of Śiva Liṅgas

Sūta said :

1. At the bidding of Lord Brahmā, Viśvakarmā made the following Liṅgas befitting the office of Devas and gave those Liṅgas to them.

2. The Liṅga made of Sapphire was worshipped by Viṣṇu. Indra worshipped that of ruby. The son of Viśravas worshipped the Liṅga made of gold.

3. Viśvedevas worshipped Silver Liṅga, Vasus the auspicious magnetic Liṅga, Vāyu the Liṅga made of brass; and Aśvins the Earthen Liṅga.

4. King Varuṇa worshipped the crystal Liṅga; Ādityas the excellent Liṅga made of copper, and king Soma the excellent Liṅga made of pearls.

5. Ananta and the other great serpents worshipped the Liṅga of coral; Daityas and Rākṣasas the ferrous Liṅga.

6. Guhyakas worshipped the Liṅga of three metals, Gaṇas that made of all metals and O excellent brahmins, Cāmuṇḍā and Mothers worshipped the Liṅga of Sand.

7. Nairṛti worshipped the Liṅga of wood; Yama that of emerald; Nīlarudra and others the pure and splendid Liṅga made of Bhasman (ashes).

8. Lakṣmī worshipped the Liṅga of Lakṣmīvṛkṣa (Bilva tree); Guha the Liṅga of cowdung. O leading sages, the sages worshipped the excellent Liṅga of Kuśa grass.

9. Vāmadeva and others worshipped the Puṣpa liṅga and Manonmanī the Liṅga made of scents. Sarasvatī worshipped the Liṅga made of jewels.

10. Durgā worshipped the Liṅga made of gold along with the pedestal. All the Mantras worshipped Ugra in the form of sacrifice with the splendid Liṅga made of ghee.

11. The Vedas worshipped the Liṅga of curds; Piśācas the Liṅga of lead. All the worshippers attained the suitable region by the favour of Brahmā.

12. Of what avail is much talk? There is no doubt in this that it was due to their worshipping the Liṅga that the universe of mobile and immobile beings could stand.

13-16. Due to the difference in the material, they say, there are six types of Liṅgas. Their subdivisions are fortyfour in number. The first type of Liṅga is called Śailaja (made of rock). It has four sub-divisions. O excellent sages, the second type is made of jewels. It has seven sub-divisions. The third type originates from metals and it has eight sub-divisions. The fourth Liṅga originates from wood and it is of sixteen subdivisions. O excellent brahmins, the fifth type of Liṅga is made of clay; it has two subdivisions. The sixth type of Liṅga is the Kṣaṇika (momentary) and it is of seven subdivisions.

17. The Liṅga originating from jewels bestows fortune; that originating from rock yields all Siddhis. The Liṅga made of metals bestows wealth and the Liṅga made of wood yields the achievement of worldly pleasures.

18. O leading brahmins, the Liṅga of clay is splendid and brings about all Siddhis. The Liṅga of rock is very excellent; the Liṅga of metals is the middling one.

19-20. Liṅgas are of numerous types. In brief, they are of nine types.

At the root of the Liṅga, Brahmā is stationed. Viṣṇu the lord of three worlds, is stationed in the middle. Above is stationed Rudra, Mahādeva, Sadāśiva who is called Praṇava. The pedestal of Liṅga is the great goddess having three Guṇas, the mother having three[659] attributes.

21-25. The goddess as well as the lord is adored by the person who worships with that pedestal. The splendid Liṅga whether of rock, or of jewel or of metals, or of wood or of clay or of momentary type, should be installed with devotion. The result is very splendid.

The person who worships the Liṅga is eulogised by Indra, Brahmā, Agni, Yama, Varuṇa, Kubera, Siddhas, Vidyādharas, the king of serpents, Yakṣas, Dānavas and Kinnaras with the sounds of the divine drum. He is a meritorious soul. Shining brilliantly with splendour he gradually occupies and passes through Bhūḥ, Bhuvaḥ, Svaḥ and Mahar worlds and then beyond Janaloka he shall go on to Tapas and Satya, illuminating them with his own brilliance. He shall unhesitatingly pierce the cosmic Egg by means of the large sword deposited in the holy path wherein the Liṅgas had been installed.

26-30. After eschewing the Liṅgas of rock, or of jewels, or of metals, or of wood or of clay or of the momentary type he shall establish his entire body in the Liṅga.

The man who instals the splendid Liṅga white as the kunda

659. **trimayā—brahma-viṣṇu-rudramayā *ST.* of the form of Brahmā Viṣṇu and Rudra.**

flower or cow's milk, in accordance with the injunctions, along with Skanda and Umā undoubtedly becomes Rudra embodied in human form. By touching him or seeing him men attain great bliss. O leading brahmins, his merit cannot be mentioned by me even in hundreds of yugas. Hence one should instal the Liṅga in the above manner.

The Sakala (one with attributes) and divinely splendid body of the lord is worthy of being conceived by all men. But the Niṣkala (attributeless) body of the lord can be conceived only by the yogin.

CHAPTER SEVENTYFIVE

Monism of Śiva

The sages said:

1. How did the lord who is niṣkala (attributeless), nirmala (pure), and nitya (eternal) adopt sakalatva (the state of being with attributes). It behoves you to tell us about this in the same manner you had learnt it formerly.

Sūta said:

2. O leading brahmins, persons who know reality recognize the lord in the form of the Praṇava, Vijñāna (perfect knowledge), after hearing about the unborn lord in the Vedāntic treatises.

3. The knowledge that has sound, etc. for its object is called Jñāna. Others say that jñāna is devoid of Error. Still others say that it is not so.

4. O brahmins, some sages say that knowledge which is pure, devoid of impurities, has no alternatives as objects and does not require a support and is made manifest through a teacher, is the real one.

5. Salvation results only from perfect knowledge. Grace of the lord is conducive to the achievement of perfect knowledge.

Both help to liberate the yogin and make him blissful.[660]

6. Some sages say that His contact can be acquired by means of holy rites. By one's own free will, the form that is conceived fancifully shall be withdrawn.

7-11. The heaven is the head of Lord, the sky[661] is his umbilicus, the moon, sun and fire are his eyes, the quarters are his ears. The nether worlds constitute his feet, the ocean is his cloth, Devas are his arms, the constellations are his ornaments, Prakṛti is his wife, Puruṣa is his Liṅga. From his face[662] issued forth all the Brahmins, Brahmā, Indra, and Viṣṇu. The Kṣatriyas issued from his arms. The Vaiśyas issued from his thighs and Śūdras from his feet. Puṣkara Āvartaka and other clouds are his hairs. The winds are born of his nose. The Śruti and Smṛti texts constitute his gait.

12. The lord in the form of Karman makes Prakṛti function by means of this cosmic body. The glorious Puruṣa is comprehensible to man through perfect knowledge, not otherwise.

13-14. Tapoyajña (sacrifice in the form of austerity) is superior to thousands of Karmayajñas (sacrifice in the form of holy rites). Japayajña (sacrifice in the form of Japa) is superior to thousands of Tapoyajñas. Dhyānayajña (sacrifice in the form of meditation) is superior to thousands of Japayajñas. There is nothing greater than Dhyānayajña. Dhyāna (meditation) is a means of perfect knowledge.

15. When the yogin stands firmly by equal elegance and sees through meditation, when he is engaged in the Dhyānayajña, Śiva becomes manifest in him.

16. All people conversant with the knowledge of Brahman are pure, thanks to that Vidyā. There is no expiatory rite or any injunction in regard to Vijñānins (knowers); nor do they have purificatory rites.

17. On consideration it is clear that there is no holy rite in

660. ānandamayaḥ—i.e. by the real knowledge and divine grace the yogin can attain the supreme bliss. Cf. "Anandamayo'bhyāsāt"—cited in *ST*.

661. kham—the world of mortals. *ST*. quotes *Viśva* in support of this meaning.

662. The divine origin of society and its division into four classes, viz. Brāhmaṇa, Kṣatriya, Vaiśya and Śūdra, can be traced as far back as the Puruṣa-sūkta of the *Ṛgveda*.

the world, there is no happiness or misery, neither dharma nor adharma, neither japa nor homa, to those who take up meditation. They come near to the 'Sat' (the existent Being).

18. The Liṅga is pure, auspicious and imperishable. It is exceedingly blissful in nature. The Niṣkala form, that is, the form devoid of attributes is all-pervasive. It is always stationed in the heart of yogins.

19. O brahmins, they say that the Liṅga is of two types viz.,—the external and the internal. O excellent sages, the gross one is the external. O brahmins, the subtle one is the internal. [So are the devotees].

20. The gross devotees are those engaged in the worship of gross Liṅgas and interested in holy rites and sacrifices. The gross idol is just for awakening knowledge of the gross devotees.[663]

21-22. The spiritual liṅga is not perceptible to the deluded person who conceives things only externally and not otherwise. The gross liṅga made of clay, wood, etc., is perceptible only to non-yogin as the subtle and eternal Liṅga is perceptible to the Jñānin.

23. Other knowers of reality say that the object, on consideration, is non-existent.[664] Therefore, everything, the Niṣkala and the Sakala is of the nature of Śiva.

24. Others say like this, O men of good holy rites—Although the ether is one, it is perceived separately in regard to separate platters. Similarly Śiva has separateness as well as non-separateness.

25. O men of good holy rites, though the sun is only one he is seen manifold in the different water-reservoirs. This example is cited in order to convince the people.

26. The creatures in the heaven and on the earth are evolved out of the five elements. Still they are seen in multiples of forms as different species and individuals.

663. **The gross (liṅga) form of the supreme lord Śiva is meant just to create a feeling of devotion in the gross-minded people. In fact, lord Śiva (like the ether) is an indivisible entity. His division into sakala and niṣkala forms, as of the ether into ghaṭākāśa and maṭhākāśa is conditioned by external factors.**

664. **arthaḥ—goal, viz. the release from the bondage of activities. Because, actually, as there is no bondage, there is no release. Cf. *Pañcadaśi*; VI. 35; also, *Mbh.* "bandhasya māyāmūlatvān na me mokṣo na bandhanam —cited in *ST*.**

27. Know that whatever is seen or heard is identical with Śiva. The difference among the people, on deliberation, is mere illusion.

28. After experiencing extensive pleasures in dream a man may be happy or miserable. But on pondering we understand that neither the pleasure nor the misery has been really experienced.

29-30. All those who have understood the real meanings of the Vedas also speak thus in regard to worldly matters. The great lord invested with attributes is directly perceptible in the hearts of the worldly-minded persons. The lord devoid of attributes appears in the hearts of yogins and is identical with the universe. He appears to the wise ones only. The physical body of the great lord is of three types.

31. O excellent brahmins, the first-one is Niṣkala, the second one is Sakala-Niṣkala and the third-one is Sakala.

32-33. Some worship the Sakala-Niṣkala form, some worship in the heart, or in the Liṅga or in the fire. Some worship the Sakala form along with their wives and sons.

34-35. Just as Śiva so also is the goddess. Just as the goddess so also is Śiva. Hence people worship the deities with the consciousness of non-difference. They worship the twenty-seven[665] principles in the body as well as outside, in the mystic diagrams of four, six, ten angles, twelve, sixteen and three sides.

36. Śiva, the lord, devoid of difference of Sat and Asat is stationed out of his own free will along with the goddess for the protection of the world.

37. Some call him one, some call him one with two Guṇas.[666] Some call him Triguṇa[667] (having three Guṇas). Some say that it is Śiva. Others, the knowers of the Vedas speak of him as the cause of the universe.

38. All Brahmins equipped with devotion and auspicious yoga are persons of special characteristics. They are interested

665. **sapta-viṁśat prabhedataḥ—In the groups of tattvas, Śiva is placed in the twentyseventh category. (Cf. 1.71.51). But this classification is only impirical, not real. However, the physical and mental worship of Śiva enjoined in the āgamas rests on the categorical basis.**

666. **dviguṇam—in the form of Prakṛti and Puruṣa.**

667. **triguṇam—in the form of Brahmā, Viṣṇu and Rudra.**

in Dharma. In the middle of the hexagon they worship the lord of yogas, having all the forms (or no form).

39. Those who perceive Śiva in the three-sided (mystic diagram), in the middle of the three principles, attain him; not the other yogins. They perceive the three-eyed[668] lord with the three Guṇas, the ancient Puruṣa along with the goddess.

CHAPTER SEVENTYSIX

Installation of Śiva's image

Sūta said:

1. Henceforth, I shall mention the benefit accruing from the installation of the idol entirely, for the welfare of the world. The idol may be in accordancc with one's own wish.

2. After making the idol of the lord seated in an elegant seat along with Skanda and Umā and after installing it with devotion one shall fulfil desires.

3. In the manner I had heard, I shall mention the benefit that a man obtains by worshipping the lord along with Skanda and Umā (even) once (but) in accordance with the injunctions.

4-7. Until the dissolution of all living beings, he becomes a yogin and sports like Śiva in aerial chariots resembling crores of suns wherein everything desirable is available and where virgins of Rudra sing and dance. In the aerial chariots where everything desirable is available he enjoys great pleasures. He then goes to the following worlds one after the other viz :— the world of Umā, of Kumāra, of Iśāna, of Viṣṇu, of Brahmā and of Prajāpati. The deity of great splendour passes through the Janaloka and Maharloka. After reaching the world of Indra he assumes the role of Indra for ten thousand years. Again, after enjoying divine and brilliant pleasure in the

668. tri-yakṣam=tryakṣam, three-eyed. See p. 280 note. 259.

Bhuvarloka, he reaches the Meru and rejoices in the abodes of Devas.

8-14. One shall attain Sāyujya (union) with Śiva by duly installing the omniscient, omnipresent lord in accordance with the injunctions of the Śāstras; the lord who has a single foot, four arms, three eyes and trident, the lord who is stationed after creating Viṣṇu from his left side and the four-faced Brahmā from the right side. The lord who created twenty eight crores of Rudras, and then the twentyfifth[669] principle Puruṣa, brilliant in all the limbs, from his heart ; the lord who created Prakṛti from his left ; cosmic intellect from the region of the intellect, the cosmic ego from his own ego and the Tanmātras therefrom. The great lord sportingly created the sense-organs from his own sense-organs. He created the earth from the root of his foot and water from the private parts. He created fire from the umbilical region. the sun from the heart, the moon from his neck, the soul from the middle of his eyebrows and the heaven from the forehead. One shall instal the image of the lord who is stationed thus after creating the entire universe inclusive of the mobile and immobile beings.

15. By making the idol of Īśāna, the lord of the sacrifices[670], who has three feet, seven hands, four horns and two heads, the devotee is honoured in the world of Viṣṇu.

16. The man will enjoy great pleasures there for a hundred thousand kalpas. He shall be happy and in due course return to his world as master of all sacrifices.

17-18. If the devotee makes the idol of the lord who rides on a bull accompanied by Umā and with the crescent moon as his ornament, he attains that merit which one usually obtains by performing ten thousand horse-sacrifices. He goes to Śiva's divine city in a golden aerial chariot having clusters of tinkling bells and he is liberated there itself.

19. In the manner I have heard, I shall mention the benefit that one attains by making the idol of the lord accompanied by Nandin and Umā and surrounded by all Gaṇas.

669. **pañcaviṁśatikam—the twenty-fifth principle, i.e., jīva (the individual soul).**

670. **yajñeśam—agnirūpam *ST.* of the form of fire.**

20-21. He will go to the city of Śiva on the aerial chariots that resemble the solar sphere, that are tied to the bulls, that are difficult of access even to Devas and Dānavas that are occupied and beautified all round by the dancing nymphs. He shall then attain the chieftainship of the Gaṇas.

22-26. I shall mention the benefit that one attains by making any of the following idols of Śiva and installing it with devotion viz :—the lord of the chiefs of Devas as in his dancing posture and accompanied by the daughter of the lord of mountains ; the omniscient lord having a thousand arms or having four arms; lord Parameśvara surrounded by Bhṛgu and others as well as the groups of goblins; the bull-bannered Īśvara accompanied by the daughter of the lord of mountain, the diety as perpetually being bowed to by Brahmā, Indra, Viṣṇu, Soma (the moon) and all other Devas; Parameśvara as surrounded by Mothers and sages. He shall attain a crore times the benefit that accrues from all yajñas, penances, charitable gifts, pilgrimages to the holy centres and visits to the deities. He shall then go to the region of auspiciousness.[671] Until the dissolution of all living beings he shall enjoy great pleasure there. When the next creation arrives be shall return to the region of mortals.

27-28. One shall attain identity with Śiva by making the idol of Śiva as follows and installing it with devotion; the lord as naked, white-complexioned, having four arms, three eyes and the serpent as girdle, with black curly hairs and holding a skull in his hand.

29-33. By making the idol of the lord as follows and installing it with devotion according to the extent of one's affluence, one surmounts all obstacles and is honoured in the world of Śiva ; the lord as tearing asunder the leading elephant [672] as accompanied by Ambā, as the bestower of all desired objects ; as smoke-coloured, red in eyes and adorned with the moon on the forehead, as having three eyes, wearing the sidelocks of hairs, holding the serpent-shaped hatchet, wearing the lion's hide as his upper garment and the deer skin as the lower one, as

671. Śiva-puram—a mythical city 'Śivapura' on the the Himālayas, particularly on the Kailāsa peak is conceived as the abode of Śiva.

672. ibhendra-dārakam—ibhendraḥ gajāsuraḥ taṁ dārayatīti—one who has slain the asura Gaya.

having sharp curved fangs and armed with an iron club, holding the skull in his uplifted hand, the lord as rendering all the quarters resonant with loud shouts of "Hum" "Phaṭ" etc., holding the tiger skin[673] and the conch[674] shell in two of his hands, laughing, roaring and drinking the black ocean[675] (poison) as dancing in the company of Bhūtas (goblins) and surrounded by Gaṇas.

34-37. There (in the world of Śiva) he enjoys great pleasures until the dissolution of all living beings. By means of deliberation he gains perfect knowledge from the Rudras there and becomes liberated.

By making the idol of Śiva as follows and installing it with devotion the devotee is honoured in the world of Śiva. The excellent lord has half of his body in female form. He has four arms wherein he holds the boon to be bestowed; the gesture of fearlessness, the trident and the lotus. He is stationed in the form of a woman as well as a man, bedecked in all ornaments. There (in the Śivaloka) he enjoys all great pleasures. He is then endowed with Aṇimā (minuteness) and other qualities. Therefrom he obtains the knowledge lasting as long as the moon and the stars and is liberated.

38-40. He who makes the idol of the omniscient lord of the chiefs of Devas, Nakulīśvara, who is surrounded by disciples and their disciples and who has uplifted his hand in expounding the principles and then instals it with devotion goes to the world of Śiva. The man enjoys extensive pleasures there for a hundred yugas. After attaining the path of knowledge he attains liberation there itself.

41-43. His abode is liked by all among Devas and Asuras. By making the idol of the lord as follows and by installing it, one is liberated from the ocean of worldly existence:—The lord shows gestures. He has the ashes from the funeral pyre for his unguent; he has the triple mark of Tripuṇḍra; he wears a garland made of skulls; he wears a single sacred thread constituted

673. Puṇḍarīkājina—one who is clad in the tiger-hide. (puṇḍarīka = tiger. Cf. "vyāghre tu puṇḍarīko nā"—*Amarakośa*.

674. Kambukam—kamaṇḍulam *ST*. a water-pot.

675. Kṛṣṇa-sāgaram—*ST*. gives an alternate meaning: kṣīra-samudram, vide ch. 29. verses 29-31.

by the hairs of Brahmā; with his left hand he holds the excellent skull of Brahmā; as Parameṣṭhin he adopts the body of Viṣṇu.

44-46a. He who repeats even once the holy mantra of eight syllables, viz., "Om Namo Nīlakaṇṭhāya (Om obeisance unto the blue-necked lord), is liberated from sins. By worshipping the lord of the chiefs of Devas by means of this mantra with devotion after using scents and other things in accordance with one's wealth, one is honoured in the world of Śiva.

46b-47. By making the idol of the lord as follows and installing it with devotion the devotee attains oneness with Śiva. The lord destroys Jalandhara who is severed into two. The lord is holding Sudarśana. By installing such images or any one of such images the devotee attains oneness with Śiva. No hesitation or doubt need be entertained in this regard.

48. By making the idol as follows and by installing it with devotion one is honoured in the world of Śiva. The Deva is the bestower of Sudarśana with the characteristics as mentioned before. He is worshipped by lord Viṣṇu who adores him by means of worship including the gift of his own eye.[676]

49-51. One shall attain oneness with Śiva by duly making and installing the idol of the lord as standing on the back of Nikumbha (a gaṇa) fixing his lotus-like right foot firmly on him and embracing the daughter of the mountain on his left side. His elbow rests on the tip of his trident. The serpents are suspended from the trident like so many tinkling bells. He is glancing at Andhaka who is standing at his side with palms joined in reverence.

52-54. He who makes the idol of Śiva, the lord of the chiefs of Devas, Īśvara the destroyer of the Tripuras, with bow and arrows in his hands, the crescent moon as an ornament, seated in a chariot accompanied by Umā and being charioteered by the four-faced lord (Brahmā), assumes that form (of Śiva) and goes to the city of Śiva. He is happy and he undoubtedly sports like the second Śiva. O excellent brahmins, after enjoying great pleasures there, as much as he desires and

676. When Viṣṇu fell short of a flower he plucked his own eye and offered it as a gift.

having obtained perfect knowledge after due deliberation he is liberated there itself.

55-58. The intelligent devotee who makes and instals these idols along with Vighneśa shall attain oneness with Śiva:—The lord is seated comfortably holding the Gaṅgā and having the moon on his coronet; the lord is accompanied by the Gaṅgā and Umā is seated on his left lap; the lord is surrounded by Vināyaka, Skanda, Jyeṣṭhā, Durgā, Bhāskara, Soma, Brahmāṇī, Māheśvarī, Kaumārī, Vaiṣṇavī, Vārāhī, Varadā, Indrāṇī, Cāmuṇḍā, Vīrabhadra and Vighneśa.

59-63. By making the idols as follows and installing them with devotion one shall attain oneness with Śiva. The unchanging lord is in the form of a Liṅga surrounded by great clusters of flames; the moon-crested Īśvara as seated in the centre of the Liṅga. The Liṅga should be made in the ether with Brahmā with folded hands in the form of a swan standing on the right and Viṣṇu in the form of a Boar standing beneath the Liṅga with his face turned down. The terrible great Liṅga is stationed in the middle of the great waters.

By making idols of the lord as the protector of the holy centre, and Kṣetrapāla as lord Paśupati and by duly installing them with devotion, one is honoured in the world of Śiva.

CHAPTER SEVENTYSEVEN

The Temples of Śiva

The Sages said:—

1-2. The meritorious acts of preparation and installation of the Liṅga and the differences among the various types of Liṅgas have been heard as described by you. It behoves you to narrate the benefit that accrues from building Śiva's temple by means of materials beginning with clay and ending with jewels.

Sūta said:—

3-6. If a devotee of Śiva is endowed with perfect knowledge he is not harassed by sons, wives, houses, etc. Then of what avail are the temples he should make for the lord? Still the devotee of the lord who is saluted by the chief of Devas and the lotus-born deity Brahmā makes divine and excellent temples or shrines even with bricks and stones. Even as a childish prank if they make the primordial Śiva's image with clay or stone or even with dust and his abode also in the same manner and worship him, they do attain identity with him. Hence, for the achievement of virtue, love and wealth, the abode of Śiva should be made by devotees with devotion, assiduously.

7. By devoutly making the abode of Rudra of the type of Kesara, Nāgara or Drāviḍa one is honoured in the world of Śiva.

8. He who makes his mansion called Kailāsa, rejoices happily in the aerial chariots of the shapes of Kailāsa peaks.

9-11. Or the devotee shall make in accordance with the injunctions the temple of Mandara, for him. He shall devoutly make it in accordance with his means. It may be of the middling or inferior type. Thereby the man goes to the beautiful city of Śiva in aerial chariots which resemble the mountain Mandara, and which have faces all round, which are occupied by groups of Apsarases and which are difficult of access even to Devas and Dānavas. He enjoys all pleasures, attains the path of knowledge and finally the chieftainship of the Gaṇas.

12-13. Even by means of great sacrifices no one attains that benefit which accrues to the person who makes the mansion called Meru. He attains all the benefits of sacrifices, penances, gifts, visits to holy centres and study of all Vedas. Like Śiva, he rejoices for a long time.

14. The intelligent devotee who makes the mansion Niṣadha with devotion attains Śiva's world and like Śiva rejoices for a long time.

15-17. O brahmins, he who makes the splendid and excellent mansion called Himaśaila, goes to the splendid city of Śiva by means of vehicles comparable to the mountain Himavat. Attaining the path of knowledge, he shall achieve the chieftainship of the Gaṇas.

I shall mention the benefit that a man obtains by making the splendid mansion named Nīlādriśikhara (the peak of the blue mountain). He need make it only in accordance with his riches. He shall dedicate it to Rudra with devotion.

18-21. He obtains all those benefits which I have mentioned to you before as the benefit of making the mansion Himaśaila devoutly [see verse 15]. Then he is bowed to by all Devas. Reaching the world of Rudra he rejoices along with them.

I shall mention the benefit that one attains by making the mansion named Mahendraśaila. He goes to the divine city of Śiva in the aerial chariot as huge in size as the mountain Mahendra, yoked to bulls. O leading sages, he enjoys all pleasures and attains perfect knowledge after deliberation with Rudras. He eschews worldly pleasures as though they were poison and attains Sāyujya (union) with Śiva.

22-23. He who makes jewel-studded mansion with gold, in accordance with the injunctions, of the type of Drāviḍa, Nāgara or Kesara or makes the peak[677] or platform square or oblong in shape attains great merit. His merit cannot be mentioned even in hundreds of yugas.

24-28. If anyone repairs or rebuilds the old, dilapidated fallen or broken temples and reconstructs them with doors, etc. or if he repairs the mansion, platform, rampart or the ornamental gateway, he derives more benefit than even the original maker. There is no doubt about this. The man who does some job in the temple of Śiva though it be for his sustenance undoubtedly goes to the heavenly world along with his kinsmen. If a man does some job in the temple of Rudra even for once and for his own pleasure he attains happiness and rejoices. Hence, O excellent sages, the man who devoutly makes the temple by means of wood, bricks, etc., is honoured in the world of Śiva.

29-32. O leading sages, for the grace of Maheśa, for the purpose of achieving virtue, love, wealth and liberation, the mansion of Maheśa should be built assiduously. O excellent sages, if one is incapable of building a mansion he shall serve the lord by means of sweeping and other activities. He who performs the sweeping job with a soft and delicate broom shall attain all desires. He obtains the fruit of a thousand Cāndrāyaṇa rites within a

677. Kūṭam—yantrarūpam *ST*. made of some mechanical device.

month. He who duly performs the rite of applying unguents to the lord with the scented cow-dung water filtered and purified by means of a cloth shall obtain the benefits of Cāndrāyaṇa for a year.

33-37. The place within the radius of half a Krośa from the Liṅga of Śiva is called Śiva-kṣetra (holy centre of Śiva). He who casts off his life (within that centre) usually very difficult to be cast off, shall obtain Śāyujya with Śiva. O sages of good holy rites, these are the measuring units of the self-born Bāṇa Liṅga. In the Svāyambhuva, O excellent brahmins, the measure of the holy centre shall be half, in the Ārṣa (pertaining to the sages) it shall be half of that. In the Mānuṣa (pertaining to human beings) it shall be still half of that. O excellent brahmins, the measure of holy centres in the abode of ascetics is thus.

O brahmins, he who casts off his vital breath in any of these places shall attain Sāyujya with Śiva viz:—Rudrāvatāra, Narāvatāra, the holy Śrīparvata[678] and its boundary line. The benefit shall be extended to his disciples and the disciples of disciples.

38-39. The same is true of Vārāṇasī[679] and particularly of Avimukta.[680] He who casts off his vital breaths in Kedāra,[681] Prayāga[682] or Kurukṣetra[683] attains extreme bliss.

40. He who dies in Prabhāsa,[684] Puṣkara,[685] Avantī,[686]

678. Śrīparvata or Śrīśaila is one of the sacred hills of the south overhanging the Kṛṣṇā river. It contains the celebrated shrine of Mallikārjuna, one of the twelve jyotirliṅgas.

679. Vārāṇasī- -see p. 97 note. 120

680. Avimukta—see p. 46 note. 64

681. Kedāra—a very sacred Himalayan peak in Garhwal. It still retains its ancient name and sanctity.

682. Prayāga—see p. 291 note 567.

683. Kurukṣetra—It lies south of Thanesar, not far from Panipat in Haryana State.

684. Prabhāsa—It is a celebrated place of pilgrimage in Saurāṣṭra the southern part of Kathiawar.

685. Puṣkara—a sacred place near Ajmer famous for the lake Puṣkara.

686. Avanti or Avantikā. It is identical with Ujjayinī or modern Ujjain.

Amareśvara[687] and in Vaṇīśailākula[688] attains the nature of Śiva.

41-45. The person who dies in Vārāṇasī is not born again. He who casts off his vital breath in Triviṣṭapa,[689] Avimukta, Kedāra, Saṅgameśvara,[690] Śālaṅka,[691] Jambukeśvara,[692] in Śukreśvara,[693] Gokarṇa,[694] Bhāskareśa,[695] Guheśvara,[696] Hiraṇyagarbha,[697] or Nandīśa[698] attains the greatest goal. He who desiccates his body by means of observances and casts it off in any holy centre of Śiva whether it is of human or divine origin, whether it is built by sages or whether it is self-born, becomes a yogin and attains oneness with Śiva. O excellent sages, if the deity is self-born or installed by Devas, no doubt need be entertained in this regard. He who worships the lord and then collects fire into which he consigns his body, attains the greatest goal.

46-49. One shall abstain from taking any sort of food whatsoever and cast off one's vital breaths in a holy centre of Śiva. O excellent sages, he shall attain Sāyujya with Śiva. He who cuts off his pair of legs and stays in the holy centre of Śiva, attains oneness with Śiva. No doubt need be entertained in this regard. The vision of a holy centre is meritorious. The entrance therein is hundred times more meritorious. The touching and the circumambulation is hundred times more meritorious. The ablution in the waters is hundred times more meritorious than that.

50. The bathing of the deity, O brahmins, in milk, is hundred times more excellent. It is mentioned that the ablution

687. Amareśvara—in Oṁkāra Māndhātā. It is a sacred place of Śaiva pilgrimage in the Nimar district in Madhya Pradeśa.

688. Vaṇīśaila—not identifiable.

689. Triviṣṭapa—not identifiable. But Triviṣṭapa or tripiṣṭaka is the heaven of Indra, said to be situated on Mount Meru.

690. Saṅgameśvara—a sacred place mentioned in Sk., VII.i.33 but not identifiable.

691-693. Śālaṅka, Jambukeśvara and Śukreśvara are not identifiable.

694. Gokarṇa : lit. 'cow's ear'. It is a place of pilgrimage sacred to Śiva, on the east coast, near Mangalore. It has the temple of Mahādeva, Śiva, supposed to have been established by Rāvaṇa. This Gokarṇa should not be confused with the town of the same name situated in Nepal on the Bhāgamatī river.

695-698. Not identifiable.

with curds has thousand times more merit. With honey it is hundred times more.

51-52. The ablution with ghee has infinite merit; that with sugar is hundred times more. One shall eschew cooked rice after reaching a river near the holy centre of Śiva and plunging into it. He shall thus cast off his body. He is honoured in the world of Śiva. All the rivers near the holy centres of Śiva are very meritorious.

53-56. The wells, tanks and lakes are Śivatīrthas (sacred waters of Śiva). O excellent brahmins, by taking his bath in those (wells, etc.) with devotion a man is undoubtedly liberated from brahmin-slaughter and other sins. O excellent sages, by taking his morning plunge in the sacred waters of Śiva, a man attains the benefit of horse sacrifice and goes to Rudra's world. By taking a single plunge in the sacred waters of Śiva at midday with great devotion a man surely obtains merit equal to that of taking bath in the Gaṅgā. By taking bath after the sunset one shall attain the auspicious region of Śiva.

57-59. Casting off his slough of sins in the holy waters of Śiva the man attains the auspicious region of Śiva. O brahmins, by taking the threefold bath once in the sacred waters of Śiva, the man obtains Sāyujya with Śiva. No doubt need be entertained in this respect.

Once a boar saw a dog on the way. Due to fright it chanced that it plunged into the sacred waters of Śiva and died. O excellent brahmins, he attained the chieftainship of the Gaṇas.

60. He who sees Śiva, the lord of the chiefs of Devas, in the form of Liṅga at dawn attains a goal superior to all.

61. By seeing Mahādeva at midday one attains the benefit of sacrifices. By seeing the lord in the evening, one attains the benefit of yajñas and is liberated.

62. He is liberated from all great sins, mental, verbal and physical; subsidiary sins occurring as a sequel.

63. By visiting lord Īśāna in the form of the Liṅga at the time of transit of the sun from one sign of Zodiac to the next, one eschews sins committed in the course of month and he attains the auspicious region of Śiva.

64. By visiting the lord at the beginning of the southern or

northern transit of the sun one dispels sins committed in the course of half a month. By worshipping the lord, at the time of equinoxes, one attains the greatest goal.

65-66. The clean and pure man who circumambulates the mansion of Śiva three times in the mode of Savya and Apasavya [clockwise and anticlockwise] and treads softly shall attain the benefit of aśvamedha at every step. He who screams and laments to Śiva, attains the auspicious abode. What else remains for him to attain ?

67-73. (After sprinkling) with scented cowdung water the devotee shall make the mystic diagram of the auspicious lotus along with the pericarp. For this purpose the dust particles of pearls, sapphires, rubies, crystals, emerald, gold or silver may be used. Those who are not sufficiently rich may use other powders similar in colour to the powders mentioned above. The mystic diagram shall extend upto ten Hastas. It should be described near Mahādeva. Mahādeva accompanied by the nine Śaktis shall be invoked therein : The devotee shall invoke the lord who bestows the desired things by means of five elements, six sense-organs and eight cosmic bodies. Again the devotee shall worship Īśāna in the ten-cornered (mystic diagram) through the eight cosmic bodies or the ten organs of sense and knowledge externally. After the worship the devotee shall bow down and offer food offerings to the lord of Devas. He shall thereby obtain the benefit of the charitable gift of earth. The indigent person shall make the mystic diagram of the lotus by means of the powdered grains of Śāli rice. Even then he shall obtain the merits as mentioned before.

74-80. The devotee shall draw the mystic diagram of twelve sides and then the excellent lotus by means of such powders as those of jewels, etc. In the middle of the mystic diagram he shall instal Bhāskara along with the twelve deities and then worship the sun surrounded by the planets. He shall attain the excellent Sāyujya (the salvation of identity) with the sun. Similarly he shall draw the six-sided figure by means of red chalk to depict deities pertaining to Prakṛti. In the middle region he shall worship the goddess of Devas, Prakṛti, in the form of Brahman. To the right he shall worship the deity of Sattva-Guṇa; to the left that of Rajo-Guṇa and in front that of Tamo-Guṇa. He shall worship the goddess Ambikā in the middle. To the right he shall worship the five elements and the five Tanmātrās. To the north he shall worship the five organs of action and five organs of sense. In the six-sided figure he shall worship the two Ātmans, viz., Ātman and Antarātman as well as the cosmic intellect and ego along with the principle Mahat. He shall then attain the benefit of all sacrifices.

81. O leading brahmins, thus the great Prākṛta Maṇḍala (the mystic diagram pertaining to Prakṛti) has been mentioned to you. Henceforth I shall mention the means of achieving all desired objects.

82-85. The devotee conversant with the mantras shall sprinkle the ground duly with water and scrub it with cow-dung. He shall then make the mystic diagram in the form of a square measuring a go-carma (i.e. 150 Hastas a side). He shall then decorate it with canopies, or charming umbrellas. He shall embellish them with globe-like bubbles or crescent-shaped trinkets made of gold or the leaves of Aśvattha tree. He shall decorate it with full blown white, red or blue lotuses; also strings of pearls shall be suspended from the extremities of the canopies. He shall embellish it with white banners and silken Vaijayantīs (Ensigns) or garlands of sprouts and fruits. There shall be white mud-pots and elegant water-jars filled with water. He shall have fifty lamps in a row and five kinds of incense.

86-94. The devotee shall make an excellent lotus with fifty petals by means of powders of different colours or only with white powder. The lotus shall extend to one Hasta in magnitude. It shall be made in accordance with the injunctions. He shall fix the lord Rudra, the lord of Devas along with the goddess in the pericarp. Beginning with the petal in the east and proceeding gradually he shall fix the syllables in the petals along with the Rudras. O sages of good holy rites, the syllables are to begin with the Praṇava and end with Namas. O excellent sages, after duly worshipping thus with scents and fragrant flowers, he shall feed fifty brahmins in accordance with the injunctions. He shall give those leading sages the charitable gifts of garlands of rosary, sacred thread, ear-rings, water-pots, seats, staff, turbans and clothes. He shall offer Mahācaru as Naivedya to Śambhu the lord of Devas and dedicate the black pair (i.e. a black cow and a black ox). In the end he shall offer the mystic diagram made of powders to the lord of Devas. He shall then offer materials of utility in a sacrifice to Śiva. The intelligent devotee shall perform the Japa of the letters one by one with Oṁkāra in the beginning. I shall briefly mention the benefit that a man attains after describing this excellent Maṇḍala amongst all with devotion.

95-98. By seeing the coloured Maṇḍala and by worshipping it one attains the same benefit as a yogin attains in the following circumstances :—When he has learned the Vedas duly along with their Aṅgas (ancillary subjects); when he has worshipped God by means of sacrifices, such as Jyotiṣṭoma etc., ending with that of Viśvajit; when (as a householder) he has procreated sons like himself; when he has adopted the stage of life of a forest-dweller with earnestness maintaining the sacrificial fire, and performing all rites such as Cāndrāyaṇa, etc.; when he has renounced all holy rites, learned Brahmavidyā assiduously and attained perfect knowledge and when with perfect knowledge he has seen what should be seen.

99-100. After scrubbing and cleaning the front yard of the shrine by any material, O excellent brahmins, if a devotee describes a mystic diagram in the form of a square to the north or south or to the west of the shrine and embellishes it with the powders, flowers, raw rice grains etc., and then worships the deity with flowers, raw rice grains, etc., he is liberated from all sins.

101-102. He, who devoutly scrubs and cleans the sanctum sanctorum all round, even once, scatters scented flowers all round, offers fragrant articles like sandal paste, camphor, etc., makes the place sweet smelling with incense of four kinds and prays to the lord Īśāna, goes to the world of Śiva.

103-104. The man enjoys pleasures for a hundred crores of kalpas. His body emits sweet fragrance like that of flowers with which he fills the temple of Śiva. Gradually he goes to the world of Gandharvas and is worshipped by the Gandharvas. He comes to this world in due course and becomes a powerful monarch.

105-106. Mahādeva is the primordial lord. He is the cause of creation, dissolution and sustenance. Sadāśiva is all pervasive and is the overlord of the worlds. The nectar of Śiva-Brahman should be known as the excellent means of salvation. One shall always worship the lord, the manifest and the un manifest being the lord beyond imagination.

CHAPTER SEVENTYEIGHT

Scrubbing and cleaning the shrine of Śiva

Sūta said:

1. O excellent sages, the holy shrine of Śiva should be scrubbed and cleaned by means of water filtered and purified with a cloth. Otherwise no Siddhi is attained.

2. O leading sages, waters that have no foam, particularly from the rivers, should be taken. When filtered with a cloth they become pure and holy.

3. Hence, O excellent brahmins, all divine holy rites should be performed by the purified waters for achieving the results in all rites.

4. Waters are mixed with minute germs. By using the unfiltered waters one attains the same sin as by killing them.

5-6. O brahmins, householders adopt violent means always while sweeping or wiping, while using fire, threshing, pounding things or while fetching water. But one shall eschew violence. Non-violence is the greatest virtue to all living creatures.

7. Hence, by all means one shall practise water purified by cloth. The meritorious and charitable gift of giving protection is the excellent of all charitable gifts.

8-10. Hence, violence should be avoided always and at all places. All violent creatures do not harm a man who abstains from violence mentally, verbally and physically. They harass one who injures others. A man who abstains from violence obtains a crore times the benefit that one attains by gifting away the three worlds to one who has mastered the Vedas. Those who are engaged in the welfare of living beings, mentally, verbally and physically and those who follow the path pointed out by kindness go to the world of Rudra.

11-15a. Those who protect persons of various sorts like a loving master or with love as if they were their own sons and grandsons, go to the world of Rudra. Hence, by all means sprinkling should be performed by means of water filtered with a cloth. The ablution should be carried out particularly. Even by killing a single person in the premises of Śiva's temple one attains the sins that accrue from destroying the three worlds. But, O excellent brahmins, violence to flowers[699] must always be pursued for the worship of Śiva, violence to the animals[700] for the sake of sacrifice. The chastisement of the wicked by the Kṣatriya caste can be pursued.

15b-17a. In the case of yogins expounding the Brahman these rules regarding what is laid down and what is forbidden are not applicable. They shall not be killed even if they resort to forbidden things. Similarly expounders of Brahman shall not be killed since they have eschewed all actions and taken to Sannyāsa, even if at times they are prone to sinful activities.

17b-18. Women are holy ones as they are born of the family of Atri. Even when they are engaged in sinful acts they should not be killed. They are to be worshipped always. By killing Ātreyīs one incurs a sin equal to the slaughter of a brahmin.

19-20. Women from any caste should not be taken up for the Yajñas at any time, by anyone or in any place, O leading brahmins. Women engaged in sinful activities, whether they be dirty or beautiful, ugly or robed in ugly clothes should never be killed by men due to the suspicion that they may be Śiva.

21. Those who practise the holy rites and conduct of life outside the pale of the Vedas, those who are excluded from the rites laid down in Śrutis and Smṛtis and those who are notorious as heretics should not be conversed with by the twice-born.

699-700. violence incurred by plucking flowers (puṣpa-hiṁsā) for Śiva's worship is not sinful, so also the slaughter of animals in propitiation of Śiva.

V-19 (below) prohibits the slaughter of women in sacrifices implying thereby that man-slaughter (nara-vali) was a common practice. ST interprets 'striyaḥ' as 'mānuṣa-striyaḥ' and explains that the restriction of slaughter did not apply to the female animals. ST. quotes a scriptural saying (śruti) in support of this view : "Sarasvatīṁ Vaśām ālabheta."

22. They should neither be seen nor touched. After seeing them one should look at the sun. Still they should not be killed by kings or other creatures.

23. O brahmins, by worshipping lord Śiva even for once, thanks to the contact with good men, a man attains Rudra's world.

24. O excellent sages, all unkind persons become miserable. So also, all men who are devoid of devotion towards the great lord.

25. Those who are devotees of Śiva, the lord of Devas, are fortunate. After enjoying pleasures here itself they become liberated.

26. The minds of men are attached towards sons, wives and houses. Just as the minds of ascetics and sages are attached towards the primordial lord. But if men turn their minds towards the lord at least once by chance the world of great Īśa is not far for them.

CHAPTER SEVENTYNINE

The mode af worship of Śiva

The sages said:

1-2. O sages of great intellect, how should the great lord, the lord of subjects be worshipped by tardy and dull-witted men who are short-lived, whose strength is trifling and whose virility is insignificant. Even after worshipping lord Śiva by means of penance for thousands of years, Devas do not see him. How then do they worship the lord ?

Sūta said:

3. O leading sages, what you have said is quite true. Still with faith the lord can be seen and pleased and even conversed with.

4. O brahmins, if even those who are devoid of devotion incidentally worship the lord, he bestows fruits befitting the emotion.

5. O brahmins, the base brahmin who worships the lord after being defiled by the leavings of food becomes a Piśāca. The man of deluded intellect who worships the lord in a fit of anger shall attain the abode of Rākṣasas.

6. The wicked man who eats forbidden food and worships the lord becomes a Yakṣa. A man who practises music and worships the lord attains the abode of Gandharvas. A person who practises dance also attains the same state.

7. The base man attached to women and yearning for fame attains the abode of the moon[701] (by worshipping the lord). A person afflicted by pride and arrogance, worshipping Rudra, shall attain the abode of Soma (moon ?)

8. By worshipping the lord by means of Gāyatrī verses one shall attain the world of Prajāpati. By worshipping by means of Praṇava one attains the abode of Brahmā or Viṣṇu.

9. By worshipping the lord with faith even for once, the devotee attains the world of Rudra and rejoices along with the Rudras.

10-22. The splendid Liṅga, worshipped by Devas and Asuras should be cleaned by the holy waters. The lord should be invoked devoutly in the pedestal. After visiting the lord duly and after worshipping him he should be installed in the conceived seat which has the splendid form of perfect knowledge, which is richly endowed with detachment and prosperity, which is bowed to by all the people, which is in the middle of the lotus of Oṁkāra and which has its origin from the moon, sun and fire. After offering Pādya, Ācamana and Arghya to Rudra the devotee shall bathe the deity with pure waters, ghee and milk. He shall bathe Rudra with curds and clean Him. Thereafter he shall bathe the deity with pure water and worship it with sandal-paste. After worshipping with yellow pigment he shall worship it with red flowers, unbroken Bilva leaves, blue and red lotuses, Nandyāvarta flowers, Mallikās, Campakas, Jāti flowers, Bakulas, Karavīras, Śamī and Bṛhat flowers, Unmattas, Agastyas, bunches of Apāmārga flowers and splendid ornaments. After offering incense of five kinds he shall offer milk pudding as Naivedya. Other food offerings shall be rice with curds, rice soaked in honey and ghee, then pure cooked rice

701. cāndram—Budha-sthānam ST. the house of Mercury.

and then Mudgānna (rice cooked green gram) of six types. Thereafter he shall offer as Naivedya five types of cooked rice along with ghee, or rice alone wherein he shall cook one Āḍhaka measure of rice. After circumambulation he shall bow down again and again in the end. After eulogising lord Īśāna and after worshipping Śiva he shall adore him by repeating the mantras of Īśāna, Tatpuruṣa, Aghora, Vāmadeva and Sadyojāta. With this mode of worship lord Maheśvara becomes delighted.

23. O excellent brahmins, those trees which are utilised in the worship of Śiva through their flowers, leaves, etc., and the cows too, attain the supreme goal.

24. He who but once worships Śiva, Rudra, Śarva, the unborn Bhava attains Śiva's Sāyujya devoid of returning here again.

25. One is liberated from all sins even by seeing but once incidentally Parameśāna, Bhava, Śarva, lord of Umā who was worshipped thus.

26. There is no doubt in this that a man attains Brahmā's world by seeing Mahādeva who has been worshipped or is being worshipped.

27-30. He who on hearing about the lord approves of it and rejoices therein attains the greatest goal. He who, for even once, offers a ghee lamp in front of the Liṅga attains that goal which is difficult of access by means of the stages in life and which is steady. By offering a tree of lamps either made of clay or of wood in the temple of Śiva one is honoured in the world of Śiva along with hundred members of his family. He who duly and devoutly offers lamps to Śiva made of iron, copper, silver or gold shall go to the city of Śiva in splendid vehicles refulgent like ten thousand suns.

31-34. He who offers a ghee lamp in front of Śiva in the month of Kārttika or he who sees the great lord being duly worshipped with faith, O excellent sages, goes to the world of Brahmā.

It is mentioned that the rites of invocation, welcome presence, installation and worship shall he conducted through Rudra Gāyatrī, the Āsana (seat) by means of Praṇava, the ablution by means of five mantras (Sadyojata, etc.), assigned to Rudra.

One shall thus perpetually worship Umā's husband, the lord of Devas. One shall worship Brahmā with Praṇava on his right side.

35-37. To his north, he shall worship Viṣṇu the lord of the chiefs of Devas by means of Gāyatrī, after performing Homa in the fire duly by repeating the five mantras and the Praṇava. By thus worshipping the lord he attains Sāyujya with Śiva. Thus, succinctly the mode of worshipping Śiva has been mentioned. After hearing this directly from Rudra, this was mentioned to me by Vyāsa in former times.

CHAPTER EIGHTY

The holy Pāśupata rite

The sages said :—

1. How is the liberation of the Paśu (Individual soul) from the Pāśa (bondage) effected on seeing Paśupati ? It behoves you to tell us how Devas eschewed their Paśutva ?

Sūta said :

2-5 Thanks to the grace of omniscient lord, formerly Devas came to him as he had stationed in his city called Bhogya[702] on the peak of the Kailāsa, for the welfare of Devas. Lord Viṣṇu, mounted on the wings of Garuḍa, came along with Brahmā. He approached the lord of Devas along with Devas. Along with Yama, Indra and the Sādhyas, they came to the splendid and excellent mountain and bowed down to the excellent mountain as well as to the lord. The Garuḍa-bannered lord Viṣṇu got down from Garuḍa and climbed the Meru along with the foremost Devas.

6-7. Meru was devoid of all sins. It bestowed each and every object of desire. It was the chief means of enjoyment. The flocks of sparrows rejoiced therein. Herds of elephants

702. Bhogya or Bhogyā. The city is located on the mountain Kailāsa.

made it resonant. There was sweet rattling music. Even the darkness was welcome to people. The region of the forest was well laid with footsteps. The waters at the borderland were sparkling and the wind was attractive. It consisted of hundreds and thousands of abodes resembling suns. It was blended with the flocks of swans adept in elegant movements. It contained trees, such as Dhava, Khadira, Palāśa, sandal, etc. and groups and flocks of excellent birds, such as the cuckoo etc. and also the bees.

8. In some places it abounded in divine trees. There were Kurabaka, Priyaka and Tilaka trees. The excellent mountain had many Kadamba trees and was surrounded by the creepers of Tamāla. The mountain had many peaks.

9. The city of lord Śiva was built by Viśvakarman on the top of this mountain for the sports of lord Śiva.

10. Devas including Indra and Viṣṇu saw that city and with great concentration and attention they bowed down from a great distance due to the power of the trident-bearing lord.

11. The great primordial lord went to the mountain Kailāsa, a part of the Meru, which is as refulgent as thousand suns, and which is great and which has thousands of virtues blended with it.

12. Then Brahmā and Viṣṇu the destroyer of Asuras reached the gateway of the city which resembled the lofty mountain and which abounded in women, horses, elephants, chariots, Gaṇas and their chiefs.

13. It was surrounded by big mansions full of gold and bedecked in jewels. It contained lofty palaces of various shapes and also ramparts.

14-20. On seeing the exterior of the city of lord Śiva along with Devas including Brahmā, Viṣṇu with beaming face became delighted in his mind. He then entered the city which had great palaces and mansions with lofty upper storeys. The second city of the lord of Devas was also splendid. It had four entrances. It was encompassed by diamonds, lapis lazuli, rubies and clusters of jewels and hanging swings. It was bedecked with bells and chowries, and resonant with musical instruments, such as Mṛdaṅga, Muraja, Vīṇā and Veṇu. It was surrounded by dancing Apsarases and Bhūtas (goblins). There were mansions charming to the eyes. They resembled the abodes of the leaders of Devas. On the tops of these palaces thousands of lady citizens stood with flowers, fruits and Akṣatas (raw rice grains) in their hands. As on the head of lord Śiva they strew these on the head of Viṣṇu from all directions. On seeing Viṣṇu, the women rejoiced immediately, danced and sang. Their eyes were roving due to inebriation and they had ample buttocks. On seeing Viṣṇu some women wore smiling faces ; their garments became loosened ; their waistbands and girdles dropped. They sang passionate songs.

21-35. Viṣṇu then went beyond those excellent cities (one within the other) the fourth, fifth, sixth, seventh, eighth, ninth and tenth. Then he reached the highly-splendid city of Śiva. It was perfectly circular and very splendid, stationed on the auspicious peak of Kailāsa. It was adorned with lofty mansions resembling the sphere of the sun. In different quarters it contained crystal Maṇḍapas and splendid platforms made of gold and different jewels. The ornamental gateways were adorned with different kinds of jewellery and many jewel-studded Sarvatobhadras (temples with openings on all the four sides). There were twentyeight fort walls of different forms and shapes. There were side doors and main doors in the interstices of the quarters, all firmly built and of diverse kinds. There were hidden apartments and houses. There were splendid abodes of Guha. O highly blessed ones, they were built in the rural model and other types. There were charming pearls too. The divine abodes of the leaders of Gaṇas were full of rubies. There were many splendid flower gardens of various shapes with sandal trees in them. There were many lakes and tanks with golden rows of steps. They were frequented by swans that had been defeated by the gaits of women. The tanks had divine and nectarine water and the water fouls (Kāraṇḍas), peacocks, cuckoos and ruddy geese heightened their splendour. There were thousands of Rudrakanyās (virgins) who were bedecked in all ornaments, who were adepts in conversation and elocution, who stooped down due to the weight of their heavy breasts, whose eyes were roving due to inebriation and who were engaged in singing and playing on instruments. There were groups of dancing nymphs. The lakes contained full-blown lotuses difficult of access even to Devas. There were excellent birds of all kinds. There were the womenfolk of Rudras lustrous as rubies, engaged in aquatic sports. There were groups of women engaged in amorous festivals of great elegance. They were passionately fond of rural notes and strains of music. On seeing these things in the abode of lord Śiva the great lord of Devas stood in surprise.

36. There itself they saw Rudragaṇas and thousands of their heroic leaders.

37. They saw the crystalline aerial chariots, lofty palaces bedecked in diamonds, lapis lazuli and golden steps.

38-41. On the tops of palaces there were delighted women with lotus-like eyes, and ample buttocks. There were Yakṣas, Gandharvas and Apsarases, Kinnaris, Kinnaras, serpents, and siddha girls. They had different kinds of dresses. They were bedecked in different ornaments. They had diverse efficiency. They were fond of pleasure and amorous dalliance. They had the lustre of the blue lotus petals. They had eyes as large as the petals of lotus. They looked resplendent by their upper garments resembling the filaments of lotus. They were bedecked in bangles, anklets, necklaces and umbrellas of variegated colours as well as attractive garments. They were fond of embellishments and they were bedecked in various ornaments also.

42. On seeing these beautiful women of the chiefs of Gaṇas, the leading Devas—Indra and others went to the mansion of the destroyer of Tripuras.

43. On seeing the first palace of the lord, that had the colour of a thousand rising suns, in the middle of the city, the groups of Devas and Siddhas beginning with Indra halted there.

44. Then all Devas with Indra at their head saw Nandin, the lord of Gaṇas standing at the doorway of the palace.

45. On seeing Nandin the leader of Gaṇas, Devas bowed down to him and said "Be Victorious". On seeing them the leader of Gaṇas replied:—

46. "O highly blessed Devas, why have you come here ? O persons of good holy rites, you who have shaken off your sins, ye the lord of all worlds, it behoves you to say.

47. They then spoke to the lord, the bestower of boons, the lord having the lustre of a lordly elephant. "For our liberation from the bondage of Paśus kindly show lord Maheśvara to us.

48. Formerly in order to burn the three cities, the Paśutva was stipulated. O you of good holy rites, now we are worried over this Paśutva.

49. The holy rite Pāśupata was mentioned by lord Śiva. O leader of Bhūtas, thanks to this holy rite, the state of Paśu ceases to exist.

50-53. By performing this excellent Vrata for twelve years, or for twelve months or for twelve days, all Paśus are liberated from the bondage of worldly existence." Nandin, the son of Śilāda, the leader of the Bhūtas showed the lord to all Devas including Viṣṇu. On seeing lord Śiva the unchanging deity accompanied by Ambā and Gaṇas, Devas were thrilled with pleasure. They bowed to the lord and eulogised him. After submitting to lord Śiva, their desire for liberation from bondage, Devas stood in front of lord Śiva bowing again and again.

54-57. After glancing at them and purifying their souls, the full-bannered lord of Devas, the great lord taught the Pāśupata Vrata to them. He then seated himself along with Umā and the sages.

Since then, all Devas are known as Pāśupatas (belonging to Paśupati). All those who consider the lord of Paśus as their direct deity are said to be Pāśupatas. Thereafter, Devas performed penance again.

58-60. The excellent Devas performed penance for twelve years and became free from bondage. They went back with Brahmā and Viṣṇu. Thus everything that had been heard from Brahmā has been mentioned to you. It had been heard by Sanat and by Vyāsa from him. The man who remains pure and hears this or narrates this to the brahmins attains a different body and is liberated from the bondage of Paśus.

CHAPTER EIGHTYONE

The holy rite for the release of Paśus

The sages said:

1-4. This holy rite that liberates Paśus (individual souls) from bondage has been mentioned by you. This holy rite of Paśupati pertaining to the Liṅga had been performed formerly by Devas. It behoves you to mention this to us in the manner you had heard it formerly.

Sūta said:

Formerly, Nandin, the son of Śilāda, was earnestly asked by Sanatkumāra. What Nandin spoke to him I shall mention succinctly. This excellent vrata called Dvādaśa Liṅga and capable of liberating Paśus from bondage had been performed by Devas, Daityas, Gandharvas, Siddhas, Cāraṇas and the highly blessed sages.

5. It yields worldly pleasures, liberation, yogic power and whatever one desires. It is auspicious, holy and conducive to perseverance and energetic efforts.[703] It destroys entanglement in worldly affairs in the case of devotees.

6. It has been evolved after churning the Vedas and their six ancillaries.[704] It excels all charitable gifts and is holier than ten thousand horse-sacrifices.

7. It is sacred, bestows all auspicious things, destroys all enemies, brings about salvation even to those creatures that are immersed in the ocean of worldly existence.

8. It dispels all sickness and destroys all fevers. It had been performed formerly by Devas as well as by Brahmā and Viṣṇu.

703. N.S. edition reads 'aviyoga-karam' for 'abhiyoga-karam'. aviyogakaram—sarvadā śiva-sānnidhyadāyakam ST. that which brings about the devotee's proximity to Śiva.

704. Ṣaḍaṅga : six ancillaries to the Veda, namely (i) Śikṣā—the science of proper articulation and pronunciation, (ii) Chandas—the science of prosody, (iii) Vyākaraṇa—grammar, (iv) Nirukta—etymological explanation of difficult Vedic words, (v) Jyotiṣa—astronomy, (vi) Kalpa—ritual or ceremonial.

9. O leading brahmins, the devotee shall make a small Liṅga and bathe it with sandal water. Beginning in the month of Caitra he shall perform the holy rite of Śivaliṅga.

10-11. He shall make an auspicious golden lotus with pericarp and filaments. It shall have eight petals duly studded with all the nine precious gems. He shall then fix the crystal Liṅga in the pericarp along with its pedestal. He shall then duly and devoutly worship it with Bilva leaves.

12-14. O sages of good holy rites, he shall worship the liṅga with thousands of white, red and blue lotuses, with white Arka, Karavīra, Karṇikāra and Kurabaka as well as with other flowers in accordance with their availability repeating the Gāyatrī. After adoring with scents, etc., with incense, with auspicious lamps and with Nīrājanas (wavings of lights) the devotee shall worship the great lord in Liṅga form. O excellent brahmins, he shall offer Aguru (agallochum) in the south by means of Aghora Mantra.

15. He shall offer the divine Manaḥśilā (red arsenic) in the west with the mantra of Sadyojāta, and sandal paste in the north with the Vāmadeva Mantra.

16-17. O excellent sages, he shall offer Haritāla (yellow orpiment) in the east by means of Tatpuruṣa. With devotion he shall offer the following varieties of incense, viz., that originating from white Aguru and black Aguru; then the Guggula dhūpa (aromatic gum resin), the excellent Saugandhika (fragrant incense) and the incense named Sitāra.

18. Mahācaru or an Āḍhaka measure of cooked rice should be offered as Naivedya. Thus, this great holy rite of Śivaliṅga has been narrated to you.

19-22. All these are common to all months. I shall mention the particular features now:—The Liṅga shall be adamantine in Vaiśākha;[705] in Jyeṣṭha it shall be made of emerald; in Āṣāḍha of pearl; in Śrāvaṇa of lapis lazuli and in Bhādrapada of rubies. O leading brahmins, in Aśvina, the Liṅga shall be made of onyx; in Kārttika of coral; in Mārgaśīrṣa of lapis

705. Vaiśākhe. For the worship of Liṅga in Caitra read V-9 ff. The crystal (sphāṭika) liṅga is recommended in Caitra. Cf. अत्र चैत्रमासेऽनुक्तत्वात्तस्मिन् पूर्वोक्तं स्फाटिकं बोध्यम् *ST.*

lazuli; in Pauṣa of topaz; in Māgha solar stone and in Phālguna of crystals.

23-24. In all months one golden lotus shall be used for worship; if that is not available a silver lotus shall be used; if that too is not available ordinary lotus shall be used.

When precious stones are not available the worship shall be conducted with gold or silver. If silver is not available it shall be made with copper.

25. The Liṅga can be made of rock, wood or clay along with its pedestal. Or he shall make a temporary Liṅga with fragrant substances.

26-27. In the season of Hemanta (early winter) one shall worship Mahādeva with Śrīpatra[706] (Bilva leaves) alone. In all the months a lotus made of gold or a lotus made of silver with golden pericarp can be used. If silver lotus is not available he shall worship with Bilva leaves.

28. If thousand lotuses are not available one shall worship with half that quantity; or he shall worship Rudra with a moiety of the said half or he shall worship with a hundred and eight lotuses.

29. Goddess Lakṣmī endowed with all characteristics is stationed on the leaf of the Bilva. Ambikā is directly present in the blue lotus and Ṣaṇmukha[707] himself is present in the red lotus.

30. Mahādeva, Śiva, the lord of all Devas occupies the lotus. Hence the learned man shall never forsake the Bilva leaf. He must employ every means to secure it.

31. He shall not forsake the blue lotus, the red lilies and particularly the red lotuses. The lotus fascinates everyone. Śilā (red arsenic) bestows Siddhi of all objects.

32-33. The incense originating from the black agallochum dispels all sins; the offering of aromatic gum, resin, etc. and the gift of lamps destroy all ailments; sandal paste bestows all

706. Śrīpatra—bilva patra. Śiva is very fond of bilva. Cf. *Śiva-rahasya* as cited in *ST*.

707. Ṣaṇmukhaḥ—(Ṣaḍānanaḥ, ṣaḍvaktraḥ, ṣaḍvadanaḥ)—six-mouthed or six-faced or six-headed, i.e., Kārttikeya. He is so called because when born he was fostered by the six Kṛttikās who offered their six breasts to him, so he became six-headed.

Siddhis; the scented incense is the means of achieving all desired objects.

34. The incense originating from white agallochum as well as black agallochum and the gentle incense Sītāri bestow salvation.

35-37. The four-faced Brahmā is present in the white Arka flower; the goddess of intelligence is well established in the Karṇikāra flower; the presiding deity of the Gaṇas is present in the Karavīra flower. Nārāyaṇa himself is present in the Kurabaka flower, the daughter of the mountain is present in all fragrant flowers. Hence, one shall devoutly and in accordance with one's means, worship the lord of the chiefs of Devas by means of these splendid flowers, incenses, etc. according to their availability.

38. Thereafter, he shall devoutly offer Mahācaru made of milk, as Naivedya along with ghee and side-dishes, prepared with all materials of diet.

39-45. Or the devotee shall offer an Āḍhaka measure or half of it of pure cooked rice or cooked with green gram dal. The devotee shall offer Cāmara (chowries) and fans to the deity. He shall also dedicate presents that had been earned by legally justifiable means. They shall be holy and befitting and of diverse kinds. They should be sprinkled with water before dedication and offered to Rudra with a devoted mind. It was from milk that nectar had been extracted by the victorious Viṣṇu for the sustenance of Devas. Everything is founded on cooked rice. By giving charitable gifts of rice to all living beings lord Śiva is delighted. Hence, one shall worship the lord with cooked rice. The vital breaths are stabilised in cooked rice. There is also pleasure in the offering of other presents; the wind-god is present in the fan. Mahādeva himself is present in all materials; the lord of waters, Varuṇa is present in the scented water; Prakṛti along with the principle Mahat is present in the pedestal. Hence, one shall worship the lord duly every month. For achieving all desired objects the Vrata should be observed on the full moon day.

46. One shall preserve truthfulness, cleanliness, kindness, quiescence, contentment and liberal-mindedness. The devotee shall observe fast on full moon and new moon days.

47. At the end of the year he shall make a gift of a cow. Particularly he shall observe the rite of Vṛṣotsarga.[708] With devotion he shall feed brahmins who have mastered the Vedas and who have sound learning.

48. The devotee shall deposit the Liṅga that he has worshipped, in the shrine of Śiva along with the materials of worship or he may give them to a brahmin.

49. O excellent sages, only he who devoutly performs this great holy rite of Śivaliṅga in all the months, is the most excellent one among those who perform penance.

50. In aerial chariots that are bedecked in jewels and that are as refulgent as crores of suns, he goes to the divine city of Śiva[709] and never returns here.

51. Or he shall perform this excellent vrata only for a month. Even then he attains the world of Śiva. No doubt need be entertained in this respect.

52. Or, if the mind of the devotee is attracted to worldly pleasures he shall observe the holy rite for a year. He will attain whatever boons he craves for and obtain Śiva.

53. The devoted man obtains Deva-hood, Pitṛ-hood, or becomes the king of Devas or the chieftain of Gaṇas.

54. He who seeks learning obtains learning; he who seeks worldly pleasures will attain them; he who seeks wealth may espy a treasure-trove and he who desires for longevity will achieve longevity.

55. One rejoices by attaining whatever desires he cherishes by performing the vrata, only for a month. In the end he will attain Rudratva.

56. This sacred and excellent vrata which is a great secret is evolved by Śiva the creator of the universe, for the benefit of Devas, Asuras, Siddhas, Vidyādharas and human beings.

57. After duly worshipping the lord who is worthy of worship, after bowing to him with head bent down along with

708. Vṛṣotsarga—a rite of letting loose a bull (or, according to some, a bull and four heifers) as a work of merit, especially on the occasion of a Śrāddha in honour of deceased ancestors.

709. A mythical city 'Śiva-pura' on the Himālayas, particularly on the Kailāsa peak is conceived as the abode of Śiva.

one's sons and servants and after assiduously circumambulating him one shall repeat the hymn "Vyapohana."[710]

58. This highly precious hymn was composed by lord Brahmā, the Creator of the Universe. For the welfare of the three worlds this was repeated by the magnanimous lord along with Devas.

CHAPTER EIGHTYTWO

Hymn of purification

Sūta said:

1-4. I shall now mention the auspicious hymn that dispels sins and bestows Siddhis. This was at first heard by the noble Kumāra from Nandin and narrated to Vyāsa and from him heard by me with great attention.

Obeisance to Śiva, the pure, the renowned, devoid of impurities ; the destroyer of the wicked. Obeisance to Śarva, to Bhava ; to the great Ātman. May the omniscient five-faced,[711] ten-armed[712] lord possessed of fifteen organs of senses, decked in all ornaments and resembling pure crystal and accompanied by Umā[713] dispel sins quickly. He is quiescent, all-pervasive stationed above all in the Padmāsana[714] posture.

5-8. May Īśāna, Puruṣa, Aghora, Sadya and Vāmadeva dispel sin quickly. May Ananta, the lord of all learning, the omniscient lord who is the bestower of everything and who is richly endowed with meditation on Śiva dispel my sin. May the subtle lord of Devas and Asuras, the lord of the universe, worshipped by Gaṇas and endowed with the sole meditation on Śiva dispel my sin. May the most excellent one among auspi-

710. vyapohana—a stotra of Śiva. See ch. 82.

711. pañca-vaktraḥ—five-faced. See p. 49 note 65.

712. daśabhujaḥ—this epithet of Śiva seldom occurs in the Purāṇas.

713. someśaḥ—Umayā sahitaḥ somaḥ, sa cāsau īśaś ca *ST*. the lord accompanied by Umā.

714. padmāsana—See p. 35 note 47.

cious ones, the great one worthy of worship, the deity engaged in auspicious meditation, the all-pervasive bestower of everything dispel my sin.

9-12. May the single-eyed lord Īśa, engrossed in auspicious worship, the lord richly endowed with meditation on Śiva dispel my sin. May lord Īśa of three forms, the inducer of Śiva's devotion and richly endowed with meditation on Śiva dispel my sin. May Śrīkaṇṭha the glorious lord of fortune, always engaged in meditation and worship of Śiva, dispel my sin. May the tufted quiescent lord, smeared with ashes from the corpse and the glorious one engaged in the worship of Śiva, dispel my sin.

13-24. May the great goddess directly dispel my sin immediately:—the goddess bowed to by the three worlds, the ancient goddess in the form of a comet, the great goddess, the daughter of Dakṣa, Gaurī, the splendid daughter of the Himavān, Ekaparṇā,[715] Agrajā,[716] the gentle one, Ekapāṭalā, Aparṇā, the goddess who bestows boons, the goddess who is interested only in granting boons, Umā, the destroyer of Asuras, Kauśikī, Kapardinī, Khaṭvāṅgadhāriṇī the Divine lady, one who plucked the sprouts by means of the tip of her hand, one who is surrounded by the four sons Naigameya[717] and others, the daughter of Menā, goddess born of water, one whose eyes resemble lotuses, one who is the mother of the noble-souled Nandin devoid of sorrow, the companion of Śubhāvatī, Pañcacūḍā, the bestower of boons, the unchanging one who attained the state of Prakṛti for the sake of creation of all living beings; one who pervades everything by means of the twentythree[718] principles beginning with Mahat; one who is perpetually bowed to by Lakṣmī and other Śaktis; the delighter of Nanda; Manonmanī, one who is fond of embellish-

715. eka-parṇā—one who lived on a single leaf, i.e., Pārvatī, Umā, better known as 'aparṇā'.

716. agrajā—the first-born.

717. Naigameya, etc. The four brothers (sons of Umā) are named (i) Kumāra, (ii) Śākha, (iii) Viśākha, (iv) Naigameya. These appear on the gold coins of Kuviṣka in the early Kushan period.

718. The twentythree principles consist of ten senses, five bhūtas, five tanmātras, buddhi, ahaṁkāra and manas. Cf. Bhāga 3.6.2 "trayoviṁśati tattvānāṁ gaṇam.

ing Mahādeva the wielder of Māyās; one who agitates and fascinates the entire universe beginning with Brahmā and consisting of the mobile and immobile beings, by means of her Māyā, one who is stationed in the heart of the yogins; one who is stationed in the world both as one and many; one whose eyes resemble the blue lotus; one who is perpetually eulogised with great devotion by all Devas beginning with the leaders of the Gaṇas, Brahmā, Indra, Yama and Kubera; the mother who on being eulogised destroys all their calamities; the destroyer of the agony of devotees; the elegant one; she who destroys worldliness; the divine deity the bestower of enjoyment of worldly pleasures and liberation on devotees without their effort. [May that great goddess dispel my sin immediately].

25. May Caṇḍa the lord of all the Gaṇas, who came out of the mouth of Śiva, the glorious one engaged in the worship of Śiva, dispel my sin.

26-29. May the lord Nandin dispel all sins; Nandin the son of Śālaṅkāyana, originating from the path of the ploughshare, the son-in-law of the Maruts, the lord of all Bhūtas, the all-pervasive, one who has eyes everywhere; the lord who is like the lord of all, may he dispel sins. He is the lord of the three worlds eulogised by Devas including Nārāyaṇa, Indra, moon, sun, Siddhas, Yakṣas, Gandharvas, Bhūtas, the creators of Bhūtas, serpents, sages and the noble-souled Brahmā. He is stationed in the harem of the lord. He is always worshipped by all.

30. May he who has great splendour and strength, he who is like another Mahādeva, the glorious one engaged in the worship of Śiva, dispel my sin.

31-35. May the auspicious elephant-faced deity surrounded by hundreds and crores of Gaṇas and engrossed in the meditation on Śiva dispel my sin. He splits and pierces the ridges and peaks of the Meru, Mandara and Kailāsa; he is worshipped by Airāvata and other divine elephants of the quarters. The seven Pātālas[719] constitute his feet; the seven continents[720] his thighs and calves; the seven oceans[721] his goads; all the holy centres

719. seven nether regions, see p. 71 note 90
720. See p. 140 note 247.
721. See p. 14 note 247; p. 181 note 282.

his belly; the firmament his body; the quarters his arms, the moon, sun and fire his eyes; the asuras like the trees are killed by him; he is great and fierce with the Vidyā of the Brahman; He is bound to the pillar of lotus-like hearts of men by Brahmā and others who act as divine mahouts and who are equipped with the ropes of yoga.

36. May the glorious tawny-eyed lord Bhṛṅgin who has a body that has brightened the quarters, and who is engaged in the worship of Śiva dispel my sin.

37-41. May the Śakti-bearing commander-in-chief of the army of Devas, the glorious destroyer of Asuras by means of his four bodies [?], the quiescent peacock-vehicled leader of the armies dispel my sin. May these forms[722] of Parameṣṭhin dispel my sin, viz.,—Bhava, Śarva, Īśāna, Rudra, Paśupati, Ugra, Bhīma and Mahādeva, who are always engaged in the worship of Śiva. The following parts of his body,[723] viz.,—Mahādeva, Śiva, Rudra, Śaṅkara, Nīlalohita, Īśāna, Vijaya, Bhīma, Bhavodbhava the lord of Devas, Kapālin and Īśa, who are all engaged in doing obeisance of Śiva. May they dispel my impurity (sin).

42-43. May these twelve Ādityas[724] dispel my impurity—Vikartana, Vivasvān, Mārtaṇḍa, Bhāskara, Ravi, Lokaprakāśaka (the illuminator of the worlds), Lokasākṣin (the witness of the worlds), Trivikrama, Āditya, Sūrya, Aṁśumān and Divākara.

44-45a. The firmament, wind, fire, water, earth, moon and Ātman are mentioned as his cosmic bodies.[725] May they dispel my sin. May they destroy my fear.

45b-47a. May Vāsava, (Indra) Pāvaka (fire), Yama, Nirṛti, Varuṇa, Vāyu, Soma, Īśāna, Viṣṇu and Brahmā all engaged in meditating on Śiva dispel my sin committed mentally and physically.

47b-48. May the Maruts (wind-god) Nabhasvān, Sparśana,

722. See p. 166 note 273.

723. See p. 167 note 275.

724. twelve ādityas, viz., dhātṛ, mitra, aryaman, rudra, varuṇa, sūrya, bhaga, vivasvān, pūṣan, savitṛ, tvaṣṭṛ and viṣṇu. These represent the sun in the twelve months of the year.

725. For detail, see *MP—A Study*, p. 63.

Vāyu, Anila, Māruta, Prāṇa, Prāṇeśa and Jīveśa, all engaged in the worship of Śiva, dispel my impurities.

49-50. The following are the Cāraṇas highly purified by his worship—Khecarin, Vasucārin, Brahmeśa, Brahmabrahmadhī, Suṣeṇa, Śāśvata, Puṣṭa, Supuṣṭa and Mahābala. May they dispel my impurities and all sins committed by me.

51-52a. May all the Siddhas the worshippers of the feet of Śiva dispel my impurities—Mantrajña, Mantravid, Prājña, Mantrarāṭ, Siddhapūjita, Siddhavatparama and Siddha. They are the bestowers of all Siddhis.

52b-53. May these lords of Yakṣas dispel my impurities—Yakṣa, Yakṣeśa, Dhanada, Jṛmbhaka, Maṇibhadraka, Pūrṇabhadreśvara, Mālin, Kṣitikuṇḍali and Narendra.

54-55. May these who constitute the ornaments in the body of Śiva dispel my sin and all poison mobile and immobile—Ananta, Kulika, Vāsuki, Takṣaka, Karkoṭaka. Mahāpadma, Śaṅkhapāla and Mahābala, all engaged in doing obeisance to Śiva.

56-57a. May the Kinnaras, Vīṇājña, Śūrasena, Pramardana, Atiśaya, Saprayogin and Gītajña, all engaged in adoring Śiva dispel my impurities.

57b-59a. May the Vidyādharas, viz., Vibudha, Vidyarāśi, Vidāmvara, Vibuddha, Vibudha, Kṛtajña, and Mahāyaśas, all engaged in meditating on Śiva, dispel all terrible impurities through the grace of Mahādeva.

59b-62a. May the following noble-souled heroes, all greatly devoted to Mahādeva dispel all fear and the dreadful asura tendency[726] :—Vāmadeva, Mahājambha, Kālanemi, Mahābala, Sugrīva, Mardaka, Piṅgala, Devamardana, Prahlāda, Anuhlāda, Saṁhlāda, Kila, Bāṣkala, Jambha, Kumbha, Māyāvin, Kārtavīrya and Kṛtañjaya.

62b-64. May the following Garuḍas the vehicles of Viṣṇu, all golden in colour and adorned with various ornaments, dispel my impurity, Garutmān, Khagati, Pakṣirāṭ, Nāgamardana, Nāgaśatru, Hiraṇyāṅga, Vainateya, Prabhañjana, Nāgāśīḥ, Viṣanāśa and Viṣṇuvāhana.

65-66. May these sages who are sanctified by Śiva and who are engaged in His worship, dispel my impurity—Agastya,

726. **āsuram bhāvam –evil thoughts created by Satan.**

Vasiṣṭha, Aṅgiras, Bhṛgu, Kāśyapa, Nārada, Dadhīca, Cyavana, Upamanyu and others.

67-68a. May the departed fathers, grand-fathers, great grand-fathers, the Agniṣvāttas, the Barhiṣadas, the maternal grandfathers and others who are devoted to meditation on Śiva dispel my fear and sin.

68b-70. May the divine mothers dispel my impurities, thanks to the grace of the lord of Devas, viz.,—Lakṣmī, Dharaṇī, Gāyatrī, Sarasvatī, Durgā, Uṣā, Śacī, and Jyeṣṭhā, who are all worshipped by Devas, the mothers of Devas, Gaṇas, Bhūtas and the mothers of the Gaṇas wherever they are.

71-73a. May the celestial damsels and the goddesses, engaged in the worship of Śiva dispel my impurities—viz., Urvaśī, Menakā, Rambhā, Rati, Tilottamā, Sumukhī, Durmukhī, Kāmukī, Kāmavardhanī and other divine Apsarases in all the worlds and the goddesses who are highly purified by doing the Tāṇḍava dance for Śiva.

73b-74. May the Sun, Moon, Mars, Mercury, Jupiter, Venus, Saturn, Rāhu and Ketu (the ascending and descending nodes) dispel all affliction from evil planets.

75-77a. May these twelve Rāśis (signs of zodiac), viz.,—Meṣa, Vṛṣa, Mithuna, Karkaṭaka, Siṁha, Kanyā, Tulā, Vṛścika, Dhanus, Makara, Kumbha and Mīna (i.e., from Aries to Pisces), all engaged in the worship of Śiva, dispel fear and sin through the grace of Parameṣṭhin.

77b-81a. May the goddesses of the twenty-seven lunar mansions always dispel my impurity. They are Aśvinī, Bharaṇī, Kṛttikā, Rohiṇī, Mṛgaśiras, Ārdrā, Punarvasu, Puṣya, Āśleṣā, Maghā, Pūrvaphālgunī, Uttaraphālgunī, Hasta, Citrā, Svātī, Viśākhā, Anurādhā, Jyeṣṭhā. Mūlā, Pūrvāṣāḍhā, Uttarāṣāḍhā, Śravaṇa, Śraviṣṭhā, Śatabhiṣak, Pūrvabhādra, Proṣṭhapadā[727] and Revatī.

81b-83. May these Pramathas, viz.—Jvara, Kumbhodara, Śaṅkukarṇa, Mahābala, Mahākarṇa, Prabhāta, Mahābhūtapramardana, Śyenajit and Śivadūta, who increase one's delight as also innumerable mothers of the Bhūtas, dispel my fear and sin through the grace of Mahādeva.

727. proṣṭapadā—uttarā bhādrapadā.

84-85a. May Himavān dispel my sin, who is engaged in the worship of Śiva, who resembles a watery expanse, who has the colour of the Kunda flower and the moon,[728] who is inimical to the submarine fire and who pierces the face of Vaḍavā.

85b-87. May the lord of bulls (Nandin) dispel my sin; the bull who has four feet, who is grey in colour like the milk ocean, who is always stationed in the world of Rudra along with the Rudras and the leaders of the Gaṇas, who holds the universe, who is the divine father of the entire universe, who is surrounded always by Nandā and other mothers and who is the suppressor of sacrifice.

88. May mother Gaṅgā,[729] the mother of the universe, stationed in the world of Rudra, a delighted devotee of Śiva, dispel my sin.

89. May Goddess Bhadrā of auspicious position stationed in the world of Śiva, the highly blessed mother of all kine, dispel my sin.

90. May Surabhi, who is auspicious all round, who is the destroyer of all sins and who is always engaged in the worship of Rudra dispel my sin.

91. May Suśilā of good conduct and glorious position, sanctified by Śiva and stationed in the world of Śiva dispel my sin.

92-95. May Senāpati (Skanda) the son of the lord of Devas dispel my sin. He is conversant with the reality of the teaching in the Vedas and Śāstras; he ponders over all actions, he is richly endowed with all attributes, he is the eldest and the lord of all; he is gentle, and has the body of Mahāviṣṇu, he is the noble commander of the army, he is the mysterious suppressor of sacrifice; he rides on the elephant Airāvata, he has black curly hairs; his limbs are black, his eyes are red; moon and serpent constitute his ornaments; he is surrounded by goblins, ghosts, evil spirits and Kūṣmāṇḍas and he is engaged in the worship of Śiva.

728. kumbha-kundendu-bhūṣaṇaḥ—omitted in translation: 'adorned with the moon-like kumbha and kunda flowers. kumbhaṁ-tatsañjñakam puṣpam *ST*. a kind of flower.

729. The river Gaṅgā, the mother of the worlds (jaganmātā), is invoked in her various forms.

96-97. May all these mothers accompanied by Yoginīs dispel all great sins:—Brahmāṇī, Māheśī, Kaumārī, Vaiṣṇavī, Vārāhi, Māhendrī, Cāmuṇḍā and Āgneyikā. They are worshipped by all the worlds and they are pure and attentive.

98-103. Vīrabhadra of great splendour is the son of Rudra. He is the leader of the armies and lord of the Gaṇas. May he dispel sin. He resembles the snow, the Kunda flower and the moon; he is terrible, his great hand closely clinging to the trident. He is omniscient and thousand-armed. He holds all weapons. The three sacrificial fires constitute his eyes. He is the lord, the bestower of fearlessness on the three worlds. He is the permanent protector of the mothers. His vehicle is the great bull. He is glorious and is bowed to by the three worlds. He is engaged in the worship of Śiva. He beheaded Yakṣa;[730] he destroyed the tooth of Pūṣan;[731] he removed the hand of the fire-god;[732] he caused the eye of Bhaga to fall down;[733] he pounded the limbs of Soma by the big toe of his foot; he is the bodyguard of Upendra, Indra, Yama and other Devas; he cut off the nose and lips of the great goddess Sarasvatī.[734] May the lord of Gaṇas dispel my sin.

104. May Mahālakṣmī the mother of the universe dispel my sin. She is the eldest, most excellent, bestower of boons and bedecked in excellent ornaments.

105. May the highly blessed Mahāmohā (the great delusion), surrounded by the great groups of goblins and engaged in the worship of Śiva dispel my sin.

106. May Lakṣmī who is endowed with all attributes, who has all the characteristics, who is the goddess that bestows all and who is omnipresent, dispel my sin.

107-108. May Durgā engaged in the worship of Śiva dispel my sin. She is the great goddess riding on a lion. She is the unchanging daughter of Pārvatī. She is Mahāmāyā of Viṣṇu constituting his slumber. She is worshipped by Devas. She has

730. The translators prefer yakṣasya to yajñasya and translate accordingly. But the legends referred to in this verse relate to Dakṣa's sacrifice. Hence in 'yakṣasya ca śiraś chettā' 'yajñasya' for 'yakṣasya' would suit the context—Editor.

731-733. For the legends, see Purāṇic Encyclopaedia.

734. This legend is not traceable.

three eyes. She is the goddess who bestows boons. She had suppressed the demon Mahiṣa.[735]

109. May all the mental sons of Satī, the Rudras who sustain the Cosmic egg, and who are worshipped by all the worlds, dispel my fear.

110. May the Bhūtas, Pretas, Kūṣmāṇḍas, the leaders of Gaṇas and of Kūṣmāṇḍas dispel my sin.

111-112. Devas eulogised the lord with this hymn and then bowed down their heads as far as the ground. O excellent brahmins, he who reads this divine hymn every month, or he who listens to this, sheds off all sins and is honoured in the world of Rudra.

113. He who seeks a virgin obtains her; he who is desirous of victory shall attain victory; he who is desirous of wealth shall attain wealth and he who wishes for sons will obtain sons.

114-116. He who seeks learning obtains learning; he who seeks enjoyment of pleasures will attain pleasures. By listening to this, a man obtains immediately whatever he desires. He will be favourite of Devas. If this meritorious hymn is read on behalf of some one, the ailments arising from gas, bile, etc., do not harass him. He courts no premature death nor is he bitten by snakes.

117-120. By repeating this hymn a man obtains many times the merit of visiting holy centres, and doing Ājñās, giving charitable gifts and performing the vratas in particular. The slayer of cows, the ungrateful wretch, the murderer of heroes, brahmins, mother and father, the slayer of those who seek refuge, the sinner who is guilty of breach of faith towards friends, all these wretched men dispel their sins and are honoured in the world of Śiva.

735. Mahiṣa—the asura from whom the country of Mysore is said to take its name.

CHAPTER EIGHTYTHREE

The holy rites of Śiva

The Sages said:

1. The meritorious vyapohana hymn has been attentively heard by us. Now mention to us the vratas pertaining to the Liṅgas.

Sūta said:

2. O excellent sages, I shall mention to you the auspicious vratas that were narrated by Nandin to the son of Brahmā.

3-4. I shall mention them to you as I have heard them from Vyāsa. On the eighth and fourteenth days of both the fortnights, the devotee shall eat only once, at night, and continue this rite for one year and worship Śiva. He acquires the benefit of all sacrifices and attains the greatest goal.

5-6. By performing this rite for one day and one night on Parvan days and by making the earth the vessel, the devotee attains the benefit of three nights on Parvan days. By performing the Kṣīradhārāvrata,[736] the devotee obtains the benefit of horse-sacrifice. He shall perform this holy rite on the two Pratipads (first day) and two Pañcamīs (fifth day) in the month.

7. The devotee shall take food only once a day at night, between the eighth and the fourteenth day in the dark half of the month. He attains all worldly pleasures and goes to the world of Brahmā.

8-9. The devotee shall perform this holy rite for a year in the night of all Parvan days. He shall be celibate, conquer anger and be devoted to meditation on Śiva. At the end of a year he shall duly feed leading brahmins. He then attains the world of Śiva. No doubt need be entertained in this respect.

10. Greater than the observance of fast is the partaking of alms and greater still is food acquired without begging. Taking

736. Kṣīradhārāvratam—the observer of this vow lives only on the milk-fluid.

food only at night is greater than Ayācita (the food acquired without begging). Hence one shall duly pursue Nakta[737].

11-13a. Food is taken in the forenoon by Devas; in the midday by sages; in the afternoon by pitṛs and at dusk by Guhyakas,[738] and others. Passing over all these times, partaking of the food at night is the best thing. The devotee who regularly takes food at night shall practice taking in only Haviṣya, bathing, truthfulness, light food, rites in the fire, and sleeping on the bare ground.

13b-14a. I shall mention the excellent vratas of Śiva for each month. These vratas function for the atonement of sins and for the acquisition of virtue, love, wealth and salvation.

14b-19.

The Vrata for the month of Pauṣa.

The devotee shall worship the lord and take food only at night. He shall speak truth and conquer anger. His food shall consist of Śāli rice, wheat and milk products. He shall assiduously observe fast on the Aṣṭamī (eighth) day in both the fortnights. He shall sleep on the bare ground. At the end, on the full moon day he shall bathe Rudra, Mahādeva by means of ghee and other material. O brahmins, after worshipping the lord duly the devotee shall feed good brahmins serving them barley cooked with milk and ghee. He shall perform the japa of Śānti mantras in particular. He shall dedicate a tawny-coloured cow and a bull to Bhava the lord of Devas, to Śiva Parameṣṭhin. O leading sages, he goes to the excellent world of the fire-god. After enjoying extensive pleasures he is liberated there itself.

20-22.

The Vrata for the month of Māgha.

In the month of Māgha the devotee shall worship the lord and take food only at night. He shall partake of Kṛśara along with ghee. He shall restrain the sense-organs. He shall observe fast on the fourteenth day in both the fortnights. On the full moon day he shall offer Rudra a black cow and a

737. naktam—A kind of ritual explained in v-12 ff.

738. guhyaka—a class of demi-gods who like the yakṣas, kinnaras etc. are the attendants of Kubera and guardians of his treasures.

black bull along with ghee and a blanket. He shall worship Śiva and feed brahmins in accordance with his means. He then attains the world of Yama and rejoices there.

23-26.

The Vrata for the month of Phālguna.

In the month of Phālguna the devotee shall take food at night with cooked rice of Śyāmāka, ghee and milk. He shall conquer anger and the sense-organs. He shall observe fast on the eighth and the fourteenth day. On the full moon day he shall bathe and worship Śiva the great lord and dedicate to the trident-armed lord, a cow and a bull having the colour of copper. After feeding the brahmins he shall pray to Parameś-vara. He then attains identity with the moon. No doubt need be entertained in this respect.

27-29a.

The Vrata for the Caitra month.

In the month of Caitra also the devotee shall worship Rudra and have night food according to his pleasure, consisting of Śāli rice cooked with milk and ghee. O excellent sages, he shall be down in the cowpen on the bare ground at night. He shall then remember Bhava. On the full moon day he shall bathe Śiva and dedicate to him a cow and a bull, white in colour. He shall feed the brahmins. The devotee then attains the abode of Nirṛti.

29b-30.

The Vrata for the month of Vaiśākha.

In the month of Vaiśākha the devotee shall take food at night. On the full moon day he shall bathe Bhava by means of Pañcagavya,[739] ghee, etc., and dedicate a cow and a bull white in colour. He then attains the benefit of a horse-sacrifice.[740]

739. pañcagavya—It consists of the five products of the cow, viz. milk, curd, butter, the liquid and solid excreta.

740. aśvamedha—a sacrifice performed by kings for the achievement of universal supremacy. A horse was turned loose to wander at will for a year, attended by a guardian ; when the horse entered a foreign country, the ruler was bound either to submit or to fight. In this way, the horse returned at the end of a year, the guardian obtaining or enforcing the submission of princes whom he brought in his train. After the successful return of the horse, the horse was sacrificed amidst great rejoicings.

31-34.

The Vrata for the month of Jyeṣṭha.

In the month of Jyeṣṭha, the devotee shall, with faith and devotion, worship Śarva the lord of Devas, Bhava the consort of Umā. He shall take food only at night consisting of red Śāli rice purified by means of honey, water, ghee, etc. For half the night he shall be engaged in serving cows. He shall sit in the Vīrāsana.[741] On the full moon day he shall worship the lord of Devas, the consort of Umā after bathing the deity. He shall offer Caru duly to the trident-bearing lord. After feeding the brahmins according to his means the devotee shall give a cow and a bull smoke-like in colour. He shall then be honoured in the world of Vāyu (wind-god).

35-37a.

The Vrata for the month of Āṣāḍha.

In the month of Āṣāḍha the devotee shall be engaged in taking food at night consisting of fried grain flour mixed with ghee, sugar candy and milk products. On the full moon day he shall bathe the deity with ghee, etc. and worship him duly. After feeding learned brahmins who have mastered the Vedas he shall give a white cow and a white bull. He shall then attain the world of Varuṇa.

37b-40a.

The Vrata for the month of Śrāvaṇa.

O brahmins, in the month of Śrāvaṇa the devotee shall take food at night consisting of Ṣaṣṭika rice cooked with milk, after worshipping the bull-bannered deity. On the full moon day he shall bathe the deity with ghee, etc., and worship him duly. He shall then feed the brahmins who have sound learning and who have mastered the Vedas. He shall offer sugarcane[742] and a cow and a bull with white toes (above hoofs). The devotee then attains identity with Vāyu and becomes all-pervasive like Vāyu.

741. Vīrāsana—a particular posture practised by ascetics in meditation, sitting on the hams. It is the same as paryaṅka.

742. pauṇḍram—citram *ST*. wonderful. *ST*. quotes *Viśva kośa* in support of this meaning.

40b-43a.

The Vrata for the month of Bhādrapada.

O leading brahmins, the devotee shall take food at night consisting of what is left over after Homa. During day time he shall resort to the root of trees. On the full moon day he shall bathe and worship Śiva, the lord of Devas. He shall dedicate with devotion a cow and a bull with blue shoulders. After feeding the brahmins who have mastered the Vedas and the Vedāṅgas he will attain the world of Yakṣas[743] and be their king.

44b-45.

The Vrata for the month of Āśvayuja.

In the month of Āśvayuja the devotee shall take food at night consisting of ghee. As before, on the full moon days he shall worship Śiva and feed the ever pure brahmins, the devotees of Śiva. By giving a blue-coloured bull with lifted chest and a cow he will attain the world of Īśāna.

46-48.

The Vrata for the month of Kārttika.

In the month of Kārttika the devotee shall take food at night consisting of rice cooked with milk and ghee after worshipping lord Bhava. On the full moon day the devotee shall bathe the deity and offer Caru as Naivedya. He shall feed the brahmins according to his means. As before, O brahmins, a cow and a bull of tawny-colour shall be dedicated to the deity. He then attains identity with the sun. No doubt need be entertained in this regard.

49-51.

The Vrata for the month of Mārgaśīrṣa.

In the month of Mārgaśīrṣa the devotee shall take food at night consisting of barley cooked with ghee, milk, etc. On the full moon day he shall do towards Śarva, Śambhu, what has been mentioned before. After feeding the poor brahmins who are masters of the Vedas he shall duly make a gift of a cow and a bull of yellowish white colour. The devotee then

743. **yakṣa-loka—Śiva's world or the region of Kubera with Alakā as the capital.**

attains the world of the moon[744] and rejoices with the moon.

52-54. The following shall be practised throughout : non-violence, truthfulness, non-stealing, celibacy, forgiveness, mercifulness, three times ablution, Agnihotra, sleeping on the bare ground, food at night only, observance of fast on eighth and fourteenth days in both the fortnights. Thus the Śivavrata for each month has been fully recounted. O brahmins, the devotee shall observe this Vrata for a year in the order mentioned or in the reverse order. He then attains identity with Śiva and obtains the path of perfect knowledge.[745]

CHAPTER EIGHTYFOUR

(*The holy rite of Umā-Maheśvara*)

Sūta said :—

1. For the welfare of men, women and other creatures, O excellent sages, I shall recount the holy rite of Umā-Maheśvara, mentioned by Īśvara himself.

2. For the period of a year the devotee shall prepare Haviṣya at night[746] on the full moon and new moon days and on the eighth and fourteenth day and worship Bhava.

3-8. The devotee shall make a splendid image of Umā-Maheśa in gold or in silver and instal it duly. At the end of the year, he shall feed the brahmins and give them gifts according to capacity. He shall take the lord of Devas to the temple of Rudra on chariots, etc., fitted with all excellent things and decorated with umbrellas and chowries. He shall dedicate the Vrata unto Śiva, Parameṣṭhin. He attains identity with Śiva. If the devotee is a woman she will attain Sāyujya (identity) with the goddess. If the devotee is a virgin or a widow she shall abstain from taking food on the eighth and fourteenth

744. Soma-lokam—Śivalokam *ST*.

745. jñāna-yoga : yoga of knowledge. Knowledge has been defined in *Kūrma* thus : यया स देवो भगवान् विद्यया वेद्यते परः । साक्षाद्देवो महादेवस्तज्ज्ञानमिति कीर्तितम् ॥ cited in *ST*.

746. naktam—a vow of night. For detail, see v-12 of this chapter.

day. She shall observe celibacy and continue the holy rite for a year. At the end of the year she shall make an idol in accordance with the injunction laid down before and instal it duly. She shall then feed the brahmins after taking the idol to the temple of Rudra. Thanks to this holy rite she rejoices with Bhavānī.

9-14. If any woman continues for a year performing the rite only on the fourteenth day in the dark half, and, O brahmins, at the end of the year she makes an idol (of Śiva) in any material whatsoever and worships as mentioned above, she rejoices with Bhavānī.

The woman devotee shall take no food on the New moon day. She shall observe all other restraints and continue the holy rite for a year.

At the end of the year she shall make a trident in accordance with the injunctions and dedicate it to the lord. After the holy ablution she shall devoutly worship Īśāna with a thousand white lotuses. He shall dedicate a silver lotus with a gold pericarp. He shall give gifts to the brahmins. That woman undoubtedly dispels all wanton sins, such as the destruction of the foetus, by means of the holy rite of the dedication of the trident. O excellent brahmins, she thus obtains the Sāyujya with Bhavānī. If a man devotee performs this holy rite, he attains Sāyujya with Rudra.

15-18a. O excellent brahmins, a man or a woman can perform this holy rite. The devotee observes fast on the full moon and on New moon day devotedly for one year. O excellent brahmins, the holy rites, Japa, Dāna (charitable gift), penance and everything else should be performed by women, only at the behest of their husbands since women are never independent. Every month she shall dedicate all scented materials. At the end of the year that lady of holy rites attains Sāyujya (identity) and Sārūpya (similarity in form) with Bhavānī. Undoubtedly I am telling you the truth and truth alone.

18b-21. The woman devotee shall take food only once on the full moon day in the month of Kārttika. She shall observe forbearance, non-violence and other restraints and be celibate.

She shall alertfully offer a Bhāra[747] weight of black gingelly seeds cooked with ghee and jaggery to Parameṣṭhin and to brahmins in accordance with her means. She shall observe fast on the eighth and the fourteenth day. That lady of good holy rites attains Sārūpya (similarity in form) and rejoices along with Bhavānī.

22-23. The common characteristics of all vratas are :—Forbearance, truthfulness, mercy, charity, cleanliness, curb on the sense-organs and the worship of Rudra. I shall succinctly recount to you the extensive holy vrata for every month in due order beginning with Mārgaśīrṣa and ending with Kārttika. This has been recounted at the outset by Nandin.

24-31. In the month of Mārgaśīrṣa the woman devotee shall duly embellish an excellent bull having all limbs in perfect condition and dedicate it to Śiva. There is no doubt about this that she rejoices along with Bhavānī.

In the month of Pauṣa after doing everything mentioned before, the devotee shall instal the trident and then dedicate it to the lord. She rejoices with Bhavānī.

In the month of Māgha, the devotee shall make a chariot endowed with all characteristics. After worshipping the lord of Devas she shall offer the chariot to the deity and feed the brahmins. That highly blessed lady shall, no doubt, rejoice with the goddess.

In the month of Phālguna, she shall duly make an image of gold or radiant silver according to her means, instal it and worship it. Then she shall deposit it in the shrinc of Śaṅkara. Undoubtedly she rejoices along with the great goddess.

In the month of Caitra the woman devotee shall duly make the idols of Bhava, Kumāra and Bhavānī in copper or other metals, and instal them duly. By offering them to Rudra, she rejoices along with Bhavānī.

32-34. In the month of Vaiśākha the devotee shall perform the excellent rite of Kailāsa vrata thus :—The shining abode

747. bhāra : a particular weight equal to 20 tulās, measuring 2000 palas of gold. *ST*. quotes *pāsupata tantra* to define bhāra : तलद्वयं तु प्रसृत तद्द्वयं कुडवं भवेत् । कुडवस्य चतुर्थं स्यात्प्रस्थमित्यभिधीयते ।। आढक तद्द्वयं प्रोक्तं तद्द्वयं शिवमुच्यते । तद्द्वयं द्रोणमित्युक्तं खारी तद्द्वयमुच्यते । खारीत्रयं च भारः स्यादाचितो नवभारतः ।।

of Kubera (i.e., Kailāsa mountain) shall be made out of silver with Īśvara and Umā therein along with the lords of Gaṇas. It must be embellished with all jewels and duly deposited in the splendid abode of Bhava, Parameśa. Thereby she attains the mountain Kailāsa and rejoices along with Bhavānī.

35-38a. In the month of Jyeṣṭha the image of Mahādeva, the consort of Umā, shall be made in Liṅga form out of copper or other metals. Brahmā and Viṣṇu should be depicted as praying with palms joined in reverence and seated on the swan and on the boar respectively. O excellent brahmins, the splendid Liṅga in the middle of which is Bhava, shall be installed duly. Thereafter she shall feed the brahmins. By duly depositing this image in an abode of Śiva for obtaining auspiciousness and by worshipping Śiva along with the brahmins the devotee will attain Sāyujya with the goddess.

38b-46a. In the splendid month of Āṣāḍha the devotee shall duly make a splendid abode with baked bricks in accordance with her means. It must be filled with all necessary seeds and liquids, with all splendid household effects and utensils, the mortar, pestle etc., and furnished with maids and men servants, with all foodstuffs, bedding outfits, clothes etc. They shall be covered with cloths all round. The lord Mahādeva, consort of Umā, shall be bathed in ghee etc. A thousand brahmins shall be duly fed. A brahmin who is richly endowed with learning and humility and who has mastered the Vedas and who is in the first Āśrama[748] shall be duly and devoutly worshipped. A virgin of good waist line, accompanied by the necessary requisites for the whole life shall be offered to him. So also a piece of land, a cow and a bull and a house shall be offered to him along with the different kinds of divine perquisites as massive as the Meru mountain. She attains the world Goloka and rejoices with Bhavānī. Undoubtedly she will become similar to Bhavānī and remain unchanged throughout the kalpas, and shall in the end attain Sāyujya with Bhavānī.

46b-48a. In the month of Śrāvaṇa the devotee shall make a hillock of gingelly seeds scattered with minerals and embellished with banners and dedicate these to Śarva. The offering

748. prathamāśramiṇam—brahmacāriṇam *ST*. one who lives a student's life.

shall be made along with the canopy, banners, clothes and all the minerals. By feeding the brahmins, everything mentioned before will happen.

48b-50a. In the month of Bhādrapada the devotee shall make a splendid hillock of Śāli rice and dedicate it to the lord along with canopy, banners, clothes as well as minerals. After feeding the brahmins duly she shall present these to them. She shall then become as resplendent as the rays of the sun and rejoice along with Bhavānī.

50b-51. In the month of Āśvayuja she shall make a massive hillock of grains along with clothes of good colour. By worshipping Śiva with this offering and feeding the brahmins she will attain all things mentioned before.

52-65. *Mahāmeru vrata*.

The devotee shall make a huge mountain with all grains, all seeds and juices. It shall have all minerals and shall be bedecked in all jewels. It shall have four peaks. Its beauty shall be enhanced by canopies and umbrellas, scented garlands and incenses of diverse kinds. There shall be dances and songs and the instruments of lute, conch, etc. of diverse kinds. It shall be rendered highly meritorious by auspicious chanting of sacred hymns. There shall be eight great banners dazzling with different flowers. It shall represent the great mountain Meru, the excellent support of the three worlds. Śiva shall be depicted on its top, in the centre, by means of minerals. In the south the four-faced Brahmā shall be duly represented. In the north the devotee shall depict Nārāyaṇa the lord of the chiefs of Devas, devoid of ailments. Indra and other guardians of the quarters shall be duly represented with devotion. After installing the deity the devotee shall bathe and worship Maheśvara. In the right hand of the lord shall be depicted the trident worshipped by Devas and in the left the noose. The lotus bedecked in gold shall be depicted in the hand of Bhavānī. The devotee shall assiduously represent the conch, discus, iron club and lotus in the hands of Viṣṇu. In the hands of Brahmā shall be placed the rosary and the excellent Kamaṇḍalu (water-pot). The respective weapons of the following shall be duly depicted: the thunderbolt of Indra; the great weapon Śakti of Agni; the staff of Yama; the sword of Nirṛti the night walker; the terrible and wondrous noose; Nāga of Varuṇa; the baton of Vāyu; the iron club of Kubera that is worshipped by all the worlds and the axe of lord Īśāna. Naivedya shall be duly offered in the above order. The great worship of Śiva shall be performed with Caru. The devotee shall worship all Devas in accordance with one's means. After performing the worship assiduously the devotee shall feed the brahmins. After performing the Mahāmeru vrata she shall offer it to Mahādeva. Attaining Mahāmeru she rejoices along with Māhādevī. Undoubtedly she will attain the Sāyujya of the great goddess for a long time.

66-72. In the month of Kārttika the woman shall make a splendid image of goddess Umā fully bedecked in all ornaments and marked with all auspicious characteristics. The image may be made in gold, copper etc. and shall be duly installed. The image of the lord of Devas shall be equipped with all characteristics. In front the fire-god shall be depicted. Brahmā shall be depicted holding the sacrificial ladle. Nārāyaṇa the munificent shall be depicted bedecked in all ornaments and surrounded by the guardians of quarters and Siddhas. The vrata shall be offered in the temple of Rudra with devotion. By observing this vrata she will attain the body of Bhavānī and rejoice with Bhava. In every month it is meritorious to have the holy rite with one meal a day. Thus, the holy rites beginning with the month of Mārgaśīrṣa and, ending with Kārttika have been observed. O excellent sages, they are for the benefit of all creatures, men or women. The devoted man will attain Sāyujya with Śiva by performing the vrata and the devoted woman will attain Sāyujya with the goddess. There is no doubt that this has been so ordained by Śiva.

CHAPTER EIGHTYFIVE

The glory of the five-syllabled Mantra

Sūta said:

1. O excellent brahmins, in all these holy rites, after worshipping the lord of Devas, the consort of Umā, the devotee shall repeat the five-syllabled[749] Mantra duly.

2. There is no doubt about this that the vratas are duly concluded only with the japa and not otherwise. Hence, one shall repeat the meritorious five-syllabled Mantra.

The sages said:

3. O highly blessed one, how is this five-syllabled Mantra? How is it powerful? Tell us. We are eager to hear the methods and means for its japa.

Sūta said:

4. I shall succinctly recount the holy things, formerly recounted to Pārvatī, by lord Rudra, the lord of Devas.

The goddess said:

5. O lord, O Maheśvara of all the worlds, O lord of the chiefs of Devas, I wish to hear factually the glory of the five-syllabled Mantra.

The lord said:

6. O gentle lady, even in hundreds and crores of years, it is not possible to recount the glory of the five-syllabled Mantra. Hence, listen to it in brief.

7-8. At the advent of dissolution[750] when the mobile and immobile beings, Devas and Asuras, serpents and Rākṣasas, all are destroyed and when everything dissolves into Prakṛti along with you also,[751] O gentle lady, only I do survive. There is no second being anywhere.

749. pañcākṣarīṁ vidyām. The five-syllabled mantra of Śiva is 'namaḥ śivāya.'

750. pralaya—dissolution of the universe at the end of a kalpa.

751. During the period of dissolution and re-creation, Prakṛti remains hidden in the body of Śiva. It again becomes manifest at the beginning of creation. Thus, the supreme lord Śiva alone is eternal and the abode of all beings, mobile and immobile.

9. At that time the Vedas and Scriptures are stationed in the five-syllabled Mantra. They do not attain destruction. They are protected by my power.

10-11. I am then present in two forms: Prakṛti and Ātman. Lord Nārāyaṇa adopts the body of Prakṛti and lies on the yogic couch in the midst of water. The five-faced Brahmā is born of his umbilical lotus.

12. Brahmā was desirous of creating the three worlds. Being incompetent for it without a helping hand, he, at the outset, created ten mental sons[752] of unmeasured splendour.

13. Brahmā requested me to grant power to create. He said: "O Mahādeva, O Maheśvara, grant power unto my sons."

14. Thus requested by him I with five faces[753] uttered the five syllables to Brahmā.

15. Brahmā, the grandfather of the worlds grasped them through his five faces[753a]. He understood Parameśvara in the form of the Being expressed by the term of expression.

16. O gentle lady, Śiva who is worshipped by the three worlds is the Being expressed by the five syllables. The great five-syllabled Mantra itself is his expression.

17. After understanding properly the procedure (for japa) and attaining Siddhi (by japa), the noble-souled five-faced deity (Brahmā) imparted to his sons the five-syllabled Mantra that was meaningful and conducive to the welfare of the universe.

18. After receiving the jewel among the Mantras directly from the grandfather of the worlds they propitiated lord Śiva the greater Being than the greatest.

19. Then lord Śiva who is greater than the three deities[754]

752. daśa mānasān putrān. Their names are : Marīci, Atri, Aṅgiras, Pulastya, Pulaha, Kratu, Pracetas, Vasiṣṭha, Bhṛgu and Nārada. Their distinctive features are brought out in many a legend related of them in the Purāṇas.

753. five heads of Śiva : See p. 49 note 65.

753a. five heads of Brahmā : When the four heads of Brahmā became thwarted in their functions because of Brahmā's erotic impulse, then out of *tapas* was produced a fifth head on the top, and that head was covered with matted locks. But later on, this head was clipped by Rudra. But against this statement, see ŚP. 1.8.8.

754. Cf. *Liṅga*. 1.71.51.

became delighted. He granted them the perfect knowledge and the eight attributes such as Aṇimā (minuteness) etc.[755]

20-24. After obtaining the boons, those brahmins, desirous of propitiating me went to the mountain Muñjavat,[756] on the beautiful peak of the Meru.[757] The glorious mountain is my favourite and is always protected by my Bhūtas. Eager in the creation of the worlds they performed severe penance for a thousand divine years near that mountain, living only on air. O gentle lady, those sages stood there for my blessings. On seeing their devotion I appeared before them immediately. With a desire for the welfare of the noble people of the worlds I told them everything about the five-syllabled Mantra, its sage, its metre, its deity, its Śakti, Bīja (seed), Nyāsa (fixation), on six Aṅgas (limbs), Digbandha (the binding of the quarters) and Viniyoga (application).

25. After hearing the glory of the Mantra, those sages whose assets were the austerities, performed activities by utilising the Mantra properly.

26-28. Thanks to its glory they created the worlds including Devas, Asuras and human beings, the different castes and their sub-divisions as well as the splendid holy rites. They heard the Vedas as before and as descended from the previous kalpas. It is due to the prowess of the five-syllabled Mantra that all these survive, viz.—the worlds, the Vedas, the pious sages, the permanent holy rites, Devas and the entire universe. Therefore, I shall mention it now to you. Listen to everything attentively.

29. This Mantra has Śiva for its Ātman. It consists of few letters but is full of great meanings. It is the essence of the Vedas. It yields liberation. It is undoubtedly proficient in commanding.

30. This is my valuable statement, accompanied by different kinds of realisation; it is pleasing to the minds of the people of this world and the divine beings; its meaning is decisive and it is majestic.

755. See p. 134 note 241.

756. Muñjavān : a peak of the mountain Meru, well known for Soma production. It is also mentioned in the *Ṛgveda* as Mūjavata.

757. Meru, see p. 98 note 127.

31. It is a Mantra that can be easily uttered by the mouth; it achieves all objects; it is the seed of all Vidyās; it is the first splendid Mantra.

32. It is very subtle and its meaning is great; it is like the seed of the holy banyan tree. It is the Veda that is beyond the three Guṇas; it is the omniscient lord doing everything.

33-34. The "Om" is the single-syllabled Mantra. The all-pervading Śiva is stationed in it. The five syllables constitute his body. He is stationed in the six-syllabled subtle Mantra in the form of the "expressed and the expression." Śiva is Vācya (the expressed) since he is comprehensible. The Mantra is his Vācaka (expression).

35-36. The relation of the expressed and the expression is a primordial one between the two. In the Vedas and in Śivāgamas the main Mantra is the six-syllabled one but for purpose of secular activities it is the five-syllabled Mantra.[758] Why should he have many Mantras and extensive scriptures?

37. If anyone has retained this Mantra in his heart he has studied the Vedas, he has heard the sacred lore; he has performed everything.

38. If a scholar performs its japa after learning the Vedas in accordance with the injunctions it is enough; the perfect knowledge of Śiva is this much; the greatest goal is thus far.

39-41a. Brahmavidyā (learning pertaining to the Brahman) is this much. Hence, the learned man shall continuously perform its japa. This Mantra consisting of the Praṇava and the five syllables is my heart, it is the greatest esoteric secret greater than all else; it is the excellent knowledge leading to salvation. I shall mention the sage, the metre and the deity controlling this Mantra, its Bīja, Śakti, Svara (vowel), Varṇa (letter), Sthāna (place of origin), letter by letter.

41b-43. The sage is Vāmadeva; the metre is Paṅkti. I, Śiva alone, am the deity of this Mantra, O lady of excellent face. The syllables "na" etc. are the Bījas; they are in the form of the five elements; know that the Praṇava is the unchanging Ātman that is all-pervasive, you alone are its Śakti, O goddess bowed to by all Devas.

758. The five-syllabled mantra of Śiva prefixed by om : "Om namaś Śivāya".

44. Something is your Praṇava and something is my Praṇava. O gentle lady, your Praṇava is undoubtedly the Śakti, of all the Mantras.

45-46. The letters 'a', 'u' and 'm' are present in my Praṇava, the letters *u*, *m* and *ā* constitute in order your Praṇava, which has three Mātrās and the Pluta tone (prolated vowel). The Svara (Note) of Oṁkāra is Udātta (high), the sage is Brahmā and the body is white.

47-54. The metre is Daivī Gāyatrī and the great Ātman is the presiding deity; the first, second and fourth letters are Udātta (high). The fifth is Svarita (neither high nor low), the middle one is Niṣāda.

The letter *n* is of yellow colour, its place of origin is the eastern face. Indra is the deity, Gāyatrī the metre and Gautama the sage.

The letter *maḥ* is of black colour, its place of origin is the southern face, the metre is Anuṣṭup, the sage is Atri, Rudra is the deity.

The letter *Śi* is of smoky colour; its place of origin is the western face; the sage is Viśvāmitra, the metre is Triṣṭup and the deity is Viṣṇu.

The letter *vā* is of golden colour, its place of origin is the northern face; Brahmā is the deity, Bṛhatī is the metre and Aṅgiras the sage.

The letter *ya* is of red colour; its place of origin is the upward face; the metre is Virāṭ; the sage is Bharadvāja and Skanda is the Deity.

I shall now mention the Nyāsa (fixing rite) that is auspicious and conducive to the achievement of all Siddhis. It is destructive of all sins too. Nyāsa is of three types; the difference being due to their connection with creation, sustenance and dissolution.

55-59. These Nyāsas belong respectively to the religious students, the householders and ascetics, i.e., the Nyāsa of Utpatti (creation) is for the religious student; the Nyāsa of Sthiti (sustenance) is for the householders and the Nyāsa of Saṁhṛti (dissolution) is for the ascetics; otherwise Siddhi cannot be achieved. The Nyāsa is of three types viz., Aṅganyāsa (the fixation of the limbs); Karanyāsa (that of the hand) and

Dehanyāsa (that of the body). O lady of splendid face, the Nyāsa of the three types relating to creation, etc. is being mentioned to you. One shall at the outset perform the Nyāsa of the hand; thereafter he shall perform the Nyāsa of the body and thereafter he shall perform the Nyāsa of Aṅgas (limbs) in the order of the syllables of the mantra. The fixation beginning with the head and ending with the feet is called the Utpattinyāsa. O beloved one, that beginning with the feet and ending with the head is the Nyāsa of Saṁhāra (dissolution). The Nyāsa of the heart, face and throat is Sthitinyāsa (that of sustenance).

60-65. O splendid lady, these Nyāsas relate to the religious students, householders and the ascetics respectively. Repeating the Mantras one shall touch the body along with the bead. That is common to all householders, religious students and ascetics.

Beginning with the thumb of the right hand and ending with the thumb of the left, if the fingers are fixed it is called Utpattinyāsa (the Nyāsa of creation). Its opposite is that of dissolution. Fixing the Nyāsa beginning with the thumb and ending with the little finger in both the hands is called Sthitinyāsa (that of sustenance). O gentle lady, it yields much pleasure to the householders. This is the common procedure—the Nyāsa of the hand is performed at first, then the Nyāsa of the body and thereafter one shall perform the Nyāsa of the limbs. Then the devotee shall perform the Nyāsa over all the limbs and then one by one with the full Mantra with Oṁkāra prefixed and suffixed[759] on all the ten fingers of the hands. The devotee shall perform the Nyāsa rite facing the east or the north after first washing the feet. He shall be clean and attentive.

66-72. At the outset he shall remember the sage, metre, deity, Bīja, Śakti, Ātman and preceptor, O lady of splendid face. Repeating the Mantra, he shall wipe off the hands and fix the Praṇava in the palms and in the first and last knots in all the fingers. He shall fix the Bījas along with the Bindus in the five middle knots. In accordance with the order of the

759. The five-syllabled mantra of Śiva prefixed and suffixed by om : "Om namaś śivāya om".

stages of life he shall perform the Nyāsa of creation, etc. with both hands and beginning with the foot and ending with the head. Repeating the Mantra with Oṁkāra affixed he shall touch the body (1) on the head, face, neck, heart and in the private parts; and, on the two feet; (2) in the private parts and in the heart and in the neck in the middle of the face and on the head or (3) he shall fix in the heart, in the private parts, on the feet, on the head, in the face, and in the neck—he shall fix with the Praṇava, etc. in three ways.

73-76. After fixing the limbs thus, the devotee shall meditate upon the faces (of Śiva). Beginning with the face in the east and ending with the face upward he shall fix the syllables beginning with *na* in due order. Thereafter he shall perform the Nyāsa rite of the six limbs in the respective places with delight. The Nyāsa shall be accompanied with the words Namas (obeisance), Svāhā, Vaṣaṭ, Hum, Vauṣaṭ and Phaṭ. The Praṇava is known as the heart; the syllable *na* the head; the syllable *ma* the tuft; the syllable "*Śi*" the coat of mail; the syllable "*vā*" the eye; the syllable "*ya*" the "Astra" (missile). After fixing the letters on the limbs as mentioned the devotee shall bind the quarters.

77-78. The deities of the four corners beginning with the south-east, are respectively Vighneśa, the mother Durgā and Kṣetrajña (?). The devotee shall fix them with the tip of the thumb fixed on that of the index finger with a beaming face. After saying "Protect ye all" he shall make obeisance to them severally.

79-80. The expert devotee shall perform the Nyāsa of the hand on the fingers beginning with the index finger with his thumb. He shall perform the Nyāsa on the middle of the neck also. This Nyāsa rite is said to be splendid and destructive of sins. It is conducive to the achievement of Siddhis. It is holy, auspicious and affords all protection.

81. When the Nyāsa rite has been performed by means of the splendid Mantra the devotee shall be on a par with Śiva, Within a moment, all the sins committed in the previous births are destroyed.

82. The intelligent devotee shall be pure in body by performing this Nyāsa rite. Steady in the performance of holy rite

he shall repeat the five-syllabled Mantra after acquiring the same gracefully from a preceptor.

83-85. O splendid lady, henceforth, I shall recount the procedure for acquiring the Mantra. Without it the Mantra is futile and with it, it is efficacious. The futile ones are the following:—Ājñāhīna (i.e. Mantra acquired without permission), Kriyāhīna (devoid of holy rites), Śraddhāhīna (devoid of faith), Amānasa (non-mental i.e. if the devotee does not devote full attention), Anājñaptam (that which has been prohibited), Dakṣināhīnam (permitted but devoid of gifts) and Sadājapta (indiscriminately repeated always).

The following Mantras are fruitful—Ājñāsiddha (achieved with permission), Kriyāsiddha (attended with rituals), Śraddhāsiddha (fully equipped with faith), Sumānasa (where the mind fully dwells) and Dakṣiṇāṣiddha (attended with gifts).

86-91. The devotee shall approach the brahmin preceptor who is conversant with the real meaning of the Mantra, who has perfect knowledge who is interested in the path of meditation and who is endowed with good qualities : With emotional purity the devotee shall assiduously propitiate him mentally, verbally, physically and monetarily. The disciple shall always worship the preceptor with all attention. If he is sufficiently affluent the disciple shall give these things devoutly to the preceptor:—elephants, horses, chariots, jewels, fields, houses, ornaments, clothes, and different kinds of grains. If he wishes for his Siddhi he shall not be stingy in spending money. O gentle lady, thereafter he shall dedicate himself along with his possessions and attendants. After worshipping thus in accordance with his capacity and not at all attempting deception, the disciple shall grasp the mantra and perfect knowledge from the preceptor, gradually.

92-95. Thus propitiated, the preceptor shall make the disciple take his bath after testing him thus. The disciple shall stay with him for a year and serve him. He shall be pure and devoid of egotism. He shall become emaciated due to constant fasts. The preceptor shall then bless the disciple with the excellent perfect knowledge of Śiva in a holy place at an auspicious hour. The place may be the shore of the sea or the bank of a river, the cowpen or a temple, or a clean place in the house itself. The time shall be a Tithi conducive to the fulfilment of desires; the constellation and the junction of planets shall be auspicious. It shall be devoid of defects in every respect. Even in the isolated place the preceptor shall utter the mantra loudly and legibly with a delighted mind.

96. The preceptor shall utter himself and make the disciple utter after him. He shall then bestow Siddhi (on the disciple) saying—"May there be auspiciousness. May it be splendid. May it be pleasing".

97. After acquiring the great Mantra and perfect knowledge from the preceptor the disciple shall repeat it every day with the due Saṁkalpa. He shall perform Puraścaraṇa too.

98-99. As long as he lives, he shall repeat this a thousand and eight times every day. Without repeating it, he shall not take food. Thus interested in it he attains the greatest goal. He who repeats this Mantra a hundred thousand times for each syllable and then repeats it four times with great attention is known as one who has made a Puraścaraṇa. He shall take food only at night. He shall be self-controlled.

100. A person who seeks for Siddhi, ere long, shall be one of these two:—either a Puraścaraṇa repeater or daily repeater.

101. If a devotee performs Puraścaraṇa and continues to be a daily repeater too, there is no one else in the world who is equally accomplished, self-controlled and competent to bestow Siddhis.

102-103. Sitting in a comfortable posture he shall be silent with his mind fully concentrated. He may sit facing the east or the north and then repeat the excellent Mantra. At the beginning of the japa and at its conclusion he shall restrain his breath. In the end, he shall repeat the excellent Bīja mantra a hundred and eight times in all.

104-105. The devotee shall restrain the breath forty times and repeat the mantra. Thus the Prāṇāyāma for the five-syllabled Mantra has been cited. Thanks to Prāṇāyāma, his sins will be destroyed soon and the sense-organs shall become controlled. Hence, one shall practise Prāṇāyāma.

106. It should be known that the japa performed in the house has ordinary benefit; that performed in the cowpen shall be hundred times more efficacious; if it is on the banks of a

river it is hundred thousand times more efficacious; if it is in the presence of Śiva it is endless.

107. The japa performed on the seashore in a divine pond, on a mountain, in a temple and in a sacred hermitage has crore times the benefit.

108. The rite of japa is commended if it is in the presence of Śiva or in front of the sun, the preceptor, the lamp, cow or water.

109-111. O lady of auspicious face, if the number of the repetitions is reckoned on the fingers it has the ordinary benefit; if lines are drawn and the number is calculated the benefit is said to be eight times more; if it is reckoned by means of the fruits of Putrajīva it has ten times more benefit; if it is calculated by means of conches and jewels the benefit is hundred times more; through coral the benefit a thousand times more; it is ten thousand times more, if the reckoning is through crystals; it is hundred thousand times more if the calculation is by pearls; it is one million times more if the calculation is by lotus-seeds; if it is calculated by gold pieces the benefit is ten million times more. The benefit is infinite if the calculation is by knots of Kuśa grass or Rudrākṣa beads.

112-115. The necklace of twenty-five Rudrākṣa beads is conducive to salvation; that of twenty-seven is nourishing, that of thirty is conducive to the achievement of wealth and that of fifty pertains to black magic.

If the devotee faces the east and performs the japa it is Vaśya (i.e. he will be able to attract others); facing the south pertains to Abhicāra; facing the west bestows wealth and facing the north is conducive to quiescence.

One should know that the thumb bestows liberation; the index finger destroys enemies; the middle finger yields wealth; the ring finger causes quiescence. O splendid lady, in the rite of japa the little finger bestows protection. The devotee shall perform japa with the thumb coming into contact with other fingers.

116. Any holy rite performed without the thumb is fruitless. Listen. The japayajña excels all other sacrifices.

117-118. All the ritualistic sacrifices, charitable gifts and austerities do not merit even a sixteenth fraction of the japayajña. The other yajñas are attended with violence or killing but japayajña has nothing to do with violence. Now the greatness of only the Vācika (i.e. chanting with audible voice) japayajña has been glorified.

119-122. The Upāṁśu (mumbling) is hundred times more efficacious than verbal and the Mānasa (mental) is thousand times more efficacious than mumbling.

If one utters the mantra clearly with highly accented or lowly accented tones or without either, that japayajña is called Vācika (verbal). If one utters the mantra with a low tone, making the lips throb slightly and making only some sounds audible, that Japa is called Upāṁśu (mumbling). If the devotee ponders over the meaning of the words letter by letter and proceeds ahead with the series of syllables that japa is called Mānasa (mental). Of the three japayajñas the latter one excels the earlier one.

123-127. The quality of the benefit varies according to the mode of yajña. If the deity is eulogised continuously by japa it becomes pleased and on being pleased it shall bestow extensive pleasures and permanent liberation. Neither the yakṣas nor the Rākṣasas, neither the Piśācas nor the terrible and evil planets even approach the person doing the japa. They are frightened all round. One shall entirely suppress by means of japa all the sins committed in a number of previous births. One wins worldly pleasures, Siddhis and liberation and also conquers death by means of japa.

After thus acquiring perfect knowledge pertaining to Śiva and after understanding the procedure for the japa the devotee shall abide by good conduct. Continuously meditating thus, he attains welfare.

I shall now mention sadācāra (good conduct) that is the perfect means of Dharma (virtue).

128. Since performance devoid of good conduct shall be fruitless good conduct is the greatest virtue, the greatest penance.

129. Good conduct is the greatest learning. Good conduct is the greatest goal. Men of good conduct shall be fearless everywhere.

130-133. Similarly men devoid of good conduct shall meet with fear everywhere.

O lady of excellent face, people attain Deva-hood and sage-hood by observing good conduct. Similarly, by transgressing good conduct they attain birth in lower and base state of society. A person who has eschewed good conduct becomes despicable. Hence, one who seeks perfect accomplishment shall scrupulously cling to the good conduct. One who is wicked in conduct and activity is sinful. He is mostly unclean. He defiles perfect knowledge.

Hence, one shall assiduously perform the holy rites prescribed for respective castes and stages in life.

134-140. One who performs the rites laid down for him is always my favourite. In the evening and in the morning he shall practise worship with a delighted mind. He shall begin the rite, clean in mind and body before sunrise and before sunset and perform it duly. A brahmin shall not transgress Sandhyā due to lust, delusion, fear or covetousness. Since by giving up Sandhyā prayers, the brahmin falls off from the status of brahminhood.

One shall not tell lies. Nor shall one eschew truth. They say that truth is Brahman. Hence, untruth defiles the Brahman. These are all causes of sins:—viz, untruth, harshness (in speech), stubbornness and back-biting, Not even mentally, verbally or physically shall one violate others' wives, or take away others' wealth or injure others.

One shall eschew the cooked rice of a Śūdra, the cooked rice that is stale, the Naivedya offering, the Śrāddha (partaking of food therein), the cooked rice for the masses and at social functions or served as the doles by the king. The purity of the character is based on the purity of food and not by means of clay or water. One can attain Siddhi only when there is purity of character. Hence, he should be scrupulous about the food he takes.

141. Even those brahmins who are the expounders of Brahman are defiled by accepting gifts from their patrons, kings, etc. There is no rebirth unto those who are defiled by taking gifts, as unto the seeds that are heated in fire.

142. Gift from kings is sinful. It is comparable to poison. After realising this at the outset it shall be avoided by a learned man as he shall avoid the flesh of a dog.

143. One shall not take food without taking bath, or performing japa or worshipping the fire. One shall not take food on the outer side of a leaf. At night one shall not take food without a lamp.

144-145. One shall never take food in a broken pot, in the open street, and in the presence of fallen people. One shall not take food partly consumed by a Śūdra nor shall one take cooked rice along with infants. One shall take in only pure food which is unctuous, emollient, consecrated and inspired with mantras. While taking food one shall remember that it is Śiva who eats. He shall keep silent and concentrated.

146. One shall not drink water, sipping standing, through folded hands, nor with the left hand or seated on a bed even with the right hand.

147. One shall not resort to the shade of Vibhītaka,[760] Arka,[761] Karañja[762] and Snuhi[763] trees, nor shall one stand in the shadow of a pillar, lamp post, human beings and other animals.

148. One shall not go on a long journey by oneself nor cross a river with one's hands; one shall never descend into a well nor climb tall trees.

149. O splendid lady, one shall never perform religious actions, japas and other holy rites with the face turned away from the sun, fire, water, Devas and the preceptors.

150. One shall not warm one's feet over the fire; one shall not touch the hand by means of legs; one shall not occupy a lofty place above the fire; one shall never cast impurities or ordure into the fire.

151. One shall never kick the water with the feet; one shall never cast the dirt of the limbs into the water. After washing the dirt on the banks one shall take one's bath.

152. The water shaken off from the tip of the nail or hairs, from the garments after bath and from the water pot, is conducive to misfortune. If one touches it, it is impure.

153. If a man of deluded mind touches husks and dust particles licked up and raised by a goat, dog, donkey,

760. Vibhītaka—the tree Terminalia Bellerica.

761. Arka—the plant Calotropis Gigantea.

762. Kārañja—pertaining to the Karañja tree Pongamia Glabra.

763. Snuhi—the milk-hedge plant.

of camel or swept off by a broom it will destroy fortune even if it belongs to Viṣṇu.

154-158. A man who keeps a cat in his house is on a par with a low caste person. If a man feeds leading brahmins in the presence of a cat it shall be considered to be similar to the act of a Cāṇḍāla. No doubt need be entertained in this respect. The wind from the buttocks, the wind from the winnowing basket, the wind coming out of the mouths of animals, all these coming into contact with a person dispel his merits.

One shall never perform japa wearing a turban or a coat of mail. If one is naked or one has loosened the knots of hairs, or is dirty or is impure or has impure hands, he shall not perform japa. He shall not perform japa while conversing with others.

All these are inimical to japa, viz.—anger, arrogance, inebriation, thirst, lethargy, spitting, yawning, seeing a dog or a base man, slumber, and prattling. When these occur one shall look at the sun and get purified.

159-161. By the sun the following are meant. The sun, fire, moon, planets, stars and constellations—these are called luminaries. When anger, etc. occur one shall perform Ācamana or Prāṇāyāma and then continue the japa.

One shall not perform japa keeping the legs stretched. One shall not sit in the cock posture at the time of japa. Nor shall one be lying down, without sitting on a seat. The repeater of the mantras shall not perform japa in the open street, or in the presence of the Śūdras or in a ground smeared with blood, or sitting in a cot.

162-165. The devotee shall mentally think about the meaning of mantra. Seated on a cosy seat he shall perform japa perfectly. He shall have any of the following for a seat:—viz., a silk cloth, tiger skin, a cotton cloth, an upper cloth or a cotton quilt, a wooden plank or a palmyra leaf. The worship of the preceptor shall be performed in all the three Sandhyās by one who wishes for welfare. He who is the preceptor is also Śiva. He who is Śiva is the preceptor. As is Śiva so is the learning; as is the learning so is the preceptor. The knowledge about Śiva is obtained from the preceptor. The benefit accrues in accordance with devotion. O fair lady, indeed he (the preceptor) is identical with all Devas; he is identical with all Śaktis.

166-172. The disciple shall bear the behests of his preceptor on his head (i. e, he shall obey him) whether he is with or without good qualities. He who seeks welfare shall not transgress, even mentally, the behests of the preceptor. One who strictly conforms to the biddings of the preceptor attains the wealth of knowledge. Whatever he does in the presence of the preceptor shall be done with the permission of the preceptor viz.—going, standing, sleeping, eating, etc. Neither in front of the preceptor nor in the presence of the deity shall he be complacently seated as he pleases, since the preceptor is the lord himself and his house is the temple of the lord. If one comes into contact with sinners one will have downfall due to their sins. If one comes into contact with the preceptor one shall incur the benefit of his holy rites.

Just as a piece of gold eschews its impurities after coming into contact with fire so also a man eschews sins due to his contact with the preceptor.

Just as the ghee in a pot placed near fire becomes melted so also the sin of a person near the preceptor becomes dissolved. Just as the blazing fire burns ordure and lumber so also the contented preceptor burns sins by means of the power of his mantra.

173-179. Undoubtedly if the preceptor is satisfied, Brahmā, Viṣṇu, Rudra, Devas and sages are also satisfied and they bless him. One shall never infuriate the preceptor physically, mentally or verbally. By his wrath are burned the longevity, fortune, wisdom and good holy rites. The sacrifices of those who infuriate him are futile. His japas and other observances are also futile. No doubt need be entertained in this respect. One shall assiduously refrain from making any statement against the preceptor. If out of great delusion he speaks it out, he will fall into Raurava hell. O fair lady, never should one falsely cheat the preceptor mentally, or verbally or physically or monetarily. If he proclaims the wicked qualities of his preceptor he will have hundred times that wickedness. If he proclaims the good qualities he will have the benefit of all good qualities. Whether directed or not, he shall always do what is beneficent and pleasing to the preceptor.

180-181. Whether within sight or out of sight of the preceptor, one shall do what is beneficent or pleasing to the preceptor. If he does anything against him mentally, physically or verbally, he goes down and revolves there itself. Hence, he should be worshipped and saluted always.

182-185. The disciple shall speak to the preceptor only after getting permission from him even when he is nearby. Otherwise he shall not look at him straight in the face. The disciple who adheres to all these rules, who is devout, who is perpetually engaged in japa and who does everything pleasing to his preceptor deserves to utilise the Mantra. I shall mention the application and the purpose of the Mantra that has been accomplished. If the devotee does not know the mode of application, the mantra becomes ineffective. That should be known as Viniyoga whereby the desired benefit is put in conjunction with the activity. It is the benefit of this world as well as of the next. The benefit arising out of Viniyoga is longevity, health, the permanence of the body [?] kingdom, royal glory, perfect knowledge, heaven and salvation.

186-193. The following rites shall be performed by repeating the five-syllabled Mantra eleven times:—Prokṣaṇa (ritualistic sprinkling with water); Abhiṣeka (ablution); Aghamarṣaṇa (praying for forgiveness for sins) and the two baths—one at dawn and one at day. The intelligent devotee shall be clean and after climbing the mountain shall alertfully repeat the mantra a hundred thousand times, or two hundred thousand times on the banks of a great river; he will attain long life. Ten thousand Homas with the following materials of worship are conducive to longevity viz:—The sprouts of the Dūrvā grass, gingelly seeds, Vāṇī (?), Gudūcī and Ghuṭikā (?). The wise devotee shall repeat the japa two hundred thousand times after resorting to the holy fig tree. By touching the Aśvattha tree on a Saturday the man obtains long life. The intelligent devotee shall touch the Aśvattha tree with both the hands on Saturdays and repeat the japa hundred and eight times. It will dispel premature death. Facing the sun and with the mind not dwelling on anything else the devotee shall repeat the japa a hundred thousand times. By performing hundred and eight Homas everyday with Arka twigs the devotee is liberated from ailments. For suppressing all ailments the man shall perform ten thousand sacrifices. By performing sacrifices the man shall be free from sickness. The devotee shall repeat the mantra hundred and eight times and shall drink water in the presence of the sun. Within a month he shall be liberated from the gastric trouble.

194-201a. One shall eat cooked rice and other foodstuffs and drink the beverages after inspiring the same with the mantra eleven times. Even if it were poison it shall become nectar. Everyday, in the forenoon, the devotee shall perform hundred and eight offerings to the fire, repeat the mantra a hundred thousand times and worship the sun. He shall attain perfect health. The devotee shall fill good pot with river water. Touching it he shall repeat the japa ten thousand times. If he bathes in that water it becomes an antidote for ailments. Everyday the pure devotee shall repeat the mantra twentyeight times and then take food or he shall perform Homa with Palāśa twigs. He will attain perfect health. During the days of lunar or solar eclipse the devotee shall be clean and observe fast at the outset. For the duration of eclipse he shall with great concentration repeat the mantra on the banks of a river flowing into a sea and after the eclipse is over he shall repeat the japa, thousand and eight times and drink the juice of Brahmī. He shall then attain in this world, good intellect capable of grasping all scriptures. His words shall be superhuman and similar to those of goddess Sarasvatī.

201b-202a. If afflicted by evil planets and stars the man shall repeat the japa devoutly ten thousand times. By performing a thousand and eight Homas, the affliction of the evil planets shall be dispelled.

202b-203a. On seeing evil dreams, the man shall take bath and repeat the japa ten thousand times. By performing hundred and eight Homas with ghee, there shall be immediate calmness.

203b-205a. During the solar and lunar eclipses the devotee shall duly worship the Liṅga. Whatever he may seek, O gentle lady, he shall perform ten thousand japas earnestly in the presence of the lord. He shall be clean and keep his mind restrained. Undoubtedly that person attains cherished desires.

205b-207a. At the advent of ailments of elephants, horses and of the kine in particular the man shall be clean and perform homa with twigs. He shall worship devoutly and duly repeat the mantra ten thousand times for a month. There will certainly be peace among them and they will flourish.

207b-208a. During uprisings and calamities as well as harassment from enemies the devotee shall be clean and perform ten thousand Homas with twigs of Palāśa. He will have peace; and disturbance, if any, will be suppressed.

208b-209a. O gentle lady, one shall perform this when there is harassment from black magic, when the power of that magic shall turn round and afflict the enemy.

209b-210. In order to create hatred the devotee shall perform eight Homas with Vibhītaka twigs or with wet blood repeating the syllables of the mantra backwards. If the devotee smears himself with blood and performs the Homa with poison it causes hatred among men.

211. I shall now recount the mode of expiation for the atonement of sins. Since the atonement of sins is the cause of enrichment in perfect knowledge, all the holy rites will be futile if sins are not properly atoned for.

212-215. Because knowledge dwindles, therefore sins must be properly atoned for. O auspicious lady, for the betterment of learning and fortune the devotee shall take handfuls of water and, meditating on me (Śiva) and repeating the mantra eleven times he shall perform ablution. For the eradication of the sin he shall take bath, repeating the mantra hundred and eight times. It has the same benefit as the pilgrimage to all holy centres. It is auspicious and it dispels all sins. If there is any break in the continuity in the Sandhyā prayers the man shall perform hundred and eight japas.

216. He shall not partake of the cooked rice touched and defiled by pigs, Cāṇḍālas, wicked people and cocks. If he eats it he shall repeat the japa hundred and eight times.

217. For the atonement of the sin of brahmin slaughter the man shall repeat the mantra thousand million times i.e. hundred crores. For the expiation of great sins he shall perform the japa to the extent of half that number. No doubt need be entertained in this respect.

218. It is ordained that in the case of those who are defiled by subsidiary sins, the japa shall extend to half that number. For the expiation of other sins one shall repeat the japa five thousand times.

219. The mantra has bearing on the knowledge of the Ātman. It is a secret and it illuminates the understanding of Śiva. He who repeats the mantra unexcitedly to the extent of five hundred thousand times shall become Śiva himself.

220-226a. Thereby, O gentle lady, the man attains an easy victory over the five vital airs. The devotee shall then restrain the sense organs with purity and repeat the japa five hundred thousand times. Thereby, O lady of excellent face, he will have victory over the five sense organs. The man who meditates well and who unexcitedly repeats the mantra five hundred thousand times attains victory over the five objects of senses. The man who devoutly repeats five hundred thousand times the mantra for the fourth time attains victory over the five elements. O lady of excellent face, he who assiduously restrains the mind and repeats the mantra four hundred thousand times attains mastery over the organs. O lotus-faced lady, by means of two million five hundred thousand japas the man attains victory over the twenty five principles. A man shall earnestly repeat the japa ten thousand times at midnight when the wind is at a standstill. O beautiful lady, he attains the Siddhi of the Brahman by means of this Vrata.

226b-228. The devotee shall, without lethargy, repeat the mantra a hundred thousand times in a place where the wind is still and where there is no sound at midnight. Undoubtedly he perceives both Śivā and Śiva. There shall be the destruction of darkness along with the bright illumination as of a lamp, both within the heart and without. The self-possessed man shall repeat the mantra ten thousand times for the achievement of all kinds of weather.

229. The devotee shall with purity and devotion repeat the mantra ten million times affixed with the Bījas. He shall attain Sāyujya with me. What else is greater than this?

230-231. Thus, the mode and procedure for chanting the five-syllabled Mantra has been recounted to you. He who reads this and listens to this, attains the greatest goal. He who narrates this mode of procedure of the japa of the five-syllabled mantra to pious brahmins at a divine rite or at the rite pertaining to the Pitṛs, is honoured in the world of Śiva.

CHAPTER EIGHTYSIX

The sacrifice of meditation

The sages said:

1. The brahmins who have destroyed their sins say that the meritorious sacrifice of meditation is better than japa for unattached and enlightened persons.

2. Hence, O Sūta, tell us today about the sacrifice of meditation suited for unattached noble souls in detail and with all effort.

3-4a. On hearing those words of the noble sages who had performed the sacrifice of long duration, Sūta recounted to them what Rudra of universal action[764] mentioned after neutralising the poison Kālakūṭa[765] and entering his cave.[766]

Sūta said:

4b-5. The sages of great discipline bowed down to Śiva who entered the cave and seated himself comfortably along with Bhavānī. All of them, then, eulogised Nīlakaṇṭha, the consort of Umā.

6. "O lord, O bull-bannered lord, the terrible poison Kālakūṭa has been neutralised by you. Hence everything has been stabilised by you."

7. On hearing their words, lord Nīlalohita, the Ātman of the Universe, smilingly said to those sages, Sanandana and others.

764. Viśva-karmaṇā—viśvaṁ karma yasya saḥ viśvakarmā tena, Rudreṇa *ST*. by Rudra of multifarious activities.

765. The poison Kālakūṭa or halāhala—a product of the churned ocean was swallowed by Śiva. The blue colour of his neck and his extreme ire are the effects of that poison.

766. guhā—i.e. Meru-guhā, the abode of Śiva.

8. "O excellent brahmins, of what consequence is this? I shall mention another more terrible poison. He who nullifies that poison is really efficient. Of what avail is this?

9. What is called Kālakūṭa is not at all poison when compared to worldly existence which is the real poison. Hence, with all efforts one shall try to dispel that terrible poison.

10-13. The mundane existence is two-fold[767] in accordance with one's rights and duties. In regard to men of deluded minds, the mundane existence is very terrible and burdensome. O sages of good holy rites, creation is caused by ignorance due to the defects of malice and attachment.[768] It is certainly due to these, that virtue and evil befall everyone. O brahmins, even in regard to things not near at hand,[769] the scripture creates desire for them even in the minds of good men in the world merely by hearing of it. Hence, the perceptible world and the world of Vedic tradition[770] and rituals both should be eschewed[771] with great effort. He then becomes Virakta (unattached person) altogether.

14. That portion of the Vedas which deals with rituals is called scripture, O brahmins. It is the principal essence of the Vedas. The benefit of the rites goes to the sages.[771a]

15. Those who do not know these things say:—"Desire is natural[772] in everyone. The opposite is not seen. It is the Veda that makes them work (for fulfilling such desires).

767. i.e. tāmasa and rājasa.

768. īṣaṇā—icchā *ST*. desire.
rāgaḥ—viṣaya-prītiḥ *ST*. attachment with the objects of senses.

769. asannikṛṣṭe—that which is beyond the scope of sense-perception.

770. dṛṣṭam—aihikam *ST*. pertaining to this world.
ānuśravikam—pāralaukikam *ST*. pertaining to the world beyond.

771. *ST*. disjoins 'ucyate bhāgam' as 'ucyate abhāgam' and construes with 'karmasu'. i.e. karmasu abhāgam—non-participation in activities. *ST*. interprets : here metaphysics (ādhyātma-śāstra) is considered to be superior to the Vedas.

771a. ṛṣīṇāṁ karmaṇaḥ phalam : here karmaṇaḥ—niṣkāma-karmaṇaḥ *ST*, i.e., participation in activities without the expectation of their fruits.

772. svabhāvaḥ—participation in activities is natural. The Vedas enjoin activities such as the performance of agniṣomīya. Cf. "agniṣomīyam paśum ālabheta svargakāmaḥ".

16. The virtue of renunciation from worldly affairs, is intended for efficient persons.[773] Hence, it is said that worldly existence is caused by ignorance of all embodied persons.

17-18a. The Digit is dried up due to Karman[774] or the nature of others (?). Individuals endowed with Kalās (?) are of three types.[775] They are devoid of perfect knowledge due to ignorance. The three types are (a) those destined to fall into hell because they commit sin; (b) those destined to go to heaven because they perform meritorious deeds and they go to heaven due to the weight of their merit and (c) a mixture of these two.

18b-19. The living beings are classified under four heads[776] viz:—Udbhijjas (germinating plants), Svedajas (born of sweat, i.e. germs and worms), Aṇḍajas (oviparous beings), and Jarāyuja (viviparous). Thus the ignorant embodied being does not get relief through Karman (?).

20. Salvation is not attained by good men through their progeny, through actions, or through wealth.[777] Liberation shall occur only through renunciation. He wanders in the world due to the absence of it (renunciation).

21. Thus due to the fault of ignorance and as a result of various Karmans, the individual soul adopts a body produced by six Kośas[778] (vestures).

22. Many miseries are to be faced by the individual in the womb, in the vaginal passage, on the earth, in boyhood, in youth, in old age and in death.

773. samarthānāṃ—viraktānām *ST.*

774. For those who are unattached activities are not unavoidable. Cf. "pravṛttir eṣā bhūtānām nivṛttistu mahābalā"—*Manu*; Or activities have no fixed goal. Cf. Bhāga. 'vedoktam eva kurvāṇo nissaṅgārpitamīśvare/ naiṣkarmyaṁ labhate siddhiṁ rocanārthā phalaśrutiḥ //

karmaṇā—niṣkāma-karmaṇā *ST.* by aimless activities. Life-seed (kalā=jīvanakalā *ST.*) becomes unproductive (śoṣam āyāti)—a fact that leads one to emancipation.

775. trividhaḥ jīvaḥ—the invidividual soul is threefold (See V-18 below).

776. caturdhā—in four ways. Cf. V-19 below.

777. Cf. *Supra* I.8.27.

778. ṣaṭ-kauśikam—snāyvādi-ṣaṭkośa-yuktam *ST.* consisting of six coverings Cf. पितृभ्यामशितादन्नात् षट्कोश जायते वपुः/स्नायवोऽस्थीनि मज्जा च जायन्ते पितृतस्तथा ।। त्वङ्मांसं शोणितमिति मातृतश्च भवन्ति हि ।

23. O brahmins, if duly pondered over, good men have to face only misery through the contact with women and similar activities. The miserable try to quell one misery only by another misery.

24. Lust is never quelled by means of enjoyment of pleasures. Just as fire blazes all the more by Havis (ghee offering) so also lust is inflamed all the more by indulging into pleasure.[779]

25-27. Hence, on pondering over, it will be seen that there is no happiness unto men even due to coitus. There is misery in earning wealth as also in preserving and spending it. O excellent brahmins, if we ponder over it, there is misery amongst the Piśācas, Rākṣasas, Yakṣas, Gandharvas, in the world of the moon, in the world of mercury, in the world of Prajāpati, in the world of the Brahman, in the world of Prakṛti and Puruṣa also. O sages of good holy rites, there are miseries due to destruction of possessions, due to one's possession being excelled by another's, etc. These cause only other miseries.

28-30. One shall eschew those impure fortunes and riches. Hence, O sinless sages of good holy rites, all kinds of pleasures are really miseries to the discriminating person in whatever way you view them, viz., eightfold or sixteenfold or of twentyfour, thirtytwo, fortyeight, fiftysix, or sixtyfour types.

31-32. The pleasures of the following types are undoubtedly miseries if pondered over properly even to those yogins who talk of Brahman:—Pārthiva (earthly), Āpya (watery) Taijasa (fiery), Vāyavya (gaseous), Vyauma (of the firmament), Mānasa (mental), Ābhimānika, (bringing pride), Bauddha[780] (intellectual), Prākṛta (pertaining to Prakṛti).

33-37. The attributes (?) of the leaders of the Gaṇas are, on reflection, causes of misery. In all the worlds there is always misery in the beginning, in the middle and in the end. The present ones are miseries, the future ones are miseries. (?) In the lands defiled by faults, there are various kinds af miseries.

779. Repeated I. 8. 25; 67, 16.

780. baudḍham prākṛtam eva ca : the intellectual enjoyment is also material.

(?) Those who consider ignorance as knowledge do not consider the past events. (?) Just as the medicine is used to dispel ailments and not for positive pleasure so also the food taken in is intended for dispelling the sickness of hunger and not for any positive happiness. In the different seasons. the embodied beings undergo miseries through chillness, heat, wind rains, etc. There is no doubt about it; but the ignorant do not consider it that way. O excellent sages, even in the heaven the same thing happens through the destruction, etc. of the merit.[781]

38. Just as the tree whose roots have been cut falls down to the ground helplessly so also the living being overwhelmed by various kinds of ailments, passion, hatred, fear, etc.[782]

39-41. Similarly the heaven-dwellers fall down to the earth due to the destruction of the tree of merit. Even for heaven-dwellers who desire for things that cause misery and who are richly endowed with pleasures that cause misery, there is terrible misery when they fall from that heaven. There is definitely misery in the hell due to the fact that even religious students resort to it when they do not perform those rites that are laid down, O leading sages.

42. Just as the deer frightened of death and uprooted from his habitation does not obtain sleep so also the noble-souled ascetic engaged in meditation and frightened of the worldly existence does not obtain slumber.

43. Unhappiness is seen even in germs, birds, animals, deer, elephants and horses. Hence there is great happiness unto a man who renounces.

44. O sages of good holy rites, there is misery unto even those officers on duty spread over the whole kalpa who move about in aerial chariots, unto Manu and others who take pride in their respective positions.

781. The activities enjoined for the attainment of heaven are not without impurities. For instance, the agniṣomīya sacrifice leads to heaven, but it is attended by violence (*hiṁsā*)—the slaughter of the animal (Cf. agniṣomīyam paśum ālabheta) for which the performer of sacrifice suffers pain (Cf. Īśvarakṛṣṇa—dṛṣṭavadānuśravikaḥ sa hy aviśuddhi-kṣayātiśaya-yuktaḥ—*SK.*); secondly, heaven is not a permanent abode (Cf. V. 88 below).

782. As soon as he has exhausted merit the heaven-dweller falls from heaven. Cf. "क्षीणे पुण्ये मर्त्यलोकं विशन्ति।"

45. Devas and Daityas undergo misery due to their desire for mutual conquest. Even kings and Rākṣasas in the three worlds undergo misery.

46-48. In fact the Āśramas bring about only misery or exhaustion (śrama) unto the different castes. People do not attain the Ātman through Āśramas (stages in life), Vedas, yajñas, Sāṁkhyas, (numerical knowledge), vratas (holy rites), severe penances, different kinds of charitable gifts, etc. But people with knowledge obtain it. Hence, with all efforts one shall perform the Pāśupata rite. In the holy rite of Pāśupata, the learned devotee shall perpetually lie on bhasman, besmeared with ashes.

49-50. The learned devotee, richly endowed with the knowledge of the five objects and having great attention towards the principle of Śiva shall adopt the yoga that causes salvation and destroys fate and karman and shall become intelligent and endowed with the yoga of five objects.[783] Thereby he attains the end of misery. The devotees understand the knowable by means of Parā Vidyā[784] and not by Aparā Vidyā.[785]

51-54. Two Vidyās (topics of knowledge) are to be known: Parā and Aparā, O excellent brahmins, Aparā consists of Ṛg, Yajur, Sāma, and Atharva Vedas. Sikṣā, Kalpa, grammar, semantics, prosody and astrology also constitute Aparā Vidyā.

What is imperishable is the Parā. It is imperceptible, incomprehensible. It has no spiritual lineage, no caste, no colour, no eyes, no ears, no hands and no feet. O excellent brahmins, it is not born. It has no past. It is not describable by words.

55-58. It has no touch, no form, no taste, no smell, no change, no support. It is perpetual, omnipresent and all-powerful. It it great and massive. O brahmins, it is unborn and identical with cit (consciousness); it is devoid of Prāṇas (vital airs); it has no mind; it is non-emollient and it is devoid of blood. It is incomprehensible; it is neither stout nor long; it is

783. pañcārtha-yoga-sampannaḥ—It can be interpreted as 'accompanied by knowledge derived from the practice of the five-syllabled mantra 'namaś śivāya'.

784. parā vidyā—knowledge of Brahma as taught in the *Upaniṣads*.

785. aparā vidyā—knowledge of the ritual as taught in the *Śrauta* and *Gṛhya Sūtras*.

not excessively clear; it is not short; it is impassable; it is bliss; it is unswerving; not open; without a second; infinite; not perceivable, and not covered; Parā is identical with the Ātman[786] and not otherwise.

59. But these Parā and Aparā are not the real. I alone am identical with the universe; the universe is in me alone.

60-61. Everything originates from me, stays within me and gets dissolved in me; there is nothing different from me. This shall be realised mentally, verbally and physically. The devotee shall with concentration see everything: the 'sat' (the existent) and the 'asat' (the non-existent), in the Ātman. One seeing everything in the Ātman does not allow the mind to stray to other objects.

62. On lowering the vision, one shall see the Ātman stationed in Vitasti above the umbilicus in the heart, the abode of the universe.

63-64. In the middle of this heart is stationed the lotus[787] with dharma for its bulbous root and knowledge for its splendid stalk. The eight accomplishments are its eight petals; vairāgya (detachment) is its white pericarp; the quarters are its pores filled with the vital airs.

65-71. It sees mostly and in due order on being united with Prāṇa, etc. O leading sages, each of the veins (Nāḍīs) carries the ten Prāṇas (vital airs). Altogether there are seventy-two thousand Nāḍīs. The Jagrat (waking stage) is stationed in the eyes, the svapna (dream stage) in the neck; the suṣupta (sleeping stage) in the heart and turīya (the fourth above the three) in the head. The presiding deity in the jāgrat state is brahmā; in Svapna Viṣṇu; Īśvara in Suṣupta and in Turīya Maheśvara. Others say as follows:—when the person is in full possession of his senses and organs it is called Jāgrat; when only the four organs, mind, intellect, ego and citta function, it is Svapna. O sages of good holy rites, when the organs and senses are merged into the Ātman

786. parā vidyā anyathā na—anya-prakāreṇa varṇitum aśakyā *ST*. Cf. "yato vāco nivartante."

The realization of Brahma cannot be described in words.

787. puṇḍarīkam—hṛtkamalam ST. the lotus-heart which is the abiding place of the mind.

it is Suṣupta. The fourth (Turīya) is different from the organs and senses. The greatest Śiva who is beyond the fourth is the prime cause.

72-79. The four states Jāgrat (wakefulness), Svapna (dream), Suṣupti (slumber) and Turīya (the fourth) have been mentioned. I shall now describe the Ādhibhautika, Ādhyātmika and Ādhidaivika terms, O leading brahmins. It should be known by the learned that all these are I myself. O great sages, the Ādhyātmika (organic) is said to be fourteen in all, viz., the sense organs (five), the organs of action (five) and the mind, intellect, ego, and will (four).

O excellent sages, the following constitute the Ādhibhautika (the extraneous matter), viz.—what should be seen, what should be heard, what should be smelt, what should be tested, what should be touched, what should be thought of, what should be understood, what should be taken pride in, what should be willed, what should be spoken, what should be grasped, what should be traversed, what should be evacuated and what should be enjoyed.

The following fourteen constitute the Ādhidaivika (the Divine factor), viz.—the sun, quarters, earth, Varuṇa (water), wind, Brahmā, Rudra, Kṣetrajña, Agni, Indra, Viṣṇu, moon, lord Mitra and Prajāpati.

80-81. The following are fourteen Nāḍīs (tubular vessels), viz.—Rājñī, Sudarśanā, Jitā, Saumyā, Moghā, Rudrā, Mṛtā, (Amṛtā), Satyā, Madhyamā, Nāḍīrā, Śiśukā, Asurā, Kṛttikā and Bhāsvatī.

82-87. There are fourteen carrying winds[788] stationed in the middle of Nāḍīs:—They are Prāṇa, Vyāna, Apāna, Udāna, Samāna, Vairambha, the important Antaryāma, Prabhañjana, Kūrmaka, Śyena, Śveta, Kṛṣṇa, Anila and Nāga.

I am the lord present in all these as the great Ātman and the devotees shall worship me. I am present, O sages of good holy rites, in the eyes, in what is to be seen, in the sun, in the Nāḍī, in the Prāṇa, (five types) in the Vijñāna, and in ānanda (bliss), in the heart, in the firmament, and within all these. I am the sole Ātman, moving within. The lord is ageless, infinite, devoid of sorrow, immortal and stable. He is the sole being

788. vāyavaśca caturdaśa—the fourteen vital airs stationed in the arteries.

moving amidst these fourteen types of objects. O brahmins, all these merge into him as there is nothing else.

88. The omniscient Being is only one. There is only one lord of all. He is the overlord of all. He is the immanent soul of great lustre.

89. On being worshipped, the eternal lord grants happiness. O excellent brahmins, if one does not worship him one does not attain happiness.[789]

90. He is being worshipped by the Vedas and other scriptures. But this omniscient lord does not go unto them for succour.

91. This visible universe is his Anna[790] (food). He does not become the Anna himself (unto anyone else). Nowhere does one devour Anna guarded by one's own self.

92. I am the food taken in by the living beings everywhere. I am the knot of the living beings and I bring about all great things. I am five-fold Ātman divided into several parts.

93. I am the soul of the living beings identical with Anna. What is taken in is called Anna. I am the soul of the sense-organs identical with Prāṇa (vital breaths). I am the soul of mental conceptions identical with the mind.

94. As Soma I am Kālātman (the soul of Time), identical with Vijñāna (perfect knowledge). As Maheśa Parameśvara I become identical with Ānanda (Bliss).[791]

95. Thus I am the entire universe and everything is stationed in me. I am independent but everything is dependent on me. This can be understood on pondering over the real form of various things.

96. Even the state of being one (i.e. ekatva) is not present

789. The lord stationed in the subtle body is the source of pleasure for others but he has no source of pleasure for himself.

790. The lord is the source of food for others but he has no source of food for himself. Cf. *Bhagavadgītā*:

अहं वैश्वानरो भूत्वा प्राणिनां देहमाश्रितः ।
प्राणापानसमायुक्तः पचाम्यन्नं चतुर्विधम् ।।

791. pañcakośa or pancakañcuka of Śaiva philosophy constitutes the five sheaths of the self-luminous lord. They are the products of āvaraṇa-śakti (power of concealment) of Māyā (lord's power of projection).

there[792] as a distinct attribute. Then, how can there be Dvaita (duality)? So also there is no mortal being. Whence can there be an immortal born of the unborn?

97. The Ātman is neither Antaḥprajña (having intellectual awareness within) nor Bahiḥprajña (having the intellectual awareness without) nor is He in both ways (Ubhayataḥprajña). He is not Prajñānaghana (solid in perfect knowledge) nor Prājña (wise being) nor Ajñānapūrvaka (having ignorance).

98-99. Brahman is not one that is known nor one to be known. In fact it is Nirvāṇa (extinction, Kaivalya, Niḥśreyasa. Anāmaya (devoid of ailments), Amṛta (immortal), Akṣara imperishable, Brahman, Parama Ātman, Parātpara (greater than the greatest), Nirvikalpa (devoid of doubtful alternatives), Nirābhāsa (devoid of fallacious appearances), Jñāna (knowledge); all these are synonyms (for perfect knowledge).

100. When it is pleased and concentrated in a single form it is known as Jñāna (Perfect knowledge). Everything else is Ajñāna (Ignorance). No doubt need be entertained in this regard.

101-104. Perfect clear knowledge certainly originates from contact with the preceptor. It is uncontaminated by lust, hatred, falsehood, anger, passion, covetousness and the like. It should be known as the bestower of salvation. Since the man has the impurity of ignorance he is contaminated. Salvation takes place only when impurity is dispelled and not otherwise, even if one takes a crore of births. Without perfect knowledge[793] neither merit nor demerit is destroyed. Hence, O most excellent ones among the knowers of the Brahman, practise knowledge alone as the means of liberation. It is only by practice of perfect knowledge that the intellect of men becomes free from impurities.

105-109. Hence, one shall always practise perfect knowledge having that as the foundation and the ultimate goal. O leading brahmins, a yogin who is satiated with knowledge

792. ekatvam api nāsti—The terms ekatva (singleness), etc., are relative and hence, they shall be avoided in regard to the exposition of Brahman.

793. Cf. "jñānād eva hi kaivalyam"—cited in *ST.*; also "ṛte jñānān na muktiḥ".

alone and who has eschewed all contacts with worldly objects has no further duty. If he has, he is no longer a knower of reality. Neither in this world nor in the other has he any duty,[794] since he is a liberated soul. Hence, the knower of Brahman is the knower of the reality of perfect knowledge and perpetually engaged in the practice of perfect knowledge. He eschews the practice of all duties. He obtains perfect knowledge alone. O excellent brahmins, if one who takes pride in his position in varṇāśrama (as Brāhmin, kṣatriya, etc.) takes pleasure in other things (other than Brahman) certainly he is deluded and ignorant, even though he might have discarded anger. Ignorance is the cause of worldly existence and adoption of physical bodies means worldly existence.

110-111. Similarly, Jñāna (perfect knowledge) is the cause of salvation. The liberated man abides in his own Ātman. O leading brahmins, there is no doubt about this that wrath etc., occur only when there is ignorance. Wrath, delight, covetousness, delusion, arrogance, virtue and evil, all these, O excellent brahmins, cause adoption of physical bodies.

112-114. There is distress and pain only when there is body. Hence, the learned shall eschew Avidyā (Ignorance, illusion). Only if the yogin eschews Avidyā by means of Vidyā do anger, virtue, evil etc. perish, O brahmins. If they perish the (Ātman) is not united further with the physical body. He is liberated from mundance existene. He is devoid of the three types of miseries.[795] Thus, O leading brahmins, the meditator cannot meditate without perfect knowledge.

115. Perfect knowledge is obtained by personal contact with the preceptor and not through words in fact. After realising the Caturvyūha[796] thus and after deep thinking, one shall practise meditation.

794. ātmānaṁ ced vijānīyād ahamasmīti pūruṣaḥ
kim japan kasya kāmāya śarīram anu saṁ jvaret
—*Pañcadaśī* VII. 1.

795. duḥkha-traya: threefold misery: (i) ādhyātmika, (ii) ādhibhautika, (iii) ādhidaivika; for detail, see Vācaspati's gloss on Īśvarakṛṣṇa's *Sāṁkhya-kārikā*, karikā I.

796. Caturvyūha—four categories of the supreme soul: taijasa, Viśva, Prājña and Turīya.

116. Like fire that burns the dry fuel quickly, the fire of knowledge burns sins whether inborn or extraneous or originating from bones and speech (i.e. physically and verbally).

117. There is nothing greater than perfect knowledge for the destruction of all sins. One shall always practise perfect knowledge after eschewing all attachment to worldly objects.

118. There is no doubt that all the sins of a Jñānin shall perish. Even if he indulges in dalliance he is not affected by sins.

119-120. As is knowledge so is meditation. Hence, one should practise meditation.[797] At the outset meditation is laid down as Saviṣaya (having an object) and then Nirviṣaya (having no object). The leading yogin shall practise meditation in six ways[798] as follows:—for the duration of two, four, six, ten, twelve and sixteen units of time in order. Certainly he shall be liberated.

121-125a. At the outset he meditates on a form as resplendent as pure gold[799] or like the burning coal without smoke, of yellow, red or white colour or having the lustre similar to that of a crore of lightning streaks.

Or[800] the meditator keeps his mind assiduously stationed in the Brahmarandhra (cerebral orifice). He shall remember that it (the object of meditation) is neither white nor black nor yellow. He shall thereby become the knower of Brahman.

He shall be non-violent, truthful in speech, and non-stealer. He shall by all means maintain celibacy and avoid gifts. He shall be stable in observing holy rites, contented richly endowed with cleanliness and always engaged in the study of the Vedas. He shall be devoted to me and practise meditation, of course, as instructed by the preceptor.

125b-127a. O excellent brahmins, after fixing his mind, the meditator does not know anything else. The yogin does not identify himself with anything else. He does not see all

797. In Śaiva system of thought, emphasis is laid upon knowledge and meditation. For detail, see *Śiva-rahasya*, section X.

798. For detail about the varieties of meditation, ibid, section X.

799. śuddha-jāmbūnada. The verse describes the form of the lord in the savikalpaka samādhi. Cf. munīnāṁ jñānadātrī ca sadaivopaniṣac chrutā kaivalya-śruti-bodhyā śrī mūrtir mama maheśvari—*Śiva-rahasya* cited in *ST*.

800. The verse describes the state of the mind in the stage of nirvikalpaka samādhi.

round nor smell nor hear anything. He has dissolved himself in his Ātman. He does not feel the touch of anything. He is then known as having acquired equal taste in everything.

127b-131a. He shall think in order thus[801] :—Brahmā in the mass of earth; Viṣṇu in the principle of water; Kālarudra in the principle of Fire; Maheśvara in the principle of Vāyu and Śiva in firmament. I am lord Paśupati, stationed in eight forms. In earth I am lord Śarva.[802] In waters lord Bhava; I am Rudra in fire; Ugra in wind; in firmament, I am Bhīma; in the sphere of Sun I am Īśāna and in lunar disc as Mahādeva.

131b-137. Everything firm and solid in body is spoken of as pertaining to the earth; what is liquid in form pertains to water; what is called colour belongs to Agni (fire); what moves about is Vāyu (wind). O excellent brahmins, what appears like a hole is the firmament.

O brahmins, perfect knowledge originating from sound is born of firmament; similarly, the knowledge of what is called "touch" originates from Vāyu; that of Rūpa (colour) from Vahni; O brahmins, what belongs to water is full of taste; and what is called "smell" belongs to the earth.

Again he shall meditate in order :—the sun in the right eye; the moon in the left eye; the lord in the heart; the principle of earth upto the knee; the sphere of water upto the umbilicus; the principle of fire upto the neck; the principle of wind upto the forehead. Beginning with the forehead and ending with the tuft is the principle called firmament; above the firmament and beyond that is the Brahman called Haṁsa. This first entity called Vyoman is stationed in the middle of firmament.

138-139. These principles including the first entity Jīva, Prakṛti, sattva, rajas, tamas, intellect, the ego, the subtle elements, the sense-organs, the elements beginning with ether are not real[803]. Because he stands steady pervading the universe he is called Sthāṇu.

801. The verse describes the method of pañcatattva-devatā-dhyāna in the savikalpaka samādhi.

802. This refers to the aṣṭa-mūrti-devatādhyāna.

803. na jīvaḥ –In fact, meditation, its varieties and ancillaries are all due to *māyā*—the lord's power of projection. Actually, meditation, meditator and the object meditated upon are all unreal, vide *Pañcadaśī* vi. 35.

140-142. It is at the behest of Bhava that the frightened sun rises,[804] the wind blows and purifies, the moon shines, the fire blazes, waters flow, the earth holds aloft and the firmament gives room. Hence, O brahmins, one shall think about all these. O excellent brahmins, all these are presided over by him alone. One shall remember Bhava, thinking that he is identical with all forms in the universe.

143. To those who are scorched by the poison of mundane existence, the only antidote is the nectar-like perfect knowledge and meditation. O excellent brahmins, no other solution has been laid down anywhere.

144. Perfect knowledge originates directly from Dharma (virtue). Vairāgya (detachment) originates from knowledge; from Vairāgya arises the supreme knowledge that illuminates the true meanings of objects.

145. O excellent brahmins, he who is endowed with knowledge and detachment attains Yogic Siddhi. One who abides by sattva guṇa attains liberation through yogic siddhi and not otherwise.

146. It is surprising that his unchanging region is covered by the words tamas and Avidyā. O brahmins, one should adopt Sattvaśakti (the power of Sattvaguṇa) and worship Śiva.

147-152a. My devotee abides by the sattva guṇa. He is engrossed in my worship. He clings to virtue in every respect. He is enthusiastic always. He is endowed with concentration. He is bold and endures all Dvandvas (mutually clashing pairs). He is engaged in the welfare of all living beings. He is straightforward by nature. He is continuously healthy and normal in his mind. He is always soft-natured. He is not arrogant. He is intelligent and quiescent. O excellent brahmins, he eschews rivalry. He is always desirous of liberation. He is conversant with virtue. He is marked with the characteristics of the supreme soul.[805] He is released from the threefold indebtedness in the previous birth and is meritorious. After becoming

804. udeti—Cf. bhiṣāsmād vātaḥ pavate *TA*.8.8.1; *TU*. 2.8.1; *Nṛp.U*. 2.4

805. ṛṇa-trayam—a man owes three debts, viz.—(i) brahmacarya 'or study of the Vedas,' to the ṛṣis; (ii) sacrifice and worship, to the gods; (iii) procreation of the son, to the manes.

an aged brahmin or even otherwise he shall serve his preceptor with sincerity[806] and avoid hypocritical attitudes. O brahmins, he reaches the heavenly world and enjoys pleasures in the proper order. Then gradually he comes to the sub-continent Bhārata and is born as a knower of Brahman.

152b-157. Thanks to the contact with a Jñānin (a man with perfect knowledge), he shall acquire perfect knowledge and become conversant with yoga. O excellent brahmins, this is the order in which one full of impurities attains perfect knowledge. Hence, O leading sages, he shall proceed along this path and be steady in his holy rite. Eschewing attachment with worldly objects he is liberated from the poison Kālakūṭa in the form of the worldly existence. Thus, succinctly, I have incidentally recounted to you the greatness of perfect knowledge that is splendid and unswerving.

O leading sages, this Pāśupata yoga mentioned by Īśvara, Śiva should not be given to anyone and everyone. It should be imparted gladly to a yogin who always clings to Bhasman. The man who reads this chapter on suppression of worldly existence or listens to it certainly attains Sāyujya with the Brahmna.

CHAPTER EIGHTYSEVEN

Suppression of delusion

Sūta said :

1. After hearing it, those sages of great intellect Sanat and others who were frightened, bowed to the Pināka-bearing lord Parameśvara who was pleased and spoke to him thus :

2. "If it is so, O Maheśvara, how do you sport about with the goddess, the daughter of the Himavān and enjoy various pleasures. It behoves you to mention this."

806. śraddhayā—with faithful devotion. Cf.
सन्तः सर्वात्मना सेव्या यद्यप्युपदिशन्ति न।
यास्तु स्वैरकथास्तेषामुपदेशा भवन्ति ते ॥—cited in *ST*.

Sūta said :

3. Thus requested, the Pināka-bearing lord, Nīlalohita laughingly glanced at Ambikā and spoke to those brahmins who stood by after bowing to him.

4-5. "I am one who can adopt any body as I choose. Hence, I have neither bondage nor liberation.[807] He who is not an agent is ignorant. The jīva is Paśu (one in bondage). The all-pervading Lord is the enjoyer. Man is only an atom. He who is bound by Māyā and disallusioned is the one who is entangled in Karmans. O brahmins, the Ātman has neither knowledge nor meditation, neither bondage nor liberation.

6-7. He too who realises this in me has none of these. This Haimavatī is Vidyā[808] and I am Vedya (one who should be known). She is Prajñā (intellect). She is Śruti and Smṛti. She is Dhṛti (fortitude) stabilized by me. She is the power of knowledge, Kriyā (rite); and Īcchā (will). She is Ājñā (Behest). Undoubtedly we are the two Vidyās.

8. This Prakṛti does not belong to the Jīva. Nor is she a Vikṛti on consideration. She is Māyā. She is not a Vikāra (effect). She is devoid of clarity of 'Sat' and 'Asat'.

9. Formerly she originated from my mouth at my behest. She is the eternal deity of five faces. She is the highly blessed and bestows fearlessness on the worlds.

10-11. After entering her the Ājñā (behest), I think about the welfare of the worlds. I am Śiva. I pervade all along with her in twenty-seven[809] forms. O excellent brahmins since then begins the work for salvation."

Sūta said :

After saying thus, Parameśvara looked at Bhavānī.

12-13. On seeing him, the unchanging Bhavānī removed the Māyā. Rid of the impurities of Māyā those sages looked at Pārvatī, became pleased and were liberated. Hence she is

807. Cf. न निरोधो न चोत्पत्तिर्न बद्धो न च साधकः ।
न मुमुक्षुर्न वै मुक्त इत्येषा परमार्थता ॥
—*Pañcadaśī* VI. 35.

808. eṣā vidyā—this Umā is identical with knowledge or with Primordial nature in association with Puruṣa.

809. Cf. p. 3 note. 12.

the greatest goal. In fact, there is no difference at all between Ūmā and Śaṅkara.[810]

14-17. There is no doubt that he is stationed after adopting the two forms. When there is a contact with Vijñāna (perfect knowledge) at the behest of Parameṣṭhin, liberation occurs within a moment and not otherwise, even with crores of holy rites. Here the order intended for the living beings is not applicable. By the grace of Parameṣṭhin liberation takes place in a trice. This is undoubtedly the vow of the lord. The creature (i.e. individual soul) is liberated, thanks to the grace of Parameṣṭhin even when he is in the womb or when he is born, or when he is a boy, a young man or an old man. By the grace of the lord of Devas every living being is liberated whether it is oviparous or a plant or one born of sweat. No doubt need be entertained in this regard.

18-22a. He alone is the lord of the worlds; Śiva is the cause of bondage and liberation. The worlds viz:—Bhūḥ, Bhuvaḥ, Svaḥ, Mahaḥ, Jana, Tapas and Satya the innumerable Cosmic Eggs as well as the eight[811] coverings of the Cosmic Egg constitute the body of the lord. Mobile and immobile beings who reside in the seven continents, on the mountains, in the forests and oceans, and in the layers of winds and in other worlds also are born from the parts of the lord. Indeed, he alone is the goal unto them all.

22b-25. Rudra is all. Obeisance unto the noble-souled Puruṣa. This universe, all living beings are born of Rudra. This goddess Ambikā is the Ājñā (behest) of Rudra. Salvation is effected through Her.

Thus, the Siddhas, the heaven-walkers proclaimed with delighted minds.

When the lord stands by and glances at them gracefully along with Ambikā the heaven-walkers attain identity with the lord.

810. In fact Prakṛti and Puruṣa are identical.

811. See p. 4 note 13, p. 11. note 18.

CHAPTER EIGHTYEIGHT

Review of pāśupata yoga

The Sages said:—

1. By what yoga do the good men obtain good attributes? How do the yogins become endowed with Aṇimā and other siddhis? O Sūta, it behoves you to recount everything in detail now.

Sūta said:—

2. Henceforth, I shall recount the yoga, extremely difficult of access. At the outset, the devotee shall remember the eternal deity after fixing him in the mind in five[812] different forms.

3-4. O excellent brahmins, he shall fix the lotus posture accompanied by the moon, sun and fire. It shall be combined with the twentysix Śaktis. Thereafter, O brahmins, the devotee shall remember the lord, the consort of Umā, in the middle first in eight ways, then in sixteen and again in twelve ways.

5-6. He shall remember the unborn lord of eight cosmic bodies,[813] accompanied by eight Śaktis, along with them Rudras of eight types and then of sixty-four types. Similarly all the Śaktis endowed with the eight Guṇas are to be remembered. After obtaining perfect knowledge gradually one shall adopt this procedure.

7. The yoga pertaining to Paśupati is one that bestows salvation. O brahmins, only he who practices the yoga does get the attributes, Aṇimā, etc. and not otherwise, even through crores of holy rites.

8. There the Aiśvarya of the yogins is said to comprise of eight[814] attributes. Understand all these being narrated in the proper order.

812. pañcadhā—in five forms i.e. Sadyojāta and others.

813. aṣṭaśakti—eight powers personified and named. Cf.

वामा ज्येष्ठा तथा रौद्री काली विकरिणी तथा ।

बलपूर्वा विकरिणी बलप्रमथिनी तथा ।।

मनोन्मनी तथा चाष्टौ— *Śiva-rahasya*—cited in *ST*.

814. See p. 134 note 241.

9-10. Aṇimā (minuteness), Laghimā (lightness), Mahimā (greatness), Prāpti (the power of obtaining anything), Prākāmyam (irresistible will); Īśitva (lordship) over everything, Vaśitva (ability to make others subservient) and Kāmāvasāyitā (when everything happens according to one's desires), these are eight types. This Aiśvarya desired by everyone should be known as of three types.

11-15. The three types are Sāvadya, Niravadya and Sūkṣma. What is termed Sāvadya is of the nature of five elements. The function of the Sūkṣma (subtle) is in respect of the sense organs, mind and ego. The function is again of the nature of five elements(?). The sense-organs, mind, will, intellect and ego—the Ātman comes into contact with all these. This threefold contact functions only in the subtle things. Again the eight attributes are laid down only in the subtle forms. I shall mention their nature as described by the lord and as they are known among all living beings of the three worlds.

16. The Aṇimā, etc. are self-evident. They are well established everywhere. They are cited as difficult of access to all living beings in the three worlds.

17-19. On attaining the first Aiśvarya, the devotee gets the power of the yogins. This will make him assume such forms that will enable him to cross or float (on water or air). The second (Laghimā) is known as the attainment of great quickness (Śīghratva) among all living beings. In all the three worlds honour among all living beings is due to one's greatness. Therefore, the third yoga (i.e. Aiśvarya) is called Mahitva (=Mahimā) in the world. Prāpti enables one to mix at one's will and pleasure with all living beings in the three worlds.

20. By Prākāmya the devotee enjoys all desired objects. It is through obstruction somewhere that happiness and misery are brought about in all living beings in the three worlds.

21. The knower of the yoga Īśitva (sixth Aiśvarya) becomes the overlord everywhere in every stage. In the three worlds consisting of the mobile and immobile beings all the living beings become subservient to him. This is Vaśitva the seventh Aiśvarya.

22. Where there is Kāmāvasāyitva (the eighth and highest Aiśvarya) forms occur and cease to be as the devotee wishes

among all the three worlds consisting of the mobile and immobile beings.

23. When all these Siddhis or Aiśvaryas are attained, sound, touch, taste, smell, colour and the mind, all function or cease to function as the devotee wishes.

24-27. He is neither born nor dies. He is neither cut nor pierced. He is neither burned nor illusioned. He is neither attracted nor afflicted by anything. He does not waste away nor does he perish. He is never depressed and he is not at all made to change or undergoes change. He is devoid of smell, taste and colour, touch or sound. He has no colour or caste. He has no tone; everywhere he is without an equal. He enjoys the objects of pleasure, but he does not become attached to any. Thanks to his being minute, he is extremely subtle. Thanks to his being subtle, he is worthy of salvation.

28. Thanks to salvation, he is all-pervasive. Being all-pervasive, he is called Puruṣa. Due to his subtle nature, Puruṣa is stationed in the greatest Aiśvarya (prosperity and glory).

29-30. The Aiśvaryas are said to be subtler and greater in ascending order all round. After obtaining the excellent yoga and the unimpeded Aiśvaryas, one shall attain salvation. That is the greatest subtle goal. O leading sages, the yoga pertaining to Paśupati should be known thus.

31-32. It bestows the benefits of heaven and salvation. It is the cause of identity with Śiva. Or, one who has no perfect knowledge may perform holy rites due to attachments. After enjoying Rājasa and Tāmasa pleasures he is liberated there itself(i.e. in this world). Similarly, he who performs meritorious deeds attains the benefit in heaven.

33-37. But the moment his merits are exhausted the excellent man reverts to the mortal world from that abode. Hence Brahman is the greatest happiness. Brahman is the best and permanent goal. One shall resort to the Brahman alone. Brahman alone is the greatest happiness. All yajñas are mere waste of energy and no good results from them. One becomes a prey to death by resorting to Yajñas. So liberation is the sole happiness. After seeing the divine Puruṣa of universal names with faces all round, the devotee, engaged in meditation, devoutly engrossed in the principle of the Brahman cannot be dislodged even in hundreds of manvantaras. The divine Puruṣa has universal feet, heads and necks. He is lord of the universe. He has universal forms (colours) and smell. The universe is his garland. He is the lord wearing the universal clothes.

38-41. The rays of the sun fall on the earth but do not go back to the sun and reproduce him.

One can see the lord only through yoga and not by the eye—the lord who is the ancient sage, who is subtler than the subtlest, who is the chastiser, who is greater than the greatest, who is the golden-coloured Puruṣa without sense-organs, who has no symbol, who is devoid of attributes, who is perpetual, who is sentient, who is present always and everywhere, who is the essence of all. Devotees who are purified by Him see the deity shining with His splendour and possessing massive refulgence. He has neither hands nor feet[815] nor belly nor sides nor tongue. He is beyond the scope of the sense-organs. He is one and very subtle. Though He has no eyes, yet He sees; though He has no ears yet He hears. He has no intellect; yet there is nothing that He does not understand. He knows everything but none knows him. So they call him the great and foremost Puruṣa.

42. The yogins who are in union with the deity see the Prakṛti of all living beings as acetanā (insentient) subtle, all-pervasive and habitually giving birth to many effects.

43. She has hands and feet all round. She has eyes, heads and faces all round. She has ears all round. She stands enveloping everything in the world.

44. One who is endowed with yoga and knows the eternal Puruṣa, the lord of all living beings, never gets disillusioned.

45. One who meditates on the unchanging, great and noble Brahman which is the soul of all living beings, and which is the greatest Ātman, does not get disillusioned.

46. Just as the wind moving amongst all bodies is perceptible so also the Puruṣa. Because he lies down in the puḥ[816] so he is called Puruṣa [puri śete]. He is too difficult to be grasped.

815. This verse is found in most of the *Upaniṣads*.

816. puri śete iti puruṣaḥ. puri=liṅga-śarīre, in the subtle body. Puruṣa is so called because he is stationed in the subtle body.

47-48. If one neglects Dharma, that man is born in the womb[817] with the residue of his activities.[818] When a man and a woman indulge in intercourse and the semen gets mixed with the blood, in due course, the sperm becomes the foetus.

49-52. In due course, the foetus becomes a bubble.[820] Just as the lump of clay assumes some form of an image on being whirled in the wheel and shaped by the potter's hands so also the physical body is evolved, endowed with organic matter and filled with vital airs. As long as the external air[820] does not touch the child in the womb he thinks thus—"when I leave off the vaginal passage[821] I shall resort to Maheśvara and worship Mahādeva. The foetus becomes a human being according to the pre-ordained form and age.

53. Wind originates from the firmament, from wind water is evolved; from water originates the vital air and the semen is generated and it flourishes through the vital airs.

54. Thirtythree parts of blood are mixed with fourteen parts of semen. When halves of these parts mix together the foetus is evolved.

55. Then the child in the womb is encircled by the five vital airs. The child's form is evolved limb by limb from the physical body of the father.

56. Through the umbilical region the child is sustained by the food taken in by the mother, by the liquid drink and by the lambatives licked.

57. For nine months the child undergoes the pain and

817. brahma-garbha —brāhmaṇa-yonau *ST*. He is born in the brāhmaṇa caste. Cf. śucīnāṁ śrīmatām gehe yogabhraṣṭo 'bhijāyate.
—*Bhagavad gītā*.

818. avaśiṣṭaiḥ karmabhiḥ.
केवलं चाशुभं कर्म नरकाय भवेदिह ।
शुभं स्वर्गाय जायेत उभाभ्यां मानुषं स्मृतम् ॥ *ŚP*:—cited in *ST*.

819. शुक्रं रजःसमायुक्तं प्रथमे मासि तद्भवम् । बुद्बुदं कललं तस्मात्ततः पेशी भवेदिदम् ॥ *Śivagītā*—cited in *ST*.

820. vaiṣṇavam—the external air which the babe breathes when he comes out of the womb.

821. Cf. एवं स्मरन् पुरा प्राप्ता नानाजातीश्च यातनाः ।
मोक्षोपायमभिध्यायन् वर्ततेऽभ्यासतत्परः ॥

strain; his neck is encircled by the umbilical cord. His body is curled up as the space within the womb is not sufficient.

58. After spending nine months in the womb the child falls down through the vaginal passage with his head downwards. Then in the course of his life on the earth he commits sins and due to these sins he falls into hell after death.

59. For example, he may fall into the hells of Asipatravana and Śālmalicchedana. There he may have to suffer being beaten, eaten or forced to partake of foeted blood.

60-61. Just as the water becomes sticky and binding together when things are cut and thrown in, so also the living beings are cut and thrown into the places of torture. They are scorched by means of the sins committed by themselves. They shall attain misery or happiness according to the residue of their actions.

62. One has to go alone after leaving off all people. One has to experience pleasure or pain all alone. Hence, one shall perform meritorious rites.

63. When he starts on his journey after death, none follows him as he goes ahead. The action performed by him follows him.

64. They function thus in the realms of Yama. When the treatment is against their liking they always groan loudly. Their bodies are dessicated by diversified tortures and surrounded by torments and agonies.

65. The practice of what one repeatedly resorts to mentally, physically and verbally influences him. Hence, one shall perform auspicious things always.

66. The uninterrupted series of previous actions of the embodied soul has no beginning : The individual soul adopts six types of terrible worldly existence full of tamaoguṇa.

67-71. From human form it adopts the form of cow (domestic animal); from that of a cow, the domestic animal, he may become a wild animal; from that of a wild animal he may attain bird-hood; from that the form of a reptile and from that he may attain the form of an immobile being. When he attains the form of an immobile being it whirls like the wheel of the potter there itself till the soul is uplifted. Thus is the worldly existence beginning from human being and ending with the immobile being. It should be known as Tāmasa. The soul revolves there itself. The existence of Brahmā, etc. is Sāttvika worldly existence. The existence of embodied beings beginning with Brahmā and ending with Piśāca should be known as existing in the heavenly abodes. The existence of Brahmā is purely of the nature of Sattva, that of the immobile being is of the nature of Tāmasa alone.

72-75. In the middle of the fourteen abodes, Rajas is that which impedes or fixes firmly even as the vital parts of the body of the embodied being who is in agony, are being cut and pierced. How can the brahmin then remember the greatest Brahman ? The worldly existence is prompted by the impression and effects of the previous Dharma and accordingly human birth is achieved. Hence one shall practise meditation always. One shall realise that the zone of the worlds is of fourteen types and so shall be frightened of it and begin to practise Dharma. Then, he changes and gradually crosses worldly existence.

76. Hence, one shall always be engaged in yoga and interested in meditation. He shall meditate on the greatest being. He shall so begin the practice of yoga that he sees the Ātman within himself.

77-78. He is the waters. He is the greatest light. He is the excellent bridge. He is the cause of all living beings by means of evolution and combination. He is the permanent one. Hence, one shall worship Maheśvara the bridge, the Ātman, the fire with faces all round, and stationed in the heart of all living beings.

79-84. The devotee shall meditate on Rudra, the lord who is stationed within who is embellished by his own Śakti who, for the sake of creation, is stationed in a series of eight[822] different forms and who is stationed in the heart by compressing the fire. With the mind contemplating the fire stationed in the heart he shall perform five offerings. He shall drink pure water silently once (in the ritualistic way) in the squatting position. He shall utter "Prāṇāya Svāhā". This is the first

822. The lord is stationed in the heart in the eight-fold way, viz., earth, etc., or in eight forms, viz., Bhava, etc., or in eight mūrtis—Vāmadeva etc.

offering. The second offering is for Apāna, the third for Vyāna, the fourth for Udāna and the fifth for Samāna. After offering these severally with the utterance of Svāhā, the devotee shall partake of the remaining offering as he pleases. He shall drink water once again and perform the rite of Ācamana. After that he shall touch the heart.

85. He shall perform the rite of satiety with this mantra :—"you are the knot of the vital airs.[823] Rudra is Ātman. Ātman is the destroyer of the subjects. Rudra, indeed, is the vital air of the Ātman."

86-87. At the time of Śrāddha he shall perform five offerings as per injunction:—(1) Indeed, Rudra is embedded in Prāṇa (2) Hence, he himself is identical with Prāṇa, (3) One performs the excellent nectar unto Prāṇa and Rudra, (4) O Śiva, O Īśa, enter me, (5) Svāhā unto Brahmātman himself.

88-90. The Homa shall be concluded with the following mantras:—You are Puruṣa. You lie down in the body, in the size of the thumb. Īśa is the great cause of all though based on the thumb.[824] May the permanent lord of all the Universe be pleased. You are the eldest of all Devas. You are Rudra. Formerly you were Indra. You are soft by nature. May this sacrificial offering unto you be our food.

Thus, everything has been mentioned with special emphasis on the attainment of good attributes.

91-93. The practice of yoga has been formerly mentioned by Brahmā himself. Thus, the perfect knowledge belonging to Paśupati should be known with effort. One shall take bath with Bhasman. One shall smear Bhasman. He who reads this, listens to this or narrates this to excellent brahmins in divine rites or in those of the Pitṛs attains the greatest goal.

823. "Prāṇānāṁ granthir asi" *TA*. 10. 31.1; Mahān. U. 16.2.
824. aṅguṣṭhmātro'yam. TA. 10. 38. 1; Mahān. U. 16. 3.

CHAPTER EIGHTYNINE

Characteristics of good conduct

Sūta said:

1. Henceforth, I shall mention the characteristics of purity and good conduct. On acting according to it the pure soul will attain the highest goal after death.

2. This has been formerly mentioned by Brahmā for the welfare of living beings. This is the summary of the implication of the Vedas. It is a collection of things expounding the Brahman.

3. It is conducive to the rise of cleanliness. It is the excellent position of the sages. The sage who does not err in this does not come to grief.

4. Honour and dishonour are two things which they call poison and nectar. Dishonour is nectar and honour is poison.

5. He, the disciple, shall live with the preceptor for a year engaged in the welfare of the preceptor. He shall always be unerring in the holy observances and restraints.

6. After obtaining his permission along with the excellent path of knowledge he shall walk over the earth [i. e. fulfil the duties of the mundane existence] without repugnance to Dharma.

7. One shall traverse the path sanctified by the eyes; one shall drink the water rendered pure by a cloth (i. e. well-filtered) ; one shall speak out words sanctified by truth; one shall practise those things that are purified by the mind.[825]

8. If one drinks impure water for a day one incurs that sin which a fisherman incurs in the course of six months.

9. On drinking impure water one shall as expiation perform five hundred japas of Aghora mantra and then attain purity.

10. Or he shall worship Śiva with elaborate details, such as ablution with ghee, etc. Then he shall circumambulate the deity three times, when he shall undoubtedly be purified.

11. The knower of yoga shall not go anywhere to receive hospitality as a guest or to partake of Śrāddhas and Yajñas. It

825. Cf. *Manusmṛti* VI. 46.

is thought that the yogin will be non-violent only in this manner.

12. The intelligent mendicant shall go in for alms to a house where all people have taken food but still there is plenty of fire without smoke. But he shall not go to the same house every day.

13. In that case people will insult him and the enemies will disgrace and humiliate him. So one shall beg for alms in the proper manner. He shall not defile the Dharma of good men.

14. One shall beg for alms in the houses of vagrant mendicants and in the houses situated in the forests. The latter shall be the better mode of sustenance.

15. O brahmins, thereafter he shall go in for alms at the places of humble householders who have faith, who have control over the sense-organs and who are noble-souled scholars of the Vedas.

16. Thereafter, he shall go in for alms in the houses of the non-defiled and not-fallen. The practice of begging for alms from people of other castes is considered the meanest of all modes.

17. Any of the following things can be received in the form of alms, viz. gruel, butter milk, milk, barley water, ripe fruits and roots, bits of grains, oil-cakes and powdered fried grains.

18. The items of food mentioned by me are those that increase the accomplishments of the yogins. If they are realised the alms are said to be excellent.

19. Of these two persons, viz. one who begs for alms by means that are justifiable and the other who, (by way of penance) drinks a drop of water by means of the tip of the darbha grass once in a month, the former excels the latter.

20. Bhaikṣya is so called because it removes the sins of one who is afraid of old age, death, rebirth, residence in hells, etc.

21. Those who are addicted to the regular use of curds or milk or those who cause wastage in the individual souls—all these do not merit even a sixteenth part of one who partakes of the alms.

22. One shall always lie down on Bhasman; with control over the sense-organs he shall beg for alms. He who wishes for the greatest abode shall perform the Pāśupata vrata.

23. The rite of Cāndrāyaṇa shall be most excellent for all yogins. According to his capacity, the devotee shall perform it once, twice, thrice or four times.

24. Bhikṣus (mendicants) have five vratas, viz:—Asteya (non-stealing); Brahmacarya (celibacy); Alobha (non-covetousness); Tyāga (renunciation) and Ahiṁsā (non-violence) which is the greatest.

25. The niyamas (observances and restraints) are the following:—akrodha (abstention from anger), guruśuśrūṣā (service to the preceptor), śauca (cleanliness), āhāralāghava (lightness of food) and study of the Vedas regularly.

26. The qualities of the seed, the vagina and bondage with the objects—are due to karmans (?). Just as in the case of the elephant in the forest so also in regard to men it is laid down.

27. All the sacrificial rites are equal to Devas. But japa is superior to sacrificial rites; perfect knowledge is superior to meditation; and meditation, devoid of attachment, is still superior to that. When that is acquired, the eternal goal is obtained.

28. Those persons whose intellects have been purified by perfect knowledge say that the following are auspicious qualities, viz:—control of the mind, suppression of the sense-organs, truthfulness, state of being free from sins, silence, straightforwardness in regard to all living beings and the knowledge of those objects beyond the scope of the sense-organs.

29. Only a noble soul who has concentration, who is devoted to the Brahman, who does not err, who is pure, who likes seclusion, and who has conquered the sense-organs shall attain this yoga. Thus, say the sages who are devoid of impurities and are above censure.

30. The devotee who has destroyed even the seeds of sins by means of this pure path, restrained by the same goad (of pure path) attains the desired places.

31. Quiescent persons engaged in good conduct and

maintaining their own Dharma conquer all the worlds and attain the world of Brahman.

32. The eternal Dharma has been imparted by Brahmā himself for the utility of the people. Listen now when I recount it to you.

33. One shall duly perform his duties such as obeisance and standing up by way of welcome towards elderly persons who have acquired instructions from preceptors and who strictly adhere to their routine (i. e. the rules relating to their Āśrama).

34. O sages of good holy rites, the brahmin and the preceptor are to be honoured by obeisance with eight limbs touching the ground with the following three set aside viz:—head-dress, upper garment and footwear and with three circumambulations.

35. All elderly persons should be respected. If one wishes for excellent Siddhi one shall never break their behests.

36. One shall avoid all these things:—Taking up iron and other metals for sustenance, living in a desert or unproductive soil[826] and using worthless mantras as means of support, snake-charming[827] and backbiting, flattery[827a] or scandal.

37-40. One shall scrupulously avoid deception, stinginess in spending money, censure of others. In the presence of preceptors and elders one shall avoid laughter, haughtiness, sportive dalliance and wilfulness. One shall never contradict the preceptor; one shall never speak unbecoming words against him. One shall scrupulously avoid mentioning things disliked by the preceptor and shall not think evil of him. One shall never touch these things with one's foot—the clothes, staff, etc., of ascetics, their sandals, garlands, places of sleep [i. e. bed-mattress etc.], vessel, shadow and the requisite things of use in sacrifices.

41. O brahmins, one shall scrupulously avoid treachery

826. bila-kṣetram—ūṣarabhūmiḥ *ST*. barren field.

827. Viṣa-grahaḥ—viṣa-yuktasarpādinām mantrādinā grahaṇam *ST*. profession of a snake-charmer. It is hazardous as well as degrading.

827a. Viḍambaḥ—anyānukaraṇam ST. mimicry.

to the deities and preceptors. If one unwillingly commits it, one shall perform ten thousand japas of the Praṇava.

42-43. If he repeats the japas a crore of times he is purified from the sins of treachery to the preceptor and the deities. For the expiation of great sins, one shall repeat Śiva's mantra in accordance with the injunction. If the sinner is, otherwise, of good conduct he is purified by half the number of japas. O sages of good holy rites, all the Upapātakins (those who commit subsidiary sins) get purified by half the number of japas.

44. A brahmin guilty of the omission of Sandhyā prayers becomes pure by repeating it thrice. If the daily routine is violated, it shall be repeated hundred and one times.

45. In the following circumstances, one is purified by repeating the mantra for thousand times. The instances are:--violating agreements, eating forbidden food and speaking what should not be spoken.

46. There is no doubt in this that if one kills birds like crows, owls and doves, etc., he is liberated from the sin by repeating the mantra hundred and eight times.

47. The excellent brahmin who knows the truth and has realised Brahman becomes pure merely by remembering the deity. No doubt need be entertained in this respect.

48. There are no expiatory rites nor injunctions regarding them in the case of the knowers of the Ātman. People who are conversant with the learning of the brahman are pure themselves (because they are engaged) in the welfare of the universe.

49. Those who adhere to yoga and dhyāna are stainless like gold. They become pure by resorting to Brahmavidyā and there is no further purification for persons already pure.

50. One shall avoid turbid water. He shall perform all rites by means of waters that have been purified by filtering through the pores of a cloth and that do not contain cold foams.

51-52. One shall avoid waters of these types:—that which has defective smell, colour and taste; that which stagnates in impure places; that which is defiled by mud and pebbles, the sea water, the water from puddles, the water mingled with moss and water that is otherwise defiled. O brahmins, one shall perform all rites equipped with the cleanliness of clothes.

53. One shall perform the rites of obeisance as well as service to the preceptors with pure and clean clothes. One devoid of cleanliness and purity in clothes is undoubtedly impure.

54. It is desired that the clothes used in divine rites should be washed every day. Other clothes should be washed when they become dirty.

55-57. O brahmins, one shall scrupulously eschew the clothes worn by others.

Woollen garments and silken clothes shall be washed by means of hard coarse substances. Woven-silk garments should be washed with white mustard seeds. Silk garments called aṁśu-paṭṭas shall be washed with bilva fruits. The peculiar type of blankets called Kutapas should be washed with soap-berry nuts. The cleansing of leather, wickerwork baskets and cane-boxes is in the same way as that of clothes. Leading sages who know the brahman have mentioned that the cleansing of bark garments of all varieties, of the umbrella and of the chowrie is like that of clothes.

58. Bell metal is purified by Bhasman, iron is purified by acid; O brahmins, copper, tin and lead are cleaned with vinegar.

59. O excellent brahmins, the pots of gold and silver can be purified by water. The cleansing of jewels, rock, conch and pearls is similar to that of metals.

60. The purity of excessively polluted things is through contact with fire and water. The cleansing of all beverages is called Utplavana.

61. Objects made of grass, wood, etc., are purified by sprinkling them with sacred water. The purity of Sruk and Sruva (the sacrificial plate and ladle) is through hot water.

62. The cleansing of the utensils of yajñas, that of the mortar and pestle and the purification of those made of horn, bone, wood and ivory is by means of poring.

63. O highly blessed ones, sprinkling is the means of purification of compact solid bodies; if the things are disjointed they shall be severally cleansed.

64. If a portion of a heap of grains not eaten, is defiled that portion is removed and the remaining part is sprinkled with Kuśa grass-water.

65. It is desirable that vegetables, roots and fruits are purified like grains. The house is purified by sweeping and scrubbing. A mud-pot is purified by heating it over fire.

66. The floor can be cleansed by scraping, digging, bedaubing, sweeping, sprinkling and by tethering cows over it.

67-68. The water stagnating over the surface of lands becomes pure if a cow drinks from there and quenches its thirst, but filth should not spread over it along with foul smell, taste and colour.

The calf is purified in a spring; and the bird by throwing a fruit at it. During sexual intercourse the mouth of the wife is pure for the loving householder.

69. The excellent knower of Dharmas shall sprinkle with Kuśa grass water, the cloth manually washed by a washerman duly, and then take it for use.

70. Merchandise spread in accordance with the division of castes and stages of life is pure. Things taken out of mines are naturally pure. A hound is pure when it catches hold of a deer.

71. All these are pure even when they come into contact with the body, viz.—shadow, drops of water, brahmins, flies etc., dust, ground, wind and fire, O excellent brahmins.

72. O brahmins, even when one is pure, one shall perform the ācamana rite after sleeping, taking food, sneezing, drinking and spitting. At the beginning of the study of the Vedas and on similar occasions one shall perform the ācamana rite.

73. If the drops of water fall on the feet while others perform the ācamana rite they shall be known as earthly things. One shall not become impure thereby.

74-75. After sexual intercourse and after touching a fallen man, cocks, pig, crows, dog, camel, donkey, post, cāṇḍāla and others, one becomes pure, just by a bath. One shall not touch a woman in her monthly course, a woman after delivery and a Śūdra woman.

76. One defiled by pollution after birth or death shall not touch their dust. If he touches he shall be pure by taking bath.

77. O sages of good holy rites, the following persons are not defiled by pollution—ascetics, forest-dwellers, religious students, life-long celibates, kings and rulers of provinces.

78. Only when there are impediments in their tasks, do kings, sages and brahmins who have fallen become impure and not otherwise.

79-80. The Āśauca of the brahmins is upto the collection of bones after cremation and they are purified merely by taking bath. Similarly for those who are initiated in the sacrifice. It has been mentioned by the self-born deity that for those who had performed sacrifices the pollution is for one day. Then for those who have studied their respective branches of the Vedas it is for four days.

81. O excellent brahmins, kinsmen do not have pollution due to birth or death beyond three days (if they hear of the birth or death) after the eleventh day.

82. If one is present at the time of death one is purified merely by taking bath. If the fact of death is known after three seasons (i.e. six months)[828] the pollution is for one day.

83-84. If the fact of death is known before seven years[829] the pollution is for three days and beyond that for the brahmins, it is for ten days. The pollution due to birth is for the first day in the case of the father. O sages, in the case of the mother it is for ten days. If the fact is known after three years,[830] the purity is attained by bath by the father as well as by kinsmen.

85. If the fact is known after eight years[831] the kinsmen become pure within a day. O sages of good holy rites, if the fact

828. ṛtu-trayād arvāk—before three seasons, i. e. before six months. if the deceased is not six months old. Editor.

829. arvāk sapta-varṣāt—if the deceased is not seven years old. Editor.

830. arvāk sapta-varṣāt—if the deceased is not seven years old. Editor.

831. aṣṭābdāt—if the deceased is not eight years old. Editor.

is known after twelve years[831a] or beyond that, the ladies will have pollution for three days.

86. Sapiṇḍatā (the state of being kinsman by way of offering the funeral rice balls) recedes in the seventh generation. If the ten days immediately after death have elapsed, one shall be impure for three days.

87. The brahmin beyond that period or after a year has elapsed, becomes pure merely by taking bath.

88. If one touches a dead body, one becomes pure after three days. It is for the sake of Dharma that ablution is enjoined in regard to the persons who cremate the dead body. If he is not a relative he need take bath alone.

89. If one follows the dead body, one becomes pure by taking bath and drinking ghee. When the preceptor dies, or when a vedic-scholar passes away, pollution remains for three days.[832]

90-92. O brahmins, if maternal uncles and their wives or brothers die, if kings and rulers die, the people become pure immediately. O excellent brahmins, the pollution of the Kṣatriyas is for twelve days. A crowned king need not observe pollution if his kinsmen die in battle. A Vaiśya becomes pure in fifteen days. A Śūdra becomes pure within a month.

Thus, the excellent mode of purification has been described to you in brief.

93. Ascetics do not have to observe pollution accruing from birth or death.

O brahmins, I shall now mention another impurity, i.e., the monthly menstrual discharge of the women.

94. Due to the nature of the yuga, in the Kṛta age, ladies gave birth but once. The blessed ones repaired to the forests along with their wives like the Kurus.[833]

95. O sages of good holy rites, the arrangement regarding the castes and stages of life began ever since the Tretā yuga.

831a. strīṣu—if the married woman who has not completed twelfth year dies (in her father's house). Cf.

विवाहितापि चेत्कन्या म्रियते पितृवेश्मनि ।

तस्यास्त्रिरात्राच्छुध्यन्ति बान्धवा नात्र संशय: *Agnipurāṇa*—cited in *ST*.

832. pakṣiṇi—a night with the two days enclosing it. Cf.

द्वावह्नावेकरात्रिश्च पक्षिणीत्यभिधीयते—cited by V.S. Apte : *The practical Sanskrit-English Dictionary*, p. 557.

833. Kuravaḥ—Kuruvarṣīyāḥ ST. the residents of Kuru varṣa.

This arrangement is observed only in the southern sub-continent of Bhārata and not in the other.

96. Dharma is observed in the following continents and sub-continents, viz. Mahāvīta,[834] Suvīta,[835] Jambūdvīpa[836] and its eight other sub-continents, and Śākadvīpa,[837] etc. and in Bhārata.[838]

97-99. In Kṛta yuga, the sustenance of people was from taking liquids; in Tretā yuga from domestic trees. But this was discontinued during the subsequent ages. The same occurred in regard to the untimely intercourse, during the menstrual discharge, due to lust of men. O Brahmins, so barley and other plants of the village and forest as well as the fourteen types of medicinal herbs were cultivated untimely and destroyed, as in the case of sexual intercourse during the menstrual period due to the passion of men.

100. Hence, one shall assiduously avoid conversing with a woman in her monthly course. On the first day, she has to be avoided like a cāṇḍāla woman.

101-102. O brahmins, on the second day, she is to be treated like a woman who has slain a brahmin. On the third day,[839] she has half that sinful nature. O sages of good holy rites, she shall take bath on the fourth day.[840] She shall then be pure within half a month. From the sixteenth day onwards the women shall observe cleanliness in regard to passing of urine.

103. If the menstrual discharge continues she cannot be touched for five days.[841] As far as twenty days she is defiled by the menstrual discharge and remains untouchable.

834. Mahāvīta—see p. 206 note 323.

835. Suvīta—not identifiable.

836. Jambūdvīpa, see p. 189 note 292a.

837. ST. does not construe 'aṣṭasu' with 'śāka-dvīpādiṣu' but takes it with 'kimpuruṣādiṣu' which it supplies since it does not occur in the verse. It explains 'śāka-dvīpādiṣu' along with plakṣadvīpāntikeṣu, on the authority of Liṅga. I. 46. 46.

838. Bhārata, see p. 186 note 289; p. 202 note 318.

839. tṛtīyā'hni—on the third day of menstruation she is as impure as the washerwoman: 'tṛtīye rajakī proktā'—cited in ST.

840. She becomes pure on the fourth day: 'bhartuḥ śuddhā caturthehni'—*cited* in *ST*.

841. If her menses do not stop after three days she remains impure for five nights. But Āpastamba considers her to be impure so long as her menses continue:

स्नानं रजस्वलायास्तु चतुर्थेऽहनि शस्यते ।
गम्या निवृत्ते रजसि नानिवृत्ते कथञ्चन ।।

104-107. A woman in her monthly course shall avoid bath, toilet, singing, crying, laughing, going in vehicles, applying collyrium, playing dice, applying unguents, sleeping during the daytime, washing the teeth, sexual intercourse, worship of deities whether mental, verbal or physical as well as bowing down. A woman in her monthly course shall avoid touching another woman in her monthly course and talking to her also. She shall assiduously avoid changing her garments. A woman in her monthly course shall not touch another man after her bath.

108. She shall look at the brilliant sun and drink Brahmakūrca or Pañcagavya or milk for self purification.

109-110. The husband shall not indulge in sexual intercourse on the fourth night after the monthly discharge has started. If he indulges thus, the child born will be short-lived. The son born of this sexual contact will be devoid of learning, depraved, deviating from the observance of holy rites, violating the chastity of other men's wives and immersed in the ocean of penury. The woman should be approached on the fifth night if he seeks a daughter.

111. If the blood is predominant, the child will be a girl; if the semen is predominant the child will be a boy; if both are equal the child will be an eunuch; if the sexual intercourse is on the fifth night the child will be a girl.

112. The blessed lady shall be approached on the sixth night; she will be the mother of a good son. The son will be excessively brilliant and he will remain dutiful as a son.

113. The word Pum means "hell" and they say that hell is miserable. She will give birth to a son who will save his parents from Pum (i.e. hell).[842]

114. The husband who seeks a daughter shall approach her on the seventh night. She will give birth to a daughter.[843] If approached on the eighth night she will give birth to a son equipped with everything.

115. He who seeks a daughter shall approach his wife on

842. Cf. *Manu*. IX. 138.

843. saiva prasūyate—Bandhyā bhavati ST. she becomes barren. ST. quotes Nirṇaya-sindhu in support of his view: "saptamyām aprajā yoṣit." But this meaning is not borne out by the text.

the ninth night; if approached on the tenth night a scholarly son will be born; if approached on the eleventh night she will give birth to a girl as before.[844]

116-117. If approached on the twelfth night she will give birth to a son who is conversant with the principle of Dharma and who will observe the holy rites laid down in Śrutis and Smṛtis. If approached on the thirteenth night she will give birth to a sluggish girl who will bring about mixture of castes. Hence, one shall assiduously avoid her on that night. If he approaches her on the fourteenth night she will be the mother of a son.

118-122. If approached on the fifteenth night she will give birth to a virtuous daughter; if approached on the sixteenth night she will give birth to a son who will be a master of perfect knowledge.

If at the time of the sexual intercourse the air passes through the left side of the woman she will give birth to a daughter; if it passes through the right side she will give birth to a boy. The time of sexual intercourse shall be free from the influence of evil planets. At the time mentioned thus the husband shall remain clean and approach the pure and smiling wife joyously.

Thus, in the context of collecting together virtuous rites of the ascetics, the good conduct of all living beings has been recounted to you.

The pure man who reads this discourse on the good conduct or listens to it or narrates this to the brahmins who have destroyed their sins will attain the world of lord Brahmā and rejoice along with the lord.

844. Construe 'purvāt' with the following verse. i. e. dvādaśyām pūrvavat (=panditavat) dharma-tattvajñam (sutam prasūte).

CHAPTER NINETY

The expiatory rites of the ascetics

Sūta said:—

1. Henceforth, I shall mention decisively the mode of expiation by asectics. This is recounted by Śiva and it makes adequate atonement for the sins of ascetics.

2. Sins are of three types: those originating from speech, mind and body. It is by these that the universe is encompassed always, by day and by night.

3. "Without activities the world cannot be sustained even for a moment", says the sacred Śruti. It is the only instrument that is conducive to longevity and sustenance.

4. It is only to the unerring that the yoga becomes accessible. Indeed, yoga is the greatest strength. There is no other auspicious thing for men that is greater than yoga.

5-7. Hence, learned men endowed with virtue praise yoga. They shall conquer (ignorance) by knowledge and attain excellent aiśvarya. After seeing the greatest being inferior to none, the self-possessed ones will attain that region. There are main and subsidiary holy rites to be observed by the mendicants (Bhikṣus). Expiatory rites are also laid down for violating any of them.

By carnally approaching a woman the mendicant incurs sin and for that the following expiatory rite is mentioned.

8. He shall perform Prāṇāyāma and observe the rite Sāntapana.[845] Then with great concentration and attention at the end, he shall perform the Kṛcchra[846] rite in accordance with the direction.

9-10. Again the Bhikṣu shall return to the hermitage and perform the rite alertfully. Learned men say that a virtuous falsehood does not injure one. Still it should not be pursued. Its mere context is terrible. The expiatory rite is fasting for a night and a day and a hundred Prāṇāyāmas.

845. sāntapanam—a rigid penance; cf. Manu. 11. 213; also *Mitākṣarā* on Yājñavalkya (prāyascitta).

846. *ST*. supplies prājāpatyam with kṛcchram. For detail, see p. 45 note 62.

11. Evil utterance and discussion shall not be pursued by an ascetic desirous of attaining Dharma. Thieving shall not be indulged in even when he is in great distress.

12-13. Śruti says that there is no evil greater than stealing. What is mentioned as "stealing" is a great violence that is inseparable from it. What is named "wealth" constitutes the external vital airs (Prāṇas). Hence, he who takes away the wealth of anyone really takes away the vital airs of that person.

14-15. A person who is wicked in mind becomes one who has transgressed the bounds of good conduct by doing so (i.e. by stealing). He becomes one who has fallen down from his holy rite. He shall repent for it again and again and perform the rite of Cāndrāyaṇa[847] for a year in accordance with the injunctions laid down in scriptures. So says Śruti. At the end of the year he shall eliminate all his sins. The Bhikṣu shall then alertfully repent and perform the rites.

16-17a. The Bhikṣu shall abstain from injury to all living beings mentally, verbally and physically. If the Bhikṣu injures animals and worms even unwittingly he shall perform the rite of Kṛcchrātikṛcchra or Cāndrāyaṇa.

17b-18a. If, on seeing a woman, the ascetic were to have involuntary emission of semen due to his weakness, he shall observe sixteen prāṇāyāmas.

18b-19a. Now the expiatory rite of a brahmin who has seminal emission during the day time, is laid down. He shall observe fast for three nights and perform hundred prāṇāyāmas.

19b-20a. If he has nocturnal emission he shall take a clean bath and have twelve Dhāraṇās. O brahmins, by means of the prāṇāyāma, one becomes a pure soul and free from sins.

20b-21. The following are forbidden foodstuffs for ascetics viz.—alms from a single house every day, honey, wine, flesh (meat), uncooked food as well as salt itself. Expiatory rites are laid down for violating anyone of these.

22-23. He is freed from that sin by the observance of Prājāpatya and Kṛcchra. In regard to other transgressions whether mental, verbal or physical he shall consult good men and perform what they lay down.

847. Cāndrāyaṇa : See p. 45 note 61.

24. One shall view a lump of clay and gold alike and perform the rites. He shall be pure and clean. He shall have great concentration and attention in regard to all living beings. By living thus he attains that stable, unchanging and great abode from where he is not born again.

CHAPTER NINETYONE

Portentous phenomena

1. Henceforth, I shall mention the Ariṣṭas (the phenomena that indicate misfortune and even death); understand them. It is by means of this special knowledge that the yogins visualise death.

2. He who is not able to see Arundhatī (a constellation among the Pleiades) Dhruva (Pole star), the shadow of the moon and the Mahāpatha (Milky Way) shall not live more than a year.

3. He who sees the sun without rays and the fire with rays will not live beyond the eleventh month.

4. He who dreams that he vomits, passes urine and evacuates stools in the form of gold and silver shall not live full ten months thereafter.

5. He who sees a gold-coloured tree, the Gandharva city, (i.e. the hallucination of an imaginary city), ghosts and spirits shall live only for nine months.

6. He who becomes stout or lean all of a sudden, i.e., he who thus moves away from his nature shall live only for eight months.

7. He whose footprint appears split in front or behind in the dust or in mud lives only up to seven months.

8. If a crow, or a dove, or a vulture or any other bird of prey perches on one's head, one shall not survive six months.

9. He who goes in the company of rows of crows or of a dust storm, he who sees his own shadow in a deformed state shall live only for four or five months.

10. He who sees lightning in a spot that is not the sky and the lightning in the southern direction or he who sees the rainbow in the water shall live for only one or two months.

11. If one is not able to see oneself either in water or in the mirror or if he sees it devoid of the head he will not live beyond a month.

12. If the body emits the odour of a dead body or of fat, his death is imminent. He will not live beyond a fortnight.

13. If immediately after the bath the heart appears to dry up or smoke is seen coming out of the head, he will not live even for ten days.

14. If the bursting wind pierces the vital parts, if the hairs do not stand on their ends on being sprinkled with water, his death is imminent.

15. If one dreams of going towards the southern direction in a chariot to which monkeys and bears are yoked, and sings and dances in the meantime, it should be known that death is imminent.

16. If in the dream, a singing dark-complexioned woman who wears black clothes leads a person to the southern direction he will not live long.

17. If a man sees a slit in his own neck in the dream, or dreams of a naked śramaṇa (Buddhist recluse), know that death is imminent.

18. 'The person sinks into the ocean of mire upto the head'. On seeing a dream like this, he ceases to live immediately.

19. A person who sees ashes, burning coal, hairs, dry river, and serpents in dream does not live for ten days thereafter.

20. He who is beaten in dream by dark-complexioned hideous persons with arms lifted up or hit by stones, ceases to live immediately.

21. If jackals howl directly at a person early in the morning, at sunrise, that person's days are numbered.

22. If the heart is excessively pained immediately after the bath and there is a morbid sensitiveness in the teeth one can say that he is sure to die.

23. If a person is extremely frightened whether at night

or during daytime and he is unable to perceive the smell of the lamp one shall know that death is imminent.

24. If one sees the rainbow at night or the cluster of stars during the day and is unable to see himself in the eyes of others, he ceases to live.

25. If one of the eyes begins to water, if the ears are dislodged and if the nose becomes bent in dream the man is sure to die soon.

26. If the tongue becomes black and rough, if the face becomes red like lotus, and if the cheeks develop red fleshy swelling, his death is imminent.

27. If a man with dishevelled hair were to come face to face in the southern direction, singing, laughing and dancing, his life ends with that.

28. If the body is frequently pale, white in colour with the lustre of white clouds or like white mustard his death is imminent.

29. If one dreams that camels and donkeys are yoked to chariots they are inauspicious. If the chariot is seen going towards the southern direction he will cease to live.

30-31. The following dreams indicate that death is imminent:—Any two of the previous portents occurring simultaneously, not hearing noise in the ear, not seeing lustre in the eye, falling into a pit, inability to rise up from the pit and closing of a door.

32. These are signs of imminent death: The eyes are turned upwards, they are not steady, they are red, they revolve, there is dryness in the mouth, there is a hole in the umbilicus and the urine is excessively hot. The person is indeed in difficulties.

33. Whether during day or night if a person is directly killed but he does not see the murderer his life is extinct. He will cease to live.

34. If at the end of a dream, a man sees that he enters fire and does not remember it at all, his life ends with that.

35. If a man sees his own white blanket as a black one, in the course of the dream or as a red one, his death is imminent.

36. If the portents are indicated in the body and that time of death has arrived, the intelligent man shall eschew sorrow and dejection and treat it with indifference.

37-39. With cleanliness and purity he shall set off in the direction of east or north. He shall sit in a steady level ground in a secluded spot devoid of creatures. He shall sit facing the east or the north and perform the rite of ācamana. He shall sit in the posture of Svastika and bow to Maheśvara. The body, the head and the neck shall be erect like a lamp in a windless spot. He shall be steady without flickering. He shall not look at anything else while practising Dhāraṇā (Retention).

40-43. The knower of scriptures shall practise yoga in the spot facing the north-east. He shall restrain lust, doubt, pleasure, happiness and misery mentally and only concentrate on clean meditation. He shall meditate on the nose, tongue, eyes, skin, ears and mind. He shall retain them in the intellect and chest. After realising the time and actions he shall retain these parts of the body in the groups perpetually. This retention of the twelve parts of the body is called yogadhāraṇā. The man shall perform hundred or fifty such Dhāraṇās on the head.

44-45. If he becomes exhausted due to the practice of Dhāraṇā, the wind begins to function upwards. He shall fill the body with the wind along with the Oṁkāra. The yogin identifying himself with Oṁkāra shall merge himself in imperishable being. He shall become imperishable thus.

Henceforth, I shall mention the characteristics of the attainment of Oṁkāra.

46. This should be known as having three Mātrās (units). the consonant in it is the deity. The first Mātrā is Vidyutī (pertaining to lightning). The second is Tāmasī [having Tamo-Guṇa].

47. The third is Nirguṇā (devoid of attributes). It covers up the imperishable Being. It should be known as Gāndhārī too, because it originates from the Gāndhāra note (the third of the seven primary notes of Indian Gamut).

48. When the Oṁkāra that is uttered recedes to the head the devotee feels the touch of the moving ant.

49-52. The yogin identical with the Oṁkāra becomes identical with the imperishable Being. Praṇava is the bow, Ātman is the arrow and Brahman is the target. It should be pierced by one who does not err. He shall be concentrated therein as in regard to the arrow. The single-syllabled word Om is hidden in the cavity. The Oṁkāra is identical with the three worlds, the three Vedas, the three sacrificial fires, the three steps of Viṣṇu, the three scriptures, viz.—Ṛk, Sāmans and Yajurmantras. It should be known that they are really the three and a half Mātras. The yogin who utters it attains identity with the deity.

53. The letter "A" should be known as Akṣara (Imperishable); the letter "U" is then along with it. Including the letter "M", Oṁkāra becomes one with three Mātrās.

54. The letter "A" is the Bhūrloka; the letter "U" is Bhuvarloka, the letter "M" is Svarloka.

55. The Oṁ represents the three worlds. Its head is the Heaven. All the worlds constitute its limbs (body). Its feet are constituted by Brahmaloka.

56. Rudra's world is the foot of the Mātrā, Śiva's region is devoid of Mātrās (i.e. above them). It is with this special knowledge that, that region is worshipped.

57. Hence, the devotee shall be interested in meditation. Indeed that imperishable Being devoid of Mātrās, should be assiduously worshipped by one who wishes for permanent happiness.

58-59. The first Mātrā is a short, the next one is long; the third Mātrā is Pluta (prolated vowel). These Mātrās should be known in their proper order. They are to be retained only as long as it is possible.

60. He who always meditates on the sense-organs, mind and intellect in the Ātman and listens to even half a Mātrā shall attain its benefit.

61. Thanks to that Mātrā, one attains the merit which a person attains by a horse-sacrifice every month, continuing it for a hundred years.

62. Neither by a severe penance nor by sacrifices with plenty of gifts can that merit be obtained which is perfectly obtained by means of the Mātrā.

63. The householder yogins shall practise only that Mātrā which is taught as Plutā (Prolated Vowel).

64. This Mātrā alone comprises the eightfold Aiśvarya beginning with Aṇimā.[848] Hence, O brahmins, be in communion with it.

848. Aṇimā, etc. Cf. p. 134 note 241.

65. O brahmins, he who knows and realises the Ātman obtains everything. He shall be endowed with yoga.[849] He shall be pure. He shall subdue the sense-organs. He shall control them.

66. Hence, the learned man shall contemplate the Ātman by means of the yoga pertaining to Paśupati. Those who know the Ātman are certainly pure beings.

67. It is through the knowledge of yoga that the brahmin, thinker on spiritual topics, attains the Ṛk, Sāman, Yajur mantras, in fact all the Vedas and the Upaniṣads.

68. He becomes identical with all Devas and devoid of all elements. He gets rid of the necessity of passing through wombs and attains the perpetual region.

69. Just as the ripe fruit falls off the tree on being tossed about by the wind, so also sin perishes by the grace of Rudra.

70. Where the obeisance to Rudra yields the benefits of all Karmans, one shall not attain those benefits through the obeisance to the other deities.

71-72. Hence, the yogin shall worship Maheśvara repeating the Praṇava twice. He who enlarges the scope of the Vedas ten times more by elaborating the Vedic texts shall meditate and then forsake the body. He uplifts three generations and attains Sāyujja salvation with Śiva.

73-76. Or after seeing any evil portent and when the time of death has arrived the man shall go to Avimukteśvara in Vārāṇasī and perform the expiatory rite. Somehow the man shall abandon his body there when, O leading brahmins, he is liberated. The man may abandon his body on the mountain, Śrīparvata.[850] He attains identity with Śiva. No doubt need be entertained in this regard. Avimukta is a greatest shrine always bestowing salvation on the creatures. The intelligent man shall resort to it always especially when death is imminent.

849. ST. defines 'yoga-jñānam' as yoga-yuktaṁ jñānam' i. e. knowledge joined with meditation. Yoga is the means for the attainment of right or perfect knowledge 'yogo hi jñāna-sādhanam.'

850. Śrīparvata—See p. 381 note 678.

CHAPTER NINETYTWO

Glory of Śrīśaila

The sages said:

1-2. O sūta of great intellect, if Vārāṇasi is so meritorious it behoves you to recount its greatness to us now. We are eager to hear in detail the excellent greatness of this holy centre Avimukta.

Sūta Said :

3. I shall succinctly mention the glory of Avimukta, of Vārāṇasī in the manner in which lord Bhava had narrated it.

4. O leading brahmins, even in hundreds and crores of years it cannot be mentioned in detail by me or by the noble Brahmā.

5-6. Formerly, after his marriage, Śaṅkara, Nīlalohita started from the peak of the Himavān in the company of the goddess the daughter of the Himavān, and the leading Gaṇas. After reaching Vārāṇasī Śaṅkara showed his Liṅga Avimukteśvara and began to stay there.

7-8. One can become an ascetic in the following places, viz., Vārāṇasī, Kurukṣetra,[851] Śrīparvata, Mahālaya,[852] Tuṅgeśvara,[853] and Kedāra.[854] But if one performs the yoga of Paśupati perfectly for a day, one becomes an ascetic. Hence, one shall eschew everything and perform the Pāśupata yoga.

9. One shall stay there in the garden of the Lord. There is an excellent garden of Śarva at that place. Rudra created mentally a splendid mansion also.

10. The lord accompanied by Nandin pointed out that divine excellent garden to the daughter of the Himavān.

11. Śaṅkara Parameśāna, Bhava mentioned to her the greatness of this holy centre Avimukta just for her pleasure.

851. **Kurukṣetra—See p. 381 note 683.**
852. **Mahālaya— See p. 95 note 115.**
853. **Tuṅgeśvara—not identifiable.**
854. **Kedāra—See p. 381 note 681.**

12. The garden was rendered beautiful by the different clusters of trees in full bloom. It was very charming due to the spreading creepers, the Priyaṅgu plants with growing flowers, and the Ketaka plants in full bloom though covered with thorns.

13. It was overspread with clusters of the Tamāla trees. It was strewn with plenty of fragrant Bakula flowers all round. Hundreds of Aśoka and Punnāga trees were in full bloom. Swarms of bees hovered round the flowers.

14. In some places the garden was resonant with the birds, Sārasas (Indian cranes), Cakravākas (Ruddy geese) and the intoxicated excellent Dātyūhas (water-crows) all round. These birds were embellished by means of the pollen dust of the full-blown lotuses. They were chirping every moment.

15. In some places the excellent garden was resonant with the crowing sound of the peacocks; in some places it was resonant with the cackling sound of the Kāraṇḍava ducks; in some places the garden was rendered noisy by the swarms of the inebriate bees accompanied by their bee-mates equally agitated due to intoxication.

16. It abounded in charming and fragrant flowers. In some places it was full of Sahakāra (mango) trees with fresh sprouts; some places (in the garden) were hidden by Tilaka trees encircled by creepers. The Vidyādharas, Siddhas and Cāraṇas sang in some places in the garden.

17. The garden contained groups of Apsarases engaged in dance. It was resorted to by different kinds of delighted birds. It was resonant with the sound of the Hārīta pigeons. It abounded in birds whose minds were excited due to the roaring sound of the lord of beasts.

18. In some places it abounded in fragrant bunches of flowers and sprouts of the Darbha grass plucked by the deer. In some places it was embellished by lakes and ponds abounding in different charming full-blown lotuses.

19. The garden was charming by the grace of the blue-necked peacocks hiding amidst the clusters of branches. It was resonant with the sounds emanating from the exuberant birds. The intoxicated bees lay hidden amidst the branches of the

trees in full bloom. The tall branches of those trees were rendered more splendid due to the lustre of the fresh sprouts.

20. In some places the beautiful creepers were chewed by the ladies of the Kimpuruṣa clan who walked in the garden in their elegant slow gait. In some places the beautiful trees were embraced by the creepers.

21. (?) The beautiful tops of the trees touched the clouds. The pigeons and doves sat on these tops and made a cooing noise. The tips of the trees had beautiful white forms that captivated the minds. The flowers that were scattered by these pigeons from tree tops disturbed the swans (in the lakes below). The garden was rendered charming by several groups of divine beings.

22. It contained number of garden lakes with full-blown lilies and lotuses spreading far and wide and these brightened up the path leading to the shrine of lord Śiva. The place was covered with different hedges and branches in combination with wonderful rows of flowers in the middle of the paths.

23. The borderlands of the garden were brightened up by charming Aśoka trees with lofty tops and with their tall branches stooping down due to the weight of branches of the flowers. There were swings on either side of these trees and the songs of the birds resting therein caused pleasure to the ears. At night these trees in full bloom became indistinguishable from the Tilaka trees in bloom, thanks to the lustre of the moon. Herds of deer lay under the cool shade of the trees, some sleeping and some awake. Some of these deer had completely nibbled the tips of the Dūrvā grass.

24. The clear waters of the lakes were spreading out due to the moving lotuses which were set in motion by the wind from the fluttering of the wings of swans. Flocks of peacocks danced elegantly on seeing the plantain trees on the banks of these lakes set in motion by the waters coming to their roots. The lands in some places appeared beautiful due to the eyelets on the feathers strewn on the ground from the tails of these peacocks. In these spots, inebriate pigeons and doves of the species called "Hārīta" lurked leisurely and rejoiced.

25. In some places the spots were beautified by the Sāraṅga (flamingo) birds. Some places were covered with

heaps of flowers of variegated colour. At other places the delighted Kinnara ladies played sweet songs on their lutes and danced.

26. The trees thickly growing there harboured the residences of the sages beneath them, with flowers strewn around. In some places the garden contained a lot of Jack trees, tall and spreading all round, with fruits growing from their very bottom.

27. The garden looked charming and resonant with the sounds of the golden anklets of the Siddhas and the Siddha women resorting to the grottos of Atimuktaka creepers in full bloom. The bees eagerly hovered round the bunches of flowers of the charming Priyaṅgu trees. Swarms of bees imbibed honey from the flowers of the mango and Kadamba trees.

28. The garden which bestows salvation on embodied beings looked charming with the water in the ponds gently shaken by the breeze and strewn with clusters of flowers. The fascinating hedges with bees humming therein beautified the garden. Herds of doves which got suddenly frightened by the gusts of wind took shelter within the thickets there.

29. The garden was heightened in beauty by the charming Tilaka trees as brindled as clusters of moon's rays; by the Aśoka trees resembling saffron of the various types such as Sindūra, Kuṁkuma and Kusumbha and by the Karṇikāra trees having the lustre of gold. These trees had large spreading branches and were in full bloom with plenty of flowers.

30. The ground was covered with flowers of various colours. In some places they had the lustre of powdered collyrium; in some places they resembled coral and in other places they were like gold.

31. Hundreds of birds chirped on the Punnāga trees. The red Aśoka trees bent down due to the weight of bunches of flowers. There were rest houses on the charming outskirts of the garden and they dispelled fatigue. The bees danced sportively on the full-blown lotuses.

32. Accompanied by the daughter of the mountain with snow-clad peaks, as well as by the friendly leaders of Gaṇas who were intoxicated, delighted, and well nourished with food, lord Śiva, the ruler of all the worlds, thus pointed out the

extremely charming and extensive garden of trees of diverse kinds, to the goddess.

33. With divine ornaments evolved out of the most auspicious flowers of the forest, Śiva decorated the divine goddess who was present in the garden. The daughter of the snow-capped mountain also devoutly embellished Śiva the lord of Devas with divine flowers that were exceedingly auspicious and beautiful.

34. After seeing the extremely charming garden, after worshipping the lord worthy of being worshipped by the leaders of the gods and after bowing down to the lord who was accompanied by the leading Gaṇas, Nandin and others the goddess spoke to the lord.

The exalted goddess said:

35. O lord, the garden equipped with excessive lustre has been seen by me. It behoves you now to recount all the qualities of this holy centre.

36. O lord of Devas, O bull-emblemed lord it behoves you now to recount the glory of this holy centre, Avimukta in every respect.

Sūta said:

37. O hearing those words of the goddess the excellent lord, the lord of Devas smelt her lotus-like face. Then he laughingly spoke to her.

The lord said:

38. This extremely mysterious holy centre of mine, viz. Vārāṇasī is the hidden cause of the liberation of all creatures.

39. O fair lady, many Siddhas have adopted my Vrata in this holy centre. They have taken up different types of Liṅgas and they always desire my world.

40-41. They are saintly souls one with the supreme spirit. They have conquered their sense-organs. They practise the greatest yoga in this garden abounding in different trees and birds and embellished by lakes abounding in lotus and lily flowers. This holy place is always resorted to by Apsarases and Gandharvas.

42-43. Why this residence appeals to me, listen. One

whose mind is fixed in me, one who is devoted to me, one who has always dedicated his holy rites to me does not attain liberation anywhere else in the same manner as here. O fair lady, a creature that dies here becomes competent to attain salvation.

44-47. This great and divine city of mine is the most mysterious of all mysterious places. Brahmā, Siddhas and others who are desirous of liberation know this. The goal in me is the greatest one. Hence, this holy centre will never be abandoned by me nor has it been eschewed by me. This holy centre, therefore, is known as Avimukta.[855] Absolution is not obtained by taking dip in Naimiṣa,[856] Kurukṣetra,[857] Gaṅgādvāra[858] and Puṣkara[859] nor by resorting to these. But it is obtained here. Hence, this excels all those holy centres.

48. Liberation may be achieved either at Prayāga or here, thanks to my adopting them. This Avimukta is more auspicious than even Prayāga which is the foremost of all holy centres.

49. Truthfulness is the esoteric principle underlying virtue; self-control is the esoteric principle underlying salvation: but excellent learned men do not know the esoteric principle underlying holy centres and sacred waters.

50. Taking food, sleeping, sporting and performing different activities as one pleases, one shall cast off one's vital airs in Avimukta. The creature is then competent to achieve liberation.

51. For men it is better to commit thousands of sins and court Piśācahood than to become Indra in thousands of births without resorting to the city of Kāśī.

52. Hence, Avimukta should be resorted to for achieving salvation. It is here that Jaigīṣavya[860] of great penance attained Siddhi.

53. The excellent cave of Jaigīṣavya is purified, thanks to

855. **Avimukta—See p. 117 note 198. For a different interpretation of the name, see verse 143 of this chapter.**

856. **Naimiṣa—See p. 1 note 4.**

857. **Kurukṣetra See p. 381 note 683.**

858. **Gaṅgādvāra—See p. 93 note 107.**

859. **Puṣkara—p. 381 note 685.**

860. **Jaigīṣavyaḥ—an ancient sage (named along with Asita Devala), Mbh. ii. ix, xii. There is a liṅga Jaigīṣavyeśvara in Vārāṇasī.**

the glory of this holy centre and by means of devotion to me. It is considered to be the abode of yogins.

54. They always meditate upon me at this place. The yogic fire shines brilliantly here. They attain the greatest salvation which is inaccessible even to Devas.

55. Here itself, salvation is attained by the sages who have the unmanifest for their symbols and who know the basic tenets. It is difficult of access anywhere else.

56. To them I expound the excellent glory of the yogic practice, the Sāyujya type of salvation of the Ātman as well as the desired abode.

57. Kubera[861] dedicated his holy rites to me at this holy centre. It is by having recourse to this holy centre that he attained the leadership of the Gaṇas.

58. Saṁvarta[862] who is yet to be born will be my devotee. O fair lady, propitiating me here alone he will attain excellent perfection.

59. The yogin sage Vyāsa,[863] son of Parāśara, will be performing here a great penance. He will be my devotee and he will inaugurate the institution of the Vedas.

60-61. O lotus-eyed lady, that leading sage will be sporting about in this holy centre. Brahmā along with the divine sages, Viṣṇu, Sun, Indra and all other noble-souled heaven-dwellers do worship me here, O lady of good holy rites.

62. Other divine yogins, noble souls in disguise, worship me here always with their minds not turning to anything else.

63. Even a man whose mind is attracted by mundane affairs and who has eschewed interest in religious piety may not be reborn in this world if he dies at this holy centre.

64. But those who are bold and free from ego, who maintain the Sattva Guṇa, who have conquered their sense-organs,

861. Kubera—also named Vaiśravaṇa. He is of deformed body (Kubera), having three legs and only eight teeth. He is regarded as the son of Viśravas by Iḍaviḍā. He is represented as the god of riches and treasure. He is the regent of the northern quarter, the chief of the Yakṣas and a friend of Rudra.

862. Saṁvarta—a muni and legislator. There are references to Saṁvarta-smṛti and Bṛhat-saṁvarta-smṛti in smṛti works.

863. Vyāsa—See p. 2. note 6.

who maintain holy rites and who have eschewed unholy ones —all these have their emotional attachment to me.

65. Resorting to me, all the intelligent persons devoid of attachment have attained salvation here due to my favour, O lady of holy rites.

66. Thanks to my favour, O lady of holy rites, one attains salvation easily here itself which a yogin might attain in the course of thousand births.

67. This holy centre Gopreksaka has been formerly established by Brahmā. O excellent lady, see the divine abode Kailāsa here.

68. Going to Gopreksaka the man shall visit me here. Thereby, he avoids evil mishaps and is released forthwith from sins.

69. The great holy Tīrtha named Kapilāhrada has been made here by Brahmā. This Tīrtha, evolved out of the milk from the udders of cows, is extremely holy and sacred.

70. Here I am known as the bull-bannered lord. O gentle lady, I am present here as seen by you.

71-72. See the deep pool of water here made by Brahmā. It is named Bhadratoya (having auspicious waters). O gentle lady, I have been propitiated in this place by all Devas saying "Be subdued, O lord" and I became calm. I have been brought by Brahmā Parameṣṭhin and installed here.

73. I was seized by Viṣnu from Brahmā and re-installed by him. Then Viṣṇu was addressed by Brahmā with a dejected mind.

74. "This Liṅga has been brought by me. Wherefore have you installed it." Viṣṇu then said to Brahmā, with anger evident in his face.

75. "My devotion to lord Rudra is extremely great and noble. Although the Liṅga has been installed by me it will be known after your name."

76. Therefore, I have occupied this place by the name of Hiraṇyagarbha. Man shall visit this lord of Devas and attain my world thereby.

77. Thereafter, Brahmā who was equipped with the greatest devotion once again duly installed this auspicious Liṅga of mine.

78. I am known here as Svarlīneśvara (the lord who has merged into the heaven). I have come here voluntarily. A man who gives up his life here is not reborn anywhere.

79-80. That goal is not attained by any one else. It is what is known as the goal of yogins. In this place a haughty powerful Daitya who was a thorn to Devas, was killed by me after assuming the form of a tiger. I am perpetually settled here and am well known as Vyāghreśvara (Tiger-Lord).

81-82. By visiting Vyāghreśvara one will avoid courting disaster. There were two Daityas Utpala[864] and Vidala[864] who were, as ordained by Brahmā previously, destined to be killed by a lady. They were therefore killed by you in a battle with a ball contemptuously thrown at them. Their bodies have occupied this place.

83. It was here that I came and settled at the outset along with the leaders of the Gaṇas. Hence, this is the greatest abode of mine. Its vision is conducive to merit.

84. These Liṅgas have been installed all round by Devas. Hence, by visiting the lord in Liṅgas man shall invariably be a Gaṇa when he dies.

85-86. Realising that this place is pleasing and beneficial to me a Liṅga has been established by your father Himavān, the king of mountains. It is known as Śaileśvara. May this be seen with respect. O gentle lady, by visiting this no men shall court disaster or become wretched.

87. O gentle lady, this river Varuṇā is holy. It liberates one from sins. It embellishes this holy centre and becomes united with the Gaṅges.

88. An excellent Liṅga has been installed by Brahmā at this confluence. It is known in the world as Saṅgameśvara, (lord of the confluence).

89. If a man shall become pure taking his bath at the confluence of the divine river and then worship Saṅgameśa whence need he fear rebirth?

90. I consider this great holy centre as the exalted abode of the yogins. I am self-born in the centre of this holy spot occupying the acme of the same.

864. Utpala and Vidala—two daityas who were killed by Śiva.

865. Varuṇā—a sacred river which joins the Gaṅges at Kāśī and has given name to Vārāṇasī.

91-92. It is glorified by all Devas and Asuras as Madhyameśvara (Lord of the centre). Indeed this is the abode of Śiddhas who observe the holy rites pertaining to me. It is the abode of yogins desirous of salvation and of those who are interested in the path of knowledge. By visiting this Madhyameśāna one will not bevail one's birth.

93-94. This Liṅga has been installed by Śukra the son of Bhṛgu. It is named Śukreśvara and is worshipped by all the Siddhas and immortal beings. By visiting this deity the man who has self-control is immediately liberated from all sins. The creature that dies here is not reborn in the world.

95-99. Formerly, an Asura who was a thorn to Devas assumed the form of a jackal. The jackal was not capable of being caught by others as he had acquired boons from Brahmā. O daughter of Himavān, he was killed by me here and so I am called Jambukeśa even today. I am known as such bowed to by Devas and Asuras. By visiting this lord of Devas one shall attain all cherished desires. These Liṅgas have been installed by the planets beginning with Śukra. See these sacred Liṅgas that bestow all cherished desires. Thus, O Pārvatī, these sacred Liṅgas wherein I reside have been recounted. Listen to another esoteric secret of mine in this holy centre. This is glorified as extending to four Krośas in every direction.

100-101. O lady of charming features, this place extending to a yojana bestows immortality after death. Know, that, by visiting me stationed in the Mahālaya mountain and in Kedāra, one attains the state of being a Gaṇa. Salvation is obtained in this place. That liberation is excellent since one attains the headship of Gaṇas.

102. O lady of excellent face, this Avimukta is known as the most sacred holy centre greater than even Mahālaya, Kedāra and Madhyama.

103. These holy centres are sacred in the Bhūrloka (earth) :—viz. Kedāra, Madhyama Kṣetra and the holy spot Mahālaya. This Avimukta is more sacred than all these.

104. Ever since these worlds have been created, this auspicious holy centre has never been abandoned by me. Hence it became Avimukta (un-abandoned).[865a]

865a. For a different interpretation of the name, see p. 498, verse 143.

105. By visiting the Liṅga named Avimukteśvara the man is immediately liberated from sins. He is liberated from the bondages of jīva.

106-108. By visiting all these holy centres, viz:—Śaileśa, Saṅgameśa, Svarlīna, Madhyameśvara, Hiraṇyagarbha, Goprekṣa, Vṛṣadhvaja Upaśānta Śiva (?) the deity residing in Jyeṣṭhasthāna, Śukreśvara, Vyāghreśa and Jambukeśvara a man is not born again in the world which is the ocean of misery.

Sūta said:

After saying thus, Mahādeva surveyed all the quarters.

109. When Maheśvara the lord of Devas stopped after surveying, that place suddenly became blazing as it were.

110-114. Then hundreds of Śiddhas who were devotees of Paśupati, who were white by being bathed in ashes, who were great souls devoted to Maheśvara and who invariably observed holy rites came there and bowed down to Maheśvara. They then observed the lord of the yogas and adopted Dhyānayoga (path of meditation) assiduously. They took to the support of the Ātman and stationed themselves as though they would merge into Maheśvara. Even as they stood by, the consort of Umā, the lord of Devas, the lord Puruṣa assumed the greatest of his physical forms. He stood as though towards the close of the worlds in order to make the entire universe present in one place. With hairs standing on their ends due to her delight, the daughter of the lord of the mountains could not look at the lord of the universe who had assumed the greatest of his physical forms.

115-118. Then she understood that that form which had not been seen before was stationed in Prakṛti, and so Parameśvarī adopted the form of the Prakṛti by means of yoga. Then she could see the form of the noble soul. Then the yogins engaged in the meditation of merging (laya) entered the heart of the Puruṣa. They burnt all the seeds of mundane existence by remembering the splendid Bīja of the five-syllabled Mantra. Then the Lord established his divine and holy form which dispels all sins and which had been revealed formerly in this Nīlalohita image.

119-121. On seeing him, the daughter of the mountains

had horripilation all over the body. She bowed down to his feet and eulogised him. Then she said:—"O lord, who are these ?" Then the most excellent one among Devas spoke to the gentle lady, the daughter of the lord of the mountains.

The lord said:

These are the best of brahmins who possess devotion to me and who resort to my vrata by practising all yogas that they have learnt. O beautiful lady, thanks to the greatness of this holy centre and their devotion to me, they are blessed by me through this physical form in the course of a single birth.

122-127. Hence, this great holy centre is resorted to by Brahmā and others, by leading brahmins well-versed in the Vedic learning and by ascetics of great accomplishments. O goddess, the deity is worshipped at Vārāṇasī on the eighth and fourteenth day in both the fortnights every month. It is particularly worshipped on solar and lunar eclipse days, especially in the month of Kārttika, during all full moon and new moon days, and during equinoctial and solstitial transits. All the Tirthas of the earth resort to the holy Gaṅgā flowing north at Vārāṇasī, the Gaṅgā that flowed out of my matted hairs, the Gaṅgā that is the daughter of your father Himavān the king of mountains, the Gaṅgā that is stationed in the holy abode and flows towards sacred quarters always. O lady of excellent face, what are these Tīrthas ? Listen.

128-133. These Tirthas accompanied by hundreds of Tīrthas flow through Kurukṣetra, Puṣkara, Naimiṣa, Prayāga where there is plenty of water, and Drumakṣetra. O fair lady, they flow through all the holy centres all round. The deities, sages, Sandhyās, seasons, rivers, lakes, oceans and the divine Tīrthas join Gaṅgā during the Parvan days. O lady of good holy rites, O goddess of Devas, by visiting Avimukteśvara and Triviṣṭapa and reaching Kālabhairava, the holy centre, men become rid of their sins during the Parvans. The sacred rivers of the earth and the great shrines and abodes enter Gaṅgā at Vārāṇasī in the course of holy Parvans.

134-139. The different shrines in and around this place are as follows:—Avimukta is the most excellent holy centre. It dispels great sins. The Liṅga that is at Kedāra, the Liṅga that is in Mahālaya,[866] the Madhyameśvara, the Pāśupateśvara, Śaṅkukarṇeśvara, Gokarṇārci,[867] Drumacaṇḍeśvara, Bhadreśvara, Sthāneśvara,[868] Ekāgra, Kāleśvara,[869] Ajeśvara, Bhairaveśvara, Iṣāna, Oṁkāra,[869a] Amareśa,[870] Mahākāla, the Jyotirliṅga, Bhasmagātraka, etc, all those holy centres of mine on the earth numbering sixtyeight and all other well-established shrines come to me at Vārāṇasī during the holy Parvans. Thus the mysterious secret has been revealed to you.

140. Therefore, the creature that dies here attains the divine immortal region if he takes ablution in the Gaṅgā and visits me, O auspicious lady.

141-143. The creature immediately obtains a benefit equal to that of hundreds and thousands of sacrifices. What is more wonderful than that? O fair lady, of all the important shrines on the earth and on mountains, Avimukta is the greatest. Understand what has been said by me. The sin mentioned in the Vedas is recounted by brahmins by the word "Avi". The holy centre is called Avimukta because it is free from Avi (i. e. sin)[871] and resorted to by me.

144-147. After saying this, the lord of all the worlds said—"O goddess of Devas, Avimukta is my abode. See it well." After saying this, the lord, the consort of Umā, pointed out the excellent Śrīparvata to her. He stayed at Avimukteśvara permanently along with her. In view of his ability to go everywhere, the lord of Devas, the soul of all, identical with 'Sat' and 'Asat' came to Śrīparvata along with the goddess. He, the lord of all living beings, pointed out to her the following holy centres and idols:

148-155. Kuṇḍīprabha; the great and divine Vaiśravaṇeśvara; Āśāliṅga; Deveśa; the divine Bāleśvara; the great Rāmeś-

866. Mahālaya—This peak of the Himālayas has not been identified so far.

867. Gokarṇa—See p. 94 note 113.

868. Sthāneśvara -See p. 144 note 250.

869. Kāleśvara—the same as Mahākāleśvara in Ujjayinī, mod. Ujjain, Greek Ozene.

870. Amareśa —the same as Oṁkāreśvara in Oṁkāra Māndhātā in the Nimar district, Madhya Pradesh.

871. Avimuktaka—For a different interpretation of the name, see verses 104-105 of this chapter.

vara[871a] that had been installed by Viṣṇu; lord Kuṇḍaleśvara at the sides of the southern gate; the excellent Tripurāntaka stationed near the eastern gate; the idol that increased in size along with the mountain and was bowed to by the chiefs of Devas; what is well known in the three worlds as Madhyameśvara; Amareśvara the bestower of boons, formerly installed by Devas; lord Gocarmeśvara; the wonderful shrine Indreśvara; the large idol Karmeśvara installed by Brahmā on purpose. O unchanging lady, the holy Siddhavaṭa is my perpetual residence. The divine splendid Ajabila is consecrated by Aja himself; there itself in my divine Bileśvara are my divine sandals. In the middle of the mountain Śṛṅgāṭa is the idol Śṛṅgāṭakeśvara installed by Śrīdevī. It is in the shape of Śṛṅgāṭaka. Mallikārjuna is my splendid residence.

156-157. The shrine Rajeśvara is installed in succession by means of Rajas; the Gajeśvara, the Vaiśākha idol, the unchanging Kapoteśvara; O fair lady, see now the splendid great Tīrtha Koṭīśvara, which was formerly resorted to by crores of the Gaṇas of Rudra and which is superior to all the other shrines.

158. A splendid rocky idol was installed by Brahmā in the south and another was installed in the north by Viṣṇu. Both these together constitute the shrine called Dvidevakula.

159. See, on the western mountain a Liṅga of huge size had been installed by me formerly. It is called Brahmeśvara, Maleśvara.

160. A shrine is remembered by the name Alaṁgṛha. The lord said thus:—"O Brahmā, this has been embellished by you at the outset, along with the sages." After saying this he stayed in the house. Hence, the shrine came to be known as Alaṁgṛha.

161. O lady conversant with the Tīrthas, see there is a Tīrtha and a Vyomaliṅga of mine there also. This is called Kadambeśvara, installed by Skanda himself.

162-164. The shrine Gomaṇḍaleśvara is installed by Nanda and others. O lady of excellent face, see these holy spots and shrines installed by Indra and his Devas on the

871a. **Rāmeśvara—one of the twelve great liṅgas set up by Rāma at Rāmeśvaram, Deccan Bhārata. It is a celebrated place of pilgrimage and contains a magnificent temple.**

borders of Devahrada. O fair lady, in the place where your necklace fell down in Hārapura,[872] the sacred pit of Hārakuṇḍa has been made by you for the welfare of human beings. O lady of good holy rites, in Śivarudrapura, the idol Acaleśvara has been installed by your father on the mountain.

165-169. Formerly, the Brahman was embellished by me along with the sages. O fair lady, the shrine Caṇḍikeśvara is evolved by Caṇḍikā—Caṇḍikeśā is your daughter—This spot is the excellent Ambikā Tīrtha.

The shrine Rucikeśvara is here. This splendid Dhārā (current of water) is tawny-coloured. O fair lady, the devotee who worships me devoutly in these different holy centres and Tīrthas, shall rejoice with me. The brahmin who abandons his body on Śrīśaila destroys his all sins. Undoubtedly he is liberated in the same splendid manner as in the holy centre Avimukta. O lady of good holy rites, he who duly performs the great holy rite of ablution named Mahāsnāna by means of ghee in these holy shrines and spots attains identity with me.

170-174. If the ablution is made with twentyfive Palas of the sacred material of worship it should be known as Abhyaṅga; if it is with a hundred Palas, it should be known as Snāna. Two thousand Palas of the material are said to constitute a Mahāsnāna (great ablution). The devotee bathes my Liṅga at the outset with cow's ghee. Then he consecrates it with the other materials. Thereafter he washes with water. The benefit of a hundred Yajñas is attained by the mere rite of wiping off the Liṅga; by bathing it the benefit of ten thousand sacrifices is attained; by worship the benefit of hundred thousand sacrifices is obtained. The benefit of those who sing and play on instruments of music is infinite. By means of the great bath eight times the benefit of bath is acquired. If the devotee wishes to perform the rite of ablution by means of water alone he shall do so by means of fragrant scented water with devotion. The unguent in every case is by means of twentyfive Palas of the material used.

175. The devotee shall use Śamī flower, Bilva leaves and lotuses duly. He can use other flowers also but he shall not abandon the Bilva leaf.

872. Hārapura—not identifiable.

176. He shall worship Mahādeva with four measures or eight Droṇas of flowers etc. The Naivedya (food offering) shall be ten Droṇas or eight Droṇas.

177. If the devotee is a brahmin devoid of wealth, he attains the same benefit and merit as with the worship of a hundred Droṇas even when he worships only with an Āḍhaka measure. No doubt need be entertained in this respect.

178-184. The devotee shall keep awake during the night by playing on various musical instruments such as Bherī, Mṛdaṅga, Muraja, Timirā, Paṭaha, etc. He shall effect other types of sounds too. He shall duly pray. Accompanied by his servants, sons, wife, relatives and kinsmen he shall circumambulate the excellent Liṅga and pray thus:—

"O lord of Devas, O Śaṅkara, it behoves you to forgive all my sins. Forgive me if my worship is devoid of the requisite materials, faith and rites."

After saying this he shall immediately perform the Japa of Tvarita Rudra and other Śānti mantras. He shall then repeat the Bīja of the five-syllabled mantra. He attains the same benefit as is obtained by visiting the holy centres and performing the sacrifices. He attains the same goal as one who dies in Vārāṇasī. Similarly, he shall undoubtedly attain Sāyujya (identity with me). For the sake of propitiating me, these rites should be performed duly by my devotees. If they neglect, certainly they are not my devotees.

Sūta said:

185-188. On hearing these words, the goddess went to Vārāṇasī. She bathed the Liṅga Avimukteśvara with milk and ghee. She worshipped Rudra the lord of Devas, the leader of the worlds. On the Mandara mountain (?) in Avimukta she propitiated the great Ātman by means of penance. She built a shrine on the Mandara that has beautiful caves. It was here that the lord blessed the great daitya Andhaka, the son of Hiraṇyākṣa. Sportively he blessed him with the offer of Gaṇa-hood.

Thus the entire story has been recounted to you in detail.

189-190. He who reads or listens to the glory of the shrines shall immediately attain those merits which one attains by visiting holy centres. He shall narrate this to all the brahmins who are clean in body and mind and who have conquered their sense-organs. That man alone shall attain the benefit of all sacrifices.

CHAPTER NINETYTHREE

The Narrative of the Asura Andhaka

The sages said :—

1-5. How did the leading Daitya named Andhaka obtain the chieftaincy of the Gaṇas from Maheśvara after being subdued in the Mandara mountain with many charming caves ? It behoves you to recount it in the manner it happened and in the way you have heard.

Sūta said :

I shall succinctly mention how Andhaka was blessed, how he was dessicated on the Mandara mountain and how he attained boons. I shall mention everything briefly. Formerly a son was born to Hiraṇyākṣa. He was comparable to Hiraṇyanayana (i.e. his father in prowess). He was well known as Andhaka. By means of penance he attained great prowess. Thanks to the grace of Brahmā, he attained immunity from death. He enjoyed the whole of the three worlds. Formerly, he conquered the city of Indra sportively and terrified Indra without any strain.

6. All Devas, Nārāyaṇa and others were oppressed, beaten, bound and struck down by him. They became frightened and entered Mandara.

7. After afflicting Devas thus, Andhaka the great Asura happened to come casually to the mountain Mandara with charming caves.

8. Then all those leading Devas including Sādhyas, approached Maheśa, the lord of all Devas and said thus:—

"We have been split and pierced by the weapons of Andhaka, the king of Daityas. We are of very little virility. Hence, we are quickly struck and split in every limb.

9-10. On hearing thus of the arrival of the Daitya through his leading Gaṇas the lord set out against Andhaka. At that place, Indra, the lotus-born Brahmā, Viṣṇu and other leading Devas and the excellent brahmins shouted victories to the lord from all sides. They kept their joined palms on their crown to show their reverence.

11-13. Redueing the entire host of the Asuras to ashes in crores and hundreds of crores, Mahādeva pierced Andhaka with his trident. On seeing that Andhaka was pierced and that his coat of mail of sin had been burnt, Brahmā, shouted in joy after bowing down to Īśa. On hearing that shout Devas bowed down to the lord and shouted. The sages danced. The Gaṇas rejoiced.

14. Then Devas showered plenty of flowers on lord Śiva. The whole of the three worlds rejoiced with delight and shouted.

15. Transfixed to the trident and burned like a dead body in fire the demon assumed Sāttvika emotions and thought thus in his mind.

16-19. "Previously, lord Maheśvara had been propitiated by me in the previous birth since I have been burned now by Śiva. Hence, this has come to pass. Otherwise, this does not fit in. He who remembers Rudra even once in his mind at the time of death attains identity with him. Why not then he who remembers many times. Brahmā, Viṣṇu, and Devas including Indra seek refuge in him. One shall certainly seek refuge in him alone." After thinking thus, Andhaka, delighted in his mind, eulogised Śiva, Īśāna who had suppressed him. It was due to the weightiness of his merit that Andhaka could eulogise thus.

20-21. On being prayed to by him, lord Śiva, the lord of Devas, the dispeller of dejection, said to Andhaka the son of Hiraṇyanetra, who was fixed to the tip of the trident. Glancing at the Dānava, the lord spoke with mercy.

22. "O dear one, I am delighted with you. Welfare unto you. What cherished desire of yours shall I fulfil. O leading Daitya, O Andhaka, choose the boons. I am known as the best-ower of boons.

23. On hearing the words of the lord, the son of Hiraṇya-nayana spoke thus to Maheśvara in words choked within, due to excess of delight.

24. O lord. O Śaṅkara, the dispeller of the agony of your

devotees, O lord of the chiefs of Devas, I crave for your devotion if a boon is to be given unto me. O Īśa, be pleased."

25-26. On hearing the words of Andhaka, the great Ātman, Bhava of great lustre granted him pure devotion which is difficult of access. He conferred on him the chieftancy of the Gaṇas. The leading Devas and others bowed down to him who had been thus established in the position as the chieftain of the Gaṇas.

CHAPTER NINETYFOUR

Uplifting the Earth

The sages said:

1-2. How was his father the terrible demon Hiraṇyākṣa, slain by Viṣṇu ? How did Viṣṇu assume the form of a Boar ? How did his horn attain the status of an ornament of Maheśa. O Sūta, it behoves you to narrate all this to us in detail.

Sūta said:

3. The brother of Hiraṇyakaśipu is known as Hiraṇyākṣa. He was comparable to Kāla the destroyer. He was the father of Andhaka the lord of the Asuras.

4. This leading Daitya defeated all Devas. He bound the earth that has the lustre of blue lotus and took it to Nether regions. He made it his prisoner.

5-8. Devas including Brahmā were oppressed, struck and bound by this cruel leader of the Daityas, Hiraṇyākṣa, the strong and wicked soul. Their facial splendour became faded. They bowed down their heads to Viṣṇu who formerly had suppressed crores of Daityas. They submitted to him the news about the imprisonment of the earth. On hearing this, Lord Viṣṇu assumed the form of Yajñavarāha[873] as at the time of the manifestation of the Liṅga. With the tip of his curved fangs he killed Hiraṇyākṣa the leading Daitya of great strength. After

873. Yajñavarāha—The boar-form of Viṣṇu. On the symbolic interpretation of Yajñavarāha, see *Matsyapurāṇa—A Study*, pp. 311-334.

killing him along with other Daityas, the lord the slayer of the Daityas shone splendidly.

9-14. Just as in the beginnings of kalpas before, he entered the Nether regions and brought the earth out of the ocean and made her seated on his lap. Then Brahmā, the best of Devas, accompanied by Indra and others eulogised Viṣṇu the lord of Devas with words choked with great emotion.

Obeisance to the perpetual Varāha with the curved fangs and the staff. Obeisance to Nārāyaṇa who is identical with all. Obeisance to Brahman the greatest Ātman. Obeisance to the maker of all. Obeisance to the holder of the earth. Obeisance to the slayer of the enemies of Devas. Obeisance to the creator and leader of the chiefs of Devas and the chastiser of all. You are Aṣṭamūrti (having eight cosmic bodies). You have infinite forms. You are the primordial Deva. You are known as Ananta (Eternal Being). Everything has been created by you, O lord of Devas, be pleased, O lord of the worlds, O Varāha, O Viṣṇu.

O Viṣṇu the fulfiller of our desires, all the important Daityas were killed in a trice by you with half of a hundred millionth part of the tip of one of your curved fangs, along with their sons and servants.

15. O lord of earth, the earth was lifted up by you and held at the tip of your curved fangs, O lord, having the lustre of clouds, O lotus-faced God, served by all the people, all the mountains, all the oceans, and by all Devas and Asuras.

16. O lord, it was by you alone that the victory of the Devas was brought about. Ha ! a boon has been given; the goddess of speech has been bestowed on the lotus-born deity, O lord, be pleased.

17. All the leading immortal beings find a place in your hairs; the moon and the sun in your eyes; the earth that had been taken to the nether worlds was placed at the pair of your feet. All the constellations find a place on your back.

18. O lord, O preceptor of the universe, the earth that had been taken to the cavity of the nether regions, has been uplifted by you without the help of any army, for the welfare of the worlds. Everything has been held by you alone.

19. Thus, the lord of speech, Prajāpati, bowed down to Viṣṇu along with Devas repeating different hymns and wor-

shipping him in different ways. From Viṣṇu he (Brahmā) obtained different boons. He was himself having the body originating from the umbilical lotus of Viṣṇu.

20. Devas and the leading sages received on their heads the earth that had been uplifted by him. In the presence of the discus-bearing lord they kept the earth on their heads and bowed down to him.

21-22. "O earth, O bestower of boons, you have been redeemed by this Varāha alone, by Kṛṣṇa, by Viṣṇu who has hundreds of hands and whose activities are not strained. O earth, you are highly blessed. O unchanging one, you are an extensive being. O earth, you are the supporter of all the worlds. Dispel our sins.

23. O lotus-eyed bestower of boons, it is by your favour that we live after our sins have been destroyed by you, mentally, verbally and physically."

24-26a. On being thus addressed by Devas the earth said:—

"O brahmins, he who keeps on his head the pinch of earth broken by the curved fangs of Varāha, repeating this Mantra, shall be liberated from sins. He shall be long-lived and strong. He shall be blessed with sons and grandsons. After leaving the earth he reaches heaven and rejoices along with Devas. At the end of his Karman he returns to the earth.

26b-27. When Varāha the lord had gone back to milk ocean after leaving off the form of the boar, the earth shook again. The curved fangs of intelligent lord of Devas, pressed down by the weight of the earth fell down there.

28-32. Bhava, the lord of the universe, who casually went that way, saw that curved fang and took it up for his own embellishment. Mahādeva kept it on his head as well as on his chest. Devas including Indra eulogised Bhava, the lord of Devas.

The earth was thus stabilised sportingly by the lord of Devas during dissolution. If the lord had not thus decorated himself with parts of Viṣṇu, Brahmā and other Devas sportingly how could the brahmins attain salvation. Hence, Maheśvara wears curved fang (Daṁṣṭrā) as his ornament.

CHAPTER NINETYFIVE

The Exploits of Nṛsiṁha the Man-lion

The sages said:

1. It is heard that Hiraṇyakaśipu the elder brother of Hiraṇyākṣa was formerly killed by Nṛsiṁha. How was he killed by him, kindly tell us.

Sūta said:

2. The son of Hiraṇyakaśipu was known by the name Prahlāda. He was conversant with virtue endowed with truthfulness, asceticism and intelligence.

3-4. Ever since his birth he devoutly worshipped the unchanging omniscient Viṣṇu who is lord of Devas, who is omnipresent, who is the cause of origin of all Devas, who is the primordial Puruṣa, who has the form of Brahman, who is the overlord of Brahmā and who is the cause of creation, sustenance and annihilation.

5-6. The enemy of Devas saw that his son was frequently repeating "O Govinda, Obeisance to Nārāyaṇa." He observed that his son was devoted to Viṣṇu. The demon of sinful intellect looked at his son as though he would burn him and said:— "O boy of wicked intellect, you don't know me the lord of all Daityas as well as Devas.

7-8. O heroic Prahlāda, O my wicked son, I am the cause of agony to the brahmins as well as Devas. Who is Viṣṇu? Who is lotus-born (Brahmā)? Who is Indra, Varuṇa, Vāyu, Soma (Moon), Īśāna or Pāvaka (Fire) to be considered equal to me? Worship me alone with devotion and never the insignificant Nārāyaṇa,

9-12. O Prahlāda, listen to me if you have any desire to be alive."

Even after hearing the threatening words of Hiraṇyakaśipu, the intelligent boy Prahlāda worshipped Viṣṇu and uttered "O Nārāyaṇa obeisance to you Obeisance to Nārāyaṇa" He taught all the Daitya boys the same excellent Brahmavidyā.

Hiraṇyakaśipu saw that his command had been transgressed by his son, the command that could not be transgressed even by Indra and others. On knowing that his behest had been violated Hiraṇyakaśipu said to Dānavas ; "It behoves you to kill this wicked son of mine who is worthy of being put to death in various ways."

13. Thus ordered by that Daitya of extremely wicked heart, Dānavas hit and struck the undaunted Prahlāda who considered himself a servant of the lord of Devas.

14. O excellent brahmins, what had been evilly perpetrated then by those Asuras on the son of the king of Daityas became futile, thanks to the brilliance of the lord who lies down in the milk ocean.

15-16. In order to kill Hiraṇyakaśipu who was furious due to his haughtiness, the lord assumed the form of the man-lion and manifested himself there itself. Glancing at the son kindly he hit the father the base Dānava. At the very same moment he split him with his sharp claws.

17. Then, the dispeller of sins killed that Daitya along with his kinsmen. Like a fire of annihilation at the close of yugas he harassed the leading Daitya.

18. O brahmins of good holy rites, the entire universe became terrified due to the terrible roar of Nṛsiṁha. All the worlds beginning with the world of Brahmā trembled.

19-21. On seeing Nṛsiṁha, Devas, Asuras, Nāgas, Siddhas, Sādhyas, Viṣṇu, Brahmā and others left off their courage and strength and went off in different directions in order to protect their lives. When they had gone, the lord Nṛsiṁha who had a thousand shapes, who had all feet and all arms, who had a thousand eyes, whose three eyes were the moon, sun and fire, who was the wielder of Māyā remained there enveloping every thing. The excellent Devas who were stationed on the Lokāloka accompanied by Brahmā, Siddhas, Yama and the Maruts, eulogised him.

Prayer

22-30. You are the Brahman that is greater than the greatest. You are the greatest of realities. You are the greatest splendour among all luminaries. You are the greatest Ātman. You are identical with the universe.

You are gross and subtle; nay the subtlest. You are the auspicious being identical with Śabdabrahman. You are beyond the scope of speech and devoid of support. You are free from Dvandvas (mutually clashing opposites) impediments and calamities.

24. You are the partaker of sacrifices of sacrificers. You are the lord bestowing fruits on those who perform sacrifices. You assume the form of a fish.[874] You are stationed in the universe after assuming the form of a tortoise.[875]

25. You have assumed the forms of the Boar and the lion for saving the kingdom of Devas by killing the lord of Daityas.

26. Under the pretext of the curse of brahmin (i.e. Bhṛgu) you sportingly incarnated on the earth. Nothing is seen as distinctly different from you. You are the whole universe consisting of the mobile and immobile beings.

27. You are Viṣṇu, Rudra, and Brahmā. You are the beginning and the end; O lord, you alone are we.

28. You alone are the universe. O lord, of what avail is mere prattling. O lord, that which is non-dualistic is stationed in manifold ways, due to Māyā.

29-30. How shall we eulogise you ? O lord of the paśus ! O lord of Devas, how you shine !"

Although the lord was thus eulogised with different hymns, with emotional feelings, O brahmins, the lord did not become calm because he was honouring the species in which he manifested himself (i. e. a lion).

He who reads this hymn pertaining to the Man-lion, or he who ponders over its meaning or he who narrates this to the brahmins, is honoured in the world of Viṣṇu.

31-34. In the meantime, Devas including Indra and Brahmā came to lord Śiva and eulogised him after informing him about the activities of Viṣṇu who assumed the form of a beast (Lion). Then Brahmā and others eulogised Parameśvara. They sought refuge in him who is the great cause, for saving their souls. Accompanied by Devas and extremely afraid, Brahmā eulogised Parameśvara Mahādeva who was staying on the Mandara mountain sporting with Umā and who was served by

874-875. **The verses 24-25 of this chapter refer to the fish, tortoise, boar and man-lion incarnations of Viṣṇu. For detail, see *H.M.* under Avatāra, pp. 33-38.**

his Gaṇas, Gandharvas, Siddhas and Apsarses. Brahmā prostrated on the ground and eulogised Parameśvara with words choked in the throat.

Brahmā said :

35 Obeisance unto you the destroyer of death; obeisance unto the wrath of Rudra; obeisance unto Śiva, Rudra; obeisance to you Śiva,[876] Śaṅkara.

36 You are Ugra (Terrible), the retainer of all living beings; you are Śiva (auspicious) unto us; obeisance to Śiva, Śarva, Śaṅkara the dispeller of dejection.

37. Obeisance to Mayaskara,[877] obeisance to Viśva, to Viṣṇu, to Brahmā ; obeisance to you the destroyer ; obeisance to the lord of Umā.

38. Obeisance to Hiraṇyabāhu (one with golden arms) ; obeisance to the lord of Hiraṇya (gold) ; obeisance to Śarva,[878] having all forms ; obeisance to Puruṣa.

39. Obeisance unto one devoid of distinction between 'Sat' and 'Asat'; obeisance unto you the cause of 'mahat'; obeisance to the permanent Being of the form of the universe that is being born.

40. Obeisance unto one born in many ways ; obeisance unto the plentiful being ; obeisance to Rudra ; obeisance to Nīlarudra ; to Kadrudra; obeisance to Pracetas.

41. Obeisance to Kāla of dark complexion ; obeisance to the destroyer of Kāla; obeisance to lord Mīḍhuṣṭama[879] (bountiful) : obeisance to you Śitikaṇṭha (blue-necked).

42. Obeisance to you the great one ; to the perpetual destroyer of Daityas ; obeisance to Tāra[880] (redeemer) and to Sutāra (the excellent redeemer); obeisance to Tāraṇa (one engaged in redeeming sinners).

876. śivāya—mokṣarūpāya *ST*. of the form of salvation. Cf. "śivam mokṣe sukhe bhadre."—Viśva.

877. mayaskarāya—sukhakarāya *ST*. the bestower of happiness.

878. śarvāya—sṛṇāti jagat hinastīti śarvaḥ *ST*. the destroyer of the universe.

879. mīḍhuṣṭamāya—sarva-varṣakāya *ST*. the best among those who grant wishes.

880. tārāya—praṇavarūpāya *ST*. of the form of praṇava (om).

43. Obeisance to Harikeśa (one with tawny hair) ; obeisance to Śambhu the great Ātman ; obeisance to you the benefactor of Devas ; obeisance to one the benefactor of living beings.

44. Obeisance to the benefactor of Umā, the daughter of Himavān ; obeisance to wrath in the form of Rudra ; obeisance to Kapardin (one with matted hair). Obeisance to Kālakaṇṭha (the blue-necked).

45. Obeisance to gold-complexioned Maheśa; obeisance to Śrīkaṇṭha; obeisance to one who is smeared with ashes; obeisance to Daṇḍeśvara (lord with the staff or rod of punishment); obeisance to Muṇḍīśvara (lord with skulls).

46. Obeisance to Hrasva (short one) ; to Dīrgha (long one); obeisance to Vāmana (dwarf), to the terrible trident-bearing lord ; obeisance to the fierce being.

47. Obeisance to Bhīma (the terrible), to one of terrible form ; obeisance to you interested in terrible activities ; obeisance to one, the foremost among the annihilators; obeisance to one who can kill from far.

48. Obeisance to Dhanvin (one with a bow), to Śūlin (the trident-bearing) ; obeisance to you the Gadin (one with an iron club), to Halin (one with) ploughshare (as weapon), to Cakrin (one with discus), to Varmin (one with coat of mail), to the perpetual destroyer of the activities of Daityas.

49. Obeisance to you, the Sadya, Sadyarūpa, and Sadyojāta ; obeisance to you the Vāma, Vāmarūpa,[881] Vāmanetra;

50-51. Obeisance to you the lord with hideous form and shape; obeisance to Puruṣarūpa; to Tatpuruṣa; to the sole Puruṣa;[882] obeisance to the bestower of Puruṣārthas (aims of life) ; obeisance to the lord, to Parameṣṭhin ; obeisance to you, to Īśāna, to Īśvara.

52-54. Obeisance to Brahmā, to one of the form of Brahman; obeisance to you, to Śiva himself.

881. **Vāmarūpāya—sundararupāya *ST*. of charming features.**

882. **puruṣaika-tatpuruṣāya—puruṣeṣu ekas tatpuruṣaḥ uttama-puruṣa-rūpa ityarthaḥ *ST*. the best among men. Cf. "uttamaḥ puruṣas tvanyaḥ paramātmetyudāhṛtaḥ"—Bhagavad Gītā**

O Śarva, Viṣṇu the maker of the universe has assumed the form of Nṛsiṁha. For the welfare of the worlds that lord himself has killed Hiraṇyakaśipu with his sharp claws along with many leading Daityas. But being in the leonine form he is harassing the universe.

O lord of Devas, kindly do what should be done in the matter.

55. You are Ugra (fierce) ; you are the restrainer of all wicked ones ; you are our benefactor. Protect us through your bodies of Kālakūṭa, etc. We have sought refuge in you.

56-58. O lord of the universe, your conduct is spotless ; we are but tools of your game. Our dissolution and rise depend upon the closing or opening of your eyes. Even when you are wide awake, O lord, we are distressed by Viṣṇu of unmeasured splendour. O Śiva, our destruction cannot happen when you are wide awake. It behoves you to curb and check Nṛsiṁha, for the welfare of the worlds.

Sūta said :

The lord who was thus addressed by them replied smilingly.

59-63. The lord offered them fearlessness saying "I shall kill him." Indra bowed to the lord along with Devas. Lord Brahmā and Devas returned to their homes. Soon after Mahādeva assumed the form of a Śarabha and approached the haughty Man-lion. The lord in the form of Śarabha took away his life and was worshipped by Devas. From the form of a lion Viṣṇu assumed his original form and went away gradually. The lord too who was thus eulogised by Devas went away.

He who reads or listens to this excellent hymn of Śiva attains his world and rejoices along with him.